The War in the Pacific

From Pearl Harbor to Tokyo Bay

Harry A. Gailey

PRESIDIO

Published by Presidio Press
505 B San Marin Dr., Suite 300
Novato, CA 94945-1340

Library of Congress Cataloging-in-Publication Data

Gailey, Harry A.

The war in the Pacific : from Pearl Harbor to Tokyo Bay / by Harry A. Gailey.
   p. cm.
   Includes bibliographical references and index.
   ISBN 0-89141-486-X
   1. World War, 1939–1945—Campaigns—Pacific Area. I. Title.
D767.G28 1995
940.54'26—dc20
                                           94-32493
                                             CIP

All photos courtesy the National Archives.
Typography by ProImage

Printed in the United States of America

To my Wife,
former Yeoman Rosalie Joy Bray (W-USNR),
in deep appreciation for over
four decades of continuous support

Contents

Preface   ix

Chapter 1 Roots of Conflict   1

Chapter 2 Isolationism and Complacency   29

Chapter 3 Japanese Military Preparations   53

Chapter 4 The Day of Infamy   71

Chapter 5 The Japanese Tidal Wave   101

Chapter 6 Java, Coral Sea, and Midway   133

Chapter 7 The Guadalcanal Ordeal   173

Chapter 8 The Tide Turns: New Guinea and Bougainville   209

Chapter 9 Plan Orange Executed   247

Chapter 10 Victory in New Guinea   271

Chapter 11 The Marianas Secured   301

Chapter 12 Return to the Philippines   337

Chapter 13 Advance to Luzon   375

Chapter 14 The Noose Tightens: Iwo Jima and Okinawa   407

Chapter 15 The Killing Time   447

Chapter 16 Unconditional Surrender   477

Selected Bibliography   499

Index   509

Maps

Japanese Attack—Pearl Harbor: 7 December 1941   93
Bataan: January–April 1942   118
Japanese Invasions: Dutch East Indies,
     January–February 1942   128
Guadalcanal: August 1942   177
Lunga Point Defenses: September 1942–January 1943   189
Papua New Guinea: 1942   211
Solomon Islands & Adjacent Areas   229
Bougainville Island   239
Betio: Tarawa Atoll   258
Western New Guinea: 1944   280
Saipan: 1944   306
Guam: 21 July 1944   326
Southern Palau Islands   342
Leyte and the Visayas: 1944   351
Luzon: January 1945   383
Iwo Jima   413
Okinawa   424

Preface

The Second World War engaged the energies of the American people for almost four years and was fought on a scale barely conceived of by even the most pessimistic prewar observers. Of the many theaters of operations, the Pacific held a unique place in the public mind, for the Japanese personified what most Americans considered to be evil. Japan, by attacking Pearl Harbor, forced the United States reluctantly to become a partner in a global conflict that was already two years old. Thus, despite the U.S. government's Eurocentric military policy, many Americans viewed the Japanese as the primary enemy. Although racism may have played a role in this, remembrances of the atrocities committed by Japanese soldiers in China, the Pearl Harbor attack, and the brutal treatment of American prisoners at the hands of their Japanese captors as exemplified by the Bataan Death March probably did more to shape U.S. public opinion.

Military historiography since the war reflects the prewar bias of U.S. policy by focusing on events in Europe. This is not to imply that the Pacific war has been completely overlooked. There is a series of excellent official and unofficial histories of specific campaigns, and biographies of the most important military commanders and reminiscences by participants abound. However, many deadly campaigns once thought to have been critical have been all but ignored. The most important of these neglected areas are the central and northern Solomons actions, the murderous Peleliu engagement, Australian and American campaigns along the thousand-mile New Guinea coast, and the Philippines conquest—the largest American operation of the entire Pacific conflict. Recently, a few monographs have dealt with these areas. However, there remains no general history of the Pacific war focusing solely on that theater. The few general works available attempt to cover the vast China-Burma-India theater in conjunction with the Pacific campaigns. In every case this has meant that neither area has received the attention it deserves.

That observation was the genesis of this work. I believe that the first task of any general history of World War II is to trace the background of the war in considerable detail since political, military, and socioeconomic forces were so important in determining the decisions for war. In this work, the reader will find a thorough presentation not only of the immediate diplomatic maneuverings but an overview of the history of Japanese-American relations. Also included is an analysis of the American and Japanese military systems, permitting the reader to evaluate the immediate and long-term capabilities of the antagonists.

By eliminating a discussion of the Asian land war and its complex geopolitical problems, I was able to give greater attention to many areas of the conflict that had previously been ignored or given only brief mention. Similarly, I have tried to present the activities of the various services and nationalities involved in both the Central and Southwest Pacific areas in a logical, coordinated manner. This was no small task as the overall conduct of the war was extremely complicated. Each campaign was composed of myriad planned and fortuitous actions. It was therefore necessary for me to relate the events of most campaigns in some detail. My hope is that these narratives will enhance the clarity of the overall picture being presented and that both military history specialists and general readers will better be able to appreciate the interrelated parts of the Pacific war that contributed to the Allies' ultimate victory.

The narratives and interpretations of the various phases of the war contained herein are based on the considerable research done for my earlier monographs on operations in the Central and Southwest Pacific theaters, as well as recently declassified materials. The most important recent secondary studies also provided valuable information on specific campaigns. A detailed listing of the sources used can be found in the bibliography.

Chapter 1

Roots of Conflict

THE ATTACK ON Pearl Harbor on 7 December 1941 was the climax of nearly a half century of rivalry between Japan and the United States in the Far East. This competition, not always clearly recognized by the U.S. government, nevertheless existed even in the most quiescent periods and was clearly understood by a succession of Japanese civilian and military leaders, particularly after World War I. This differential attitude toward domination of the vast land areas of Asia was one factor that predetermined the first years of the conflict during World War II. America's isolationism, general ignorance of the situation in the Far East, arrogance, and—in the late 1930s—concern with developments in Europe all contributed to its woeful lack of preparation to meet the well-planned and executed simultaneous attacks against preselected targets by the Japanese military.

Japanese and American planners in the first part of the twentieth century viewed the Pacific region as an adjunct to the main area of concern. It was obvious to Japanese military planners that at some future date the United States might interfere militarily and endanger Japanese goals on the Asian mainland. In such an eventuality it would be necessary for the Japanese navy to intercept and destroy any American Pacific fleet units near Japanese home waters.

American plans regarding the Pacific were never as clear. Most of the United States's Far Eastern and Pacific military and diplomatic activities could be called mere posturing. The earliest example of this was the dispatch of the Great White Fleet on its around the world cruise in 1907, a blatant announcement that the United States had become a major power. Certainly one of President Theodore Roosevelt's goals was to overawe Japan, the new Asian military power. Although not as obvious, much of the American government's activity in the Pacific in the following years was confused, and the amorphous goals enunciated from time to time were not backed by a military presence that could assure their realization if opposed by another major power.

Much of the antipathy between the United States and Japan prior to Japan's invasion of Manchuria in 1931 was synthetic. There were no areas where Japanese interests in Asia and the Pacific, either economic or military, conflicted directly with those of the United States. Despite this, feelings of distrust and suspicion continued to grow after the Japanese victory over Russia in 1905. Japanese expansionists believed that the very presence of the United States in the Far East would prevent Japan from dominating China and Manchuria. To bolster this logical construct, increasingly vitriolic anti-American propaganda was spouted in government circles and in the media. The Washington disarmament conference, which assigned Japan only three-fifths of the capital ship tonnage of Britain and the United States, was seen as further evidence that Japan was being purposely kept weak so that the Western powers could thwart Japan's aims in Asia and the Pacific.

The Japanese government's defensive attitude prior to World War II had some substance in history, although Japanese leaders later overexaggerated American and European hostility. Japan, a divided feudal kingdom closed to the outside world for centuries, had—in a single generation after being forced to deal with foreigners—become the most technologically advanced state in Asia. The Meiji Revolution produced a centralized state and in 1889 established the framework of a Western style parliamentary regime with a two-house legislature and a ministry appointed by Emperor Mutsuhito. Copying the best examples available in Europe and the United

States, the government helped entrepreneurs create a firm modern industrial base.

Three Italian-made looms imported in 1868 gave rise to lucrative textile manufacturing in Japan, which was for many years the nation's basic industry. Over the next two decades chemical, iron, and machine-tool industries were brought to Japan. By 1895 there were more than six thousand factories in the islands, and more than twenty thousand by the eve of World War I. The organization of these businesses followed the German model: they were large holding companies (*zaibatsu*) controlled by important families, run by professional managers, and backed by massive government support. The imperial family was a major stockholder in the Bank of Japan, as well as many of the major industries.

By the early twentieth century, the foreign commerce of the newly industrial Japan was worth $250 million, a tenfold increase from the mid-1870s. Japanese exports were thus in competition for markets with those from Europe. Needing secure markets as well as raw materials, the Japanese turned to the Asian mainland as the logical place to secure both. In so doing, this newfound Japanese economic imperialism was not only resisted by the Chinese government, but collided with the more well established European powers, which had rendered the moribund Peking aristocracy almost helpless.

The Japanese were excellent imitators in diplomacy as well as in the more mundane areas of industrial and economic development. They recognized that past European economic goals had been assured by the threat of and blatant use of military force, so they decided to emulate the Europeans in this regard. One important aspect of the Meiji Revolution was the transformation of a feudalistic warrior society into one in which men of all classes were expected to serve the state. Importing the best instructors from continental Europe, the Japanese government created a national army whose training and tactics were copied from the Germans. In 1871, a general staff modeled upon the Prussian system was created. The new army purposely retained many of the rules of honor and devotion that had governed the samurai. Officer training was provided by the Department of Military Training. The officer corps was dominated by young aristocrats of the Choshu and Satsuma clans, and this dominance would continue until after World War I, when more sons of shop-keepers and small farmers rose to higher rank. The new army, highly disciplined and totally obedient to the purported wishes of the emperor, had grown to 180,000 regular and 600,000 reserve soldiers by 1904. This army, modern in weaponry and tactics, was unique in its adherence to the more archaic concepts that had motivated an earlier warrior society.

The Japanese government realized that to carry out expansionist plans, or even to defend the home islands, a navy would be necessary. It was an age when the ideas of the American naval theorist, RAdm. Alfred Thayer Mahan, had great favor with military planners throughout the world. The Japanese eagerly accepted the notion that to be a great power in an increasingly industrialized world, a state needed a powerful navy. As with the army, the Japanese turned to the most advanced European state for assistance. The British provided instructors for the new naval academy and the Japanese modified British training methods to meet their special needs. Furthermore, British shipyards at first provided naval vessels for Japan, then later helped the Japanese construct shipyards, gun factories, and the hundreds of supporting industries needed to build complex, modern fighting ships. After depending upon Britain for its merchant ships and warships in the early stages of armament, by 1900 Japan had modern facilities at Yokosuka capable of building and repairing large modern ships. Its gun factory could manufacture 12-inch naval rifles.

The 1890s witnessed naval construction at an unprecedented rate in all western states. The drive for an efficient blue-water U.S. Navy began at this time, and even Great Britain, the dominant naval power, began to enlarge and modernize its fleet. It would have been surprising if Japan had not responded in some fashion to this arms race. However, Japanese naval construction and purchases far outstripped, on a per capita basis, all other countries. By the beginning of the Russo-Japanese War, Adm. Marquis Heihachiro Togo would command a fleet of six modern battleships, eight armored cruisers, eighty torpedo boats, and nineteen destroyers.

Despite the size and modernity of its army and navy, there was considerable skepticism among European military men as to the battle effectiveness of Japan's military. Nor were the Europeans completely convinced by Japan's easy victory over the Chinese in the Sino-Japanese conflict of 1894. The locus of that conflict was Korea, where Japanese businesses, backed by the military, wanted a state independent of Chinese control. China sent troops to protect its suzerainty over the area, and the Chinese commander promised quick victory over the Japanese "dwarfs." In less than six months, the Japanese had driven the Chinese out of Korea, invaded Manchuria, and captured Port Arthur. The war showed clearly that Japanese imperialism was a force to be reckoned with; no longer would European states have a totally free hand in Asia.

The Treaty of Shimonosiki, signed in April 1895, sent a signal to all states with interests in the Far East, particularly Russia. The victorious Japanese, demanding a large indemnity, forced the Chinese to cede Formosa. But the most crucial part of the agreement was the cession of the Liaotung Peninsula including the fine harbor of Port Arthur. This latter clause frightened and enraged the Russians, who believed Manchuria, Korea, and the Liaotung Peninsula to be within their sphere of influence. With the cooperation of the German and French governments, the Russians forced Japan to evacuate Port Arthur and the peninsula. This loss was made worse to Japanese officials by the blatant land grabs of those same powers in the next five years. The Germans secured the Shantung Peninsula on a long lease, and the French gained concessions near Hainan. But the Russian moves were the most damaging. They loaned the Chinese government money and in return were granted the right to extend the Siberian Railway across Manchuria to Vladivostok and to maintain infantry and cavalry units there, ostensibly to protect the line. The final insult was the long-term lease of Port Arthur granted to the Russians. It is difficult to know precisely when the Japanese began to view Europeans, and by extension Americans, as potential enemies. However, the reaction to their victory over China indicated to them that there were two sets of rules for imperial expansion in Asia—one for the Europeans and the other for the Japanese.

Japan viewed Korea and southern Manchuria as areas whose control was absolutely vital for Japanese economic expansion. This ran directly counter to Russian ambitions, and at the beginning of the twentieth century, Japanese diplomats attempted to reach an agreement with the Russians over spheres of influence. The Russian government, inefficient in St. Petersburg where it was far removed and ignorant of the issues, was nonresponsive. Diplomatic negotiations ceased in January 1904. By that time, the Japanese government had decided that war was the only way to gain dominance in Korea and Manchuria and ordered preemptive naval strikes at Chemulpo and Port Arthur. Without a declaration of war, Japanese naval units attacked on 8 February, and then imposed a blockade on Russia's major Far Eastern bases. Hampered by a divided command structure, incompetent commanders, and a long supply line, the Russians never could seize the initiative from the Japanese. The Japanese First Army landed in Korea on 8 February, captured Seoul, drove the small Russian force back, and reached the Yalu River by 3 April. Soon afterward, Japan had three other armies in Korea and the Liaotung Peninsula. The Third Army settled in for the long bloody siege of Port Arthur, which capitulated on 5 January 1905. The First, Second, and Fourth Armies invaded Manchuria. The ensuing conflict was the first modern war to utilize most of the weapons that would later become so familiar in World War I. The Japanese offensives and Russian defensives employed huge numbers of men, the battles were fought out over lines many miles long, and the casualties were horrendous. As the Russian commander, Gen. Aleksey N. Kuropatkin, fell back slowly toward Mukden, he was continually outmaneuvered by his Japanese counterparts. He attempted to break the winter stalemate by launching a major offensive in early March 1905 on a forty-seven-mile front. It proved to be a disaster. Although the Japanese suffered heavily, their lines held and the ensuing counteroffensive resulted in 50 percent casualties to the 380,000-man Russian army. Mukden fell shortly after that, and the Russian government, bothered by social unrest in its large cities, began to search for ways to end the unprofitable war.

The nature of the land fighting and the costly Japanese victories before Mukden were largely ignored by westerners, who had few military and civilian observers on the scene. This was not true of the Japanese naval victories, which caught the imagination of readers in Europe and the United States. Admiral Togo, whose triumphs over the Russian Baltic and Pacific fleets were unexpected and devastating, was viewed as a modern-day Nelson. The Japanese fleet's early successes at Chemulpo and Vladivostok and the bottling up of powerful Russian units at Port Arthur were nothing compared to Togo's victory at Tsushima. The Russian Baltic fleet, after an epic seven-month voyage from Europe, was confronted by the Japanese blocking the Straits on 27 May 1905. Admiral Togo accomplished the dream of all naval commanders: bringing the full weight of his guns to bear on the enemy's lead ships. Togo executed the maneuver—known as crossing the T—not once but twice. Seldom in history has a victory been so one-sided. Of the thirty-eight Russian vessels involved, twenty were sunk and five were captured. The Japanese lost three torpedo boats.

After the twin disasters of Tsushima and Mukden, and faced with threats from dissatisfied citizens in St. Petersburg demanding a change in the government, the czar and his ministers finally decided to accept President Roosevelt's offer to mediate. The Japanese, although everywhere victorious, had suffered huge losses and were eager to end the conflict while they were still winning. The exhausted armies limited themselves to skirmishes during the peace negotiations. Finally, on 5 September 1905, the Treaty of Portsmouth, New Hampshire, was signed. Japan gained the objectives enunciated in government councils before hostilities began. Russia surrendered its lease on the Liaotung Peninsula and Port Arthur, ceded the southern half of Sakhalin Island to Japan, withdrew from Manchuria, and recognized Korea as a Japanese sphere of influence. Assuming control first of Korea's foreign policy and later police, military functions, and economy, Japan by 1910 had made Korea totally subservient to its will. Later, Manchuria was secretly divided into Russian and Japanese spheres of influence, and in 1928 Russia renounced its desire to dominate its sphere economically or politically. Although nominally ruled by China, Manchuria—even before the Mukden incident of September 1931—was in reality a Japanese protectorate.

The Russo-Japanese War was a watershed in modern Japanese history. It proved the worth of the Japanese military and gave rise to the myth of invincibility held by many senior military and political leaders. Field Marshal Iwao Oyama and Admiral Togo became heroes worthy of emulation by generations of young patriotic Japanese.

The territory gained and political and economic influence exercised in Korea and Manchuria provided the raw materials for Japan's industry and markets for its products.

It is well to note that certain concepts existing in embryo form in 1904 became solidified and would not change even during World War II. One fact was the obvious direction of Japan's expansion. Little thought had been given to the vast reaches of the Pacific. Dominating the Asian mainland was the single-minded goal of Japan's government. The invasion of Manchuria in 1931 and the eventual war with China begun in 1937 were but a continuation of this earlier ambition. Although Japan's defeat in World War II came about largely because of its losses in the Pacific, the largest portion of Japan's army remained in mainland Asia to the very end.

The second fact to emerge from the war was the growing influence of the army. Although Admiral Togo may have gained the lion's share of publicity in the world press, even he recognized that the navy's role, however vital, was still secondary. Some British observers faulted Togo for not destroying the Russian fleet at Port Arthur when he had the chance. This was a misreading of Togo's mission, which was to keep the sea-lanes open. The defensive role assigned to the navy in 1904 did not change until the eve of World War II. The primary reliance upon the army to carry out the fundamental goals of the emperor and his government resulted ultimately in the dominance of army leaders in the councils of state. Naval commanders tended to be less parochial and more knowledgeable of the world outside Asia, and most were not in favor of policies that might bring the great powers into conflict with Japan. Many senior generals had no such scruples and instead favored a forward imperialistic policy without fear of consequences. By 1941, the army, successful in all its major undertakings, believed itself invincible. Its two clashes with the Soviet Union in the late 1930s, which resulted in humiliating defeat for elements of its Manchurian forces, were dismissed as aberrations.

During the two decades prior to World War I, the U.S. government thrust itself more openly into Asian and Pacific affairs. This was a reflection in part of the increased value of American business, particularly in China. Americans had been active in the China trade for more than half a century; much of the wealth of some New England seaport towns had been gained in that trade. Whalers, having nearly exhausted the easy harvests in the Atlantic, had even before 1850 rounded the Horn to pursue the different varieties of whales found in the Pacific. Some American entrepreneurs found it easy to make their fortunes in the Hawaiian Islands and eventually to dominate the government there, finally engineering the overthrow of the monarchy in 1893.

Nevertheless, American imperialism in the Pacific and Asia had less to do with the hope of increased economic gain than with the more intangible ideas expressed in such phrases as "Manifest Destiny" and "White Man's Burden." The media and many influential businessmen and politicians had convinced themselves it was necessary for the United States to be recognized as a great power. The last two decades of the nineteenth century saw the major European states divide the huge African continent between them, quarrel over Asian possessions, and claim most of the Pacific islands. Americans came to believe that to gain the power and prestige that were their due, the United States should emulate Britain, France, and Germany. This desire had obvious corollaries, one of which was building a modern navy capable not only of protecting commerce, but of demonstrating the power of the United States throughout the world.

American imperialism, like its European counterpart, was fostered by a few highly placed men who firmly believed that it was the nation's destiny to expand its political and moral influence worldwide. At first, theirs was a minority opinion in government. Witness the action of President Grover Cleveland, who denounced the Hawaiian coup and refused the offer of the American adventurers to annex the islands. Gradually, the desire for expansion gained momentum. Fueled by the same moral fervor that spawned the concept of manifest destiny half a century before, the government, media, and general population came to fully support the expansionists' program. Yet few Americans envisioned an American empire in the Pacific. Instead, cloaked in moral platitudes, the McKinley government intervened directly in the rebellion in Cuba. Led by activists in Washington, and spurred on by lurid accounts in the Hearst and

Pulitzer newspapers, an accommodating president led the nation into a welcomed war with Spain—a war ostensibly to free the Cuban people from Spanish tyranny.

Theodore Roosevelt, a key figure in pre-World War I imperialism, was most responsible for securing the basis for an American foothold in the Pacific. As undersecretary of the navy, even before war was declared on Spain, he had taken advantage of the absence of the navy secretary to wire instructions to one of his most trusted senior officers, Commodore George Dewey, commander of the Asiatic Fleet, to proceed to the Philippines as soon as hostilities began and destroy the small ancient Spanish fleet in Manila Bay. Ostensibly this was to be done to free the Filipino people from Spain.

Once the destruction of the Spanish fleet had been accomplished, the government rethought its position and decided that the glory of victory in Cuba and Manila Bay was not enough; neither was the knowledge that the Filipinos had been liberated. The Filipino leader, Emilio Aguinaldo, was abandoned, and an American army led by Maj. Gen. Wesley Merritt occupied Manila and its environs. This set off a tragic war of pacification lasting almost five years. "Civilize 'em with a Krag" became a popular saying. It was obvious many Filipinos neither wanted nor appreciated the moral mandate felt so deeply by President William McKinley and his advisers, who decided to keep the Philippines until they were certain the Filipinos could govern themselves. It is doubtful if even such an ardent imperialist as Roosevelt had planned for the annexation; certainly McKinley had not. At the beginning of the war, he had not even known where the Philippines were located, but he concurred in their annexation after listening to arguments proclaiming it America's duty to bring Western civilization to the islands. That American expansion in the Pacific was not welcomed by a significant number of the power brokers is shown by the acrimonious debates over the Spanish peace treaty in the Senate. It is doubtful that the annexation of the Philippines and Guam would have been approved had it not been tied directly to the general peace settlement. The Senate simply did not want to reject the entire treaty. America thus acquired one of its two major Pacific possessions not by Machiavellian manipulation, but rather by default.

The ambivalence of American official opinion with regard to overseas imperialism had been shown earlier by the peace commissioners. The Spanish government was in no position to refuse U.S. demands concerning its Pacific possessions, so the Caroline, Marshall, and Mariana Islands were there for the taking. But U.S. representatives made no such demands. Guam was reluctantly claimed because some naval officials believed it would serve as an advanced coaling station. Furthermore, the Americans did not protest when the German Foreign Office, taking full advantage of Spain's weakness, concluded treaties giving Germany possession of islands that would cost the United States dearly in blood and treasure four decades later.

American interest in Asia proper continued to be important for a few entrepreneurs, but hardly enough to bring the government in conflict with the Japanese. China, stumbling toward revolution and near chaos, would have been an easy victim for the extension of foreign control inward from European coastal bases. The Boxer Rebellion had demonstrated the ineffectiveness of the government dominated by the dowager empress. The American proposal of an "Open Door" succeeded only because it suited the concerned European states and Japan and did not mean a great increase in American investment in that troubled land. President William Taft's "Dollar Diplomacy" ultimately failed because it was seized upon by his political opponents and because it aroused the enmity of Britain and Germany who feared, without much reason, for their local monopolies. Important for the future of Japanese-American relations, however, was the missionary activity in China. Although efforts to Christianize large numbers of Chinese failed, hundreds of American and European missionaries experienced localized success. The missionaries reported their achievements—as well as their trials and tribulations—to their home societies. Later they and some of their converts would play crucial roles in reporting the depredations of Japanese armies in the years immediately prior to American entry into World War II.

The onset of World War I presented Japanese expansionists with unique opportunities. As early as 1902, the government had allied itself with Britain. Almost immediately after the war started, Japanese expeditionary forces landed on the all but defenseless German Pacific holdings and mounted what was to be a successful attack upon Tsingtao, the main German base on the Chinese mainland. Having secured these coveted areas, the Japanese were not content to wait out the war to secure permanently further advantages in Asia. China, deeply divided between rival revolutionary factions, was in no position to resist militarily Japanese ambitions as stated in the famous Twenty-One Demands of January 1915. Had these been granted, Japan would have severely compromised China's sovereignty and wrecked America's celebrated Open Door policy. Backed by the warring allied powers, the United States was able to curb the Japanese demands. However, during the summer of 1917, Viscount Kikujiro Ishii, on a special mission to the United States to discuss the full range of questions related to China, secured from Secretary of State Robert Lansing recognition of Japan's "special interests" in China.

The next overt move by the Japanese was at the Versailles peace conference. Japan's delegates wanted to have their de facto occupation of the ex-German territories and their paramount economic position in Shantung Province recognized. Their request followed Italy's demand for Fiume. Both were anathema to President Woodrow Wilson because they violated his ideas of self-determination. But the Japanese had gained Britain's support for their position with a secret agreement calling for Japanese support of Britain's claim to other ex-German territories in the South Pacific. Faced with the possibility that the peace conference might collapse if Italy and Japan walked out, Wilson and the American delegation backed down. American observers did not forget, however, and the more extreme newspapers were filled with stories concerning the "yellow peril."

The Japanese were not paragons of virtue. Many of their officials, particularly army officers, were aggressive and overbearing. Their maltreatment of Chinese civilians in the 1930s was reprehensible in the extreme, and the savage pillaging of Nanking remains one of the most brutal acts perpetrated by a victorious army. Those atrocities were yet to come, but the American press in the 1920s, particularly the Hearst papers, inflamed the public with horror stories hinting at a Japanese conspiracy to dominate Asia and warning of a possible attack on the United States. This mythmaking went far in creating in the minds of readers a fear of Japanese goals. Generally ignorant of world affairs, particularly Asian problems, they were prepared to believe the newspaper accounts. Thus, even when Japanese actions were reasonable—or at least no more reprehensible than those of other nations—many American opinion makers maligned Japanese motives.

From the perspective of the Japanese government, it seemed that the United States was unnecessarily intervening in affairs in which it had little specific, concrete interest, and was arbitrarily opposing legitimate Japanese goals. Another factor alienating the two states in the 1920s was the overt racism evident in Japanese-American relations. California was at the forefront of actions to limit Japanese immigration. In 1907, San Francisco school boards refused to permit Japanese children to attend classes. The ensuing Japanese protests eventually led to the so-called Gentleman's Agreement, a series of communications between the two governments in which the Japanese ceased to issue passports to citizens hoping to emigrate. But the issue was far from dead. In 1913, a major crisis developed when California proposed state legislation barring Japanese from owning land. This, coupled with personal affronts to many Japanese residents, caused giant protest movements to be organized throughout Japan, and the Japanese government appealed to the new Wilson administration to take action. Despite Washington's pleas to the contrary, an exclusionary law was passed, although it was worded in such a way that it appeared not to be directly aimed at the Japanese. But it was, and Japanese officials knew it. Their communications to Washington clearly showed how much they resented the California legislation.

The immigration question simmered for another decade, until the debates on the proposed new federal Immigration Act of 1924. Although the legislation would allow foreign nations to send 2 percent of the number of their citizens who had entered the United States in 1890, the act proposed to bar completely the entry of "aliens ineligible for citizenship." Ambassador Masanao Hanihara was invited to share with Congress his understanding of the Gentleman's Agreement and his thoughts on how the Japanese should be treated.

Some unfortunate harsh language in his note was seized upon by the anti-Japanese press, however, and Congress, reflecting the same attitude, refused to compromise on the exclusionary segments of the legislation. Japanese exclusion was passed overwhelmingly by both Houses and signed into law by President Calvin Coolidge. The government and people of Japan viewed the Immigration Act of 1924 as a deliberate insult, the Japanese press denounced the "outrageous enactment," and a move to boycott American goods was begun. The day the law became effective was declared a day of national humiliation. Millions of Japanese citizens would never forgive this affront, and it became a part of their long list of grievances against the United States.

Grievances with more substance than the racism implicit in U.S. immigration laws were those involving allowable comparative strengths of the world's major navies as determined by the Washington disarmament conference. Convened at the behest of Secretary of State Charles Evans Hughes, the conference opened on 12 November 1921 and concluded its business the following February. The focus of the conference was the reduction of the massive naval forces that had been built up since the launching of the British battleship *Dreadnought* fifteen years before. Of almost equal importance, however, was the need felt by the United States to establish order and stability in Asia and the Pacific. The Japanese actions directed toward China during and immediately after the war appeared to the State Department to be a real threat to the Open Door policy. The Anglo-Japanese Treaty, which was scheduled to be renewed in 1922, also seemed to many to compromise the U.S. position in the Pacific, and it had the potential to disturb America's newfound friendship with Britain.

The Washington conference was a major success for the United States, although it resulted in the scrapping of more than twenty of its capital ships. Parity in major naval vessels between Britain and the United States was maintained. The other major powers were assigned lesser numbers despite the arguments of their representatives. The ratio was to be five to three between the United States and Japan.

The Japanese representatives protested most vigorously over their inferior allotment. Their government and military planners could foresee a possible alliance between the United States and Britain—which in the case of war would give these allies parity, if not outright superiority, over the Japanese navy in the central and northern Pacific. To partially compensate Japan and ease fears, Britain and the United States agreed not to fortify any of their Pacific island bases. An exception was demanded and granted in the case of Hawaii. This less publicized agreement gained greater security for the Japanese. Americans critical of the pact pointed out that the Japanese navy was recognized as dominant in the Pacific and said the agreement not to fortify U.S. Pacific bases left them vulnerable. Admiral William S. Sims noted disgustedly that someone could spit on the Philippines and the United States would be unable to stop them. Despite this obvious practical advantage, senior Japanese naval and even army officers never forgave the United States for the alleged slight of being forced to accept the naval clause.

A further blow to Japan was the proposed Four-Power Treaty, which—under pressure from the United States, Britain, and France —Japanese representatives reluctantly accepted. This agreement allowed the British government to withdraw gracefully from the Anglo-Japanese pact without seeming to abandon Japan. The treaty provided that the four powers would respect one another's rights in the Pacific and refer future disputes to a joint conference. Although vaguely worded, this section seemed also to imply the possibility of joint concerted action. Despite the injury to Japanese feelings, the Four-Power Treaty was but a reiteration of the older Anglo-Japanese agreement, strengthened by the addition of France and the United States.

Of more import to future relations between the United States and Japan was the Nine-Power Treaty proposed by the British, sponsored by the United States, and aimed at maintaining the Open Door in China. Signed in February 1922, the treaty bound the signatories to respect the sovereignty, independence, and administrative integrity of China. Japan agreed to sign only after great pressure had been exerted by Britain and the United States. The weakness of the pact was that no means was spelled out for enforcing its provisions. Its validity rested on the good faith of each of the powers. However, it appeared at that time that Japan had been reconciled with China. Two days before signing the Nine-Power Treaty, the dispute over Shantung—the major problem between the two states—had apparently been resolved. Japan also had withdrawn the more objectionable of its earlier Twenty-One Demands, evacuated Siberia, and agreed to U.S. demands for cable rights on the island of Yap. After all the quid pro quo, it is understandable why moderate diplomats on both sides of the Pacific considered most of the real differences between the two states settled.

Except for the limitation of naval power and agreement on fortification of the islands, the vast Pacific region was given little consideration by the discussants in Washington. One of the reasons for this was the general feeling by all participants that the disposition of these islands had been settled when those once controlled by Germany passed to the League of Nations's control. There was little opposition to Japan's request to have its military occupation of these islands confirmed with only nominal, perfunctory oversight by the League. Annual reports were filed and inspection teams would occasionally visit. For the most part, as with mandates throughout the world, these territories were ruled directly by and, for all practical purposes, belonged to Japan.

The Japanese, unlike their predecessors, saw in the islands a source of food and raw materials. Very soon after World War I, Japanese fishing boats began to mine the rich waters off some of the islands, and Japanese experts in many fields began to investigate how to maximize their agricultural potential. The South Sea Bureau was established in the early 1920s, thus providing a civil government for Micronesia. Development funds were provided in considerable amounts for some of the more promising areas. There the Japanese improved the docking and harbor facilities, poured miles of breakwaters, paved the main roads, and constructed two- or three-story permanent buildings to house administrative and scientific research activities. They erected fish canning factories on some islands, and on others, such as Angaur in the Palau group, they built a refinery and a railway to exploit mineral deposits. In all this, the Japanese, while utilizing some of the native people for labor, tended to leave those in the interior regions relatively alone. Instead, thousands of Japanese were resettled. The one exception to the almost purely commercial activity of the Japanese was Truk, whose lagoon provided an important natural harbor. By the mid-

1930s, they had constructed a major naval base, which in the early stages of World War II would become the most important forward anchorage for the Combined Fleet.

In the United States, a number of influential government and military officials became convinced that all Japanese activities in the Central Pacific area violated the mandate. Some of the more sensational newspapers and periodicals ran articles and commentaries pointing to the danger of the alleged Japanese military buildup. These reports increased in number after Japan's attack on Manchuria, which fueled charges of warlike intentions on the part of the Japanese government. The Japanese did nothing to challenge such reports. Almost immediately after the League of Nations confirmed the mandate, the Japanese drew a veil of secrecy over the islands. Their attempts to exclude foreign visitors, combined with their warlike posture in Asia, appeared to confirm the worst suspicions of the anti-Japanese press.

As early as the 1920s, some Americans attempted to penetrate the supposed fortresslike islands. A marine lieutenant colonel, Earl H. Ellis, posed as a traveler and visited the Palaus in 1923. He was taken into custody by the Japanese and subsequently died in the jail at Koror. This provided more grist for American journalists, who were never satisfied with the Japanese explanation that Ellis had died of a fever. An even more sensational set of stories circulated when Amelia Earhart disappeared in 1937 near the Marianas. For the next fifty years a plethora of articles and books speculated that she was on a government-authorized spy mission that was discovered by the Japanese, who somehow managed to capture her and hold her prisoner on Saipan, where she subsequently died.

Although the press may have sensationalized Japanese activity in the Pacific, most Americans in the two decades before Pearl Harbor were blissfully unaware or uncaring. Their representatives in government were also generally unconcerned. The heady days of the postwar years gave way to the depression era, and the president and Congress were almost totally committed to domestic policies. Those few members of Congress and the executive branch who took time to glance at the Pacific did not feel in any way threatened by Japan. They were convinced that the Washington treaties had solved the basic problems between the two countries, and many could see no reason to maintain a hold on the Philippines—the one place where it was most likely for the Japanese to attack. Secure in the vast distances between the United States and Japan and in the supposed superiority of the U.S. Navy, the government, despite its moral support of China in the early 1930s, was clearly unworried. What the Japanese may or may not have been doing in the mandated islands was never crucial. This is clearly shown by the lack of action by the United States and Britain when Japan withdrew from the moribund League of Nations in 1935. Japan continued its administration of those islands as if nothing had happened.

Two interconnected factors dictated American policy in the interwar period: neoisolationism and domestic economic concerns. Combined, they produced a generally quiescent foreign policy and extreme cuts in military expenditures. Thus it was not only the restrictive clauses in the Washington Treaty that kept the United States from developing more secure defenses for its Pacific possessions. Little was done even in the Philippines, and the government welcomed the move toward Philippine independence not only for moral reasons, but also because it would eliminate a financial burden as well as a potential cause for disagreement with Japan. There was some discussion about improving the defense capabilities of the islands, but it was not until 1939 that any significant amounts of money were appropriated for this purpose. Guam, Wake, and Midway were prized in the years prior to the war primarily because they were necessary links in the transpacific air traffic pioneered by Pan American Airways. By 1938, however, President Franklin D. Roosevelt and his advisers had become seriously concerned with European developments. From that time forward, despite protestations over Japanese depredations in China, the United States had a Eurocentric foreign policy. The State Department, while monitoring Japanese activity in the Far East, showed little concern with affairs there until after the disastrous events in Europe in 1940 and Japan's joining the Axis powers with the signing of the Tripartite Pact.

While events in America in the two decades before the war dictated a quiescent policy, domestic developments in Japan during the same period were even more crucial in determining Japan's foreign policy and its ultimate decision to attack the United States. Japan had reached the apogee of its economic growth by the close of World War I. During the 1920s, while the United States was enjoying unprecedented prosperity, Japanese industry was moribund; the country ran a consistent trade deficit. If it had not been for its huge colonies in Formosa, Korea, China, and the Pacific mandate, the country would have had little economic growth. As it was, with a population of more than 70 million, with a rigid class system, and with its government in turmoil, Japan was even less prepared than Western states to meet the crisis of the worldwide depression. Although Japan's population was largely made up of small farmers, there was a significant urban population that suffered greatly during the early 1930s. Both peasants and the depressed working class generally welcomed the expansionist policies enunciated by the military, which had come to dominate the government.

The government, as with so much in Japanese society, was an uneasy blend of traditional and Western. At the center of all affairs was the emperor, who was not only the head of state, but also considered divine. Japanese of all classes gave him unstinting, unquestioned loyalty. But Emperor Yoshohito, and to a greater extent his successor, the young Hirohito, was content to allow his ministers to determine domestic and foreign policy. In much the same way as the king of England, he reigned but did not rule. This was not necessarily constitutionally determined, but was rather a matter of choice. Hirohito chose not to exert his executive or divine prerogatives to check what his government was doing. Japan's foreign policy was thus dictated by an oligarchy, despite the dual fiction of a divine emperor and a legislature patterned on Western models. This is not to suggest that there was not a strong liberal movement in the ruling circles of Japan, but in the upheavals of the 1920s and early 1930s, the liberals were largely silenced by the militarists.

The emperor's silence on key issues allowed every self-proclaimed patriot to decide for himself what Hirohito wanted. An oriental version of national socialism called *Kodo-Ha,* "the Way of the Emperor," thus developed. Superpatriots, mainly junior officers in the army and navy, who came from lower middle-class backgrounds joined secret societies whose aims were to restore military supremacy over the liberals at home and to continue Japanese conquests abroad. These sons of the middle class vied with the descendents of the samurai in promoting Bushido, the ancient warrior code. Theoreticians such as Ikki Kita gave a modern underpinning to the ancient concept of warriors conquering for the good of the emperor. He proposed a number of radical programs, the most important being the abolition of parliament, the dominance of the army, and freeing Japan's Asiatic brethren from white domination. Japanese hegemony over Asia would ultimately lead Japan to dominate the world. Such ideas were eagerly absorbed by young officers who came to believe that anyone who opposed the military, particularly the army, was an enemy of the emperor. American actions during the Versailles peace conference and the Washington disarmament conference, coupled with passage of the Immigration Act reinforced the Japanese belief that their destiny ran counter to American policy. To them, the United States was already the enemy.

The decade after parliament's refusal to provide sufficient funds for the army, which had caused it to withdraw from Siberia, was a time of ferment within the armed forces. Elements within the army planned a coup against the liberal ministry responsible for the Japanese retreat from Siberia and acceptance of the inferior naval ratios presumably dictated by the Western powers. However, the great earthquake of 1923 interrupted those plans. Western aid in the wake of that disaster assured a brief period of good feelings among most Japanese, but the onset of the depression brought the extremists in the army once again to the fore. One idea prevalent among right-wing elements was that Japan's future was tied directly to expanding its control over Asia. They wanted to begin by ridding Manchuria of China's tenuous influence. General Senjuro Hayashi, commanding Japanese forces in Korea, was in full agreement. Despite orders to the contrary, he moved his army into Manchuria in September 1931 in the wake of a bomb explosion on the tracks of the South Manchurian Railway. Even the War Department was not informed of what was going on in Manchuria. Ultimately the Foreign Office, believing it had no other viable choice, accepted the military action. Since a state of war with China existed, this gave the military constitutional control over the government. From that time onward, the real rulers of Japan were the ultraconservative military officers, most of whom were army men. Naval officers were never as rabid, nor did they have the power that senior army officers came to possess.

The Manchurian episode was the beginning of full-scale Japanese aggression in Asia. As a result, Japan became increasingly isolated in the world community. The United States took the lead in condemning Japan. Secretary of State Henry L. Stimson stated in January 1932 that America would never recognize any treaty or agreement gained by force. The Japanese responded by creating a puppet regime in the so-called nation of Manchukuo, and retaliated against the Chinese boycott of Japanese goods by landing troops in Shanghai. Having vented themselves on the Chinese troops and civilians there with a savagery that would later become well known, the Japanese troops were withdrawn in May. The League of Nations received the report of its special commission in September, which branded the Japanese as aggressors. In reaction, the Japanese government withdrew from the League in March 1933.

At the same time that the Manchurian affair was unfolding, the ultramilitarists were further consolidating their power in Tokyo by assassinating those persons within the government believed to be hostile to Japanese expansion. The minister of finance, the manager of the Mitsui interests, and, surprisingly, seventy-five-year-old Prime Minister Tsuyoshi Inukai were all killed. This method of intimidation was repeated again in February 1936, only with more high-level government officials targeted. Once again the trigger was the refusal of the finance minister to increase army appropriations to support Japanese aggression in China. The lord privy seal, the army inspector general, and a number of lesser officials were killed. The main target—the prime minister, Adm. Keisuke Okada —escaped when assassins shot his brother-in-law by mistake. The American ambassador, Joseph Grew, had also been marked for death but escaped unscathed. The conspirators hoped that by killing him they could precipitate war with the United States.

Most Japanese in the government who might have opposed more military expenditures and the planned all-out attack on China were intimidated. After two brief cabinets failed to form a consensus, Prince Fumimaro Konoye was called upon to be prime minister.

Although he personally disagreed with the plan to attack China, like his emperor he did nothing to stop the militarists. Conversion of industry to war production was sped up, tax forgiveness was given to producers of heavy equipment, government loans were made available to manufacturers, and a five-year program of warship construction was begun. On 7 July 1937, when the army was finally ready, it precipitated a clash between Japanese troops on maneuvers and a Chinese outpost on the Marco Polo Bridge near Peiping. The militarists had finally achieved what they wanted. But as events were to prove, the war begun by design and without provocation would prove to be one of the main reasons for Japan's eventual defeat. Not only would Japanese action there predispose the United States to react in ways that led to the attack on Pearl Harbor, but Japan could never extricate substantial forces from China and Manchuria during the subsequent conflict with the United States.

China, deeply divided politically, was in no condition to effectively resist the well-trained Japanese armies. Chiang Kai-shek's army, even the elite "Generalissimo's Own" three-hundred-thousand-man force, proved no match for the Japanese. By December 1937, the Kuomintang had virtually abandoned all five provinces north of the Yellow River to the Japanese. The one place that Chiang established a major defense was at Shanghai, and it took the Japanese three months and the loss of more than forty thousand men to capture the city and district. They then proceeded up the Yangtze Valley and, after a desperate fight, took the city of Nanking. There the victorious general rewarded his troops by allowing them to run amok, raping and murdering, for more than a month. The Western world, not yet jaded by the wanton acts to come, watched in horror as more than a quarter of a million innocent civilians were slaughtered. Following the loss of Nanking, the Nationalists lost most of their major coastal cities in 1938, including Hankow, Chenchow, and Canton. The Japanese armies of the north and south had linked up by the late summer, but Chiang refused to surrender. With the forces still available, he fell back into the deep interior and established a new capital at Chungking. Although the Japanese had gained the most productive areas of China, final victory was thus denied them. The stalemate would continue to the end of World War II.

The actions of the Japanese armies in China, a portent of things to come, were unnecessarily brutal. These were reported in detail by Western observers—particularly missionaries, the majority of whom were American. The Japanese controlled the air, and attacks upon defenseless cities that caused thousands of civilian casualties appeared at the time to be but an extension of an innate barbarity. Despite the feeble efforts of the Japanese Foreign Office to dissuade the army from attacking American missions, by 1940 hundreds of churches, hospitals, and schools had been bombed. It appeared as if there was a concerted plan to drive Americans out of China.

The most blatant attack on Americans in China occurred in December 1937. On the eleventh, the USS *Panay,* one of five gunboats maintained by the U.S. Navy on the Yangtze River, took on board the last members of the diplomatic staff in Nanking and slowly made its way upriver escorting three Standard Oil Company barges. It was taken under fire by Japanese shore batteries, then attacked the following day by a flight of more than twenty planes and sunk. The planes even strafed the lifeboats after the *Panay* was abandoned. Two oil barges were also sunk. They, like the *Panay,* plainly flew the American flag. The pilots of the strafing planes obviously knew that the ships were not Chinese, as the Japanese government later insisted. Three Americans were killed and eleven seriously wounded. The survivors were taken on board other ships, and within hours the U.S. government and media learned of the attack.

In a strange scenario, the United States, which had suffered from the unprovoked attack, did nothing to avenge the bombing. This disappointed the more militant Japanese expansionists. Men who belonged to the *Kodo-Ha* movement had hoped for a war that would give the military an excuse to wipe away the last vestiges of civilian participation in the government. Much to the chagrin of some American newspaper publishers, all that President Roosevelt demanded was an apology and indemnification for the attack. He accepted the Japanese explanation that the attack was a mistake.

From the moment of Japan's assault on China, the United States had taken the lead in trying to resolve the war. Soon after hostilities began, delegates from the United States and eighteen other nations met in Brussels to consider ways to end the conflict. The conference, without a Japanese representative present, issued a declaration affirming the Nine-Power Treaty and asking for a suspension of hostilities and mediation to find an equitable settlement. Not surprisingly, Japan refused to consider these suggestions, reiterating that the "China Incident" was its exclusive affair. As the war dragged on, the American government increased its support, directly and indirectly, to China. Economic support generally took the form of large loans. President Roosevelt refused to invoke the Neutrality Act, thus making possible the delivery of increasing amounts of munitions and other war materiel over the long, tortuous Burma Road. American sympathies for China were expressed in a variety of ways. One of the most romantic, yet practical, was the formation of the American Volunteer Group (AVG), the famed Flying Tigers, whose pilots, flying P-40 fighter aircraft, gave China an air force capable of challenging the dominant Japanese bomber formations.

The growing sympathy for China and increased materiel support, however, did not mean stopping the shipment to Japan of vast amounts of scrap iron, petroleum products, and other raw materials that could be converted into weapons. Ambassador Grew repeatedly cautioned Washington not to cut off Japan's access to petroleum, iron, tin, and other strategic materials. He was convinced that if that occurred, Japan would seriously consider sending its armies into the Dutch East Indies and Malaya to obtain them. President Roosevelt and Secretary of State Cordell Hull obviously agreed. Even though the 1911 commercial treaty with Japan had lapsed by January 1940, the U.S. government did not attempt to embargo exports. However, on 25 July 1940, the president announced a ban on the export of oil and scrap metal except by firms licensed by the government. Five days later, the sale of aviation gasoline was restricted to the Western Hemisphere. Although not specifically aimed at the Japanese, these restrictions were the first steps toward a complete embargo of trade with Japan.

What had changed the president's mind? In January he was in favor of continuing the two-decades-old policy of appeasement, but six months later he restricted trade of strategic materials in a way that could only damage the Japanese war effort. The answer appears to be the unexpected success of Axis forces in Europe during the spring and summer of 1940—combined with Roosevelt's limited success in improving America's military posture. A factor that remained constant during the decade after 1935 was the Eurocentric nature of U.S. policy. Although ostensibly isolationist and neutral, Americans viewed the actions of Italy and Germany with growing alarm. Once the war in Europe had begun, the government began inching slowly away from a strict neutralist stance. Hitler's lightning war in the west leading to quick victories over Belgium, Holland, and France in the spring of 1940 was an important catalyst for speeding up industrial production in the United States intended to help Britain stave off defeat.

The German victories also had a profound effect upon Japanese foreign policy. Prince Konoye, who had been out of power, returned as prime minister in July. Within four days of its formation, the cabinet unanimously approved a new national policy whose general aim was a "new order in Greater East Asia." The most dominant members of Konoye's government were Lt. Gen. Hideki Tojo as minister of war, and the brilliant, but erratic militant Yosuke Matsuoka as foreign minister. Matsuoka believed that Britain was on the verge of defeat and that Japan should take every possible advantage from the fall of France. The hapless Vichy French government in Indochina was pressured to sign a convention in Hanoi allowing Japan to set up air bases in the northern part of the country. The United States became fully aware of Japanese sub-rosa activities in Thailand, and at the same time, the Japanese ambassador in Washington queried the State Department concerning the future of the Dutch East Indies.

For President Roosevelt, Britain's desperate situation dictated speeding aid to that beleaguered nation. Loopholes in the law were found enabling large amounts of World War I equipment, including badly needed airplanes, to be transferred to Britain. In September 1940 the United States gave fifty old four-stack destroyers to the British in exchange for ninety-nine-year leases on naval and air bases in the Caribbean and Newfoundland. Although Roosevelt had to move slowly since the basic temper of the American public was still isolationist, he had set the nation directly on a confrontational course with Germany. His close, friendly association with Prime Minister Winston Churchill, which became such a dominant feature of decision making later on, was already formed.

Meanwhile, the United States was belatedly beginning to repair the damage to its armed forces caused by twenty years of neglect. Congress, hesitant to stir up public opinion, had nevertheless voted more than $17 billion for rearmament. In September 1940, after heated debate, Congress also agreed to the first peacetime draft in the history of the United States. In December, Roosevelt went much farther in his support of Britain by proposing the Lend-Lease Act, which was approved the following March.

The final linkage between Japan and the Axis was the work of Matsuoka. He was convinced that Germany would soon win the European war, and he wanted to quickly work out a reasonable agreement with Hitler that would allow Japan a free hand in Asia. On 27 September 1940, he concluded the Tripartite Pact, which Secretary Hull interpreted as a bluff. Nevertheless, it was obvious that the pact was aimed at the United States.

Matsuoka followed that triumph with lengthy negotiations with the Soviet Union that culminated in the Neutrality Pact signed in April 1941. This latter pact was absolutely necessary to prevent a possible Soviet attack on Manchuria if the Japanese decided to move into the Dutch East Indies or Malaya. Japan had every reason to fear the Soviet Union after border clashes in 1937 and 1939 had demonstrated the power of Russia's Far Eastern army.

Still, China remained the major stumbling block between Japan and the United States. The United States was firmly committed to the financial support of China. In early December 1940, Congress made $50 million in credits available to Chiang's government to stabilize the currency. At the same time, Japan recognized a puppet regime in Nanking as the de jure government of China. The Japanese government and news media denounced U.S. aid to China and bluntly advised America to mind its own business. Thus, at the beginning of the crucial year of 1941, the two nations were much farther apart than in previous years, although the only new factor was Tokyo's adherence, at least in form, to the Axis. However, the rhetoric had become more strident, and Japan's ambition to dominate Asia was at last openly avowed.

The closer alignment of the United States to Britain and the Dutch government in exile made President Roosevelt and his secretary of state more concerned than ever about a possible attack upon their

Far East possessions. While coveting those mineral and petroleum rich areas, the Japanese knew that such an attack in all probability would mean war with the United States—a war that, despite the posturings, few in Japan wanted. How each government managed to compromise the complex differences during 1941 would determine whether the fitful peace in the Pacific would endure or whether, despite protestations on both sides, there would be war. If it came to the latter, the vast Pacific region that had played such a minor role in bringing on the conflict would assume primacy. The armed forces in both Japan and the United States had envisioned such a war as one in which their navies would have a leading role, and each had increased its military expenditures for that branch. But if there was any consensus among the naval commanders on both sides, it was that there would be no war. The actions of both governments, particularly in the summer and fall of 1941, negated those expert opinions. For the Japanese, war became the most viable option.

Chapter 2

Isolationism and Complacency

THE AGGRESSIVE DIPLOMATIC stance taken by the United States after the defeat of France in 1940 belied its weak military position. The chief reason for this unpreparedness was the decade-long depression that had so intensely focused government and public opinion on the country's many domestic problems. Requests for increased military appropriations were postponed as the deeply troubled nation sought to repair its economic system. Supporting these fiscal attitudes was the assurance by many of the nation's leaders that, protected as they were by two wide oceans, Americans need not fear invasion.

As late as the eve of World War II, the prevalent attitude was that all would be well if the government would simply refrain from unwarranted interference in European and Asian affairs. Important blocs in both the Senate and the House of Representatives opposed most of the government's feeble attempts to upgrade the armed forces during the 1930s. Charles A. Lindbergh, later ostracized for his views, echoed the prevailing public opinion when he opposed U.S. involvement in the world's troubled areas.

The army bore the brunt of the neoisolationism in the two decades following America's rejection of the Versailles Treaty. Its authorized strength in 1940 was only 150,000 men, placing the

United States on a par with Portugal in terms of the size of its army. Economics aside, few Americans saw a need for a large standing force. The public was imbued with a deeply ingrained belief that citizen soldiers, not professionals, had won American independence, conquered Mexico, and preserved the Union. World War I further bolstered that belief. The draft had provided in a matter of months over four million men. A million of them, after minimal training, performed admirably in France, defeating the presumably professional, Junker-led German army at Soissons, Château-Thierry, Saint-Mihiel, and in the bloody Argonne Forest.

Forgotten in this reasoning was the shortage of American-made equipment, Allied efforts, and Germany's decline. Doughboys had generally carried British rifles and depended upon French automatic weapons and artillery. Tanks and combat aircraft were also borrowed from the Allies whose huge armies bore the heaviest share of the fighting. Finally, there was the condition of the German army itself—worn down as it was by four long years of fighting. The German units facing the American First and Second Armies in 1918 were far from the efficient fighting machines that had marched so confidently into France.

Despite the obvious examples of American weakness prior to the war and its dependence for arms on its Allies, the myth of the natural superiority of a citizen army persisted. Government penury during the interwar years almost killed military research and development in such vital areas as aircraft and tanks. Thus the army in 1940 was in much the same poor condition it had been prior to its entry into World War I in April 1917.

Although America's 1898 war with Spain had clearly shown the need for close coordination between the army and navy, no serious effort was made to combine the separate war and navy departments. A joint army-navy board was established in 1903 to attempt to reconcile differing military plans, but it was so ineffectual that by 1914 it ceased to function. Yet it was resurrected after World War I. Nevertheless, interservice rivalry continued to plague war planners until the conditions encountered after Pearl Harbor dictated that a means be found to coordinate war policy.

The most far-reaching reforms in the military prior to World War II were those instituted by Secretary of War Elihu Root in 1903.

The basic structure of the army command system resulting from those reforms remained relatively unchanged until the pressures created by complex, worldwide commitments forced modifications after Pearl Harbor. Root's 1903 reforms, supplemented by others in 1916, did away with the post of commanding general of the army and substituted a chief of staff subordinate to the secretary of war. This abolished the direct command relationship between the military chief and the president that had caused so many problems in the last third of the nineteenth century. The once powerful administrative offices of the Adjutant General, Inspector General, Quartermaster General, Medical Department, Payroll Department, Signal Corps, and Corps of Engineers were retained, but the chief of staff "supervised" these bureaus. Almost immediately the bureaus, which had oftentimes functioned at cross purposes, found that supervision meant control. By the end of the 1930s, the chief of staff's office was not only responsible for providing war plans, but had assumed the function of controlling all army activities. The chief of staff's term of office was tied directly to that of a serving president to avoid any inherent conflict between the army command and an incoming chief executive.

The army reforms, born in part from the debacle of the Spanish-American War, proved durable and flexible. Legislation and practice in the nearly four decades after they were proposed by Secretary Root had solidified the overall army command system. Although the army during World War II would expand greatly in size, its fundamental organization remained unchanged. Under the direction of one of its most able leaders, Gen. George C. Marshall, the army met the severe challenges of the most complex, far-flung war in the nation's history.

An important strength of the interwar army was its officer corps. Denied adequate funds to modernize the forces or even to keep abreast of second tier military powers, those few, dedicated men, most of whom were West Point graduates, took every opportunity to improve their skills on both the practical and theoretical levels. Fortunately, due to pressures generated in the late nineteenth century for more professionalism, a series of branch schools had been established. A junior officer who expected to advance in the ranks had to plan on attending the schools in his field. The Army War

College was established in 1901, and the Command and General Staff School later was set up at Fort Leavenworth, Kansas. Both schools provided graduate-level instruction. Numerous specialist schools were established, the most important located at Forts Belvoir, Virginia; Sill, Oklahoma; and Benning, Georgia. Flight training was centered at Randolph and Kelly Fields in Texas for the army, and Pensacola Naval Air Station, Florida, for the navy and marines.

Rotation from the line to staff duty or teaching positions kept officers abreast of the latest thinking in their respective branches. In the 1920s, far-seeing leaders such as Brig. Gen. Douglas Mac-Arthur broke the exclusivity of the service academies by inviting brilliant, qualified nonacademy graduates to teach at West Point, Annapolis, and the higher-level service schools. A few of the brightest were selected to attend such foreign schools as France's École de guerre or Germany's Kriegsakademie. Promotions were distressingly slow. It took Eisenhower, Bradley, Patton, and many others almost twenty years to regain the rank they had held temporarily at the end of World War I. Yet despite all the financial and professional problems that might have distracted its members, the army officer corps at the beginning of World War II was the most professional in the nation's history, and provided the senior commanders for the largest force ever fielded by the United States.

Still, the army had a number of problems unrelated to the low level of financial support provided, although that remained crucial. Perhaps the most important inhibiting factor was the conservative nature of most senior officers. This can be seen clearly in their attitudes toward the use of tanks and aircraft. They tended to be suspicious of new weapons or tactical innovations. Perhaps it was inevitable that they would dictate training regimens, plan for a future conflict, and request funds based upon their experiences and those of the Allies in the most recent war. Since that war apparently had been won by a combination of infantry assaults backed by massive artillery preparations against stationary defenses, it was natural that these two combat arms were considered to be key to victory in any conflict that might arise. Because of this, most senior officers overlooked the important part played by British and French tanks in the war's final offensives and assigned a low priority to tank development. Even more serious was their downplaying of the role of armor in a future conflict. The National Defense Act of 1920 specifically prohibited the creation of a separate tank corps. Proponency for tanks was given to the infantry branch. Later, Brig. Gen. Adna R. Chaffee Jr., the most vocal proponent of armor in the 1930s, lobbied for better equipment and select officers imbued with the goal of ultimately establishing a separate armored force. In the former he was only moderately successful. Only a comparative handful of lightly armored, undergunned American tanks were built during the 1920s and 1930s. The bulk of the U.S. tank force during that period, especially in the twenties, was made up of surplus World War I British heavy tanks and American-made copies of the French Renault light tank. This failure to design and construct more advanced tanks meant that even after rearmament sped up in late 1940, manufacturers did not have the facilities to construct tanks equal to those used by the Germans. The best example of this inadequacy was the placement of the main gun in a hull-mounted sponson on the General Grant tank because the machinery needed to build a larger turret was not available.

Chaffee did, however, manage to inspire a cadre of dedicated officers and men, mainly from the cavalry, who would lead the early armored units in World War II. As late as March 1940, despite General Marshall's support, the army staff recommended against the creation of a separate armored force. The formation of the first armored units on the eve of World War II was directly attributable to Marshall overriding his G3. The Armored Force was thus born, and Chaffee was promoted to major general and commanded it until his death in August 1941.

The American army, professional though its junior and midrange officers might have been, was severely handicapped not only by inferior armored equipment, but also because too few men had been trained in such vital areas as infantry-tank cooperation in the attack. Although a serious handicap, the lack of attention to tank warfare in the United States was paralleled by similar attitudes in France and Britain, where policy makers turned a deaf ear to such vocal proponents of mechanization as Charles de Gaulle, B. H. Liddell Hart, and Maj. Gen. J. F. C. Fuller. It was not until Hitler, a military amateur, gave his support to Gen. Heinz Guderian and other experimentalists that senior German officers became committed to swift-striking armored attacks. The methods they used to crush Poland and later France finally awakened American military planners to the need for better equipment and tactics. The army then attempted to build competitive tanks and to organize and train two armored divisions in a critically short period of time.

Conservative generals, believing that infantry and artillery would win any future war, argued that tanks and airplanes were fads. Because of this, the equipment they provided to the tankers and aviators was far from adequate. The basic weapons issued to most infantrymen in 1940 were the same as those carried in France two decades before. The standard rifle was a 1917 adaptation of the .30 caliber British Enfield, although many units retained the dependable .30 caliber 1903 Springfield. The semiautomatic .30 caliber M1 Garand, which became the workhorse of the infantry in World War II, was in the development stage until 1936, when it was adopted as the replacement for the older bolt-action rifles. Unfortunately, as late as 1941, many units had not received the new weapon. Automatic fire was provided by the Browning Automatic Rifle, a 1918 vintage weapon, and the reliable .30 caliber Browning M1917AL water-cooled machine gun. The sidearm authorized for officers was the .45 caliber M1911 automatic pistol, which had great striking power but questionable accuracy.

The French 75mm gun, the mainstay of the light artillery in World War I, had by 1940 been phased out except in a version modified for use as a pack howitzer. By then the army had developed the 105mm M2 medium howitzer and the heavier 155mm M2 "Long Tom" gun. Yet, as late as the autumn 1940 maneuvers, many units had to make do with simulated field pieces made of wood.

Another crucial area where conservative thinkers shortchanged the military during the interwar period was in their lack of vision regarding the importance of airpower in future wars. Military planners in the 1920s and early 1930s chose to be very selective in their analysis of the previous conflict. While the various important land battles of World War I were intensely studied at West Point, the War College, and in the Command and General Staff School, the role of aircraft was minimized or entirely ignored.

The fragile, slow-moving airplanes of 1914 had evolved within four years into fast, maneuverable pursuit planes capable of speeds well over 100 mph. Observation, which had at first been the airplane's primary task, had been vastly improved by the development of better cameras and trained cadres of observers. Nor had the design of bombers been neglected. Two-, and even four-, engine bombers were available to all Allied forces in considerable numbers before the 1918 summer offensives began. More importantly, what had once been simply a sporting game between knights of the sky had become very serious business. Pursuit squadrons after 1916 had altered their tactics to minimize lone wolf heroics and to mass large numbers of aircraft over a given sector. Commanders like England's Air Marshal Hugh M. "Boom" Trenchard and America's Brig. Gen. William "Billy" Mitchell saw the airplane as a type of flying artillery whose major tasks were direct support of an attack and striking deep behind enemy lines at strategic targets. Mitchell, in support of the Saint-Mihiel offensive in mid-September 1918, had a force of more than fourteen hundred American-manned aircraft borrowed from the Allies, but the fledgling Army Air Service saw its numbers dwindle rapidly during October in the bloody Meuse-Argonne campaign.

The combination of a penurious government and a conservative military struck directly at the army's air arm during the interwar period. While commercial aviation was making great advances and individual exploits seized the nation's interest, the equipment supplied to the Army Air Corps was old and outdated. The clash between army leaders, bolstered by the prestige of Gen. John J. Pershing, and the modernists came to a head in 1925 when Mitchell, reduced in rank to colonel for his outspoken criticism, invited a court-martial by accusing his superiors of treason.

Mitchell felt driven to this by the attitude of both army and navy senior officers who had ignored what he and his men had done two years before. Challenged to show that aircraft could sink capital ships, Mitchell conducted an experiment in which his planes sank a destroyer, a cruiser, and the supposedly unsinkable German battleship *Ostfriesland*. He followed up this demonstration with successful attacks on other old capital ships, showing clearly the vulnerability of large warships to air attack. The dilatory attitudes of his superiors convinced Mitchell he should publicize the folly of current military policy. The furor raised by his court-martial, however, did not produce a verdict favorable to him or provide more and better equipment for the Air Corps. He was found guilty and discharged from the service. General MacArthur, a member of the court-martial board and no great supporter of airpower at the time, was the only officer to vote against his conviction.

Nevertheless, Mitchell's protégés carried on the frustrating task of upgrading the air arm. The government's decision to have military flyers carry the mail resulted in a number of crashes and drew attention to the outdated equipment. By the mid-1930s, although the Air Corps's size remained miniscule, frontline aircraft types were significantly better. Some of the prototypes not yet accepted were comparable to the best in the world. The Air Corps managed to convince Congress to appropriate money for the development of a long-range heavy bomber by using the argument that such a plane would be basically defensive, extending the distance from America's shores where an enemy fleet could be located and destroyed. This decision resulted in contracts that led directly to not one, but two four-engine bombers, the Boeing B-17 Flying Fortress and the Consolidated B-24 Liberator, that would carry the brunt of offensive action during World War II.

As with the ground forces, the air arm was blessed with an officer corps that compared favorably with the best in the world. The training regimen devised by Mitchell and his successors had three parts: primary, basic, and advanced. Standards for entry into flight school were very high because budget constraints permitted only a limited number of volunteers to be admitted. By the time a cadet had successfully completed his training at Randolph and Kelly Fields and been assigned to a bomber or fighter squadron, he was already an accomplished pilot. The record of Army Air Corps units, despite inadequate equipment in the early phases of World War II, was a testament to the thorough training program. Despite the manifold increase in the size of the army's air arm during the war, the basic pattern of training established during the interwar period was not significantly altered.

America's first-line aircraft at the outset of World War II in Europe were, with the exception of heavy bombers, generally inferior to those of the other major powers. Germany's Messerschmitt Me 109, Britain's Supermarine Spitfire, and Japan's Mitsubishi A6M2 Zero each could outperform the pursuit aircraft flown by U.S. Army pilots. The best army fighter of the period, the Curtiss P-40 Tomahawk, succeeded in China largely because of the skill of the AVG's pilots and the fact that they intercepted mostly Japanese bombers and second-class fighters. The Bell P-39 Airacobra and Brewster F2A Buffalo both operated at a handicap in later combat against the Japanese. The Douglas B-18 bomber was slowly being replaced by the B-17 which, after many significant modifications, became the backbone of the strategic bomber force during the war.

The Air Corps was blessed by the existence of a healthy, growing civilian aircraft sector. There was a quantum leap in the airframe and powerplant industries during the 1930s, and the recently established airlines took full advantage of these developments. Planes such as the long-range "China Clipper" and the Douglas DC-3, destined to become the workhorse of the army's Air Transport Command, had allowed the establishment of air transport routes throughout the United States. Overseas travel also became commonplace. Thus the technology to build larger and faster aircraft was already in place. All that was needed was to shift this technology to the mass production of a wide variety of military aircraft. By the end of the 1930s, this was already taking place. Urged on by a concerned government, private firms had begun to develop superior aircraft of all types. Prototypes of the Lockheed P-38 Lightning, Republic P-47 Thunderbolt, Grumman F4F Wildcat, Martin B-26 Marauder, and North American B-25 Mitchell had all been test flown. Although few in number, these and other models were already available and there was no need in many cases for the long period necessary to design and test them. All that was needed was a signal from the government to proceed to large-scale production.

Although tight budgets had a definite effect upon the development and construction of naval vessels and equipment, the navy was far better prepared for war in 1940 than was the army. The main reason was that ever since President Cleveland's first administration, the navy had been viewed as America's first line of defense. Ships were seen by the nation's leaders as an extension of the coastal defense system established in the late nineteenth century. Construction of a first-class navy had been given top priority by Theodore Roosevelt, who was committed to making the United States an imperial power. After the Great White Fleet had been rendered obsolete by the construction of the newer *Dreadnought*-class battleships, Congress agreed to expend vast sums to upgrade the navy. By the end of World War I, America had almost achieved parity in capital ships with Great Britain.

The navy's actions in the war with Spain were neither heroic nor efficient. However, the destruction of the outmoded and outgunned Spanish fleets at Manila Bay by Commodore Dewey and off Santiago in Cuba by RAdm. William T. Sampson caught the imagination of the American public and helped mask the urgent need to upgrade the navy's command system. Thus, while Secretary Root was making fundamental changes in the army's organization, the navy did little to correct its own until 1915. Even then, the change was minimal. The main question was the relative power of the technocrats, who controlled important boards such as the Bureau of Ships, and the line officers, who in many cases had to accept critical decisions with which they did not agree. The General Board, established in 1900 and given primary responsibility for making war plans, encroached upon the technocrats' preserve, and the debate over relative authority went on for more than thirty years. It was not resolved until after Pearl Harbor.

An act of Congress in 1915 created the position of chief of naval operations (CNO). Although this in some ways improved the naval command structure, it did not eliminate all of the problems. The chief of naval operations, unlike his army counterpart, did not have wide-ranging powers. The CNO's authority was limited to planning and executing naval operations in preparation for war and ostensibly supervising the various bureaus. But his authority overlapped that of the bureau chiefs and the commander in chief of the U.S. fleet. The latter was a line commander who supervised the commanders of the Pacific and Atlantic fleets. Generally, the commander in chief exercised his authority only when he was present at major fleet maneuvers. It was assumed that in time of war he would exercise more direct control of both fleets. During peacetime this system worked well since there was little stress on the cumbersome, complex command system. But soon after Pearl Harbor it became obvious that the posts of commander in chief and chief of naval operations needed to be combined. In March 1942, Adm. Ernest J. King assumed both positions.

Not until well into the interwar period did anyone in authority seriously question the supremacy of the battleship in any future confrontation. In this, U.S. naval tacticians were no different than their counterparts elsewhere. Britain's launching of the fast, heavily armored big-gun *Dreadnought* class of battleships made all previous capital ships obsolete and precipitated an arms race. After much debate, Congress in 1914 authorized the construction of three new battleships to replace the pre-*Dreadnought* ships of the same name. These were the 32,000-ton *New Mexico, Idaho,* and *Mississippi.* The following year it approved the construction of the *California* and *Tennessee.* Their main armament was twelve 14-inch guns. President Wilson urged Congress in 1916 to appropriate still more funds for capital ships with the ultimate goal of having an even larger navy than Great Britain. Congress complied, and ultimately the *Colorado, Maryland,* and *West Virginia,* each mounting eight 16-inch guns, were built. Wilson's administration also gained approval for the complementary construction of cruisers and destroyers.

The postwar Washington disarmament conference resulted in the United States scrapping fifteen battleships and battle cruisers in which some $300 million had already been invested. Furthermore, all signatories to the pact agreed on a ten-year moratorium on capital ship construction. The London Naval Treaty of 1930 extended this construction hiatus for another five years.

The recalcitrance of the Japanese at the 1936 London naval conference, more than anything else, caused the failure of that international meeting to limit further ship construction. Their representative announced that by the end of that year, Japan would no longer be bound by the limits imposed by the Washington Treaty. This immediately resulted in the rapid construction of newer and larger ships by both Japan and the United States. Congress was by then more willing to listen to naval experts worried that the fifteen-year lapse in ship building had impaired the navy's ability to provide adequate defenses for a conflict in both the Atlantic and Pacific zones. The first major response to Japan's actions was the authorization in August 1937 to build the *North Carolina* class of updated battleships. The *North Carolina* and its sister ship, the *Washington,* were commissioned in the spring of 1941. In 1938 a different design of a 35,000-ton battleship, the *South Dakota,* was authorized, and in the following year construction was begun on the *Indiana, Massachusetts,* and *Alabama,* which were completed in mid-1942. Despite the earlier naval restrictions, the United States had seventeen battleships by mid-1941, the majority of which were on station in the Pacific.

There was also considerable development of smaller surface craft. American diplomats at the Washington conference had pressed for and secured a 10,000-ton limit for cruisers. American designers at first preferred building up to that limit. The first of these heavy cruisers, the *Pensacola* and *Salt Lake City,* each mounting ten 8-inch guns, were launched in 1924. This continued to be the favored configuration in the United States until the early 1930s. Other nations preferred smaller light cruisers with a main armament of 6-inch guns. However, beginning with the *Brooklyn* class, which was the counterpart of the Japanese *Mogami* cruisers, the navy ordered the construction of both heavy and light cruisers. Destroyer construction recommenced with the *Farragut* class. These vessels mounted five 5-inch guns and had eight 21-inch torpedo tubes. By the time the Japanese attacked Pearl Harbor, the U.S. Navy had 171 destroyers, of which all but 71 were of post-World War I design.

Considered by many observers to be the more conservative of the services, the navy proved to be more receptive to developing an aerial capability than was the army. Although many senior officers saw airpower as only a useful adjunct to the main battle group, during the two decades following the Versailles Treaty, the Bureau of Aeronautics oversaw the development of a series of sturdy, serviceable fighters, and torpedo and dive-bombers. In 1941 the standard shipboard offensive aircraft were the Douglas TBD Devastator torpedo bomber, the SBD Dauntless dive-bomber, and the Grumman F4F Wildcat fighter. These planes carried the burden during the first year of combat, after which they were gradually replaced by planes that had been in various stages of development when the war began.

The development of aircraft carriers was slow not only because of military and civilian opposition to the cost, but also because of the technical difficulties involved. Although a navy pilot first successfully landed on a ship in 1911, a suitable type of arresting gear was not developed until the early 1920s. This was used on the first American aircraft carrier, the *Langley,* a converted collier with a wooden flight deck built above the hull. There was storage space below the deck for a maximum of thirty-four planes. The *Langley* was accepted by the navy in 1925 after three years of trials and continued to serve as a carrier until 1937, when it was converted into an aircraft tender. The navy's next two carriers were larger and incorporated many advances discovered while operating the *Langley.* These were the *Lexington* and *Saratoga,* converted from incomplete battle cruisers. These almost identical ships were fast, with a maximum speed of thirty-three knots, and displaced 33,000 tons. Their main armament was four twin 8-inch guns. Their normal complement was seventy-eight planes, but in actual practice each could carry as many as ninety.

The first ship designed specifically as a carrier was the *Ranger.* In 1927 the General Board announced a plan to build six new carriers, one every year after 1929, each with a displacement of 13,800 tons. This would give the navy nine carriers and still be within the tonnage limits specified by the Wasington Treaty. The depression killed the plan, however. Only the keel of the *Ranger* was laid, and then not until 1931. It eventually displaced 14,500 tons and could make only twenty-nine knots, but it could handle seventy-five planes. Many problems were discovered with the design after its completion, and *Ranger* was the only one of its type built.

The next two carriers were authorized in 1932. Funded by the Public Works Administration, the 19,800-ton *Yorktown* and *Enterprise* were completed in 1937. Each was designed to handle eighty aircraft and could move at a maximum speed of thirty-three knots. Defensive armament consisted of twelve 5-inch guns and sixty-eight antiaircraft guns. The 14,500-ton *Wasp,* launched in 1939, was a smaller scale version of the *Yorktown* and *Enterprise.* By sacrificing some speed, the *Wasp*'s design enabled it to handle as many airplanes as its larger sisters. The Naval Expansion Act of 1938 provided for two more carriers of approximately 20,000 tons each. After much discussion and preliminary planning, the design for the *Hornet* emerged. The last American carrier to be built prior to Pearl Harbor, *Hornet* displaced 26,000 tons, had a top speed of thirty-three knots, and could carry ninety aircraft.

By mid-1940, the world situation had convinced all but the most die-hard isolationists that the United States should not only provide war materiel for Britain, but that it should try to improve its own armed forces, especially the navy. Congress, ignoring the statutory limit on tonnage, passed an 11 percent fleet expansion bill and a "two-ocean navy" bill. The former authorized the immediate construction of three new 27,100-ton carriers. The first of these *Essex*-class carriers became available to Adm. Chester W. Nimitz in 1943 and served as the core around which he built the huge fleet that destroyed Japanese naval power in the Central Pacific.

Naval planners and designers had provided the United States with another potent weapon whose value was proven during World War I. During the latter stages of the war, the United States had constructed a number of submarines classified as S-type boats. These small 650- to 1,000-ton boats were constructed primarily for coastal defense and had a very short range. Interior space was at a minimum and the lack of air-conditioning made the air rancid during any prolonged underwater travel. These original S types fully deserved the title "pig boats." By the 1930s, considerable advances had been made in boat design so that those longer-ranged boats ordered by the Bureau of Ships were not only larger, but substantially more livable. The first of the boats ordered during the thirties were also classified as S boats. However, submarines such as the *Squalus, Salmon,* and *Sargo* were much larger and faster than the earlier type. Additional improvements were also made in the P-type boats of 1,320 tons, which had a surface speed of twenty knots and a cruising range of twelve thousand miles. By 1934, ten boats of this type, including *Pike* and *Perch*, had been constructed. Further refinements were made in the *Tambor* and other T-class submarines, and by 1940 thirty T-class boats were under construction. The final American attack submarine designed prior to World War II was the G type. Boats such as the *Gato, Gar,* and *Grampus* were 308 feet long, displaced 1,525 tons, had ten torpedo tubes, and a surface speed of twenty knots. The G class, and later modifications that resulted in the *Albacore* class, were the standard long-range submarines produced by all American shipyards during World War II.

By 7 December 1941 the navy had 113 submarines, but only 40 were of the newer type; 64 were older boats built during World War I and 9 were unreliable cruiser-type boats dating to the mid-1920s. The majority of available submarines were deployed in Atlantic waters. Only twenty-two submarines were assigned to the Pacific in mid-1941. Fortunately, sixteen of these were the modern fleet type. In the first months after Pearl Harbor, these few American submarines played a vital role in taking the war to the enemy. However, the effectiveness of all submarine classes was severely undercut by the inadequacy of the torpedoes they carried. The steam-driven U.S. torpedoes tended to run too deep to trigger their magnetic detonators, and the alternate detonators, a contact type, also had a high failure rate. Until these defects were corrected, many otherwise successful attacks on enemy shipping proved fruitless. The unreliability of the torpedoes was also a major factor in the failure rate of American torpedo bombers until improved models arrived in the Pacific in early 1943.

Another major resource in the navy, one that would leave its mark on the war in the Pacific, was the Marine Corps. Initially formed in the eighteenth century, the corps was designed to provide a trained force capable of defending American ships engaging an enemy. Later, an additional responsibility was added: providing an amphibious force that could assault enemy coastal strongholds. In the Mexican War the marines were utilized not just in these specialized roles, but as elite infantry. The Marine Corps continued to perform these multiple roles during the Civil War and the Spanish-American War. A greatly expanded Marine Corps participated in World War I primarily as infantry. A marine, Maj. Gen. John A. Lejeune, commanded the army's 2d Division—including the Marine Brigade, which won widespread acclaim for its heroic stand in Belleau Wood.

America's aggressive diplomatic policy during the first third of the twentieth century was carried out largely by Marine Corps units dispatched to Haiti, Honduras, and Nicaragua. In these so-called banana wars, later Marine Corps legends such as Lewis B.

"Chesty" Puller, Merritt A. "Red Mike" Edson, and Herman H. Hanneken learned valuable lessons about small-unit combat in tropical surroundings.

Always small, the Marine Corps had been even more sharply curtailed in the interwar period. By mid-1939 there were only 18,052 active duty marines. As a part of the buildup after the war in Europe began, the number authorized was steadily increased. In September 1940, twenty-three reserve battalions were activated, bringing the size of the corps to over thirty thousand men. In February 1941, the 1st Marine Brigade at Quantico, Virginia, was designated as a division with three regiments—the 1st, 5th, and 7th Marines. At the same time, the 2d Brigade at Camp Elliott also became a division, with the 2d, 6th, and 9th Marines in its ranks. The corps also had its own aviation groups. These dated to the pre-World War I period. Their function, and in this marine aviators were far beyond their army counterparts, was to directly support the action of ground troops. The various groups were integrated in July 1941 into two wings, the 1st at Quantico, and the 2d in San Diego, California.

Marine Corps leaders, supported by a few senior naval officers, had in the 1930s begun to look carefully into the problems of amphibious warfare. The Marine Expeditionary Force was redesignated as the Fleet Marine Force in 1933 and its three thousand men were made an integral part of the U.S. fleet. In the following year, planners collected their recommendations on amphibious warfare into the *Tentative Manual for Landing Operations*. Four years later, the navy issued a revised version, FTP 167, *Landing Operations Doctrine*. These manuals spelled out doctrinal concepts developed by men such as Col. Holland M. Smith and others responsible for conducting landing exercises in the Caribbean. From 1935 onward the marines conducted annual fleet landing exercises. Later in 1941, the army issued its own field manual on the subject, almost identical to the 1938 navy edition.

Despite these developments, senior navy commanders were slow to approve Marine Corps requests for improved landing craft. The 1930s exercises featured landings made using standard ships' boats. These were not designed for heavy surf conditions or for crossing coral reefs. Most restrictive was their size. Each could hold only a few troops. The marines argued that using these boats made it impossible to put enough men on shore to establish and hold a beachhead. A behind-the-scenes struggle over the design of better landing craft ensued. Some Marine Corps officers had been working with Andrew Higgins since 1934 on a small, shallow-draft boat that could easily carry a complement of men up to a presumably hostile beach. Higgins had developed such a craft in 1927 for use by oilmen in the Louisiana bayous. By 1939 these LCVPs (for Landing Craft, Vehicle and Personnel) were fitted with bow ramps that expedited the unloading of troops and materiel. This early design became the model for a whole series of landing craft developed during World War II. However, there were few available when the war began, and as late as the Guadalcanal landings, many marines were still being ferried to shore in ships' boats.

Like their Air Corps counterparts, the marines thus benefited from actions in the civilian sector. In forcing a reluctant naval command to accept the realities of amphibious warfare, the Marine Corps had an effect on World War II far beyond its numbers or its localized Central Pacific theater of operations.

How to conduct a war in the Pacific had occupied much of the time of naval planners, and, to a lesser extent, their army counterparts during the four decades prior to Pearl Harbor. The question of how best to defend America's new Pacific possessions arose almost immediately after the Spanish-American War. No answer that would satisfy the politicians and the senior army and naval officers was ever found. A joint army and navy board consisting of five officers was convened in 1903 to promote cooperation between the services. This board was responsible for creating contingency plans for wars in several different theaters against several possible foes. The code name given to the plan for a possible war against Japan was Orange. The earliest version, very sketchy in nature, was based largely on the probability of a naval war in which the American fleet would take the offensive against the Japanese. However, the plan gave few details of exactly how victory would be accomplished. There was an early consensus between the leaders of the armed services that it would be impossible to hold the Philippines against a concerted Japanese attack. After Japan's victory in the

Russo-Japanese War, the joint army and navy board could at least identify the most likely enemy, but that was as far as realistic planning progressed.

Various plans were proposed to make Guam a major naval base, but differences within the naval high command negated all such proposals. Army and navy leaders quarreled over the choice of a major base in the Philippines. The navy preferred Olangapo, whereas the army spent considerable sums building defenses around Manila—although the troops available were too few to provide an adequate defense even of adjacent areas on Luzon. Before World War I, the only general agreement was on Hawaii as the major forward naval base—despite the fact that it was more than five thousand miles from the scene of any planned action.

Japan's position in the Pacific was greatly strengthened after World War I by its acquisition of the former German islands. The joint board, revitalized because of the war, was given the task of reviewing this new situation and making suggestions to update and modernize the faulty Orange Plan. Its conclusion, however realistic, was shocking: the members believed that the Philippines could not be defended. It was a simple matter of logistics. The bulk of the American fleet was at Pearl Harbor, far from the threatened islands. Even had there been sufficient army personnel in Hawaii to reinforce the fewer than twenty thousand troops in the Philippines, the Japanese would be able to land more than twice that number on Luzon within a week—long before American reinforcements could arrive.

Although this pessimistic conclusion was obvious, it was too bitter to be accepted fully. General Leonard Wood, then governor-general of the Philippines, warned against publicizing America's inability to defend the islands. Neither he nor any other senior commander of either service in the 1920s was able to offer any solution to the defensive dilemma. The Orange Plan adopted in 1924 ignored the details of how its major objective of establishing offensive operations in the western Pacific was to be accomplished and, specifically, how American possessions were to be held. The one clear dictate of the Orange planners, bowing to the reality of fighting a war over the ocean's vast stretches, was that the offensive war would be primarily a naval affair.

Despite its flawed nature, Plan Orange remained the basis of planning for a future Pacific war. Details of the plan were revised on almost a yearly basis without serious modification. Perhaps the most significant change was made in 1935 when the navy insisted that relief of the Philippines would be contingent upon U.S. occupation of the Marshall and Caroline Islands, a move that would delay Philippine rescue operations. The following year, the army's mission on Luzon was restricted to holding only the entrance to Manila Bay.

The navy accepted the broad outlines of the various Orange plans, and every year the War College conducted games designed to instruct future leaders on how to implement them. But, given the realities of the situation in the Pacific in the 1930s, much of this was wishful thinking. Nevertheless, the exercises prepared Central Pacific staff planners for the plan's implementation when it was possible in 1943 for the United States to take the offensive. Admiral Nimitz later stated that after the thorough chart and board exercises he participated in at the War College, nothing that happened during the war was unexpected or strange to him.

The festering debate between the army and navy over Pacific strategy came to a head in 1938 when Lt. Gen. Stanley D. Embick, the chief of the army's War Plans Division, faced the realities of the situation and recommended that America, in case of war, retire behind a line running from Panama to Oahu to Alaska. From this presumably impregnable position, the army and navy could effectively protect the continental United States. The navy reacted by defending the older precepts of the Orange Plan calling for immediate offensive operations undertaken mainly by naval forces. The joint board sought a solution amenable to both services and commissioned Embick and his naval counterpart, RAdm. James O. Richardson, to work out a compromise. Their solution was prophetic. The modified plan called for an initial defense along a line suggested by Embick while the army and navy prepared for offensive action against the Japanese mandated islands and ultimately the Philippines. By implication, the plan suggested that the Philippines and the other minor American possessions could not be held. The key to the implementation of the offensive phase was the naval base at Pearl Harbor. Even the most pessimistic observer of the situation in 1939 could agree that as long as the Pacific Fleet was present in Hawaii, the defensive line could be held even if the Philippines were sacrificed.

The attention of most political and military leaders was firmly fixed on Europe as war, so long delayed, finally erupted in September 1939. The world reeled as the German *Wehrmacht* overran first Poland and then, in the spring of the following year, occupied Denmark and Norway, brushed aside the feeble resistance of the Dutch and Belgian armies, and conquered France in a scant few weeks. After evacuating their beaten army from Dunkirk, the British alone confronted Hitler's potent war machine. At the same time, Adm. Karl Dönitz's small submarine fleet was beginning to wreak havoc on British shipping, an attack that would grow in intensity until it threatened to isolate Britain from the goods and supplies so necessary for it to continue the war.

Although President Roosevelt had been deeply concerned by European developments long before the fall of France, that event finally focused the attention of a hesitant Congress on the inadequacies of the American military. The legislators responded by appropriating $10.5 billion for defense. After the navy's General Board warned of the necessity of building ships to the utmost capacity of the shipyards, Congress, by July 1940, had voted to spend over $5 billion. This allocation allowed shipbuilders to more than double the output of the previous two decades. The president's advisers also began to talk of a fifty-thousand-plane air force, and the army began to plan for a massive manpower buildup. Congress responded by reluctantly approving the first peacetime draft in the nation's history.

In June 1940 the Eurocentric attitude was made a general policy of the government. Later contacts between Roosevelt and Churchill and the fear of Britain's defeat inspired the revision of the neutrality acts, the Lend-Lease Act, the near outright gift of fifty aged destroyers, and ultimately the provision of U.S. naval escorts for British convoys. By the fall of 1941 the United States was involved in an undeclared sea war with Germany.

This flurry of activity did not lead to any substantial change in planning for a possible Pacific war. The Rainbow plans drawn up by the Joint Planning Board in 1939 would remain the basis for

U.S. action throughout World War II. Rainbow 2 and Rainbow 3 concerned the Pacific. The former assumed an alliance with Britain that would give the Allies numerical superiority and allow for the offensive action contemplated by the navy. Rainbow 3 reiterated the basics of the earlier Orange Plan, with the provision that priority be given to defense of the Western Hemisphere. In all this generalized planning, however, emphasis was given to implementing Rainbow 5, which called for joint action with Britain in the European and African theaters.

Although American foreign policy became increasingly hostile to the Japanese, little was done to improve American naval, air, or ground capabilities in its Pacific possessions. The consensus in Washington was that stationing the main elements of the U.S. Pacific Fleet in Hawaii in May 1940 would do two things. It would show the Japanese how serious the differences were between the two powers, and it would locate this powerful naval force, the major U.S. offensive threat, much closer to the area of projected action. However, even with the fleet based in Hawaii, the only significant factor in favor of American forces was distance. Senior commanders did not believe that any attacker could approach the islands without being detected. This was the major reason for complacency among high-ranking officials. Even the Pacific Fleet's commander in chief, Adm. Husband E. Kimmel, although pressing hard for more ships and equipment, was not unduly alarmed by the growing disparity in naval forces with Japan. While he had rough parity in battleships, Kimmel was far outnumbered in cruisers and destroyers. Furthermore, Japan had ten carriers that could be deployed, whereas Kimmel had but three. On 7 December only two were available because the *Saratoga* was on the West Coast undergoing refitting.

It was not until mid-1941 that any serious thought was given to reinforcing America's outlying garrisons and updating their weaponry. Guam, despite a report by RAdm. Arthur J. Hepburn's committee in 1939, was considered to be of no strategic value, so nothing was done to bolster its small complement of 153 marines and 271 sailors. Admiral Kimmel saw Wake Island as an important outpost, and in August the first contingent of marines arrived there. However, there were fewer than four hundred men on Wake when

Japan struck. By complete chance, Wake and Midway played a pivotal but unplanned role in thwarting Japanese plans in the early stages of the war. Kimmel's two available carriers, the *Enterprise* and *Lexington,* were not at Pearl Harbor on 7 December because they had been sent to deliver fighter aircraft and pilots to marine units on the two island outposts.

The most significant change from the original Orange plans concerned the Philippines. This change of attitude was primarily the work of one man, the charismatic former army chief of staff and sometimes field marshal of the Philippines, Douglas MacArthur. He argued that with time he could prepare ten Filipino divisions. Then, combined with the American garrison, his two-hundred-thousand-man force would defend not only Manila Bay, but all the other islands. As the crisis with Japan deepened, this optimistic evaluation from one of the army's most respected senior officers was exactly what Secretary of War Stimson and the army chief of staff, General Marshall, wanted to hear. In retrospect such strategic and tactical projections appear at first glance to be sheer bombast, but closer inspection shows them not to be that far-fetched if there had been time to implement them.

MacArthur based his revised plans on two factors that most Americans in mid-1941 believed to be correct. The first was that Japan would not dare to attack the United States. MacArthur, while not quite as sanguine, did not believe that war would come until at least mid-1942. He hoped that would give him time to transform raw Filipino troops into a reasonable fighting force. The second factor was the belief that the U.S. Navy would be able to keep the sea-lanes to the Philippines open. Supplies and reinforcements would thus be forthcoming if MacArthur could maintain a force in being to guard Manila. Neither of these assumptions proved to be correct.

In July 1941 MacArthur was recalled to active duty and given command of American as well as Filipino troops. Two months later, General Marshall assured MacArthur that the Philippines had been given the highest equipment priority. In fact, a considerable number of modern weapons, including Ml Garand rifles, modern radar, and 105mm howitzers, had been dispatched or had already arrived in the

Philippines by the time Japan struck. High priority was also given to beefing up MacArthur's air force with B-17 heavy bombers. The huge Boeings were believed to be capable of intercepting an enemy force hundreds of miles at sea and either destroying or dispersing it. General Henry H. "Hap" Arnold, the Air Corps chief, eventually planned to have three hundred B-17s in the islands with P-40 pursuit aircraft serving as escorts.

All this planning was for naught. Given the neglect of defenses prior to mid-1941, MacArthur and his associates could not stem the Japanese tide when the invasion was mounted. Time had simply run out. On 8 December MacArthur had only 130,000 men, of whom 107,000 were Filipinos. They were generally ill trained and ill equipped. The heart of his ground defense was the 22,400 U.S. regulars and 12,000 Philippine Scouts. Far from having the three hundred Flying Fortresses envisioned by General Arnold, MacArthur's air commander, Maj. Gen. Lewis H. Brereton, had only thirty-five. The bulk of the bomber force consisted of obsolete Douglas B-18 aircraft. Even the token U.S. Asiatic Fleet commanded by Adm. Thomas C. Hart, which consisted of one heavy and two light cruisers, thirteen destroyers, and twenty-eight other craft, would not be available to intercept the invading force. Expecting the major naval action to be in the Dutch East Indies, the Navy Department had ordered the majority of Hart's ships southward to Java.

Continual lethargy on the part of military and civilian leaders, combined with a lack of time to repair two decades of neglect, cost the United States and its allies dearly during the first months of the war. The only hopeful sign as war drew near was that American cryptanalysts had broken the Japanese diplomatic code. All high-level transmissions between Tokyo and the Japanese embassy in Washington were continually monitored, and select members of the U.S. government were thus privy to this information. This ability, along with continual monitoring of radio messages between Japanese fleet elements, gave American commanders good information on generalized fleet movements. However, as the crucial time for the implementation of Adm. Isoroku Yamamoto's plan drew near,

American leaders with all the information available of a massive Japanese buildup in Southeast Asia and in some Central Pacific islands were fooled as to Japan's intentions.

American leaders had finally awakened to the danger of aggression in Europe and Asia and were attempting to reverse the pattern of military neglect. Huge sums of money were made available to contractors who already had begun production on a small scale of war materiel targeted to aid Britain in its struggle. Most of the senior officials in the War and Navy Departments who would be responsible for the major decisions during the coming war were in place. Generalized plans, although not addressing the very serious strategic questions of time and place, had been approved. Although 7 December 1941 found the nation still ill prepared for war, decisions had already been made to correct many of the deficiencies and America's awesome production potential would soon be realized. Japan at Pearl Harbor did not disturb a sleeping giant, but rather one already slowly awakening from its isolationist dreams.

Chapter 3

Japanese Military Preparations

IN 1941, JAPAN'S armed forces had already been at war with China for four years, and although not completely mobilized, the nation was fully prepared for a continuation of the Sino-Japanese conflict. The disturbances of the pre-China war period had consolidated political power in the hands of ultranationalist military leaders occupying high government positions or operating behind the scenes to influence government policy.

Japan, to a foreign observer, represented a series of dichotomies. In the late nineteenth century, Emperor Mutsuhito and his advisers launched the Meiji Revolution, which utilized European political systems as models in creating a government of shared powers. There was a two-house parliament and a professional civil service. The ministry, like the German model, was not responsible to the legislature, but the presumption was that the prime minister and his associates, before carrying out a particular policy, would seek the legislature's support. Japan, however, was far from being a nation in which the government depended on popular support. The traditional nobility and the great industrial magnates dominated Japanese political life. Most Japanese unhesitatingly followed the decisions of those leaders partially because of police actions, but mostly because the structure of Japanese society had changed very little since the nineteenth century. One noticeable shift had been to transfer the martial attitudes of a small warrior class to the population at large. After World War I, the officer ranks were opened to the middle class and these young men were indoctrinated in the ancient code of Bushido, the code of the warrior. Thus, on the surface, Japan was a well-organized and in many ways modern industrial state, but it was driven by men loyal to ideas dominant in the previous century. The martial qualities of the samurai had been mobilized for the national good, particularly as exemplified by the armed forces.

At the apex of the Japanese political system was the emperor. As with so much in Japanese society, the immediately apparent was not necessarily the reality. In theory the emperor was a god and was worshiped as such by millions of his subjects. Even the best educated and those most closely associated with Hirohito, emperor since 1924, felt an attachment to his person far beyond that reserved for mere mortals. This exalted position, combined with the practical structure of Japanese government, gave Hirohito potentially more power to shape events than totalitarian leaders in Europe. However, Hirohito chose not to dominate his government, but rather was dominated by it. Beginning during his father's reign, the emperor became in practice a constitutional monarch, allowing his ministers to make policy. This quiescent attitude suited the personality of Hirohito, a gentle man and respected marine biologist, whose slight build and thick glasses made him look less like the lord of a warlike nation than a meek university professor. He would interfere directly in the normal decision-making process only twice—the first time in 1928 in reaction to the army's assassination of Marshal Chang Tso-lin, and the last to bring an end to the war his ministers had begun. Otherwise, although he had grave doubts about his subordinates' policies after 1937, he never used his supposedly divine authority to restrict their actions. Rather, he lent himself to the growing militarism of his government and people.

Long before General Tojo became prime minister, the armed forces had dominated the central government. The spate of assassinations in 1932 and 1936 had not been carried out by senior officers dissatisfied with civilian domination of the government. They were instead conducted by superpatriotic junior officers who believed that their leaders, mainly retired admirals and generals, were too cautious and conservative. The junior officers pushed the Japanese government to adopt a bold policy that culminated in the war with China, two border clashes with Russia, and ultimately a pact with the European Axis powers.

The Japanese for the most part were parochial. Few had any significant knowledge of Europe or the United States, and they were inordinately proud of their armed forces—which had not been defeated in the modern era. One major reason for this success was the indoctrination and training given to the young men who either volunteered for or, after 1930, were conscripted into the army and navy. Most of the conscripts in the 1930s were very young. They became eligible for two years of active service upon reaching seventeen years of age.

Army training, measured by Western standards, was extremely harsh, and private soldiers were often brutalized by their noncommissioned officers. Soldiers became hardened by long marches with heavy packs under the most adverse conditions. Training stressed the offense—based in part on the successes of the Russo-Japanese war, when massed infantry assaults many times succeeded against superior forces. Defensive tactics received only minimal attention. Emphasis was given to the idea that in war the soldier's life belonged to the emperor, and thus it was a great honor to die for him. A soldier would shame himself, his family, and the emperor if he did not fight bravely without giving thought to surrender no matter what the odds. Such training produced an army of tough, fatalistic troops who could be almost invincible in the attack. Yet these same troops lacked individual initiative and, although tenacious in the defense, had a tendency to unnecessarily choose death rather than retreat.

The training of sailors in the naval rank and file was in its own way as harsh and unyielding as that of their army counterparts. Fleet exercises were conducted in remote training areas located almost exclusively in the Northern Hemisphere, where the weather was cold and the seas normally ran high. The standards of proficiency demanded of ordinary seamen roughly paralleled those expected of their officers. Thus, at the beginning of World War II,

Japan had superbly trained seamen who believed firmly in their emperor and their leaders, and who were convinced they had the finest equipment in the world.

Most army line officers traditionally were graduates of the Central Military Preparatory School or had passed a required examination after completing middle school. Students at the preparatory school were selected from the ranks of young men who had completed three years of training at a local military school. Beginning pupils at such schools ranged from thirteen to sixteen years of age. Training for the various combat arms branches at the preparatory school lasted for twenty-one months, after which the cadets were commissioned. The demands of a greatly expanded army after 1937 were met partially by doubling class sizes and speeding up course work. After the war with China began, it became popular to have reservists take an examination or for noncommissioned officers with good records to be recommended for commissioning. In December 1938 an air academy was created for the aviation branch. Subsequent education and training was provided for qualified officers at one of thirty-four military schools. The General Staff College was at the apex of this system of advanced officer training.

Training of naval officers followed a similar pattern, although the requirements tended to be more rigorous. Most of Japan's senior naval commanders were graduates of Eta Jima—the Japanese equivalent of Annapolis—in Hiroshima. Entrance into the academy by young men between the ages of sixteen and twenty was by competitive examination in ten subject areas. Successful candidates were then required to complete three years of training in seamanship, navigation, gunnery, higher mathematics, and engineering. After passing their final examinations, cadets were given eight months of additional sea training under difficult conditions before they were finally commissioned. Specialist schools and staff college training were provided for the more senior officers. This demanding regimen produced a cadre of senior commanders who, although handicapped by the navy's ultraconservative attitudes, were technically as good as their counterparts in other navies.

Although presumably dedicated to the same goals, the Japanese army and navy were continually at odds. Interservice rivalry was noticeable in the armed forces of all nations, but the differences between the two branches in Japan were far more serious because most disagreements were political or ideological. Naval leaders tended to be less doctrinaire and some, by Japanese standards, were quite liberal. One reason for these attitudes was that more naval officers had traveled and seen other nations firsthand, whereas very few of the army's senior commanders had had the same opportunities. Army leaders were therefore more given to underestimating the strength of a potential enemy. Even before October 1941, when General Tojo became prime minister, the army leadership dictated not only military, but also foreign policy. Naval leaders—including the chief of the naval staff, Adm. Osami Nagano, and the commander of the Combined Fleet, Admiral Yamamoto—although consulted, were helpless after 1937 to alter fundamentally the actions of the army-dominated government.

Prior to 1937, the army and navy commands had been totally separate, each fashioned to a considerable degree upon European models—the British for the navy, the German for the army. The army was divided into line and staff, each segment ostensibly controlled by the minister of war, who in most cases was either a serving or retired general. The chief of staff and his deputies had considerable autonomy for planning and executing war plans. The general staff was divided into sections, each responsible for a specific task such as supply, intelligence, and operations. The First Bureau, responsible for operations, was the most important. Field armies were organized under an overall commander, who was given great latitude with regard to tactics by the central administration. He was aided by a large staff section responsible for planning and executing tactical operations. A field army was composed of several divisions, each of which prior to World War II was made up of men from a specific part of Japan.

The navy's organization was similar to that of most Western fleets. The minister of marine, a cabinet officer, was responsible, in conjunction with the naval staff, for mobilization planning and defense of the homeland. He was in charge of seven bureaus and four separate departments. A curious factor in the hierarchy of command was the position of the chief of the naval general staff. He had direct access to the emperor and thus was in many ways not directly subordinate to the marine minister, but instead cooperated with him on an almost equal basis.

By 1941 all ships except those in the naval force in China were assigned to the Combined Fleet. The commander of this large force, because of the prestige and importance of the position, was able to convince the staff to alter basic strategy despite being subordinate to the chief of staff. Admiral Yamamoto's concepts regarding war with the United States were thus adopted in 1941 and the long-standing defensive posture advocated by the naval staff was abandoned.

The Combined Fleet on the eve of World War II contained all available ships with the exception of a few under separate command of naval forces in China. It was divided into a number of sections, with most of the ships of each kept in harbor in Japan. The strongest element was the First Fleet, or Battle Force, commanded by Admiral Yamamoto. Its strength lay in the ten battleships and six cruisers normally at anchor in Hiroshima Bay. The Second Fleet, the Scouting Force, composed primarily of cruisers, was based at Hainan. The bulk of the Third Fleet, the Transport Force, was located in Formosa. Japan maintained its Fourth Fleet, a small detachment of four cruisers, eight destroyers, and sixteen submarines, at Truk under the command of VAdm. Shigeyoshi Inoue. Even fewer ships comprised the Fifth Fleet at Ominato. The main submarine force, composed of forty I-class boats with their tenders, was sited at Kwajalein. A powerful adjunct to these separate fleets was the Carrier Fleet, consisting of six fleet and four light carriers based at Kure under the command of VAdm. Chuichi Nagumo. In addition, the navy had more than twelve hundred planes in a combined air force, most of which were based in Japan, Formosa, and Indochina. Like any major navy, the size and composition of these units changed with their mission or the situation.

In order to create a more unified command structure, the Imperial General Headquarters was established in 1937. This headquarters was composed of the ministers of war and the navy, the chiefs of staff of the army and navy, and their principal advisers. It normally convened twice a week on the grounds of the Imperial Palace. When joint actions between the army and navy were required, general agreement had to be achieved before orders were issued.

Yet even when joint action was necessary, each service maintained its integrity. There was no overall commander of a given operation, naval and army leaders were simply instructed to cooperate with one another. Army and navy commanders on the eve of Pearl Harbor retained operational control over their forces in the field. Each service had its own air force, its own procurement program, and designated its own weapons systems—and the services jealously guarded these prerogatives. This rivalry continued into World War II, where in some instances rival leaders refused to cooperate with one another even under the threat of immediate destruction by Allied forces.

A further attempt to secure unity in policy making was the creation of the Liaison Committee, a group composed of the prime minister, the minister of foreign affairs, the ministers of war and the navy, and the service chiefs of staff. Its function was to provide a forum for the discussion of all phases of foreign policy, allocation of resources, and war strategy. It met twice weekly in a room in the Imperial Palace. When very important matters were being discussed, the emperor would also attend. Sitting at the head of the conference table, he would listen quietly while the service chiefs or their ministers made presentations. In keeping with his policy of not unduly influencing policy, he rarely spoke—and even more rarely made clear his personal feelings. Although the Liaison Committee did not halt destructive interservice rivalry, it did provide a means for making the emperor aware of the major problems confronting the nation. As such, it became Japan's most important policy agency during World War II.

Japan had been involved in a major war with China for more than four years when the decision to attack Pearl Harbor was made. Although there was an increase in nationalistic propaganda and quasi-military training for Japanese youth in 1941, there was no need to switch to a wartime economy. The five-year plans had already done that. The army, whose normal size was a quarter of a million men, had by October 1937 been expanded threefold, giving Japan twenty-four ground divisions and an air service of more than ten thousand men. By 1941 Japan had fifty-one divisions, many of which were on assignment in Manchuria and China. The war with

China had at first exceeded the most optimistic expectations. The huge, ill-trained Chinese armies were cut to pieces and the ever-victorious Japanese occupied the coastal areas and much of northern China. The Japanese infantry's reputation for ferocity and unwarranted savagery was also established. The bombing of civilian targets and the murder of Chinese civilians caused extreme negative reactions throughout Europe and the United States.

The victories over the Chinese were not without cost. Casualties had been heavy, particularly in the Shanghai area in the fall of 1937. In April 1938 a Japanese force of more than sixty thousand men ambushed at Taierchwang lost one-third of its number killed. However, the army's overall success bred a sense that it was invincible and led army leaders to hold fast to the status quo, especially with regard to weapons development. The army's standard weapons, the Nambu .25 caliber rifle and .30 caliber machine gun, were dependable, but their designs were old. Japan had nothing to match the Garand rifle or .50 caliber heavy machine gun then available to U.S. forces.

The most significant failure of the Japanese army, however, was in the design and use of armored vehicles. Japan created armored regiments very late, but these were normally attached to larger infantry units. The tanks were seen simply as mobile artillery that could support infantry in the attack. This system had worked well against Chinese units, which generally had no armor. Japan's main tanks were the Type 95 light tank and the Types 94 and 97 medium tanks. These remained the army's standard tanks throughout World War II. Both were lightly armored, slow, and undergunned. The best was the Type 97 *Chi-Ha,* which was based on an early 1930s British design. At first it had a short-barreled 57mm main gun and two 7.7mm machine guns. Later, after the clashes with the Russians, the main armament was changed to a longer 47mm weapon with improved range and accuracy. The improved Type 97 tank was no match for the American Sherman tank with its 75mm gun, however, and even the earliest version of the bazooka could destroy Japanese tanks.

The conservative, almost smug, attitude of the Japanese army high command could be clearly seen in the reaction to the Manchurian border clashes with Russia in 1938 and 1939. The most serious of these was the Nomonhan Incident in mid-1939. Of the 15,140 Japanese troops engaged, 11,124 were either killed or wounded. The Russians, commanded by Gen. Georgy Zhukov, were clearly superior, and their tanks outran and outgunned the Japanese. The army high command reacted to this stunning defeat by dismissing the senior officers held responsible for the defeat but did nothing significant to correct the army's deficiencies. They preferred to look at the Chinese examples, where Japanese dominance was apparent, rather than react positively to the hard lessons of the Manchurian debacle.

The negative aspects of Japan's victories over Chinese armies were also reflected in its air forces. Very early in that conflict Japan gained almost total aerial supremacy after destroying the bulk of the Russian planes supplied to Chiang Kai-shek. This unequivocal success masked the deficiencies in Japanese aircraft design and production. Japan's planes in 1941, both army and navy, were generally good aircraft that could stand up well to harsh flying conditions. But their performance would prove inferior to aircraft that would become available to the United States after it recovered from the shock of Pearl Harbor. Not surprisingly, Japanese manufacturers, reacting to military specifications, designed their bombers for theater utilization with the knowledge that the air force controlled the skies over China. Thus they never developed a four-engined bomber capable of flying long distances with a heavy bomb load. Japan's basic medium bomber at the start of the China conflict was the Mitsubishi G3M2, which was given the Allied code name Nell. These were phased out in 1942 by a larger Mitsubishi bomber, the G4M Betty, which was developed after 1937. The backbone of the army's bomber force was the Kawasaki Ki-21 Sally. Both the Betty and Sally carried a small bomb load (only twenty-two hundred pounds) and, because of their short range, could be used effectively only when Japanese forces controlled land bases relatively close to the target areas.

Army fighter aircraft had some of the same qualities as their bombers: they were well built, simple, and easily serviceable, but had a short range. They were light and highly maneuverable, the designers sacrificing heavier aluminum frames, sheeting, and armor plate in exchange for better performance. A variety of fighters were available to the army by 1941. The Nakajima Ki-27 was the first standard monoplane fighter. The first of these was produced in 1935 and saw considerable action in China, but its slow speed and light armament (two machine guns) made it obsolete by 1941. Its performance against the American Volunteer Group's Curtiss P-40 Tomahawks in late 1941 showed its vulnerability. Nevertheless, thirty-four hundred Ki-27s were produced. The best army fighter of the period was the Nakajima Ki-43 Oscar. A radial-engine craft that first flew in 1939, it was very agile and had a top speed in excess of 300 mph. At first it was superior to all the Allied aircraft it faced, dominating the skies over Malaya, Burma, Java, and Sumatra. Although at a disadvantage later in comparison to newer Allied fighters, its production continued throughout the war, with more than fifty-nine hundred being built.

The fact that Japan's attack in December 1941 was a gamble without proper preparation for a drawn out conflict with the United States can be seen clearly by viewing the aircraft industry. Like all segments of Japanese industry, its potential was far less than that of its projected enemies. The production figures for all types of aircraft bear out Japan's inferior airpower position if engaged in a prolonged war. In 1940 total aircraft production for both the army and navy was only 4,768, and by the crucial year 1941 had risen to only 5,088. The projected number of aircraft to be produced by the United States just for the navy in 1942 exceeded total Japanese production of all types for both services. Furthermore, as the war dragged on, Japan found it difficult to halt production of its standard aircraft in order to begin producing in quantity the better planes needed to meet the challenge of its enemies' superior aircraft. The United States could afford the luxury of phasing out obsolete designs to make way for improved bombers and fighters. The Japanese could not, except in rare instances. Although by 1945 Japan had a few more advanced planes such as the Kawasaki Ki-61 Tony and the Mitsubishi A7M2, successor to the famous Zero, there were not enough of them to affect the outcome of the air war. For all practical purposes, Japan was forced to fight the entire Pacific war with the planes it had available in 1941.

The quality of navy aircraft was generally superior to those flown by the army. This was due in part to the demands on planes operating at sea, where they had to withstand the shock and strain of carrier landings. It was also due to the early recognition by far-sighted planners such as Admiral Yamamoto that the greatest burden of a war with the United States would be borne by the navy and its aircraft carriers. The navy operated not only carrier-based aircraft, but large land-based bombers, the most important being the twin-engined Mitsubishi G3M Nell and its successor, the G4M Betty. The planes that most concerned Allied pilots were the Aichi D3A Val and Nakajima B5N Kate dive and torpedo bombers. The Val prototype first flew in 1938, and by the end of the war more than fifteen hundred had been built. It proved to be one of the best weapons in Japan's naval arsenal. Complementing it was the Kate, which was, until the introduction of the American Gruman TBF Avenger, the best torpedo bomber in the Pacific. Over eleven hundred were produced before Japan's carrier losses made its continued production impractical.

The finest of all naval aircraft during the early months of World War II was the Mitsubishi A6M2, which the Americans code-named Zeke but which was better known by its navy designation, Zero. Designed by Jiro Horikoshi, one of Japan's foremost aeronautical engineers, it became operational in 1940 and was immediately put into mass production. Over ten thousand of various models of the Zero were produced during the war, and they were utilized on all fronts by the army as well as the navy. It was fast, the earliest versions having a top speed of 320 mph, and could outclimb and outmaneuver every Allied fighter. It would retain that superiority until the closing days of World War II. In the hands of well-trained Japanese pilots, the Zero was a formidable weapon despite its lightweight construction and lack of armor plate. Even though American pilots by late 1942 had devised tactics to counter the Zero's superior performance, they could ill afford to engage in a conventional dogfight with one.

Japan entered World War II with approximately twenty-five hundred navy and thirty-five hundred army pilots. These were superbly trained men, a credit to rigorous training regimens that blended the best features of Western programs with the discipline inherent in Japanese military schools. Because Japan had been at war for four years, many pilots had combat flying experience. A typical army pilot in 1941 had over five hundred hours flying time, whereas many of those in the navy had more than eight hundred hours—plus the benefit of having trained under the arduous conditions dictated by Admiral Yamamoto.

These advantages allowed Japan to maintain air superiority in all theaters of operation during the first year of the war. However, the Japanese high command had not planned for a prolonged war of attrition and had not provided the facilities for training replacements. The pilots lost in the air battles of 1942 could not be replaced quickly, and Japan's policy of not rotating their best, most experienced pilots home to aid in training ultimately meant that in the crucial battles of 1943–45, Japanese pilots were invariably inferior to their Allied counterparts.

Japan's navy was far better prepared to conduct a war against a major power than was its army, although most naval commanders were adamantly against any conflict with the United States. Despite the restrictions imposed by the Washington Treaty, Japan had the most powerful navy in the Pacific.

Traditional naval wisdom in the interwar period had assigned the battleship the major role in any future war, and in 1941 Japan had ten of these, the oldest of which were four *Kongo*-class vessels constructed between 1913 and 1915. The newest were the *Nagato* and *Mutsu*, completed just before the limitation on tonnage went into effect after the Washington conference. These two ships were fast, with a top speed of twenty-six knots, and each mounted eight 16-inch guns, an improvement over the 14-inch guns of the earlier battleships. Even before the Washington Treaty lapsed, Japan began reconstruction of the two *Nagato*-class ships, doubling their horsepower, increasing the thickness of the armor plate, and adding many antiaircraft guns. The same was done for the four *Kongo*-class battleships— the *Kongo, Hiei, Haruna,* and *Kirishima*—which had their speed increased to slightly more than thirty knots.

In 1937, the Japanese high command, responding to a perceived need for larger battleships with heavier caliber armament, authorized construction of what were to be the world's largest battle-ships. The *Yamato*'s keel was laid in November 1937 and construction was completed in December 1941. Its sister ship, the *Musashi*, was begun in March 1938 and finished in early 1942. Each of these monsters displaced 72,800 tons loaded, and had nine 18.1-inch guns backed by twelve 6-inch guns. The 18.1-inch guns fired a 3,200-pound projectile, twice the weight of a 16-inch shell. The ships' maximum speed was twenty-seven knots. The keels for two more of the huge ships were laid in 1940, but they were later converted into aircraft carriers. Plans were made for even larger battleships mounting 20-inch guns, but the war revealed the vulnerability of battle-ships, and these behemoths never got past the preliminary design stage.

Japanese cruisers, particularly their heavy cruisers, were justifiably considered by observers to be almost without peer. The *Titibu*-class ships were very large, almost the equivalent of a pocket battleship. They had a maximum speed of thirty knots and mounted six 12-inch guns. The *Atago*-class cruisers launched in 1932 could reach thirty-four knots and had ten 8-inch guns, as did the older *Nati*-class heavy cruisers. Japan's light cruisers, varying in displacement from 7,000 to 8,500 tons each, had 6-inch main batteries and could reach speeds of over thirty knots.

The Imperial Navy's destroyers were equally well built. The *Fubuki* class (1928–33) led the world in modern design, boasting six 5-inch guns enclosed in twin mounts.

The submarine service had a variety of modern boats varying in size from 20-ton midgets to giant submersible transports of 3,500 tons. Their combat submarines were divided between the smaller RO class, designed primarily for use in coastal waters, to the 1,000-ton I class, which was roughly comparable to the *Pike-* and *Perch*-class boats in the U.S. Navy. Large four-hundred-foot-long transport submarines were also built and used effectively later in the war to ferry troops from one island to another.

The relative failure of Japan's submarine service in World War II was not because of inferior equipment but rather a strategic concept at variance with the offensive potential of submarines. Except in rare instances, Japan never used its submarines in an appropriate offensive role. No serious attempt was made in 1942 to interdict the

Allies' long Pacific supply lines. One wonders what the German submarine commander, Admiral Dönitz, would have done in similar circumstances. This failure to use the submarine properly is even more difficult to understand since Japan had by far the world's best torpedoes. By 1933 the Japanese had perfected their oxygen-fueled Type 95 torpedo, which delivered a 1,200-pound warhead fifty-seven hundred yards. The Type 95 played an important role in devastating the American fleet at Pearl Harbor. Japanese pilots could drop the Type 95 from a thousand feet at speeds upward of 200 mph and expect good results. Japan also had developed the Type 93, which could travel at forty-nine knots and had a range of twenty-two thousand yards. By contrast, the standard torpedo available to the United States had a range of only forty-five hundred yards.

The same debates over the future role of aircraft that divided American naval leaders during the interwar years were also carried on in Japan. Although conservatives maintained that aircraft would always play a subsidiary role to that of the fast, heavy-gun battleships, Japan nevertheless began to build aircraft carriers in the early 1920s. It was not until March 1923 that the first pilot landed on the decks of the experimental carrier *Hosho.* In an effort to get around provisions of the Washington Treaty that required Japan to scrap a number of ships still under construction, the Japanese followed America's lead and converted two of their proposed 41,000-ton battle cruisers into aircraft carriers. These large, heavily armed carriers, the *Kaga* and *Akagi,* each with a capacity of ninety-one planes, joined the fleet in 1927. The Japanese also saw merit in the design of America's small carriers, and constructed the 8,000-ton *Ryujo* in 1929. This prototype was the only one of its class built.

By the early 1930s, naval airpower gained an important champion in the fast-rising Admiral Yamamoto, who had commanded the First Air Fleet and who became the vice minister of the marine in 1937. Respected and vocal, he pushed his generally reluctant colleagues into approving the design and construction of newer planes and larger, faster carriers. In 1934 the keel for the *Hiryu* was laid, and the following year work on its sister, *Soryu,* was begun. Each ship displaced 19,000 tons, carried fifty-three aircraft, and was capable of steaming at thirty-four knots. In 1937, at Yamamoto's urging, work was begun on two large, fast carriers, the *Shokaku* and *Zuikaku,* each weighing 26,000 tons, handling seventy-two aircraft, and able to reach a speed of thirty-four knots. The *Kaga* and *Akagi* were also modernized, giving Yamamoto the carrier superiority that he desired in the Pacific. In addition, the navy began converting three 17,000-ton luxury liners in 1940. When completed, these ships—the *Taiyo, Chuyo,* and *Unyo*—each carried thirty aircraft, but had the slow speed of only twenty-one knots. The last of the prewar-planned carriers were the 24,000-ton *Hiyo* and *Junyo,* which were begun in 1941.

The Japanese navy on the eve of World War II was by far the largest and best equipped naval force in the Pacific, outnumbering the combined British, Dutch, and American fleets. The question thus posed to naval planners was how this powerful force should be used. All their plans concerning a war with either one or both potential Pacific enemies had been defensive. The Japanese were aware of the various Orange plans and intended to use U.S. strategy to defeat its navy. The planners did not preclude landing army units in the Philippines since possession of those islands would provide good anchorages for the Japanese fleet. Nevertheless, they believed ultimate victory depended on luring the enemy's fleet into an open battle and then decisively defeating it, as Admiral Togo had done at Tsushima.

These plans were rudely upset by diplomatic developments after World War II began in Europe, bringing new problems and challenges to the government and the military. During the first six months of the European war, the Japanese government steered a neutral course. Its major preoccupation was with Russia in Mongolia, where explosive border disputes had triggered two armed confrontations.

In 1940 a combination of developments allowed the militaristic faction within the government to move toward an alliance with the Axis powers. One major factor in this was the stiffening of the U.S. attitude toward Japanese excesses in China and what appeared to be its designs on other areas in Asia. An indication of this was the permanent transfer of the bulk of the U.S. Pacific Fleet from the West Coast to Hawaii in May 1940. This action prompted Japanese militants to overthrow the ministry of moderate Adm. Mitsumasa Yonai. He was succeeded by the vacillating Prince Konoye, who appointed the mercurial Yosuke Matsuoka as foreign minister. The quick German victories culminating in the defeat of France convinced Matsuoka to seek a rapprochement with Hitler. With the reluctant blessings of others in the government, Matsuoka successfully concluded negotiations and signed the Tripartite Pact on 27 September 1940. This brought Japan on a collision course with the United States, which by then was an open ally of Great Britain. The linkage of Japan's concept of a "New Order in Asia" with Germany's European war aims intensified the already strained relations between the United States and Japan. In December the American government, deeply disturbed over the increasingly belligerent attitude of the Japanese, imposed an embargo on the sale of scrap iron and war materiel to Japan.

Six months earlier, Admiral Yamamoto had been considering an offensive role for the navy in the event of war with the United States. He, more than any other government official, understood Japan's military situation compared with the industrial potential of the United States. His focus always came back to the presence of the large American fleet anchored at Pearl Harbor. It was at this time that, upon being queried by Prince Konoye, he uttered his oft-quoted prophecy concerning a possible war with the United States: "I shall run wild considerably for the first six months or a year, but I have utterly no confidence for the second and third years." Although an opponent of the Tripartite agreement and a vocal member of the peace group, Yamamoto was charged with protecting Japan in case of war. He had no confidence in the earlier plans to use a large part of the navy to cover the invasion of the Dutch East Indies while the rest of the fleet stood on the defensive awaiting an American counterattack. The successful British strike on the Italian fleet at Taranto in November 1940, where air-dropped torpedoes launched in forty-two feet of water had sunk three battleships, proved that a torpedo attack in shallow water could be successful. Inspired by this, Yamamoto ordered one of the foremost naval aviators, RAdm. Takijiro Onishi, to examine the problems associated with an attack on Pearl Harbor. By April 1941 a detailed plan was submitted to Yamamoto. Onishi and Yamamoto's chief of staff,

RAdm. Shigeru Fukudome, were not optimistic about the success of the proposed attack.

Relations between Japan and the United States worsened during the first six months of 1941 largely because of Japan's expansion in Southeast Asia. Immediately following the defeat of France, Japan forced a subservient Vichy government to allow the landings of troops in northern Indochina. In July 1940 Japan succeeded in forcing Britain to close the Burma Road. The arrival of Japanese warships at the port of Haiphong two months later effectively closed off another supply route for China. After much debate, the Japanese agreed in March 1941 to mediate a dispute between Thailand and Indochina. By helping the Thai regain lost territory, Japan secured a mutual defense treaty with Thailand that was much to its advantage.

By mid-1941 Japan had gained virtually complete control over Indochina. The threat to Malaya and Singapore was obvious, and the United States, reacting to the potential loss of this great naval base, decided to strike directly at the most vulnerable part of Japan's economy. Japan had to import its raw materials, the most crucial of which was petroleum. On 26 July, President Roosevelt froze all Japanese assets in the United States and announced an embargo on the shipment of all petroleum products to Japan. Britain and Holland quickly followed suit. This action threatened to choke Japanese industry and the military. Japan had been stockpiling oil for some time, but the military had at most enough for one year of war. Unless there was a substantial change in either Japan's expansionist policies or in the United States's embargo, war between the two powers was inevitable.

The six months prior to the attack on Pearl Harbor witnessed furious attempts on the part of moderates in Japan and the United States to find some way of avoiding the conflict. Although Gen. Hajime Sugiyama and Admirals Nagano and Yamamoto had input into Japan's policy making, they were more concerned with putting Japan on a wartime footing and drawing up plans for a future conflict. Already 1.5 million reservists had been called up. Army headquarters had selected the Dutch East Indies as the primary target; the Philippines and Malaya were secondary in its plans. Only eleven divisions could be spared for this southward drive since most of Japan's army was deployed in China and few troops could be withdrawn from there. Also, despite the neutrality treaty with the Soviet Union signed in April, the high command decided to keep the Kwantung Army in Manchuria at full strength. Manchuria had become even more vulnerable after Japan's ally, Germany, attacked the Soviet Union in June. Japanese planners would not feel safe from a Russian attack until later in the year.

Admiral Nagano and his staff believed that the navy should protect troops landing in Java and the Philippines and intercept the American battle fleet either near the Marianas or northward in the Sea of Japan and then destroy it. Yamamoto disagreed. Despite criticisms leveled by Onishi and Fukadome, he believed that an attack on the U.S. fleet at Pearl Harbor was not only possible, but if properly delivered would give Japan the time necessary to complete its conquests without fear of retaliation. He was convinced that Japan had enough carriers to support the southern invasions and still strike at Pearl Harbor. In this belief he stood almost alone. The naval general staff was firmly opposed to the plan, arguing that its success depended upon surprise. Failure to achieve this could be disastrous. Even Admiral Nagumo, commander of the carriers that would lead the attack, was opposed. He argued that his force would be vulnerable to counter–air attacks.

On 6 September the argument within the naval establishment ceased to be academic when the Liaison Committee announced its decision to go to war with the United States when necessary. Nevertheless, the debate continued throughout September and October, with the naval staff and Admiral Nagumo attempting to dissuade Yamamoto. At the end of October, Yamamoto sent his deputy, RAdm. Kameto Kuroshima, to present final arguments to the naval staff. When they wavered, Yamamoto instructed Kuroshima to deliver an ultimatum—either they accept Yamamoto's offensive plan or he would retire and return to civilian life. His prestige was such that Admiral Nagano, upon being informed of Yamamoto's threat, immediately approved the plan. It was 3 November. Only a month remained for the navy to work out the final details of Yamamoto's plan and prepare for the attack that would bring war to the Pacific.

Chapter 4

The Day of Infamy

THE DIPLOMATIC AND military developments during the last year before the war have given rise to various interpretations as to why the Japanese attacked Pearl Harbor and why the attack came as such a surprise to America. The reasons for the differing interpretations, even the allegation that President Roosevelt conspired to bring on the war, are not hard to find. The diplomatic maneuverings on all levels in Tokyo and Washington are difficult to follow and their very complexity tends to mask how fundamentally simple was the disagreement and how the respective positions taken by the two governments by mid-1941 made any peaceful settlement extremely difficult. This central fact was recognized by the highest level Japanese and American officials. American intelligence agents, utilizing logical deductions, devised a code-breaking machine they named "Magic" to break the Japanese diplomatic code. Thus President Roosevelt and selected advisers in the war and navy departments were kept fully abreast of presumably secret information that was passed from Japan to Washington. Given this advantage, one need not be a severe critic of the Roosevelt-Hull policy to ask how it was possible for the disaster at Pearl Harbor to have occurred. To answer this question one must look at the sequence of events immediately preceding and following Japan's occupation of Indochina on 24 July 1941.

Japan's concern over the reaction of the United States to its aggressive policy led to new diplomatic incentives in the spring of 1941. A new ambassador, bearlike former admiral Kichisaburo Nomura, known as a moderate, was sent to Washington to resolve the differences between the two nations. His initial proposal, presented on 11 May, was that the United States should cease aiding China and resume normal trade with Japan. Secretary of State Hull found these conditions totally unacceptable as they ran directly counter to American policy. However, at this stage, direct negotiations in Washington continued in a friendly and open manner.

Germany's attack on Russia late the next month precipitated a crisis in Tokyo—Foreign Minister Matsuoka wanted Japan to launch an immediate coordinated attack on Russia while at the same time keeping pressure on China and attacking Singapore. Such an aggressive policy was too much for even the war and navy ministers, and in a gesture partially designed to appease American opinion, Prime Minister Konoye replaced Matsuoka on 16 July with Adm. Teijiro Toyoda, another moderate. Thus, by the middle of July, Konoye's government—without retreating from its stated position regarding China—had in key positions men who were far more flexible than their predecessors. Unfortunately, the actions of the Liaison Committee, which authorized the army to seize bases in Indochina, negated any goodwill that these changes may have engendered.

President Roosevelt's preoccupation with Europe did not blind him to Japanese aggression. Matsuoka's earlier diplomatic coups aligning Japan with Germany and Italy and negotiating the neutrality pact with Russia had brought the United States's concerns with Europe and Japan together in a single package. Now Japan, taking advantage of the French defeat in Europe, had bolstered its military position in Southeast Asia. Roosevelt and his advisers believed they could not ignore this maneuver. On 25 July, Roosevelt did what Chiang Kai-shek had long been hoping for: the president froze all Japanese assets in the United States and proposed that Indochina be declared neutral. This was not well received by the Japanese, and on 1 August Roosevelt ordered an embargo on high octane gasoline and crude oil exports to Japan. Britain immediately joined in these punitive actions. The Dutch government in exile was also persuaded to refuse Japanese requests for a long-term arrangement to provide petroleum products from its East Indies fields.

If any one decision can be called the "irrevocable act" that made war inevitable, it was Roosevelt's pronouncement. This and Secretary Hull's refusal to moderate the economic ban placed the Japanese military leaders in a position where they believed they had to act to secure adequate oil supplies. Their petroleum stocks were very low, having fallen from 51 million barrels in 1939 to only 40 million by mid-1941. These reserves were totally inadequate to sustain Japan in a war with a major power. Even the war with China could not be concluded satisfactorily with the oil supplies then on hand. Almost all the Japanese leaders, civilian as well as military, agreed that unless Japan wanted to become a second-rate power bowing to the demands of the United States, the oil fields of the Dutch East Indies would have to be seized. The army already had developed plans for this operation, and in the next few weeks both services came to agree that in order to protect the supply lines, a concurrent operation would have to be mounted against Malaya and Singapore. How to deal with the potential threat from the U.S. Navy prompted Admiral Yamamoto to force the Pearl Harbor plan on his recalcitrant colleagues.

Konoye believed that the United States was playing a dangerous game and that Hull was simply playing for time. He thought that he could make Japan's position clear and also thwart the extremists in his government if he could meet with President Roosevelt. On 28 August he proposed such a face-to-face meeting with the president. The American ambassador, Joseph Grew, concluded after several conferences with Konoye that there was little chance the premier could influence the militarists in his government to retreat from their stated position. Nevertheless, he counseled Washington to accept Konoye's invitation. Secretary of War Stimson, deeply suspicious of Japan, advised Hull to maintain a hard-line attitude toward such overtures. The secretary of state in turn advised Roosevelt to decline the proffered meeting. Konoye realized by this time that war was inevitable unless one side or the other was willing to make concessions. He met with the war minister, General Tojo, and explored the possibility of ending the war in China. But Tojo refused to consider giving up any part of what had been won in four years of fighting. Thus the impasse continued, with neither side willing to compromise.

The attitude of both army and navy leaders toward diplomatic maneuvering to end the impasse was the same. They would continue to prepare for a war with the United States and Britain while the discussions were going on. Hopefully the diplomats could secure Japan's objectives; if not, Japan was prepared to seize what was needed. The Liaison Committee on 3 September decided that if a suitable diplomatic solution was not reached by mid-October, it would meet again and decide whether or not to go to war—and if so, when. On 6 September the committee leaders met with the emperor and informed him of their decision. Although Hirohito pointed out the potential dangers and expressed his desire for peace, the time line for diplomacy to succeed was maintained. On 9 August the army high command had made its decision. It would not take advantage of a weakened Russia nor would it order new offensives in China. Instead, the oil fields of Sumatra would be seized. The operation was to be mounted before the end of 1941 because Japan's oil stocks would be too low if the seizure was postponed longer.

Konoye had needed some movement from the United States in order to maintain his uneasy control over the army and navy. As the mid-October decision date approached, he was informed by the foreign, army, and navy ministers that he must prepare for war. Tojo stated that if Konoye was not prepared to do so, he should resign. After considering the situation for four days, the prince tendered his resignation to the emperor on 17 October and suggested that Tojo be appointed premier. As a part of this shake-up, Adm. Shigetaro Shimada became navy minister. The detailed planning for army operations was sped up and Yamamoto's Combined Fleet began to prepare in earnest for the strike on Pearl Harbor.

Discussions at the highest level had given Yamamoto much of what he wanted. He had from the first demanded six carriers, but the army had opposed that, maintaining that most of the naval force was needed to cover the southern invasions and that the numbers of carriers for the Pearl Harbor venture be limited to three. By Sep-

tember, Yamamoto and his associates had convinced General Headquarters to allow Nagumo's First Air Fleet to have the extra three
carriers that all the air officers considered necessary for success.
Training for the attack had begun in July. Pilots from the *Soryu*
and *Hiryu* were trained near Izumi, while the rest were trained at
Kagoshima. The training squadrons, both torpedo and high-level
bombing, were provided with the same plane, the Nakajima B5N2
Val. Torpedo bomber pilots had the most difficult task because they
had to fly precise routes, keep close formation while flying as low
as 150 feet, and practice releasing the torpedo at exactly the right
spot. At first, practice torpedoes were not available, so the pilots
had to simulate releasing them. These rigorous practice attacks continued for ten to twelve hours a day.

A great element of risk was inherent in Yamamoto's plan. Maximum secrecy was essential, and the high command could only hope
that if agents observed increased fleet activity, they would conclude
that the navy was preparing for supportive action to the south. Then
there was the thirty-seven-hundred-mile distance, probably in heavy
seas, separating Japan from the Hawaiian targets. Two further problems subsequently developed that threatened the success of the entire venture.

The first of these concerned the type of torpedoes to be used.
Commanders Minoru Genda and Mitsuo Fuchida, the major air attack planners, believed that the most effective weapon against the
U.S. fleet would be torpedoes; bombing would be secondary. The
most inexperienced pilots, those of the 5th Carrier Division, were
assigned this latter role. But the standard Japanese Model II torpedo
had to be modified. Technicians worked furiously at the test station
at Yokosuka and finally discovered that by adding wooden stabiliz-
ers to the fins they got successful results at Kagoshima in forty feet
of water. However, the modification took time, and it appeared that
only eighty torpedoes would be available by 31 October. The last
one hundred would not be ready until 30 November, too late for the
projected Pearl Harbor operation. Without informing Mitsubishi as
to the reason why all the modified torpedoes had to be delivered by
mid-November, the naval general staff was able to impress on the
executives the need for overtime work. Mitsubishi met the time

limit; the last of the ordered torpedoes were delivered on 17 November and were loaded on the *Akagi* and *Kaga*.

The second major technical problem concerned fueling the ships for the long voyage to Oahu. Only the carriers *Kaga, Shokaku,* and *Zuikaku,* the battleships *Hiei* and *Kirishima,* and two heavy cruisers could make the long voyage to Hawaii without refueling. This meant that the *Akagi, Soryu,* and *Hiryu,* as well as most escort ships, would have to take on fuel at sea. Special permission was obtained from the naval general staff to void the rules and allow storage of extra oil in vacant areas of the large ships. This extended the range of the three carriers. Refueling procedures were also modified. The largest ships would be refueled with the tankers positioned astern of the carriers and battleships. Practice refueling operations in October convinced the commanders that the eight tankers accompanying the strike force would be able to provide enough fuel to ensure the mission's success.

Meanwhile the high command, still not totally secure in its decision to strike Pearl Harbor, carefully studied a variety of reports sent by the consulate in Honolulu. It was an open secret during the year prior to the Pearl Harbor attack that the Japanese consulate was a center for espionage. The consul was deeply involved in supporting the activities of a number of his employees who spied upon military and naval activities in Hawaii. They moved freely around Oahu even during the crucial month of November. Secretary Hull did not want to close the consulate while the high-level negotiations were going on. Thus the Japanese continued spying until the eve of the attack. Information was relayed by a fairly simple code so that Tokyo knew almost everything about troop and ship dispositions and movements. The final pieces of information on Pearl Harbor and Hickam Field were provided to Admiral Nagumo by Lt. Comdr. Suguru Suzuki who spent two weeks in Honolulu observing the location of the Pacific Fleet's ships in Pearl Harbor. His 23 November report on the usual lack of American activity on Sundays and the facts that the bulk of the fleet was present at Pearl Harbor and no major ships were at Lahaina reassured the skittish Nagumo. A detailed message from the consulate was relayed to Nagumo on board the *Akagi* on 29 November giving the exact location of individual ships, and the last message confirming the number of ships in the harbor was received by the Japanese task force at 0120 on 6 December.

Nomura's chief of staff, RAdm. Ryunosuke Kusaka, in early September had created a study group headed by Commander Genda charged with examining various alternative approaches to Hawaii. They considered a number of different routes. The group rejected the southern ones because they required the fleet to rendezvous at Wotje in the Marshall Islands and then proceed eastward in well-traveled shipping lanes where it could be easily spotted. The study group then looked carefully at possible central approaches, using Chichi Jima as a rendezvous point. This route was rejected because of the likelihood of detection either by submarines or air patrols from Midway. Eventually the group concluded that the best route was a northern one, and it selected an approach that began at a rendezvous point far to the north in the Kurile Islands. The task force would proceed eastward until it was approximately nine hundred miles northwest of Oahu, then turn southeastward for the final approach to Pearl Harbor. The major advantages of this route were that fewer commercial ships would be met, and that the storms and heavy seas that would be encountered along the way would cause the Americans not to expect an attack from that direction.

Indicative of how divided was the thinking among Japan's senior military officers at this time was Nagumo's reaction. He did not like the plan, arguing that complete surprise would be impossible. He wanted to use the shorter southern route where he could expect calmer seas. In this way, even if detected, he could still achieve substantial damage. It was weeks before Kusaka, Genda, and others who believed in the plan were able to convince Nagumo to accept it.

General Tojo, who as war minister was so critical of Konoye as premier, was not prepared immediately to sanction war. Tojo and the Liaison Committee had met almost continuously during the two weeks following Konoye's resignation, looking carefully at all ramifications of Japan's position. Most of the older members had counseled caution and wanted to allow time for diplomacy to work. The army representatives were unanimous in demanding war with the United States. Tojo understood that Japan's precarious oil

supply, combined with the notorious bad weather, would make the
Pearl Harbor attack almost impossible if postponed past the target
date of 8 December (7 December Hawaii time). Still, he refused to
give the order to go, deciding to allow the diplomats until 25 November to solve the problem. However, army and navy preparations were far advanced before that date. The actual war orders
were issued on 5 November. The advance screen of sixteen submarines, five of them carrying midget submarines, left port
headed eastward toward Hawaii. On 17 November the ships of
the Pearl Harbor task force began to slip away from their anchorages and head north to the cold waters of Tankan Bay in Etorofu,
the largest of the Kurile Islands.

While high-level Japanese officials had been confronting the
hard choices of peace or war and their armed forces were preparing
for conflict, their American counterparts seemed blissfully unaware
of the potential consequences of President Roosevelt's embargo.
The administration's concern with supporting England had the effect of downgrading the Japanese problems. It is difficult to ascertain exactly what Secretary Hull hoped to achieve in his dealings
with Ambassador Nomura, who had accurately conveyed the senti-
ments of his government. Again and again Hull and his assistant,
Sumner Welles, insisted upon a complete Japanese withdrawal from
both China and Indochina. Perhaps the proposed meeting between
President Roosevelt and Premier Konoye would, as Hull claimed,
settle nothing, but America's refusal indicated that the State Department did not even wish to try to reconcile the differences. As early
as his first meeting with Nomura on 8 March, Hull was aware that
his policy might lead to war with the Japanese. Later it was obvious
to Secretary of War Stimson and the U.S. chief of naval operations
(CNO), Adm. Harold R. Stark, that only a Japanese withdrawal
from China would have averted war.

Perhaps it is too much to say, in retrospect, that anyone in the
U.S. government wanted war with Japan, but obviously little was
done to avert it. At the same time that the hard-line diplomatic
policy was being pursued there was complacency at all levels in
Washington and Honolulu. This is the only explanation for why the
Japanese consulate in Hawaii was allowed to operate unimpeded

throughout the crisis months of negotiations. The bulk of the information concerning the U.S. military on the islands came from agents operating there. The reason the State Department gave for not closing the consulate was that it did not want to anger the Japanese while talks were underway. This is hardly a credible reason, however, since relations with Japan in the last four months of 1941 could hardly have become worse.

The potential advantages gained by having broken the Japanese diplomatic code were dissipated through layers of bureaucracy and false security. The fear that the Japanese would learn that their code had been broken led to restrictions on who could receive decoded material. The army's list included only the secretary of war, the chief of staff, the chief of war plans, the G2, and the president's military aide. The navy directed the messages to the equivalent officers. The commander of the Pacific Fleet, Admiral Kimmel, charged with overall responsibility in the Pacific if war was declared, was not routinely provided with the key translations. Kimmel first learned of the so-called Purple code on 3 December when a message from Washington mentioned the color. He was assured by his chief intelligence officer, Lt. Comdr. Edwin T. Layton, that the word meant nothing. This reaction was a normal one given the nature of the message. Earlier in April, Layton had requested information from other intelligence sources in Washington and was told that "information of a political significance" would not be routinely submitted to the fleet unless it was directly concerned. Long dispatches from Admiral Stark paraphrasing the intercepts were no substitute for the messages themselves. As war drew nearer, some of the phrases used in Stark's communications led Kimmel to downgrade the need for security at Pearl Harbor. Unfortunately, those persons in Washington most concerned about what they learned from monitoring the flow of information from Japanese sources had neither the rank nor the authority to translate their fears into action.

Kimmel had available other sources of information about Japanese ship movements, however. These were the radio intercepts that Layton and his staff monitored. They had identified the call signals of more than two hundred ships. By strict surveillance and some intelligent guesswork, they could locate specific ships and by back plotting could in general determine a ship's movements. Thus they had been able to pick up the movement of submarines and the transfer of ships southward. On 1 December the Japanese changed their radio calls. This was routinely done at six-month intervals. Since the codes had been changed on 1 November, Layton saw this as significant and so informed Kimmel. He also had to admit that he had lost track of the carriers. But neither the admiral nor Layton considered this anything to be alarmed about since it had happened before. The presumption was that the carriers were on the move to support whatever mischief the Japanese were planning in either the Dutch East Indies or Malaya.

One of the best examples of the general complacency with regard to Japanese intentions was the so-called bomb plot message of 24 September sent from the foreign ministry to the Honolulu consulate. This message was different from previous ones in that it created a grid system for the port facilities. Japanese agents were specifically asked to report on the presence of U.S. warships and whether they were at anchor or tied up at wharves. The message clearly indicated a great interest in the specific location of particular ships. One would have imagined that American intelligence officers, particularly the Office of Naval Intelligence (ONI), would immediately have seen some significance in this request. This was not the case. It was not translated until 9 October. At that time, Col. Rufus S. Bratton, an army intelligence officer who was already very concerned about Japanese activities, passed on the information—along with his concern—to his superior, Brig. Gen. Sherman Miles. Miles saw nothing sinister in it, just a normal request for details of naval traffic in Honolulu. Bratton also sent the message to General Marshall and to the chief of the War Plans Division, Brig. Gen. Leonard T. Gerow, without eliciting a response. Bratton did not have the authority to do more. Lieutenant Commander Alwin D. Kramer of the ONI sent the message through normal channels to his superiors. He also prepared a comment on the bomb plot translation but did not give much importance to the Japanese message. In any event, Kimmel never received the translation indicating that the Japanese wanted exact locations of all ships under his command.

The American intelligence service decoded a whole series of messages sent from Tokyo to its envoys warning that 25 November was a deadline for successful conclusion of the Washington negotiations. On 22 November a message was decoded that indicated that the deadline had been extended to 29 November, after which things would automatically happen. The State Department understood even before Japan's special envoy, Adm. Saburo Kurusu, arrived on 15 November that the Japanese government was likely to implement its long-promised expansion plan. Kurusu, the former ambassador to Germany who had signed the Tripartite Pact for Japan, was a career senior diplomat whom Nomura had requested in April. His arrival in the United States, although heralded by the media as a sign of a possible breakthrough in negotiations, was largely window dressing since the Pearl Harbor strike force was already gathering at Tankan Harbor.

A new Japanese foreign minister, Shigenori Togo, had been appointed, and he submitted a proposal to Washington on 7 November that the State Department found to be totally unacceptable. It called for the embargo to be lifted and Japan to be given a free hand in China for at least twenty-five years. Hull, Stimson, and Welles did not move from their inflexible position first enunciated in June. On 20 November, Kurusu presented a softer, more conciliatory note containing Japan's promise not to seize any of the oil-producing islands if the United States promised not to interfere with the China war. The Japanese also asked that the United States provide oil until arrangements could be made for the Dutch to supply them with what was needed. If this was done, Japan promised a phased withdrawal from Indochina.

Secretary Hull's negative reply on 26 November reiterated the previous U.S. demands and, given the military preparations of the Tojo government, war became inevitable. In Tokyo on 27 November, despite efforts by Konoye and other elder statesmen on the Liaison Committee to extend the deadline for discussions, war was decided upon. The emperor attended the committee meeting of 1 December and by his silence confirmed the decision. The next day orders were sent to the various army and navy commands to expect war on 8 December. Far to the north, on the *Akagi*, a previously reluctant Admiral Nagumo received from Yamamoto the coded message "Niitaka Yama Nobore" [Climb Mount Niitaka] ordering him to weigh anchor for Pearl Harbor.

Admiral Kimmel and his army counterpart, Lt. Gen. Walter C. Short, conferred often, and there was constant interchange between members of their staffs. They understood each other and the respective roles assigned them. The defense of Hawaii against invasion and sabotage was the army's responsibility. Short shared the belief of most senior officers that Japan would not invade the islands, thus most of the activities of the army units involved training exercises that had little direct relation to the growing crisis with Japan. Army planes were utilized for only short-range operations; long-range surveillance was left to the navy.

Returning to his office after a conference with Kimmel on 27 November, General Short received a dispatch he believed to be from General Marshall, although it was later determined that it was prepared by Marshall's staff. The message—framed to alert Short that the negotiations with Japan, for all practical purposes, had been terminated—noted that the government wanted Japan to commit the first hostile act. Short was instructed to place the army in a defensive posture and to carry out reconnaissance without alarming the civilian population. Short was further ordered to take measures against sabotage. If war did come, the Rainbow 5 Plan was to be implemented.

Later that same day, Short received a message from General Miles specifically warning against subversive activities by the Japanese. Instead of plainly stating that war was imminent and that Short should place his troops on a war alert, these dispatchs emphasizing espionage confirmed Short's own views. He had concluded that air attack was highly unlikely because Japan had no long-range bombers that could reach Hawaii from Japanese bases and return. Short therefore reacted in a predictable way to make sure that all the army bases were secure from what he considered the greatest danger—sabotage. Among other things, Short directed that all army aircraft be brought in from their dispersal areas to central locations at each airfield where the planes could be more easily guarded. He believed that with thirty minutes' warning they could be dispersed if the need arose.

Antisubmarine patrols were left to the navy. However, Short never asked Kimmel if the navy had enough of the proper planes to perform long-range reconnaissance. If Short had, he would have discovered how lax the navy's patrols were and perhaps could have offered the use of some of the army's long-range B-17s.

Admiral Kimmel's duties were more complex than were his army counterpart's. All the war plans devised since World War I had placed the Pacific Fleet in the forefront of any successful counterthrust against the Japanese. He was fully aware of this awesome responsibility and the shortcomings of the Pacific Fleet. Throughout 1941 he had bombarded Washington with pleas for more ships and planes. He had been particularly frank with Admiral Stark while arguing against transferring an aircraft carrier and two battleships to the Atlantic, which was presumed to be the more threatened theater. Kimmel looked to Washington to be candid with him and give him up-to-date advice. What he received only confused him.

Kimmel got a long dispatch from the CNO's office on the same day that Short received the messages from Marshall and Miles. Although revised after consultation with Stark and others and approved by Navy Secretary Frank Knox and the president, it was mainly the work of RAdm. Richmond Kelly Turner, chief of naval war plans, a man not known for mincing words. The message began: "This dispatch is considered a war warning." It then went on to give the navy's best appreciation of Japanese intentions. Washington was aware of the movement of Japanese troops and ships southward and had concluded that either the Philippines, Borneo, or perhaps even Thailand was their objective. The CNO ordered Kimmel to undertake "appropriate defensive deployment" preparatory to carrying out the basic naval plans in case of war.

Washington authorities believed that sufficient warning had been given to both Kimmel and Short and that they would place their commands on full alert. This was not the case. Kimmel's staff examined the CNO's dispatch carefully and concluded that if there was a war, it would not immediately concern Pearl Harbor. The admiral saw no reason to change the orders that he had issued in

October regarding security aboard ships. He further decided against increasing security and readiness measures on the vessels within Pearl Harbor. Nor did Kimmel order any long-range aerial scouting missions. Presumably he believed that RAdm. Claude C. Bloch, commandant of the 14th Naval District and whose chief responsibility was the naval defense of Hawaii, would take that action.

However one wishes to sympathize with Kimmel, it is difficult to comprehend why a seasoned flag officer who had been told that a dispatch was "a war warning" failed to take such basic precautions. One possible explanation is that, confident in his preparations, he ignored the fact that during fleet exercises in 1928 and again in 1932 and 1938, successful air attacks had been launched against Hawaii by American planes acting as aggressors. Nor was Kimmel alone in his overconfidence. In a conversation with his chief of staff, Capt. Charles H. McMorris, Kimmel was reassured that the chance of a surprise attack was nil.

Kimmel's most positive defensive action came on 1 December when he ordered a squadron of Marine fighters to be delivered by the carrier *Enterprise* to Wake Island. Four days later the *Lexington* steamed from Hawaii with a squadron of fighters for Midway. These ships were under orders to patrol aggressively and notify Pearl Harbor of anything out of the ordinary. Vice Admiral William F. Halsey Jr., aboard the *Enterprise,* believed hostilities were imminent and put the carrier on war alert. Because of the movement of these carriers, the southwest approaches to Hawaii were reasonably well covered by planes from the two task forces. However, nothing was done to cover the northwest approaches—which in previous naval air exercises had been considered the most important sectors. This nonchalance existed despite the fact that the navy had available eighty-one twin-engine PBY patrol craft, of which fifty-four were the latest types.

Meanwhile, in Washington, neither Secretary Hull nor the Japanese had modified their positions. Kurusu and Nomura met with Hull on 1 December and were told flatly that the United States would not be in league with the Japanese military. Although not the last contact, this for all practical purposes brought an end to negotiations. Kurusu had suggested earlier that the president send a cable directly to the emperor appealing for peace. After considering the proposal carefully, Roosevelt decided not to go over the heads of the Japanese envoys in Washington.

There was much confusion in the upper military echelons in Washington in the week prior to Pearl Harbor. They knew that Japanese diplomats in London had been ordered to destroy their codes and to prepare to close down. This clearly indicated a possible break with Britain. The intelligence services also had received indications that perhaps the Japanese were planning something besides a descent upon the East Indies or Malaya. One such indicator was the reception of the so-called Winds Messages. The last and operative message was sent to Nomura on 29 November. It advised him that, in case of emergency, he would be notified by one of three messages informing him which state—Russia, Britain, or the United States—was affected. The messages would be injected into the noon radio broadcasts. The code name for the United States was "East Wind Rain"; for Russia it was "North Wind Cloudy"; for Britain it was "West Wind Clear." On 5 December the issue for American intelligence officers was complicated by the signal "North Wind Cloudy." This message did not fit with various other intelligence reports indicating that Russia was not the target. It took time to conclude that this phrase was not a code but simply a part of the regular weather report. There is no proof that Japan ever used the code since normal channels of communication remained open until after the attack on Pearl Harbor.

Colonel Bratton of army G2, who had been closely monitoring the Japanese messages, was concerned whether or not naval officials at Pearl Harbor had been sufficiently alerted. He was assured that they had, and that the fleet had put out to sea. The fact is, Washington authorities, particularly navy leaders, were even more certain than Kimmel that the Pacific Fleet was in no danger. Bratton's counterpart in naval intelligence, Lieutenant Commander Kramer, and his superiors, although following events in the Pacific, continued to be unconcerned about the war status of Hawaii.

Japan's official reply to Hull's 26 November response was a very long fourteen-part message to Washington presenting in detail the Japanese position. The first thirteen parts were intercepted by American intelligence and were translated by early evening of

6 December. Copies were delivered personally by Kramer to the president and Navy Secretary Knox. Roosevelt, after reading the material, although it was a prosaic recitation of past events, concluded that war was imminent. Kramer also informed his superior, RAdm. Theodore S. Wilkinson. Wilkinson was hosting a dinner party that included General Miles among the guests. Neither did anything with the information. Colonel Bratton read the army translation and concluded it should be delivered to the State Department. He personally delivered a copy of the intercept to the night duty officer at State and asked that it be given to Secretary Hull as soon as possible. He then went home. Before leaving his office, Bratton concluded that the fourteenth message was not likely to be received. However, his assistant, Lt. Col. C. C. Dusenbury, continued on duty with instructions to deliver the intercepts to Stimson, Marshall, Miles, and Gerow. The fourteenth message came in just after midnight. Dusenbury concluded that it was not important and decided against waking the senior officials. General Marshall and the senior army officers were thus unaware at that juncture of the contents of the Japanese communication. Dusenbury's decision meant that eight or nine precious hours were lost. General Gerow, the chief of war plans, later testified that had he received the intercepts, he would have immediately asked Marshall to send another preemptory warning to Short.

The key passage of the fourteenth message was the last sentence, which stated that the Japanese government believed that further negotiations would be fruitless. This was not a declaration of war, just a statement that a break in relations was imminent. The translation of this final message was known to Admirals Stark and Wilkinson before 0800, and the president had it by 1000 on 7 December. Roosevelt correctly surmised that the Japanese were going to sever relations, but he did not believe that they would declare war. The War Department delivered copies of the fourteenth message to the State Department before 0800. Soon afterward, Colonel Bratton received an intercept of a short message to the Japanese embassy from Foreign Minister Togo. The dispatch instructed Nomura to present the official reply to the secretary of state no later than 1300 on 7 December. Bratton later said this convinced him that the Japanese were going to attack some American installation. None of his superiors were in their offices that Sunday morning. Knowing that only Marshall could issue a command message, Bratton called him at home at 0900. He was told that the general was out riding. Marshall did not call back until 1030 and decided to go to his office, where he saw the intercept a few minutes after 1100.

Marshall agreed that the last message was significant. After conferring with Miles and Gerow, he called Stark and suggested sending a joint message. The admiral demurred, fearing that the many messages already sent to Kimmel had confused the warning issue. Instead he asked that Marshall simply notify the navy of the contents of any message the chief of staff might send. Marshall then hastily scribbled a short note informing field commanders that the Japanese envoys were going to destroy their code machines and present an ultimatum at 1300. "Just what significance the hour set may have we do not know but be on alert accordingly," he concluded. Marshall instructed Bratton to carry the note to the message center for dispatch to the Caribbean Defense Command, the Philippines, and Hawaii—with precedence given to MacArthur's command.

Bratton encountered difficulties at the message center when the clerk could not read Marshall's writing. It had to be deciphered before it could be encoded for transmission. All this took valuable time. The message went out at noon to the Caribbean Defense Command, and a few minutes later it was sent to the Philippines. The time thus wasted from the point when Bratton read the short intercept became crucial even for MacArthur as it took more than half an hour to be decoded and delivered—perilously close to the deadline mentioned in Togo's dispatch. Even worse, the message to Short could not be sent because atmospheric conditions had made it impossible to get through to Hawaii. Rather than try using navy facilities, the officer in charge of the message center decided to send it by Western Union to San Francisco and thence on to Hawaii. All of these delays meant Marshall's crucial warning was not received in Honolulu until thirty minutes before the attack. Even then it was not marked for priority delivery, but was simply put with other routine messages for Fort Shafter. It was not delivered until Monday morning.

The diplomatic charade in Washington was about to end. Nomura and Kurusu, ignorant of their nation's plans and equally ignorant that their diplomatic code had been broken, prepared to call on Secretary Hull at 1300 as instructed. However, the transcription of Tokyo's fourteen-part message, the same one that American intelligence officers had had in their possession for hours, was taking more time than planned. Nomura asked Hull to delay their meeting. At about 1340 Secretary Knox informed the president of the attack on Pearl Harbor. Notwithstanding this knowledge, Roosevelt advised Hull to receive the Japanese envoys. Less than an hour later, Nomura presented the long dispatch, which Hull slowly read. He then lectured them, concluding with the observation that the document was crowded with "infamous falsehoods and distortions on a scale so huge that I never imagined until today that any Government on this planet was capable of uttering them." The shocked and surprised envoys left the State Department. Only after returning home did they discover the reason for Hull's anger.

Despite the general knowledge among senior naval officers at Pearl Harbor that the crucial discussions in Washington had all but foundered, nothing had been done to place the ships on an alert footing. Pearl Harbor continued to be fully lit during the last night of peace, a tempting target for any enemy. The situation in retrospect was potentially more dangerous than normal since *all* the battleships in the fleet were at anchor. This was the result of Admiral Halsey's departure to ferry planes to Wake Island. Normally the battleships in his squadron would have rotated with those of VAdm. William S. Pye, whose squadron had just returned from its tour at sea. Thus all of Kimmel's major ships except the two carriers were in port. Kimmel had not felt it necessary to have an alternate commander take Halsey's ships out for their routine sea duty.

General Short's sabotage alert had been implemented by the evening of 6 December. At Hickam Field, where the bombers were based, all the planes that could fly—six B-17s, twelve A-20s, and seventeen B-18s—were grouped together in the open under guard. The most excitement on the field early on the morning of 7 December was the projected arrival of the twelve unarmed B-17s that General "Hap" Arnold had sent to replace the outdated B-18s. At Wheeler Field, the army's fighter base, the planes, including sixty-two new P-40s, were lined up in neat rows. This was also true at Bellows Field in eastern Oahu, where two squadrons of planes were also neatly aligned. At Kaneohe Naval Air Station all the PBY patrol planes were either in the hangars or at anchor—with the exception of three that were on patrol duty. The major exception to this somnolent attitude was at the tiny west island airstrip at Haleiwa, where Lieutenants George Welch and Ken Taylor, survivors of an all-night poker game, were awake and arguing about going for a swim.

Meanwhile, Admiral Nagumo's task force was drawing nearer to its launch point. It had been protected by the northern route it was following and also by bad weather, which further limited the chance of detection. The seas had been so rough on 4 December that refueling operations were canceled after a number of unfortunate seamen were washed overboard as the smaller ships were tossed about. Nagumo, never an enthusiastic supporter of the plan, continued to worry about the location of the American carriers. Nevertheless, he had made it clear in his message to the fleet on the previous day that the attack would proceed even if it were detected. By 1550 on 6 December, the task force had reached a point approximately six hundred miles north and slightly west of Oahu. The ships refueled one last time before the tankers broke away to take up rendezvous positions for after the attack.

As the Japanese fleet neared the launch point, Nagumo ordered speed increased to twenty-four knots. By that time submarines had surrounded the Hawaiian Islands, lurking approximately three hundred miles offshore. However, those that were to launch midget submarines were much closer. It was one of these that was detected on the afternoon of 5 December by an American destroyer. The destroyer squadron commander dismissed the soundings as reflections from a "big black fish." Nagumo continued to receive reports from the Japanese consulate in Hawaii, relayed from Tokyo, on changes in the location of the American battleships and cruisers. The last message, received at 0200 on 7 December, reported that no barrage balloons were aloft anywhere on Oahu and that no torpedo nets had been observed.

Morale was high on all the carriers, particularly among the air officers. Genda and Fuchida could hardly contain their eagerness. After breakfast there were final briefings and last minute instructions. Earlier, the Z flag flown by Admiral Togo at Tsushima had been raised on the flagship, *Akagi*. At approximately 0530 the cruisers *Tone* and *Chikuma* launched their scout planes. Without waiting for their reports, the carriers, at a point 220 miles north of Oahu, turned to port and prepared to launch their planes. The heavy seas delayed the launching, and the takeoff of the first strike group was very dangerous. At 0610 the first of the Zero fighters lifted off, followed by the high-level bombers and the torpedo bombers. It took several minutes for all the planes to get airborne and form up. Then, at 0620, Fuchida gave the signal to take up the attack course.

The first wave of 140 bombers and 50 fighters had been specifically assigned targets at five airfields and the capital ships moored in Pearl Harbor. Immediately after the last planes of the first wave were airborne, crews began preparing to launch the second wave. The rough seas hampered raising the planes from the hangar decks to the flight decks. Finally, at 0705, the task force turned eastward and again launched aircraft. The second strike force was composed of 213 planes. The 54 horizontal bombers were assigned to follow up the strikes at Hickam, Kaneohe, and Ford Island. The 78 dive-bombers were to target all the ships in Pearl Harbor, while some of the fighters were to provide top cover and others were to strafe targets of opportunity. After the final plane took off, Nagumo left the launch area at high speed to take up a preset position approximately 175 miles north of Oahu.

A series of encounters by the American destroyer *Ward* on patrol duty outside Pearl Harbor should have alerted higher headquarters to take immediate precautions. At shortly before 0400 the tender *Condor* had sighted a submersible object and reported it to the *Ward*'s commander, Lt. William W. Outerbridge, who declared general quarters. At about the same time, the gate to the torpedo net was opened for normal traffic. It would remain open until 0840, allowing one midget submarine to enter the harbor undetected. Outerbridge meanwhile continued the search for the midget reported by *Condor*'s lookout. At shortly before 0640, observers on the *Ward* spotted a black object just in front of the open torpedo gates. The pilot of a PBY had also seen the submarine. Fearful that he might be attacking an American boat, Outerbridge nevertheless attacked and sank the intruder with depth charges. This first action of the Pacific war was immediately reported to the naval district headquarters at approximately 0650. Once again communication problems combined with lethargy to prevent quick, definitive defensive action. At 0715 Admiral Bloch received a report that the *Ward* had dropped depth charges on a submarine operating in the defensive area. But it did not indicate that the boat had been sunk. Confusing the issue further was a report from a patrol plane that it had sunk a submarine. Bloch and his chief of staff spent some time trying to understand the messages. Bloch asked for confirmation and then decided to await developments. Kimmel's headquarters had also been notified, but the duty officer made a series of phone calls to try to ascertain exactly what had happened before finally deciding to call the admiral at 0740. During all this time, no one thought to inform General Short's headquarters of the events outside the harbor.

A further chance of alerting the military of the approaching danger was lost by the nonchalant way reports from the Opana radar station were handled. This most remote of five such stations was manned by two privates, both of whom were familiar with the operations of their radar set, which had a maximum range of 130 miles. Hardly any traffic had been observed that morning and the men prepared to close down the operation until 1100. They were in no hurry since their breakfast truck had not arrived. They were relaxing, watching the radar screen, when at 0702 they picked up a blip larger than any they had ever seen. After checking to make certain the set was operating properly, they contacted the information center at Fort Shafter. The officer in charge of operations that morning was a pursuit pilot who had never been involved with the identification and plotting systems before. All the other personnel, with the exception of the switchboard operator, had left for breakfast at 0700. The lieutenant, unimpressed by the report, did nothing. Another message from Opana arrived at 0715. This time the blips indicated at least fifty planes only ninety-two miles distant. One of the radar operators finally talked directly with the lieutenant, who assured the soldier that what he was seeing was either the B-17s due to arrive from the West Coast or planes from one of the aircraft carriers. The last sighting report was made at 0739, when the planes entered the dead zone and could not be tracked any farther.

Flying at ten thousand feet, Fuchida's air armada approached Oahu from the northwest. After confirming that the island was in sight, he ordered all planes into attack formation and then, at 0740, fired a signal flare. A mix-up occurred when the dive-bomber leader misunderstood the signal to mean that the Americans were alerted. He therefore began his attack on Hickam Field and Ford Island. This placed the torpedo bombers out of sequence from the original plan. Fuchida had no choice but to order his torpedo bombers in as quickly as possible. At 0749 they began their runs. Fuchida need not have worried. The Japanese had achieved complete surprise. Even before the first explosions, Fuchida radioed the code words "Tora, Tora, Tora," indicating that the U.S. forces had been caught totally unaware.

The American capital ships were berthed very much as the consulate reports had indicated. The northernmost ship on the east side of Ford Island was the *Nevada*. At equal distance in line were anchored by twos the *Arizona*, next to the repair ship *Vestal,* followed by the *Tennessee, West Virginia, Maryland,* and *Oklahoma.* The *California* was anchored at the extreme eastern end of the island. Four cruisers were anchored south of the island, and the *Pennsylvania* sat nearby in dry dock. On the opposite side of the island was the old *Utah,* then in use as a training ship. The ships moored outside to the east were the most vulnerable to torpedo attack.

The first attackers over the harbor were the dive-bombers and at about 0755 a bomb struck the minelayer *Oglala,* then occupying the *Pennsylvania*'s normal berth. Rear Admiral William R. Furlong—commander of Battle Forces Pacific, which was basically a service organization—was by chance on board the *Oglala* and gave the alarm for all ships to sortie.

By this time the torpedo planes were making their runs. One torpedo passed under the *Oglala* and struck the cruiser *Helena.* Even more damaging was a three-plane attack on the *Oklahoma.* All scored hits. Shortly thereafter, a fourth torpedo slammed into the *Oklahoma,* which then slowly turned over. At about the same time, torpedoes struck the *West Virginia* and Pye's flagship, the

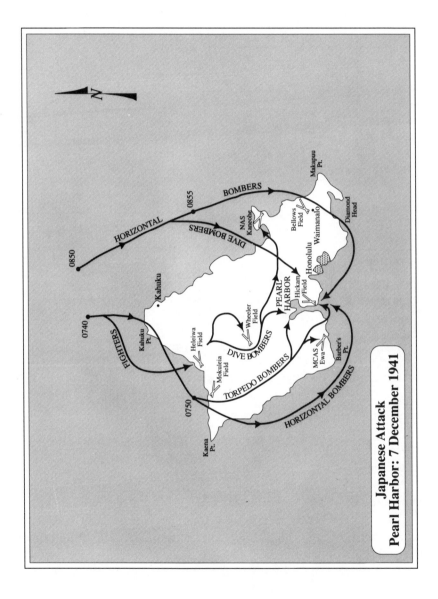

Japanese Attack
Pearl Harbor: 7 December 1941

California. The *California* lost all power and began to list. It, too, was in danger of capsizing. On the other side of the island, the *Utah* was sunk. The *Nevada* and *Arizona* had also been struck by torpedoes, and the *Tennessee* had a turret torn off by a bomb from a dive-bomber. By 0805 the high-level bombers had arrived with their modified armor-piercing bombs. The bombadiers zeroed in on the *Maryland* and *California* with deadly accuracy. The *West Virginia* took six torpedoes and two bombs but stubbornly refused to sink immediately. The most devastating single hit was made on the *Arizona*, where an armor-piercing bomb sliced through several decks to explode in the forward magazine at 0810, causing the ship to explode. Forty-seven officers and 1,056 men were killed or later listed as missing.

Although less dramatic, the dive-bombers and fighters assigned to other military targets were also uniformly successful. At 0758 the first bombers arrived over Hickam Field from the south. They were soon joined by planes that had attacked the ships in Pearl Harbor. They dive-bombed and strafed the hangars and the neat rows of planes without opposition. Troops at Wheeler Field could hear the first explosions but were left alone until 0802, when the first group of dive-bombers and fighters appeared. Caught totally by surprise, personnel at Wheeler watched the systematic destruction of their planes and equipment. Two pilots, the poker-playing fliers Welch and Taylor, ran a gauntlet of fire to reach their planes located at Haleiwa. The Zeros strafed Schofield Barracks, receiving only small-arms fire. Twenty-one Zeros descended on the Marine Corps field at Ewa and destroyed thirty-three of the forty-nine planes there. Even worse hit was the naval air base at Kaneohe, where only three PBYs survived the attack.

At 0820 pilots of the first wave, having dropped their bombs and exhausted their ammunition, formed up for the flight back to the carriers. They left behind scenes of destruction at all American military installations that delighted the operation's planners. The first minutes of their attack had found a thoroughly confused enemy. Army personnel believed the navy was conducting exercises and naval officers and men thought the army was guilty of disturbing the peace of that somnolent Sunday morning. However, after the message "Air Raid, Pearl Harbor, This is not a Drill" was broadcast and the explosions from the ships confirmed that war had begun, officers and men of all services began to sort things out. Despite the continuing desperate attempts to save the ships and those trapped inside, what was left of the fleet took up defensive positions, the men manning antiaircraft and machine guns. The same pattern was followed at the air bases.

The second wave of Japanese planes, launched mainly from the *Shokaku, Zuikaku,* and *Soryu,* approached Oahu from the east at about 0900. The dive-bombers, flying in four groups, concentrated on the ships in the harbor, while the horizontal bombers struck the airfields. The Zero fighters provided top cover and strafed at will. However, the defenders at all the stations were better organized and the Japanese were met with a hail of antiaircraft fire. Welch and Thomas flew into the midst of the Japanese formations and claimed the destruction of seven planes. Their success serves as an indicator of what might have occurred had General Short not been so preoccupied with sabotage. However, despite the defenses, the second wave inflicted considerable damage on Wheeler and Hickam Fields and severely damaged the battleship *Pennsylvania* and the destroyers *Cassin* and *Downes,* which were also in drydock. A damaged Japanese plane crashed into the seaplane tender *Curtiss,* and the cruiser *Raleigh* took a direct bomb hit. The *Honolulu* and *New Orleans* lost all power and were defenseless. Of the cruisers, only the *St. Louis,* moored next to the *Honolulu,* was able to get under way and move out into the channel.

Earlier, in the midst of the carnage caused by the first attacks, seamen on board the targeted ships saw a strange but inspiring sight. The battleship *Nevada* was moving out. With both the captain and executive officer on shore, the senior officer on board was Lt. Comdr. Francis Thomas. Thomas decided that he could get under way with only two boilers operating. Swinging clear of the doomed *Arizona* without a tug, the huge ship began to make its way past Battleship Row toward the channel. The sight of *Nevada* drew concentrated attacks by the Japanese, who hoped to sink the ship and block the channel. *Nevada* took hit after hit, yet still continued to move. By the time it was opposite the floating drydock, senior officers on land had seen the drama and, understanding how important it was to keep the channel open, ordered Thomas to stay clear of it. He reluctantly obeyed orders and grounded the *Nevada* near Hospital Point. It was now 0900 and the immobile *Nevada* was struck with three more bombs.

Suddenly it was all over. At 1000 the Japanese attackers formed up and set course for Nagumo's waiting carriers. All over Oahu the survivors at the various military installations were frantically trying to repair equipment that could be immediately salvaged. For the navy, the first priority was the grim business of trying to rescue the men trapped in the fleet's battered ships. It would be some time before the full extent of the disaster was known.

Yamamoto's plan had succeeded beyond the wildest dreams of the Japanese high command in Tokyo. The task force had lost only twenty-nine planes, one large submarine, and five midget submarines. Only fifty-five fliers had been killed. On the opposite side of the ledger, his airmen had sunk the battleships *Arizona, Oklahoma,* and *Utah,* as well as the destroyers *Downes* and *Cassin.* This was not the full story, however. The battleships *West Virginia, Nevada,* and *California* and the minelayer *Oglala* were sunk but later raised and repaired. The battleships *Tennessee, Pennsylvania,* and *Maryland,* the cruisers *Honolulu, Helena,* and *Raleigh,* the destroyer *Shaw,* and the service ships *Vestal* and *Curtiss* were all damaged. The navy also lost ninety-two planes and had an additional thirty-one damaged. A total of 2,008 navy personnel were killed and 710 wounded. The Marine Corps had 109 killed and 69 wounded. There were 103 civilian casualties, including 68 dead.

The army also suffered heavily. Only fourteen planes took off from Wheeler Field—all of them obsolete P-36s, which were easy prey for the Zeros. Almost the entire stock of P-40s fell victim to the Japanese. In all, 96 army aircraft were destroyed and 128 damaged. Army casualties numbered 218 killed and 364 wounded. Hangars and storage facilities at all the airfields were either destroyed or badly damaged. Few military operations in history have had such devastating results in such a short period of time. Nevertheless, army and air corps losses were replaced easily, and in just a few months their offensive potential was greater than before 7 December.

Despite heroic salvage efforts, it was more than a year before some of the damaged ships were returned to active service. However, in retrospect, the navy's inability to immediately implement the Orange Plan was less due to the Pearl Harbor attack than the lack of adequate preparation prior to it. Most of the ships seriously damaged or sunk were battleships. Conventional wisdom had held that these would be the main components of any naval offensive. Pearl Harbor and later encounters in the Coral Sea and at Midway showed that the aircraft carrier had become the major factor in naval warfare. On 7 December the United States had only two carriers operating in the Pacific, and both fortunately escaped Nagumo's planes. The fact remained that even at Midway, six months later, Japan would have a two to one advantage in carriers. Victory in the Pacific would depend upon control of the air. Battleships would later be relegated to supporting amphibious landings or escorting carriers.

When Fuchida returned to the *Akagi* he found admirals Nagumo and Kusaka and other staff members in serious discussion about what the fleet's next move should be. The admirals were concerned about the location of the American carriers. Nagumo was fully satisfied that his major objective of supporting the southern invasion force had been accomplished and did not want to risk further losses. He was supported in this by his chief of staff. Fuchida ardently argued for another strike on the dockyards, fuel tanks, and whatever ships had not been put out of action. Genda agreed fully with Fuchida that the forces on Oahu were paralyzed and that the American carriers were too far away to interfere. Even if they were close, the aviators insisted they would be no match for the overwhelming superiority that the Japanese could muster from Nagumo's six carriers. Nagumo then made his most fateful decision of the entire war. There would be no further attacks. Instead, he ordered his task force northward at twenty-five knots. Later he would rendezvous with Admiral Yamamoto near Midway Island. At a conference on board Yamamoto's flagship the morning following the attack, the Combined Fleet commander decided to support Nagumo's decision to withdraw. In retrospect, what Nagumo and Yamamoto did at this early date was to hasten the defeat of their nation. Had the United

States lost its oil tank farms and maintenance facilities, serious operations in the Pacific would have been postponed for more than a year. Yamamoto later stated categorically that he had made a great mistake by not ordering a follow-up strike.

At Pearl Harbor, except for the immediate efforts to save the trapped men, all was confusion. Rumors abounded, including one that had the Japanese landing on Oahu. Rear Admiral Milo F. Draemel led four cruisers from Pearl Harbor to search for Nagumo's force. Fortunately for the small squadron, he was searching in the wrong direction. Despite every indication that the Japanese planes had come from the north, the American search was concentrated south of Oahu and was shifted northward only after it was too late to intercept the Japanese. This was partially the fault of a mistranslated message from the cruiser *Minneapolis,* which had been ordered to investigate the sighting of ships south of Barber's Point. Its message of "no carriers in sight" was delivered as "two carriers in sight." Given the nature of the search, it was fortunate that scout planes did not damage or sink any American ships. A B-17 found the *Enterprise* and the pilot momentarily believed it to be Japanese. The cruisers *Minneapolis* and *Portland* were almost bombed, and some of Halsey's planes nearly attacked Draemel's small cruiser force. Farther away, the *Lexington* task force also turned south in hopes of intercepting the Japanese. All of these poststrike actions illustrate the confusion existing at all levels in Hawaii.

In retrospect, it was fortunate that the *Enterprise* and *Lexington* were searching 180 degrees away from Nagumo's force. In the months ahead they would be America's major offensive weapons. Had either of them discovered the Japanese fleet, they most likely would have been sunk.

The confusion in Hawaii continued into the night of the seventh. The men manning antiaircraft guns throughout the island would fire at anything believed to be an enemy. The worst case involved six *Enterprise* dive-bombers directed to Hickam Field after searching for the Japanese. Four were shot down by trigger happy gunners.

In Washington the shock and surprise over the Japanese attack, although of a different order, were as great as in Hawaii. The first reaction of both military and civilian leaders was incredulity. When informed that the Japanese had attacked Pearl Harbor, Navy Secretary Knox was certain that the message was wrong. It had to be the Philippines. When assured that the information was correct, he phoned the president. The call was taken by Roosevelt's trusted friend and adviser, Harry L. Hopkins, who reacted by saying that the information had to be a mistake. The president immediately called Gov. Joseph B. Poindexter in Honolulu. While Roosevelt was on the phone, Hawaii was struck by the second wave of Japanese planes. The president and his chief advisers met that evening with shocked and angry congressional leaders who focused most of their outrage on Secretary Knox, who could not explain why Pearl Harbor had not been on the alert. Roosevelt informed them that he expected to go before Congress the next day and ask for a formal declaration of war.

The following day, precisely at noon, President Roosevelt arrived at the Capitol and thirty minutes later entered the chamber. He was met with resounding applause from even those who had long opposed him. His speech was short, only six minutes long. The most memorable part of it was the opening: "Yesterday, December 7, 1941—a date which will live in infamy—the United States of America was suddenly and deliberately attacked. . . ." Less than an hour later, Congress declared war on Japan. Three days later, Hitler, in a colossal blunder, honored the Tripartite Pact and declared war on the United States. All pretense of neutrality regarding the war in Europe was gone. America would fight the two-front war U.S. planners had envisaged in their worst-case scenario. Japan's success at Pearl Harbor had united America as never before.

Chapter 5

The Japanese Tidal Wave

THE SHOCK OF the surprise attack on Pearl Harbor, combined with the misinformation concerning the location of Nagumo's task force, minimized any effective counteraction against the Japanese until it was too late. The defensive mode adopted by U.S. army and navy commanders immediately after the strike was replaced on 9 December by a hastily planned offensive action directed at protecting Wake Island. Earlier in the year Admiral Kimmel, in one of his dispatches to Washington, maintained that the defense of Wake was of great importance because it would force the Japanese to deploy a part of their fleet and this could lead to a decisive naval action. Although his fleet was badly damaged, Kimmel, who had been informed of the first Japanese attacks on Wake, was still convinced that the island could be defended and that, at the very least, the enemy fleet committed to the invasion could be brought to action.

Kimmel planned to employ three task forces to relieve Wake, each to be organized around a carrier. Vice Admiral Wilson E. Brown would lead Task Force (TF) 11 with the *Lexington* and three cruisers to strike at Jaluit in the Marshall Islands in order to pin down enemy naval forces believed to be there. Kimmel assigned the major role, delivering reinforcements to Wake's beleaguered defenders to TF 14, built around the carrier *Saratoga*. Although

Kimmel understood that time was important, there was nothing he could do to speed the arrival of the *Saratoga* from California and its subsequent refueling. The refueling was finished at midday on 16 December. Admiral Halsey, on board the *Enterprise,* had to wait until the *Saratoga* battle group finished before his TF 8 could put to sea. Task Force 8 was assigned a primarily defensive mission: it was to operate west of Johnston Island as a screen for Oahu.

This excellent plan was marred at its inception by faulty intelligence information and a poor decision by Kimmel. The *Lexington* task force's initial mission proved a waste of time because there were no ships of any consequence at Jaluit. On 20 December Admiral Brown was instead ordered to head north at full speed to aid in the defense of Wake. Kimmel's decision to appoint RAdm. Frank J. Fletcher to command the *Saratoga* task force was, in retrospect, a needless mistake. The senior officer aboard the *Saratoga* when it reached Pearl Harbor was RAdm. Aubrey W. Fitch, an aviator with considerable experience operating carrier forces. Kimmel replaced him with Fletcher largely because Fletcher was senior to Fitch by a few months. Unfortunately Fletcher had no experience commanding aircraft carriers; most of his experience had been in cruisers. His lack of experience would have a crucial effect on later events. It is also probable that had Kimmel not considered the defense of Oahu paramount, he would have used the aggressive Halsey to command the Wake relief efforts. Not only later events, but his whole previous career showed how offensive minded was the man given the defensive role in Kimmel's plan.

All this planning came to nothing largely because of the actions of Secretary Knox and President Roosevelt. Official Washington was reeling from the shock of Pearl Harbor, and members of Congress and the press demanded to know how the disaster could have happened. Knox was accused by many of laxity and, when queried, he had no specific answers. He decided to go to Hawaii to investigate the situation for himself. He made the long, tiring trip with the president's blessing, arriving in Oahu on 11 December. He then flew back almost immediately, conferring for hours with Roosevelt on 15 December. While in Hawaii Knox had a number of long discussions with Kimmel and Short. It was apparent that he had believed that Kimmel had more direct information about Japanese intentions than the admiral had actually received. Knox believed that Admiral Stark had provided the warning of 6 December— which had in reality been authored by General Marshall and not delivered until 8 December.

Sometime between Knox's departure from Washington and his conference with the president, they decided to relieve Kimmel. This rush to judgment was based partially on good military grounds and partially on the need to identify a scapegoat. Kimmel was duly informed of the secretary's decision and relinquished his command on 17 December to Admiral Pye, who acted as commander in chief, Pacific (CINCPAC) until the arrival of Kimmel's replacement, Admiral Nimitz. Although Nimitz had been only a rear admiral, junior to many, he was the president's personal choice for the post. His appointment was one of the most sagacious moves made during the early stages of the war. Nimitz assumed command at Pearl Harbor on the last day of 1941.

Also on 17 December, relying in large part on Secretary Knox's reports, the army relieved General Short, whose successor, Lt. Gen. Delos C. Emmons, was in California. Other subordinate officers were soon shifted out of their old positions. The navy shake-up began on 20 December when Adm. Ernest King, commander of the Atlantic Fleet, was appointed naval commander in chief (COMINCH). The last major figure in Washington to be ousted was Admiral Stark who in March 1942 was sent to Europe as commander, Naval Forces Europe. King then was appointed CNO, combining for the first time what had been two separate positions.

Secretary Knox's investigation and Kimmel's subsequent relief had a devastating effect on the defenders of Wake Island and possibly robbed the United States of a much needed early victory that might have helped bolster morale following the Pearl Harbor disaster.

The segment of the Japanese fleet detailed to capture Wake Island was vulnerable to attack in the days immediately before and after its conquest. Whatever chance of relieving the beleaguered marines on Wake and enabling them to hold the island was lost by the dilatory attitude of Admiral Fletcher. By early evening of 21 December, TF 14 was within six hundred miles of the island. Had Fletcher pressed on at top speed, he would have met the Japanese invasion force just as its troops were landing early in the morning on the twenty-third. Instead, he decided to refuel on the twenty-second. Difficulties with the fueling operation made him turn the ships northward away from Wake.

Meanwhile, at Pearl Harbor, Admiral Pye was having second thoughts about following through with Kimmel's plan. He was understandably uncomfortable because he had been even more convinced than Kimmel that the fleet was safe from attack. Pye was not encouraged by his superiors in Washington who, without knowing the full circumstances, had ordered an almost totally defensive stance. On the day that TF 11 was ordered north to Wake, Pye received a dispatch from Admiral Stark stating that both he and Admiral King believed Wake Island to be a liability. But they left it to Pye to either continue the relief operation or call it off. Pye's communications to Fletcher were equally ambivalent. On the evening of 21 December, Pye received information about the reinforcements Nagumo had sent to aid in the attack on Wake that proved to be only partially correct. That was the excuse Pye needed; he did not want to present the incoming CINCPAC with another long list of casualties. On 22 December he ordered Brown and Fletcher to return to Pearl Harbor. In any event, because of Fletcher's time-consuming refueling operation, it was probably too late to catch the naval task force that had supported the Wake invasion.

Much has been written about the Marine Corps in various Central Pacific actions. Some of those reports have been accused of exaggerating the Corps's role in the Pacific victory. But there were some desperate actions in which both officers and enlisted marines performed what appears to have been superhuman feats. The first of these confrontations with the Japanese occurred at the tiny outpost of Wake Island.

When the Japanese bombed Pearl Harbor, the newly arrived commander on Wake, Comdr. Winfield Scott Cunningham, had only 449 marines available for action. The first of these troops had arrived only in August. There were also 1,146 contract workers, 70 Pan American employees, and 5 army communications personnel. Some of the civilians would later aid in the defense of the islands. The marine ground detachment was commanded by Maj. James P. S.

Devereux. The air detachment, VMF-211, which reached the island on 4 December after being ferried across the Pacific by Halsey's *Enterprise* task force, was commanded by Maj. Paul A. Putnam. Putnam's squadron was equipped with Grumman F4F Wildcat fighters instead of the older Brewster Buffalo, which proved to be a deathtrap elsewhere in the early stages of the war.

Wake Island is shaped like a horseshoe with the open end pointed northwest. The sides of the horseshoe are broken, forming two islands at the tips—Peale to the north and Wilkes to the south. The main part forms Wake, the big island, on which were located the airfield and most of the service facilities. Despite the small complement of men, Wake was defensible and, if aid had been forthcoming, it perhaps could have been held. Aside from Putnam's aircraft, the most important weapons Devereux had were the three 5-inch gun batteries. Battery B was located on the extreme northwestern side of Peale; Battery L, on Wilkes, protected the seaward approaches to the lagoon; and Battery A was sited at Peacock Point on the southern tip of the main island. Located near these larger guns were three batteries, each with four 3-inch rifles.

The Japanese invasion force consisted of three cruisers, six destroyers, and four transports commanded by RAdm. Sadamichi Kajioka. A part of the Fourth Fleet at Truk, it arrived on 4 December off Roi-Namur in the Marshall Islands. Kajioka's plan was simple. As soon as the war began, bombers from the 24th Air Flotilla would attack Wake's facilities and destroy the small fighter force there. After the island defenses had been neutralized by the air bombardment, he would land his 450 special naval troops. The admiral, leading his small force in the light cruiser *Yubari,* did not expect too many difficulties in overrunning the island. He was fully aware of how inadequate a force opposed him. Unlike most other Japanese commanders at this stage of the war, he was supremely confident that all would go according to plan.

Cunningham and Devereux learned of the attack on Pearl Harbor by 0630 (Wake time) on 8 December and immediately ordered all personnel to their posts. Putnam put up an eight-plane patrol. Just as at Pearl Harbor, the air search was in the wrong direction—in this case to the north.

A rain squall masked the first air attack. At about noon, thirty-six

Japanese bombers from Kwajalein Atoll, six hundred miles away, struck the main island with devastating effectiveness. Seven of the twelve VMF-211 fighters being refueled were destroyed on the ground. Most of the hangars, tools, and general support equipment were also lost in this one raid. Twenty-three marines from the air squadron were killed, as were ten civilians at the Pan American terminal area. Lacking suitable air cover, it was obvious to Cunningham on the first day of the war that, unless help arrived, Wake could not be held. The Japanese bombers returned at about the same time the next day. They were intercepted by three of Putnam's serviceable Wildcats, which shot down one bomber. Antiaircraft fire destroyed another and damaged several more. The hospital was hit during the strike, killing four marines, several navy corpsmen, and fifty-five civilians. Twenty-seven bombers struck on the tenth, targeting the gun emplacements and strafing the causeway to Wilkes. One lucky bomb struck a civilian supply dump, causing a terrific explosion when over a hundred tons of dynamite detonated. However spectacular the visual effect of this raid, casualties were light and marine Capt. H. T. Elrod shot down two more bombers.

At daybreak on 11 December Kajioka's force was about four miles off Wake following a northerly course when it turned for a run parallel to the south shore of the island and shelled the installations for forty-five minutes. He ordered the troops, despite heavy seas, into the boats for a landing on Wilkes. At 0615, Battery A at Peacock Point opened fire on the *Yubari* at a range of about fifty-five hundred yards, scoring two direct hits near the cruiser's waterline and forcing it to retire. At about the same time, the destroyer *Hayate* closed to within four thousand yards. It was caught broadside by a salvo from the two guns of Battery L and blew up. The gunners there also scored hits on another destroyer and a transport. This portion of Kajioka's force escaped under a smoke screen. A few minutes later, three destroyers attacked Peale Island and Battery B's guns scored a hit on one before the ships retired southward. Putnam sent his four remaining planes, which had jury-rigged bomb release systems, after the retreating enemy ships. They scored hits on the two light cruisers, *Tenyru* and *Tatsuta*. The most devastating blow was delivered by Captain Elrod, whose 100-pound bomb landed on extra depth charges being carried by the destroyer *Kisaragi*. The entire crew was lost when the destroyer blew up.

Far from being the easy task envisioned by Kajioka, his abortive assault had cost Japan two destroyers sunk. The marine gunners also damaged all the cruisers, a destroyer, and a troop transport. An estimated seven hundred Japanese were either killed by gunfire or drowned. The marines had every right to be jubilant. A PBY flying boat flew into Wake on 20 December to inform Cunningham and Devereux about Fletcher's relief force. Unfortunately, the marines' situation grew more desperate with each passing day. While Kajioka's damaged ships were being repaired at Kwajalein, land-based bombers struck Wake again and again, normally arriving near noontime. In the mornings and evenings, four-engined flying boats also raided the island. The two remaining U.S. planes valiantly intercepted the bomber formations until they were shot down on 22 December by carrier-based Zeros.

Admiral Shigeyoshi Inoue, commander of the Fourth Fleet at Truk, was taking no further chances in the second attempt to conquer Wake. Although embarrassed, Kajioka remained in command. He had all the surviving ships from the first abortive try plus four heavy cruisers, covering destroyers, and a seaplane carrier. Most important, and giving an indication of just how important the Japanese considered this attempt, was the assignment of the carriers *Soryu* and *Hiryu* to support the invasion. The second landing would be made by some two thousand Special Landing Force troops—the Japanese marines.

The Japanese began their assault in the early morning hours of 23 December with simultaneous landings on the south shore of Wake and on Wilkes. A force of about a hundred picked men from the Special Landing Force was met on Wilkes by seventy marines commanded by Capt. W. M. Platt. After a bitter four-hour battle, almost all the Japanese were killed. Meanwhile, on Wake, the Japanese rammed their landing craft on beaches that could not be covered by the 5-inch battery. By 0500 there were approximately a thousand Japanese on the island confronting only eighty marines. The Japanese had taken most of the airfield, although fighting around the 3-inch guns to the south continued as Putnam, Elrod, and the men of VMF-211 fought until only one marine remained unwounded. Devereux had established a line north of the field across the base of the northern leg of Wake manned by just forty men. An air strike by planes from the Japanese carriers hit the

American positions at 0700. By then Devereux had lost contact with Wilkes. He erroneously believed the marines there had been overrun. Earlier, at about 0320, he had been informed by radio from Pearl Harbor that the two submarines in advance of Fletcher's task force had been ordered back. His last communication with Hawaii at 0500 was terse: "The enemy is on the island. The issue is in doubt." When Devereux informed Cunningham that he could not hold for long against such overwhelming force, the commander decided to save as many lives as possible. At 0730 Devereux hoisted a white flag over his command post and Cunningham surrendered to the Japanese. Because of poor communications, Devereux had to personally visit all the outlying posts. The victorious marines on Wilkes did not lay down their arms until midafternoon.

The marines at Wake Island did not, as a victory-starved media reported, communicate the message: "Send us more Japs." They did, however, sink two Japanese destroyers and inflict far more damage than anyone might reasonably have expected of such a small garrison. The Japanese lost more than 1,500 dead in the two landings on Wake. American losses amounted to 49 marines, 3 sailors, and 70 civilians killed in action. Commander Cunningham surrendered 470 officers and men to Kajioka on 23 December. More than 1,100 civilians were also taken prisoner. All of the American prisoners except for about 100 civilians were evacuated to mainland Japan on 12 January 1942.

There was no such heroic struggle for Guam, the largest and potentially most defensible of the Mariana Islands. Four decades of fruitless haggling over defensive appropriations for the island had produced nothing. Navy captain George J. McMillin, the island's governor, had available only 271 sailors, 152 marines, and 246 men of the Guam Insular Guard, an ill-equipped militia unit, for the defense of the island. There were no heavy guns protecting Apra Harbor; the largest gun was a small-caliber antiaircraft weapon on board the ancient patrol vessel *Penguin*. McMillin had been informed on 6 December that the Pacific situation was so serious that he should destroy his code books. Military dependents had all been taken off the island by November. Admiral Thomas Hart's message, delivered just before 0600 on 8 December, informing McMillin of the beginning of the war thus came as no surprise.

Overall command for the Guam operation fell to Admiral Inoue on Truk; tactical control was exercised by RAdm. Aritomo Goto, whose task force departed the Bonins on 4 December. It appears at first glance that the Japanese were guilty of overkill since the army unit to be utilized was the five-thousand-man South Seas Detachment commanded by Maj. Gen. Tomitaro Horii. However, the Japanese considered Guam to be but a way station for these troops, who were scheduled to participate later in the occupation of the territory adjacent to Rabaul on New Britain.

Hostilities began at about 0830 on 8 December with air raids by 18th Air Group planes from Saipan. These attacks, directed primarily at the major town, Agana, and the Piti Naval Yard, continued for two days. Then, just before dawn on 10 December, an advanced landing force of four hundred men stormed ashore. There was little fighting. A larger force soon followed, landing at Agat, south of the marine barracks on the Orote Peninsula. The most serious resistance was concentrated in the center of Agana, where members of the Insular Guard put up a twenty-five-minute fight against overwhelming odds. In all, twenty-one service personnel and civilians were killed. McMillin surrendered at 0700 on 10 December and the island remained under Japanese control until liberated in July 1944. The native Chamorros suffered brutal treatment by their conquerors.

However important the Japanese offensive in the Central Pacific was to the overall goals of the planners in Tokyo, it was secondary to their major objectives of the Dutch East Indies, the Philippines, and the associated mainland areas of Southeast Asia. The overall commander of Southern Area Operations was Gen. Count Hisaichi Terauchi, who operated with the Fifteenth Army in Burma and Thailand. The Twenty-fifth Army, led by Lt. Gen. Tomoyuki Yamashita, was assigned the difficult task of conquering Malaya and Singapore. China command was ordered to detach the 38th Division to capture the British base in Hong Kong. The task of securing the Philippines was given to Lt. Gen. Masaharu Homma, who had the 16th, 48th, and 61st Divisions and the 65th Individual Brigade—a total of about sixty-five thousand troops—at his disposal.

The main landing force aimed at Lingayen Gulf was composed of seventy-six transports, which picked up 48th Division troops at the Pescadores and Formosa. The 16th Division boarded twenty-four transports at Amami-O-shima. Its target was Lamon Bay on the eastern side of Luzon. A smaller force shipped out of the Palaus with the mission of seizing Davao in the south, thus assuring the Japanese a base from which their aircraft could support the proposed invasion of the Dutch East Indies.

The Japanese committed an overwhelmingly superior naval force to the invasion. Vice Admiral Nobutake Kondo's Second Fleet, built around two battleships and two heavy cruisers, acted as a distant covering force. Close-in support was given by VAdm. Ibo Takahashi's Third Fleet. He had available the aircraft carrier *Ryujo,* five heavy cruisers, five light cruisers, and twenty-five destroyers divided into four attack forces.

Admiral Hart, commander of the U.S. Asiatic Fleet, had only four destroyers, thirteen submarines, six gunboats, a handful of assorted support craft, and some PT boats at Manila. The heavy cruiser *Houston* was at Iloilo, and Hart had commandeered the light cruiser *Boise* from the Pacific Fleet. The closest thing he had to an aircraft carrier was the old *Langley,* which had been converted into a seaplane tender. The aircraft available to him were patrol planes —mostly PBYs. Patrol Wing 10 had twenty-eight of these. For Hart to contemplate a direct confrontation with Takahashi's invasion force was to invite immediate destruction.

The importance of the Philippines in Japanese planning can be seen in the air support planned for Homma's invasion. Primary support was to be provided by the Eleventh Naval Air Fleet based on Formosa. The fleet had 308 planes of all types, including 144 bombers and 110 long-range Zero fighters. The army air force on Formosa would contribute 54 light and 17 heavy bombers and 72 fighters. Despite the superiority in numbers of planes, Japanese air commanders were deeply concerned about the Americans' capabilities, which on paper were indeed formidable. General Lewis Brereton, MacArthur's Air Corps commander, had 277 planes available, most of which were at Clark and Nichols Fields. The buildup of American airpower, which had been designed to provide MacArthur with 75 B-17 Flying Fortresses by the spring of 1942, had begun just a few weeks prior to the war. Only 35 of these heavy bombers had reached the islands. Although manned by young, green crews, the long-range B-17s, if handled properly, could have caused great damage to fixed installations on Formosa. Of the fighter aircraft, 107 were P-40E Warhawks, not as maneuverable as the Zero, but more heavily armed. An earlier version, the P-40B Tomahawk, had run up an enviable record against the Japanese with the American Volunteer Group in China.

MacArthur, despite his upbeat communications with Washington during the last six months of 1941, must have realized the hopelessness of his task. The very geography of the Philippines works against the defender. The archipelago has more than seven thousand islands with a combined coastline longer than that of the United States. The chain is dominated by two large islands, Luzon in the north and Mindanao in the south; between them are the nine larger Visayans. The bulk of the population and the economic center of the Philippines were concentrated around Manila Bay on Luzon. All plans for the defense of the Philippines therefore concentrated on that island. However, its size and its geographic features made this difficult. Luzon is approximately 400 miles long from north to south and 140 miles across at its widest point. A central plain runs from the Lingayen Gulf in the north to Manila Bay. Bordering this wide plain on the east are the Sierra Madre Mountains. To the west are the Zambales Mountains, the southern end of which are in the rugged Bataan Peninsula, which extends into Manila Bay.

Although few in Washington believed even before Pearl Harbor that MacArthur could defend Luzon, the operative plan, War Plan Orange 3 (WPO-3), was designed to give American and Filipino forces a chance of defending the Bataan Peninsula until help could arrive. That plan envisaged that the defenders would have to hold out for up to six months. However, typical of the prewar planning process, the army made little coordination with the navy, which considered that it would be at least two years before a significant relief force could be landed in the Philippines. MacArthur did not approve of WPO-3 because of its defensive nature, and he convinced his superiors that he could meet and defeat the Japanese on the beaches. Much of this reasoning had to be for Washington's consumption because MacArthur, since assuming command of U.S. forces in the Philippines, had continually pressured Marshall and

Arnold for more men and planes. He erred by attempting to implement his offensive plans long before he had sufficient manpower. On 8 December he had only thirty-one thousand U.S. Army troops. Another fifteen thousand were in Air Corps units, manning harbor defenses, or service troops. The American regulars generally formed the core of the Philippine divisions. Only the 31st Infantry Regiment and the 4th Marines were composed of all U.S. troops, and MacArthur, despite his later praise, did not like the marines and assigned them to guard duty. The most thoroughly trained of the Philippine units was the Philippine Division, which was composed mainly of Philippine Scouts complemented by the U.S. 31st Infantry.

MacArthur placed Maj. Gen. Jonathan M. Wainwright's North Luzon Force consisting of the 11th, 21st, and 31st Philippine Divisions, with the 71st in direct support, in position to block the expected Lingayen landings. Two other divisions, the 41st and 51st, made up the South Luzon Force, which was supposed to defend the southeastern beaches. MacArthur retained command of the Reserve Force, made up of the Philippine Division and the 91st Division, the best-trained troops in his command. A separate command with three of the weakest divisions was deployed on Mindanao and the Visayans.

Although MacArthur's chances of successfully carrying out his plan were slight to begin with, the loss of a large portion of his aircraft on the first day of the war rendered the task impossible. The first news of the Pearl Harbor attack was received by Admiral Hart's command at 0300 on 8 December. Hart immediately placed his ships on wartime alert and within the hour had notified MacArthur and his chief of staff, Maj. Gen. Richard K. Sutherland. MacArthur and his Air Corps chief thus had eight hours before the first major Japanese air strike, yet that attack caught the planes at Clark and Nichols airfields totally unprepared.

What occurred between MacArthur and his Air Corps chief during this interval is still a matter of contention. MacArthur later claimed that he gave Brereton full authority to take whatever measures he felt necessary. Sutherland added that Brereton had been encouraged for weeks before the attack to move his B-17s to Del Monte Field on Mindanao. Brereton contradicted MacArthur's statement with a detailed description of his plans for a daylight strike at Formosa—plans he said were communicated to Sutherland, who promised to get authorization from MacArthur. Brereton said he waited almost two hours before he was informed that he was to take no offensive action without definite approval. Bombs were not even to be loaded on the B-17s. It was not until after 1000 that he received permission for a reconnaissance flight over Formosa. False alarms of incoming Japanese planes had caused most of the Luzon-based aircraft to scramble; the B-17s were also ordered on patrol. Similar reports left the American command confused throughout the morning. The official documents indicate that it was not until approximately 1100 that Brereton received orders to attack Formosa. But by then the planes had been recalled, and by 1130 all U.S. aircraft based on Luzon were back on the ground, the B-17s being refueled and loaded with bombs at Clark. By noon the pursuit planes at Nichols, Iba, and Del Carmen were standing by for orders.

These events, sketchily reported and confusingly remembered after the war, are nevertheless extremely important because the procrastination caused the immediate loss of almost half of MacArthur's aircraft. The weight of evidence supports Brereton. MacArthur, for whatever reason, wasted valuable time before freeing up his air commander to take offensive action. This was the first of MacArthur's major errors in defending Luzon. At this juncture, like so many senior army generals, he did not understand the full implications of airpower. In his defense, one can speculate that MacArthur might have been concerned that bomber losses in a Formosa strike would cripple his air units and make it impossible to bomb the expected Japanese landings. A heavy fog early in the morning over Formosa was perhaps another reason for delay. MacArthur's staff officers also believed that Clark and its secondary fields were located too far away for Japanese bombers to reach them. But they were wrong. Compounding the problem was the fact that facilities for dispersing aircraft even at Clark were primitive. Money had not been available to build such facilities in the months before the attack. That failure meant that when the planes landed to be serviced, they were clustered together as the ground crews rushed to get as many as possible ready for the projected attack on Formosa.

At 1245, while the air crews relaxed or went to lunch, the Japanese struck all the airfields on northern and central Luzon. This one raid gained for them aerial superiority throughout the Philippines. The Japanese had fully expected to meet heavy resistance. Surely, they reasoned, the Americans had been informed of the Pearl Harbor strike and were prepared to fight. But that was not the case. The pursuit squadron detailed to cover Clark Field had not taken off because of a localized dust storm. Thus when a large force estimated at over fifty high-level bombers with accompanying fighter cover arrived over Clark, it found no opposition. Attacks on other fields also encountered little resistance. Although the bombers did little damage to the B-17s, they destroyed shops, barracks, and, most important, the communications center. Fighters coming in for low-level strafing attacks did the most damage. The Japanese destroyed twelve B-17s and damaged five others; fifty-five of the P-40s were lost either in combat or on the ground, and only fifteen of the obsolete P-35s remained operational. Further losses were sustained on the tenth when an estimated sixty bombers and fifty fighters struck at Cavite Naval Base and Clark, Nichols, and Iba Fields. The Americans could scramble only twenty P-40s and fifteen P-35s. Although there were individual heroics, such as those of 1st Lt. Boyd D. "Buzz" Wagner, who became one of the first U.S. aces, the Japanese set ablaze the entire naval base and much of Cavite town. Another aviation disaster occurred on the eleventh when most of the navy's long-range PBY patrol planes were destroyed. By 12 December the few B-17s left were operating out of Mindanao, and Brereton had only thirty-five fighters left on Luzon.

MacArthur's plans to stop the Japanese on the beaches were perhaps wishful thinking even before the disastrous air attacks. Nevertheless, he was committed to keeping the Japanese from reaching Luzon's coastal plain. The first Japanese landings were on 8 December, when a small force seized the nearby island of Batan. However, no landings were attempted on Luzon until the Japanese had seized control of the air. Then, on the morning of 10 December, they struck at three separate locations. The Aparri Force in the extreme north went ashore opposed only by one company of the Filipino 11th Division. An attack by five B-17s managed to hit only one minesweeper. The Japanese soon accomplished their first mission by capturing the Aparri and Cumulankigan grass airfields. Finding that these fields were not suitable for medium bombers, the advance columns pushed southward. At the same time, on the west coast, the 2d Attack Force, consisting of forty-four hundred men, landed at Vigan. Brereton's planes sank another Japanese minesweeper and seriously damaged two transports. Despite this attack and extremely bad weather, the Japanese by 11 December had established a beachhead in the Vigan area and continued to put men ashore. Far to the south, adjacent to the San Bernardino Strait, a major landing force from Palau, protected by four cruisers and the aircraft carrier *Ryujo,* seized Legaspi.

The main landing came on 21 December at Lingayen Gulf. Because of the proximity to Formosa, the same troop transports were used for this operation. By this time the token support given by Brereton's air units was minimal because most of the B-17s had been ordered south to Darwin, Australia. As at Vigan, the landings were very difficult due to bad weather. The transports had to be dispersed, and at one point the ships were stretched out over a distance of twenty miles. This provided a golden opportunity for Admiral Hart's submarines. However, once again the Americans were caught off guard despite the sure knowledge that Lingayen would be the main landing area. Hart's five submarines arrived from Manila Bay too late to attack the majority of the transports in deep water. Only one transport was sunk. The following day a small freighter was also torpedoed. As mentioned earlier, the submariners were plagued by another problem that was not resolved until mid-1943: ineffective torpedoes. For example, on the fourteenth the *Seawolf* fired four torpedoes at a seaplane tender; the only torpedo that hit proved to be a dud.

The defenders offered little opposition to the Japanese landings. Wainwright committed the 11th Division to check the invaders around Santo Tomas, but aggressive action by the Japanese forced the green Filipino unit to retreat. Despite this success, the heavy surf made the landings a nightmare. However, by the evening of the first day, most of the infantry of the Japanese 48th Division was ashore and consolidating their hold on the beaches. Their tanks and artillery were ashore by the twenty-fourth, and a concerted advance southward began.

During this dark period, one of the great myths of the war was created by a government that desperately wanted to provide heroes. Captain Colin P. Kelly, piloting one of the few B-17s still flying, attacked the Lingayen invasion force and mistook the heavy cruiser *Ashigara* for the battleship *Haruna*. He dropped his bombs, but they missed the warship. Kelly's B-17 was badly shot up and he ordered his crew to bail out over northern Luzon while he stayed aboard, hoping to nurse the plane back to Clark Field. He did not make it; the crippled bomber crashed in the mountains.

The story correspondents heard was quite different. They were told that Kelly crashed his battered plane into the battleship and sank it. Kelly was posthumously awarded the Distinguished Service Cross, and for years the American public believed the story concocted for the press.

The harsh fact was that, by 24 December, the Lingayen forces had linked up with the Vigan group. They had driven the Philippine Scouts from Damoritis and attacked the key road junction of Rosario, battering the 11th Division still further. Wainwright deployed the 71st around Sison on the twenty-second, and he ordered the 91st north to support it. A Japanese air strike destroyed the bridges over the Agno River and the 91st could not advance quickly enough. The 71st was broken by attacks by three Japanese regiments, and its remnants retreated south of Pozorrubio. General Homma had secured all the narrow coastal plain, defeating some of the best of the Filipino and American troops, and now confronted them in strength as they scrambled to cover the wider expanse of the plain.

MacArthur, realizing he was threatened with envelopment, decided to implement WPO-3, the plan he had earlier opposed, and move all available troops into the rugged Bataan Peninsula. On 23 December he ordered Maj. Gen. George M. Parker Jr. to create a Bataan Defense Force to secure the area and prepare for the arrival of the frontline units. Within two days the 31st Division and what was left of the 26th Cavalry Regiment were in place. They were soon joined by the 41st Division and the Philippine Division.

Meanwhile, on the twenty-fourth, a regiment from the Japanese 16th Division landed at Lamon Bay on Luzon's east coast. The Filipino 51st Division had already been removed from the area, so the landing was unopposed. The Japanese were now in an excellent position confronting MacArthur's weak South Luzon Force and threatening Manila from the east. By the twenty-seventh, the Lamon landing force had joined troops from Legaspi and broken through the American defenses at Tayabas Bay.

The retreat to Bataan was a tactical masterpiece. It had been designed earlier by MacArthur and, as implemented by Wainwright and Maj. Gen. Albert M. Jones, it completely baffled Homma. The South Luzon Force was fortunate that the Japanese air force did not destroy the key bridges. Although MacArthur had declared Manila an open city on the twenty-seventh, Homma believed the movement from Manila northward was the disorganized flight of residents. In reality, 14,000 of the original complement of 15,000 troops reached Bataan safely. The Northern Force retreated in an orderly, planned fashion. The concept was to set up a series of five defensive lines roughly one night's march apart. These would be maintained during the day and then the troops would slip away during the night to the next one south. By 6 January MacArthur had established his northern defense line on Bataan. Within the peninsula's confines he had 65,000 troops and 26,000 civilians ensconced in a very defensible position.

At the time, MacArthur's actions were viewed by the American public as laudatory in the extreme and would be cause for the president to award him the Medal of Honor. In retrospect, his actions during the first weeks of the war were at least as poor as those of Admiral Kimmel and General Short, who were speedily relieved of their commands. At the outset, MacArthur's headquarters had almost eight hours warning of the impending attack. His dilatory attitude toward the use of airpower led directly to the loss of a large portion of it without inflicting any damage on the enemy. The planning for the defense of Bataan was an administrative nightmare. MacArthur had not liked WPO-3, and therefore did not order the withdrawal to Bataan until it was obviously the only viable course of action. The tactical brilliance of the withdrawal masked the fact that food and supplies were left behind in warehouses all over Luzon. At one depot alone there was enough rice left to feed the soldiers and civilians on the peninsula for five months. The troops were forced to go on half rations as soon as they reached

Bataan. Clothes, other food supplies, and drugs were also left behind, as were a half million rounds of artillery ammunition and
more than three million gallons of gasoline. All these articles would
soon be in desperately short supply.

One can thus reasonably ask what the difference was in the
government's perception of MacArthur and of those dismissed for
the Pearl Harbor debacle. The answer seems to be that MacArthur

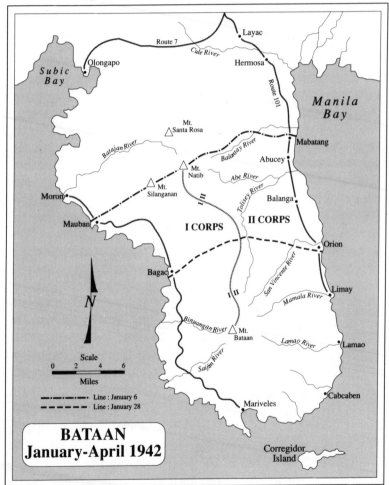

BATAAN
January-April 1942

was already a hero, the senior American general in terms of service, and he was in the midst of a battle presumably against overwhelming odds. The nation needed heroes; it did not need to know that MacArthur had made disastrous mistakes in his handling of the Philippine crisis.

As recognized years before, Bataan was extremely defensible. Its rugged terrain included two extinct volcanoes and varied from dense jungle to large swampy areas. The defense of Bataan, like that of the central plain, was based on a series of lines, the first of which was the Abacay-Mauban line hinged in part on Mt. Natib and Mt. Silanganan near the center of the line. Wainwright commanded the Mauban sector in the west, while General Parker conducted the defense of the Abacay area.

Imperial Headquarters, reflecting the general optimism on 2 January, removed the 48th Division, the best in Homma's command, for action in the Dutch East Indies. Its replacement, the 65th Brigade, was inferior both in numbers and combat experience. Nevertheless, on 9 January Homma attacked the Abacay-Mauban line with a series of frontal assaults. Slowly Parker's forces gave ground. Fearing they might be flanked, the American command ordered a retreat to the second defense line on the Pilar-Bagac road. MacArthur, who had ignored Homma's call for surrender, informed Washington that this was his final line. There would be no withdrawal, he would halt the Japanese advance there. Removed from the rigors of the fighting on Bataan, MacArthur on Corregidor still believed that aid was forthcoming. He was encouraged in this by General Marshall, and the president's announcement on 8 February that there would be no surrender underscored MacArthur's hope for relief.

It appeared that MacArthur's optimism was justified. Throughout February his troops blunted all Japanese attacks, wiped out attempts to flank the line, and destroyed large bodies of isolated enemy troops with limited offensives. Homma was forced to withdraw to a better defensive position while he regrouped. Japanese forces had suffered casualties from combat and disease that would have rendered units in most armies totally unfit for combat. Sickness was rampant, and their primitive medical system was not prepared to handle the thousands of casualties. Homma's 16th Infantry Division was reduced to only seven hundred men, and the army was only a shadow of its size the month before. His chief of staff argued that no strategic advantage could be gained from resuming the offensive. He suggested that simply allowing disease and hunger to take their toll on the Americans and Filipinos would force their surrender. But Homma, feeling pressure from the army high command, wanted a military solution. By the time he resumed his offensive, many of his tired and sick troops had recovered and he had received substantial replacements. Four thousand men of the 21st Infantry Division were sent to bolster his force, as was a large part of the 4th Infantry Division from Shanghai.

The American and Filipino forces at the beginning of February were in no worse condition than the Japanese, but as the months passed, their situation became more desperate. They had already eaten all the cavalry horses and mules, and most troops were on one-third rations of rice. They were plagued by a full measure of tropical diseases, including fevers and intestinal disorders. For all their ailments, there were few drugs. Occasional visits at night by submarines did little to ease supply problems. These factors, as much as the renewed Japanese offensive, finally resulted in the decision to capitulate. Another factor that determined the fighting capacity of the Allied troops was morale. Even before the withdrawal to Bataan, there had been many desertions by the previously untested Filipino troops. They and their American counterparts understood how desperate was their situation. The actions of their supreme commander certainly did nothing to boost morale. MacArthur never visited his troops on Bataan; he was content to stay in the relative security of his Corregidor headquarters with his wife, son, and immediate staff. This gave rise to jokes about MacArthur and earned him the nickname "Dugout Doug." Although unfair, since no one could ever seriously question his personal bravery, that appellation would follow him throughout the war. The average soldier's opinion of MacArthur was reinforced when the general, acting on orders from the White House, left Corregidor for Australia by PT boat on 12 March. It was fortunate for the general's wartime reputation that the half-million-dollar award President Manuel

L. Quezon paid to MacArthur in mid-February for his "magnificent defense" was not made public until many years later.

After MacArthur's departure, command of the Philippines fell to General Wainwright, who moved his headquarters to Corregidor after passing command of the field forces to Maj. Gen. Edward P. King Jr. MacArthur's actions with regard to Wainwright in the ensuing weeks were petty and, even given MacArthur's ego, his plans for continued control of Philippine operations from three thousand miles away were, in retrospect, ludicrous. The army eventually sorted out the command situation by promoting Wainwright to lieutenant general and confirming him as commander, but it also required him to take instructions from MacArthur.

In late March, Wainwright reported that even with the restrictions on rations, there was only enough food to last until mid-April. MacArthur contradicted this estimate, stating that when he left there were enough stores to last until 1 May. He then expressed his complete opposition to surrender and ordered Wainwright to "prepare and execute an attack upon the enemy" if food ran out.

On Good Friday, 3 April, Homma began a renewed general offensive with a five-hour artillery bombardment and continuous air attacks. His main infantry attack was in the center, where the Allied line was weakest. Within two days the Japanese had all but destroyed the 41st Division and cracked the 21st. Despite the defense line falling apart, Wainwright, under orders from MacArthur not to surrender, ordered counterattacks. General King, realizing how exhausted his troops were, concluded that nothing could be gained by prolonging the fight. He decided to disobey orders and asked the Japanese for surrender terms. The reply was unconditional surrender. Believing he had no other alternative, King capitulated on 9 April. The victory had cost the Japanese 3,000 killed and 5,000 wounded.

Following the surrender there occurred one of the most infamous episodes of the war, one which, along with the Pearl Harbor attack, convinced Americans of the barbarity of their enemy. In part, the so-called Bataan Death March resulted from poor planning. The Japanese command had expected to have to deal with 25,000 prisoners. In fact, they had more than three times as many. The prisoners, already malnourished and many of them ill, were forced to walk the sixty-five miles from Mariveles to the railhead at San Fernando. This would have been a hard march for healthy men given the temperature and humidity and the fact that the Japanese did not provide food or water. Nor did Japanese officers exercise control over their men, who had only contempt for anyone who surrendered. Beatings were commonplace, and many of the weakest men were bayoneted as they fell by the wayside. The exact number who died on the march will never be known. The best estimates place the toll at between 7,000 and 10,000 of which 2,330 were Americans. General Homma, who had shirked his responsibility to ensure that prisoners were treated humanely, was executed after the war for the brutal actions of his men.

The Japanese could not be secure in their possession of Manila Bay as long as their enemy held the key offshore islands. The largest of these was Corregidor, three and one-half miles long and one and one-half miles wide. In the period prior to World War I, a number of coast artillery batteries had been emplaced on the island. At the time, that was enough to protect the bay's main entrance. However, because of the terms of the Washington Treaty, few improvements had been made during the interwar years—with the exception of adding some antiaircraft batteries to the island's defenses. Most of the work during this period had been devoted to building a very comprehensive tunnel system in Malinta Hill. The main tunnel was thirty feet wide and fourteen hundred feet long. Power generators, a hospital, and considerable storage space for food and water were also located inside the hill. The addition of a number of American troops and Philippine Scouts beefed up the normal complement on the island. Also present were the remnants of the 4th Marine Regiment, which despite being relegated to guard duty by MacArthur, had performed well. From his headquarters on Corregidor, Wainwright was in direct communication with both Washington and MacArthur in Australia.

Attacks on Corregidor began while the struggle for Bataan was still in progress. In March there were sixty air raids that did little damage but forced most of the defenders underground. The fall of Bataan allowed the Japanese to bring up their heavy artillery, much of which outranged the island's guns, and begin a constant bombardment that did extensive damage. The troops in the tunnels could do nothing in retaliation. Some broke under the strain; most simply endured the situation, although with each passing day, their morale suffered. By the end of April they were on half rations and there was a growing water shortage. On 3 May, Wainwright informed MacArthur that his situation was desperate. That evening a submarine took off twenty-five persons—key members of Mac-Arthur's staff and several army nurses.

After pounding the island for over a month, the Japanese finally sent in their infantry on the evening of 5 May. The defenders came out of the tunnels to counterattack and there was fierce close combat. Wainwright, who had earlier considered his situation hopeless, decided to surrender. Unlike King, he did not disobey orders. He had been given authority to capitulate by his superiors in Washington. Even so, MacArthur found a way to exercise a last bit of pettiness. The message from Washington was relayed through his Australian headquarters and he simply did not pass it on to Wainwright. When it became apparent the message had not gotten through to Wainwright, Washington finally contacted him directly. Wainwright then conferred with MacArthur, who told him that the decision to surrender had to be Wainwright's. On 6 May, Wainwright attempted to surrender only those forces in the Manila Bay area, transferring overall command in the rest of the Philippines to another American commander. The Japanese would not accept this and Wainwright was forced to surrender all remaining troops in the islands. During the following weeks the Japanese accepted the capitulation of most Filipino and American troops on the central and southern islands. However, many refused to give up, and retreated into the hills and jungles to form the guerrilla forces that would continue to plague the Japanese for the next two and one-half years.

During the desperate fight for Luzon, the Japanese also moved to secure the strategically important area of southern Mindanao. It was a stepping stone on the path to conquest of the Dutch East Indies, particularly Borneo and its rich oil fields. Fear of a concentration of U.S. airpower on Mindanao had prompted a major attack on

Davao on 8 December by planes from the carrier *Ryujo*. But few Americans were there and, given the strength of Air Corps units in the Philippines, after the first day of the war there was little the Japanese had to fear from Davao.

The Davao invasion fleet commanded by RAdm. Raizo Tanaka left Kossol Roads in Palau on 17 December. This southern force was composed of five transports escorted by a cruiser, six destroyers, and the carrier *Ryujo* and the seaplane carrier *Chitose*. Nine B-17s attacked the convoy on the twentieth, but they did no serious damage. The landings were otherwise unopposed and by the evening of the twenty-third the airstrip was ready to receive fighter planes. This released the covering carriers for operations elsewhere. Almost immediately, a four-thousand-man invasion force left Davao on nine transports to secure the island of Jolo in the Celebes Sea. By noon on Christmas Day, that island was secured and work began on establishing a naval station there. Thus, long before Homma could claim victory on Luzon, the Japanese were moving toward one of their main objectives: the oil of the Dutch East Indies.

The complex Japanese operations in the Dutch East Indies were an adjunct to their mainland objectives. The story of Allied attempts to defend these islands, although involving ships and men of the U.S. Army Air Corps and Admiral Hart's Asiatic Fleet, more properly belongs to a survey of Japanese and Allied actions in Southeast Asia. That fact is reflected by the command structure hastily assembled to meet the Japanese threat. The American, British, Dutch, and Australian Command (ABDACOM) was one of the creations of a series of meetings between Churchill and Roosevelt and their military advisers between 22 December 1941 and 14 January 1942. This conference, code-named Arcadia, was one of the most important of the many that were held during the war. It was responsible for defining the Anglo-American alliance's major goal as the defeat of Germany first, and from it was issued the Declaration of the United Nations. The informal discussions between senior military officers later became institutionalized in the Combined Chiefs of Staff headquarters in Washington. But the overriding military problem that needed to be addressed was how to stop the

Japanese from further advances in Asia and the Pacific. This was the imperative that led to the creation of ABDACOM.

Proposed by General Marshall, ABDACOM was a desperate measure to try to organize scattered Allied units under a unified command. The Dutch were hardly consulted, and the plan was presented to the Australians as something of a fait accompli. Despite the political bickering, the plan was accepted and, at Marshall's suggestion, Field Marshal Sir Archibald P. Wavell, then commanding the Indian army, was chosen to serve as supreme commander. Wavell, fresh from a near impossible, thankless task in the Middle East, was thus handed a command that had little chance of succeeding. Distance alone made Wavell's job extremely difficult. The limits of ABDACOM stretched from Burma to the north coast of Australia, and then eastward to the 141st parallel. An Australia–New Zealand Command (ANZAC) under Australian control extended eastward from there past the Fiji Islands and was not a part of Wavell's responsibilities.

Upon his arrival in Batavia, Wavell established a command system that attempted to balance national rivalries. He chose as his deputy an American, Lt. Gen. George H. Brett. An Englishman, Gen. Sir Henry Pownall, became chief of staff. Major General Brereton, fresh from the Philippine debacle, was appointed commander of the air forces, and a Dutchman, Maj. Gen. Hein ter Poorten, took command of the land forces.

The naval command was also a mixed bag. Although technically under the command of the British admiral in charge of the Eastern Fleet, VAdm. Conrad Helfrich, commander of Dutch Pacific naval forces, had exercised an all but independent command in the East Indies. When Admiral Hart arrived in Batavia on 1 January, he took over ABDACOM's naval flotilla (ABDAFLOT), which included the U.S. Asiatic Fleet and the Dutch naval forces. On 30 January Hart's deputy, William A. Glassford, was promoted to vice admiral. At the same time, Hart's Asiatic Fleet was deactivated and Glassford became commander of all U.S. naval forces in the Southwest Pacific. Hart remained in command of ABDAFLOT. While this complex command system might appear logical on paper, it proved to be a nightmare when confronting the Japanese invasions.

Those in Washington who created ABDACOM obviously had some idea of the difficulties of blending together four separate army and navy systems, particularly when senior commanders could not even understand one another. Leaving aside all the technical problems related to this type of forced integration, the major difficulties faced by Wavell and his field commanders in all areas were a shortage of trained troops, lack of good equipment, and a disastrous shortage of aircraft. Most of the fighter planes available were obsolete and thus no match for the Japanese Zeros and Oscars flying cover for the bombers.

An inherent weakness of ABDACOM was tying defense of the East Indies to operations on mainland Asia. Field Marshal Wavell was most concerned with developments in Malaya, where Japanese troops under General Yamashita outmaneuvered the numerically superior British and Commonwealth forces in a series of lightning strikes. By the end of January, the last Allied troops had crossed the bridge to Singapore from Johore, and on 15 February Lt. Gen. Arthur E. Percival surrendered the supposedly impregnable Far Eastern naval base and more than 130,000 men to the victorious and slightly incredulous Yamashita.

Earlier, on 10 December, Japanese planes attacked the modern battleships *Repulse* and *Prince of Wales* as VAdm. Tom Philipps rashly led his task force too close to land-based Japanese planes. Operating at extreme range, eighty-eight bombers and torpedo planes based in Indochina sank both the great ships. This disaster, coupled with later operations by Nagumo's carrier group in the Indian Ocean, forced the British navy to fall back first to Ceylon and then to seek haven in Madagascar. Thus the defenders of the East Indies could expect no assistance from what had before the war been considered a formidable force operating from Singapore.

The Japanese conducted their complex operations in the East Indies with overwhelming superiority in ships, men, and planes, and proceeded with calm efficiency to move first into Borneo, then to Celebes, Amboina, and finally Sumatra and Java—always making certain that their amphibious operations did not outstrip the available air cover.

The first target was Tarakan Island on the northeast coast of Borneo, the site of a major oil field. On 10 January 1942 sixteen troop transports carried a regimental combat group and a special landing force from Davao. Landing on the morning of the eleventh, the attackers quickly overwhelmed a battalion of Dutch troops there. Before they surrendered, the Dutch were able to set the oil fields and a hundred thousand tons of stored oil on fire. At the same time, a smaller convoy left Davao and crossed the Celebes Sea and landed at Menado on the northern end of Celebes Island. The Japanese planned a double envelopment and a parachute drop to overcome the resistance of the fifteen hundred troops there. Once again the Dutch resistance was minimal, although the defenders badly damaged the airfield in an effort to deny its use to the Japanese. Nevertheless, the airfields at Tarakan and Menado were operational within twenty-four hours. Landings at Brunei on 6 January, Jesselton on the eleventh, and Sarawak on the twenty-third secured the western coast of Borneo for the Japanese and paved the way for a major operation against Balikpapan on the island's eastern coast.

The Eastern Striking Force, composed of sixteen transports covered by six destroyers, left Tarakan and, screened by bad weather, arrived off the port on the afternoon of 23 January. The Dutch commander of the tiny garrison ordered the oil fields set afire before he led his two hundred men into the interior, where they surrendered weeks later. At the same time, a smaller task force left Menado for Kendari at the southern end of Celebes and landed on the twenty-fourth. The Dutch surrendered after a slight skirmish, giving the Japanese another airfield from which planes could control ship movements through the Molucca and Flores Seas.

Despite having air and naval superiority, the Japanese suffered considerable losses in their invasions of Borneo and Celebes. The Allied air force was generally ineffectual partly because of the quality of its planes, but also because the potentially most effective plane, the B-17, was used only for high-level bombing. Unfortunately the vaunted Norden bombsight, designed for stationary targets, was not able to score hits on moving ships from over fifteen thousand feet. Still, there were isolated cases where the bombers were effective. On 4 January they struck Davao and seriously damaged the heavy cruiser *Myoko* and caused lesser damage to a destroyer and the seaplane tender *Chitose*. On the twenty-third Dutch pilots strafed, bombed, and sank a transport in the Makassar Strait.

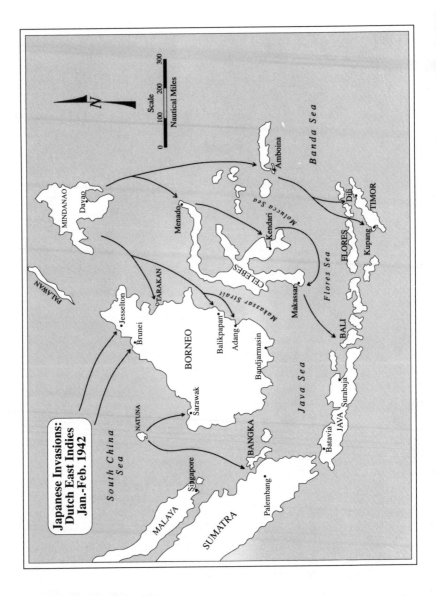

Japanese Invasions:
Dutch East Indies
Jan.-Feb. 1942

Far more effective than Allied airpower were the submarines of Admiral Hart's flotilla. Despite all the difficulties of operating out of Surabaja on Java thousands of miles from their supply and repair base at Darwin, and oftentimes with defective torpedoes, the submarines managed to sink a number of Japanese vessels. On the night of 23 January the *Sturgeon* sank a transport off Balikpapan. The same night, the *Swordfish* sank a transport off Kendari and damaged a destroyer and another transport. A Dutch submarine sneaked past the picket boats and sank a 7,000-ton transport while the Japanese were unloading troops at Balikpapan. Before hostilities in the East Indies ended in March, American submarines had sunk twelve ships totalling over fifty thousand tons, while losing just four boats from all causes.

Admiral Glassford, commanding the American portion of ABDAFLOT, was at Kupang Bay on Timor on 20 January when he learned of the Japanese movement toward Balikpapan. He decided to intercept with his two light cruisers, *Boise* and *Marblehead,* and four destroyers, *Pope, Ford, Parrott,* and *Paul Jones.* The *Marblehead* had only one turbine operating and could make only fifteen knots, and in the first part of the movement north, the *Boise* hit an uncharted rock. Glassford ordered both cruisers to turn back while the old four-stack destroyers proceeded up the Makassar Strait. They evaded the Japanese destroyer screen and caught a dozen transports anchored about five miles off Balikpapan. Commander Paul Talbot in the *Ford* led his destroyers in a complex series of attacks against the ships silhouetted against the backdrop of the burning oil fields. The Japanese naval commander cooperated by leading his destroyers on a mad chase out to sea rather than staying close to the transports. In an hour-long attack the old American destroyers sank four transports and a patrol ship. Talbot broke off the action after expending all his torpedoes. This Battle of Balikpapan was the first American surface action of the war, and it would have been much more successful had it not been for the torpedoes, many of which proved to be duds.

The next target for the Japanese was Amboina, a small island 350 miles east of Kendari. The Dutch, against the advice of Admiral Hart, left some of their best troops, along with an Australian battalion, on the island. Field Marshal Wavell, preoccupied with events elsewhere, decided to let General ter Poorten have his way. The Japanese brought the carriers *Soryu* and *Hiryu* within range and began to soften Amboina's defenses on 24 January. Then, in a two-pronged attack from Menado and Davao, they brought eleven transports guarded by two heavy cruisers, destroyers, and the seaplane carriers *Chitose* and *Mizuho* down the Molucca Sea. Their first amphibious assault was mounted on 31 January and, after some heavy fighting, the Japanese had secured Amboina town by 3 February. All the Dutch and Australian troops were either killed or taken prisoner.

Rear Admiral Karel W. F. M. Doorman, in command of the Combined Striking Force on 4 February, was informed of a large naval force of three cruisers, destroyers, and twenty transports coming down the Makassar Strait. He decided to try to intercept despite the fact that to do so would place him in range of Japanese bombers. His surface force was formidable, consisting of the Dutch light cruisers *De Ruyter, Tromp,* the American heavy cruiser *Houston* and light cruiser *Marblehead,* and four destroyers. The squadron was attacked by thirty-six navy bombers north of Bali, and Doorman's flagship, the *De Ruyter,* sustained some damage. But the most successful of the attacks was on *Marblehead,* which was hit a number of times, jamming its rudder. The cruiser eventually limped back to base by using its engines to steer. Also hard hit was the *Houston.* After vigorous maneuvering and destroying a number of attackers, the big cruiser was hit by a single bomb that knocked out the aft gun turret, killing more than fifty sailors. Doorman decided to give up his plans to intercept the Japanese and beat a hasty retreat through Lombak Strait and thence along the south coast of Java to safety. Without fear of further interference from the Allied surface fleet, the Japanese proceeded to send in a large force mounted from Kendari and took Makassar on 6 February after a brief skirmish. The American submarine S-37 exacted some retribution when it torpedoed and sank the *Natsushio,* one of the covering destroyers. Bandjarmasin, the largest town on the south coast of Borneo, fell on 16 February to a small contingent of Japanese.

By early February the Japanese had secured the huge island of Borneo with its oil fields, as well as Celebes and Amboina, and their navy and air force dominated the Flores Sea and the islands

east of Java. The Allies' only safe anchorage in the East Indies was
the crowded port of Tjilatjap on Java. But the vise was closing
around Java, the seat of government and the island which from the
beginning had handled the concentration of Allied ships and men.
However, before Java could be invaded, the Japanese needed to
seize Sumatra. General Yamashita's success in Malaya had freed the
Japanese fleet based in Indochina from action there, so on 9 February VAdm. Jisaburo Ozawa led a powerful naval force of six cruisers, destroyers, and the carrier *Ryujo* south from Camranh Bay
guarding twenty-five transports carrying two infantry regiments.
The target was Bangka Island, the source of much of the world's
tin, and Palembang, capital of Sumatra. The Japanese dropped approximately five hundred paratroopers on Palembang on the morning of 14 February to seize its two airfields and the oil installations.
They captured one airfield and held it despite counterattacks by one
of the eight Dutch battalions deployed in southern Sumatra.

ABDACOM headquarters was aware of the movement of Ozawa's
fleet, and Wavell, however pessimistic, knew that southern Sumatra
had to be held if Java was to be defended. He therefore ordered
Doorman to again try to intercept the Japanese. By the fourteenth,
Doorman had assembled all available ships, the most powerful of
which was the British heavy cruiser *Exeter*. The *Exeter* aided in the
destruction of the German pocket battleship *Graf Spee* in 1939.
Doorman also had three Dutch and one Australian light cruisers and
four Dutch and six American destroyers. His excursion northwest
through Karimata Strait caused Ozawa to order his advance force,
which had already landed, to move farther up the Molei River to
safety. Ozawa then turned his transports back and proceeded southward to meet Doorman.

Land-based bombers struck the ABDA force in the afternoon
but did little damage. Doorman, who had lost two of his destroyers
to a reef collision, decided to turn back although his fleet was un-
hurt by the air attack. In retrospect, although he was criticized for
it, this was the proper move; any one of Ozawa's cruisers outgunned his most powerful ship. Had there been an engagement, all
evidence points to the destruction of the Combined Striking Force.
Without the fleet's protection, and despite attacks on the enemy by
Allied aircraft, the Dutch army commander on Sumatra decided to

abandon the capital. It was not an orderly retreat; the Dutch left behind a great amount of usable equipment. Most of the Dutch troops safely crossed the Sunda Strait to Java by the evening of 17 February, giving the Japanese control of Sumatra after only three days. This victory, combined with the earlier occupations of Borneo and Celebes, sealed Java's fate. Wavell recognized that fact and ordered the evacuation of British troops from the ABDA area on 20 February. He followed them out five days later. General Brereton withdrew what was left of the U.S. Air Corps units on Java to India. General Brett had already left for Australia. ABDACOM was no longer a viable force.

Although the fate of the East Indies was generally known by February, there was infighting between the Allied naval commanders. Admiral Hart wanted the ABDA naval forces to pursue more aggressive operations and was openly critical of Admiral Doorman's actions in the abortive attempt to intercept the Makassar invasion fleet. There was also friction between Hart and Admiral Helfrich, whose semipolitical position made it difficult for Hart to operate efficiently. Helfrich also resented being under the command of an American admiral when defending Dutch territory. Thus, at this crucial moment in the naval defense of the islands, there was animosity at the highest levels. The Dutch ambassador in Washington protested the ABDACOM relationships, and his arguments were bolstered by Churchill's influence with the president. Partially from a conviction that the East Indies were already lost, Roosevelt finally decided to give in to the Dutch demands. The Combined Chiefs in turn ordered Wavell to let Hart keep the title of ABDAFLOT commander, but give operational control of the force to Helfrich. This was not sufficient for Hart, who left Java on 16 February. He deserved better from the two masters he had been forced to serve—MacArthur and Wavell. Given the many problems of supply and service facing Hart's understrength Asiatic Fleet, it had performed exceedingly well. What was left of that command continued to serve proudly in the desperate sea battles that marked the final stages of the conquest of the East Indies.

Chapter 6

Java, Coral Sea, and Midway

THE KEY TO Field Marshal Wavell's defensive strategy was the fortress and naval base at Singapore. He had hoped that by holding that base he could build up reinforcements for an eventual counter-attack against the Japanese in the East Indies. However questionable this idea was in light of the inferior land and air forces available, it was impossible after the capture of the great bastion on 15 February 1942. The loss of Singapore and the 130,000 men who surrendered there was a blow from which the Allies would not soon recover. More importantly for the defenders of northern Sumatra and Java, it meant that Japan could concentrate even more ships and men on those islands. Wavell informed Governor-General A. W. L. T. van Starkenborgh-Stachouwer on 21 February that Java could not be held. Wavell and the American air commanders, Brett and Brereton, began to plan for the evacuation of as many of their men as possible.

However obvious this decision might have been, the governor, Admiral Helfrich, and General ter Poorten believed they had no choice but to resist the Japanese for as long as possible. On paper it might appear that the defense force available on Java was formidable. The Dutch in their three regional commands—East, Center, and West—had more than 90,000 troops. They were reinforced by

5,500 British and 2,900 Australian infantrymen. The American contribution was very slight—an artillery battalion of approximately 500 men. To guard the approaches to Java, the Dutch had a naval force commanded by Admiral Doorman composed of a number of submarines, one heavy cruiser, seven light cruisers, and more than twenty destroyers. In reality, this force of Dutch, British, and American ships was in sad need of repair, and oil and ammunition supply problems were an ever-present limiting factor. Although Admiral Glassford and his British counterpart, RAdm. A. F. E. Pallister, cooperated fully with the Dutch, they all had difficulty coping with the different codes, signals, and even tactics of the three navies.

Before invading Java, the Japanese decided to sever its lines of communication with Australia. Their first move in this direction was to dispatch a naval landing force to Timor. The Allied high command had not yet written off the East Indies, and thus decided, ill-advisedly, to reinforce the Timor garrison. Four transports carrying American and Australian troops left Darwin on 15 February escorted by the cruiser *Houston,* one destroyer, and two Australian sloops. ABDACOM finally called off the operation, but not before the *Houston* had fought off a series of attacks by Japanese land-based bombers. The convoy returned to the presumably safe harbor in Darwin on 18 February. Meanwhile, Admiral Kondo boldly sailed into the Timor Sea with two battleships, three heavy cruisers, and Admiral Nagumo's four carriers. This was the most powerful Japanese armada to be brought together since Pearl Harbor. The task force, aided by land-based bombers, struck Darwin on the nineteenth. More than two hundred planes systematically worked over the harbor, airfield, and town. Eight Allied ships were sunk, nine were damaged, and the airport was rendered useless. Darwin was abandoned as a naval base and the town itself was temporarily evacuated. The only positive news was that the *Houston* left port before the attack.

To support the attacks in the east, the Japanese, as noted earlier, sent a small task force to seize the rich oil center of Palembang in southern Sumatra. They immediately began constructing airfields there in order to threaten the major cities of western Java. On the eighteenth, the Japanese loaded elements of their Sixteenth Army, then at Makassar, for an invasion of Bali. Allied intelligence knew of these plans ten days before the landings, but Admiral Doorman's ships were so widely scattered that he could not respond quickly enough and the Japanese were unloaded at Sanur Roads without incident. This delay was unfortunate. For one of the few times during the sea engagements in the East Indies, Doorman would have had superior firepower as the Japanese escort consisted of only eight destroyers. Instead, the Dutch admiral decided to employ a three-echelon attack on the Japanese force anchored off Bali. The strike should have destroyed most of the ships left there since he was operating with two cruisers and five destroyers against only two destroyers (later augmented by three others). A tragicomedy of errors allowed the transports to escape, and the Japanese destroyer captains fought well, sinking one Dutch destroyer. With the occupation of Bali in the east and southern Sumatra in the west, Java was the only island in the region remaining under ABDACOM's control.

The Japanese had no such problems as those facing the ABDA-COM commanders. Their invasion of Java was to be the largest amphibious operation of the war to that point. They decided upon a three-pronged attack on east, central, and western Java. On 18 February Admiral Ozawa led the main western force of fifty-six transports escorted by three cruisers and six destroyers south from Camranh Bay. The next day, RAdm. Shoji Nishimura's eastern force of forty-one transports sailed from Jolo in the Sulu Sea guarded by seven cruisers and nineteen destroyers. Ozawa's western attack group was later joined by seven more cruisers, additional transports, and the aircraft carrier *Ryujo*. The Japanese ultimately committed ninety-seven troopships to the invasion.

From the beginning the Japanese had superiority in ships, men, and aircraft. The Dutch had lost three light cruisers and fifteen destroyers to a variety of causes before the invasion. The ABDACOM air force, never large, had been reduced to only a handful of Brewster Buffalo fighters and patrol craft when Brereton ordered the few American planes left to fly either to India or Australia on the twenty-fourth. Admiral Doorman, if he were to intercept the invasion fleet, would face two to one odds in ships—and he was without air cover.

The Java defenders' need for aircraft led to a desperate attempt to bring in fighters from Australia. After the loss of the Timor airfield, the only way this could be done was by sea. The first

American aircraft carrier, the thirty-year-old *Langley,* long since converted into an auxiliary, was chosen to ferry thirty-two P-40s and pilots. Accompanying the *Langley* was the freighter *Sea Witch,* which carried twenty-seven more crated P-40s. The ships left Freemantle on 22 February in a convoy headed for Bombay. The original plan for the approach to Java was changed by Admiral Helfrich, who ordered the two ships to proceed on a shorter route to Tjilatjap harbor. The *Langley*'s captain wanted to make the run into the harbor at night, but once again Helfrich overrode him and ordered the ships to make full speed to deliver the planes before the Japanese invasion force landed. This meant they would be exposed to Japanese daylight surveillance. The *Langley* and its two-destroyer escort were sighted by Japanese patrol planes on 27 February, and nine bombers operating from Kendari were soon over the ships. The *Langley* took five hits and was set on fire. It was soon dead in the water and the crew abandoned ship. The destroyer escort rescued survivors and then scuttled the *Langley.* Ironically the *Sea Witch,* which had been left behind by the *Langley*'s commander in his haste to comply with Helfrich's request, made harbor safely. Another tragic irony was that the crated planes could not be assembled in time for the invasion and had to be destroyed by the Dutch to keep the Japanese from getting them.

Admiral Doorman used all available ships to sweep the northern coast of Java but failed to locate the enemy. He returned to Surabaya on the twenty-sixth to refuel and discovered a message from Helfrich ordering him to put to sea again as soon as refueling was completed. At the same time, a relatively strong British force of four cruisers and two destroyers was searching for the Japanese far to the west. Unable to find any sign of the enemy, the British task force was ordered to Ceylon. Doorman thus lost a force almost as large as his own for the crucial naval battle in the East Indies.

On 27 February, Doorman's small fleet—composed of the light cruisers *De Ruyter, Exeter, Perth,* and *Java,* the heavy cruiser *Houston,* six British destroyers, and five American destroyers—deployed to meet the Japanese eastern covering group. This force, commanded by RAdm. Takeo Takagi, had two heavy cruisers, the *Nachi* and *Haguro,* one light cruiser, and seven relatively new destroyers. Takagi also had the distinct advantage of having spotter planes to help direct fire.

The ensuing Battle of the Java Sea began at 1600 and resulted in the destruction of half of Admiral Doorman's force. The guns on Takagi's cruisers could outrange any of the Allied guns—with the exception of the *Houston,* which went into the fight with only two-thirds of its 8-inch guns operating as its aft turret was still inoperative due to the earlier bomb hit. The first hour of the battle consisted of aimless sparring. The Japanese, despite having spotter planes, failed to score any hits. Nor were torpedo attacks by their destroyers successful. The Allied ships could not get close enough to the Japanese to make their smaller caliber guns effective.

A few minutes after 1700 the *Exeter* was hit, lost power, and turned sharply left. The other ships' commanders—with the exception of the *De Ruyter,* which carried Doorman on board—thought it was a planned maneuver and followed. In the ensuing confusion, a Japanese torpedo struck the Dutch destroyer *Korteneer,* which sank almost immediately. Subsequent Japanese torpedo attacks during the second and third hours of the battle were unsuccessful. An attack by the four American destroyers on the heavy cruisers also failed because of the fuse settings and the distances involved.

By 1900, Doorman's ships were unable to communicate effectively. The coming of darkness further hampered the Allied admiral, who was vainly trying to reach the Japanese transports. It didn't matter, Takagi had already ordered them north. When Doorman finally changed course and headed along Java's northern coastline, his movements were tracked by Japanese aircraft that dropped illuminating flares. During this maneuvering, the British destroyer *Jupiter* struck a mine laid earlier by friendly forces and sank at about 2125. Approximately thirty minutes later, Doorman tried to slip by the Japanese screen to get to the transports. He failed and for a time the two fleets ran parallel to one another about eight thousand yards apart. The Japanese launched a wide spread of torpedoes, several of which this time found their mark, striking the *De Ruyter* and the *Java.* Both were quickly engulfed in flames and soon sank. Admiral Doorman, along with a large portion of the crews of the two ships, was lost. The captains of the *Houston* and the *Perth,* who had previously been ordered not to stand by, made their way back to port to report the loss of a significant part of Java's major defense element.

With the ABDA fleet all but destroyed, Admiral Glassford and his British counterpart decided to try to save what was left of their ships. The wounded *Exeter*—escorted by two destroyers, the British *Encounter* and the old American four-stacker *Pope*—tried to make it to the Sunda Strait and thence into the Indian Ocean. They were intercepted early on the morning of 1 March by Admiral Takagi's victorious cruiser force. After an unequal two-hour battle, the *Exeter* was sunk and the *Encounter* was dead in the water. The *Pope* managed to escape but was sunk by land-based bombers an hour later. The *Houston,* accompanied by the Australian light cruiser *Perth* and the destroyer *Evertsen,* also made a breakout attempt. They left Batavia headed for the Sunda Strait on the twenty-eighth and, approaching Banten Bay just before midnight, located what the ABDA commanders had been searching for: the Western Force transports unloading troops. Detected at about the same time as the lookouts saw the Japanese transports, the cruisers evaded a torpedo attack. Ironically, the Japanese torpedoes struck two of their own troopships. Before attempting to flee northward, the *Houston* and *Perth* sank one large transport outright and caused three others to run aground. One of the survivors of the sinkings was the commander of the Japanese land forces, Lt. Gen. Hitoshi Imamura.

However gallant the fight by the officers and men on the Allied cruisers, their fate was sealed. The Japanese sent planes after them, launched from the carrier *Ryujo,* and four heavy cruisers closed on the ships. Two of these, the *Mogami* and *Mikuma,* intercepted the *Houston* and *Perth.* In the running battle that followed, one Japanese destroyer was hit and an 8-inch shell damaged the *Mikuma.* However, shortly after midnight, the *Perth* was struck by torpedoes and shells from the guns of the two cruisers and quickly sank. The *Houston* fought on alone, its captain killed and the decks strewn with dead, until all ammunition was expended. Only then was the ship abandoned. At about 0045 on 1 March the *Houston* sank. Only 361 of its complement of more than 1,000 men survived the desperate one-sided fight.

On the positive side, a British convoy of twelve transports bringing almost 11,000 Australians home from the Middle East stayed far to the west and escaped detection.

The loss of the ABDA fleet left Java virtually defenseless. The size of the island made any defense plan difficult, and the Dutch and British Commonwealth defenders were spread thin in order to try to counter all Japanese landing attempts. Without air cover, the troops were at the mercy of Japanese planes—and even the rank and file knew of the naval defeats. Morale was therefore low, and the Dutch were uncertain of the loyalty of the Javanese, many of whom were actively hostile to the colonial regime.

The 6th Infantry Regiment, augmented by three reserve battalions, defended the eastern part of the island. In the center were the weak 2d Infantry Division and two cavalry squadrons. The bulk of the Dutch force, consisting of the 1st Infantry Division, two additional regiments, and a composite Allied organization called Black Force after its commander, Brigadier A. S. Blackburn, was concentrated in the west. The Dutch commander had deployed his army to give maximum protection to the three major cities: Surabaja, Bandung, and Batavia.

While the opposing fleets battled in the Java Sea on the last day of February, the Japanese off-loaded their troops at three widely separated points on the north shore of the island. At Kragen, ninety miles west of Surabaja, the 48th Division and the 56th Regimental Group landed virtually unopposed and, without consolidating the beachhead, drove inland and along the coast toward the major port city. At Ereta-Wetan, 130 miles northeast of Bandung, the 230th Infantry Regiment struck inland and by 1 March had captured the Kalidjati airfield. The main concentration of Japanese troops was at Banten Bay, a few miles northwest of Batavia. The strong Japanese 2d Infantry Division landed there after suffering most of the losses inflicted during the bombardment by the *Houston* and *Perth* on the evening of the twenty-eighth. At no place during the short campaign were the Allied forces able to check the Japanese advance, although Maj. Gen. G. A. Ilgen held up the 48th Division long enough for demolition experts in Surabaja to blow up much of what would have been of value to the Japanese. Nevertheless, Japanese elements entered the city on 7 March.

The story was the same in central Java. The Japanese divided their force and one group pushed westward along the north coast while the other thrust through the mountains toward the port of Tjilatjap on the southern coast. That city fell on the same day as Surabaja. Meanwhile, in the west, Dutch demolition of roads and bridges held up the 230th Regiment only briefly. Major General

Willem Schilling, faced with double envelopment by troops from the 48th Division and the 230th Regiment, evacuated Batavia on 5 March. Black Force fought a successful delaying action that allowed troops of the Dutch 1st Regiment to escape from Batavia, and Schilling prepared to fall back to the Bandung plateau to continue the fight. Rather than defend, however, he instead launched an attack aimed at recapturing Kalidjati airport. Its failure, probably more than anything else, convinced Governor Starkenborgh-Stachouwer and General ter Poorten that the situation was hopeless. Hoping to spare Bandung and save the lives of soldiers and civilians, they met with General Imamura on 8 March and surrendered unconditionally. General ter Poorten broadcast the surrender to all Allied troops the following day.

The final major operation in the East Indies was the invasion of northern Sumatra on 12 March. After accepting the surrender of the last Allied troops in the region, the conquerors interned them. They would spend more than three miserable years in captivity.

The Japanese in just sixty days had mounted more than a dozen amphibious landings and destroyed the bulk of the American and Dutch Asiatic fleets. Despite the efforts of the retreating Dutch, the Japanese captured intact most of the strategic oil production and storage facilities in the region. Their need for those supplies was the major reason they had attacked U.S. bases and brought on the Pacific conflict. Japanese land, sea, and air victories in Malaya and Burma gave them access to much of the raw material needed to maintain their war effort. But, faced with growing American naval power, their problem quickly became how to get those precious goods safely back to the home islands.

Japanese successes in the Philippines and the East Indies were duplicated in the Southwest Pacific, where the defense situation in the islands north of Australia was even worse than elsewhere. Australia is a huge continent, but in 1941 it had a population of only seven million persons, most of whom lived in the south near Sydney or Melbourne. Despite a patriotic populace, the government could not field a large army, and its navy was also very small. The bulk of the Australian army had served with distinction in the Middle East. At the outset of the Pacific war, its 6th, 7th, and 9th

Divisions were with the Western Desert Force in Egypt. Most of the 8th Division had been sent to defend Malaya and the East Indies, but its men were lost when the Japanese overran those territories. Few trained soldiers remained in Australia; most of the defense force was composed of militia units. Not until early March 1942 did almost eleven thousand regular troops return to Australia from North Africa, their convoy having eluded the Japanese.

Because of the shortage of trained troops, the Australian government decided early in the war not to reinforce the token units on New Britain in the Bismarck Archipelago or New Georgia in the Solomons. The battalion stationed at Port Moresby in New Guinea was reinforced, however, bringing the garrison there to three thousand men. The battalion of the 8th Division guarding Rabaul on New Britain with approximately fourteen hundred men was all but abandoned. Except for a few coastwatchers, the only other Australian forces outside the country were in a small detachment, the 1st Australian Independent Company, in northeast New Guinea. Too weak to defend Lae and Salamaua, it retired into the Bulolo Valley to defend a small mountain airstrip.

This litany of weakness extended to the air force and navy. Nine squadrons of the Royal Australian Air Force (RAAF) were in the European theater, and even if more planes had been available, there were too few pilots. In addition, almost nine thousand Australians were serving in the Royal Air Force (RAF). The entire Australian bombing force available in the Pacific was twenty-nine Hudson medium bombers and fourteen PBYs. The fighter squadrons, equipped with obsolete Brewster Buffalos, had been sent to Malaya where they were destroyed by superior Japanese fighters. Australia's air defense thus hinged on a handful of Wirraways—a domestic version of the American advanced trainer, the AT-6 Texan. The navy, which was in better condition than the other services, had only three light cruisers at the core of its fleet.

It was obvious to both the Allied and Japanese commands that Japan could take any of the areas in this vast region whenever it wished. Nevertheless, Imperial Headquarters did not take chances. On 4 January, General Horii, commander of the five-thousand-man South Seas Detachment that had taken Guam, was ordered to move southward to capture Rabaul. On 16 January the detachment left

Guam guarded by elements of the Fourth Fleet, to which had been added the aircraft carriers *Kagi* and *Akagi*. A naval landing force whose objective was Kavieng on New Ireland joined the convoy at Truk. The naval troops easily overwhelmed the small Australian garrison at Kavieng.

On the night of 22–23 January 1942, the South Seas Detachment landed at three places along Simpson Harbour and, after a few fierce firefights, took Rabaul and its two small airfields. Some four hundred Australian soldiers escaped and reached New Britain's south coast, from which they were later rescued. Japanese construction crews immediately began improving the airfields. The Japanese ultimately had five airfields at Rabaul, which soon became the nerve center for all southern operations for both the army and navy.

After the fall of Rabaul, the Japanese were in a position to move on Port Moresby and the Solomons. Aware that the southeast islands in the Solomons chain were undefended, the Japanese moved in a leisurely fashion to occupy them. They seized key points on New Ireland in February, and by the end of March had made landings on both sides of Buka Passage and on the eastern coast of Bougainville.

Meanwhile, the Allied command situation in the Pacific was becoming chaotic. There was confusion over the boundary of Nimitz's command and whether the admiral's authority extended to army units. Then another player was added when, to meet the growing threat to Australia, the ANZAC Force was created on 24 January. General Brett continued to command the few U.S. ground troops and aircraft in the region, and command of the ANZAC Force was given to another American, VAdm. Herbert F. Leary. The most important elements available to him were the Australian cruisers *Australia, Canberra,* and *Hobart,* and the U.S. cruiser *Chicago*. Washington also provided Leary with a squadron of B-17s flown in from Hawaii. Another strong Allied naval force began operating in the South Pacific in mid-February. This task force, composed of the carrier *Lexington,* four heavy cruisers, and ten destroyers, answered directly to Admiral Nimitz.

The tasks of the Japanese Fourth Fleet and the South Seas Detachment were outlined in an order issued on 2 February. Joint army and navy operations were first to secure Lae and Salamaua on the west side of New Guinea's Huon Gulf. Later they, with reinforcements, were to take Port Moresby, and still later occupy Tulagi and the southern Solomons.

The New Guinea landings were postponed when a task force commanded by Admiral Fletcher moved to break up the Japanese troop concentration on Rabaul. The Japanese were alerted to the task force's presence and, when it was about three hundred miles distant, sent a number of land-based bombers to intercept the Americans. Thanks to effective air cover and good evasive action, none of the U.S. ships were hit; the Japanese lost eighteen bombers in the attack. The American task force was low on oil and Fletcher, reluctant to risk his precious carrier, retired northward.

Finally, in the early morning hours of 8 March, Japanese army troops landed unopposed at Salamaua and a naval landing force occupied Lae eighteen miles to the north. The Japanese immediately began to improve the airfields there. However, before the first fighters from Rabaul landed on 10 March, the Americans, in an unusual show of strength, struck the landing areas. This was by far the largest task force yet assembled by the United States in the southern Pacific. It was built around two large carriers, *Yorktown* and *Lexington,* supported by eight heavy cruisers and fourteen destroyers. The target for the attack had at first been Rabaul, but was shifted to the Lae and Salamaua beachheads. Approaching northeast from the Gulf of Papua, VAdm. Wilson Brown launched 104 planes. The pilots flew northward at seven thousand feet through a pass in the Owen Stanley Mountains and caught the Japanese by surprise. The carrier strike was followed by attacks from ANZAC B-17s and Hudsons. In all, three ships were sunk, four were damaged, and the Japanese suffered almost four hundred casualties. Another attack by ANZAC pilots the next day further damaged facilities at both locations. These attacks, a portent of things to come, did little to slow the consolidation of Japanese control in the western segment of the Huon Gulf.

A new figure surfaced in Australia during this crucial period. General MacArthur, his family, and his staff, after a harrowing journey by PT boat and B-17, arrived on 17 March. Soon after, without authorization, he issued his famous "I shall return" promise, giving

the impression that authorities in Washington had given the reconquest of the Philippines high priority. MacArthur's presence did
what Australian Prime Minister John Curtin had hoped—the general's optimism and flamboyance bolstered morale.

At first, MacArthur had no specific command in Australia. It was
not until 30 March that the Allied joint chiefs decided on a division
of responsibilities for operations in the Pacific theater. Although
later commentators have pointed to the lack of consultation with the
Australian government in many matters, MacArthur's appointment
as commander in chief of the newly created Southwest Pacific Area
(SWPA) was welcomed by Curtin and his government. MacArthur
was given responsibility for action against the Japanese in the
Solomon and Bismarck Islands, Australia, New Guinea, the Philippines, and all the waters in between. The vast reaches of the Pacific
north of latitude 20 degrees north and generally east of longitude
160 degrees east were assigned to Admiral Nimitz, whose title,
Commander in Chief, Pacific Ocean Areas (CINCPOA), aptly described the far-flung nature of that command. Nimitz's territory was
later further subdivided with the creation of the South Pacific Area,
which was defined as the region extending from the equator to the
South Pole. Vice Admiral Robert L. Ghormley moved to Noumea,
New Caledonia, on 17 May to take up this command. After the
Battle of Midway, the North Pacific Area, which included Alaska
and the Aleutians, was established as part of Nimitz's command.

Although disappointed with the few troops available—he had
expected more—MacArthur immediately made his presence felt.
Australian military and political leaders were convinced that Port
Moresby could not be held, and they did not want to repeat the earlier mistake of sending reinforcements to an area that was already
doomed. MacArthur disagreed. He believed that the defense of
Australia depended upon maintaining a foothold in New Guinea.
Furthermore, that huge island was the first step toward the eventual
conquest of the Philippines. MacArthur's concept prevailed and he
soon began to receive the means with which to hold Port Moresby.
At the end of March, just as he assumed command, the 41st Austra-
lian Division and the headquarters of the U.S. I Corps reached
Adelaide. Early in April, the U.S. 41st Infantry Division arrived at
Melbourne, and a few days later the 32d Infantry Division landed at
Adelaide. The Australian 19th Brigade Group was sent to reinforce

Port Moresby where engineers were busy enlarging the port and improving its airfields. At the same time, a series of new airfields were built at Moreeba, Cooktown, and Coen along the Cape York Peninsula. What would become a flood of new airplanes began to arrive for General Brett's depleted air force. These included B-17s, the versatile B-25 and B-26 medium bombers, and P-40 and P-39 fighter aircraft.

MacArthur's command structure, however slanted by political considerations, was in place by April. Major General Richard Sutherland, brilliant, overbearing, and to some obnoxious, continued to serve as MacArthur's chief of staff. General Sir Thomas A. Blamey, the veteran Australian commander recently arrived from the Middle East, was appointed as ground forces commander. Admiral Leary relinquished his ANZAC post to become commander of Mac-Arthur's naval forces. The land forces on New Guinea were led by Australian Brigadier Robert Van Volkenburgh. Friction soon developed between Sutherland and Brett, and this controversy soon involved MacArthur. The result was that Brett was replaced in July by Maj. Gen. George C. Kenney.

Almost immediately after arriving in Australia, MacArthur began complaining that the Pacific theater was being neglected in favor of the buildup of forces in Europe. He was joined in this by Admiral King, the chief of naval operations. These two, who would later be at odds over strategy, continued throughout the war to press for more men and materiel for the war against Japan. However correct their complaints were, an unbiased view of the first six months of the war showed that the Pacific was not being neglected. By the beginning of May, Nimitz had four carriers available, and although it would be another year before his fleets would be able to dominate the Japanese, he had enough strength to begin offensive operations. The need to secure the long shipping route from Hawaii to Australia and New Zealand resulted in the establishment of new bases in the Tonga Islands and at Efate in the New Hebrides. At the same time, existing bases in Fiji, Samoa, and New Caledonia were expanded. By mid-1942 more than 245,000 troops were stationed on key islands along the supply route.

Meanwhile, in Japan, serious discussion at the highest levels had been ongoing throughout the month of March concerning the next targets for the army and navy. Yamamoto, in retrospect, made a serious error by dispatching Nagumo's carrier striking force into the Indian Ocean in hopes of destroying what remained of British naval forces in those waters. Admiral Sir James F. Somerville, who had no intention of confronting such overall superiority, withdrew his ships to Madagascar. The only positive result of Nagumo's foray was a major attack on Ceylon on Easter morning. However, by the time Nagumo's force returned to Japan, its ships were in sad need of repair.

Yamamoto, still very concerned about the American carriers, argued with members of his staff who wanted to deploy all available forces to cut the American supply line to Australia by occupying the southern Solomons, the New Hebrides, and New Caledonia. Instead, he sought a showdown with the American fleet. Once it had been rendered totally ineffectual, there would be ample time for the operations his staff wanted. He would strike at Midway, calculating that Nimitz would commit his carriers to keep the Japanese from occupying the island. As with the Pearl Harbor plan, Yamamoto's reputation carried the day. It would be Midway. This decision meant that all other planned operations would have to proceed with the forces already available. Nagumo's carriers would be needed to strike the final blow against the American fleet.

Yamamoto's fears were not unfounded. Although the U.S. command had adopted a generally defensive posture in the Central Pacific in the three months following the Pearl Harbor debacle, in March Nimitz allowed Admirals Brown and Fletcher to use their precious carriers to attack Rabaul.

A further show of American aggressiveness was the decision to bomb Japan. Lieutenant Colonel James H. Doolittle, a prewar aviation pioneer who gained fame piloting fast, experimental aircraft, organized a group of Air Corps adventurers and trained them in Florida for very short takeoffs with twin-engined B-25 bombers. In April, sixteen B-25s and their crews were transferred to the *Hornet* and, with Halsey aboard the *Enterprise* commanding the task force, they left on what amounted to another nuisance raid. The plan was to launch the bombers about 350 miles from Japan. This would give the pilots enough fuel to reach China after hitting their targets. Unfortunately, the task force was detected on 18 April while still 650 miles out to sea. Halsey ordered the planes launched immediately. Each of the heavily loaded bombers followed Doolittle safely off the *Hornet* despite the pitching of the carrier in the rough seas. Thirteen B-25s bombed Tokyo, and the remaining three hit targets in Nagoya, Osaka, and Kobe. The crews arrived over Tokyo in the midst of an air defense drill, so many Japanese were not even aware they were being bombed. Physical damage from the bombing was insignificant, and most of the planes crash-landed in China. One landed safely in Russian territory, where the crew was interned. The Japanese, duplicating actions that had become commonplace, executed three of the eight men who came down in Japanese-held territory and were captured. The psychological impact of the Doolittle raid was another thing entirely. American morale soared when President Roosevelt announced the raid, insisting that the bombers had come from Shangri-la, an allusion to a faraway, mystic place referred to in a popular 1930s novel. The raid also quieted critics of Yamamoto's plan to destroy the American fleet at Midway.

While Nagumo's carriers were being readied and detailed plans for the complex Midway operation were being drawn up, the high command belatedly decided to improve the Japanese position in New Guinea and the Solomons. The main objective of this so-called MO Plan was Port Moresby, although a smaller invasion force was sent to seize Tulagi for use as a seaplane base. As with most Japanese naval plans, the MO Plan was too complex. Instead of relying on superior force, with the transports being protected by one main support group, it called for five separate elements. Admiral Takagi, with the carriers *Shokaku* and *Zuikaku* escorted by two heavy cruisers and six destroyers, would supply the long-distance cover for the landing force being moved in eleven transports. Direct support would be provided by a support group built around a seaplane carrier protected by two light cruisers and three gunboats. A further subdivision of the attack force was Admiral Goto's covering group, which consisted of four heavy cruisers and the slow light carrier *Shoho*.

Admiral Nimitz became aware of the concentration of Japanese shipping at Truk and Rabaul on 17 April. He correctly concluded that the objective would be Port Moresby. Nimitz had available two task forces, the largest of which was TF 17 commanded by Admiral Fletcher operating out of Noumea. The centerpiece of this force was the carrier *Yorktown,* supported by three cruisers, six destroyers, and the tanker *Neosho.* The other carrier group, TF 11, was built around the *Lexington,* which would ultimately have five cruisers attached when RAdm. John C. Crace of the Royal Navy joined up. Five destroyers and the oiler *Tippecanoe* were also in TF 11, which was commanded by RAdm. Aubrey Fitch. Task Force 11 had recently undergone three weeks of refitting at Pearl Harbor, and Fitch, who replaced Admiral Brown on 3 April, was ordered to move south and rendezvous with Fletcher at a point west of the New Hebrides. Nimitz's orders to Fletcher, who would be in overall command of the combined force, were very broad: he was to patrol the Coral Sea and use his discretion concerning tactical moves.

Fitch's task force joined Fletcher's early on the morning of 1 May approximately 250 miles east of Espíritu Santo and was redesignated TF 17.5. Fletcher immediately began refueling from the *Neosho* and was finished the next day. He ordered Fitch to refuel and then join up at a prearranged point on the fourth. Fletcher then led the *Yorktown* group out in search of the Japanese. When he learned of the Japanese presence at Tulagi, Fletcher headed directly for the landing beaches there. Fletcher's action depleted his attack force, which was very vulnerable if the Japanese mounted a large-scale attack against TF 17.5. However, luck was with him: the major covering force had retired from the vicinity of Tulagi, Admiral Chuichi Hara's carriers were still north of Bougainville, and the Japanese invasion group was just leaving Rabaul. Fletcher's force then ran into the northern edge of a cold front that would screen his planes as they attacked Tulagi.

At 0630 on 4 May, Fletcher launched the first of three attacks on the invasion force. The attackers irreparably damaged a destroyer and sank three minesweepers. The following two strikes managed to sink just four landing barges. Three aircraft were lost during this phase of the Coral Sea operation. Admiral Nimitz later showed his disappointment when he said that very little was accomplished considering the amount of ammunition expended. After the Tulagi attack, Fletcher's force rendezvoused with Fitch's and Crace's on the fifth and again refueled.

Meanwhile, the Japanese Port Moresby invasion group was sailing toward the Jomard Passage, which separated New Guinea and the Louisiade Archipelago. Fletcher calculated that the convoy would be fully committed there by 7 or 8 May. Admiral Takagi's escorts and Hara's carriers had rounded the east end of San Cristóbal Island, entered the Coral Sea, and turned west. Fletcher meanwhile had reorganized his forces into three groups. Rear Admiral Thomas C. Kinkaid commanded an attack group of four heavy and one light cruisers and five destroyers. A support group of three heavy cruisers and two destroyers was commanded by Admiral Crace. Fletcher's major offensive weapons, the carriers, constituted the air group, which was controlled by Fitch. Fletcher's full force departed for the Jomard Passage on 6 May hoping to intercept the Japanese invasion group.

A U.S. land-based patrol discovered the Japanese covering force, and at midmorning on the sixth a group of B-17s attacked the troop ships without success. By that evening the Japanese troop convoy was ready to enter the passage. Both Takagi and Fletcher were operating blind in these opening stages of the battle—Fletcher because he could not depend on land-based, long-range patrol craft, and Takagi because he surprisingly did not order such searches. Thus neither side realized that on the sixth, the two forces were only seventy miles apart before Takagi turned north to protect the convoy.

Early on the morning of the seventh, Admiral Hara ordered a search to the south of his carriers. The pilots reported back that they had sighted a carrier and a cruiser. In reality they had spotted the oiler *Neosho* and its escort, the destroyer *Sims,* which Fletcher had detached from his main force. Hara immediately launched bombers and torpedo planes. The American ships took evasive action and avoided being hit in the first two attacks. A third attack by thirty-six dive-bombers at midday was more successful. The *Sims* took a bomb and sank immediately. The *Neosho* was hit seven times, lost power, and drifted westward. Its crew was rescued on the eleventh and the crippled oiler was scuttled.

The Japanese concentration on these two ships drew their attention away from the main body of TF 17.5. In the meantime, Fletcher took another gamble, reducing his antiaircraft defense by detaching Crace's group to proceed northwest in an attempt to intercept the transports. The Japanese spotted Crace's battle group in the early afternoon and launched three strikes in a five-hour period. To add insult to injury, friendly B-26s also attacked Crace's cruisers.

On the evening of the seventh, Admiral Inoue, troubled by conflicting reports from Takagi and Hara, ordered their transports north out of harm's way until the main American force could be dealt with. The Port Moresby invasion was postponed for two days. Upon learning that the Japanese transports had moved away, Crace turned south.

Earlier on the seventh Fletcher's patrol planes had alerted him to the presence of what he thought was the main Japanese fleet. Unfortunately his scouts, like their Japanese counterparts, misidentified the enemy ships. They were actually two light cruisers and two gunboats from the support group. At 0930 Fitch launched ninety-three aircraft. Although *Lexington*'s attack group did not locate the ships that had been reported, they did find the *Shoho* and the rest of Admiral Goto's covering group. Joined by planes from the *Yorktown,* the attackers pounded the *Shoho,* which took thirteen bomb and seven torpedo hits before sinking. Fitch decided against any further sorties after the planes landed. Not so his Japanese counterpart. Admiral Hara ordered a very risky night operation. He selected twenty-seven pilots with night flying experience and gave them the mission of finding and attacking the U.S. ships in the dark. American fighters vectored to the attacking planes managed to shoot down nine, but others located Fletcher's carriers. Mistaking the American flattops for their own, however, they tried to land. Of the twenty-seven Japanese planes launched, only six returned safely.

On the morning of 8 May the Americans and Japanese sent off their scout planes at about the same time—0815 to 0845. At 0930 the Americans located the Japanese carrier force some two hundred miles northeast of Fletcher's position. Fitch immediately launched twenty-four dive-bombers, nine torpedo bombers, and six fighters from the *Yorktown.* The *Lexington* attack group was airborne ten minutes later. *Yorktown*'s SBD Dauntless dive-bombers found the enemy at 1030 and waited for the slower TBD Devastator torpedo bombers to arrive. By that time the *Zuikaku* had moved into hiding in a rain squall, so the attackers concentrated on the *Shokaku.* The slow-moving and defective torpedoes were ineffectual, but the dive-bombers scored two hits on the carrier, causing a serious fuel fire. Its aircraft were transferred and Hara detached the *Shokaku* to return to Truk for repairs.

Japanese scout planes located TF 17.5 at 1115 and the first wave of enemy torpedo and dive-bombers soon followed. The *Yorktown,* able to take effective evasive action, was struck by only one bomb, which caused considerable damage but in no way threatened the ship. The *Lexington,* not nearly as maneuverable, took two torpedoes on the port side and was also struck by two bombs.

By noon the carrier battle was over. Admiral Nimitz, who had received radio reports of the action, feared further attacks on his carriers. The *Saratoga* had been hit by a torpedo on 11 January and was on the West Coast for repairs. Knowing that half of his Pacific carrier force had been damaged, he ordered Fletcher to retire southward. Nimitz's counterpart, Admiral Inoue, believing the reports of Hara's pilots that the two American carriers had been sunk, ordered Takagi back to Truk. Admiral Yamamoto in Tokyo overruled Hara and ordered Takagi to seek out and destroy whatever elements of the American fleet were left. Takagi complied, but it was too late to intercept the American fleet, which was well on its way to Noumea and Tonga.

When the fighting ended, the Americans appeared to have won a small tactical victory. Of Hara's 122 available planes, 43 were lost as compared to U.S. losses of 33 planes from a total of 121. In addition, TF 17.5's planes sank the light carrier *Shoho,* a destroyer, and several minelayers, and seriously damaged the fast carrier *Shokaku.* The Japanese in turn sank only the *Neosho* and the *Sims.*

The scales tipped in favor of the Japanese with the sinking of the *Lexington,* however. The great carrier emerged from the battle well under control and with only a 7-degree list. Damage control specialists believed that all was well. Then, at about 1245, there was a tremendous internal explosion caused by a fire in a generator that ignited fuel vapors. The ensuing blaze raged out of control until 1445 when another explosion brought the *Lexington* to a dead stop. The crew was evacuated and at 2000 the destroyer *Phelps* torpedoed and sank the "Lady Lex."

Despite this tragedy, the Coral Sea battle was a strategic victory for the United States. Fletcher, although making certain questionable decisions, had successfully carried out his main mission, which was to protect Port Moresby. A Japanese invasion flotilla would not soon threaten the Allies' major base in New Guinea. Secondarily, the losses of planes and pilots from both Japanese carriers and the extensive damage to the *Shokaku* prevented them from taking part in Yamamoto's great plan to draw out the American fleet at Midway.

The Coral Sea battle was the first naval engagement in which the ships involved never got close enough to use their gun batteries. It was the first of a new style of naval battles dominated by carriers. Henceforth the battleship, believed to be the true measure of sea power, would be relegated to a backup role. The Coral Sea battle was also important because it marked the first time in the Pacific war that the Japanese had been thwarted. It would not be the last.

The setback in the Coral Sea forced the Japanese to revise their plans to secure all of Papua New Guinea. However, Japanese planners were not overly concerned with the outcome partially because they still had superiority in ships and planes in the southern region. More specifically, the naval high command was deeply involved in putting together Yamamoto's grand design to force the remnants of the U.S. Pacific Fleet into a decisive battle.

Yamamoto's plan for the Midway operation, like all Japanese naval plans, was extremely complex. The main blow at the permanent installations on Midway and against the American fleet was to be struck by Admiral Nagumo's lst Mobile Force. However, he had available only the carriers *Akagi, Kaga, Hiryu,* and *Soryu.* The other two fleet carriers that had been a part of the Pearl Harbor attack, the *Shokaku* and *Zuikaku,* were undergoing repairs at Truk. Nevertheless, the lst Mobile Force was still very powerful, having a total of 279 planes about equally divided between fighters, dive-bombers, and torpedo bombers. To cover his carriers and provide antiaircraft protection there were two battleships, the *Haruna* and *Kirishima,* two heavy cruisers, and twelve destroyers. Nagumo's major objective was to draw out the American fleet by first attacking the island installations and thus prepare the way for the landing forces.

An integral part of Yamamoto's plan was a ruse he hoped would lure a large portion of the fleet from Pearl Harbor before Nagumo struck Midway. Yamamoto reasoned that Nimitz might be decoyed into believing that the main Japanese objective was the Aleutians. He thus ordered VAdm. Boshiro Hosogaya to seize the islands of Kiska, Adak, and Attu after eliminating the U.S. defenses at Dutch Harbor. For these landings Hosogaya's 2d Mobile Force had four transports carrying twenty-five hundred troops. These were directly covered by the two small aircraft carriers *Ryujo* and *Junyo,* three heavy and two light cruisers, and nine destroyers. Although more than sufficient for the occupation of the islands, the force was too weak if Nimitz took Yamamoto's bait and dispatched the major portion of his fleet to the Aleutians. To counter this, Yamamoto detached an Aleutian screening force from his main body. This element would spring a trap on any U.S. force risking an attack on Hosogaya's mobile force. The screening force was built around the battleships *Ise, Hyuga, Fuso,* and *Yamashiro.*

The Midway occupation force was divided into two parts. The transport group sortied from the Marianas with twelve transports carrying the 5th Special Naval Landing Force and the Ichiki Detachment—a total of five thousand men. Accompanying the transports to give close support were four heavy cruisers and two destroyers. The covering group consisted of the battleships *Kongo* and *Hiei,* four heavy cruisers, and a screen of seven destroyers.

Yamamoto planned to control the battle from the *Yamato,* the most powerful battleship in the world and the flagship of the fleet's main body. In addition, the main body consisted of two other battleships, the *Mutsu* and *Nagato,* one light carrier, two seaplane carriers, and twelve destroyers.

This complex organization suggests two things. The most striking is the number of ships committed to the Midway operation. Except for skeleton forces and damaged ships, all of Japan's available capital ships were committed. This shows how concerned Yamamoto was by the potential threat from the American navy. He was convinced that with such overwhelming superiority he could crush any force that Nimitz might dispatch either to protect the Aleutians or Midway. The relatively small number of troops allotted to capture Midway indicates that Yamamoto viewed capturing the island to be of secondary importance. It was merely bait, as was the Aleutian attack force.

Yamamoto was partially correct in this assessment. Nimitz could not afford a Japanese presence on Midway, which is only eleven hundred miles west-northwest of Hawaii. He would indeed commit all the forces available to prevent the loss of the island. Nimitz was less concerned that the Japanese might attempt to gain a foothold in the Aleutians.

The first part of Japan's grand armada to move was the carriers and covering cruisers of the task force assigned to attack Dutch Harbor. These ships sailed from Ominato at the northern tip of Honshu on the night of 25–26 May, followed two days later by the transports loaded with the troops that would occupy Kiska, Adak, and Attu on 5 June. Next to leave home waters was Nagumo's mobile carrier force, which left the Yashiro Jima anchorage on the inland sea so as to be in position to begin the air attacks on Midway by dawn on 4 June. Yamamoto led the main body, accompanied by Kondo's covering group and Admiral Takasu's Aleutian screening force, out to sea on the twenty-eighth. Takasu's powerful battleship force soon diverged from the main body to take up an intercept position south of the Aleutians. The Midway occupation group from Guam would rendezvous with Kondo's heavy ships, which had taken up position southwest of Midway. Yamamoto's force, proceeding on a direct line to Midway, would lag approximately two hundred miles behind Nagumo and be in a position to destroy any surface force that Nimitz sent out and which managed to escape Nagumo's planes. To calm the fears of some of his subordinates, including Nagumo, Yamamoto planned to have Pearl Harbor thoroughly reconnoitered by seaplanes operating from French Frigate Shoal. This tiny spit, located 490 miles northwest of Oahu, had been a staging base for seaplane attacks on Hawaii on 3–4 March and on Midway on 10 March. Yamamoto also sent out two cordons of submarines to take up station north and west of Hawaii by 2 June. A third group of submarines was ordered to patrol the sea-lanes between Hawaii and the Aleutians.

It must have appeared to Yamamoto's logical mind that he had considered every eventuality and had taken steps to counter any aggressive move Nimitz might make. What he did not know was that Nimitz had information indicating Yamamoto's objectives and his time table. The Japanese commander believed that Nimitz would not be aware of the presence of Japanese forces until after they had struck Midway. According to this scenario, Nimitz's response would be too late and those elements sent out would then be destroyed by Japanese air and surface forces.

Unfortunately for Yamamoto, Commanders Layton and Joseph J. Rochefort and their cryptographers at Pearl Harbor had broken the Japanese naval code to the extent that a portion of the Japanese messages sent by long-range radio could be understood. Together with complicated analysis of the fleet message traffic, a reasonable approximation of Japanese intentions could be deduced. On 14 May Nimitz declared a state of "Fleet Opposed Invasion" and ordered all of the ships involved in the Coral Sea operation back to Hawaii. Nimitz fully accepted his intelligence officers' conclusions that Midway was the objective despite some opposition from those in Washington who believed that the Japanese were planning an attack on the West Coast. The staff estimate issued on 23 May as to the size of the Japanese force and its plan of attack later proved to be uncannily accurate.

Nimitz correctly concluded that Admiral Pye's battleships would not be an asset in the coming battle and ordered them to remain on the West Coast. He realized that the crucial factor was the availability of the American carriers. The *Saratoga,* which had earlier been torpedoed, was repaired but was still in San Diego training new air crews. Halsey's TF 16 built around the *Enterprise* and its veteran air group, and the *Hornet,* which had been sent south to support Fletcher in the Coral Sea, arrived back at Pearl Harbor on 26 May. The following day, Fletcher's TF 17 arrived with the battered *Yorktown.* It was immediately placed in drydock and more than fourteen hundred workers scrambled to make emergency repairs. The civilian and naval technicians performed a near miracle, making in only two days extensive repairs that would normally have taken weeks. The *Yorktown* sailed at 0900 on 30 May with a new air group made up of pilots from three different carriers. They would operate together for the first time during the battle.

Although Nimitz had fewer ships in every category compared to the huge Japanese armada, he could count on near parity in the most important category. Nagumo had four aircraft carriers with a total of 272 planes of all types. The three U.S. carriers had 233 planes. In addition, Midway Island itself could be considered a large aircraft carrier. The navy had 32 PBY Catalina patrol bombers and 6 TBF Avenger torpedo bombers there, the marines could muster 27 dive-bombers and 27 fighters, and the army had 4 B-26 medium and 19 B-17 heavy bombers.

Immediately prior to the departure of the carrier task forces, Nimitz had to make a critical command change. Halsey, who by seniority would have commanded both forces, had developed a very serious skin condition and, despite his opposition, was hospitalized. At Halsey's recommendation, Nimitz chose RAdm. Raymond A. Spruance, who had previously commanded Halsey's cruisers, to take over TF 16. This proved to be one of the most astute decisions Nimitz made during the war. Nimitz also had a command problem involving Admiral Fletcher. There was criticism in Washington, particularly from Admiral King, over Fletcher's handling of the Coral Sea engagement. After thoroughly investigating his actions, Nimitz concluded that the allegations were groundless and gave Fletcher overall command of the two Midway-bound task forces. However, the need to repair the *Yorktown* meant that Spruance took TF 16 out of Pearl Harbor on 28 May and, until Fletcher's force joined him on 2 June, exercised tactical command of the operation. By previous design, Spruance positioned his two carriers, six cruisers, and nine destroyers 350 miles northwest of Midway at "Point Luck" and waited for Fletcher.

On 30 May the navy headquarters on Midway ordered round-the-clock searches by long-range PBY patrol planes. On 3 June one of these located a large number of ships some seven hundred miles west of the island. This enemy force was strung out in two long lines with an arrowhead-shaped screen moving in front. The observers and Midway command believed this to be the main attack force, although it was actually the Midway occupation group. Nine army B-17s attacked the Japanese flotilla and, the pilots' claims of hitting two battleships or cruisers and two transports notwithstanding, hit nothing. Early the next morning, four PBYs armed with torpedoes located the enemy force again and attacked it in the dark. They caused only minimal damage.

Admiral Fletcher, meanwhile, was convinced that the main Japanese force was much closer than had been reported. He moved his two carrier task forces to the southwest during the night of 3–4 June to a position roughly two hundred miles north of Midway. At 0430 on 4 June, Fletcher launched ten SBD scout planes from the *Yorktown* to search north, south, and west in a hundred-mile arc. In addition, the Midway-based PBYs continued their surveillance.

While the Americans and Japanese sought each other around Midway, Admiral Hosogaya's decoy force approached Kiska, Adak, and Attu in the western Aleutians. He planned to land five hundred Special Naval Landing Troops and seven hundred construction workers on Kiska, and twelve hundred army troops on Attu. Although the main purpose of the expedition was to draw off American naval forces that could be used to defend Midway, there was a further reason for the landings. The westernmost island, Attu, was only 650 miles from Paramushir in the Kuriles, where the Japanese had naval and air bases. Occupation of the Aleutian Islands would prevent air attacks on Paramushir.

Japanese intelligence was faulty due largely to the difficulty of observation because of the extreme cold and persistent fog in the region. The Japanese believed that Kiska was defended by more than two hundred marines and that Attu had a radio station, observatory, and a garrison of unknown size. In reality, the only Americans there were a ten-man weather crew on Kiska and a married missionary couple on Attu. Equally wrong was the Japanese assessment of the defenses at Dutch Harbor, the main American base in the Aleutians. Instead of the full division believed to be there, the army and navy together could muster only about fifty-five hundred personnel. Furthermore, the effectiveness of the few army and navy planes based at Cold Bay was limited by the continual foul weather and the pilots' inexperience in flying under such conditions.

The defenses throughout the Alaska area were deplorable, particularly those adjacent to the Aleutians. To counter the Japanese move toward the islands, Admiral Nimitz had collected a force of five cruisers and four destroyers from various areas in the Pacific and placed them under the command of RAdm. Robert A. Theobald. Not all of these ships joined up until after the first Japanese attack on Dutch Harbor. Theobald himself did not arrive in Kodiak until 27 May, at which time he organized his small TF 8 into a number of groups. The air striking group was composed of eighty-five planes at Kodiak, Cold Bay, and Umnak. A surface strike group consisting of a few patrol craft, nine destroyers, and six submarines was assigned the task of defending Dutch Harbor. Theobald planned to remain with the main body of cruisers and destroyers and set off in search of the Japanese invasion fleet. This posed a problem, however. Theobald believed that Hosogaya's objective was Dutch Harbor, and he feared the loss of this major base to the Japanese. He thus ignored Nimitz's suggestion, received the day Theobald arrived at Kodiak, that the Japanese were aiming for Kiska and Attu. On 1 June, Theobald left Kodiak to rendezvous with the rest of his command four hundred miles to the south so that he could intercept the invasion fleet he believed was headed for Dutch Harbor. This decision took him out of the forthcoming engagement.

Rear Admiral Kakuji Kakuta, commanding Hosogaya's carriers, planned for air strikes on Dutch Harbor to keep the Americans there from resisting the invasions. Aided by foul weather, he evaded detection and slipped to within 165 miles of his target. Early on the morning of 3 June, Kakuta launched fourteen bombers against Dutch Harbor. They were moderately successful, their bombs hitting an oil tank farm, barracks, and a radio station. On their return they were intercepted by P-40s from Umnak, which shot down two attackers and damaged several others. Later that morning Kakuta launched a second strike aimed at the American destroyers of the surface strike group, but the weather was so bad that the pilots could not find their targets. After recovering his planes, he headed westward and then reversed his course for another attack on Dutch Harbor. This time his force was observed and army bombers attacked the fleet. But, as with most such land-based bomber attacks, they hit nothing. The Japanese did considerable damage to the hospital and a hangar, blew up four big new storage tanks, and killed eighteen persons. The attackers lost six planes to the P-40s. One development from this attack that had a far-reaching effect was the crash landing of a Zero fighter on Akutan Island. The plane was recovered intact by the Americans and restored to flying condition. Studied for the next eighteen months by aeronautical engineers, it yielded a wealth of data that was then factored into improving the design of American fighters.

*   *   *

Far to the south, the main battle for Midway was about to begin. The weather had been kind to Nagumo's force. A weak stationary front created fog so thick that at one point the admiral lost visual contact with his own ships and had to break radio silence to instruct them to change course. The fog hid the strike force from the American search planes from Midway. The PBYs were not yet fitted with radar, so Nagumo was able to approach the island undetected. Early on the morning of 4 June, he prepared to launch an attack on it. Nagumo did not ignore the American fleet. At 0430 he ordered a search by planes from the carriers *Kaga* and *Akagi,* the cruisers *Tone* and *Chikuma,* and the battleship *Haruna.* A malfunction in the catapult on *Tone* kept its search aircraft from being launched until 0500. This seemingly trivial occurrence had tragic consequences for the Japanese since the American carriers were approximately 215 miles away in the search area assigned to *Tone*'s aircraft.

The Japanese on board the carriers were preoccupied with preparing their aircraft for the attack on Midway. The strike force consisted of thirty-six Kate torpedo bombers, each carrying a 1,770-pound bomb; thirty-six Val dive-bombers; and thirty-six Zero fighters. The air fleet took off at about 0430, and the carrier launch crews immediately began lifting the remaining planes to the flight decks in preparation for a second launch. Although the American ships had not been sighted, Nagumo was certain that they soon would be and decided to load his Kate aircraft with torpedoes.

Midway radar picked up the Japanese attackers at 0553 at a distance of about ninety miles. Bombers and patrol planes were ordered into the air with instructions to the pilots to stay away from the attack area. The twenty-six marine fighters intercepted the Japanese planes thirty miles out at twelve thousand feet and immediately attacked. The Brewster Buffalo and Wildcat fighters were no match for the Zeros, although some got through to the bombers and shot several down. The marines lost seventeen planes and pilots and seven fighters were badly damaged.

The Japanese bombers were met by a hail of antiaircraft fire, but they methodically destroyed oil tanks, the seaplane hangar, the marine command post and mess hall, and damaged storehouses, the hospital, a powerhouse, and the gasoline supply system. However, when they departed at 0650, the runways were relatively undamaged. Casualties from the raid were minimal. The leader of the attack, Lt. Joichi Tomonaga from the *Hiryu*, concluded that another strike would be necessary to neutralize the island's defenses.

The ability of the defenders to strike back was shown by the attack of six TBF Avengers and four army B-26s on the Japanese carriers at 0710. They went in without air cover, and the poorly functioning torpedoes carried by the TBFs once again spelled failure for this near-suicidal mission. Only one Avenger and two B-26s escaped to crash-land back at Midway. However fruitless this attack may have seemed, it helped convince Nagumo that a second strike on the island was necessary.

While the Japanese strike force was on its way to Midway, the crew of a navy PBY sighted Nagumo's carriers through a break in the clouds at approximately 0530. Zeros sent to intercept the patrol bomber lost it in the clouds and, fifteen minutes later, another report of "carriers in sight" came through from the PBY to Admiral Fletcher. However, the observers did not give their location or the number of ships sighted. This information was not received until 0600, placing the Japanese carriers two hundred miles southwest of the *Yorktown*. Since *Yorktown*'s scouts were still out, Fletcher ordered Spruance to intercept the Japanese and attack the enemy carriers as soon as their location could be pinpointed. Spruance complied and ordered the *Enterprise* and *Hornet* and their protective screen to break away from TF 17.5 and proceed southwest at twenty-five knots. This established, for all practical purposes, a dual tactical command situation for the Americans.

Meanwhile, Admiral Nagumo had made the first of a series of decisions that would ultimately contribute to the Japanese defeat. At 0715 he decided to heed the advice of his strike commander and ordered another attack on Midway. This meant that the Kate bombers on the *Kaga* and *Akagi* that had been loaded with torpedoes had to be removed from the flight decks and refitted with bombs. This was hard, time-consuming work and could not be completed quickly. Then, at 0728, Nagumo received the first message indicating that there might be American carriers within striking distance. The search plane launched late from *Tone* reported sighting ten ships and gave their distance and heading from the Japanese carriers, but did not give the composition of the naval force. Nagumo, fearing the presence of carriers a scant two hundred miles away, agonized for fifteen minutes before finally giving the order to stop loading bombs and to replace them with torpedoes. It was not until 0810 that the dilatory observers aboard the *Tone* scout plane reported that the American force consisted of five cruisers and five destroyers.

Although this report was a relief to the worried Nagumo, he had more pressing problems to deal with. His carriers were under attack by land-based aircraft from Midway. Fifteen B-17s dropped their bombs from twenty thousand feet while navy and marine dive and scout bombers came in at low level. Evasive action and Zero fighters prevented hits from being scored on any of the Japanese ships. However, Nagumo had scrambled all his fighters to deal with the attackers, which meant that if he launched another attack on Midway immediately, his bombers would be without escort. To add to the confusion in the Japanese force, an American submarine, the *Nautilus,* one of a dozen protecting Midway, fired several torpedoes at one of the battleships. Although the attack was not successful, it forced the battleship and cruiser screen to try to hunt down the intruder at the same time the fleet was maneuvering to avoid the air attacks. Then, at about 0820, Nagumo received the message that dashed his hopes of completing the attack on Midway before any serious opposition developed: an enemy carrier task force was in the vicinity. At this juncture the planes from the Midway strike returned, some damaged and all short of fuel. Nagumo rejected the advice of his subordinate, RAdm. Tamon Yamaguchi, who wanted to launch the planes on deck immediately. Instead, Nagumo ordered them below and began to take aboard Lieutenant Tomonaga's aircraft. The operation lasted for more than forty-five minutes.

Meanwhile, Spruance's TF 16 continued at full speed to intercept the Japanese. He had calculated that it would be 0900 before the enemy would be within reasonable striking distance, and decided to gamble by launching his planes early, hoping to catch the Japanese as they were landing the planes from the Midway action. At 0752 a force of thirty-seven SBD dive-bombers led by Lt. Comdr. Wade McClusky took off and was ordered to proceed without waiting for the torpedo bombers or fighter cover. He set a course southeast toward Midway. Very soon, all available aircraft were on what was believed to be an intercept course. However, due to the hurried nature of the launches and the cloudy weather, the initial attack broke down into four separate groups. The most serious result of this was that the torpedo squadron from *Enterprise* had no fighter escort.

Arriving at what was believed to be the intercept point, the American pilots discovered no ships in sight. After taking on Tomonaga's planes, Nagumo had altered course northeast to close with the American carriers. This course change saved the Japanese from immediate detection. Lieutenant Commander Samuel G. Mitchell, leading thirty-five dive-bombers and their F4F Wildcat fighter cover from the *Hornet,* chose to continue southeastward. Running low on fuel after a fruitless search, most of the SBDs later landed on the *Enterprise,* although thirteen sought refuge on Midway. All of the fighters crash-landed in the ocean. Mitchell's entire group was thus never a factor in the developing battle.

Lieutenant Commander John C. Waldron, leading *Hornet*'s Torpedo Squadron 8, opted to search in a northerly direction. At approximately 0925 he sighted the Japanese fleet. His lumbering TBD Devastators had been without air cover since just after takeoff, when the fighters assigned to protect them lost sight of the squadron in the clouds. Despite the certain knowledge that a run at Nagumo's carriers in all probability could not succeed, Waldron began his attack. The squadron was intercepted by the Zeros covering the fleet and then met by a curtain of antiaircraft fire from the cruiser and destroyer screen. One by one the TBDs were shot down. A few managed to release their torpedoes at short range, but without effect. Of the thirty pilots and crewmen in Torpedo Squadron 8, only one man survived. Ensign George H. Gay, his radioman already dead, launched his torpedo just before his rudder pedal was smashed, causing him to crash. Gay managed to escape from the plane and hid under a seat cushion. From this vantage point, he observed the subsequent attacks on the Japanese fleet. The following afternoon he was sighted by a PBY and rescued.

Hardly had the Japanese destroyed the *Hornet*'s TBDs than Lt. Comdr. Eugene E. Lindsey of the *Enterprise*'s Torpedo Squadron 6 began his attack, concentrating on the *Kaga.* Lindsey's squadron also had no fighter escort since the Wildcats assigned to it had erroneously accompanied Waldron's squadron before losing contact with it. Once again the slow-moving Devastators were caught by nimble Japanese fighters and shot from the sky. Ten of the fourteen attackers were destroyed, including Lindsey's plane. None of their torpedoes hit the target.

Shortly after this slaughter, at about 1000, Torpedo Squadron 3 from the *Yorktown* made an appearance. Admiral Fletcher, after taking in his scout planes, had quickly followed in TF 16's wake and very cautiously launched a portion of *Yorktown*'s aircraft. Torpedo Squadron 3's planes, accompanied by Lt. Comdr. John S. Thach's six Wildcats, followed their leader, Lt. Comdr. Lance E. Massey, in a low-level attack on *Soryu*. The escort was driven off by a swarm of Japanese fighters, and Massey's attack, which duplicated the bravery of the other torpedo runs, was unfortunately no more successful. Only five of the TBDs were able to drop their torpedoes, which hit nothing, and seven aircraft, including Massey's, were shot down in flames.

The torpedo attacks had been disastrous. Of the forty-one planes involved, only six returned. However, their near-suicidal attacks contributed directly to the eventual destruction of Nagumo's carrier force. They had caused the Japanese fleet to take severe evasive action, which prevented the launch of more planes. More importantly, the attacks had drawn the Japanese fighter cover down low to deal with the torpedo attacks, leaving no high-level protection for the carriers.

Throughout the melee, the Japanese continued to refuel and rearm their planes. The carrier decks were crowded when Nagumo finally gave the order to launch the strike force. As the carriers turned into the wind to comply, the American dive-bombers appeared.

These bombers were from two different carriers. Lieutenant Commander Maxwell F. Leslie, leading Bombing Squadron 3, had accompanied Massey's ill-fated torpedo bombers from the *Yorktown* and was jockeying for an attack on *Soryu*, the easternmost of Nagumo's carriers. About four miles to the west was *Kaga*, and two miles to the northeast was *Akagi*. These would be the targets for Lieutenant Commander McClusky and his thirty-seven planes from the *Enterprise*. McClusky had proceeded to the expected intercept point only to find nothing. Fortunately, he spotted the destroyer

Arashi, which had been left behind by the mobile force to try to locate and destroy the American submarine *Nautilus*. It was now hastening to rejoin the main fleet, and McClusky correctly deduced that by following the *Arashi*'s heading, he would find the carriers. Thus at almost the same time that Leslie began his attack on *Soryu,* McClusky's group swooped down on *Kaga* and *Akagi*. Only three planes attacked the *Akagi,* the remainder concentrating on the *Kaga,* but these three did their job well. One 1,000-pound bomb missed, but the other two scored direct hits. The first hit the afterdeck in the middle of the parked planes causing a huge blaze to erupt. The second struck just opposite the bridge, penetrated the deck, and exploded in the main hangar, detonating the torpedoes stored there. Almost immediately the carrier was out of action.

Admiral Nagumo, unable to conduct the battle from the burning carrier, was literally dragged from the bridge by his subordinates, who eventually convinced him to transfer his flag to a cruiser. The *Akagi*'s crew continued to fight the fires into the evening before the captain ordered all hands to abandon ship. Drifting out of control, the *Akagi* was scuttled early the next morning by a Japanese destroyer.

While this drama was unfolding on the flagship, the *Kaga* took four hits. One struck just in front of the bridge, killing everyone there, including the captain. The other three bombs landed among the planes on the flight deck and penetrated into the hangar area below. There they started a similar train of explosions as those that destroyed the *Akagi*. Within minutes the *Kaga* was a mass of flames, and many of the officers and men hastily abandoned ship. The drifting, burning wreck sank shortly before the *Akagi* went down. Meanwhile, Commander Leslie's seventeen dive-bombers from *Yorktown* were attacking *Soryu*. Divided into three groups, the planes attacked in intervals from three directions and scored three hits. One bomb penetrated into the hangar area while the others blew apart the planes waiting to take off and started fires. Within twenty minutes the captain ordered the carrier abandoned by all except demolition control parties. Escorted by two destroyers, the *Soryu* was moving at very slow speed and the fires appeared to be under control when the submarine *Nautilus* appeared. At about 1400, its captain, Comdr. William H. Brockman, fired three torpedoes, all of which hit home. *Soryu* sank within four hours.

The dive-bombers, in attacks lasting just five minutes, had helped redress the naval balance in the Pacific. Not only had they sunk three fleet carriers, but most of Japan's experienced carrier pilots were lost. The Japanese would never again be able to put into the air such well-trained, experienced pilots. By noon on 4 June it was apparent that the Japanese had been dealt a disastrous blow— more severe than that visited on the American fleet at Pearl Harbor.

Japanese fighters and a miscalculation of "Point Option," the intercept point for the returning planes, caused further American aircraft losses. By noon those losses stood at 14 of 37 dive-bombers, 10 of 14 torpedo bombers, and 1 fighter from *Enterprise*. *Hornet* lost all 15 of its torpedo bombers and 11 of 12 fighters. *Yorktown* lost 12 of 13 torpedo bombers, 2 dive-bombers, and 3 fighters. The air battle, however, was not over. The Japanese still had one operable carrier, the *Hiryu*, which had possibly been out of position far ahead of the other carriers.

Admiral Nagumo relinquished tactical control of the carrier strike force to RAdm. Hiroaki Abe, commander of the battleship screen, while he transferred his flag from the doomed *Akagi*. When Abe learned the *Yorktown* had been sighted he ordered Admiral Yamaguchi on the still undamaged *Hiryu* to attack. They had concluded that the Americans most likely had only one carrier and saw this as the chance to tip the balance in their favor. Admiral Yamamoto, on board the *Yamato*, also began to concentrate his conventional force. He ordered Admiral Kondo to speed north with the supporting force and detached the smaller aircraft carriers *Ryujo* and *Junyo* from the Aleutian force. They were to rendezvous with Yamamoto as soon as possible to continue the battle.

Yamaguchi sent off his first attack group, eighteen dive-bombers and six fighters, at approximately 1100. They were led by the scout planes that had located *Yorktown*. As soon as they left, ten torpedo bombers and six more fighters were launched. Fletcher had a combat patrol of twelve Wildcat fighters out searching and was refueling a previous patrol while Leslie's dive-bombers circled, waiting for permission to land. Shortly before noon, *Yorktown*'s radar picked up the Japanese planes while they were still some distance away. Leslie was waved off and preparations were made to minimize bomb and fire damage. The Wildcats intercepted and either destroyed or damaged ten Vals so badly that they could not drop their bombs. Antiaircraft fire destroyed two more, but the remaining dive-bombers got through and scored three hits. The most serious put out the fires in all but one of the boilers. By 1220 *Yorktown* was dead in the water. With his radar and other communications knocked out, Fletcher transferred his flag to the cruiser *Astoria*. Before the *Yorktown* could be taken in tow, the damage control teams managed to get the fires extinguished and four boilers operating. Less than an hour after the attack, the carrier was under way at twenty knots and refueling fighters when the captain was notified that another enemy force was approaching.

Only eight fighters could be launched to join the four others on patrol. They were unable to stop the Japanese, who broke through to attack the carrier from four directions. A wall of antiaircraft fire from the carrier and its screen could not prevent four Kates from getting through to release their torpedoes. Two of these missed, but the others struck *Yorktown* on the port side, knocking out all power, rupturing the fuel tanks, jamming the rudder, and causing flooding that resulted in an immediate 15-degree list. By 1515 this had become an alarming 30 degrees. The captain, when informed that power was needed for counterflooding to correct the list, ordered the ship abandoned. The destroyer screen moved in to pick up survivors.

The saga of the *Yorktown* continued long after the battle was over. Attempts to save the carrier resumed on the fifth when a large salvage party boarded the ship twenty-four hours after it had been abandoned. By midafternoon on the sixth, the crew appeared to be making good progress. Protected by four destroyers and drawing power from the destroyer *Hammann* lashed to its starboard side, the carrier was being towed slowly to safety. However, a Japanese float plane located the *Yorktown* and Yamamoto ordered the submarine I-168 to intercept and destroy it. The submarine commander successfully penetrated the protective screen and fired four torpedoes at about 1330 on 6 June. Two went under the *Hammann* and struck the carrier; a third hit the destroyer, which sank almost immediately with heavy loss of life. Despite the two new hits, the captain intended to continue salvage operations, but at 0600 on 7 June the *Yorktown* sank, the last victim of the Japanese at Midway.

Admiral Spruance had been given de facto command of the operation at 1300 on 4 June when Fletcher radioed from the *Astoria* that he would conform to Spruance's movements. Before this, Fletcher had ordered scout bombers out to try to locate the *Hiryu*. They found the carrier with its escort at about 1445 and radioed a very complete description. Although the *Yorktown* was in no condition to respond, being at that time under heavy attack, Spruance could. At 1530 he sent out twenty-four dive-bombers, led by McClusky without fighter escort, to intercept Nagumo's lone remaining carrier. They found the *Hiryu* at 1700 and immediately attacked. The carrier took four hits that destroyed all communications, the bridge, and began uncontrollable fires. *Hiryu* did not sink immediately, but drifted. A number of attacks by aircraft from Midway did little more damage to the stricken carrier. Resisting many attempts by Japanese destroyers to sink the hulk, *Hiryu* finally went down at 0900 on 5 June.

At dawn on the fourth, Yamamoto had been some three hundred miles behind Nagumo, too far away to aid in either the strike on Midway or the defense of the carriers. By so distancing himself and by insisting on strict radio silence, he had effectively relinquished command to Nagumo. He had no contact with Nagumo's force for almost two hours after the air action began. Then, at 1050, a message from the cruiser *Tone* informed him of the fate of the three carriers that had been sunk. That was just before Yamaguchi launched *Hiryu*'s planes to attack *Yorktown*. Even then, Yamamoto was certain that all was not lost. He still believed that he could force the Americans to commit all their available ships to a decisive battle. Once again he made a serious miscalculation. Nagumo's strike at Pearl Harbor and the sinking of the British battleships the previous December had shown how helpless were the former titans of the sea when confronting aircraft. The American victory at Midway simply confirmed this. Yet Yamamoto believed he could provoke a night action, although he was actually too far away for this. Admiral Kondo on his own initiative had begun at 1400 to close on Midway with two battleships, the carrier *Zuiho*, and a destroyer squadron. Yamamoto had earlier ordered the small carriers *Ryujo* and *Junyo* away from the Aleutians to join the main Midway force. With the old aircraft carrier *Hosho* accompanying the main body and the *Zuiho* coming up from the southwest, Yamamoto could put more than a hundred planes in the air if he could bring the carriers together in time. The *Yamato* and its escorts were under way by early afternoon, but were slowed by fog.

To a large extent, Yamamoto's moves after being informed of the losses were simply wishful thinking. The carriers *Ryujo* and *Junyo* could not arrive under the best of circumstances until the afternoon of the eighth, and the main body was still eight hundred miles from Midway. Even if Admiral Kondo, who had replaced Nagumo in command, found Spruance's ships, he would be facing planes from the *Hornet* and *Enterprise* backed by all the available army and navy aircraft on the island. This scenario was very unfavorable to the Japanese. Believing that the American ships were still heading westward, Yamamoto changed course to intercept them. Spruance, however, decided to avoid a night action and retired to the east, about 250 miles northwest of Midway.

At 2030 on the fourth Yamamoto also ordered the submarine I-168 to proceed to Midway and begin shelling the island preliminary to being joined by Adm. Takeo Kurita's four heavy cruisers. The submarine commander, faithful to his orders, sent six rounds toward the island at 0130 on the fifth. These did little more than make the garrison even more edgy. Even before the I-168 bombardment, Spruance began moving his ships at full speed back toward Midway. At 2250 an observer in a scout plane launched by the cruiser *Chikuma* saw two American carriers just before his aircraft flew into a cloud bank. When it came out, he observed the same carriers, but believed them to be different ships. Knowing the *Yorktown* was still afloat, he reported that the Americans had five carriers, four of which were steaming toward Midway.

Armed with this information, and after considerable discussion with his staff, Yamamoto reluctantly decided to call off Kurita's attack and abandon the Midway enterprise. He rejected a plan by some of his advisers to continue the attack, and at 0255 on 5 June ordered a general retirement. Without air cover, he knew he would be courting an even greater defeat. All elements of the invasion force were ordered back either to Japan or to the bases from which they had sailed. The great, overly complex enterprise to destroy the American fleet was almost over, having been halted by only five minutes of attacks by American dive-bombers.

But the Midway battle was not yet over. When Spruance was informed by observers in land-based aircraft that Yamamoto was retreating, he ordered all available planes to attack. Earlier, while responding to Yamamoto's withdrawal order, two of the Japanese heavy cruisers in a force of four proceeding toward Midway had rammed each other. The *Mogami* struck the port side of the *Mikuma,* damaging its bow and puncturing the *Mikuma*'s oil tanks. This accident lowered their speed to only sixteen knots. Leaving behind a destroyer screen, Admiral Kurita proceeded westward at full speed with his undamaged ships. The American submarine *Tambor* sighted and began tracking the crippled cruisers. Several B-17s from Midway searched the area for them, but their pilots could not locate the ships. Then, at about 0745 on the fifth, a marine attack squadron of twelve planes picked up *Mikuma*'s oil slick, followed it, and attacked it unsuccessfully—except for the crash of the squadron leader's plane on *Mikuma*'s aft turret. The crippled cruisers managed to hide until they were spotted early the next day by scout planes from the *Enterprise.* Three separate air strikes by planes from the *Hornet* and *Enterprise* further damaged the *Mogami.* After the last attack it limped slowly back to Truk, where it spent a year undergoing repairs. The *Hornet*'s planes meanwhile had zeroed in on the *Mikuma;* one bomb detonated its torpedoes and the cruiser sank later that evening.

Yamamoto still had not given up entirely. From the reports of the cruiser action, he believed he could still lure Spruance into a trap. He formed a new task force of six heavy cruisers and their destroyers to proceed to the aid of the *Mogami* and *Mikuma.* He hoped that such action would draw the Americans close enough to Wake Island for land-based aircraft to hit them. Late in the afternoon of 6 June, Yamamoto ordered his main body and the Second Fleet south to intercept Spruance if all went as planned. Spruance did not take the bait. He instead stopped TF 16's westward pursuit and awaited the arrival of replacement aircraft from the *Saratoga,* which had reached Pearl Harbor on the sixth. Nimitz briefly toyed with the idea of sending TF 16 north to engage the Japanese in the Aleutians, but canceled the operation on 11 June.

While the main battle was going on, Admiral Hosogaya was confused by conflicting messages from Yamamoto. At first, on 4 June, he was ordered to break off action and take his attack squadron south.

That order was canceled after it became obvious to Yamamoto that time and distance militated against the squadron being of use. Hosogaya was then ordered to proceed with the invasion. When Kusaka's carriers joined up on the fifth, Hosogaya decided against attempting to take Adak and instead concentrated on Kiska and Attu.

On 7 June the Japanese bumbled ashore at Holtz Bay on Attu, marched overland through the snow, and captured thirty-nine Aleuts and the two missionaries. There was no opposition on Kiska, and the ten-member weather crew was taken prisoner. Army and naval air attacks meant to disrupt the Japanese landings proved fruitless. The occupation of these two small islands was the only positive outcome of Yamamoto's grandiose plan. Although the American media made much of the Japanese threat stemming from the loss of these islands, in reality their possession added nothing to Japan's strength. Rather, their defense drained Japanese men and materiel from the major theaters of war. However plausible an invasion of the Alaskan mainland was beforehand, it was totally impossible after the Midway disaster.

The confrontation at Midway was one of the most important naval battles of the war. Yet some observers have assigned greater significance to the American victory than the facts allow. Yamamoto still had naval superiority in the Central and South Pacific arenas. His surface force was relatively untouched, and even with the loss of four fleet carriers, there were more Japanese carriers available than Nimitz could muster at that time. A sober assessment of Midway underscores the fact that it was a great tactical victory for Spruance and Fletcher, who clearly outmaneuvered their opposites. It ended the active threat to Midway and, by extension, the Hawaiian Islands. With such security, Nimitz could begin to assemble what would ultimately be the overpowering Fifth Fleet. He could later pick his objectives without fear of Japanese attack. Hawaii thus became the main supply base for the Pacific war. The Japanese commanders in turn became defensive, not willing to risk the main elements of the Combined Fleet in another major engagement. This led them to abandon plans for the conquest of Fiji, New Caledonia, and New Zealand. There would be other critical naval engagements before the end of the war, but none with the disastrous potential that a victory by Yamamoto's grand fleet would have posed. The defensive stance taken by Admiral Yamamoto and his successor, Adm. Mineichi Koga, meant that until mid-1944 most Japanese naval actions would involve only their cruisers and destroyers. Very soon, victorious Japanese army units would also be forced on the defensive throughout their newly won empire.

Chapter 7

The Guadalcanal Ordeal

DURING THE FIRST months of 1942 the attention of VAdm. Jin'ichi Kusaka, commander of the Southeast Area Fleet, and his army counterpart, Gen. Hitoshi Imamura of the Eighth Area Army, was firmly fixed on New Guinea. They were aware that no Allied force was available to protect the many islands stretching over six hundred miles southeastward from Rabaul, the main Japanese naval and air base on New Britain. There seemed to be no pressing reason for rushing to occupy any of these islands as long as the goal of capturing Port Moresby had not been achieved. The Japanese commanders, therefore, leisurely sent small detachments to key areas in New Ireland in February 1942, followed by landings adjacent to the Buka Passage and eastern Bougainville in March. Then, on 26 April, Admiral Goto's support force for the invasion of Port Moresby stopped briefly at deserted Tulagi Harbor and informed higher headquarters of its desirability. One week later the Japanese sent troops and construction workers to Tulagi, and within weeks there was a functioning radio station there. Very soon, long-range reconnaissance seaplanes and twelve Zero floatplanes were operating from the island.

The decision to occupy Tulagi was a reflection of the Japanese high command's strategic compromise. As noted earlier, serious debates preceded the Midway debacle. Although Admiral Yamamoto won out, others in the navy and army who wanted to launch a major effort designed to interdict the long, vulnerable Allied supply line to Australia and New Zealand were given the green light to engage in secondary efforts to take New Caledonia, Fiji, and Samoa. The operation to take Port Moresby was also to be sped up. Unfortunately for the Japanese, the Coral Sea encounter briefly thwarted these latter plans.

On 28 May the local commander at Tulagi, acting on his own initiative, sent patrols across Sealark Channel to Guadalcanal, twenty miles away. Even then, no serious thought was given to establishing a permanent base there. The patrols were looking for a possible source of meat for the Tulagi garrison, as well as for native laborers. The reports from these patrols convinced the Japanese that a flat area on the old Lunga Plantation between the Ilu and Kukum Rivers was suitable for an airfield. A survey party was sent to Guadalcanal on 19 June, and on 1 July an advance party of four hundred men was sent from Tulagi. Within a week, almost three thousand men from Japanese construction battalions were at work on the airfield.

Admiral King, the most ardent proponent of diverting men and materiel to the Pacific, was well aware of the threat the Japanese posed to the vital supply line between Hawaii and Australia. In March 1942 he proposed an offensive operation that would secure the Solomons and thus deprive the Japanese of the land bases from which to strike at the Allied lifeline. At the very least he wanted to seize Tulagi. This recommendation could not be implemented because of the critical shortage of men and materiel available.

General MacArthur, faced with General Horii's drive across the Owen Stanley Mountains toward Port Moresby, was also pressing hard for more men. In a show of bravado probably to call attention to his needs, MacArthur promised to take Rabaul within three weeks if given the necessary troops backed by a naval task force with at least two carriers. His promise, given the state of Allied forces, was absurd—and was treated as such by the service chiefs in Washington. Still dominated by the Europe first strategy, they believed that the Pacific was receiving all that could be spared from the main effort. In fact, by March, MacArthur had already received more than eighty thousand troops, as well as increasing numbers of planes for his soon to be christened Fifth Air Force. Within three months additional forces would be available. The 37th Division had arrived in Fiji, the Americal Division's regiments were scattered in New Caledonia, and the 147th Infantry Regiment was at Tongatabu. However, at this juncture, none of these could be spared from guard duty to undertake an offensive. Nevertheless, it was generally agreed that although an immediate assault upon Rabaul was out of the question, some limited offensives should be launched.

Long discussions between army and navy planners in Washington—with input from MacArthur's and Ghormley's headquarters—finally resulted in an agreement on 2 July concerning the major immediate objectives. The news of Japanese activity on Guadalcanal spurred planning for these operations, which ultimately resulted in wresting Rabaul from the Japanese. Code-named Operation Watchtower, the plan was divided into three tasks. The first was to occupy the Santa Cruz Islands and recapture Tulagi with forces controlled by Admiral Ghormley. To accommodate this, the eastern boundary of MacArthur's command was moved westward, making the southern Solomons operation the ultimate responsibility of Admiral Nimitz. The second task was to halt the Japanese push toward Port Moresby, then advance Allied troops up the northern New Guinea coast. At the same time, other Allied units would move up the Solomons chain. When these tasks were completed, MacArthur would be free to launch an assault on Rabaul.

The report that the Japanese had sent construction workers to Guadalcanal and were busily constructing an airfield caused the Americans to initiate the first phase of Watchtower. If the Japanese completed the airstrip, their bombers could attack Allied bases on Espíritu Santo, Efate, or perhaps even New Caledonia. Thus invading Guadalcanal before the airfield became operational was added to the objectives of the first task. Admiral Ghormley protested the time frame established by Washington. He was joined by MacArthur, who in a reversal of his earlier optimism, declared the proposal too risky.

There was good reason for their pessimism. MacArthur could not spare any units for the Guadalcanal landings because he was busy preparing for his New Guinea operation. The separate regiments of the Americal Division were needed to garrison the islands adjacent to the key sea-lanes leading to Australia. The only unit of sufficient size to carry out the Guadalcanal operation was the lst Marine Division. Its lead regiment, the 7th Marines, did not arrive in Samoa until April, and the other two infantry regiments and supporting elements were still on the way to New Zealand in June. The division commander, Maj. Gen. Alexander A. Vandegrift, had been assured by higher authority that his division would have time to train and would probably not be used until early 1943. Instead, Vandegrift was forced to plan for the Guadalcanal landings while a large part of his division was en route to New Zealand. This second echelon did not arrive until three weeks before the proposed date for the invasion. The planning for one of the most crucial campaigns of the Pacific war was thus done in haste.

Although the Australians had plantations along the north coastal plain before the war, little was known to the planners about the interior areas except that it was generally rain forest interspersed with patches of kunai grass. The temperature and humidity were uniformly high, and malaria was epidemic. Despite these obvious problems and the time constraints imposed on Ghormley's and Vandegrift's staffs, Admiral King brushed aside all objections to the operation. The only concession Washington made was to postpone the proposed landings three days. D day would be 7 August.

Vandegrift's staff, lacking detailed intelligence of the island, planned to land "where the enemy was not"—east of the Ilu River about eight thousand yards from the airstrip. Two combat groups would land on the two-thousand-yard-wide Red Beach. The first, Combat Group A consisting of two battalions of the 5th Marines, would land, move into the immediate interior, and establish a perimeter. Combat Group B, Col. Clifton B. Cates's lst Marines, would then pass through the 5th Marines's lines, and move westward to capture the airfield. If this part of the plan appeared simple, other aspects were definitely unclear. Rear Admiral Richmond Kelly Turner was appointed the amphibious commander, but his actual authority over tactical affairs after the marines landed was not defined. Rear Admiral John S. McCain was assigned to command land air operations, but he was not made subordinate to Turner. This meant that in order to coordinate air strikes, he would

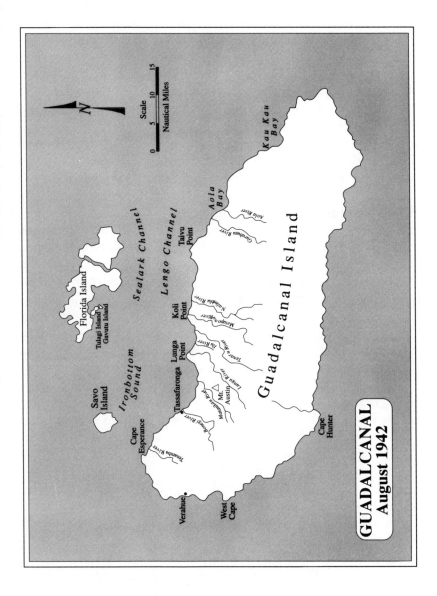

GUADALCANAL
August 1942

have to initiate a request and wait for confirmation—which might have to come from Ghormley's headquarters in Noumea. Nor was the problem of what to do with the airfield once it was captured well thought out. Ghormley had only a few planes available and, even after two marine fighter squadrons had been designated to operate from the field, they were based far away. It would take time for them to become operational from Guadalcanal. This would force the marines to depend upon the navy for air cover until their own air units arrived.

Still another problem complicated preparations for the invasion. The second echelon of the 1st Marine Division arrived in Wellington during heavy rains. New Zealand labor union leaders, oblivious to the fact of the war, refused to allow their workers to unload the ships during inclement weather. The dock workers were ordered away by the police while the marines, working eight-hour shifts in the downpour, did the best they could to sort out the equipment and supplies needed for the operation. All extraneous personal gear had to be stored and all bulk supplies, such as food and lubricants—in many cases inadequately packaged—were cut to a sixty-day supply. Ammunition was reduced to only a ten-day supply. Despite the lack of time, bad weather, poor packaging, and uncooperative dock workers, the supplies were sorted out and those considered most necessary were reloaded onto the assault ships.

On 22 July, Turner's invasion fleet left Wellington. The importance Nimitz's headquarters attached to the Guadalcanal operation can be seen in the naval support supplied. Admiral Fletcher, who was in overall tactical command, had a large part of the Pacific Fleet's available offensive weapons. His attack force, TF 61, was built around the carriers *Saratoga, Wasp,* and *Enterprise.* They were supported by the new fast battleship *North Carolina,* five heavy and one light cruisers, and sixteen destroyers. Turner's amphibious force, TF 62, was guarded by an additional eight cruisers and a destroyer screen.

This armada of seventy-six ships, the largest naval force assembled by the United States up to that time, rendezvoused off Koro, a small island in the Fiji group, on 26 July. There Vandegrift and Turner conferred with Fletcher and received a further shock. Admiral Ghormley had not suitably briefed Fletcher on Operation

Watchtower, leaving Fletcher considerable leeway in defining his role. Fletcher, who did not believe wholeheartedly in the Guadalcanal operation, had earlier expressed to Nimitz his opposition to the landings. Aware that he controlled three-quarters of America's carrier strength in the Pacific—and that any carrier sunk could not be replaced for months—Fletcher decided that he could only support the landings for two days. Despite vociferous protests by Vandegrift and Turner, Fletcher was determined to get his carriers out of harm's way as quickly as possible.

General Vandegrift was further discouraged by the poor performance of the combined rehearsal for the attack. The coral off the rehearsal beaches prevented good landings, and mechanical failures stopped many of the assault boats dead in the water. The air and naval support was also erratic and ineffective.

Despite such negative portents, the transports and Fletcher's TF 61 were fortunate that their movements were undetected by the Japanese. Rain squalls had kept the Japanese search aircraft at Rabaul and Tulagi grounded. The transports off-loaded the 5th Marines as planned, and at 0909 on 7 August the first boats ground to a halt on Red Beach. Soon after, the three battalions of Cates's lst Marine Regiment landed and began to advance southwest toward Mount Austen. Meeting no resistance, the 5th Marines cautiously moved toward their first day's objective: Alligator Creek, two miles west of the landing beach. They reached it before nightfall.

The heat and humidity took their toll on the heavily laden marines, particularly members of the lst Marines, who found they could not reach their first day's objective. Vandegrift ordered them to halt, dig in, and in the morning proceed westward to the Lunga River to envelop the airfield from the south. Both regiments continued to advance the next morning, and patrols from the lst Marines, moving slowly through the tangled growth, reached the north end of the field by midafternoon. They were soon joined by the main elements of the 5th Marines, who pushed on to take the Kukum village. Not surprisingly, the Japanese construction workers and their naval force protectors had fled into the jungle.

Meanwhile, Turner was frantically unloading his vulnerable transports. He understood very well that as soon as the Japanese were aware of the landings they would concentrate their bombers on the beaches and transports. One major problem was the small number of men in the shore parties. Vandegrift could not spare extra men from his combat units, so naval personnel were used to unload the ships. They simply dumped supplies of all types on the beach with no semblance of order. Red Beach soon became so jammed that another beach farther to the west was designated to receive supplies and, later in the afternoon, some sailors were dispatched to help sort out the mess.

As expected, the Japanese sent a major force of twenty-seven two-engined bombers escorted by eighteen Zero fighters to strike at the invasion fleet. Warned by coastwatchers on Bougainville, Fletcher provided fighter cover over Savo Island and Turner's ships prepared to meet the attack, which began shortly after 1100. Those Japanese planes that got past the fighters bombed erratically, causing only minor damage to one destroyer. The antiaircraft gunners on the transports had a field day against the low-flying aircraft.

Another interruption in the landing operation occurred in mid-afternoon when a dozen dive-bombers were reported over Bougainville headed for Guadalcanal. They, too, caused no damage. Of the fifty-one planes dispatched from Rabaul on D day, only twenty-one returned.

At the same time as the Guadalcanal landings, marine units commanded by the assistant division commander, Brig. Gen. William H. Rupertus, hit Florida, Tulagi, and the smaller islands of Gavutu and Tanambogo. The 1st Battalion, 2d Marines, landed on the tip of Florida Island and met no resistance. This was not the case with the 1st Raider Battalion assaulting Tulagi or the 1st Parachute Battalion at Gavutu. The Raiders, after securing their beachhead and advancing into the town, were hit with heavy mortar and machine-gun fire. During the night of 7–8 August, they beat back four major frontal attacks, then systematically cleared most of the caves of the surviving Japanese the next day. By sunset, Tulagi was secured.

The fighting for Gavutu was even more fierce. The marines, despite close-in naval support, were briefly pinned down on the beach. Finally breaking out, they secured the high ground but then had to root the Japanese from caves. A narrow causeway connected Gavutu to Tanambogo, and fierce Japanese fire repeatedly halted the marines trying to cross over it. Air strikes did not help. Many of the bombs fell short, causing some marine casualties. Admiral Turner finally released a battalion of the 2d Marines to replace the paratroopers. Close-in bombardment by a destroyer allowed them to cross the causeway, and the Japanese retreated to caves where they managed to hold out for days.

By D-plus-2, the marines had eliminated the key small islands adjacent to Florida and secured a toehold on Guadalcanal. No one at that juncture could have imagined how desperate the fight for Guadalcanal would become—or that the struggle to hold the initial gains would determine in large part the fate of the overexpanded Japanese empire in the South Pacific.

The air raids on the Guadalcanal beachhead were but a harbinger of the Japanese reaction. When he learned of the American landings, VAdm. Gun'ichi Mikawa, commander of the Eighth Fleet, alerted all available combat ships to sortie toward Guadalcanal. His was a significant force of five heavy and two light cruisers and a destroyer, but it was more than matched in numbers by the Allied fleet. Mikawa decided to risk a daylight run in the narrow passage between Santa Isabel and New Georgia, which came to be known as the Slot. He planned to be in a position to attack the transports early on the morning of the ninth. His force was spotted by an Australian patrol plane, but the observer misidentified what he saw, reporting that the main elements of the Japanese force were two seaplane tenders. The torturous communications net then operating caused the erroneous message to be delayed eight hours before it finally reached Turner, who erred in thinking that the Japanese ships were heading for Santa Isabel Island to set up a seaplane base.

Believing that his ships were in no danger that evening, Turner ordered his second in command, British RAdm. Victor A. C. Crutchley, to Guadalcanal to confer on how to handle the crisis that had been thrust upon them by Admiral Fletcher. Turner's communications staff had earlier intercepted a message from Fletcher to Ghormley asking permission to immediately withdraw TF 61 from the operation. Fletcher cited plane losses, low fuel, and the presence of many enemy planes as the reason for his request. Fearful of losing any of his carriers, he began withdrawing before receiving Ghormley's approval. Thus Turner's ships were without air cover on the ninth. This unforeseen decision, harshly criticized by both Turner and his superiors, seriously jeopardized the success of the plan so hastily put together at Admiral King's insistence.

Admiral Crutchley had formulated no detailed battle plan before leaving the Savo Island area for the conference on board his flagship, the *Australia*. Turner had approved the disposition of the Allied naval force into three separate formations to guard all possible approaches to the invasion beach. Rear Admiral Norman Scott patrolled the eastern area between Tulagi and Guadalcanal with two cruisers. Crutchley's western force was deployed just east of Savo Island, divided into two sections so as to block the entrances to Sealark Channel. The southern section consisted of the *Canberra* and *Chicago*. In Crutchley's absence, Capt. H. D. Bode on the *Chicago* had assumed operational command of the entire force. The northern group included the *Vincennes, Astoria,* and *Quincy*.

Both segments of the western force were unaware of the Japanese approach. Although on alert, they were caught almost totally unprepared by Mikawa. The Japanese flotilla slipped past the picket destroyer just after midnight, closed with *Canberra*, and, at 0138 on 9 August launched a string of "long-lance" torpedoes. By the time these struck, the Japanese cruisers had closed to within a mile and their very accurate gunnery blew the *Canberra* apart. Captain Bode on the *Chicago* mistook a destroyer for one of the enemy cruisers and set off in pursuit, taking his ship out of the battle without giving adequate warning of the Japanese presence. Mikawa then divided his force and, hidden by a sudden rain squall, bore down on the other three Allied cruisers. Their guns were still pointed to the front when the Japanese struck their flank. The Japanese cruiser *Chokai* attacked *Astoria* at 0150 and quickly reduced it to a burning shambles that sank the next morning. The *Quincy,* next in line, was struck by fire from both Japanese columns. At approximately 0235 it rolled over and sank. The captain of the leading cruiser, the *Vincennes,* was also surprised, but managed to deliver a few salvos, striking one Japanese ship before being hit by three torpedoes and gunfire from both sides. The *Vincennes* sank shortly after the *Quincy*.

In just thirty-two minutes, Mikawa had administered the U.S Navy its worst surface defeat. The Battle of Savo Island cost the

Allies four cruisers, 1,270 men killed, and more than 700 wounded. Mikawa had opened the way to Turner's transports but, fearing retaliation by Fletcher's carriers, he gathered his scattered force and retired to Rabaul.

The disaster off Savo Island left Admiral Turner with no choice; he had to get his transports and cargo vessels out of harm's way. Despite the danger, he continued unloading ships until noon before ordering the operation to cease. Only half of the needed supplies were off-loaded. As the last of his ships disappeared eastward through Lengo Channel, Turner left more than sixteen thousand marines on their own without naval or air cover. Vandegrift, without bemoaning his fate, ordered his staff to sort out the chaotic supply system, speed up work on the airstrip, and improve the beach defenses.

After Tulagi was cleared, most of the marines there were moved to Guadalcanal. On 15 August three destroyer transports brought in bombs, .50-caliber ammunition, gasoline, and aircraft spare parts in addition to a small complement of Marine Corps air operations personnel. The airfield, christened Henderson in honor of a marine dive-bomber pilot killed at Midway, was ready to receive planes after the fifteenth. Five days later, the escort carrier *Long Island* brought in a marine squadron with twelve SBD dive-bombers and another with nineteen F4F Wildcat fighters. These reinforcements meant that the ground troops would not be completely at the mercy of Japanese aircraft.

Japanese commanders at Rabaul and in Tokyo lost their best opportunity to dislodge the marines in those confused days following the landings. The reasons for their sanguine reaction are partially explained by the army's ignorance of what the navy had been doing in the eastern Solomons and its need to depend upon its sister service for intelligence. Five days after the invasion, the Rabaul command still believed the Guadalcanal operation was just a probe and that only a few thousand Americans were there. On 10 August Tokyo ordered Lt. Gen. Haruyoshi Hyakutake, then at Truk, to send the 35th Infantry Brigade, reinforced by two additional regiments, to recapture Tulagi and Guadalcanal. Japanese overconfidence is apparent as they decided to dispatch a smaller force to the large island with the hope of recapturing the airfield before the main Japanese elements arrived. This thousand-man force, commanded by Col. Kiyono Ichiki, embarked at Truk and planned to land at Taivu Point, about twenty miles east of the Ilu River. Later, an additional seventeen-hundred-man force would be brought in to reinforce Ichiki.

Ichiki's force, carried aboard six destroyers, landed early on the nineteenth and immediately began moving west along the coastal plain toward the Ilu. When the marine commanders learned of the landing, they registered their artillery on all the approach routes and moved a number of 37mm antitank guns into position to support the 2d Battalion, 1st Marines, which manned the river defense line. Early on the morning of the twenty-second, the Japanese assaulted the marine lines but were beaten back. Two more such attacks were also halted.

Vandegrift had meanwhile brought up the 1st Battalion, 1st Marines. Attacking northward, they completed the encirclement of the Japanese. In twelve hours of fighting, the combined fire of artillery, small arms, and light tanks almost completely destroyed the Japanese detachment, killing more than eight hundred men. Colonel Ichiki, who escaped to Taivu Point with a few survivors, burned the unit's colors before committing suicide. The marines' success boosted morale and shattered the myth that the Japanese infantryman was invincible.

Perhaps realizing that he might be presented with another opportunity to destroy main elements of the American fleet, Admiral Yamamoto ordered Admiral Kondo to sortie with two battleships and four heavy cruisers from the 2d Fleet, rendezvous with Nagumo's three carriers, and then proceed to the Solomons area. Their first priority was to find the American carriers known to be in the theater. Secondarily, they were to protect the landings of Maj. Gen. Kiyotake Kawaguchi's 35th Brigade. At the same time, RAdm. Raizo Tanaka was to proceed down the Slot ahead of the main force with four converted destroyers and a large transport carrying the 5th Naval Landing Force and that part of Ichiki's force that had been left behind.

On the American side, Admiral Fletcher commanded the most powerful U.S. fleet yet assembled in the South Pacific. In addition to the huge new battleship *North Carolina*, he had three carrier groups built around the *Saratoga, Enterprise,* and *Wasp.* After reports of the Japanese movement reached Admiral Ghormley in Noumea, he ordered Fletcher to intercept. Fletcher did not expect an immediate confrontation with the Japanese, and on the twenty-third he dispatched the *Wasp* group to be refueled. This decision reduced his force by one-third.

On 24 August a PBY spotted the *Ryujo* approximately 280 miles distant. Admiral Kondo had detached the small carrier and one cruiser from his main force in order to lure the Americans into attacking. This ruse was successful; Fletcher launched most of his torpedo and dive-bombers in the early afternoon. Learning of the presence of the major elements of the Japanese fleet, he tried to redirect the attack against the *Shokaku* and *Zuikaku.* Poor communications prevented this, and the torpedo and dive-bombers concentrated on *Ryujo.* Struck a number of times, the small carrier sank later that evening.

Admiral Nagumo, believing he had an open invitation to strike Fletcher's carriers, launched his attack groups shortly before 1600. These were intercepted by fifty-three F4Fs, which fought through a swarm of Zero fighters and destroyed twelve Val dive-bombers from a force of thirty-six. The remaining Vals concentrated on the *Enterprise,* which was struck by three bombs that ruptured the decks. Good damage control saved the carrier. The *North Carolina* beat off all attacks, its antiaircraft gunners destroying fourteen planes. No enemy planes reached the *Saratoga,* but a small number of its aircraft discovered the seaplane carrier *Chitose,* attacked, and severely damaged it. At approximately 2000 Fletcher broke off the action and moved his ships southward to take on fuel. Kondo tried to catch the American ships but gave up just before midnight. The main action in the naval battle of the eastern Solomons was over, a tactical victory for Fletcher whose force had suffered damage only to the *Enterprise* and the loss of seventeen aircraft.

By early morning of the twenty-fifth, Admiral Tanaka's force had reached a point approximately one hundred miles north of Guadalcanal. It was soon located and a mixed flight of Henderson-based SBDs and *Enterprise* dive-bombers struck the Japanese flotill. One bomb hit Tanaka's flagship, the cruiser *Jintsu,* causing severe damage; another hit the 9,000-ton transport *Kinryu Maru* with a 1,000-pound bomb. Tanaka had just ordered two of his old destroyers to begin picking up survivors when eight B-17s from the New Hebrides suddenly appeared. Their attack was very successful in contrast to previous high-level strikes on Japanese ships. Five 500-pound bombs hit the destroyer *Mutsuki*, which sank immediately. Another destroyer, *Yayoi*, was damaged. With *Jintsu* burning, Tanaka was likely relieved when he got the order to retire to the Shortlands.

The first Japanese attempt to land significant reinforcements on Guadalcanal had failed. A postscript to the carrier battle on the twenty-fourth occurred a week later when the Japanese submarine I-26 torpedoed *Saratoga* and caused damage that took three months to repair.

Air action over Guadalcanal was just as desperate. The Japanese, with air bases near the island, could muster far more fighters and bombers than the Americans. In the weeks following the landings, the Japanese made daily raids, mainly against the dispersed planes and primitive facilities of the so-called Cactus Air Force at Henderson Field. They paid a heavy toll, as the marine fighter pilots registered a kill ratio of better than five to one.

On 30 August the last two squadrons of Marine Air Group 3, VMF-234 and VMSB-231, arrived, as did fourteen P-400s—the export version of the Bell P-39 Airacobra—belonging to the army's 67th Fighter Squadron. Four days later a new air commander, Brig. Gen. Roy S. Geiger, was assigned; his optimistic attitude reinforced Vandegrift's. Nevertheless, by 10 September the constant action and mechanical breakdowns had reduced marine fighter strength on the muddy airstrip to only eleven F4Fs. The P-400s, lacking turbo superchargers, were inadequate for combat above fifteen thousand feet. After only one week of action, the 67th could muster just three serviceable aircraft, and Geiger restricted their use to ground support missions. As a result of frantic requests from Vandegrift and Turner, Admiral Ghormley detached twenty-four Wildcats from Fletcher's carrier group. They arrived on the late afternoon of the tenth.

Meanwhile, Admiral Tanaka took full advantage of the fact that from dusk to dawn the Japanese navy controlled the waters around

Guadalcanal. He was convinced that he could supply troops and material to the island by using older, troop-carrying destroyers. The first attempts at this were unsuccessful. On 27 August four destroyers whose departure had been delayed by orders from Rabaul were caught trying to off-load troops at dusk. Dive-bombers from Henderson Field sank one and badly damaged two others. Tanaka had also planned to transport Kawaguchi's 35th Brigade by destroyer, but the general demurred. He wanted to carry more supplies to support his men after landing and insisted on moving them by barge. A compromise was reached whereby Tanaka would move a thousand troops by destroyer to a staging area near Taivu Point. The remaining men would follow later in forty-eight slow-moving barges.

Kawaguchi arrived by destroyer and established his headquarters in advance of the rest of his brigade, much of which never arrived. The barges left Santa Isabel Island on 4 September, ran into heavy seas that further delayed them, and were spotted the next day by American planes. The SBDs and F4Fs had a field day strafing and bombing the vessels. Some managed to escape to Savo Island; others continued on to unload their troops near Cape Esperance. In this one operation, Kawaguchi lost more than four hundred men. However, Tanaka learned from these mistakes and continued to deliver men and materiel each night. After landing troops under cover of darkness, his destroyers lingered to bombard the marine lines before withdrawing.

While at Rabaul, General Kawaguchi, with no knowledge of Guadalcanal's terrain or climate, had planned a very complex three-pronged attack on Henderson Field. The main thrust would be delivered from the south by a force of nearly three thousand men led by the general himself. The fault with this detailed preliminary plan was soon evident. The march of his three-mile-long column was through putrid jungle, where heat and humidity slowed the advance. Leaving on 6 September, it took six days for his force to get within striking distance of its target. In the meantime, Col. Merritt Edson's Raiders struck behind Kawaguchi's forces less than two miles south of the field. There they dug in and waited. Brigadier General Pedro A. del Valle, commanding the artillery, zeroed his howitzers in on the approach routes to Edson's position on Lunga Ridge. Meanwhile, Kawaguchi, even before reaching the jump-off point, received heavy preliminary support. On the eleventh and twelfth, Japanese planes dropped bombs and strafed the marines, and on the evening of the twelfth a cruiser and three destroyers bombarded the ridgeline.

By the evening of 13 September, Kawaguchi was in position. His first attack was preceded by a heavy bombardment of the field and ridgeline by seven destroyers. At 2100 two Japanese battalions surged forward, but General del Valle's artillery devastated the attackers before they reached the dug-in marines. Edson's lines bent back on the flanks but did not break. Kawaguchi pulled back and launched another assault at midnight. Once again the attackers were halted by artillery and small-arms fire. Edson pulled his troops back to a final position only a thousand yards from the field. There the marines received Kawaguchi's final assault at 0200 on the fourteenth. This attack also was beaten off. Kawaguchi, finally admitting defeat, began his retreat. Henderson Field was saved. The Japanese had lost more than five hundred men killed in their assaults on what was fast becoming known as Edson's Ridge.

At the same time Kawaguchi was being repulsed, a secondary attack against marine positions along the Ilu River was also halted. Kawaguchi's third planned strike never materialized; its commander never moved from his start line. The main force, carrying four hundred wounded, retreated toward the Matanikau River and thence northward. Eight days later, the remnants of Kawaguchi's force—disease ridden, on the verge of starvation, and without their heavy weapons—finally arrived in Japanese-held territory.

Kawaguchi's failure to take Henderson Field produced a crisis at Rabaul. General Hyakutake, determined to succeed, sought additional troops for a massive follow-up attack on 17 October. He got them by ordering a halt to offensive operations on New Guinea, stopping General Horii's advance within sight of Port Moresby. Hyakutake also alerted the major elements of Lt. Gen. Masao Maruyama's 2d "Sendai" Division, and Admiral Tanaka delivered some of these units to the Cape Esperance region between 11 and 14 September. The rest of the division followed in early October. Meanwhile, Lt. Gen. Tadayoshi Sano's 38th Division was ordered to move as rapidly as possible to the Shortland Islands as a backup to the 2d. Hyakutake displaced the headquarters of his Seventeenth

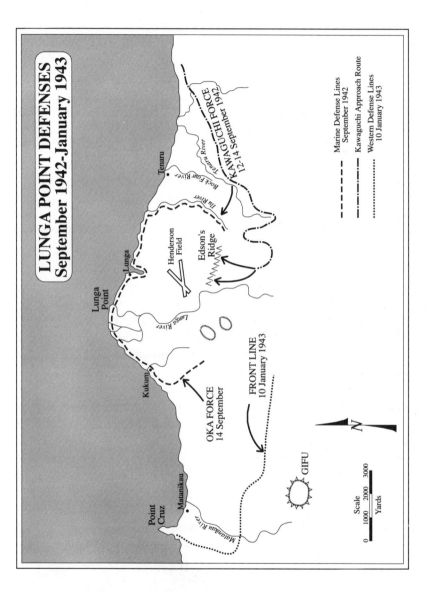

LUNGA POINT DEFENSES
September 1942–January 1943

KAWAGUCHI FORCE
12–14 September 1942

Bock Four River

Tenaru River

Ilu River

Tenaru

Lunga

Henderson
Field

Edson's
Ridge

Lunga
Point

Lunga River

Kukum

OKA FORCE
14 September

FRONT LINE
10 January 1943

Point
Cruz

Matanikau

Matanikau River

GIFU

N

Scale
0   1000 2000 3000
Yards

Marine Defense Lines
September 1942

Kawaguchi Approach Route

Western Defense Lines
10 January 1943

Army to Guadalcanal on 9 October and prepared to take personal command of the operation.

What had begun as a meeting engagement in the Solomons was fast escalating. The Japanese had decided to make control of Guadalcanal the major issue in their South Pacific plans.

Meanwhile, the American high command appeared paralyzed. Vandegrift had only two-thirds of his division, few supplies, no tanks, and only thirty operational aircraft. He had requested but not received Wildcat fighters stationed elsewhere in the South Pacific. All plans for sending high-performance P-38 Lightnings had been shelved by the army. The navy was conspicuous by its absence. Tanaka's "Tokyo Express" operated in the Slot with impunity. Admiral Ghormley in Noumea was being bombarded with pessimistic assessments about the situation on Guadalcanal. Lieutenant General Delos Emmons, commanding U.S. Army forces in the Pacific, concluded after an inspection trip that Guadalcanal was a lost cause. This assessment was shared by MacArthur, and later by the chief of the Army Air Forces, General Arnold, who conferred directly with Ghormley in late September.

But Ghormley could not imagine abandoning Vandegrift, and finally released the 7th Marines from garrison duty in Samoa. They were loaded on five transports on 14 September and, along with two supply ships, began the hazardous run to Guadalcanal. Ghormley also ordered his carrier group, built around the carriers *Hornet* and *Wasp,* to provide long-range cover. This latter decision, while necessary, proved disastrous when two Japanese submarines attacked the task force on the fifteenth, torpedoing the *Wasp,* the battleship *North Carolina,* and the destroyer *O'Brien.* Struck by three torpedoes, the *Wasp* was soon a burning hulk and later had to be scuttled. This loss left only one operational American carrier in the South Pacific. Meanwhile, Admiral Turner, over a hundred miles away, had taken evasive action, and on 18 September delivered the 7th Marines—along with tanks, rations, ammunition, aviation fuel, and sorely needed aviation ground crews and specialized equipment—to Guadalcanal.

The reinforcements allowed Vandegrift to establish a strong, horseshoe-shaped defensive perimeter anchored in the east by the Ilu, in the west by the ridgeline west of Lunga, and in the south by what had become known as Edson's Ridge. The marines worked feverishly to improve the defenses, building coconut-log-roofed dugouts, laying wire, and clearing fields of fire in the kunai grass and jungle undergrowth. Not content to stand entirely on the defensive, Vandegrift twice tried to dislodge the Japanese from strong points along the Matanikau. One battalion of the 7th Marines probed the interior on the twenty-third, while another attempted to establish a command post near the mouth of the river. Both units ran into heavy opposition from a portion of the four-thousand-man Japanese force holding the west bank of the river. The marines were briefly trapped and extricated only with great difficulty.

On the last day of September, Admiral Nimitz visited Guadalcanal on his way to Noumea, where he heard Ghormley's pessimistic assessment. Soon afterward Nimitz received a more positive memorandum on the situation from Maj. Gen. Millard Harmon, commander of Army Air Forces' units in the South Pacific. Harmon, noting the precarious nature of the situation, nevertheless urged reinforcements and a more active naval role to intercept Tanaka's Tokyo Express. He also recommended that the plan to seize Ndeni in the Santa Cruz Islands be called off and that troops and equipment earmarked for the operation sent to Vandegrift. Nimitz, on the basis of his own observations and bolstered by Harmon's memorandum, ordered the American Division's 164th Regiment to prepare for embarkation.

On the seventh, Vandegrift launched a five-battalion attack against the Japanese strong points along the Matanikau. While three of the battalions struck due west across a sandbar, two others crossed the river to the south and then swung north. Lieutenant Colonel Lewis Puller's lst Battalion, 7th Marines, surprised a large Japanese force in bivouac. He set up a defense line along a ridge, called in artillery fire on the enemy, and blasted those who tried to escape. In all, more than seven hundred Japanese were killed. It appeared that a trap was about to be sprung on an even larger group when Vandegrift, informed of an impending all-out Japanese attack against the perimeter, called off the operation. Nevertheless, the marines had forced General Maruyama to pull his line back two miles to the west.

Both sides were in a race to bring in men and supplies, and

in early October the Japanese were winning. Tanaka's Tokyo Express and the slower barges had completed the transport of the 2d Division, many of the units of the 38th, sixteen tanks, and eight 8-inch howitzers, which were emplaced west of the Matanikau. Vandegrift desperately needed reinforcements to man his extended perimeter. The men in the first battalions ashore were exhausted, and most had malaria. Dispatch of the 164th Regiment from Noumea was imperative.

On 8 October Admiral Turner took on the army troops and headed for Guadalcanal screened by TF 64—two heavy and two light cruisers and five destroyers commanded by Admiral Scott in the *San Francisco*. On the evening of the eleventh, Scott learned that a Japanese force covering troop landings was headed down the Slot. Scott surprised his Japanese counterpart, Admiral Goto, and nearly destroyed the Japanese force. In a very confused action beginning at about 2330, the Americans sank the cruiser *Furutaka,* the destroyer *Fubuki,* and severely damaged the heavy cruiser *Aoba.* In return, Japanese fire badly damaged the *Boise* and later sank the destroyer *Duncan.* This American victory off Cape Esperance was tempered by the fact that the Japanese managed to land fresh troops and artillery pieces at Tassafaronga. What remained of Goto's force was in no position on the thirteenth to prevent Turner from landing 3,000 men of the 164th RCT, as well as seventy days' of supplies and general equipment and ammunition. The addition of the 164th gave Vandegrift a total of 23,000 men on Guadalcanal, with an additional 4,500 available on nearby Tulagi Island.

Admiral Yamamoto, in charge of the main elements of the Japanese fleet north of the Solomons, detached a major force built around the battleships *Kongo* and *Haruna* whose task was the destruction of planes and equipment at Henderson Field. Early on the morning of 14 October they bombarded the field and all adjacent areas for over an hour. Then the cruisers and destroyers continued the bombardment for another hour. The 14- and 8-inch shells destroyed much of the steel matting on the field and damaged or completely wrecked all of the fighters and most of the torpedo bombers. In addition, the shelling wrecked the tent area, struck the hospital, started fires in the fuel dumps, and killed sixty marines. Two days later the heavy cruisers returned. This time their bombardment was supported by air strikes from Rabaul and Buin. The patched up Wildcats of a recently arrived marine fighter squadron fought off most of the attackers, but many still broke through, adding to the devastation.

The continual bombardment by Japanese heavy artillery and evidence of a large troop buildup drew Vandegrift's attention to the west, to the Japanese positions along the Matanikau. That was exactly what Hyakutake wanted. His plan was to launch his main attack against the airfield from the south. The plan called for General Maruyama to cross the river with seven thousand men, swing south, and be in position to strike the southern end of the marine lines on 22 October. The four days' march was through very rough jungle terrain, and the heat and humidity slowed the men. This forced postponement of the main attack for forty-eight hours. However, news of the delay did not reach the Japanese commanders responsible for the supporting attacks. General Tadashi Sumiyoshi sent his tanks ahead across the Matanikau sandbar leading the infantry. They ran into marine antitank guns, which destroyed all of them, and the infantry was dispersed by accurate artillery fire. Maruyama's attack, which had been rescheduled for 1700 on 24 October, was disrupted by a heavy thunderstorm that turned the jungle into a swamp, broke up communications, and prevented the right flank units from being in place on time. Maruyama then made a fateful mistake. Instead of waiting, he attacked with only his left flank units. The American positions along Edson's Ridge were held by only two battalions, Puller's 1st Battalion, 7th Marines, and the yet untested 2d Battalion, 164th Infantry Regiment. In the fiercest fighting yet on the island, the marine and army units hurled back every assault that evening. As the marines braced for further attacks, Vandegrift took advantage of his central position and began shifting troops to the south, where more than a thousand Japanese dead were stacked in front of the marines' lines.

Maruyama was not yet finished. He reorganized his spent troops for a final effort. Soon after dark on the twenty-fifth, the Japanese assault began. The slaughter continued until even Maruyama realized the futility of it all. The Sendai Division was shattered; half of its officers were dead, and the hungry, tired, dispirited survivors were forced to retrace their steps.

Another part of Hyakutake's plan called for a third attack against the marine lines in the west. But Col. Akinosuka Oka, the Japanese commander in that sector, had not reconnoitered the terrain and his troops were in no position to support Maruyama's main attack. Nevertheless, Oka ordered his men forward early on the morning of the twenty-sixth. They were thrown back with heavy losses by a group of cooks, bandsmen, and runners hastily assembled by Lt. Col. Herman Hanneken.

The failure of the Japanese offensive was due not only to the courage of the marines and army personnel, but also to the rigidity and overconfidence of the Japanese commanders. The senior officers, who had gained battle experience either in China or earlier in the war against vastly outnumbered green Allied troops, no doubt felt contempt for the Americans and believed that the raw courage of their infantry combined with aerial and naval superiority would assure easy victory. It didn't work out that way. Hyakutake's ambitious plan failed to take into account Kawaguchi's earlier failure, Maruyama launched frontal attacks with tired troops before all his men were in position, and Colonel Oka did not send out reconnaissance patrols to study the terrain. In the final analysis, the Japanese commanders had destroyed one of their finest infantry divisions for absolutely no gain.

The situation at Guadalcanal was overshadowed by preparations for the Allied invasion of North Africa. Thus, despite pleas from Ghormley and Vandegrift, only a trickle of men and supplies reached the embattled marines. Ghormley remained pessimistic, bombarding Nimitz with requests for more men, equipment, and ships than were available in the theater. Despite his Eurocentric policy, President Roosevelt on 24 October indicated to the service chiefs that he expected all possible assistance to be given to Vandegrift. Navy Secretary Knox also stated that he expected that the marines, with reinforcements, would hold their lodgment. Perhaps jostled by the president's concern, the service chiefs alerted the 25th Infantry Division, commanded by Maj. Gen. J. Lawton Collins, to prepare to leave Hawaii for Guadalcanal. The 37th Division's 145th RCT, earlier slated for Ndeni, the 8th Marines from Samoa, the 2d Raider Battalion, and an advance party from the 43d Division were also ordered to move as quickly as possible to the island. In addition, new fighter and bomber aircraft were flown to Henderson Field to replace those that had been lost. It was absolutely necessary if the ground troops were to hold on that the Japanese be denied control of the air. Despite the heroics of the pilots of the Cactus Air Force, Geiger had only twenty-nine battered planes left on 26 October.

Nearly as important as the new personnel who would soon arrive was the change in command. Rear Admiral Thomas Kinkaid replaced Admiral Fletcher as commander of the main naval strike force. Even more important, however, was the replacement of Ghormley. He has perhaps been too harshly condemned for his lack of aggressiveness, forced as he was to confront the Japanese with only minimal tools. Nevertheless, he had been opposed to the Guadalcanal operation from the start, and he was very timid in committing his naval force to protect the marines' enclave. The new commander in chief of the South Pacific Area was VAdm. William Halsey, who arrived at Noumea on 18 October for a familiarization tour and was given a message from Nimitz announcing Ghormley's relief and handing him this "hot potato." It was soon apparent that Halsey was far different from his predecessor. He ordered Vandegrift to fly to Noumea as soon as the situation allowed. On the twenty-third, a high-level conference was held on Halsey's flagship. In addition to Vandegrift, Turner, Harmon, Maj. Gen. Alexander M. Patch Jr., commander of the Americal Division, and the Marine Corps commandant, Lt. Gen. Thomas Holcomb, attended the meeting. After listening to the various presentations, Halsey promised Vandegrift all the support he could muster. Nothing would be held back.

Halsey's nerve would soon be tested. Admiral Yamamoto, despite some misgivings about the army's performance, still believed it possible to destroy the remnants of the American fleet while helping the army capture Henderson Field. He assigned two fleets to this task. Nagumo, commanding the main force, had the fleet carriers *Shokaku* and *Zuikaku* and the light carrier *Zuiho,* with the battleships *Hiei* and *Kumano,* five cruisers, and twelve destroyers as escorts. The second force, commanded by Admiral Kondo, consisted of the carrier *Junyo* escorted by the battleships *Kongo* and *Haruna,* seven cruisers, and twelve destroyers. While General Maruyama was vainly attempting to crack the marine lines, these strong naval forces moved just north of the Santa Cruz Islands, approximately 850 miles from Noumea.

The American forces available to counter the Japanese were woefully inferior in numbers. Kinkaid, in command of TF 61, had available the *Enterprise,* the battleship *South Dakota,* two cruisers, and eight destroyers. When joined by RAdm. George D. Murray's TF 17, Kinkaid added the carrier *Hornet,* four cruisers, and six destroyers to his flotilla. Just after midnight on the night of 25–26 October, a PBY patrol craft located the Japanese fleet. Despite the disparity in numbers, Halsey's orders to Kinkaid were simply to "Attack, Repeat, Attack." Thus began the aerial clash that became known as the Battle of the Santa Cruz Islands.

Dive-bombers from the *Enterprise* were the first to strike. Locating Nagumo's force just before dawn, two SBDs attacked the *Zuiho* and registered a pair of hits that damaged the flight deck and started numerous fires. However, Nagumo had already launched a sixty-five-plane strike against the American task force. A ring of antiaircraft fire and the carriers' fighter cover were not enough to keep them from drawing blood. Concentrating on the *Hornet,* the Japanese dive and torpedo bombers registered a number of hits. By 0930 the carrier was dead in the water. Meanwhile, planes from the *Hornet* located the Japanese and planted six bombs on *Shokaku*'s deck, effectively removing the carrier from the battle. Some of the dive-bombers attacked the heavy cruiser *Chikuma,* damaging it so severely that it was forced to limp back to Truk. The *Enterprise,* which had at first been screened from attackers by a heavy fog bank, next came under attack. For an hour and a half, the "Big E" maneuvered and fought off a series of attacks. One 500-pound bomb ripped through the *Enterprise*'s flight deck and exploded, tearing a gaping hole in the port side. During this phase the *South Dakota* was also hit, and the cruiser *San Juan* and the destroyer *Smith* were badly damaged. Earlier, at about 1130, the *Hornet* was struck by *Junyo*'s planes while under tow. A similar attack in midafternoon resulted in the decision to abandon ship. The *Hornet* resisted all attempts by American destroyers to sink it and was finally finished off by Japanese torpedoes just after midnight.

Admiral Kondo sent his fast vanguard group ahead to try to locate the *Enterprise*, but Kinkaid had wisely broken off action by midafternoon on the twenty-sixth and retired beyond the area the Japanese considered safe. Despite their advantage, they did not press forward, partially because of two torpedo attacks by PBYs early on the twenty-seventh. After maneuvering around north of Ndeni, Kondo finally decided to retire to Truk.

The Japanese had won a tactical victory off the Santa Cruz Islands. The loss of the *Hornet* meant that Halsey had only one serviceable aircraft carrier with which to confront the Japanese. It was, however, a strategic victory for the Americans. The two Japanese admirals, Nagumo and Kondo, by not being more aggressive, took some of the pressure off Halsey, whose main objective was the defense of the Guadalcanal perimeter. The Japanese did not escape unscathed—two of their carriers and one cruiser were so badly damaged that they would be out of action for months. More importantly, they had lost 69 of the 212 planes in their attack group. In a period of just two months beginning on 1 September, the Japanese had lost nearly 500 planes in the Guadalcanal battles. The planes could be replaced, but the pilots could not. The Japanese were sacrificing their finest air crews in a vain attempt to regain control of Guadalcanal.

Meanwhile, Vandegrift planned to push his perimeter beyond the village of Kokumbona, eight thousand yards to the west. If successful, he planned to further extend it to the Poha River. On 1 November the 5th Marines crossed the Matanikau River on bridges constructed by the engineers and pushed forward on a fifteen-hundred-yard front. At the same time, a composite group crossed farther upstream and provided flank protection. The offensive was supported by division artillery and the heavy guns of the cruisers *San Francisco* and *Helena*. Airacobras, SBDs, and a flight of B-17s also pounded the Japanese positions. Within a day the marines had trapped a large number of the enemy in a pocket at Point Cruz. By 3 November this pocket had been eliminated; more than 350 Japanese were killed. Meanwhile, elements of the 2d Marine Division and a battalion from the Americal passed through the 5th Marines' lines and got within two miles of Kokumbona before meeting stiffening resistance. At that point Vandegrift called off the offensive. A portion of the 5th Marines dug in at Point Cruz, and the rest of the force pulled back to the Lunga perimeter.

The reason for the halt was that Vandegrift had learned that a Japanese force had landed east of the perimeter at Koli Point. He simply did not have the manpower to defend in the east while continuing the Poha River offensive. One reason for this was that Admiral Turner, against the advice of engineers, had convinced Halsey to build another airstrip fifty miles to the east of the Lunga River at Aola. Before the project was canceled, it had absorbed all available Seabees, a battalion of the 147th Infantry Regiment, half the 2d Raiders, and artillery from the Americal. Fearing a Japanese landing to the east, Vandegrift on 2 November had sent Lieutenant Colonel Hanneken with a battalion of the 7th Marines to establish a blocking position near the mouth of the Metaponu River. There they could only observe the landing of approximately fifteen hundred troops sent by Hyakutake to hold the area while Japanese engineers built a new airstrip. Hanneken's force fought a delaying action until he was reinforced by another battalion from the 7th Marines and the 164th Infantry.

The Japanese were pounded by successive air attacks from Henderson and by steady bombardment from American cruisers and destroyers offshore and from land-based 155mm howitzers. By 8 November the Japanese were nearly surrounded. They lost more than four hundred men in the pocket and, as the remainder retreated southwest into the jungle, they were harried by Raiders brought in from Aola. Fewer than half the Japanese who landed were able to join the main force near Mount Austen.

Vandegrift resumed his offensive in the west on 10 November with five battalions from the newly arrived 2d Marine Division and one army battalion. The Japanese were determined to hold Kokumbona because it was both Hyakutake's command post and the terminus of the main supply trail to Japanese positions around Mount Austen. After halting the American attack, Hyakutake planned to strike their left flank with a force of five thousand men. Vandegrift, unaware of this threat, again called off the offensive and pulled his troops east of the Matanikau River, destroying the bridges. The reason for the halt was news that the Japanese were preparing to send large troop convoys to Guadalcanal before launching a major offensive in mid-November.

The Japanese army and navy planners had at last decided to do what Admiral Mikawa had suggested in August—smash the Americans with a massive combined effort. To accomplish this, Yamamoto committed two aircraft carriers, four battleships, eleven cruisers, forty-nine destroyers, and fourteen thousand men under the command of Admiral Kondo. Admiral Tanaka commanded the troop transport section sortieing from the Shortlands. They were to land at Tassafaronga on 13 November after Henderson Field and its environs had been bombarded night and day. This task was assigned to RAdm. Hiroaki Abe's battleship force, which would pound the defenders the night before, followed by Admiral Mikawa's cruiser force during daylight on the thirteenth. Admiral Kondo, with the carriers *Hiyo* and *Junyo* and the battleships *Haruna* and *Kongo,* would cover the operation from about 150 miles to the north.

To oppose this formidable assemblage, Halsey had at Noumea only the crippled *Enterprise,* two battleships, two cruisers, and eight destroyers. Admiral Turner, who had delivered the 182d Infantry Regiment on the morning of 12 November, had an escort consisting of three heavy and two light cruisers and eight destroyers off Lunga Point. In order to protect Henderson Field and the marines from another devastating bombardment such as that delivered by Admiral Kurita a month before, Turner ordered RAdm. Daniel J. Callaghan on board the *San Francisco* to intercept Abe's battleships with the covering force.

The first action of the naval battle of Guadalcanal occurred at about 0145 on 13 November just northwest of Lunga Point. The leading destroyers of Callaghan's force almost ran into Abe's van. Turning sharply to avoid a collision, they threw the ships behind them into confusion. Poor radar readings on board the American cruisers delayed firing, and the Japanese struck first, torpedoing the cruiser *Atlanta* and taking it out of the fight almost immediately. Despite the heroic efforts of salvage crews, it sank that evening. An earlier salvo had torn away its bridge, killing RAdm. Norman Scott. The battle disintegrated into a melee, with the lighter American ships valiantly attacking the Japanese battleships. Within minutes two destroyers, the *Laffey* and *Cushing,* were sunk, but the Japanese battleship *Hiei* had been hit by torpedoes at close range. *San Francisco* was next battered into uselessness, the light cruiser *Juneau* was knocked out of action by a torpedo, and *Portland*'s stern was hit, jamming the steering mechanism and forcing it to turn in circles. Later the destroyer *Barton* was sunk and the *Monssen* severely damaged. Despite the battering the out-gunned Americans sustained, they gained the strategic advantage that Turner had sought. At 0200 Admiral Abe ordered his two battleships to break off the action and steam north. Henderson Field was spared from a battering by the Japanese fleet. Had Abe continued, it is possible the plan to smash the airfield's perimeter might have succeeded.

The naval battle did not end with the disengagement of the main forces however. The remnants of Admiral Callaghan's covering force retired southeast toward the New Hebrides without their commander, who died on the *San Francisco*. At about 1050, the Japanese submarine I-26 torpedoed the light cruiser *Juneau,* which sank almost immediately. Nearly seven hundred men, equal to the number of marines killed on Guadalcanal, were lost. Admiral Kondo, approximately 250 miles to the north, decided to press his advantage in planes and guns to support the planned landings. He would assimilate the undamaged part of Abe's fleet and, with planes from his two carriers providing cover, protect Tanaka's transports. Meanwhile, Admiral Kinkaid with TF 15 organized around the damaged *Enterprise* and two big-gun battleships was proceeding at full speed from Noumea. Kinkaid decided to share his planes with the marines at Henderson and sent off nine TBF Avengers and six Wildcats. They found the *Hiei* badly shot up from the night action. The wounded battleship attracted dive and torpedo bombers from Henderson and B-17s from Espíritu Santo. They pounded the battleship for hours before it sank at 1800 northwest of Savo Island.

Admiral Mikawa, whose six cruisers and six destroyers were supposed to deliver a secondary blow to the marine perimeter, now headed the main Japanese naval effort. Halsey ordered Kinkaid to send his two battleships ahead to intercept them, but was surprised to learn that RAdm. Willis A. "Ching" Lee Jr. could not reach the Savo area before 0800 the next day. Mikawa had a clear path to Henderson. Shortly after midnight on the night of 13–14 November, Mikawa sent two heavy and one light cruisers ahead and began a two-hour unopposed bombardment. Satisfied that he had put the field out of commission, Mikawa retired toward the Shortlands. But the field was still operational, and only eighteen planes were destroyed. Showing a typical lack of coordination, Kondo had not sent planes to protect Mikawa's retreat. Aircraft from Henderson found Mikawa's ships early the next morning and torpedoed one heavy cruiser, which was later sunk by planes from the *Enterprise*. They also seriously damaged three of Mikawa's remaining cruisers.

Admiral Tanaka, taking his transports on the direct route through the Slot, was vulnerable to attack by planes from Henderson and *Enterprise* and B-17s from Espíritu Santo despite some fighter cover from *Hiyo*. The attacks began at noon, while Tanaka was still 150 miles from Guadalcanal, and continued until sunset. As the Wildcats and Airacobras, joined by newly arrived twin-boomed P-38s, staved off *Hiyo*'s Zeros, dive and torpedo bombers wreaked havoc on the transports. Tanaka's eleven destroyers were also helpless; all they could do was take off as many troops as possible from the burning, sinking transports. By nightfall he had only four transports left, and had lost most of the men of the Special Naval Landing Force and half of the 38th Division. Still obsessed with landing the remnants of this force at Tassafaronga, he retired northward, planning to try again the next day after Admiral Kondo bombarded Henderson Field.

After dividing his force into three parts, Kondo raced south to protect Tanaka's transports. In the lead was the distant screen of one cruiser and three destroyers, then the close screen of one heavy cruiser and six destroyers followed by the main element of two heavy cruisers and the battleship *Kirishima*.

Meanwhile Admiral Lee, who had earlier been detached from the *Enterprise* group, headed north to intercept the Japanese transports. Cruising west of Guadalcanal, he took his flotilla of four destroyers and two battleships, *South Dakota* and *Washington*, into Ironbottom Sound. At approximately 2315 they made radar contact with Kondo's distant screen and Lee's four destroyers opened fire. But the Japanese ships were screened by the cliffs of Savo Island, so the Americans did no damage. Shortly thereafter, the Japanese launched their dreaded long-lance torpedoes and scored hits on three of the American destroyers. The *Preston* and *Walke* sank soon afterward;

Benham did not go down until the next day. During the attack the *South Dakota* inexplicably lost electrical power and soon was caught in the searchlights of the Japanese ships, which concentrated their fire on it. Struck by forty-two large-caliber shells, it was soon out of the fight, although in no danger of sinking. By concentrating on *South Dakota,* the Japanese allowed Admiral Lee in the *Washington,* using the latest radar, to zero in on the *Kirishima* at a range of eighty-four hundred yards. Hit by nine 16-inch and forty 5-inch shells, the big Japanese battleship was left wrecked and burning. It sank at 0320 on 15 November.

Both sides, after some skirmishing, disengaged and concentrated on getting their damaged ships to safety. Always tenacious, Tanaka escorted his four transports to Guadalcanal and beached them. The next day, American air and naval forces destroyed the vessels. For all their trouble and losses, Tanaka was able to land fewer than twenty-five hundred troops.

Vandegrift and Halsey were jubilant. They considered the worst to be over. With the waters around Guadalcanal firmly in American hands, they could go over to the offensive. Vandegrift resumed his earlier push in the west, first to secure the ridgelines east of the Poha River, then extending the perimeter to the river itself. He shifted the bulk of General del Valle's artillery to where it could blast these areas with preparatory fires. Brigadier General Edmund B. Sebree of the Americal Division commanded the assault force, which was made up of the 182d and 164th Infantry Regiments and the 8th Marines, and had the 1st Marines in reserve.

On 18 November the lead battalions of the 182d crossed the Matanikau, one in the interior and the other near the mouth, with a gap between them. The Japanese soon counterattacked through this gap and threatened to flank the army units in the north. Sebree plugged the gap with the 164th Infantry and later brought up the 8th Marines. At one point he pulled his advance troops back three hundred yards so that the artillery could pound the Japanese' positions. Despite the desperately poor condition of the Japanese troops, they contested every yard. Finally, on the twenty-third, Vandegrift halted any further advance and ordered his men to dig in. This was the beginning of the stalemate along the American perimeter.

* * *

Despite already frightful losses, the Imperial General Headquarters concluded that Japanese forces on New Guinea and Guadalcanal must hold on. To accomplish this, they made several major command changes. On 16 November Admiral Nagumo was relieved and replaced by VAdm. Jisaburo Ozawa. General Hyakutake relinquished control of the New Guinea operation but retained command of the Seventeenth Army and once again was charged with the responsibility of defeating the Americans on Guadalcanal. His immediate superior was Lt. Gen. Hitoshi Imamura, commander of the recently activated Eighth Area Army headquartered at Rabaul. A new army was also to be formed to reinforce the troops in New Guinea. The Japanese belatedly decided to build more airfields within range of Guadalcanal and to commit the army air force, which had not been used previously.

The main problem with the plan was that the units needed to reinforce Hyakutake were scattered from the East Indies to Malaya. On arrival at Rabaul, Imamura concluded that the new offensive could not begin until 15 January. Meanwhile, Hyakutake, with more than half of his thirty-thousand-man force sick or wounded, would simply have to hold ground.

Sweeping changes were also made on the American side. On 9 December General Patch replaced Vandegrift as commander of the expanding force on the island. The 25th Division was sent directly from Hawaii, its first elements arriving on 17 December, and the ragged, weary 1st Marine Division was evacuated by the end of the month. In all the fighting the division had lost 774 men killed and 1,962 wounded, but over 5,400 had been stricken by malaria. Patch's command was designated the XIV Corps, and by the first of the year consisted of two regiments of the 2d Marine Division, the Americal, and the 25th—a total of more than 50,000 men. However, many of these men—like the departing marines—were sick from malaria and a variety of jungle diseases.

The Cactus Air Force was in the best condition since the beginning of the operation, having more than 150 planes of all types operating from Henderson and its auxiliary fighter strip. No longer were the ground troops at the mercy of Japanese air attacks. Instead, American planes were striking Munda and the Shortlands regularly.

One last major naval confrontation occurred before the Japanese high command decided to cut its losses and evacuate the island. This involved eight destroyers led by the indefatigable Tanaka and a much superior American force sent to halt his Tokyo Express. By the last weeks of November, the Japanese on the island were in dire straits since no regular supply ships could reach them during the day because of American air superiority. Tanaka had developed a way to off-load supplies by putting them in drums and throwing them overboard at night from destroyers speeding close to shore. He was engaged in one such operation on the evening of 30 November when he was surprised by TF 67, a force of five cruisers and six destroyers commanded by RAdm. Carleton H. Wright, who had taken command from Kinkaid only two days before. Wright adopted Kinkaid's plan in every way except one: he failed to send out an advance destroyer screen. Wright brought his force into Ironbottom Sound with four destroyers in the van followed by his cruisers in line. At about 2300 he surprised Tanaka, and his destroyers fired their torpedoes. As was the case in so many actions, the American torpedoes did not have the range or efficiency of the Japanese models. They missed, but Tanaka's tenacious destroyers did not. They turned toward the Americans, launched a barrage of torpedoes that ripped into the cruisers *Minneapolis, New Orleans, Pensacola,* and *Northampton,* and then beat a hasty retreat.

Tanaka lost only one destroyer, and the *Northampton* sank at 0240 on 1 December. The other cruisers limped into Tulagi Harbor for repairs. They did not return to action for nearly a year. In all, four hundred U.S. sailors died. Clearly, American commanders still had much to learn about the deadly efficiency of the long-lance torpedo.

As part of the reorganization of his South Pacific command, Admiral Halsey made General Harmon his deputy and gave him overall responsibility for quashing Japanese resistance on Guadalcanal. Harmon and Patch planned for a major westward offensive in January, but first sought to eliminate the Japanese positions on and around Mount Austen. The few reports of Japanese activity there seemed to indicate that those were lightly held, so on 16 December Col. Leroy E. Nelson of the 132d Infantry Regiment was ordered to commit one company to take this excellent observation post. It was soon discovered that the Japanese were in force not on Mount Austen itself, but in a horseshoe-shaped line between two hills to the northwest. Nelson gave two battalions the task of rooting them out. The heat and humidity took their toll on the soldiers, many of whom were not acclimated, and the Japanese in the heavy jungle growth fiercely resisted their advance. Nevertheless, by 23 December Mount Austen was secured.

Nelson then turned his attention to a strong point the Japanese called "Gifu." They had constructed forty-five mutually supporting interconnected pillboxes, each with at least one machine gun, and had more than five hundred men defending the position. The American assaults began on Christmas Day and, despite heroic actions and heavy air and artillery support, they were repulsed day after day. Patch agreed to release a fresh battalion from the corps reserve. This enabled Nelson to take a strategic hill adjacent to Gifu, but the main line held. Finally, on 3 January, the offensive was called off and the troops ordered to dig in. The battered 132d, having suffered 380 battle casualties in the eighteen days of jungle fighting, was replaced by elements of the 25th Division.

The continued losses of men and materiel, combined with evidence of the growing Allied strength in the Solomons, convinced Imperial General Headquarters to evacuate the island. Admiral Nagano and the army chief, Gen. Hajime Sugiyama, conferred with the emperor and obtained his permission to withdraw the troops from Guadalcanal. When informed of this decision, Imamura and Kusaka protested and briefly considered continuing the operation. However, the emperor's order prevented such disobedience. The courier from Rabaul on 14 January encountered similar resistance from Hyakutake and his subordinates. They wanted to order banzai charges and thus give their lives gloriously for the emperor. But they, too, decided to obey the distasteful order and began preparing for the proposed evacuation. The decision to withdraw was a secret kept from all but a few senior officers.

Meanwhile, General Patch prepared for an offensive aimed at driving the Japanese from their key inland strong points. This was to be the most ambitious operation undertaken on Guadalcanal. He called on General Collins's relatively fresh 25th Division, supported by elements of the American and 2d Marine Division, to conduct the attacks. The 35th Infantry Regiment was to strike west of Gifu and hold a line approximately two miles west of Mount Austen, while the 27th Infantry moved to seize a mass of seven hills to the north called Galloping Horse, because of its appearance in aerial photographs. With very heavy artillery and air support, the 27th began its attack on 10 January 1943 and took all its objectives within three days. In the south, the 35th seized a key highland position and pushed its patrols a mile beyond. This sealed the western approaches to Gifu. Concentrating one regiment of the American in the northwest, Collins began reducing Gifu on the thirteenth. Despite heavy artillery support and the use of tanks, the redoubt held out for ten days. The stubborn defense climaxed with a banzai charge by more than a hundred Japanese on the night of the twenty-second.

While the army was securing its objectives in the interior, the 6th and 8th Marines were conducting offensive operations in the Point Cruz area adjacent to the coast. Slowed by Japanese resistance and heavy rains and mud, the marines nevertheless killed more than six hundred Japanese and advanced their lines almost a mile in five days of fighting.

As soon as supplies could be brought up, Patch planned to continue his offensive with the 25th Division striking north from the recently captured hill locations toward the village of Kokumbona. Meanwhile, the newly created Composite Army-Marine (CAM) Division would continue to advance west along the coast. This offensive began on 22 January and by evening, elements of the 25th had reached the hills overlooking the village. Kokumbona fell the next day, and three days later most of the Japanese operating east of the Poha River were trapped and wiped out.

Patch ordered a quick pursuit of the retiring Japanese; however, word of a concentration of newly arrived Japanese troops at Rabaul, along with coastwatcher reports, made him halt the 25th Division to counter a possible new enemy landing. Most of the Japanese units withdrew to the cape in an orderly fashion, and evacuation began on 23 January. The bulk of the Japanese were taken off by destroyers during the nights of 1, 4, and 7 February. When the 2d Battalion,

132d Infantry, which landed at Verahue on the northeast coast, met the advance elements of the CAM Division at Tenoro, they found that the Japanese were gone. Except for mopping up, the battle for Guadalcanal was over.

Perhaps, as General Hyakutake claimed after the war, a more rapid pursuit by all American elements would have prevented the evacuation and completely destroyed his army. However, even with the escape of approximately 13,000 Japanese, the victory was still gratifying. Tactically, marine and army leaders had completely outmaneuvered their enemies and, despite the appalling environment, the vaunted Japanese jungle fighters had been resoundingly beaten.

Of the estimated 36,000 Japanese who fought on the island, more than 14,000 were killed and another 9,000 perished from disease. The American ground force casualties, however large, were less than originally expected. The totals were approximately 1,600 killed and 4,300 wounded. The navy, although badly battered in a half-dozen battles, also carried out its main tasks of supplying and protecting the ground troops. The vital supply line to Australia and New Zealand was secure.

The Guadalcanal victory cannot be assessed simply in numerical terms or tactical advantage. It was a stunning blow to the Japanese. They not only lost an island that would later serve as one of the main staging grounds for further offensive action in the South Pacific, but their preoccupation with Guadalcanal prevented them from improving their situation on New Guinea. Their losses of approximately six hundred planes could be replaced; not so their trained naval fliers. Japanese expansion in the Pacific stopped at Guadalcanal.

Chapter 8

The Tide Turns:
New Guinea and Bougainville

NEW GUINEA BY the spring of 1942 had become the focus of attention for both Japanese and American commanders. Soon after his arrival in Australia, MacArthur made it clear to Prime Minister Curtin that he believed the battle for Australia had to be fought in the Papua area of New Guinea. However, he was without the men and materiel necessary to do anything except stand on the defensive and hope his inadequate forces would be able to protect Port Moresby, the vital base in southern Papua.

MacArthur's complaints and requests to Washington for more support were met with assurances that in light of the demands of the European theater, he was receiving all that could be spared. Vice Admiral Arthur S. Carpender, MacArthur's new naval commander, had only five cruisers, eight destroyers, and twenty submarines during the crucial month of August. General Brett, the air commander, had few planes and, at first, few airfields to operate from. This shortage would be alleviated during the summer months by the rapid construction of three airstrips on the Cape York Peninsula, one at Milne Bay, and by building or improving four fields in the Port Moresby area. By September the Port Moresby garrison had grown to twenty-eight thousand men with the arrival of two brigades of the 7th Australian Division. All Allied forces in New

Guinea were put under the command of an Australian, Maj. Gen. Sydney F. Rowell, who by that time was busy feeding reinforcements up the Kokoda Trail, the only link over the Owen Stanley Mountains between Port Moresby and the villages of Buna and Gona on the northeastern shore of Papua.

The Japanese were equally convinced of the importance of Papua and of seizing Port Moresby. They had occupied Lae and Salamaua on the Huon Gulf early in March, but their plans for taking Port Moresby were set back by the Coral Sea debacle. In June, General Hyakutake, commanding the Seventeenth Army, received the go-ahead from higher headquarters for the assault on Port Moresby. This was planned as a two-pronged movement: an attack over the Kokoda Trail and landings at Milne Bay on the eastern end of the island. From there, land-based aircraft could dominate the sea-lanes westward into the Gulf of Papua. To facilitate the overland assault on Port Moresby, the Japanese had to seize Buna and Gona, and by the end of July the expedition commander, Maj. Gen. Tomitaro Horii, had landed more than eleven thousand troops at these two points.

General MacArthur's headquarters was surprised by this Japanese maneuver. His staff had planned to seize the two key villages and the coastal plain at Dobodura in order to construct an airstrip there. The Japanese landings, which began on 21 July, forestalled this operation. Even so, MacArthur's staff discounted the possibility of an overland assault on Port Moresby. His intelligence officers were convinced that the Kokoda Trail, difficult enough even for natives, would prove too much of a deterrent for any large-scale troop movement. They had every reason to be surprised when Horii's troops began to move south. The trail was narrow and in the lowlands bordered by nearly impassable jungle in which troops were subjected to extremely high temperatures and humidity. The ascent to the pass at seven thousand feet was very steep, the weather at that altitude was cold, and there were few opportunities for either the defenders or attackers to try flanking movements. The Japanese forward elements, despite these conditions, pushed ahead and captured the village of Kokoda on 26 July. At the time, the only Allied element in the Kokoda area was a company from the Australian 39th Battalion. General Rowell immediately began to shift all

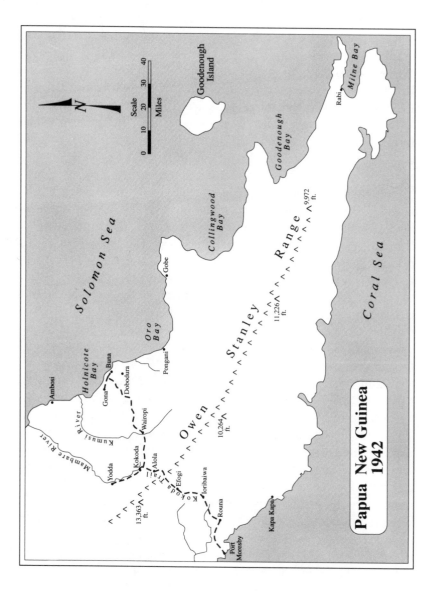

Papua New Guinea 1942

available troops northward to block the Japanese advance, including the 21st Brigade, which had just arrived from Australia.

The South Seas Detachment, the backbone of the Japanese Kokoda Trail operation, reached Buna on 7 August, the same day the marines landed on Guadalcanal. As noted earlier, the American landings there altered Japanese plans because units designated to support Horii had to be shifted to the Solomons. Nevertheless, Horii resumed his advance from Isurava village, six miles south of Kokoda, on 26 August.

Despite heroic resistance by the Australians, they were constantly flanked and forced to retreat. Their supply problem was very difficult. All ammunition, food, and equipment had to come from Port Moresby more than a hundred miles to the south—most of it carried by Papuan native porters. Allied air gave what assistance it could, although it did not make up for the three to one numerical advantage of the Japanese. The three Australian battalions gave way in a fighting retreat until, by 7 September, Horii had moved south of the divide and was poised to take the last strong point outside Port Moresby. MacArthur's intelligence section reported all along that the Australians had numerical superiority, so the general could not understand why they kept falling back. Peremptory inquiries by his staff on this point raised the Australians' ire and served as an early example of the strained relations between MacArthur and his Australian subordinates.

Meanwhile, the Japanese had initiated the second phase of their offensive, the landings at Milne Bay. Located at the extreme southeastern tip of New Guinea, the bay is approximately twenty miles long by ten miles wide. It is flanked on either side by dense jungle leading almost immediately to mountains ranging to four thousand feet in elevation. The narrow corridor leading from the head of the bay inland is very swampy thanks to the over two hundred inches of annual precipitation. This would restrict Japanese movements toward the main Australian position in the area, located at what had been a coconut plantation before the war. The base had one functional airstrip, and American engineers were in the process of building two other airfields, one west and one east of the headquarters.

MacArthur's staff had early determined the importance of Milne Bay, and on 21 August the Australian 18th Infantry Brigade was sent to join the 7th Brigade already in position there. Including service troops, Maj. Gen. Cyril A. Clowes, a veteran of combat in North Africa, had nearly seventy-five hundred men available to defend the installations at Milne Bay. In addition, he was supported by P-40s from Milne Bay's Airfield No. 1 and could call in B-17s from Port Moresby.

The original Japanese plan was for the Aoba Detachment in the Philippines to occupy Milne Bay. However, Admiral Mikawa, commander of the Eighth Fleet, acting on intelligence reports that estimated only two Australian companies were there, decided not to wait for the detachment. Instead, he put together two separate naval landing forces, one from Kavieng and a smaller one from Buna, totaling roughly fifteen hundred men. The smaller force was to land on the northern side of the bay and march overland, while the larger went in about three miles from the main wharf area and proceeded westward to capture Airfield No. 1.

As D day approached, things began to go wrong almost immediately for the Japanese. On 24 August RAAF P-40s caught the smaller force resting on Goodenough Island and destroyed its landing craft, leaving the troops stranded. The main Japanese landing the evening of the next day, although successful, was at the wrong place—five miles farther east than planned. Then, on the twenty-sixth, RAAF planes destroyed most of the Japanese supplies on shore and U.S. B-17s damaged one transport. Nevertheless, the Japanese force was augmented by 1,100 more men later that day and by another 750 on the twenty-ninth.

General Clowes thus faced a dilemma. Unaware of the total Japanese strength at the north end of the bay, he was afraid to commit too many troops to that sector until he could be certain that the enemy was not going to land more men to the south. He therefore had sent forward only one battalion, and this force was not sufficient to halt the Japanese, who advanced past the mission station and reached the Gama River on 29 August. That same day, MacArthur ordered Clowes to clear the north end, a further example of how uninformed MacArthur's headquarters was of the situation on New Guinea. Clowes had every intention of destroying the Japanese, but he was not going to speed up his operation to please MacArthur and Sutherland.

On 29 August the Japanese, who had struggled through the dense undergrowth plagued by continual rain and the fierce Australian rear-guard action, arrived at Airstrip No. 3. The strip had been only partially graded, but it offered a good defense line over two thousand yards long. Clowes had positioned two battalions of the 7th Brigade there, aided by U.S. engineers and an airborne antiaircraft unit equipped with 37mm guns. He also had his medium artillery zeroed in on the strip. Thus, when the Japanese made a frontal attack on the field on the evening of the thirtieth, they were cut to pieces. By early morning they were in full retreat, pursued by elements of the 18th Brigade.

Admiral Mikawa briefly considered sending reinforcements to establish a defensive perimeter until the Aoba Detachment could arrive, but instead decided to evacuate what was left of his landing force when informed that the troops at Milne Bay could not hold on. The remnants were taken off the island on 4 and 5 September.

The Japanese lost about 600 killed, and those who were evacuated were so crippled by wounds and disease that it would be many months before they would be effective. The Australians in turn lost 122 men killed and 198 wounded in these actions, but they had secured southeastern New Guinea. From that time forward, Allied naval units, combined with the growing fighter and bomber strength at Milne Bay, would preclude any further Japanese landings there.

After braving the concerted resistance of the two Australian battalions and the almost impassable terrain of the Kokoda Trail, by 12 September General Horii's troops were ready to assault Ioribaiwa village, just forty miles north of Port Moresby. However, Horii faced a number of tactical problems. His troops were exhausted, many were ill, and the closer he came to Port Moresby the more difficult his supply problems became. Allied planes constantly harassed the Japanese with low-level strafing and bombing attacks. Two brigades of the Australian 6th Division had arrived on New Guinea and General Rowell immediately sent the 25th Brigade ahead to reinforce his battered frontline elements. Nevertheless, Horii still had the initiative, and on 16 September the Japanese took Ioribaiwa and prepared to assault the Australian defenses in the Imata Range only a day's march from Port Moresby.

The Japanese would advance no farther. On 29 August Horii was ordered to go on the defensive as soon as his troops reached the southern foothills. He could expect no reinforcements. The demands of Guadalcanal were such that offensive operations both there and on New Guinea were too much for the limited resources of the Seventeenth Army. Soon after the capture of Ioribaiwa, Horii's orders were again changed. The terrible defeat administered to the Kawaguchi Detachment in its attempt to take Henderson Field convinced the Japanese high command to declare Guadalcanal the first priority. This meant abandoning the Port Moresby operation until after Guadalcanal was taken. On 18 September the Japanese began to withdraw from their advanced positions, and within a week the Australian 25th Brigade launched an attack on Ioribaiwa and forced Horii's rear guard from the village.

Even before the Japanese withdrawal, MacArthur had initiated a plan—to be executed by American commanders whom he felt he could trust—to drive the Japanese from their Buna-Gona positions. On 7 August Maj. Gen. George Kenney replaced Brett as theater air commander and head of the newly designated U.S. Fifth Air Force with responsibility for operations on New Guinea. The RAAF was given the secondary role of defending Australia proper. A month later, Maj. Gen. Robert L. Eichelberger arrived and took command of the recently formed I Corps, composed of the 32d and 41st Infantry Divisions. MacArthur had been critical of the Australians' long retreat down the Kokoda Trail and rarely consulted with General Blamey, ostensibly his chief lieutenant in charge of ground forces. Blamey later would be shunted aside in favor of American generals. But, for the time being, because only Australian troops were engaging the Japanese, MacArthur had to depend upon Blamey and the new commander of Allied forces in New Guinea, Lt. Gen. Edmund F. Herring, who had succeeded Rowell.

MacArthur planned to reinforce the Australians at Port Moresby with two regiments from the U.S. 32d Division, a National Guard unit commanded by Maj. Gen. Edwin F. Harding. This decision to commit the 32d was not based on readiness but rather upon convenience. The 41st Division was farther advanced in training, but the 32d was located in an area near Brisbane too restricted in size and needed to be moved. Since the 32d had to be relocated anyway,

General Eichelberger chose to deploy the 32d Division to open the American offensive in Papua, although none of the units had received proper jungle warfare training. The plan called for a battalion from the 126th Infantry to cross the Owen Stanley Mountains while lead elements of the 128th were airlifted to a makeshift airstrip sixty-five miles from Buna. From there they would be transported in small boats to Pongani, twenty-three miles from the objective, where a new landing strip was to be constructed. Once it was built, the remainder of the 126th would be flown there.

Because of the nature of the terrain, all of the division's artillery and most of its heavy mortars were left behind when the first troops moved from Port Moresby on 6 October. After an arduous five-week march, the 2d Battalion, 126th Infantry, reached Bafu. There it linked up with the rest of the regiment, which had flown ahead to Pongani. The 128th reached the airstrip at Wanigela Mission on 18 October and then moved by sea to Pongani. By 15 November both regiments were ready for the advance to Buna. To secure Hunt Strait before the attack on Buna, elements of the Australian 18th Brigade had occupied Goodenough Island on 23 October.

While the 32d Division was preparing to attack Buna, the Australians continued to bear the brunt of the offensive along the Kokoda Trail against the stubborn Japanese rear guard. The 25th Brigade secured Templeton's Crossing on 8 October but was held up a week at Erora Creek when the Japanese made another stand. The 16th Brigade then took over the pursuit as the Japanese fell back to Oivi village. The 25th resumed the offensive there and on 2 November captured Kokoda with its vital airfield. This meant that the Australians' forward units could at last expect a steady flow of supplies delivered by C-47s.

By this time Horii and his subordinates were operating with a main force of about a thousand men. The rest were scattered through the jungle, small units making their own way to the coast. Horii's retreat had become a rout. On 9 November the Japanese evacuated Oivi, abandoning a considerable amount of supplies and ammunition there. Colonel Kiyomi Yazawa led the main elements across the Kumusi River and followed it to its mouth before heading southeastward to Gona. On the thirteenth the Australians bridged the river. The troops of the two Australian brigades finally reached the Japanese defenses around Sanananda on the coast, but after two months of continuous marching and fighting they were badly worn down. Their best hope for relief was the two still untried American regiments. General Harding, just beginning his attack on Buna, could spare only one battalion from the 126th Regiment to support the Australian advance on the Soputa-Sanananda road.

The Sanananda beachhead was triangular, with its base along the coast and the apex approximately three and one-half miles inland. On 20 November, Col. Yosuka Yokayama, who assumed command of Japanese forces on New Guinea after General Horii drowned trying to cross the Kumusi River, had barely three thousand survivors of the Port Moresby attack to defend the perimeter. On 2 December he received almost a thousand men from Rabaul. A second detachment of almost the same size arrived from Rabaul less than two weeks later. By mid-December he had more than five thousand men dug in and supported by artillery. The Allies were forced by the terrain to move along the main roads, so Yokayama established a series of strong roadblocks along these routes. An Australian patrol had earlier stumbled into Gona, the western cornerstone of the Japanese defenses, but was too weak to hold it. Only when fresh troops from a new brigade, the 21st, were flown in was it possible to capture Gona on 9 December. None of the 650 Japanese defenders there survived.

Meanwhile, beginning on 19 November, the 16th Brigade launched a series of frontal attacks along the Soputa-Sanananda Road only to be driven back by defenders of the main roadblock. However, three companies from the 126th Infantry working around the flank established their own block north of the Japanese on 30 November. For the next three weeks they would beat off counterattacks from all directions. It became obvious to Maj. Gen. George A. Vasey, commander of the Australian 7th Division, that reduction of the roadblocks and destruction of the Sanananda lodgment would have to wait until the Americans took Buna.

The optimism in MacArthur's headquarters for a quick capture of Buna was based on faulty intelligence reports and almost total ignorance of the actual terrain, weather, and health conditions. The Fifth Air Force, although vital to the ultimate success of the operation, did not totally control the air. General Kenney at that time did not have enough planes to operate against the airfields at Lae, Salamaua, and Rabaul and at the same time provide adequate cover for the Allied operations at Buna. The 32d Division, untested in jungle warfare and without adequate artillery support, was expected to overcome quickly the few Japanese presumed to be there. However, there were eighteen hundred fresh combat troops defending two positions widely separated by swamps. The first, to the east of Buna, was centered on an airstrip still under construction. Approximately three thousand yards to the west was the main defensive perimeter, which extended a thousand yards southeast of Buna village. There were only four trails that the attackers could use, and the Japanese simply emplaced most of their force around them in an interlocking defensive system made up of coconut-log bunkers and trenches. By this time, with the situation worsening on Guadalcanal, Japanese officers at Buna realized that there would be no massive reinforcements and prepared to hold the lodgments until the bitter end.

The first attack, conducted by two battalions of the 32d, was on the eastern flank of the Japanese defenses around the new airstrip. They were halted without gaining even a glimpse of the Japanese positions. The following day, two more battalions staggered through the swampy terrain to strike the main Japanese defenses. That attack also failed. From that time forward, the battle would be fought on the flanks; there would be no center. The 32d Division's left-flank units, code-named Urbana Force, attacked the southern part of the Japanese defenses south of Buna village on the twenty-fourth without success; all that was learned was that future attacks should be launched from the west. On Thanksgiving Day, Harding again sent his right-flank units, by then known as Warren Force, against the new airstrip. Again they gained no ground. Before the next attack the weary infantrymen finally had adequate artillery support; ten 105mm howitzers had been landed. These and badly coordinated air attacks were a prelude to the resumed offensive of 30 November. However, this attack produced only one positive result—communications between Buna village and Sanananda were cut.

MacArthur's planned two-pronged offensive ground to a halt because of a combination of factors. Heat, humidity, and disease had worn down the infantry. Furthermore, the extent of the Japanese defenses, manned by dedicated troops, was still largely unknown to the officers of the 32d. MacArthur and his staff in Brisbane, blissfully ignorant of the conditions into which they had thrown green troops, concluded that the main reason for the slow advance was poor leadership. MacArthur, in his usual melodramatic way, dispatched the I Corps commander, General Eichelberger, to the front with the admonition to take Buna or not come back. After tramping the front lines, Eichelberger sadly concluded that Harding and two of his senior commanders should be replaced, and on 1 December he took direct command of the operation.

Eichelberger's assumption of command did not physically alter the 32d Division's situation. The only definite improvement was in the area of supplies. Much of what Harding had earlier requested began arriving on small coastal ships or by air at Dobodura. Even more important to the ultimate success of the operation was the arrival of fresh troops and equipment, including tanks. However, before any significant reinforcements arrived, Eichelberger ordered a general advance on 5 December. Despite air support, the attack on the Warren front was again halted with no gain. However, on the Urbana front, a platoon from the 126th Infantry reached the sea, driving a wedge between the Japanese at Buna village and the mission. Reinforced, the infantrymen held tenaciously to their positions. By the twelfth, a fresh battalion from the 127th Infantry had arrived by air and, two days later, following a heavy mortar barrage, succeeded in capturing Buna village.

The veteran Australian 18th Infantry Brigade arrived from Milne Bay on 8 December, reinforcing the worn out 126th and 128th Regiments. Equally important, the Aussies brought seven light tanks. The 18th's commander, Brigadier George F. Wootten, ordered an attack along the coast after taking command of the Warren Force. The Australians, their tanks in the lead, drove a wedge between the main Japanese defenses and the sea. Later, a combined attack from the west by one Australian and two U.S. battalions finally cracked the Japanese defenses in the plantation area. On 2

January 1943, an Australian battalion crushed the last enemy strong point.

Meanwhile, advances by the Urbana Force were also proceeding slowly because of the lack of supporting firepower. Nevertheless, by the twenty-ninth, a wedge had been driven between the mission and Giropi Point, cutting off the enemy in the mission area. The final push by a company from the 127th Infantry drove the remaining enemy into the sea, many of whom attempted fruitlessly to swim for their lives.

It took forty-five days, but the Japanese had been cleared from the Buna region. Over 1,450 of the defenders were killed or captured. Allied casualties amounted to 620 men killed and more than 2,000 wounded. The Australian 18th Brigade suffered more than 850 casualties. These figures, although comparable to the 1st Marine Division's losses on Guadalcanal, tell only a part of the story. The 32d Division was shattered: more than 2,900 men were in the hospital at Buna, suffering from a variety of tropical diseases.

With the fall of Buna, renewed efforts were made to oust the Japanese from the Sanananda area. By the end of December, the U.S. 41st Division's 163d Infantry Regiment was flown into Dobodura and Popondetta and almost immediately sent to relieve the Australians in their blocking positions. The 127th Infantry moved north along the coast while the Australian 18th Brigade and its tanks took up positions in front of the southernmost Japanese road-block. On 9 January attacks began to drive back the Japanese along the southern portion of the Soputa-Sanananda road. The positions there were cleared by the sixteenth, opening up the Killerton Trail to the west. The Australians quickly moved toward the coast and then swung to the east. They were followed by the 163d Regiment, which veered east toward the main trail halfway to the coast. In the meantime, the 127th managed with great difficulty to cross Konombi Creek, thus almost closing the Japanese line of retreat. By the evening of the sixteenth the operation was completed. All that was left was to systematically destroy the many strong points still held by the sick and starving, but still deadly, survivors. Attempts to rescue the bulk of the trapped Japanese who had fallen back to

Giruwa failed when Allied artillery drove off most of the rescue boats. Nevertheless, an estimated twelve hundred Japanese escaped by sea and another thousand reached safety farther to the west. Giruwa finally fell on 22 January.

General MacArthur, in a press release announcing the victory in Papua, stated that Allied losses were low because time was not a factor. The statement was false on two counts. First, MacArthur had relieved General Harding and was constantly after Australian commanders for not moving as fast as he believed they could. Second, the casualties sustained were quite heavy. All together, the Australians had committed seven infantry brigades and had suffered over 2,100 casualties by 16 November. The Australian casualties for the entire campaign amounted to 8,546, of whom 3,095 were killed. American losses were 847 killed and 1,918 wounded. There were 2,700 more Allied casualties in the six-month struggle for Papua than were suffered at Guadalcanal. The Japanese lost more than 12,000 killed during the Papua campaign.

MacArthur, who never visited the New Guinea front while the struggle was unfolding, has been criticized sharply for his impatience, forcing his commanders to make frontal attacks against strong defenses. His relief of Harding was completely unjustified; Eichelberger could do no better, and MacArthur's implicit criticism of the Australians was totally without merit. Still, the campaign was a strategic success. Port Moresby was saved, the Japanese had been chased from Papua, and MacArthur had gained airfields from which Kenney's bombers and fighters could strike at Rabaul and cover subsequent attacks on Japanese strong points along the New Guinea coast. Furthermore, the bloody debacles at Buna and Sanananda had taught MacArthur that in the future, unless forced to, he should not order frontal attacks without adequate artillery and air preparation.

While the long and costly battle to defeat the Japanese at Buna and Sanananda was proceeding, MacArthur received more men and materiel, although his theater was still near the bottom of the priority list of the Combined Chiefs of Staff. By 1 July 1943 he had available in Australia and New Guinea four U.S. and six Australian and New Zealand divisions, along with a number of specialized troops such as the 503d Parachute Infantry Regiment. Three of these divisions, the 7th and 9th Australian and the U.S. 41st, were in New Guinea.

MacArthur's supply situation also had vastly improved. Convoy after convoy brought vital materiel to Australia and New Zealand, and the means to deliver men and supplies to the New Guinea front far outstripped the dreams of the engaged infantry units a few scant months before. Although far from satisfactory, the naval units available were strong enough to support future operations on New Guinea. The PT boats, once the mainstay of the navy during the Buna operation, had been joined by cruisers and destroyers. These larger ships could operate in the dangerous waters off northern New Guinea because of improved hydrographic charts. Nevertheless, most supplies brought by sea came in small coastal steamers, many belonging to the Dutch KPM shipping line. Rear Admiral Daniel E. Barbey, an expert on amphibious operations, arrived in Australia on 8 January to take command of VII Amphibious Force. Before the war was over he would oversee fifty landings. But in early 1943 he had few landing craft even for practice; the demands of Europe and the projected central Solomons campaign took precedence. However, by June 1943 he had enough boats for operations in the Trobriand Islands.

The most obvious change in the status of Allied forces was in the fortunes of the Fifth Air Force. At the beginning of 1942 only 19 heavy bombers and 101 fighters were available to General Brett. By the end of the year there were 81 heavy and 83 medium bombers and 238 fighters. These operated from five airfields near Port Moresby and from advanced strips clawed out of the jungle at Milne Bay, near Buna, and later from Woodlark Island. The most important of these forward strips was at Dobodura. At that time there were two bomber groups—one equipped with B-25s and the other with B-26s—and a P-40 fighter group based there. Within weeks another fighter group equipped with long-range P-38s arrived. At Port Moresby, Kenney had two heavy bomber groups, a medium bomber group, and three fighter groups—in addition to the Australian fighter and medium bomber elements already operating there. The Fifth Air Force, which would continue to grow, would be used with devastating effect, first with continuing raids on the main Japanese naval and air bases at Rabaul, and then in direct support of MacArthur's operations against Lae, Salamaua, Wewak, and Hollandia.

After the capture of Buna and Sanananda there was a lapse in the ground campaign as the battered Australian and U.S. units rested and refitted. The only serious activity was near Wau on the Owen Stanley escarpment, a few miles inland from Lae, where the Australians controlled a small airfield.

In early January 1943 the Japanese landed a regiment at Lae and Salamaua. The Japanese commander there subsequently mounted a series of attacks against the Australians at Wau and in the Bulolo Valley, but was unable to capture the village or the airfield. When he complained of the shortage of men, General Imamura and Admiral Kusaka decided to send the 51st Division to Lae. This was in keeping with the Japanese plan to hold firmly to the major operative areas in northern New Guinea. Kenney's pilots had observed the concentration of ships at Rabaul, so MacArthur was aware that the Japanese planned to reinforce one of their garrisons. The logical place was Lae. Imamura believed that Japanese planes would be able to give sufficient air support to the slow-moving convoy. But he had totally underestimated the growing strength of the Fifth Air Force. On 28 February the convoy of eight transports carrying sixty-nine hundred troops left Rabaul escorted by eight destroyers. It proceeded on a westerly course north of New Britain, its movement shielded in part by a severe tropical storm. After being sighted by a B-24 on 1 March, the convoy disappeared. It was picked up again the next morning off Cape Gloucester when the weather cleared. Twenty-nine American heavy bombers were sent to attack the flotilla. They sank one transport and damaged another. Nine hundred and fifty survivors were picked up by the destroyer escorts and delivered to Lae.

Imamura's plan for fighter cover broke down because the weather over eastern New Britain at first prevented the Zeros from taking off. When they were able to join other fighters from Wewak high above the convoy on 3 March they were engaged by P-38s and P-40s of the Fifth Air Force and RAAF. Even had they not been intercepted, it is doubtful they could have prevented the convoy's destruction since the main American bomber attacks were delivered at very low levels using skip-bombing techniques that were totally new to the Japanese. After delivering their bombs at almost sea level, the A-20s and B-25s, some of which had been modified to carry eight .50-caliber machine guns in their noses, strafed the hapless transports. Later, PT boats attacked the transports and destroyers that remained afloat. The slaughter continued through 5 March. When it was over, more than three thousand Japanese troops had been killed and all twelve of their ships sunk.

This unheralded Battle of the Bismarck Sea was one of the most important engagements of the Pacific war, not only because of the heavy Japanese losses, but because of the reaction of the Japanese high command. It would never again send large ships into waters off New Guinea covered by the Fifth Air Force. Japanese troops in Papua became more and more isolated, having to depend on small coastal vessels or submarines for supplies. The proposed campaign to drive the Australians from Wau never materialized, and it became a major base for support of MacArthur's plan to capture Lae and Salamaua.

Airpower played a decisive role in the Pacific war, and nowhere was it more important than New Guinea. The size and nature of the island made it imperative that land operations not outstrip air cover. Rabaul, the great Japanese bastion on New Britain, was the major target of both MacArthur's and Halsey's actions largely because of the air bases there. The Japanese, although they kept feeding aircraft into Rabaul, were handicapped because the actions of Allied forces in the Central Solomons forced them to fight a two-front air war. Thus, although the Japanese mounted attacks against Allied advances in New Guinea, they were never as great as those launched against the Solomons landings. Also, the increasing strength of the Fifth Air Force created a third air front—that over Rabaul itself. Kenney's planes, although concentrating on Rabaul, were increasingly active against the Japanese airfields at Lae, Salamaua, and Wewak, and in western New Britain. The air campaign against the Japanese was so effective that by the end of April 1943, the Lae and Salamaua fields were hardly usable.

MacArthur's next step after the Buna campaign was to take Lae, Salamaua, and Finschhafen and thus control the Huon Gulf area 150 miles northwest of Sanananda Point. To better secure the entrance to the Solomon Sea, Admiral Barbey landed troops on Woodlark Island on 22 June, and four days later another amphibious landing was made on Kirwana. Both of these Trobriand Islands were secured without opposition. Ultimately, sixteen thousand men were stationed there, and an airfield was constructed on Woodlark. Another preparatory move was the landing of elements of the 41st Division at Nassau Bay, just a few miles south of Salamaua, on 30 June. This provided a permanent base for delivering supplies by water to the target areas instead of the much more difficult delivery by air to Wau and then by native bearer to the front. Also in early June an old airstrip was discovered at Tsili Tsili, approximately forty miles inland from Lae. By the middle of the month, infantry and engineers had been shuttled there and fighters were operating from the field within a week. A secondary or dummy field was also built at Bena Bena to help confuse Japanese air surveillance.

General Blamey's plan was to converge on Lae and Salamaua from three directions. Elements of the 3d Australian Division joined the U.S. 41st at Nassau Bay, and, although operating in extremely bad conditions, had pushed the Japanese back to the outskirts of Salamaua by the end of July. This offensive drew many of the defenders from the Lae area. The second prong of the offensive was to consist of forces from east of Wau that would cooperate with paratroops dropped into Markham Valley. The third was to be an amphibious landing on two beaches east of Lae. Before these last two parts of the offensive began, the Japanese high command decided to wipe out the air threat from Tsili Tsili and Bena Bena. Believing that Wewak was too far away for an Allied counterstroke from Dobodura, they concentrated almost two hundred planes there and in western New Britain. However, Kenney's planes found them on 17 August and destroyed seventy aircraft on the ground. This disaster, combined with the demands to defend Rabaul and the central Solomons, meant scant air protection for the Japanese in the region.

On 4 September VII Amphibious Force landed the first elements of the Australian 9th Division fifteen miles east of Lae. Within two days, seventy-eight hundred troops were ashore and moving westward along the north shore of Huon Gulf. The next day Kenney put more than three hundred planes in the air in order to deliver the 503d Parachute Infantry Regiment over the inland village of Nadzab, nine miles east of Lae. In this first air drop of the Pacific war, seventeen hundred parachutists seized the airstrip there, and by the next day C-47s were using the field to fly in the first of thousands of Australians. After regrouping, the combined force marched down the Markham River against only slight resistance, and by 14 September had reached the outskirts of Lae. The Japanese commander there, RAdm. Kokichi Mori, decided to evacuate the area and retreated northward, harried by the Australians. After a month of hard marching over the rugged Huon Peninsula, a smaller duplication of General Horii's earlier debacle in Papua, fifteen hundred survivors reached Sio. In the meantime, Salamaua's defenders were cleaned out by Australians and Americans advancing along the coast.

Blamey did not wait long after capturing Lae and Salamaua before moving to secure Finschhafen. He brought up the Australian 26th Brigade and its tanks to reinforce the planned amphibious attack led by Brigadier Victor Windeyer. The Japanese commander, Maj. Gen. Kunitaro Yamada, had correctly concluded that Finschhafen would be the next target, but he believed the attack would come from inland. He therefore left only a thousand men to defend the village and beach area and displaced three thousand more to cover the possible inland routes. But the main effort came from the sea, with landings south of the village on 22 September. Taken by surprise, Yamada could not mount a counteroffensive until the twenty-eighth, but by then the Australians were at full strength and expanding the beachhead. Despite the efforts of Japanese Special Landing Force troops, Finschhafen fell on 2 October 1943.

Meanwhile, in the interior, General Vasey and the Australian 7th Division had the difficult task of clearing the Markham and Ramu Valleys. After the Australians captured the Kaiaput airfield, the 21st and 25th Brigades were flown in from Nadzab. Vasey's patrols soon reached as far north as the outskirts of the Japanese base at Madang. Amidst this checkerboard of opposing troops, Yamada, with reinforcements from Madang, attempted a major attack on Finschhafen on 17 October. After a week of fighting, his sick and exhausted troops retreated, leaving behind 679 dead. For all practical purposes, the Allies controlled Markham Valley and the Huon Peninsula.

Although the Japanese naval air force at Rabaul was still powerful, the Japanese high command's attention was focused on protecting Rabaul and trying to save Bougainville from the fate that had recently befallen the Japanese on New Georgia. And, with the northeast New Guinea coast cleared of Japanese, MacArthur was finally in a position to shift the axis of his advance northward to New Britain.

Long before the Lae operation there was high-level disagreement on the next moves in the South Pacific Area. Much of what had been outlined in the Joint Chiefs' directive of 2 July 1942 had been accomplished—Guadalcanal was secure and the Japanese were on the defensive in New Guinea. Believing an invasion of New Britain would be necessary to eliminate Rabaul, MacArthur did not want to attempt any further advance in the Solomons until more forces were available. A contrary opinion was expressed by Nimitz and Halsey, who wanted to use the considerable forces available to them to take New Georgia with its vital airfield at Munda before landing on Bougainville. An airfield on Bougainville would bring Rabaul within 250 miles of Allied planes.

The disagreement between MacArthur and Halsey over timing prompted the Joint Chiefs to convene a Pacific military conference in Washington on 12 March 1943. General Sutherland, MacArthur's representative, brought with him a completed plan code-named Elkton II—and a request for five more divisions and a substantial shift of naval power to the Southwest Pacific in order to implement it. General Harmon, Halsey's representative, pointed out that the Japanese were on the defensive, the Russell Islands had been seized in February, and that Halsey had enough forces available to seize New Georgia without any additional troops. Given these choices, the Joint Chiefs accepted Halsey's plan and issued a directive on 28 March authorizing the seizure of New Georgia followed by landings on Bougainville. They avoided the thorny question of command— the central Solomons were in MacArthur's command area but the forces available were all from Nimitz's theater. They compromised by giving Halsey tactical command under MacArthur's strategic guidance. What could have been a difficult situation was avoided by Halsey's diplomatic handling of his position and the fact that MacArthur and Halsey liked each other. MacArthur's headquarters issued a revised plan for the subjugation of Rabaul, Elkton III, which brought the earlier plan in line with the 28 March directive.

Halsey had available for the central Solomons venture a considerable force—in sharp contrast to the situation when he had assumed command only nine months before. His army commander, General Harmon, now had four divisions—the 25th, 37th, 43d, and the Americal—in addition to the 1st and 3d Marine Divisions. With service troops, this constituted a force of 275,000 men. There were more than 400 aircraft based throughout the South Pacific. Immediately available for action in the New Georgia campaign was Air Command Solomons (AirSols), a composite force that included Marine Corps, navy, and New Zealand air units, and heavy bombers from the Thirteenth Air Force. Its commander, Admiral Fitch, could call upon more than 200 fighters and 250 bombers of all types. Although Halsey did not have a large naval force permanently attached to his command, Nimitz normally provided whatever Halsey requested to carry out a specific mission. In the spring of 1943, this included Turner's amphibious force, TF 32, and two cruiser-destroyer forces, TF 67 and TF 68, with a total of eight cruisers and sixteen destroyers. In addition, there were two carrier task forces built around the *Saratoga* and *Enterprise*. Halsey could also call upon Admiral Lee with four new battleships, and RAdm. Harry W. Hill's flotilla of two resurrected older battleships and three *Sangamon*-type escort carriers.

While planning for the New Georgia campaign was just beginning, AirSols delivered a stunning blow to the Japanese high command. Nimitz and Halsey learned that Admiral Yamamoto was planning to visit forward bases in the South Pacific. After being assured by Washington and members of his staff that none of Yamamoto's subordinates were of the same quality, Nimitz authorized an attempt to intercept and destroy Yamamoto's aircraft. The specifics of the task were turned over to the new commander of AirSols, RAdm. Marc A. Mitscher. He in turn ordered Maj. John W. Mitchell, commander of the 339th Fighter Squadron on Guadalcanal, to do the job. It was decided that when they learned of Yamamoto's takeoff from Rabaul, long-range P-38s would attempt an air interception.

Yamamoto and many of his senior staff left Rabaul for the Kahili airfield on Bougainville in two Betty bombers at midmorning on 18

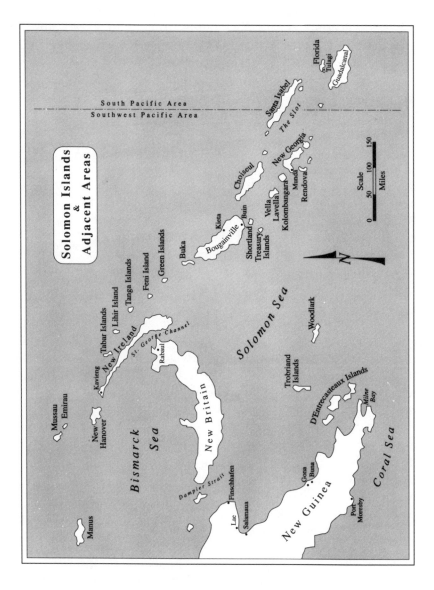

April 1943. The bombers were protected by nine Zeros. The P-38 pilots, sweeping in low over the water, engaged the bombers just as they were making their landing approach—and after the Zeros had turned back. Captain Thomas G. Lamphier Jr. was credited with shooting down the first bomber, which crashed in the jungle, while Lt. Rex Barber got credit for destroying the other. In all probability Yamamoto was in the first bomber. Most of his staff also perished, although his chief of staff, VAdm. Matome Ugaki, survived.

When the news was relayed to Guadalcanal—and later Pearl Harbor—there was a general consensus that this stroke was equivalent to a major naval victory. Later assessment somewhat modified this feeling, since it is doubtful that Yamamoto could have done any better than either of his successors, Adm. Mineichi Koga or Adm. Soemu Toyoda, to retrieve Japan's fortunes. Nevertheless, Yamamoto's death was keenly felt in Japan. After the war, VAdm. Shigeru Fukudome, one of the key Japanese commanders, summed up this feeling of loss when he said that Yamamoto's death was "an unbearable blow to the morale of all the military forces."

The plan developed in Halsey's headquarters for seizure of the vital Munda air base on New Georgia was simple. The 43d Division, commanded by Maj. Gen. John H. Hester, would land on suitable beaches east of the airfield and proceed quickly to break through whatever defenses the Japanese had constructed along the trails to the field. At the same time, twenty-six hundred marines under Col. Harry B. "the Horse" Liversedge would go ashore near Rice Landing on the north coast and drive southwest to secure Bairoko Harbor, thus preventing the Japanese from using the port for evacuation. Even before these landings, a regiment would seize the northern part of nearby Rendova Island, from which batteries of artillery could support the troops advancing toward Munda. General Hester would be in charge of the entire operation.

The first part of the plan worked well despite repeated air attacks by Japanese planes from airfields at Munda and on Kolombangara and Bougainville. The Marine Corps's 4th Raider Battalion landed south of Segei Point on 21 June and overcame sporadic opposition to secure Viru Harbor by 1 July. Seabees soon followed and began work on a fighter strip near Segei. Later, a battalion from the 103d

Infantry seized Vangunu Island, which was directly on line with the supply line from the Russell Islands. The 172d Infantry landed on Rendova on 30 June and very quickly secured that island. Most of the 172d later joined the main force, which on 2 July landed on Zanana Beach, three miles farther east than the more favorable Laiana Beach. Hester had rejected this latter landing point because he believed it to be too heavily defended. Once the beachhead had been consolidated, two regiments began moving toward Munda. They were halted almost immediately by the Japanese.

The Japanese commander, Maj. Gen. Noboru Sasaki, had established a series of fortified defense lines and roadblocks east of Munda. Controlling more than five thousand troops and having the advantage of central position, he pinned the 43d Division's advance down in front of his first line. The first break in the line occurred when Hester shifted the 172d Regiment south and finally captured Laiana Beach. But Sasaki cut its communications with the 169th Infantry on the Munda Trail and interposed a battalion between the two American units. The 169th was up against a well-designed defense system bristling with automatic weapons. Supplies for the beleaguered attackers were intermittent, and the troops soon became tired and dispirited as they made little headway with their frontal attacks.

The situation elsewhere also belied the optimistic hopes of the American planners. A combination of miserable terrain and stubborn Japanese resistance had slowed the marines moving to capture Bairoko Harbor. They did not reach Enogai Point until 11 July, five days behind schedule. Bairoko remained open for Japanese reinforcements and later for the withdrawal of Sasaki's troops. Without reinforcements of his own, Liversedge could not move any farther south.

Even the navy support task groups were having problems. Although the American naval forces by then outnumbered the Japanese in the waters around New Georgia, the Japanese still possessed an equalizer in the form of the long-lance torpedo, which remained far superior to American torpedoes. Task Group (TG) 36.1, commanded by RAdm. Walden L. Ainsworth, rediscovered this fact so painfully learned in the naval battles around Guadalcanal.

After bombarding Vila and Bairoko, Ainsworth was alerted on 4 July to the movement of ten destroyers carrying supplies and men down the Slot. Ainsworth's task group had three cruisers and four destroyers, so theoretically his force outgunned his opponent. The Japanese commander had divided his ships into three sections: one to provide cover, the other two to land the reinforcements. Ainsworth intercepted the Japanese at approximately 0200 on 6 July in the Kula Gulf north of Kolombangara, and the fire from his cruiser's 6-inch guns at first sank one destroyer and damaged two others. But a spread of three torpedoes struck the cruiser *Helena*, which soon sank. Later, confusing contacts between American and Japanese destroyers resulted in serious damage to one of the Japanese ships. Navigating in the dark, another Japanese destroyer ran aground. Unable to get it off the reef, it was abandoned and sunk the following day by American planes. In addition to the loss of the *Helena*, Ainsworth failed to prevent the off-loading of supplies and sixteen hundred men at Vila to support Sasaki's defense of Munda.

American planes soon spotted an updated version of the Tokyo Express leaving Rabaul heading for New Georgia. This flotilla, built around the light cruiser *Jintsu*, had five destroyers and four destroyer transports containing an additional twelve hundred men. Ainsworth, who had been reinforced, had overwhelming superiority with three cruisers and ten destroyers. He rushed northwest from Tulagi to intercept. Just after midnight on 13 July, radar picked up the Japanese ships off Kolombangara and a few minutes later the leading American destroyers loosed their torpedoes. They had no effect. Then the radars on the three cruisers locked on the *Jintsu*. At least ten 6-inch shells struck the cruiser, which went dead in the water. A torpedo from one of the destroyers finished it off. If the action had stopped there it would have been a considerable victory, but Ainsworth followed the retreating Japanese destroyers, which took advantage of a rain squall to rearm their torpedoes. Doubling back, the Japanese launched their feared torpedoes, and at 0215 one struck and blew up the destroyer *Gwin*, and two others hit the cruisers *St. Louis* and *Honolulu*. The two cruisers limped back to Tulagi where repair work kept them out of the war until November.

After the action, a rueful Ainsworth admitted the fallacy of sending cruisers after Japanese destroyers. The action at Kolombangara did, however, prevent reinforcements from reaching Sasaki. They were off-loaded at a harbor on the west coast of Kolombangara instead.

Admiral Halsey and General Harmon were perplexed at the slowness with which the 43d Division was moving, and on 11 July sent XIV Corps's new commander, Maj. Gen. Oscar W. Griswold, to investigate. In his report, Griswold was very critical of Hester's dual command. He found the troops dispirited, exhausted, and suffering from low morale, and expressed concern that the 43d would fold up if reinforcements were not sent immediately. Harmon responded to this report by placing Griswold in overall command, relegating Hester to only divisional command. Harmon ordered Maj. Gen. Robert S. Beightler, commanding the 37th Division, to embark his 145th and 148th Infantry Regiments and General Collins, commanding the 25th Division, to immediately transport his 161st Infantry—to be followed shortly by the 27th Infantry. By 20 July the size of the American force on New Georgia was thus doubled—bringing the number of troops available to what it probably should have been in the original plan. American commanders throughout the Pacific war tended to underestimate Japanese resistance, and thus committed too few troops initially to adequately carry out a specific mission.

General Griswold moved the 37th Division north of the 43d, where he hoped that it would envelop Sasaki's line and force a general withdrawal. The new offensive began on 25 July in the 43d Division's zone. Artillery, air, and naval gunfire had knocked out many of the fixed defenses, and within days of the beginning of the offensive the Japanese—after suffering heavy losses—fell back to other prepared defenses. Eighth Fleet headquarters at Rabaul then ordered Sasaki to retreat into a narrow perimeter around Munda Point. Sasaki reluctantly obeyed, giving up the airfield, which was captured on 5 August. Meanwhile, elements of the 27th and 161st Regiments were plodding northwest across hills and through jungle, clearing their own trail with the goal of cutting off Sasaki's escape route. On 9 August they made contact with Liversedge's troops. However, they were not able to capture Bairoko Harbor until the twenty-fifth. During that interval, Sasaki successfully evacuated the bulk of his remaining forces to Kolombangara and the adjacent island of Baanga. The latter was taken by units of the 43d on 21 August.

The New Georgia campaign ended with the capture of Arundel Island in September. The surprisingly hard-fought campaign had cost 1,094 killed and 3,873 wounded. Japanese losses are unknown, but in all probability were many more than the 2,500 dead reported by XIV Corps headquarters. Far more important than the Japanese casualty count, however, was the seizure of the vital airfield at Munda.

With twelve thousand troops on Kolombangara, General Sasaki, after receiving reinforcements, had expected to reinvade New Georgia. All such plans were overruled by his superiors at Rabaul after the naval action in Vella Gulf on the night of 6–7 August. There, three Japanese destroyers carrying troops and supplies escorted by another destroyer were caught by Comdr. Frederick Moosbrugger's six destroyers. The outcome differed significantly from that of earlier clashes with Japanese destroyers, as Moosbrugger's ships torpedoed and sank three of Japan's newest destroyers off the northwest coast of Kolombangara. Some fifteen hundred Japanese soldiers and sailors perished in the engagement.

Even after this disaster, Sasaki expected the Americans to invade Kolombangara to secure the important Vila airfield. Halsey, however, had no intention of engaging in another slugging match on the well-fortified island. Instead, he ordered RAdm. Theodore Wilkinson, who had replaced Turner in command of TF 32, to transport and land six thousand 25th Division troops on the southern tip of Vella Lavella. Surprisingly, this island—located roughly fifty miles northwest of Kolombangara—was not garrisoned. The Japanese had used it only as a stopover for their interisland barge traffic. Approximately 250 stragglers found at the landing site were quickly overcome. This maneuver rendered Sasaki's position on Kolombangara untenable, and Imperial Headquarters ordered his troops evacuated to southern Bougainville. In a major operation involving thirty-eight landing craft and eighty army barges protected by eleven destroyers and heavy air cover, the Japanese made three night runs—despite being intercepted by American destroyers. The

Japanese lost twenty-nine landing craft, one submarine, and had one destroyer damaged before the operation was completed on 2 October, but most of the troops escaped. When advance elements of the 27th Infantry landed on Kolombangara on 6 October they found only abandoned Japanese equipment and a few stragglers. That same day, the Japanese committed nine destroyers and four submarine chasers in an attempt to rescue some six hundred men still on Vella Lavella. During the night three American destroyers intercepted the Japanese and torpedoed and sank one destroyer. However, the Japanese sank the *Selfridge,* and the other two U.S. destroyers ran into each other, causing considerable damage. Both sides eagerly withdrew, the Americans because of damage, the Japanese because their rescue attempt had succeeded. While the destroyers were engaged, the sub chasers slipped into Marquana Bay and took off the waiting Japanese troops.

The capture of the important Vila airstrip gave Maj. Gen. Nathan F. Twining, the new commander of AirSols, four functioning airfields in the central Solomons. The way to Bougainville and beyond had been cleared for the shorter-range Allied land-based aircraft to support the next step in MacArthur's Elkton plan.

In March 1943 MacArthur had told Halsey to begin planning for the invasion of Bougainville. The major question confronting Halsey's staff was *where* to land. The obvious target was the Buin-Kahili area in the south, where the two largest Japanese airfields were located. In addition, Tonoley Harbor was an excellent port. However, by the end of July, Halsey's staff had rethought its plan to land on southern Bougainville. More than half the estimated thirty-five thousand Japanese on the island were located there and it appeared that trying to seize a lodgment in that area would present even more problems than those encountered on New Georgia. Halsey then considered seizing the Shortland Islands off the southern tip of Bougainville. From there, artillery could render the airfields and harbor useless for the Japanese. Later information indicated that there were no good areas on the Shortlands for airfields, so Halsey then gave thought to capturing the lightly held Treasury Islands and Choiseul, building airfields there, and thus negating the Japanese presence on Bougainville. MacArthur disapproved this plan and instead suggested occupying the Treasuries and, some time after 1 November, seizing a beachhead at Empress Augusta Bay on the west coast of the 125-mile-long island of Bougainville. Halsey adopted this suggestion, believing such a landing would be a complete surprise to the Japanese. It was known from coastwatchers that there was only a small force located there, and, given the hills, swamps, heavy jungle, and lack of good roads, it would take time for the Japanese to bring up reinforcements.

The date for the Empress Augusta Bay operation was set for 1 November. The landing would be carried out by the 3d Marine Division with attached parachute and Raider elements. Major General John R. Hodge's Americal Division would remain in reserve on Fiji. Five days before the Bougainville landing, the 3d New Zealand Division's 8th Brigade was to seize the two Treasury Islands. Backing up the amphibious operation off Cape Torokina were over five hundred AirSols fighters and bombers operating from the Russells and New Georgia. Task Force 38, built around the carrier *Saratoga* and soon to be joined by the *Princeton,* and TF 39 with its fast cruisers and destroyers provided naval support. A diversionary move was to be made on 28 October by a battalion of the 1st Marine Parachute Regiment on the large island of Choiseul in hopes of confusing the Japanese as to the actual point of attack.

The operations proceeded as planned. On 27 October men of Brigadier R. A. Row's 8th Brigade embarked on thirty-one ships, bound for Mono, the largest of the Treasury Islands. The landings there—and later on smaller Stirling Island—were barely contested by the small Japanese garrison. Within a day, the bulk of Row's four-thousand-man assault force was on shore and fanning out to search for the few Japanese who had taken to the bush. Both islands were declared secure by 4 November. The New Zealanders, with few casualties, had secured a good port at Blanche Harbor and sites for future radar stations only seventy-five miles southeast of Cape Torokina.

Another attempt to confuse the Japanese as to American intentions was the raid on the big island of Choiseul. Lieutenant Colonel Victor H. Krulak and 656 men of the 2d Parachute Battalion landed after dark on 27 October at Voza, located in the extreme northwest part of the island. From there they struck at lightly held Japanese positions north and south of their perimeter, destroying some stores and killing a few enemy soldiers. The raiding party had drawn the attention of the Japanese commander on the island, who dispatched troops to counter what he believed was the prelude to an invasion. On 3 November, before the Japanese could reach the Voza area, Krulak and his men were withdrawn.

It is questionable whether the raid fooled General Hyakutake, commander of Japanese forces on Bougainville, but a chart the marines discovered during the raid showed the location of the Japanese minefields off the island's coast. The chart was a definite aid to naval units operating in support of the Torokina landings.

Air preparations for the Bougainville operation were impressive. The task of keeping Japanese airpower at Rabaul busy fell to the Fifth Air Force. Photos of the four airfields there taken on 11 October showed 128 bombers and 145 fighters. The following day Kenney launched the largest air strike of the Pacific war: 213 heavy and medium bombers escorted by 128 P-38s. Three large merchant vessels and many smaller ships were sunk, ammunition dumps were blown up, and, most important, an estimated 100 planes were destroyed. This massive strike was followed by an 18 October raid on which 54 B-25s almost destroyed Tobera airfield. When the weather improved, the Fifth Air Force again struck at Rabaul with low flying B-25s, and on 29 October Kenney sent 53 P-38s and 37 B-24s to hit the already seriously damaged port and air facilities there.

An estimated 200 Japanese planes were destroyed either in the air or on the ground at Rabaul during the month of October, forcing Admiral Koga, Yamamoto's successor, to strip most of the planes from his big carriers then at Truk and send them south in order to keep the huge Japanese base operational. In the meantime AirSols, composed of the 1st and 2d Marine Air Wings and the Thirteenth Air Force staging from Guadalcanal and the new airfields in the central Solomons, hammered the Japanese fields on Bougainville. AirSols's planes were active for twenty-one days in October, and by D day, Bougainville's airfields were virtually useless.

The main assault on the Japanese at Empress Augusta Bay was to be carried out by the 3d and 9th Marines, aided by two marine Raider battalions. After practice runs at Efate and Espíritu Santo in the New Hebrides, the 12,500 marines were loaded on the amphibious force's transports and rendezvoused with other support elements off Guadalcanal on 28 October before proceeding to Bougainville without incident. Its accompanying destroyers briefly bombarded the landing beaches, followed minutes before the landings by thirty-one bombers, which strafed and bombed the beach areas. The 9th Marines landed on five northern beaches at 0730 on 1 November. The 3d Marines landed on three beaches to the south, and the 2d Raider Battalion, aided by a battalion from the 3d Marines, had the task of neutralizing the main Japanese defenses at Cape Torokina. The long beach area west of Cape Torokina varied from ten to fifty yards deep and was backed by swamp and jungle. High surf in the 9th Marine's sector wrecked a large number of landing craft. Before the landings were completed, sixty-four LCVPs and twenty-two LCMs were wrecked. Once ashore, the 9th Marines discovered that the beach rose sharply for ten yards and then fell off into a nearly impassable swamp. Nevertheless, by nightfall they had pushed inland and established a strong outpost south of the Laruma River. The 3d Marine Regiment battalions assigned to the beaches south of the Koromokina River experienced fewer problems with the high surf and met only minimal Japanese resistance.

The worst fighting was at Cape Torokina, where the bulk of the Japanese force—estimated at three hundred men —manned twenty-five log and earthen pillboxes with interconnecting trenches. Naval gunfire and air strikes failed to damage this defense system, so the 1st Battalion, 3d Marines, had to make a series of frontal assaults. The pillboxes were not taken until late afternoon. Most of the Japanese defenders were killed, but a few escaped into the jungle. The 12th Marines's medium artillery was on shore by the evening of 2 November, by which time the marines had extended their perimeter inland and were firmly entrenched and fully prepared to expand their lodgment into the interior.

The response of the Japanese high command to actions in the central and northern Solomons was complicated by the need to share resources with New Guinea. Admiral Koga repeatedly refused Admiral Kusaka's requests for reinforcements for Rabaul. Finally, the losses of planes and pilots became so serious that Koga was forced to relent and send additional support. The need to stand on the defense in both the Central Pacific and the southern areas meant that Koga also had to split his surface forces. The Japanese reaction to the Bougainville invasion was thus confused and slow to develop.

On 31 October the Japanese learned of the impending invasion. Believing the Shortland Islands to be the objective, the high com-

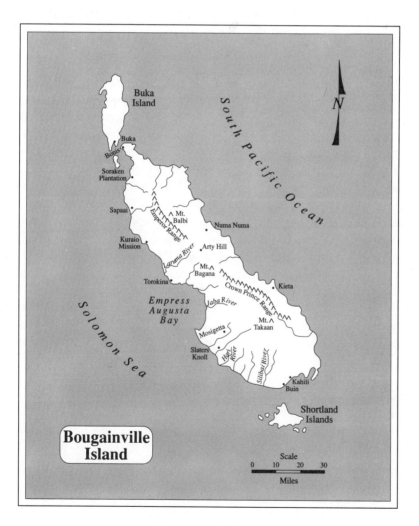

mand ordered RAdm. Sentaro Omori, commanding two heavy and two light cruisers and two destroyers, to intercept. A combination of bad weather and searches away from Empress Augusta Bay frustrated Omori, who was surprised to learn of the marine landings after his return to Rabaul on 1 November. Later that day he again sortied from Rabaul, his force augmented by eight more destroyers, five of them carrying a thousand men for a counter invasion at Cape Torokina. In the meantime, RAdm. A. Stanton Merrill's TF 39, composed of four new light cruisers and eight destroyers, took up a position to protect the beachhead after bombarding airfields and installations in southern Bougainville.

In the early morning hours of 2 November, the two forces collided off Empress Augusta Bay. Before the action began, Omori sent the troop-carrying destroyers back to Rabaul. The Japanese, in contrast with earlier actions, fought a very disorganized battle. Two of their destroyers ran into each other and another smashed into Omori's flagship. Concentrated fire from the American light cruisers sank the Japanese cruiser *Sendai,* and the destroyer *Hatsukaze* was later blown to pieces. Merrill's force escaped with only two destroyers damaged. A furious Japanese air attack followed the surface engagement but was fruitless: the inexperienced Japanese pilots proved no match for AirSols's fighters.

Omori's failure convinced Admiral Koga to commit major elements of his as yet undamaged Second Fleet. He believed that by doing so he could lure the major American naval units in the Solomons into battle and destroy them. He dispatched seven heavy and one light cruisers to Rabaul, believing that Halsey would have only light cruisers with which to oppose this force. It may be that Halsey exaggerated when, after the war, he claimed this was his most desperate moment. Nevertheless, the situation had all the makings of a disaster. A transport group had left Guadalcanal for Empress Augusta Bay with thirty-five hundred men of the 21st Marines. Another batch of reinforcements, the army's 148th Infantry Regiment, was scheduled to leave on the seventh. To protect the lodgment and the convoys, Halsey had Merrill's TF 39 and Sherman's TF 38. Although Sherman had two carriers, the conventional wisdom was that they should not operate within range of land-based aircraft. Neither of the American task forces had heavy cruisers.

Halsey decided to go against accepted doctrine and ordered Sherman to move his carriers close enough to strike Rabaul on the morning of the fifth. Kenney's Fifth Air Force was asked to hit the port three hours after Sherman's planes. At 0900 on the fifth, Sherman launched ninety-seven planes, denuding his task force of air cover and forcing him to rely on planes from Vella Lavella for support. Although his strike did not sink any ships, it badly damaged three of the heavy cruisers and convinced Koga to recall all of the Second Fleet's ships to Truk. Counterattacks against Sherman's carriers proved futile. No ships were damaged, and the fighters providing air cover claimed twenty-five planes destroyed. Kenney's follow-up attack with twenty-seven B-24s further damaged Rabaul's port and warehouse facilities. The marine and army reinforcements the fleet had been protecting landed without incident at the Cape Torokina beaches.

Admiral Nimitz finally decided to reinforce Halsey, and sent RAdm. Alfred E. Montgomery's TF 50.3 to the South Pacific. This group was organized around the fast carriers *Essex* and *Bunker Hill* and the light carrier *Independence*. Halsey planned a three-pronged air strike against Rabaul for 11 November to be carried out by Sherman and Montgomery in conjunction with the Fifth Air Force. Bad weather over New Guinea prevented Kenney's planes from participating. Sherman's planes made it to the target through heavy fog, and their attack damaged a light cruiser in the harbor. Montgomery launched 105 aircraft, which sank one destroyer and seriously damaged another. Both attacks also resulted in still more extensive damage to the port facilities. Montgomery's task force in turn beat off prolonged counter air attacks without damage to any ship.

Koga's plans thus came to nothing. Not only had his ships failed to engage the Americans, his air losses were devastating. Of the carrier-based planes loaned to Rabaul, 43 of 82 Zeros, 38 of 45 dive-bombers, and 34 of 40 torpedo planes were destroyed. Rabaul never recovered from the week's devastating attacks.

A final engagement, the last of fifteen naval battles in the Solomons, was fought on 25 November when a Japanese convoy of three destroyer-transports and two escorting destroyers was intercepted by two American destroyer divisions commanded by Capt. Arleigh A. Burke. In yet another departure from previous actions, the Americans surprised the Japanese, torpedoed and sank the two escorts, and sank one of the destroyer-transports in a running gunfight.

The ultimate payoff for the air and naval engagements in early November was the elimination of Rabaul as a significant threat to Allied plans. Future air raids on the American perimeter on Bougainville would be of the nuisance variety. Finally, the isolation of Rabaul ultimately convinced General MacArthur that there was no need to invade New Britain.

On Bougainville, Maj. Gen. Allen H. Turnage, commander of the 3d Marine Division, was in tactical control until General Geiger arrived on 9 November to take command of the I Marine Amphibious Corps. Geiger's immediate problem was to reorganize his forces and move inland along the Mission and Piva Trails to establish a firm position in case the Japanese launched a serious counterattack.

The Japanese were slow to respond, however. General Hyakutake believed that the landings at Cape Torokina were a ruse to draw substantial troops north. He was convinced the main landings would come in the Buin area in the south. Even when pressured by his superiors in Rabaul to take more offensive action he misjudged the size of the American force. He believed that the Americans had landed at most five thousand troops, whereas Turnage on 5 November had more than twenty thousand men ashore. This faulty information explains why Hyakutake sent only a reinforced battalion to land at Koromokina, north of the marine lines, on 6 November. The small force was to attack the flanks while a larger group consisting of two battalions from the Japanese 23d Infantry Regiment struck westward down the Piva River. Although these attacks isolated some marine units and caused headquarters a few anxious moments, they were contained. By 8 November the Japanese had been driven back to their hill lines with a loss of more than eight hundred men.

The first elements of General Beightler's 37th Division landed on 8 November and were deployed to the north of the marines. The army troops would eventually hold half of the expanding beachhead. On the thirteenth, a battalion of the newly arrived 21st Marines was sent north to block the Numa Numa and East-West Trails.

Work had already begun on a fighter strip at Cape Torokina, but it was decided to investigate the possibility of building one and perhaps two longer fields farther inland. This meant that the perimeter had to be expanded and the Japanese driven from their positions in the Piva Forks area. To accomplish this, on the eighteenth the marines initiated the most serious engagement they would fight on Bougainville. Corps and division artillery knocked out most of the Japanese artillery on the high ground to the east and butchered the Japanese as they mounted counterattacks from their bunkers. By the twenty-fourth, most of the Japanese strong points had been taken and their 23d Infantry Regiment ceased to exist as a fighting unit after losing more than eleven hundred killed.

The marines moved into the Piva Forks area on 28 November. Three days before that, 37th Division troops occupied their final perimeter lines so Seabees and engineers could safely begin work on two bomber fields. The perimeter was then expanded to the southeast to secure hills from which the Japanese might threaten the airstrips. This was the last offensive maneuver by the marines on Bougainville. By the end of December the Americal Division was moving on line to relieve the 3d Marine Division. General Griswold, still commanding XIV Corps, succeeded General Geiger on 15 December. By then there were more than fifty thousand troops manning a continually strengthened defense line that stretched over twenty-three thousand yards.

General Griswold, satisfied with the extent of the perimeter, was mainly concerned with making certain that no major Japanese attack could seriously threaten it. For the next two months forward troops built log and sandbag pillboxes and trenches all along the line. They cut down timber and burned grass to clear fields of fire, set out mines and booby traps, and placed barbed wire in front of key positions. Behind the lines, Griswold had six 105mm howitzer battalions, five batteries of 155mm guns, and six cannon companies equipped with 75mm field guns.

The major offensive actions during January and February 1944 were constant patrols up the trails and along the river valleys. These were normally made by company-size units that struck at Japanese positions far in advance of the perimeter. Among the more successful missions were those undertaken by the 1st Battalion of the Fiji Regiment, which would penetrate the Japanese defenses, set up a

base, and proceed to destroy outposts and supply dumps and interfere with the enemy's communications. In some cases a jungle airstrip would be hacked out and supplies flown in on small observation aircraft belonging to the artillery.

Meanwhile, the air war against Rabaul continued unabated. General Kenney's Fifth Air Force operated exclusively against targets
in New Guinea, leaving Rabaul to AirSols. General Mitchell's force
had begun operating from the three Bougainville fields and the new
airstrip on Stirling Island, further tightening the noose around
Rabaul. On 15 February 1944, the 14th New Zealand Brigade occupied the Green Islands, only fifty-five miles east of New Ireland,
and construction of an airfield there made the ring complete.

Admiral Koga was in a dilemma. He did not wish to abandon the
five airfields at Rabaul despite the mounting plane and pilot losses.
In late January, therefore, he once again stripped his 2d Air Squadron at Truk to provide planes to defend Rabaul. By that time,
AirSols could bring more than 50 bombers over the harbor in a
single raid and Mitchell had 200 first-line fighters to protect them.
The inexperienced Japanese pilots were no match for the Americans
and Koga's reinforcements did little to protect Rabaul. The last
major dogfight over Rabaul occurred on 19 February, when 145
American planes were met by 50 Japanese fighters. These were
quickly overcome with minimal loss to the Americans.

By April the objective of neutralizing Rabaul had been accomplished without an invasion. The ninety-thousand-man garrison on
New Britain was isolated. General Hyakutake's men on Bougainville were even more so. From mid-February 1944 the only way
they could be supplied was by submarine.

Long after it was possible to drive the Americans from their
lodgment, General Hyakutake nevertheless attempted it. He shifted
approximately ten thousand troops from the 6th Division, notorious
for their actions during the rape of Nanking, northward to reinforce
the units already holding the hills east of the American perimeter.
This movement was extremely difficult, particularly for his artillery
units, because of the lack of good trails, the hilly terrain, and the
many streams that had to be crossed.

By mid-February most of his units were in place. The field commander, Lt. Gen. Masatane Kanda, divided the attacking forces into three sections each named for its commander. Beginning early on the morning of 9 March, the 4,200-man Iwasa Unit, hidden behind Hill 1111 in the center, was to drive directly against Hill 700, which was held by the 37th Division's 148th Infantry. Once that hill was secure, the Japanese believed the way to the beach would be open. On the Japanese right, the 4,300-man Magata Unit, taking advantage of the confusion expected to be caused by the Iwasa attack, was to break through the 37th Division's 129th Infantry on 12 March and then follow the Laruma River to the bay. On the left, the smaller Muda Unit, with only 1,350 men, was to seize Hill 260 from the American's 182d Infantry and then join the Iwasa Unit to destroy the surviving American units.

Hyakutake's plan was doomed from the beginning. He had no air cover or naval support units, and his artillery was outranged and outgunned. He had also underestimated the number of American troops and the strength of their defenses. By mid-February, General Griswold was aware of the impending attack, so the element of surprise was lost. Major General Shun Iwasa counted on the shock value of large numbers of massed infantry to secure a major breakthrough. This did not occur; only seven pillboxes were captured and the riflemen of the 148th contained the attack. The Americans counterattacked on 12 March and forced a general retreat in Iwasa's sector.

That same day, Col. Isashi Magata launched his frontal attack against the 129th Infantrys even better defenses. Although the Japanese assaults resulted in minor gains, these were soon reversed by combined tank, artillery, and infantry attacks. In the American sector, Col. Toyhorel Muda was more successful on 10 March, seizing a projection of Hill 260 nicknamed South Knob. The Japanese held tenaciously to the ground until 20 March, despite repeated infantry attacks and artillery concentrations. But again the Japanese lacked the men and firepower to exploit their success.

General Kanda, after the blunting of his offensive, pulled his troops back to the hill lines, regrouped, and on 23 March struck at the 129th Infantry's lines once again. The Japanese were cut to pieces by artillery concentrations from seven 105mm battalions and all of the 129th's mortars before they reached the American positions. Most of what was left of the Japanese infantry was destroyed by rifle and machine-gun fire from the fixed defenses. Kanda finally pulled back what was left of the 6th Division and attached units and began an orderly retreat southward, harried by air attacks and pursuit by three American battalions.

Hyakutake's poorly conceived plan had failed totally. Although there was never an accurate accounting of Japanese losses, after the war Japanese and American researchers estimated 5,500 men died in the abortive attacks. By contrast, XIV Corps had only 263 men killed in the two-week action.

American aims on Bougainville had all been achieved even before the Japanese March offensive. Planes flying from the three airfields constructed there aided in the destruction of Rabaul, the major Japanese naval and air base in the South Pacific. Once Rabaul ceased to be a threat there was no reason to continue to seize more territory on Bougainville except to expand the perimeter slightly to provide a more secure defense. The Japanese airfields were unusable and their navy's presence was a nocturnal one, limited primarily to submarines bringing in some supplies. From March 1944 onward, the Japanese struggled to simply stay alive; the bulk of Hyakutake's troops spent most of their time planting and cultivating huge garden plots to provide the minimal daily ration of food. Aside from continuing aggressive patrols by both the 37th and Americal Divisions, there was little offensive action throughout the rest of 1944.

Even before Hyakutake's abortive attack, the focus of Allied attention had been shifted to the Central Pacific theater, and Bougainville and the rest of the Solomon Islands became a backwater. Henceforth, their main function would be to serve as the staging ground for planned offensive operations in the Gilbert, Marshall, and Mariana Islands.

Chapter 9

Plan Orange Executed

ADMIRAL NIMITZ HAD been forced on the defensive for the first eighteen months of the war. Except for scattered naval and marine raids, there had been little offensive action in the vast area of the Central Pacific. The major concern of Nimitz and his staff had been to check the Japanese threat in the Solomons. By mid-1943 the reversal of fortune was obvious, and Nimitz planned to take the offensive in both the Aleutians and the Gilbert Islands. Nimitz agreed with Admiral King that defeating Japan would require implementing an updated version of the prewar Plan Orange. Thus, throughout the difficult battles for Guadalcanal and New Georgia, Nimitz rationed out his support for Halsey's efforts in MacArthur's theater and began building a great blue-water fleet whose responsibility would be to carry out the Central Pacific offensives.

In March 1943, Admiral King established a new system for identifying American naval forces. Halsey's South Pacific force was redesignated as the Third Fleet, and by August Nimitz had received enough new ships to reconstitute the Central Pacific force as the Fifth Fleet. He selected his chief of staff, Admiral Spruance, to command this force.

Nimitz had encountered considerable opposition from General Marshall and other senior army officers, who believed MacArthur should have overall command of Pacific theater operations. Under-lying their argument was the belief that there should be only one Pacific theater—and it should be under army control. Although Admiral King successfully fought off all attempts to make the navy secondary in importance to the army, army criticism of the loose organization of Nimitz's command led Nimitz to reorganize his headquarters in September 1943. A joint CINCPAC staff divided into four sections—Plans, Operations, Logistics, and Intelligence—was created. Two of the staff sections were commanded by army officers.

Spruance, as Fifth Fleet commander, had operational command of the theater's combat forces. The fleet had three components: the assault force commanded by Turner, the fast carriers commanded by RAdm. Charles A. Pownall, and shore-based aircraft under RAdm. John E. Hoover. Lieutenant General Robert C. Richardson Jr. was commander of Army Forces, Central Pacific. He was re-sponsible for training and supplying all army ground and air units in Nimitz's theater. Central planning for and control of army units in combat fell to either Nimitz's staff or the amphibious corps commander.

Throughout the war the army was dissatisfied with the second-ary role assigned to it. Nor were army commanders the only ones dissatisfied with Nimitz's reorganization. The senior Marine Corps officer, Maj. Gen. Holland Smith, complained throughout 1944 about the interference of naval commanders, particularly Admiral Turner, in ground operations. Admiral Nimitz preferred to use Marine Corps units in his offensive operations, but he did employ army divisions as a backup in most campaigns. This, cou-pled with differences of command philosophy and offensive strat-egies, resulted at times in open conflict between marine and army commanders.

Even within the navy there was dissatisfaction with Nimitz's choice of personnel to command air operations. Vice Admiral John H. Towers was the most vociferous critic of placing nonaviators in command of carrier task forces. Despite all these criticisms, Nimitz held to his reorganization and gave unstinting support to the offi-cers he appointed. The subsequent Central Pacific offensive vindi-cated his choices.

*   *   *

In mid-1943, Nimitz began to receive a steady flow of new ships. The most important were the new fast *Essex*-class carriers. These were 28,000-ton ships bristling with antiaircraft guns ranging in size from 20mm to 5-inches, and carrying the latest radar. Each carried almost a hundred aircraft. By October, Nimitz had ten of these fast carriers, as well as seven 11,000-ton *Independence*-class escort carriers. He also had two more new battleships, eight heavy and four light cruisers, and sixty-six destroyers—of which twenty were in the 2,100-ton class.

The new carriers featured the latest aircraft: Grumman F6F Hellcat and Chance-Vought F4U Corsair fighters, Curtiss SB2C Helldiver dive-bombers, and Grumman TBF Avenger torpedo bombers—each better than any comparable Japanese aircraft. In addition, the army's Seventh Air Force, headquartered in Hawaii, had a growing fleet of long-range B-24 heavy bombers. The navy also finally acquired reliable torpedoes when, after many tests, a faulty firing pin was discovered to be the cause of misfirings. All ships were supplied with proximity fuses for antiaircraft defense. These enabled a better defensive shield to be raised against attacking aircraft.

By the fall of 1943, Nimitz, handicapped only by a shortage of long-range transports and cargo vessels, was prepared to carry out the modified Orange Plan.

Churchill and Roosevelt had approved Nimitz's plan at the Trident meeting in New York in May 1943. With the North African campaign successfully completed, much of the discussion had focused on the future use of men and materiel against the Axis. The major disagreement was between British and American planners over where to open Stalin's long-sought "second front." Churchill wanted to strike at what he called Europe's soft underbelly—Sicily and Italy—partially in hopes of delaying a cross-channel invasion. In such an atmosphere, Admiral King's pleas for the diversion of significant resources to the Pacific had little chance of being adopted. Nevertheless, more support was promised, and the navy's proposal for the seizure of bases in the Gilbert Islands, code-named Galvanic, was approved as a preliminary to moving into the Marshall and Caroline Islands.

MacArthur argued against the entire Orange concept both before and after its approval. He believed that the plan called for amphibious frontal attacks against a series of islands of questionable value supported solely by carrier-based planes. He believed that more men and materiel should be entrusted to him to speed up the advance along the north coast of New Guinea and ultimately to the Philippines. The debate between MacArthur and the navy over Pacific strategy became so heated that General Marshall flew to Australia after the Teheran conference to confer with the SWPA commander. Marshall explained once again the reasons behind approval for the Central Pacific offensive, but mollified MacArthur by promising continued support for his Southwest Pacific operations. Although the argument persisted, Nimitz prepared to undertake the first major offensive in the Central Pacific, beginning planning for the Gilberts operation even before the New Georgia campaign was completed.

There was one area of operations that, although not a top priority, had to be cleared before any other major offensives could be launched in the Central Pacific: the Aleutians. The Japanese occupation of Kiska and Attu, although never a serious threat to mainland Alaska, had caused considerable concern in the United States. That concern was kept alive by fanciful media accounts of the potential for invasion of the United States from the north. Therefore, throughout 1942, there was a continual flow of men and materiel to Alaska.

The command situation in the Aleutians was complicated by the fact that naval units answered to Nimitz, whereas army forces were controlled by Lt. Gen. John L. DeWitt, head of the Western Defense Command. Unlike the South Pacific, where MacArthur and Halsey cooperated well in the subjugation of the Solomons, there was a personality conflict in Alaska. Rear Admiral Theobald, commander of the North Pacific Area, and Maj. Gen. Simon B. Buckner Jr., head of the Alaskan Defense Command, did not like each other. Buckner, whose Eleventh Air Force was the major air weapon in the theater, did not believe that Theobald was active enough in bombarding the Japanese-held islands or in intercepting Japanese transports. Theobald, on the other hand, did not want to risk his small fleet in what he considered useless operations. Despite the distances involved and the foul arctic weather, naval units had struck at both Kiska and Attu with little effect. Under pressure from Washington, Nimitz removed Theobald from command—despite arguments raised in his favor. In January 1943 Admiral Kinkaid took command of the North Pacific Area, bringing an end to the interservice quarrels.

Operations of all kinds in the Aleutians were conducted in some of the world's worst weather. Temperatures during most of the year were normally in the subzero range. Storms were a constant menace and the high winds and fog made flying particularly hazardous. Despite these problems, the Eleventh Air Force continually attacked Japanese installations on both islands. Sometimes the attackers were lucky, as they were on 5 January 1943, when they sank two large transports. But normally it was difficult to assess bomb damage. Despite continuing foul weather, the number of air strikes increased in February. Kinkaid also ordered RAdm. Charles H. McMorris, the new commander of TG 16.6, to establish antishipping patrols to halt Japanese attempts to reinforce the garrisons.

American intelligence officers considered Kiska to be the main objective because there were more than twice the number of troops there than on Attu. Admiral Hosogaya had also begun building an airfield there. But Kinkaid, commanding TF 16, did not have enough shipping to transport the troops believed necessary to take Kiska. He therefore decided to retake Attu first. The invasion was set for 7 May 1943. In preparation, a small army force was landed on Amchitka, only ninety miles east of Kiska and between that island and Attu. This maneuver convinced VAdm. Shiro Kawase, commanding the North Area Force at Paramushir, that the Japanese must either reinforce their Aleutian garrisons or abandon them. The Japanese high command belatedly decided to keep its foothold in the western Aleutians and to heed Admiral Hosogaya's pleas for more men and supplies. On 22 March a U.S. Navy flotilla of two heavy and two light cruisers and four destroyers intercepted a convoy off the Komandorskiye Islands. In a three-hour surface battle fought at distances of up to eight miles, the outgunned American force prevented the Japanese from landing the much needed reinforcements. Admiral Hosogaya inexplicably broke off the action and retired, thus abandoning the twenty-five hundred men on Attu.

Rear Admiral Francis W. Rockwell was appointed to head the

Amphibious Force Northern Pacific with a joint army and navy staff whose major combat component was the 7th Infantry Division. The 7th, commanded by Maj. Gen. Albert E. Brown, left San Francisco in late April 1943 and reached its rendezvous point, Cold Harbor, in early May. It was greeted with extremely bad weather— hundred-knot winds, heavy seas, and bad fog. Admiral Nimitz had allocated two battleships, the *Idaho* and *Nevada,* and the escort carrier *Nassau* for the operation. They joined McMorris's augmented force of three heavy and three light cruisers and nineteen destroyers, which gave the Americans overwhelming naval superiority.

The landings were postponed because of the bad weather but were finally made on 11 May after heavy naval and air bombardment on the thirty-five-mile-long by fifteen-mile-wide island. Because of the high mountains and muskeg valleys, one landing was made west of the main Japanese installation at Holtz Bay and another to the south at Massacre Bay.

An advance reconnaissance group of four hundred men landed at a selected spot in the north. They became lost and never reported back on the trail conditions leading to the bay. Finally, Col. Frank L. Culin, commander of the 32d Infantry Regiment, pioneered the way directly to the bay. By that evening more than fifteen hundred men were ashore. The Japanese made no attempt to block them. The southern landings, delayed at first because of fog, began in the afternoon. By the end of the day, two thousand troops from the 17th Infantry Regiment had landed on the two designated beaches.

Japanese Imperial Headquarters in Tokyo reacted too late to the stepped up U.S. activity in the Aleutians. Admiral Koga moved a significant part of the Combined Fleet from Truk to the home islands, but by the time it arrived, it was already too late to help Col. Yasuyo Yamazaki and his men on Attu. Realizing his situation, he had withdrawn from the beaches and set up strong defensive positions in the valley connecting Holtz and Massacre Bays.

Even with close air and naval gunfire support, the 17th Infantry made little headway against these defenses. During the first two days the regiment advanced only four thousand yards. The slowness of the advance and General Brown's negative attitude led Kinkaid to relieve him, and on 16 May Brig. Gen. Eugene M. Landrum took over the division. As with so many forced changes of command, this had little to do with ultimate victory. That was more directly related to the Americans' nearly five to one superiority in manpower and total air assets.

On 15 May, Colonel Culin's troops broke through to Holtz Bay and the lost pathfinder group finally caught up with the main elements. However, the Japanese in the south fought a desperate rearguard action before being forced onto a fishhook-shaped ridge commanding the entrance to Chichagof Harbor. Yamazaki, despairing of continuing the defense, prepared his remaining troops for a massive banzai charge. He led them down from the hills at approximately 0330 on 29 May. The Japanese assault broke through the 17th's lines, overran two command posts, and reached the hospital area before it was halted. Hundreds of defeated Japanese soldiers then committed suicide.

The conquest of Attu was complete, although with heavy cost to the 7th Division, which suffered six hundred killed. The Japanese lost the entire garrison; only twenty-eight prisoners were taken.

By July enough transports were available to launch the long-delayed assault on Kiska Island. Major General Charles H. Corlett, the 7th Division's new commander, would have, in addition to his unit, a variety of attached and service units, giving him a total of more than thirty-four thousand troops. His counterpart on Kiska had only fifty-one hundred men and, as on Attu, the Japanese had no air cover. The high command in Tokyo decided against sending any of Koga's capital ships to the Aleutians, and Admiral Kawase was expressly ordered *not* to seek an engagement in Aleutian waters.

The Japanese on Kiska were pounded almost daily by Eleventh Air Force planes guided through the fog by radar. To Kawase and his superiors, the only logical solution was to evacuate the garrison. At first he sent in big I-class submarines to run the American blockade. However, between 26 May and 21 June, seven of the thirteen submarines making the hazardous run were sunk. Kawase then called off the operation and planned a bold evacuation. Evading the American blockade under cover of the almost continuous fog, he brought two cruisers and six destroyers into Kiska Harbor on 28 July 1943. In less than an hour, the entire garrison was boarded. Three days later they were in Paramushir.

One reason for the Japanese success in running the blockade was the phantom battle fought by American naval units south of Kiska. They were reacting to radar contacts that indicated a large enemy naval force was in the area. After firing for some time at these targets it was discovered that the radar signals were faulty.

Before leaving Kiska the Japanese set fire to or blew up all of their installations. American photo reconnaissance credited this destruction to continued bombing by the Eleventh Air Force. Corlett and other high-level observers still believed the Japanese were present in force. Even when the landings on the western side of the island were unopposed, they concluded that the Japanese had retired into the interior. Not until 22 August did they finally realize that the Japanese had managed to rescue the entire garrison. There was thus no reason for the embarrassment that followed this discovery. Given the weather conditions and the naval blockade, the logical conclusion was that a large Japanese force was present and was as committed to defending the island as its Attu counterpart had been.

With the successful conclusion of the Aleutian operation, and later the securing of the central Solomons, Nimitz could concentrate on beginning the much delayed modified Orange Plan. The most exposed portion of the Japanese defense ring was the Gilbert Islands, and Nimitz's headquarters decided even before the Trident meeting to seize several islands for bases there. Looking toward that end, men of the 5th Marine Defense Battalion in early October 1942 occupied Funafuti Atoll in the Ellice Islands, seven hundred miles southeast of Tarawa. Construction battalions subsequently built an airfield there capable of handling bombers. By the time the Japanese discovered it in April 1943, the Americans had a functioning base from which land-based bombers could strike Tarawa, the main target in the Gilberts.

From the beginning, navy planners viewed Tarawa as the primary objective there. Nauru had at first been considered as a secondary target, but the belief that it would take a very large force to overcome the considerable Japanese garrison there forced the cancellation of that operation. Instead, Makin—located about a hundred miles northwest of Tarawa—was chosen because the small Japanese force there could be overcome without significantly affecting the main effort on Tarawa.

Contrary to widespread belief, the Japanese had done little before the war to develop the military potential of their Central Pacific bases. Most of that work had been concentrated on Truk and at Kwajalein. Even after Pearl Harbor, little was done to improve the islands' defenses. But the ill-conceived October 1942 raid carried out by Lt. Col. Evans F. Carlson's marine Raiders on Butaritari Island at Makin alerted the Japanese to the need to improve the defenses of their other island possessions. By mid-1943 they had constructed three airfields on Roi, one on Kwajalein, and others at Mili, Maloelap, and Wotje—all islands in the Marshalls chain. Despite the growing threat of American submarines, the Japanese also increased the garrisons on the main islands and provided supplies needed to construct coastal defense emplacements, radio facilities, and, in some cases, advanced radar stations. The Japanese devoted similar attention to the Gilberts. They built an airfield on Nauru and a seaplane base at Makin, and—after January 1943—had a functioning airstrip on Betio, the main island in the Tarawa group. The four-thousand-foot runway on Betio took up most of the available space on the tiny island, which was only thirty-eight hundred yards long and five hundred yards wide.

Rear Admiral Keiji Shibasaki commanded a force of 4,836 men on Tarawa that included approximately 1,500 men from the elite 7th Naval Special Landing Force and 3d Special Base Force. His combat troops, augmented by construction units made up largely of Koreans, built what he considered to be an impregnable defense that could not be broken in a thousand years.

Betio is only one island of the many comprising Tarawa atoll, but it is the one nearest the break in the reef guarding the entrance to the lagoon. The axis of the 350-acre island is generally east to west, with the widest part in the east. It is surrounded by reefs located eight hundred to a thousand yards offshore. The Japanese placed boat obstacles made of logs just off the beaches and covered the approach lanes thus created with artillery. Admiral Shibasaki emplaced fourteen coastal defense guns ranging in size from five and one-half to eight inches on the corners of the island and had twenty-five 37mm and 75mm field guns in coconut-log and concrete pillboxes. These later were backed by dug-in tanks. The Japanese also had huge, reinforced concrete bunkers scattered around the airfield. These served both as command posts and defensive bastions. Covered with sand, they were difficult to detect and proved impervious to naval gunfire and air attacks. The only part of the Japanese defense plan not completed was the mining of the lagoon.

Makin, in contrast, was relatively unprepared. The main island and the target for invasion there was Butaritari, a T-shaped island much larger than Tarawa. It is eleven miles long and about three miles across at its western end. However, most of the island is only some four hundred yards in width. The Japanese built no complex defenses there; the most important obstacles were two tank traps built just east of the main settlement on the north side of the island. The Japanese had approximately 800 men on Makin commanded by a senior lieutenant. Of this number, 275 were construction workers; only 400 belonged to the Special Landing Force or the Pioneers.

Admiral Turner was responsible for seizing both atolls. He divided the attackers into two amphibious groups—the northern and the southern attack forces. Command of the Southern Force, responsible for taking Tarawa, was given to RAdm. Harry Hill. Turner himself—with four battleships, four cruisers, thirteen destroyers, and two large and three escort carriers—also directly controlled the Northern Force. He elected to do this because there was a chance that the Japanese would send part of their fleet to aid in the defense of the islands. Remaining in the north would leave him in a better position to intercept them.

The task of taking Tarawa was assigned to the veteran 2d Marine Division, commanded by Maj. Gen. Julian C. Smith. The Makin operation was given to the army's 165th Infantry Regiment, reinforced by a battalion from the 105th Infantry Regiment, both part of the 27th Division. Its commander was Maj. Gen. Ralph C. Smith. The clash of personalities at the highest level led to the senior Marine Corps commander in the Pacific, Maj. Gen. Holland Smith, whose staff largely planned the operation, being excluded from command of any part of the operation. Instead, he went along as an observer on Turner's flagship, the battleship *Pennsylvania*.

At 0640 on 22 November, the three battleships of Turner's Northern Force began the systematic bombardment of the western section of Butaritari. They were joined immediately by fire from the cruisers and destroyers. Then planes from the carriers worked over Red Beach, where the 27th Division men were to land. The first waves of the lst and 3d Battalions of the 165th Infantry were soon on shore. By noon the western area was secure and supplies were piling up on the beaches. The 2d Battalion landed just before 1100 on the lagoon side, near the middle of the island. The few Japanese defenders, with the exception of snipers, made a stand at each of the tank traps but, outnumbered ten to one, they were unable to stop the army battalions. Realizing this, Ralph Smith chose not to rush the operation. By keeping to the timetable agreed upon in the planning sessions, he in all probability saved many lives. He declared the island secure at 1030 on 23 November, and radioed Turner, "Makin taken." American casualties were very low: only 64 killed and 150 wounded, largely by sniper fire.

The capture of Makin was relatively unimportant in the unfolding strategy of the Pacific war. Yet it became a sore point because of events totally unconnected with the army's performance. General Holland Smith, sent by Turner to observe the operation on the second day, proceeded to criticize directly and indirectly Ralph Smith's handling of it. Although unfair and without merit, his remarks widened the gulf between the services.

Later Holland Smith and some senior naval officers blamed the army for the sinking of the *Liscombe Bay,* although it happened twenty-four hours after Ralph Smith declared an end to hostilities on Makin. The tragedy occurred at dawn on the twenty-fourth, when the Japanese submarine I-175 torpedoed the escort carrier twenty miles southwest of Butaritari. Despite heroic rescue efforts, 644 men drowned, ten times the number of 27th Division men killed in action.

The more important assault on Tarawa was conducted at the same time as the Makin operation. The plan called for two 2d Marine Division regiments to land on the north (lagoon) side of the island after a suitable period of naval and air bombardment. The marines would land on three beaches designated from west to east as Red 1, Red 2, and Red 3. The dividing line between Red 2 and 3 was a long pier, which, aside from the airfield, was the most noticeable man-made feature on the island. The assault troops in the first wave were the 3d Battalion, 2d Marines on Red 1; the 2d Battalion, 2d

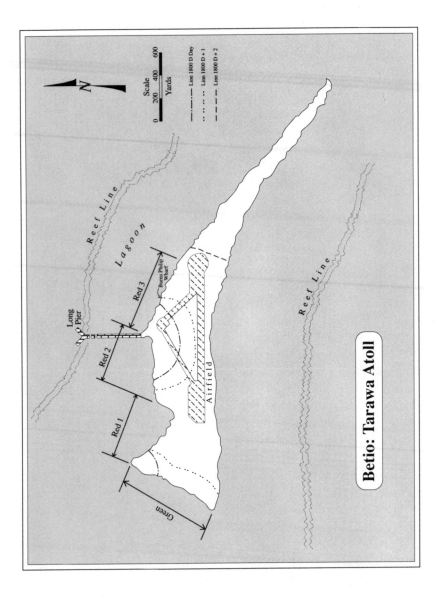

Betio: Tarawa Atoll

Marines on Red 2; and the 2d Battalion, 8th Marines on Red 3. They would be carried to the beaches aboard a hundred LVT-2 amphibious tractors.

During the planning sessions in Hawaii, Holland Smith had fully justified his nickname "Howlin' Mad" with his fight for these amtracs. The navy argued that they were not needed, that the assault could be made with ship's boats. If that had been the case, given the difficult tides and treacherous reefs, it is doubtful if the marines could have effected a landing. As events proved, even this number of LVTs was too few for the task.

One suggestion put forward by army officers during the planning session was ignored. They recommended seizing lightly held Bairiki Island east of Betio and emplacing howitzers there. They argued that the howitzers' high-angle fire would be more accurate than naval gunfire. Later analysis of the battle showed the wisdom of this suggestion. But naval and marine planners overestimated the effects of naval gunfire and aerial bombardment and underestimated the Japanese will to fight to the last man. Tarawa would not be the last Central Pacific island that would be assaulted with too few men and inadequate preinvasion bombardment.

At dawn on 20 November two battleships and four cruisers began pounding the small island. After forty-five minutes, the shelling lifted and planes from three aircraft carriers struck at targets of opportunity for ten minutes. The ships resumed their bombardment for another eighty minutes, lifting fires just before the marines landed. Two destroyers led the way into the lagoon followed by the amtracs carrying the assault troops. Finally, at 0915, after various problems that caused H hour to be postponed had been resolved, the first LVTs touched the beach.

Unfortunately, the delay allowed the Japanese time to shift men from the interior to the beach areas. The Japanese at Red 1 waited until the 3d Battalion was within a hundred yards of shore before opening up with artillery of all kinds. Many LVTs were knocked out before they could land their troops. At Red 2, heavy fire from the coconut-log emplacements pinned the marines down on the beach. Colonel David M. Shoup, commanding the landing force, had to establish his command post just out of the water near the long pier. The 2d Battalion, 8th Marines, landing at the east end of the pier, was not heavily opposed at first, but the Japanese soon shifted men there who kept the marines pinned down at the waterline.

The riflemen were alone—the division artillery did not land until that evening, and the light tanks that came in with the fifth wave were soon knocked out. Colonel Shoup called for more naval and aerial support and committed his reserve, the 1st Battalion, 2d Marines. General Julian Smith, responding to Shoup's urgent request, sent in half the division reserve—the 3d Battalion, 8th Marines— just before noon. The tide was out, causing the reserve force to wade the last 700 yards. By that time most of the amtracs had been knocked out, and Julian Smith requested that the corps reserve be released to support the five thousand marines clinging to the beaches. Despite sustaining losses of more than fifteen hundred killed or wounded, the marines, using flamethrowers and TNT, had managed by evening to slightly expand their holdings in two areas. In the center they held a strip 700 yards long by about 300 yards deep and at the end of Red 1 another lodgment 150 yards long by 500 yards deep.

General Smith sent in the rest of the division reserve the next day. No landing craft could float over the reef, so the men of the 1st Battalion, 8th Marines had to wade ashore, taking very heavy casualties. During the morning, whenever possible, planes from the carriers would support the marine attacks on strong points, but the closeness of the fighting meant that pilots could not effectively strafe the areas. In the early afternoon the tide came in, and with it the corps reserve—the 6th Marines—which began landing at Green Beach at the extreme west end of the island. At the same time, men of the 2d Marines reached the southwest part of the island. Light tanks landed at Red 2 and joined the riflemen and artillery in reducing the pillboxes and bunkers. By 1600 the Japanese defenders had been split into two groups, with the central area around the pier firmly controlled by the marines. By the time that Col. "Red Mike" Edson went ashore that evening to take command, the operation was clearly a success. Earlier fears that the issue was in doubt had been laid to rest.

By the evening of the third day, the marines had cleared most of the southern section of the island. At the western end, only the area around the big bombproof structure remained in Japanese hands.

The advance continued toward the east during the day with a noticeable slackening of enemy resistance. That evening, elements of the 6th Marines repulsed three counterattacks. The Japanese lost more than three hundred men in these futile charges.

The entrenched Japanese continued to inflict casualties on the twenty-third, but by midafternoon the 3d Battalion, 6th Marines had reached the eastern end of the island. At about the same time, another team of two battalions combined to reduce the still-strong defenses behind Red 1. The destruction of these interlocking positions around the large concrete bunker spelled the end of organized Japanese resistance on the island. Sporadic fighting continued during the day as lone Japanese were hunted down. Only 146 men surrendered, and all but 17 were Koreans. Almost the entire Japanese garrison, a total of 4,690 men, was killed.

The press covered the Tarawa operation more thoroughly than any previous campaign. The reports of 980 marines and 29 sailors killed in just seventy hours, coupled with pictures of dead marines in the surf, shocked the nation. There was immediate criticism of the planning and execution of the affair, leading to a debate that continued long after the war. Critics of the Tarawa operation, including Holland Smith, point to the fact that the island proved later to be unimportant as the action moved westward. The airfield's runway was too short to handle long-range bombers, and the continued superiority of the Fifth Fleet made the need for land-based bombers secondary.

But even if taking Tarawa was strategically unnecessary, the lessons learned there were invaluable. The LVTs were a huge success, and they would be necessary in greater numbers for future landings. Problems with communications equipment that prevented higher commanders from knowing the onshore situation would be largely rectified later by better equipment, and an amphibious command ship packed with communications gear was made available for the assault on the Marshall Islands. Training programs quickly incorporated the lessons of Tarawa, with particular attention devoted to small-unit operations, the use of flamethrowers, and tank-infantry cooperation. The preinvasion bombardment, however intense, was too short, and the navy promised longer, more sustained preparations in the future. At Tarawa, the problem was partially due to the man-made and natural defenses of the Japanese held islands, but subsequent failures to silence defenders with naval gunfire and aerial bombardment were due as much to misplaced belief in the efficacy of the support as to the strength of the defenses. Although the preparations for amphibious landings were better after Tarawa—at least from the rifleman's point of view—they still needed improvement.

An intangible but nevertheless important result of the Gilberts operation was the fact that the Americans had succeeded in breaching the eastern defensive perimeter of the recently expanded Japanese empire. The Japanese high command surely realized after Tarawa fell the vulnerability of all its Pacific island possessions.

The next objective in Admiral Nimitz's plan was the Marshall Islands, the possession of which would advance American air support more than five hundred miles from Tarawa into the heart of Japan's oceanic empire. The main target was Kwajalein, the world's largest coral atoll, composed of more than ninety islands. The most important of these were seventy-mile-long Kwajalein Island and, forty miles to the north, the twin islands of Roi and Namur. Capture of these was once again the responsibility of Admiral Turner, who had the army's 7th Infantry Division and the yet untried 4th Marine Division as assault elements.

Code-named Flintlock, landings on these islands were scheduled for 1 February 1944. The marines, commanded by Maj. Gen. Harry Schmidt, would assault the northern islands while General Corlett's army units were assigned to capture Kwajalein Island. Admiral Turner chose to command the Southern Attack Force, and he appointed RAdm. Richard L. Conolly, a veteran of the Sicilian landings, to command the Northern Attack Force. Holland Smith's headquarters again was deeply involved in the planning, but he had little to do with the success of the operation. General Corlett made it clear from the outset that he expected no interference from Smith once the 7th Division landed on Kwajalein.

Before the main invasion began, a battalion from the 27th Division's 106th Infantry Regiment landed without opposition on Majuro Island south of Kwajalein. Majuro was garrisoned immediately and its large lagoon soon became a major assembly point for dozens of Allied ships. The airstrip at Dalop was soon functioning and planes from there joined in the attack on neighboring islands. Rear Admiral Hoover's planes flew a number of softening-up missions from distant bases against islands in the southeast Marshalls. B-24s based at Canton Island and Funafuti Atoll flew the longest one-way missions of the war, over fifteen hundred miles, to strike at Jaluit, Maloelap, and Kwajalein. Despite these large-scale raids by the Seventh Air Force, the Americans still did not control the air over Kwajalein. The Japanese had an estimated 150 planes there, mostly at Roi. Then, on 29 January, TF 58, the fast carrier force commanded by RAdm. Marc Mitscher, struck. The task force was divided into four task groups, each organized around a large carrier. Rear Admiral John W. Reeves's *Enterprise* group pounded Roi-Namur and effectively destroyed all Japanese aircraft there. Rear Admiral Alfred Montgomery's *Essex* group and RAdm. Forrest P. Sherman's *Bunker Hill* group struck repeatedly at Kwajalein's installations. Rear Admiral Samuel P. Ginder's *Saratoga* group hit Wotje, and then pulverized Engebi islet far to the north. By D day, the Japanese defenders on the targeted islands had no air cover, and Admiral Koga at Truk, seemingly caught unaware, was in no position to provide surface ships to aid in their defense.

On 31 January, the Northern Force, which included Admiral Conolly's bombardment group of older battleships and cruisers, shelled the four smaller islands flanking Roi-Namur before three battalions from the 25th Marines landed. Very shortly, marine howitzers were sited on these islands, and by late afternoon they joined the naval guns saturating Roi-Namur. Unlike at Tarawa, where the planners had disdained such support, the plunging fire from the howitzers did tremendous damage to installations and personnel.

Early the next morning, men of the 23d and 24th Marines landed on the southern beaches of both islands. The dazed defenders on Roi fell back, and by 1600 the marines had reached the north side of the island. Within another two hours it was declared secure. The 24th Marines on Namur encountered heavier resistance and had not reached the north side by evening. The heaviest casualties sustained during the day occurred when a huge storage blockhouse blew up, killing a number of marines. The Japanese launched several attacks in the western sector during the night, but all were futile. By the afternoon of 2 February, Namur was also secure—but not until most of the thirty-five hundred Japanese garrisoned there had been killed. The next day debris was cleared from the airfield, and Admiral Hoover's planes began using it.

Meanwhile, on 30 January, the Southern Force began occupying twenty-seven islets. The most important of these—Gea, Enubuj, and Nini—were located only a few miles from Kwajalein. Opposition was slight, and by 1 February most of the 7th Division's artillery, as well as twelve 155mm howitzers from corps, was registered on Kwajalein. The preinvasion bombardment group for Kwajalein included seven battleships, and air strikes were made by planes from three escort carriers. This massive force raked the island over and over in the days preceding the landing. The Japanese commander of the Marshall Islands, RAdm. Monzo Akiyama, had more than four thousand men on the boomerang-shaped island, but the defenses were not as well prepared as they had been on Betio. The preinvasion bombardment destroyed many of his positions.

The first wave, carrying the 7th Division's 184th and 32d Infantry Regiments, landed at the extreme western end of the island without incident. Within an hour tanks joined them ashore, and the infantry quickly proceeded to cooperate with them in reducing enemy strong points. The army units moved methodically, bringing maximum firepower to bear on each enemy position. By the end of the day, the regiments had reached their goals—taking few casualties in the process.

The following day they had moved halfway up the island and Corlett, despite proddings from Holland Smith, kept to his planned timetable. The heaviest fighting occurred on 3 February when units reached the blockhouse area in the north. Heavy bombardment reduced most of these positions to rubble, but even this provided the enemy with good defensive positions. The Japanese in turn launched a series of night attacks that were beaten off. On the fourth, after heavy naval gunfire and artillery bombardment, the infantry, aided by tanks, advanced against the small area left to the Japanese. By 1530 the advance units reached the northern tip of the island. The following days were devoted to mopping up positions that had been bypassed earlier. At the same time, the 17th Infantry and parts of the 184th occupied twenty other islets in the atoll.

The Kwajalein operation showed how far interservice cooperation had progressed since the debacle in the Gilberts. Even Holland Smith agreed that all branches performed satisfactorily. The Japanese lost more than 7,800 men, whereas U.S. forces suffered a relatively low 1,954 casualties, including 372 men killed. This was in stark contrast to the costly Tarawa campaign.

There was never any question about the overall importance of the Kwajalein operation. As a result of the four-day action Nimitz had gained an excellent harbor that could be used as a forward staging area for further advances. The bomber field on Roi was soon operative, and another airfield was later completed on Kwajalein. The growing strength of U.S. naval, air, and ground forces made it clear that however desperate a defense the Japanese mounted on any of the Central Pacific islands, they could expect little help from their navy—and their air units later proved to be no match either in numbers or quality to those of the Americans.

The relative ease with which Kwajalein was taken led Admiral Spruance to suggest that the date for the Eniwetok assault be moved up. Nimitz concurred.

The 22d Marines and the 27th Division's 106th Infantry were immediately available for the operation. Admiral Hill was given overall command, and he, Maj. Gen. Thomas E. Watson, the proposed ground commander, and Admiral Turner met aboard Turner's flagship several times to put the finishing touches to the plans formulated by their staffs. The operation, code-named Catchpole, was rescheduled to begin on 18 February. The 22d Marines would land on Engebi, the most important and believed to be the most heavily defended island in the large, circular atoll. The 106th would simultaneously attack the southern island of Eniwetok. Finally, Parry, the other major island in the Eniwetok group, would be occupied. Unlike earlier operations, General Watson would assume direct control of land operations as soon as the troops hit the beach. This had been a major point of contention between the navy and ground-force commanders, particularly in operations in which Turner was the amphibious force commander. He had insisted on trying to run the entire operation from aboard ship.

Before the attack on Eniwetok could safely begin, it was believed that airpower at the main Japanese base on Truk, only 650 miles away, had to be dealt with. Admiral Spruance decided on a full-scale air and naval attack on the so-called Gibraltar of the Pacific as a precautionary measure. Truk was a drowned mountain range with a coral ring providing a huge lagoon area that protected the islands and fleet anchorages from naval gunfire. The Americans' perception of Truk as a major stumbling block to Central Pacific expansion led to high-level discussions concerning the possibility of invading the atoll. It was not until March 1944 that Nimitz decided to bypass Truk. As a result of Spruance's and Mitscher's attack on 17–18 February, this decision was the only logical choice.

At the beginning of February the superbattleship *Musashi,* two carriers, six heavy and four light cruisers, twenty destroyers, and a variety of smaller ships were anchored at Truk. Alerted by increasing American air activity, Admiral Koga ordered most of his ships to safety in Palau while he left for Japan on board the *Musashi.* Thus, when the first attack was launched, the American fliers found only two light cruisers, eight destroyers, and a number of smaller ships present in the harbor. The American attack group showed off the might of the Fifth Fleet. Admiral Mitscher commanded three fast carrier groups built around five large carriers. Spruance—with the two new fast battleships, *New Jersey* and *Iowa,* and carrier and cruiser escorts—took up a position to intercept any ships attempting to flee.

The first attack on Truk was made by seventy fighters launched at dawn on 17 February. These destroyed two-thirds of the estimated 360 Japanese planes either in the air or on the ground. The fighters were followed by torpedo and dive-bombers, which targeted the airfields. In the early afternoon Mitscher launched half of his available planes against the remaining ships in the harbor. They destroyed two auxiliary cruisers, one destroyer, two aircraft tenders, six tankers, and seventeen transports. Although most of the capital ships escaped, the sinking of so many transports dealt a severe blow to the Japanese merchant fleet in the Central Pacific. Mitscher continued the attacks on the eighteenth, hitting hangars, ammunition dumps, and service facilities.

Meanwhile Spruance, the task force commander on board the

New Jersey, accompanied RAdm. Willis Lee's battleships as they cruised off the atoll. On the seventeenth the battleships intercepted a few Japanese ships attempting to escape and sank one destroyer and two transports in a short, uneven battle.

The actions of 17–18 February ended Truk's importance to the Japanese. A raid conducted in April simply confirmed this. Admiral Koga had already dispersed the ships of his Combined Fleet, and he later moved his headquarters to Koror in the western Carolines. The Combined Fleet would not come together again until the naval actions off Leyte later in the year. Of more immediate importance to Hill and Watson, the air strikes against Truk meant that the Eniwetok operation could go on without fear of interference from Japanese naval or air units.

The occupation of the main islands at Eniwetok proceeded with few problems. The navy saturated Engebi with a heavy preinvasion bombardment. Two small islands were seized close to Engebi and artillery was emplaced there on D day to provide the marines with more direct and accurate fire support. The 22d Marines landed on two beaches the next day and met little opposition. There were few fixed defenses, and the air and naval attacks had destroyed most of these. Within six hours the island was declared secure. Only sixteen prisoners were taken from a garrison of more than twelve hundred.

The 106th Infantry's landings on the north side of Eniwetok Island were more difficult. The Japanese had fooled American intelligence officers into believing that Eniwetok and Parry were unoccupied. The navy did not deliver a heavy preinvasion bombardment, so the army units encountered heavy fire from a bluff that had been ignored by invasion planners. This defense line was eventually broken and two battalions moved to secure the western part of the island while the rest of the regiment, augmented by a battalion of marines, drove eastward. By the evening of the twentieth the western area was secure, and by midday on the twenty-first troops had reached the island's eastern tip. More than eight hundred Japanese were killed in this action, whereas the army and marines lost only thirty-seven men.

Parry Island, where more than thirteen hundred Japanese were located, proved even more difficult than the other two islands. However, heavy gunfire from three battleships and three cruisers, as well as coordinated attacks by naval air, made the marines' job easier. Tanks were also brought ashore very quickly, and the two marine battalions crossed the island before moving to reduce Japanese resistance to the east and west. Parry was secure by the evening of the twenty-second, but it cost the marines twice the number of men as had been killed on Eniwetok.

By the end of April small detachments of marine and army units had occupied more than twenty more small islands in the Marshalls. The only serious fighting occurred on Ailinglapalop, where the survivors of an aerial attack on their landing craft disputed the landing.

Nimitz's headquarters had earlier opted to bypass four larger islands—Jaluit, Mili, Wotje, and Nauru. Instead, heavy bombers from the Seventh Air Force continuously bombed them. Later, when the B-24s moved on to Kwajalein and Eniwetok, fighters and navy bombers from Makin, Tarawa, and Abemama took over the task of harassing the Japanese garrisons. By midyear they were virtually cut off from outside aid, and the majority of the Japanese troops there were forced to farm and fish just to stay alive. More than one-third of the garrisons died from disease or starvation on these bypassed islands before the war ended.

Combined with the negation of Rabaul and the destruction wrought on Truk, the Marshalls campaign cracked the Japanese outer defense ring. Together, these losses were a visible sign of Japan's growing weakness and caused a major shake-up in the highest levels of command. Admiral Nagano was replaced as chief of the naval staff by the more compliant Shigetaro Shimada. Nagano's counterpart, General Sugiyama, was also removed and his duties assumed by the premier, General Tojo. These changes did little to rectify the situation; the Japanese could respond only with difficulty to later American actions in the Central Pacific.

In contrast, the Americans gained possession of three large harbors, each of which became a major fleet anchorage and staging area for future offensives. The Japanese airfield on Engebi was lengthened and improved, and new, larger airstrips were constructed on Eniwetok and Kwajalein. Another airfield was built at Majuro, and planes from these bases harassed the Japanese on the bypassed atolls. The successful Marshalls operations thus set the stage for the next step in the revived Orange Plan: the conquest of the Mariana Islands.

The metamorphosis of the U.S. Navy from a battered force standing on the defensive to one that could dominate the Pacific is well illustrated by the submarine service. The few operative submarines in the Asiatic and Pacific fleets after Pearl Harbor, as with other branches of the Allied war machine, were forced to retreat before the overwhelming Japanese assaults. Two submarine bases in Australia—one at Brisbane in the east, and one at Freemantle in the west—were established early in 1942. Submarines based in Brisbane were concerned with the area off the coast of Australia and in the Solomon Islands, and later operated in the Bismarck Sea. Those operating from Freemantle patrolled the South China Sea.

The major base for submarine action in the Pacific, however, was Pearl Harbor. In early 1942 Nimitz began receiving a steady supply of fleet boats of the *Tambor* class, and his submarine commanders began to use some boats to operate aggressively in the broad areas of the Central Pacific and even in the waters close to Japan. Another base was established in the Alaska region, where six boats, mostly obsolete S-class types, operated mainly in a defensive capacity. Before being withdrawn in October 1943 they had sunk only four small ships. Throughout 1942, American submarines in all areas were generally delegated to coastal defense and blockading. The 350 war patrols that year did not cause extreme damage to the Japanese lifeline southward, although the boats sank 180 ships displacing a total of approximately 725,000 tons.

By 1943, RAdm. Charles A. Lockwood in Hawaii and his counterparts, Captains James R. Fife in Brisbane and Ralph W. Christie in Freemantle, had begun to get fleet boats with the most advanced sonar systems as well as improved torpedoes. Just as important was the Allies' code-breaking success, which gave senior commanders vital information on Japanese convoy and troop movements, allowing them to direct attacks on known targets. This became even more important when, beginning in October, the Americans began employing the wolf pack tactics so successful for the Germans in the Atlantic war. However, most of the patrols in 1943 were made by single boats assigned to specific cruising sectors, with crews staying out for thirty to fifty days. The Freemantle command sent out a maximum of six boats a month, and during 1943 these claimed 105 ships displacing over 600,000 tons. An equal number of boats from Brisbane claimed 61 ships totaling 350,000 tons. The biggest score was racked up by boats operating from Pearl Harbor. More than twenty-five boats each month cleared the harbor, and these claimed a total of 277 ships with a combined total of 1,890,000 tons. All this was accomplished with the loss of only twelve boats in all operational areas.

The examination of Japanese high command archives after the war indicated that these claims were inflated in some cases by 100 percent. Even if one accepts the lower Japanese figure, however, the "silent service" struck a heavy blow to the Japanese supply lines. At the beginning of 1943 Japan had 5.2 million tons of shipping, excluding tankers. By the end of the year this had fallen to 4.1 million tons. Another telling statistic is that in 1942 Japan imported 19.4 million tons of bulk commodities. The following year that total was only 16.4 million tons.

As Japan's empire shrank in size in 1944, the number and efficiency of American submarine attacks increased so that not only were supplies absolutely vital to Japanese industry reduced to a trickle, but it also became virtually impossible to move men and equipment to counter American attacks in the Philippines and the Marianas. The submarines thus played an important role in isolating Japanese garrisons and forcing their commanders into making do with inferior numbers of men and equipment against ever-increasing Allied might.

Gen. George C. Marshall,
U.S. Army chief of staff.

Adm. Ernest J. King, chief
of naval operations.

Gen. Douglas MacArthur, commander, Southwest Pacific Area.

Lt. Gen. Richard K. Sutherland, MacArthur's chief of staff and later deputy commander of the Southwest Pacific Area.

Gen. Sir Thomas A. Blamey, the Australian who served as MacArthur's ground forces commander in the Southwest Pacific theater.

Lt. Gen. George C. Kenney, MacArthur's air commander in the Southwest Pacific theater.

Lt. Gen. Robert L. Eichelberger, I Corps commander on New Guinea and Eighth Army commander in the Philippines.

Lt. Gen. Walter Krueger, commander, Sixth Army.

Lt. Gen. John R. Hodge, commander of the Americal Division on Bougainville and XXIV Corps in the Philippines.

Maj. Gen. Robert S. Beightler, commander of the 37th Division on New Georgia, Bougainville, and in the Philippines.

Maj. Gen. Oscar W. Griswold (*center*), commander of XIV Corps on New Georgia and in the Philippines, confers with Admiral Halsey (*left*).

Adm. Chester W. Nimitz, commander of the Pacific Ocean Areas, which included the North, Central, and South Pacific Areas.

Adm. William F. "Bull" Halsey, commander of the South Pacific Area and later the Third Fleet.

Adm. Raymond A. Spruance, who rose to command the powerful Fifth Fleet.

VAdm. Charles A. Lockwood, commander of submarine forces in the Pacific, 1943–45.

Lt. Gen. Holland M. "Howlin' Mad" Smith, who finished the war as commander of Fleet Marine Forces, Pacific.

From left: VAdm. Thomas C. Kinkaid, commander of North Pacific Area forces, briefs RAdm. Francis W. Rockwell, commander of TF 51; Maj. Gen. Charles H. Corlett, commander of the Assault Force; Lt. Gen. Simon B. Buckner Jr., commander of the Alaska Defense Command; and Lt. Gen. John L. DeWitt, commander of the Western Defense Command, on the Sitka operation in August 1943.

From left: Maj. Gen. Roy S. Geiger, commander of III Amphibious Corps, Adm. Spruance, Lt. Gen. Holland Smith, Adm. Nimitz, and Lt. Gen. Alexander A. Vandegrift, the Marine Corps commandant, meet at Geiger's headquarters on Guam in August 1944.

Lt. Gen. Vandegrift (*left*), congratulates Maj. Gen. Allen H. Turnage, commander of the 3d Marine Division, for his part in the retaking of Guam.

Maj. Gen. Ralph C. Smith, commander of the 27th Division on Makin and Saipan.

Lt. Gen. Robert C. Richardson Jr., commander of U.S. Army forces in the Central Pacific Area (*right*) and Maj. Gen. M. Sanderford Jarman, commander of U.S. forces on Saipan, chat with a Chamorro tribesman at an internment camp on the island in July 1944.

Maj. Gen. Andrew D. Bruce, commander of the 77th Division on Guam, in the Philippines, and in the Okinawa campaign.

Gen. Hideki Tojo, Japanese prime minister from 1941 until shortly after the fall of Saipan in the summer of 1944.

Adm. Isoroku Yamamoto, architect of the Pearl Harbor operation and commander of the Combined Fleet from 1941 until his death in the Solomons in 1943.

VAdm. Chuichi Nagumo, commander of the Japanese carrier fleet.

Field Marshal Count His-aichi Terauchi, commander of the Southern Army.

Gen. Tomoyuki Yamashita commanded the Twenty-fifth Army in 1942, earning the nickname "Tiger of Malaya." He later moved to the Philippines, where he commanded the Fourteenth Army in 1944–45.

Lt. Gen. Takeshi Takashina (*right*), commander of Japanese forces in the Marianas, discusses the defenses on Guam during an inspection tour.

Chapter 10

Victory in New Guinea

GENERAL MACARTHUR CONTINUED to be dissatisfied with the amount of support he was receiving, as well as what appeared to him to be unwarranted enthusiasm for Nimitz's Central Pacific plans. To a certain extent his complaints were warranted. His Seventh Fleet was but a shadow compared to the powerful Fifth Fleet. The Seventh had no aircraft carriers, and most of its capital ships were from Admiral Crutchley's Australian contingent of cruisers and destroyers. Of much real concern was the shortage of landing craft with which to carry out the many planned amphibious operations.

A problem of a different kind also bothered MacArthur and his all-American staff in Brisbane: what role General Blamey should play in plans for further conquest in New Guinea and beyond to the Philippines. As ground force commander, Blamey should have been in charge of all field operations. This, however, would have put the more numerous American divisions under his command—something MacArthur did not want. Furthermore, MacArthur, lacking an appreciation of the terrible conditions in New Guinea, had continually been critical of the Australian field commander, particularly of the action around Finschhafen. MacArthur addressed the issue in two ways. The longer-term problem of assuring that American troops would be commanded only by American senior officers was partially solved by the creation of the Alamo Force in the spring of 1943. This organization, which included most of the American troops in the theater, was commanded by Lt. Gen. Walter Krueger, who reported directly to MacArthur. From that time onward General Blamey would command only Australians. In addition, on 3 October 1943, MacArthur ordered Blamey to shake up the Australian senior command in New Guinea by appointing Maj. Gen. Sir Leslie Morshead to command New Guinea Force and Maj. Gen. Frank H. Berryman to take charge of the Australian II Corps.

Unlike Nimitz's mixed staff, MacArthur's senior staff officers were all army. Air, naval, and Australian officers served simply as technical advisers, although Admirals Kinkaid, commander of the Seventh Fleet, and Barbey, the fleet's amphibious force commander, had increasing impact on planning. MacArthur's style was to issue broad directives to his staff. These would outline objectives and the general means to achieve goals. He then allowed his staff and subordinate commanders to fill in the details—subject to his final approval, of course. For example, General Kenney and his able assistant, Maj. Gen. Ennis C. Whitehead, were generally left alone to carry out the air campaign against first Rabaul and later selected targets in New Guinea.

MacArthur's plans for further operations along the New Guinea coast were approved in December 1943 by the Combined Chiefs of Staff during their meeting in Cairo. He had proposed to have the Australians continue to pressure the Japanese inland while U.S. forces staged amphibious assaults on select coastal locations. This would either isolate large numbers of Japanese or force them into long, hazardous retreats as they fell back on their major bases. He also proposed to secure the Vitiaz and Dampier Straits separating New Guinea from New Britain by establishing a secure perimeter in the Cape Gloucester area of western New Britain. The means available to him to carry out these plans were considerable. By the early spring of 1944 he had available seven U.S. Army and one Marine Corps divisions, as well as three separate regiments. Australia provided him with five infantry divisions and several separate brigades, the equivalent of two more divisions. He finally chose the reconstituted 1st Marine Division, whose task would be to secure the lodgment at Cape Gloucester, for the main New Britain operation.

The Japanese had an estimated seventy-five hundred men in western New Britain, but these troops were, for all practical purposes, cut off from the main base at Rabaul, with its more than ninety thousand army and navy personnel. The lack of roads, the terrain, and Allied sea and air superiority meant that the U.S. Army and Marine Corps units could operate without fear that the enemy at Cape Gloucester would receive appreciable reinforcements.

The invasion was postponed until new airfields could be built in New Guinea's Ramu and Markham Valleys in order to supply fighter cover for the assault troops. The initial plan called for a landing at Gasmata on the south coast of New Britain, but in late November this was abandoned for a plan to seize Arawe, which was considerably closer to Cape Gloucester on the island's west end. Planners believed that the harbor there would be useful to support the main landings, and later as a PT boat base after the Cape had been seized. The 1st Cavalry Division's 112th Cavalry Regiment was selected for the Arawe invasion.

After heavy aerial bombardment and support from destroyers, the cavalrymen landed on 15 December. The Japanese, operating from Wewak and Rabaul, mounted heavy air raids against Barbey's invasion fleet, but with little success. By the end of the day, more than two thousand troops were ashore.

The Japanese brought up additional troops on the twenty-sixth, but by then the Americans had established a strong perimeter and were able to beat off all attacks. The Japanese commander soon abandoned his attempts to dislodge the cavalrymen there and instead began to concentrate his forces for an expected larger invasion. Unfortunately, the harbor was too shallow for any but small-draft boats, so it was never used by Allied naval forces.

Between the Arawe and Cape Gloucester landings, General Krueger decided to push Allied control farther up the New Guinea coast. On 2 January 1944, Admiral Barbey's ships convoyed a regiment of the 32d Division to Saidor, where the Japanese had constructed an airfield. The town and the air base were seized without serious opposition. Construction crews followed the assault troops and quickly repaired the damaged airfield.

On 16 January the 126th Infantry Regiment was brought in to

help defend the perimeter. There was initial concern that the Japanese retreating along the coast in front of Maj. Gen. George Wooten's Australians would attempt to retake Saidor. However, the Japanese headquarters at Rabaul decided to write off the entire area and ordered Lt. Gen. Hatazo Adachi to withdraw by an inland route to Madang. Elements of the Australian 7th Division, which had engaged the Japanese for a month in conditions reminiscent of the earlier Kokoda Trail actions and had fought over the Finisterre Range and secured the Markham and Ramu Valleys, reached the coast on 10 February and linked up with the Americans just north of Saidor.

By March, General Adachi had conceded a vast area to the Allied forces, and was forced to concentrate the fourteen thousand men of his Eighteenth Army at Madang and Wewak.

Although the capture of the Huon Peninsula probably made the Cape Gloucester campaign unnecessary, intelligence reports had convinced MacArthur that he could not afford to move toward the Admiralty Islands until both sides of the straits between New Guinea and New Britain were safely under Allied control.

On Christmas Day, after reconnaissance patrols over New Britain found two small beaches north of Silimati Point on Borgen Bay suitable for landings, Admiral Barbey's amphibious units set out with the lst Marine Division. The marines landed there and on the Dampier Strait side of the island, six and one-half miles southwest of Cape Gloucester. For three days prior to the assault, Fifth Air Force units hit Madang, Wewak, and Cape Gloucester, while Air-Sols struck Kavieng and Rabaul. Major General Iwao Matsuda had approximately seventy-five hundred men under his command in western New Britain to counter the Americans. However, fewer than half were combat troops, and all had been operating on short rations. Many suffered from a variety of tropical diseases. He deployed about a thousand men near the landing site, but these were pinned down by the guns of the Australian destroyer escorts and by rocket fire from LCIs.

The first wave of the 7th Marines landed at 0800 on 26 December and had little difficulty overcoming local Japanese resistance. By the end of the day, the marines had more than twelve thousand troops ashore and an additional fifteen hundred on the Dampier side of the island. This smaller contingent was to march overland and assist the main force in taking the airfield, the major objective of the operation. Despite an initial poor response, the Japanese air commander at Rabaul sent twenty Val dive-bombers with fighter cover to attack the landing sites in the afternoon. The new destroyer *Brownson* was repeatedly hit and soon sank. Fortunately for the Americans, bad weather and the escalating attacks on Rabaul by AirSols kept the Japanese from mounting nothing more than a few nuisance raids.

The marines found the terrain and weather to be formidable foes. Although not as deadly as the Japanese, it was nevertheless something for which their training had not prepared them. The terrain around the landing beaches was generally swampy, and the only way supplies could be moved forward was by amphibious tractors. The problem was compounded when, on 29 December, a monsoon storm hit western New Britain. As much as fifteen inches of rain fell in one day. Although the weather kept the Japanese planes grounded, it made the marines' task doubly difficult. Nevertheless, the marines took the airfield on the thirtieth and overran Cape Gloucester the following day.

Just as at Cape Torokina on Bougainville, it was necessary to expand the perimeter in order to make the lodgment more defensible. General Matsuda had entrenched his still considerable force on the western side of Borgen Bay in positions anchored by two fortified hills. It took the 5th and 7th Marines almost two weeks to regroup and move through the swampy jungle and kunai grass to get in position to attack the most important objective, Hill 660.

The attack was contained by the Japanese and by 13 January the marines had been pushed back until they controlled only the south slope, which was partially protected by ravines. Despite the terrain and continuing rain, the 3d Battalion, 7th Marines, attacked the next day and clawed its way up the last section of the hill. The marines took the defenders by surprise and thus broke Matsuda's line. The remnants of his command retreated into the jungle, pursued by marine patrols.

After a torturous retreat, Matsuda finally reached Rabaul with only 1,000 men remaining from his command. Marine casualties numbered more than 1,000, including 248 men killed in that "green hell," which most 1st Marine Division veterans considered to be worse than Guadalcanal.

With the occupation of Cape Gloucester, MacArthur had no reason to fear any serious Japanese resistance from the east side of Dampier Strait. Just as important was the further isolation of the more than ninety thousand Japanese at Rabaul. The jungle-clad mountains of the interior protected the Cape Gloucester enclave, and Allied planes based there joined in harassing the once dominant bastion. By then it was apparent to MacArthur's headquarters that no direct land attack was needed. Furthermore, MacArthur was able to shelve plans to put pressure on Rabaul by taking Kavieng on the northern tip of New Ireland.

With Rabaul neutralized, MacArthur began considering the bold move of bypassing Wewak and landing in the Hollandia area of Netherlands New Guinea, 450 miles up the coast. To do so, he would need assistance from Admiral Nimitz, who had consistently denied MacArthur direct control over carrier forces, because Hollandia was beyond the range of Kenney's land-based planes.

Before moving on Hollandia, however, MacArthur decided to occupy the Admiralty Islands. Located two hundred miles north of New Guinea, they appeared to be the perfect base from which the Seventh Fleet could support the Hollandia invasion. Manus, the largest island, forty-nine miles long and sixteen miles wide, was volcanic and heavily forested, but could be used for military installations to support further movement north to the Philippines. The eastern-curved island of Los Negros abutted Manus, and together they enclosed Seeadler Harbor, one of the finest in the Pacific. Moreover, airfields on these islands would deny any Japanese countermove toward the Bismarck Archipelago and could be the center for a major air web projecting American airpower far to the north. Reconnaissance of the islands indicated that they were weakly held with few good fixed defenses. Initially scheduled for 1 April, MacArthur moved up the date for landing at Hyane Harbor on the east coast of Los Negros to 29 February. The planned reconnaissance in force became the actual invasion.

Unfortunately, intelligence officers underestimated the size of the

Japanese garrison. There were approximately two thousand Japanese on the island, and the elements of the army's 1st Cavalry Division that landed found themselves outnumbered two to one. As usual, preliminary air strikes were made on Los Negros by Fifth Air Force B-25s and P-38s, and the eastern side of the island was pounded by American and Australian destroyers. The landings met little opposition because the Japanese commander had expected the invasion on the Seeadler Harbor side of the island. Within three hours, the unused Momote airstrip had been captured and a defensive perimeter established. General MacArthur and Admiral Kinkaid went ashore later that afternoon to inspect the situation. Fortunately, the Japanese had not recovered sufficiently to launch counterattacks that might have threatened the general's party. Brigadier General William C. Chase, commanding the cavalrymen, found that by evening most of the naval support had left. Chase pulled his troops back into a smaller, more defensible perimeter east of the airfield. During the next two days, aided by the Fifth Air Force, the cavalrymen beat off successive piecemeal attacks launched by Col. Yoshio Ezaki.

The rest of the 5th Cavalry Brigade, along with more than four hundred Seabees, landed on 2 March. The latter worked on repairing the air and docking facilities and helped man the defense line against continuing but generally uncoordinated attacks. With the arrival of the 7th Cavalry on 4 March, Maj. Gen. Innis P. Swift, the division commander, could launch his own offensive. By the ninth, the Japanese were in full retreat into the rugged jungle of western Los Negros. It took the cavalrymen ten days of heavy fighting to advance the three-fourths of a mile toward the key hill defenses there. These movements were coordinated with advances by the 12th Cavalry to the west. The Japanese, caught in the middle, abandoned their positions, leaving the cavalrymen the dangerous task of mopping up.

The Japanese on little Hauwei Island west of the main entrance to Seeadler Harbor were neutralized by naval gunfire and the island was occupied on 13 March. Two days later, an amphibious force from Los Negros crossed the harbor and landed on Manus west of Lorengau airfield. The bulk of the Japanese defenders, nine hundred strong, were concentrated there. By the eighteenth, the village and airfield had been captured and the surviving Japanese driven down the coast to a village called Old Rossun, where they made their last stand. For the next few weeks, cavalry patrols through the eastern jungle hunted down individual Japanese trying to escape. Although the important portion of Manus was occupied, a number of Japanese continued to live in the jungles of the central and eastern parts of the island. Later, American troops staging there for action farther north would practice against these stragglers. The last Japanese stronghold in the Admiralties, Pityilu Island, was taken on 31 March by troopers from the 7th Cavalry.

The earlier intelligence miscalculations as to the number of enemy present had not been disastrous. The outnumbered men of the 1st Cavalry had performed beyond all expectations on 1 and 2 March. After reinforcements arrived and the full weight of Allied airpower was brought to bear, surviving troops of the Japanese garrison were lost. MacArthur's gamble had paid off. He secured an excellent harbor and two airfields that not only contributed to his campaign in New Guinea, but also extended the Allies' air reach far to the north.

After further debate between MacArthur's headquarters and Nimitz over jurisdiction, the Joint Chiefs decided that Halsey's South Pacific command would be in charge of expanding base facilities in the Admiralties, although the area remained in MacArthur's zone of command. Much to MacArthur's chagrin, they deferred until later the final decision on whether to underwrite completely his proposals for the recapture of the Philippines. He was merely directed to prepare for possible landings on Luzon in February 1945. However, his plan to bypass Wewak and Hansa Bay and capture Hollandia was approved. The navy's general plan to bypass Truk and invade the Marianas on 15 June was also approved, and Nimitz was instructed to prepare plans for an invasion of Formosa possibly to be undertaken sometime in early 1945.

The plan for the Hollandia landings, code-named Reckless, called for the Army's I Corps, commanded by Lt. Gen. Robert Eichelberger and consisting of the 24th and 41st Divisions, to land in the Humboldt-Tanahmerah Bay region on 22 April. The 24th would land at Tanahmerah Bay and, using a native track, maneuver around the Cyclops Mountains to take the three airfields sited on the plain to the south. Meanwhile, the 41st would land at Humboldt Bay and move toward airfields located fifteen miles to the west.

Because the landings would be made beyond the range of land-based fighters, Nimitz agreed to allow Admiral Mitscher's TF 58 to give immediate support. Task Force 58 began interdicting the Japanese in the Carolines in late March with air strikes on Truk and Koror. An estimated one hundred planes and seventeen freighters and tankers were destroyed, and considerable damage was done to fixed installations. Even more important, Adm. Soemu Toyoda, who had been forewarned of the raid, removed most of his combat vessels to safety. They were thus in no position to interfere with the Hollandia operation.

The need for a fighter base closer to Hollandia convinced MacArthur's headquarters to plan for a simultaneous landing at Aitape, 125 miles southeast of Hollandia. There was a small airfield there and, as soon as the area was secure, the P-40 equipped Australian 78th Fighter Wing would move in to support the main landings. The task of securing the Aitape plain was assigned to the 41st Division's 163d Infantry Regiment. Immediate close air support would be provided by TF 78, which included of a number of escort carriers loaned to Admiral Kinkaid by Nimitz.

The Japanese situation in Netherlands New Guinea was grave but not hopeless. The Japanese Second Area Army, headquartered at Manokwari on the Vogelkop peninsula, deployed approximately 170,000 troops, the bulk of which were in New Guinea. General Adachi's Eighteenth Army had three understrength divisions, roughly twenty thousand men, mostly in the Madang area. Lieutenant General Fusataro Teshima, commander of the Second Area Army, decided to abandon both Madang and Wewak and concentrate his forces in the Hollandia region. On 25 March he ordered General Adachi to break off action and begin moving the Eighteenth Army to Hollandia. Adachi, convinced that the next Allied landing would be in the Wewak area, reluctantly began to move slowly westward from Hansa Bay with his army spread out over many miles. He planned to reach Hollandia in June. This decision, so fortunate for Allied plans, was buttressed by various ploys, including

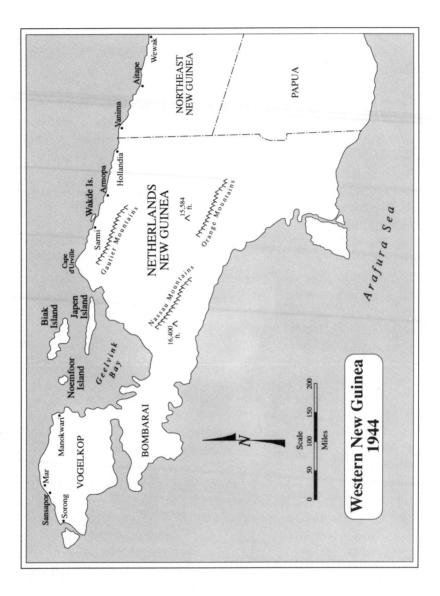

air strikes and feints by the Allies to keep Adachi's forces in the Wewak area.

The Japanese Southern Army Command in Singapore also ordered an additional one hundred planes from the First Air Fleet to be sent south to Hollandia to join those of the 6th Air Division, which had been withdrawn from Wewak. These preparations were a part of Admiral Koga's Z Plan, which sought to establish a new defense line from Hollandia to Timor, Palau, and the Marianas. The most important garrisons would be reinforced and, as soon as a major landing either in the Philippines or Palau was undertaken, the Combined Fleet would sally forth to destroy the American Fifth Fleet. Admiral Koga, who had moved his headquarters temporarily to Koror, was lost on a flight to the Philippines on 31 March. His successor, Adm. Soemu Toyoda, accepted Koga's plan, changing only the code word for the operation—to A-Go. He believed that the next major operation would be in Palau. Preparations for such an action meant that the Japanese fleet was in no position to interfere with the Hollandia landings.

Preliminary to those landings, all the Japanese bases in western New Guinea, Biak, the Moluccas, and Palau were hit by long-range B-24s of the Thirteenth Air Force, which was being shifted from the South Pacific to the Southwest Pacific theater, and by medium bombers from Kenney's Fifth Air Force. On 30 March, Kenney put more than three hundred planes into the air, striking at Wewak, Wakde Island, and the Hollandia airfields. A particularly successful raid by B-25s and A-20s against Hollandia surprised the Japanese and destroyed more than a hundred planes on the ground. Continuous raids against Japanese targets contested by Japanese pilots led to the destruction of all but a few of the 6th Air Division's planes. Thus, when the Hollandia and Aitape landings took place, there was no appreciable hostile air activity. Task Forces 58 and 78 flew protective missions, but the full might of this massive naval air operation was not needed. As with so many areas in the Pacific, the Japanese infantryman would be forced to fight alone without naval or air protection.

The plan for landings at Tanahmerah Bay on 22 April called for the 24th Division's 19th and 21st Infantry Regiments to land on two beaches on the east side of the bay and then move rapidly over trails toward nearby Lake Sentani. After the usual bombardment by Australian cruisers and destroyers, the infantry landed at 0800, only to find that the planners, working with faulty intelligence, had put the main effort on Red Beach 2, which was backed by a nearly impassable swamp that began only a few yards inland. Men and materiel, including heavy artillery, stacked up on the beach, and the tanks that were brought in were never used. The situation at Red Beach 1 was better, and Maj. Gen. Frederick A. Irving, the division commander, shifted as many troops there as possible aboard tracked vehicles. The troops at Red 1 found the trail to the lake to be only a winding path, but by nightfall patrols had penetrated more than five miles into the interior.

It soon became obvious that the main effort against the Japanese could not be launched from the Tanahmerah area, and on the twenty-third General Eichelberger and Admiral Barbey decided to concentrate on Humboldt Bay, where the terrain was better. General Irving and his two regiments would remain at Tanahmerah and press on along the narrow, winding trail toward the airfield. Fortunately, there were few Japanese in the vicinity of the beaches and the American troops strung out along the trail encountered only sporadic resistance. Despite the many difficulties, advance elements reached the westernmost airfield on 26 April, where they met 41st Division troops advancing from Humboldt Bay.

At the same time as the Tanahmerah landings, the 162d and 186th Infantry Regiments from Maj. Gen. Horace H. Fuller's 41st Division landed on the west side of Humboldt Bay after a long bombardment by destroyers and cruisers. Major General Masazumi Inada was completely surprised by the assault, and most of his seven-thousand-man garrison fled into the interior. Unusual for Pacific operations was the number of Japanese prisoners taken. By the end of the campaign, more than six hundred men had been captured. All the major objectives set for that day had been achieved by midafternoon with only minor losses. By the close of the next day, the town of Hollandia was captured and elements of the 162d had moved halfway to Lake Sentani. A single Japanese plane bombed the congested beach area at 2045 on 23 April. One of its bombs hit a large Japanese ammunition dump, and the ensuing explosion spread fire and destruction along the beach, killing twenty-four men and destroying 60 percent of all the rations that had been unloaded. The supply situation for the next few days was critical. The men of the 162d endured the hardship of half rations as they moved to seize the airfields. On the twenty-fifth, engineers supporting the division used amphibious tractors to ferry elements of the 152d across Lake Sentani, thus bypassing a Japanese trail block. The next morning the regiment captured the Cyclops airfield, and by evening had taken Sentani, the second airfield, and made contact with the 24th Division.

General Teshima at Manokwari planned to send two regiments from the Wakde area to help Inada, whose units had reassembled about fifteen miles west of Lake Sentani. This plan was vetoed by his superiors in the Philippines. Nevertheless, he dispatched three battalions, which slowly made their way eastward. Allied landings near Wakde in mid-May threatened this relief effort, and the Japanese commander decided to retreat back to the Sarmi area. Meanwhile, General Inada decided on the twenty-sixth that his only course of action was to do the same. Disease, wounds, and lack of food took a terrible toll. By the time the straggling Japanese arrived at what they believed was a safe area, Allied landings at Sarmi threatened the thousand or so survivors. They were all that remained of the nearly eleven thousand men defending the Hollandia region in March.

Meanwhile, the third phase of MacArthur's plan, the seizure of Tadji airstrip at Aitape, had gone even better than planned. The 41st Division's 163d Infantry, which landed in nine waves early on 22 April, had met little opposition. The Japanese garrison fled into the jungle, and the Americans reached the airstrip by midday. Very soon, RAAF engineers were at work on the field, and the next day twenty-five RAAF P-40s landed on the repaired airstrip. The 32d Division's 127th Infantry Regiment also landed on the twenty-third, and helped expand the perimeter. Task Force 78's escort carriers, which had received few calls for aerial support, were released on the evening of the twenty-fourth and sent to the Hollandia area. The 163d Infantry was ordered from Aitape to prepare for the Wakde operation, and Maj. Gen. William H. Gill brought in the rest of his

32d Division to defend the perimeter and keep watch on General Adachi, whose troops at Wewak some ninety miles to the east had been bypassed.

General Adachi, whose broad interpretation of his orders to pull back verged on disobedience, was able to convince his superiors to approve his plan for an offensive against the American perimeter along the Driniumor River a few miles east of Aitape. Despite his near desperate supply situation, he had managed to bring together almost twenty thousand troops for the attack.

Allied intelligence units had kept a close watch on the Japanese at Wewak. Increasing contact with the enemy at Yakamul, east of the Driniumor, at the beginning of June confirmed the information in plans captured in May. Alerted to the main outlines of Adachi's plan, General Krueger ordered the 43d Division and the 112th Cavalry and 124th Infantry Regiments to Aitape. These units, along with the 32d Division, were constituted as the XI Corps under the command of Maj. Gen. Charles P. Hall, and the main line of resistance along the Driniumor was strengthened. Hall held back six battalions near the airfield and kept the newly arrived 124th Infantry in reserve. He deployed five 32d Division battalions and two cavalry troops under Brig. Gen. Clarence A. Martin, whose covering force was to hold the Driniumor line.

Just before midnight on 10 July, Adachi launched a series of frontal attacks with three regiments, most of their weight falling on the 32d Division. By early morning these near-suicidal assaults had ripped a three-quarter-mile-wide gap in the American lines and the Japanese crossed the river, separating the 128th Infantry Regiment from the 127th farther south. General Martin was forced to pull his units back east of the river.

At the same time, a Japanese coastal attack force made a series of uncoordinated assaults on the 128th Infantry. By early morning of 14 July the Japanese commander withdrew what was left of his battered force. There was little subsequent action in this swampy area. Despite the problems created by the gap in the American positions, the Japanese made no further penetration of the main defense line, and by 18 July elements of the 124th Infantry and the 112th Cavalry had closed the gap. The Americans then concentrated on clearing out the Japanese forces that remained east of the river.

This complex task had not been completed when Adachi again attempted to breach the line on 22 July by sending one of his regiments against the 124th Infantry south of the now all but closed gap. This attack was also halted. The action coincided with attacks from Japanese west of the river trying to escape. In the confused fighting a special force of two Japanese battalions began an attack on the extreme southern part of the American line and by 19 July had forced the cavalrymen holding the village of Afua back to a new defense line two-thirds of a mile north.

The arrival on 20 July of the first elements of the 43d Division gave General Hall enough men to begin to plan for a counterattack—despite the fact that the 43d had been so hurriedly put on board ships that there was no combat loading. Furthermore, many of the 43d's automatic weapons were old and nonfunctional. However, the new regiments could at least be plugged into the least dangerous areas.

The bulk of the fighting during the last week of July was in the vicinity of Afua, where Brig. Gen. Julian W. Cunningham, commanding the South Force consisting of the 127th Infantry and 112th Cavalry, had been forced to withdraw. Beginning on the twenty-third, his troops succeeded in relieving some of the units cut off by earlier attacks. He then began an offensive west and south against the thousand-man Miyake Force. This number swelled to more than three thousand by the twenty-sixth as Adachi passed troops around the Americans' flanks. Despite some success in clearing the ridgelines, the situation became critical and General Cunningham ordered Afua abandoned. The 127th Infantry and 112th Cavalry beat off a number of Japanese attacks on 28 and 29 July. South Force had by then suffered more than a thousand casualties, but its ordeal was about over. General Adachi ordered what was left of his 41st Division south to reinforce his troops striking at Cunningham's command. On the morning of 1 August, with Adachi in command, four thousand sick, tired, and hungry Japanese charged the American lines. They were halted with heavy losses. Sporadic attacks continued during the night and early morning of the second with little success. Then, at 1900 on 2 August, approximately three hundred Japanese assaulted the 127th's line in four separate waves. They were cut to pieces by accurate artillery, mortar, and machine-gun fire. The Japanese continued to batter themselves against the American lines the next day before General Adachi decided to break off the offensive. Early on the morning of the fourth, Adachi launched a series of attacks to cover the withdrawal of other Eighteenth Army elements. These small, suicidal assaults were totally unsuccessful, and the Japanese lost more than two hundred men.

Even before Adachi began his withdrawal in the south, General Hall had begun a counteroffensive in the north. On 30 July, four battalions code-named Ted Force struck eastward and reached Niumen Creek, some three thousand yards away, by 1 August. Hall then turned his units south to strike the main east-west trail before turning westward in an effort to trap as many of Adachi's troops as possible. Battling heavy rains and almost impassible undergrowth and a few strong defensive positions, the wide envelopment reached the Driniumor on 6 August. The offensive continued for two more days before Hall decided that all objectives had been reached. Approximately eighteen hundred Japanese were dead. Meanwhile the South Force commander, General Cunningham, ordered three battalions to clear the Afua area before pushing southward to join Ted Force.

By 9 August, General Hall was aware that resistance along the Driniumor and in the Afua area had ceased, and he began relieving the units that had fought the month-long battle. During the next three weeks, patrols from the 43d Division operated far to the south and east in areas where no American troops had been for three months. Finally satisfied that the Eighteenth Army posed no further threat to the Aitape region, General Krueger declared the Aitape campaign over on 25 August.

When General Adachi finally disengaged, his regiments had been reduced to an average of approximately 150 men each. Almost all the field grade officers were dead. The Eighteenth Army lost more than 9,000 men killed in the period after 1 June. The battle for Aitape also claimed 3,000 American casualties, of which 440 were killed in action. This second most-costly battle of the New Guinea campaign was unnecessary. It had no effect on the outcome of the campaign because even before Adachi decided to attack the Driniumor line, Allied forces had already taken the next step on the long road to the Philippines by capturing Wakde Island, 275 miles north-west of Aitape.

After the battle, General Adachi and the remnants of his army fell back on Wewak. American forces continued to patrol the interior until the last unit, the 43d Division, was replaced by the Australian 6th Division in late November. The next month the Australians, disdaining the idea of simply maintaining a perimeter, began a slow advance toward Wewak through some of the worst jungle and mountainous terrain in north central New Guinea. The Japanese put up heavy resistance and it was not until 10 May 1945 that Wewak fell.

As they had on Bougainville, General Blamey and his subordinates, feeling left out, carried out an unnecessary offensive that did little more than showcase the valor and determination of the Australian soldier. The four-month-long Wewak campaign resulted in the deaths of more than 7,000 Japanese at a cost of 451 Australians dead.

MacArthur and his senior advisers were handicapped in a number of ways as they attempted to carry out the general's strategic goal of returning to the Philippines. One ever-present problem was the availability of landing craft. Admiral Barbey, a master of amphibious operations, and his able lieutenant, RAdm. William M. Fechteler, were forced to plan dozens of landings with inadequate materiel. Another limiting factor was the fact that Nimitz controlled all the aircraft carriers, and by early 1944 he believed he needed them for his own Central Pacific operations. Without carriers, MacArthur had to advance along the coast of New Guinea in a step-by-step fashion, securing air bases from which Kenney's planes could cover the next move. This was the situation that resulted in the Wakde-Sarmi campaign.

MacArthur's ultimate goal in New Guinea was to seize bases from which he could dominate Geelvink Bay, a two-hundred-mile-deep indentation that helps define the bird's-head shape of the extreme western end of the island, aptly named the Vogelkop (Bird's Head). In order to do this, MacArthur decided to seize Biak, one of the Schouten Islands, 325 miles northwest of Hollandia and just north of Geelvink Bay. However, before attempting a landing on Biak, the planners wanted to take the main island in the Wakde group, which had an excellent airfield. The many plans prepared for this venture included seizing a lodgment on the mainland near Sarmi to secure two other fields. Ten days after these objectives had been taken, Alamo Force would land on Biak.

On 17 May the reinforced 163d Infantry Regiment, code-named Tornado Force and commanded by Brig. Gen. Jens A. Doe, landed on the mainland near the village of Arare opposite Wakde Island. By then the Allies had total air superiority. Australian and Dutch squadrons struck southwest of the Vogelkop, the Fifth Air Force struck the Wakde and Biak areas over and over, and the Thirteenth Air Force continued its bombing campaign against targets on New Britain and in the Carolines. The landings near Arare went as planned, the infantry battalions moving immediately into the interior and along the flanks so that by the close of D day, more than nine thousand men held seven and one-half miles of coastline.

On the eighteenth, after intense artillery and aerial bombardment, four companies from the 163d, supported by four Sherman tanks, crossed to Wakde Island. The island, only two miles long by three-fourths of a mile wide, was dominated by a single feature—the airfield. It was defended by only eight hundred troops who had constructed hundreds of bunkers of varying size. By the end of the first day, the airstrip had been seized. The following day the remaining Japanese were forced into the northwest corner of the island where, after a small but spirited banzai charge, they were quickly annihilated.

Engineers went to work on the airfield before the island was secure, and the first fighter planes landed on 21 May. The runway was later extended so that medium bombers could operate from it.

The decisions of General Krueger to widen the lodgment centered on Arare, and the Japanese commander in the Sarmi area, Lt. Gen. Hachiro Tagami, to destroy it precipitated a month-long, hard-fought campaign. Japanese Imperial Headquarters had already written off that part of the New Guinea coast and ordered the Second Area Army to hold a line from Manokwari to Biak.

The order stemmed in part from the loss at sea of the major portion of two divisions sent from China to reinforce the western New Guinea sector. One of the regiments was decimated when its transport was sunk by an American submarine in the South China Sea. Later, three more ships in the convoy were sunk in the Celebes. The Japanese 32d Division could land only two understrength regiments, while the 35th was reduced to four shattered battalions. These submarine attacks were more devastating to the Japanese than many of the land actions.

As was the case in so many Pacific campaigns, General Tagami, with his supplies low, nevertheless ignored the odds and decided to attack the Americans with two infantry regiments and three battalions from the battered force that had fallen back from the Hollandia area. Dividing his eleven thousand men into three sections, he planned a double envelopment of the Americans at Arare.

Meanwhile General Doe, commanding the Tornado Force, waited until Wakde Island was secure before extending the lodgment. Reinforced by the 158th Infantry Regiment, he began a cautious move across the Tor River with the objective of taking Sarmi, sixteen miles to the west. Japanese resistance stiffened as the lead units reached the edge of Lone Tree Hill, which guarded the approach to Maffin airfield. By 27 May the 158th had sustained three hundred casualties, most from heat exhaustion. Nevertheless, an infantry company reached the crest of the hill the next day. General Krueger, however, withdrew the 163d Infantry to prepare for the Biak assault, leaving only the 158th to defend twelve miles of coastline.

General Doe became the assistant commander of the 41st Division and was replaced by Brig. Gen. Edwin D. Patrick. When informed of a possible Japanese attack, Patrick pulled his advance elements in the west back more than a mile. The American hold on the narrow belt was not continuous, but rather on 30 May there were twenty-one noncontiguous perimeters when the first of Tagami's attacks materialized. Fortunately for Patrick's troops these were uncoordinated and, with the aid of artillery and air support, were beaten back. By employing these piecemeal tactics, the Japanese missed their best opportunity to at least severely damage the American position. On 10 June, after having suffered heavy losses, the Japanese began to retire to new positions in the west. They were pursued by the 158th, which reached Maffin Bay the next day.

General Krueger decided to withdraw the 158th Infantry in order to prepare for a later assault on Noemfoor Island. It was replaced by the 6th Division's untried 20th Infantry Regiment. Within a week another of the division's regiments, the 1st Infantry, arrived and the new commander, Maj. Gen. Franklin C. Sibert, was ordered to destroy the Japanese west of the Tor River and take Sarmi as soon as possible. The offensive, backed by low-flying P-47s from Wakde, began on 20 June and the 6th Division GIs took Lone Tree Hill the next day. A Japanese counterattack briefly cut off several units, and from natural defensive positions launched attack after attack. The Americans bypassed much of this resistance by crossing the Tor River, and by 25 June the two 6th Division regiments had destroyed most of the defending Japanese. All that was left was to mop up as the western border of the perimeter was extended to the Woske River.

The 6th Division, scheduled for the Biak invasion, was pulled out on 30 June and replaced by the 31st Division. By then an estimated thirteen hundred Japanese had been killed in the Sarmi operation. Disease and starvation also continued to take a heavy toll on Tagami's men. American estimates on 1 September concluded that there were fewer than two thousand effective Japanese troops in the Sarmi area. By contrast, the Americans in the Wakde-Sarmi area had acquired excellent airfields and good staging areas for the planned future attacks on Biak, the Vogelkop, and ultimately the Philippines.

With the battle for control of the Sarmi region barely begun, MacArthur and Krueger moved to implement their next step, the occupation of Biak Island some one hundred miles east of the Vogelkop, partially blocking the entrance to Geelvink Bay. The island, roughly shaped like a woman's shoe, is forty-five miles long by about twenty miles wide, and is composed of a series of broken coral terraces covered by dense rain forest. Only on the southeastern shore are there beach areas suitable for amphibious landings. The Dutch had improved this area, and the main town, Bosnik, is located there. The beaches in the area are paralleled by a high, narrow coral ridgeline. The Japanese had constructed three airfields along this coastal plain. Mokmer, eight miles west of Bosnik, was the easternmost, and two miles farther west was Borokoe Field. A smaller field was built near the coast at Sorido. These were the main targets for Operation Hurricane, which MacArthur hoped would provide bases for long-range bomber support for the planned Central Pacific offensive as well as for further action in New Guinea. The invasion of Biak was scheduled for 27 May 1944 and was to be commanded by General Fuller, who would have only two regiments, the 162d and 186th, from his 41st Division.

Biak proved to be one of those operations that did not show MacArthur, Krueger, and their staffs at their best. Their main fault was again underestimating Japanese strength. Radio intercepts had kept MacArthur generally well informed as to the location and strength of the Japanese as his forces moved up the coastline. The reports indicated that there were at least seven thousand Japanese on the island. MacArthur, however, instead chose to believe the estimates of his own intelligence officers, who placed the number at only twenty-five hundred. The recent successes on the mainland led him to believe that two infantry regiments with supporting tanks and artillery would be able to seize the airfields quickly. Another problem not appreciated by higher headquarters was the terrain. Planners based decisions on aerial photographs that did not show the many caves dug into the ridgelines dominating the coastal plain. The situation that thus developed on Biak was reminiscent of MacArthur's handling of the Buna operation in November 1942: too few forces were provided at first, and higher headquarters never appreciated the difficulty of the task given to General Fuller.

The Japanese high command viewed Biak as critical to holding back the Allied advance toward Halmahera, Morotai, and ultimately the Philippines. In December 1943, Gen. Korechika Anami sent the 36th Division's 222d Infantry, a veteran of campaigns in China, to Biak. This brought the number of Japanese troops to more than eleven thousand, of which some four thousand were fully trained infantry. The garrison commander, Col. Naoyuki Kuzume, decided he could not prevent an American landing; Allied naval and air forces were simply too powerful. He decided to use the natural terrain features, disperse his forces in open country, and dig in along the ridgelines and in caves. His plan was to pin down the invaders on the beach and use his artillery to deny them the airfields. He had three strong points in the terraces above Mokmer Field. One, the West Caves, consisted of three large sumps surrounded by bunkers, pillboxes, and interconnected trenches. In the center was the Ibdi Pocket, and the East Caves controlled the eastern part of Mokmer Field. Each of these positions had bunkers backed by mortars and mobile artillery. Colonel Kuzume, in tactical control, was joined just before the invasion by the chief of staff of the Second Area Army, Lt. Gen. Takazo Numata. Neither officer had any intention of wasting troops in futile banzai charges. Instead, they planned to exact a heavy price for each strong point.

Operation Hurricane began early on 27 May with a major foul-up. Advance elements of the 186th Infantry were to land on four beaches around Bosnik. But the currents proved swifter than expected and carried the landing craft one and one-half miles west, where they deposited the first waves in a mangrove swamp. Later waves compensated for the currents, and by evening more than twelve thousand infantry, a tank company, and a battalion of medium artillery were ashore.

Elements of the 162d Infantry began moving northwest toward the airfields as the 186th pushed east of Bosnik. This relatively successful start was halted by the thin screen of Japanese defenders south of the ridge and by heavy fire from the higher elevations. By the twenty-ninth, despite some local gains, it was obvious to Fuller that the airfields could not be used until the Japanese had been cleared from the ridges.

Even at this early stage, high temperatures and humidity were taking their toll on the 41st Division troops. There was no fresh water on the island, and for the first few days many frontline units went without. Fuller established a defensive perimeter and requested more troops. Krueger responded by sending two battalions from the 163d Infantry near Sarmi. They arrived on 1 June. He also prodded Fuller to move forward and carry out his mission quickly.

Feeding the reinforcements into the line, Fuller, after a heavy artillery preparation, moved the 186th north to try to flank the Japanese positions. But the drive soon slowed down because of the very rugged terrain along the main ridge and degenerated into a number of small-unit actions. Supply continued to be a problem, and the Japanese remained firmly in control of their major defenses.

Krueger ordered Fuller to shift his assault once again in the direction of the airfields, and on 7 June elements of the 186th took Mokmer Field. Engineers were brought in and the field was repaired by the fifteenth, but it could not be used as the Japanese controlled the heights. Heavy counterbattery fire from the division's 105mm howitzers managed to knock out many of the Japanese mobile guns and most of Kuzume's tanks were destroyed in futile attacks against the heavier, more powerful Shermans. From 7 to 10 June, all attempts to gain control of the low ridge north of the airfield failed. Beginning the next day, the 162d fought its way along the coast to Borokoe Field and a mile beyond to Sorido. Two battalions then moved north to the low ridgeline and the West Caves, where Fuller discovered he had too few exhausted troops to clear the Japanese from their strongholds.

General Krueger, reacting to pressure from MacArthur's headquarters, repeatedly pressed Fuller to speed things up. The presumed need for another airfield led to the occupation of Owi, a neighboring small island, on 2 June. Within two weeks engineers had constructed a fighter strip there, and two squadrons of P-38s began to operate from it on the twenty-first. However, Alamo Force headquarters still wanted the three functioning airfields on Biak. Fuller had explained his situation and need for reinforcements. He was certain that the Japanese were sending in fresh troops. Krueger did send another regiment, the 24th Division's 34th Infantry, which arrived at Biak on 18 June. Finally, on the fourteenth, Krueger decided to relieve Fuller of overall command and replace him with the I Corps commander. Fuller, justifiably believing that higher headquarters did not understand or appreciate his problems, asked for a transfer out of the theater. His request was approved, and he was later assigned to Adm. Lord Louis Mountbatten's Southeast Asia Command.

Fuller was partially correct. The Japanese did try to reinforce Biak. In May, aware of the probability of attacks on the Marianas, Admiral Toyoda planned for a final showdown with the U.S. fleet and began to mass the Combined Fleet for it. However, he wanted to use part of the fleet to support Biak. To accomplish this, the Japanese gathered an amphibious force of four thousand men guarded by one battleship, three cruisers, and six destroyers. The convoy was scheduled to arrive at Biak on 4 June. MacArthur discounted all reports of reinforcements even after the convoy was sighted. He believed that they were headed instead for Halmahera. Fortunately for the Americans on Biak, planes from the Japanese scouting force erroneously reported sighting a large Allied naval force that included carriers just off the island. Fearing a confrontation with such a large force, the convoy commander ordered it to return to base.

The Japanese made two other major attempts to reinforce the Biak garrison. The second convoy sent was even larger than the first, but it was intercepted by American planes that sank two destroyers and damaged three others. The convoy commander, again fearful of encountering a major Allied naval force, aborted the mission. The last relief expedition was canceled because all available ships were needed to counter the 15 June invasion of Saipan. Fewer than twelve hundred Japanese troops reached Biak, and those were sent mostly by barge from Noemfoor.

General Eichelberger, who had taken over from Fuller, began a general advance on 18 June. The 186th and 162d Infantry Regiments bypassed the West Caves, which were finally taken on 27 June. Meanwhile, the 34th Infantry advanced along the coast and seized the Borokoe and Sordido airfields, and the village of Sordido farther west.

The last major areas of Japanese resistance were the East Caves and the Ibdi Pocket. Continuous probing attacks, combined with heavy artillery concentrations, were directed against the caves, and air strikes by B-25s and P-38s put tremendous pressure on the defenders. On 3 July the surviving Japanese fled into the open jungle to the north. The Ibdi Pocket was repeatedly attacked by the 162d Infantry, and later the 163d, supported by tanks and artillery. The area was cut off from all reinforcements after 10 June, and one by one the caves were either neutralized or sealed off. Nevertheless, the pocket was not cleared until 22 July.

By 24 June, the estimated four thousand Japanese still on the island had been deprived of their main defenses and were reduced to wandering the interior searching for food. The three regiments of the 41st Division continued to scout the interior as late as mid-August, hunting down the surviving bands.

MacArthur finally had his three airfields, but it had taken far more time than he had allotted. The cost, too, was relatively high: 400 killed, 2,000 wounded, and over 7,200 nonbattle casualties.

The entire Japanese garrison, except for 800 prisoners, was ultimately destroyed. By August, Mokmer Field had been lengthened to handle heavy bombers, and Biak became a major supply base that provided logistical support to more than seventy thousand men.

Looking ultimately to establish lodgments on the Vogelkop peninsula, MacArthur next decided to occupy the island of Noemfoor. Located seventy-five miles due west of Biak, Noemfoor is roughly circular, approximately fifteen miles in diameter. Most of the terrain is low lying, with the highest elevation barely over six hundred feet. The interior is covered with heavy jungle and bush. Noemfoor is surrounded by coral reefs that protect most of the coast, and the only good landing beaches are in the northwest sector near Kamiri. The Japanese had built three airfields near the coast, Karnasoren and Kamiri in the north, and Namber in the south.

Alamo Force's G2 section for once overestimated Japanese troop strength. Planners guessed that approximately 3,000 men, including from 1,600 to 2,000 combat troops, were on the island. In reality, Colonel Shimizu had only 2,000 men—of whom only 900 were effective infantry.

The 158th Infantry, which would conduct the assault, was moved from the Sarmi area to prepare for the operation. On 1 July eighty-four B-24s and forty-eight medium bombers pounded the island, and a similar force struck the next day just before the 158th landed. Admiral Fechteler, commanding the amphibious operation, had available one of the largest covering forces for any New Guinea invasion. His three cruisers and eighteen U.S. and Australian destroyers delivered a heavy preinvasion bombardment just before the first wave landed early on the morning of 2 July. There was no opposition, and the Kamiri airfield was quickly secured and advance elements pushed into the interior to establish a secure perimeter. By evening seven thousand men were ashore, the medium howitzers had been registered, and an engineer battalion was already at work on the airfield.

General Patrick, commander of the expedition, was informed by his intelligence section that a captured prisoner reported that more than three thousand men had landed on 25 June to reinforce the Japanese garrison. The report later proved to be untrue, but Patrick nevertheless asked for reinforcements despite the scant Japanese resistance. Krueger agreed and alerted the reserve force, the 503d Parachute Infantry Regiment (PIR) at Hollandia, as well as the 34th Infantry at Biak. The 503d PIR dropped 1,424 paratroopers from very low altitude on 3 and 4 July. Their target was the airstrip, and many men were hurt as they landed on parked heavy equipment, boulders, and jagged tree stumps. In all, the 503d sustained 9 percent casualties.

Although in retrospect this exercise in American air superiority was not needed, the extra troops did enable General Patrick to end the active phase of the campaign much sooner than expected.

Most of the Japanese resistance to the expanding perimeter came from hilly areas, particularly Hill 201 southwest of Kamiri Field. Those positions were taken on 4 July. Early the next morning Colonel Shimizu responded with a major unsupported infantry attack against the 158th's lines. Artillery, mortars, and machine guns aided the infantrymen in destroying the attackers within an hour. After that, the Japanese withdrew into the interior.

An amphibious landing by elements of the 158th Infantry on the sixth secured Namber, and aggressive patrols from the 158th and the 503d PIR pursued the retreating Japanese. There were a number of small-scale actions as Shimizu's force of approximately four hundred men retreated from hill to hill.

Kamiri Field became operational for fighters on 16 July, and the engineers soon lengthened Karnasoren Field's runways to accommodate B-24s, which began bombing oil-producing areas in the Dutch East Indies.

The American forces on Noemfoor encountered a situation that later became all too common as more Japanese-held territory was liberated. The Japanese had brought in more than 3,000 Indonesians and 900 Formosan laborers to build roads and airfields. They had been treated with appalling savagery—overworked, starved, beaten, and beheaded for the slightest infractions. By the time they were liberated, only 403 Indonesians remained alive, and one-third of the Formosans were dead. Such discoveries fueled the conviction already held by most U.S. infantrymen that the Japanese soldier was not only insane, but a vicious animal that deserved to be killed. By the time General Krueger declared the operation over on 31 August, 1,730 Japanese were dead. Given the savagery of the campaign, a surprisingly large number, 186, were captured.

Neutralizing the substantial Japanese force in the Vogelkop had always been part of MacArthur's overall plan. He hoped to isolate large numbers of the enemy while at the same time gaining territory for more airfields to support his return to the Philippines.

The first tentative plan called for a lodgment near the village of Sorang in the extreme northwest part of the "bird's head." One reason for choosing this location was the belief that the oil fields at nearby Klamono could be put into operation and thus provide the Allies with much-needed petroleum products. Although a special thirty-three-hundred-man engineering unit was formed in California to operate the fields, the project was canceled in late May because studies showed that the fields could not be profitably operated before 1946. MacArthur had earlier asked Krueger to investigate the possibility of landing near the north coast villages of Mar and Sansapor. Negative reports from reconnaissance teams convinced Krueger that the proposed operation should be canceled, but MacArthur insisted that it be carried out. One of the reasons for Krueger's conclusion was that Mar was located on a swampy plain, and the prospects for building an airfield there seemed questionable.

The plan as developed was for two regiments from the 6th Division to land at Mar and also on the offshore islands of Middleburg and Amsterdam on 30 July. Admiral Fechteler's attack force would consist of three cruisers and twenty destroyers for the operation, code-named Typhoon. Five engineer battalions would follow the initial assault forces in order to begin work quickly on the proposed airfield. Planes from the Fifth Air Force, aided by Australian and Dutch squadrons, struck at Manokwari and Sorong in the Vogelkop, as well as the Halmahera area, in the days before the landing.

The amphibious landings went off as planned early in the morning on 30 July. There was no opposition at Mar or on the offshore islands. Despite the soft soil conditions, which caused problems for wheeled vehicles, the division artillery was ashore and registered by 1100 and infantry units were pushing inland to establish a defensible perimeter. The few Japanese in the area simply fled into the interior.

The next day, the 3d Battalion, lst Infantry Regiment, was loaded on landing craft and landed at Sansapor village nine miles southwest of Mar. There was no opposition to this landing, either. General Sibert, the 6th Division commander, ordered the expansion of both perimeters and aggressive patrolling beyond the lines.

The desperate food situation had convinced the Japanese Second Area Army commander even before the Mar landing to shift the bulk of his force southward to areas where natural foodstuffs were available. This movement meant that the American patrols in the Sansapor area encountered more Japanese during the next two months. By early October, when control of the area passed to the newly formed U.S. Eighth Army, the Japanese had lost nearly seven hundred men killed in a series of sporadic firefights. The Japanese never made a serious attempt to oust the Americans from their lodgments.

The advance party of the 13th Air Task Force, which later took over a portion of the aerial action, decided to construct a fighter strip on Middleburg Island and develop a bomber field west of Mar. The Middleburg airfield was operational by 17 August, and a sixty-five-hundred-foot runway was finished at Mar in early September in time for the bombers to aid in preparatory strikes against Morotai.

The occupation of the Mar-Sansapor area was the final American operation in New Guinea. MacArthur and his lieutenants could be criticized for not foreseeing some of the tactical problems that developed, such as the underestimation of Japanese strength at Biak. But the strategic planning was impeccable, and cooperation between naval, air, and ground forces was superb. In just nine months, admirals Barbey and Fechteler had superintended fourteen major amphibious landings as Allied forces bypassed the Japanese strong points of Hansa Bay, Wewak, and Manokwari. This thousand-mile advance neutralized thousands of Japanese while providing air bases and staging grounds for further advances. The isolated Japanese were generally ignored and they spent the remainder of the war desperately trying to stay alive.

MacArthur's New Guinea campaign had a twofold purpose. The first was to defend American and Australian bases from attack. The second was to proceed methodically to secure bases from which to support his return to the Philippines. Until the spring of 1943, the Joint Chiefs in Washington could offer MacArthur only empty words of encouragement. However, the success of MacArthur's New Guinea operation, coupled with Nimitz's invasion of the Marianas, meant that a decision had to be reached on whether the Philippines should be targeted or bypassed.

Admiral King was the most ardent exponent for a policy of neutralizing the Philippines with air and naval forces without committing a large ground force to what could be an interminable series of island conquests. Instead, King proposed seizing Formosa, an island much closer to Japan proper. He believed that Chiang Kai-shek would be willing to provide many of the ground units necessary for its conquest. King was also guarding what he believed was the navy's turf. He wanted to ensure that the final steps toward the ultimate conquest of Japan remained under his and Nimitz's control. If the Philippines became a primary objective, he was certain that MacArthur and the army would be given the dominant role there.

While the action in northern New Guinea was still under way, MacArthur was ordered to Pearl Harbor for a conference with President Roosevelt, his advisers, and Nimitz and his senior officers. Whether the president believed it was time to meet his Pacific commanders and attempt to settle their strategic differences, or whether, as MacArthur believed, the president's decision to come to Hawaii was politically motivated, is still debatable. In any event, the meeting between a reluctant MacArthur and the commander in chief on 26–27 July, although not finally settling the question of Luzon or Formosa, did show that Roosevelt favored MacArthur's plan. No minutes were kept, but both the president and MacArthur later discussed what had occurred with others.

Contrary to MacArthur's suspicions, the president conducted the formal sessions with impartiality, listening critically to both Nimitz's and MacArthur's presentations. At the conclusion of the meeting, Roosevelt told MacArthur that he personally favored an invasion of the Philippines and would use his influence to see that it was so ordered. As MacArthur recalled, it was not just the military argument that won the president's support, but the general's reminder of America's moral obligation to the people of the Philippines.

Another factor in MacArthur's favor was the success of the Japanese Ichigo offensive in eastern China, which cast doubt on the possibility of Chiang's support for a Formosa venture.

Admiral King in the months ahead continued to press for the abandonment of MacArthur's Philippine plan, but when President Roosevelt left Pearl Harbor on board the *Baltimore,* MacArthur could reasonably expect the navy's opposition to be ignored by the president and the Joint Chiefs. MacArthur could at last prepare for assaults on Morotai, Leyte, and Luzon.

Chapter 11

The Marianas Secured

THE ULTIMATE GOAL of the Central Pacific command had always been the occupation of the major islands in the Marianas chain. Admiral Nimitz, ably supported by his superior, Admiral King, believed the conquest of Saipan, Guam, and Tinian was vital for three interconnected reasons. First, possession of these islands would give the navy forward bases for an eventual assault on the Japanese home islands. Second, naval planners in Hawaii and Washington also believed that the Saipan landings would bring out the long-quiescent Japanese Combined Fleet for a final showdown. Finally, and perhaps even more crucial, the possession of these islands would provide air bases from which a new heavy bomber, the Boeing B-29 Superfortress, could more easily operate against Japanese cities a scant twelve hundred miles away.

The latter consideration gained for the navy an important ally in high-level discussions on Pacific strategy. General Arnold, commander of the Army Air Forces, desperately wanted the Marianas bases so he could shift his B-29s from unsatisfactory airfields in China. The main prize was Aslito Field, located on the southern coastal plain of Saipan. It would require little effort to make it operational, as engineers believed that simply extending the runways would make it suitable for heavy bombers. In addition, there was a fighter strip at Chalan Kanoa, and the Japanese were building another at Marpi Point in the north.

Although General MacArthur continued to oppose Nimitz's plans, the Marianas operation was approved by the Combined Chiefs of Staff at the Sextant meeting in Cairo in November 1943. The goals outlined for Admiral Nimitz in 1944 included seizure of bases in the Marshalls in January and February, capturing Truk in July, and the invasion of the Marianas on 1 October. Admiral Nimitz modified this schedule in his December 1943 directive, postponing the invasions of Saipan and Tinian until 1 November 1944 and that of Guam until 15 December 1944.

The ease with which Kwajalein and Eniwetok were taken, combined with Admiral Mitscher's successful strike at Truk in February 1944, convinced Nimitz to abandon plans to seize the huge Japanese base and move up the invasion dates for the Marianas. Nimitz's staff guide of 20 March, although changed in some details, remained the key document for planners.

Admiral Spruance, whose massive Fifth Fleet would cover the landings, was given overall command of the Marianas operation. The target date for the Saipan assault was moved forward to 15 June. Admiral Turner, operating with a relatively free hand, commanded the expeditionary forces and would continue, as Northern Attack Force commander, to be in direct charge of the Saipan landings. The original plan called for the invasion of Guam three days after the assault on Saipan. A Southern Task Force commanded by Admiral Conolly was given this mission.

The units designated for the Saipan operation were the veteran 2d Marine Division of Tarawa fame, commanded by Maj. Gen. Thomas Watson; the 4th Marine Division, commanded by Maj. Gen. Harry Schmidt; and the army's 27th Division, commanded by Maj. Gen. Ralph Smith. The 27th was in reserve, and planners never clearly defined its mission. Depending upon the situation, it was to be used either on Saipan, Tinian, or Guam. Major General Ralph Smith's staff prepared a total of twenty-one plans to cover all foreseen eventualities. Ironically, none of them were ever implemented.

"Howlin' Mad" Smith was in overall charge of land operations. He also commanded the V Amphibious Corps, which was assigned to conduct the assault on Saipan. Ground operations on Guam were to be controlled by marine Maj. Gen. Roy Geiger, commander of the III Amphibious Corps.

Planning for the Saipan operation revealed one of the major flaws common to many Central Pacific operations. Lacking good maps of the island and with faulty intelligence estimates of the number of defenders, Smith's staff assumed that two divisions would be adequate for the task. Early in May, intelligence officers believed that the Japanese had only 10,000 combat troops on Saipan. This figure was later adjusted to between 15,000 and 18,000 personnel. In reality, however, there were nearly 23,000 army troops and 7,100 sailors—including 800 men from the Special Landing Force. Thus, if the 27th Division was routed to the Tinian or Guam operations, there would be rough parity between the attackers and defenders.

There is every indication that the planners, perhaps emboldened by the relative ease of the Marshalls operation, had concluded that Saipan would not present too much of a problem. Nevertheless, despite American air and naval superiority in most previous campaigns in the Southwest and South Pacific Areas, the Japanese soldiers had displayed a ferocity and tenacity that should have indicated to Holland Smith that Saipan would be defended fanatically.

The island's geography was also an indicator of potential danger, if not disaster, for any invader. Saipan is quite small: less than fifteen miles long and seven miles across at its widest point, narrowing to three miles in the vicinity of Magicienne Bay. High cliffs dominate the eastern and northern sides of the island, dropping sharply to the ocean in places. By contrast, the western part of the island is a low-lying plain with few obstacles to troop movement. The bulk of the Japanese and Chamorro population lived in towns along the west coast. The most important were Chalan Kanoa in the south and Garapan, the capital, in the middle of the island. Fifteen-hundred-foot Mount Tapotchau and two smaller hills, Mount Tipo Pale and Hill 789, dominate the central part of the island. Approximately a thousand yards east of Tapotchau is a relatively flat expanse later called Death Valley. A series of hills separate the valley from the east coast. The terrain in the highlands is rugged, etched by a number of draws and bluffs intersecting the main ridges. In the extreme southeast is the Nafutan Peninsula, whose gullies and heavy vegetation made its defense relatively easy. The east coast, except at a few places in Magicienne Bay, is devoid of coral reefs, whereas the west coast is almost completely ringed by reefs.

The Japanese situation on Saipan was desperate. The high command, understanding the island's importance, had rightly concluded that it would be a target. However, most officers believed that an invasion there would not come until after the Allies assaulted the Palau Islands. Nevertheless, the Japanese made two major attempts to reinforce Saipan and the western Carolines. On 29 February, the American submarine *Trout* sank a large troopship carrying forty-one hundred men off Saipan; only seventeen hundred reached the island. Another attempt at the beginning of June also resulted in disaster when five small transports from a convoy of seven ships were sunk with a loss estimated at a thousand troops. All of the Japanese 118th Regiment's heavy equipment and artillery was lost, and the survivors were landed at Saipan and Guam, many without weapons.

An indication of how thoroughly the U.S. Navy dominated the Pacific in mid-1944 is seen in the fate of Lt. Gen. Hideyoshi Obata, the senior Japanese commander in the Marianas and Carolines. Obata was on an inspection tour at Koror when the Saipan invasion began. He tried to return, but got only as far as Guam. The defense of the island thus fell to Lt. Gen. Yoshitsugu Saito, commander of the 43d Division.

Saito divided the island into five districts, each defended by the equivalent of a regiment. Fortunately for the marines, both Saito and Obata had earlier agreed that the most likely place for an American invasion was Magicienne Bay. The beaches there were free of coral reefs, and an invader would have relatively easy access to central Saipan. Acting on this belief, Saito placed a mixed brigade, backed by most of his available tanks and much of the heavy artillery, in position to defend that vital region.

The American planners, despite their lack of detailed knowledge of Saipan's defenses, correctly judged that the Japanese would expect a landing at Magicienne Bay. They decided instead to mount the invasion on eleven beaches on the western side of the island, stretching from Agingan Point in the south to a spot just north of the main cross-island road. The 2d Marine Division was scheduled to land on beaches in the north, and the 4th Division was assigned the beaches south of Chalan Kanoa.

The major obstacle to the landings, the coral reef, would be overcome by using forty-eight troop-carrying LVTs for each division. These tracked vehicles would be accompanied by eighteen LVT(A)s located on either flank and by twenty-four LCIG gunboats for close-in support. Seven older battleships and five cruisers provided naval gunfire support, and RAdm. Gerald F. Bogan had seven light carriers with a total of 166 planes for air interdiction and close air support.

Lurking farther offshore was the heart of Admiral Spruance's Fifth Fleet: seven each of fleet carriers, light carriers, and fast battleships. His major task was to give additional protection to the landings, but all concerned secretly hoped that the Japanese Combined Fleet would finally decide to come out of hiding.

On the afternoon of 11 June, Admiral Mitscher's TF 58 launched two hundred aircraft from a position two hundred miles west of Saipan to strike at Saipan, Tinian, and Guam. The Japanese at Aslito airfield were taken completely by surprise, and an estimated fifty planes were destroyed on the ground and in the air. This left the Japanese with few planes to aid in the island's defense.

The next day, the fast battleships moved in closer and battered the west coasts of Saipan and Tinian for seven hours. Admiral Turner's older battleships, cruisers, and destroyers continued to pound the island on the fourteenth. Aircraft from Admiral Bogen's light carriers, unchallenged by Japanese planes, flew with impunity through the poorly aimed antiaircraft fire and hit any target that appeared to be of use to the enemy. The bombardment and air attacks destroyed many of the fixed defenses and upset General Saito's plans to halt the invasion on the beaches.

Despite three and one-half days of intense bombardment, most of the concealed Japanese artillery and tanks were still operational. The dug-in infantry, particularly in the hilly areas, also were untouched. Despite all the explosives directed at the island, the navy did not hit the flanks of the invasion beaches hard enough. The Japanese there survived the bombardment with machine guns and mortars intact, and were ready to pour enfilading fire on the invaders. As with so many Central Pacific assaults, what had appeared from aboard ship to be totally devastating fire did not prevent the first waves of marines from taking heavy casualties.

On D day, Admiral Turner's battleships, cruisers, and destroyers began their final preinvasion bombardment at 0700. Planes from the light carriers had even earlier begun to make strafing runs along the

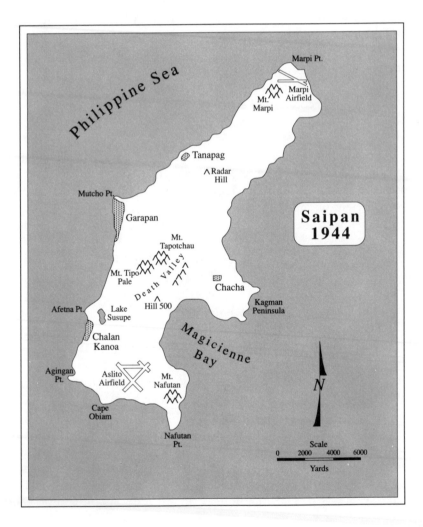

beaches and their approaches. The first waves of the marine assault force were ordered into the LVTs just before 0600, and elements of the 2d Marine Division hit Red Beach north of Afetna Point at 0845. Minutes later, the first waves of the 4th Division landed south of Chalan Kanoa.

There was considerable confusion in the 2d Division area when two battalions of the 8th Marines went ashore too far north. It took much of the day to sort out that problem. Meanwhile, the Japanese 75mm and 105mm guns sited on the reverse slopes of the hills overlooking the beaches blasted the men and machines piling up on the shoreline. The initial plan to have the LVTs drive inland so the marines could quickly seize key interior objectives was thus thwarted.

In the south, 4th Division units were pinned to the beach until midmorning. Naval covering fire was ineffective because there was little direct communication with fire control personnel on the beaches. Shortly after noon the 25th Marines took Agingan Point with the aid of tanks, eliminating the enfilading fire that had nearly paralyzed the right flank. The 23d Marines then secured most of the devastated town of Chalan Kanoa, but the regiment was halted by fierce artillery and small-arms fire along a ridgeline not shown on the marines' maps.

In the 2d Division sector, men of the 6th and 8th Marines were able to move ahead only a few yards. By nightfall, the marines held two small lodgments with a gap between the two divisions. They had advanced only halfway to the overly optimistic first day's objectives, and had sustained more than three thousand casualties getting there.

General Saito, believing the landings on the western beaches to be a feint, refrained from ordering any major counterattacks on D day. He thus passed up his best opportunity for victory. Nor did he order a serious attack on the gap between the two marine divisions that night. Instead, local commanders launched uncoordinated attacks on the beachhead. The most serious, at 0300, was against the 6th Marines. It was finally halted after two hours of close-in fighting.

The 4th Division, in an effort to turn the enemy's flank, began to penetrate inland and along the south coast the following day. The capture of Afetna Point ended the menace of enfilade fire from there. Meanwhile, elements of the 2d Division in the north closed the gap between the two divisions by noon.

As fast as division and corps artillery units landed, they engaged in fierce counterbattery operations against the concealed Japanese guns. By nightfall on D-plus-1, the beachhead had been expanded two thousand yards inland in places and despite still not reaching the first day's objectives, the marines were unlikely to be dislodged from their positions. It was then that Saito decided to launch a major attack. Fortunately for the marines, his orders to his subordinates were unclear; the attack, which should have begun at 1700 on 16 June, was not launched until about 0300 on the seventeenth.

Japanese infantry, with forty-four light tanks leading the way, stumbled toward the 2d Division lines. Star shells illuminated the unfortunate tanks, and artillery of all calibers ripped them apart. As many as thirty tanks were destroyed. Saito's counterattack was a miserable failure, and the marine position was stronger than ever.

From the beginning of the war, the Japanese naval high command had a fixation on bringing the U.S. fleet into one climactic, decisive action. Although relatively quiescent during 1943, the Japanese Combined Fleet was still a potent force. It had been reorganized in March 1944 into a mobile force built around carriers, much like Admiral Mitscher's TF 58. In June, VAdm. Jisaburo Ozawa's First Mobile Fleet had available five fleet carriers, four light carriers, seven battleships, and thirteen cruisers. The heart of the force was its almost five hundred planes. All in all, he commanded 90 percent of Japan's seapower.

Ozawa still believed in the possibility of a cataclysmic victory similar to the fabled destruction of the Russian fleet at Tsushima in 1905. His plan to achieve such a victory was code-named A-Go. Ozawa and his army colleagues believed the next major American operation would be in the western Carolines. A-Go was thus designed to intercept the Fifth Fleet in the Palau region. When it became obvious that the Marianas were the Americans' next target, Ozawa was authorized to modify his plan and seek a decisive confrontation off Saipan.

The First Mobile Fleet left its anchorage on 13 June, proceeded through the San Bernardino Strait and into the Philippine Sea, all the while being tracked by American submarines. Admiral Matome Ugaki, commanding the flotilla sent to aid Biak, was ordered to rendezvous with the main elements on 17 June. By then, Ozawa knew fairly well the Fifth Fleet's general location.

Submarine reports convinced Admiral Spruance that the Japanese would be in a position to attack by the evening of the seventeenth. This posed a major problem: What to do with the vulnerable transports and Admiral Bogan's lightly protected Carrier Support Group? Even more serious was the need for the 27th Division on Saipan, where the two marine divisions had suffered very heavy casualties.

Because the 27th Division was the reserve force for both Saipan and Guam, the Guam invasion scheduled for 18 June would have to be postponed indefinitely. The nearest reserve force available to back up the marine units scheduled to land there was in Hawaii. Spruance canceled the Guam operation and ordered the transports carrying the 3d Marine Division and the 1st Marine Provisional Brigade back to their anchorages at Kwajalein and Eniwetok. Then, aware of the approaching Japanese fleet, Spruance decided to send the 27th ashore immediately. He communicated his decision to Turner and Holland Smith on 16 June. Spruance wanted to choose the time and place of the major naval battle he envisioned, so he ordered the transports and less powerful covering elements to move eastward out of harm's way. Turner continued to unload supplies until late on the seventeenth, then moved all of his ships to rendezvous points some three hundred miles east of Saipan.

Considering the latest statements made by Holland Smith, it is important to note that the 27th Division's Ralph Smith was not notified of Spruance's decision until late on the sixteenth—well after Holland Smith and Turner got the word. All the advanced planning for the way his division was to be used went for naught as one foul-up by the corps staff and the navy followed another in the attempt to land the 165th Infantry, the first regiment Ralph Smith chose to send in.

The 4th Marine Division commander, General Schmidt, who took command of the 165th in the midst of a difficult situation on shore, was never given the appropriate information to enable him and his staff to plan for orderly insertion of the army regiment into the line. The army troops were kept on alert for hours. Then, just before midnight on 16 June, they were finally loaded into boats. Most of them bobbed around for hours because the commanders of the navy picket ships had not been alerted that an army regiment was to land in the dark. The snafu snowballed when many of the units were landed on the wrong beaches. Some of the key officers of the first two battalions ashore did not land until 0400. In a very real sense, the 165th was literally thrown onto the beaches.

Somehow, despite the series of blunders, the scattered troops were collected and inserted on the right side of the 4th Marine Division's line and participated in the general attack at 1100 on the seventeenth. The third battalion of the 165th was ashore before noon, and men from the 105th Regiment began landing on Blue Beach. However, congestion of boats at the reef line limited the landing of the 105th's support equipment and other supplies. When the order for all ships to clear the harbor was issued at 1700, the regiment was left to make do until the supply ships returned on 25 June. The 106th Infantry, the 27th Division's third regiment, landed on the twentieth, the day after the shattering naval victory over the Japanese First Mobile Fleet.

Admiral Spruance, meanwhile, had calculated that Ozawa's force would not be in a position to attack until the eighteenth. He thus did not cancel the scheduled strikes against Iwo Jima and Chichi Jima by the *Hornet* and *Essex* task groups. Their planes hit the two islands on the sixteenth, destroying an estimated seventy planes. Both groups rendezvoused with the main fleet by noon on the eighteenth.

Spruance had made it clear to Mitscher and his other subordinate commanders that he considered his first duty to be the protection of the Saipan beachhead and the relatively defenseless transports and service vessels. He was concerned that the Japanese commander would divide his force and send part of it after the beaches and the transports. At midnight on the seventeenth, the submarine *Cavalla* reported sighting the Japanese fleet eight hundred miles southwest of Saipan. Mitscher wanted to turn his powerful carrier force in that direction and close on the Japanese. Spruance, in keeping with what he considered his main task, twice denied this request, preferring to stand on the defensive.

Despite having fewer ships and aircraft, Admiral Ozawa did have one advantage. His planes lacked armor protection and self-sealing gas tanks, and so weighed less than their heavy American counterparts. This gave them a normal radius of action of 550 miles compared to the maximum of 350 miles for American aircraft. He also counted very heavily upon assistance from land-based aircraft, particularly from Guam, and he planned to use Orote Field for his carrier-based planes to land, rearm, and take on fuel after their first strikes. But RAdm. Kakuji Kakuta, commanding the Japanese air units on Guam, had misled Ozawa into believing that a significant number of planes would be available from Guam, Saipan, and Yap. In reality, Kakuta could muster only fifty planes, and these would play no important role in the battle.

By the afternoon of the eighteenth, Ozawa had pinpointed the location of the American fleet. Like his counterpart, he had to restrain an aggressive subordinate, RAdm. Sueo Obayashi, the commander of one of his carrier divisions. He feared a night engagement, as did Admirals Spruance, Mitscher, and Lee, who commanded the American battleship line. So the two fleets spent an anxious night waiting for daylight.

Admiral Ozawa had divided his force into two carrier groups moving northeast. By 19 June his van, consisting of the carriers *Chiyoda, Zuiho, Chitose,* and supporting elements, was a hundred miles ahead of the main fleet, which was built around the carriers *Junyo, Hiyo, Ryujo, Taiyo, Zuikaku,* and *Shokaku.* Mitscher had arrayed TF 58 approximately a hundred miles northwest of Guam in an inverted *F* formation moving in a northerly direction. Rear Admiral Joseph "Jocko" Clark's *Hornet* group was in the lead, followed by RAdm. John Reeves's *Lexington* group twelve miles to the south. This in turn was followed by RAdm. Alfred Montgomery's *Bunker Hill* group, another dozen miles behind. About twelve miles west of Clark's force was RAdm. William F. Harrill's *Essex* group. The midpart of the *F* bar was filled by Admiral Lee's fast battleships, steaming fifteen miles west of the *Lexington.* The opening engagement in the Battle of the Philippine Sea did not, however, involve a confrontation between the naval air units. Instead, Mitscher, responding to what appeared to be land-based planes from Yap en route to Guam to augment the Japanese forces there, ordered an 0700 strike on the island. In the ensuing air action, F6F Hellcat fighters from the *Belleau Wood* destroyed most of Kakuta's Guam-based air force. This dashed one of Ozawa's main hopes for assistance even before he launched his first attack on TF 58.

At approximately 0730, Japanese search planes located Mitscher's fleet. The sighting was confirmed a few minutes later by a second air patrol. Knowing his planes had greater range, Ozawa immediately ordered Admiral Obayashi, commanding the carriers in the van, to launch a major attack. Soon, sixty-one Zeros, forty-five carrying bombs, and eight torpedo planes were in the air. They were picked up by Admiral Lee's radar when they were 150 miles distant, and Mitscher turned his carriers into the wind and began to launch his fighters.

One great advantage the American commanders had was their advanced air search radar capability—and an efficient organization to exploit it. Each carrier had a fighter director on board, and Lt. Joseph Eggert on the *Lexington* acted as the task force fighter director. These directors controlled not only the direction of intercept but also the number of fighters necessary for optimum use. A Japanese language specialist monitored the Japanese air coordinator's frequency, as the latter circled and gave directions to his pilots. Within seconds the fighter directors had detailed information on enemy strength, altitude, and intentions.

The first major encounter with Japanese aircraft occurred when *Essex*'s combat air patrol (CAP), already operating between seventeen thousand and twenty-two thousand feet, attacked the Zeros in Ozawa's first wave. The outnumbered *Essex* pilots were soon joined by thirty more Hellcats from other carriers, and the combined group destroyed an estimated twenty-five planes. Some of the attackers managed to break through and strike Lee's battle line. *South Dakota* was hit, but the damage was not serious enough to keep the fast battleship out of the battle. None of the planes from this first strike got through to the American carriers, and forty-two of the sixty-nine aircraft sent fell to the fighters and Lee's antiaircraft gunners. This first engagement showed clearly the superiority of the American pilots and planes. The F6F Hellcat, in the hands of a skilled pilot, was more than a match for Zeros operated by green, relatively untrained pilots.

Thirty minutes after Obayashi dispatched the first wave of planes from the van, Ozawa launched a massive attack from his own carrier force. Eighty bombers and dive-bombers escorted by forty-eight Zeros made up this second wave. Long before they approached the American fleet, eight aircraft developed engine trouble, and ten were either damaged or destroyed by antiaircraft fire from Admiral Kurita's ships by overanxious gunners who believed the planes were American. Then, at about 1140, while still some sixty miles from the *Lexington,* the Japanese encountered a swarm of Hellcats from the central carrier group. In the ensuing dogfight an estimated seventy Japanese planes were destroyed. A few attackers did break through, but they were met by a hail of fire from ships of the battle line. The gunners' effectiveness had been considerably improved by the newly developed proximity fuse, which exploded antiaircraft rounds without them having to hit a target. Both Montgomery's and Reeves's task groups were attacked by small numbers of planes, but there was only minimal damage from near misses to the *Wasp* and *Bunker Hill.* Of the 128 planes Ozawa ordered into the air at 0900, only 31 returned.

But the Japanese were not yet finished. Obayashi sent off another forty-seven aircraft at about 1000, and these were directed to a contact point north of the leading American task group. They found nothing, so most of the force returned to the carriers. A few pilots did sight Lee's battleships, but they were intercepted before they could inflict any damage.

The final Japanese attack occurred when the bulk of Ozawa's remaining planes, eighty-two in all, were launched at 1100. Most of them searched in the wrong direction and were directed to Orote Field on Guam. They were intercepted over the island by fighters from *Cowpens, Essex,* and *Hornet,* which destroyed thirty of the unfortunate carrier-based planes. Ozawa's final attempt to attack the American task force had cost him dearly—seventy-three planes.

Unable to continue offensive operations, he was forced to think primarily about saving the rest of his fleet so that he could reorganize his depleted forces for a strike on the twentieth.

In this, the greatest of all carrier battles of World War II, the Japanese lost 330 planes and had fewer than 100 operational aircraft left for action the following day. The "Marianas Turkey Shoot," as it became known, was a disaster from which Japan would never recover.

Ozawa also lost two carriers on the nineteenth. Spruance had twenty-six submarines operating in the vast area from the Philippines to the Bonin Islands. Four were sent to patrol an area in the Philippine Sea through which RAdm. Charles Lockwood, the sub commander, believed Ozawa's fleet would pass. One of these, the *Albacore,* sighted Ozawa's flagship, the *Taiyo,* Japan's newest and, at 33,000 tons, largest carrier. The *Albacore* fired six torpedoes at the *Taiyo* just after Ozawa launched its planes for the second strike. One torpedo struck the carrier, rupturing its fuel tanks. Efforts to contain the fumes were not successful and shortly after 1500 the ship blew apart. It sank two hours later with a loss of more than sixteen hundred men. Ozawa managed to escape, and transferred his flag first to a heavy cruiser and eventually to the *Zuikaku.*

Three hours after *Albacore*'s attack, another submarine, the *Cavalla,* encountered the Japanese van and fired six torpedoes at *Shokaku.* Four struck the carrier, causing similar damage as that done to the *Taiyo.* Fumes spreading throughout the ship were ignited, and the resulting fire caused a bomb magazine to explode. Shortly thereafter, *Shokaku,* a veteran of Pearl Harbor and the Coral Sea action, went down. Both *Albacore* and *Cavalla* survived sustained depth-charge attacks by the carriers' destroyer screen.

Despite the air victories on the nineteenth, Mitscher still did not know the exact location of the Japanese fleet. Night searches were instituted, and the next day search planes from all the task groups fanned out in all directions. None made contact until, at about 1600, a plane from *Enterprise* sighted the Japanese fleet 275 miles away. Later reports placed the Japanese a crucial sixty miles farther out.

Only three hours of daylight remained at the time of the sighting, and the enemy fleet was at the extreme range of the American fighters. Nevertheless, Mitscher ordered an immediate launch—knowing full well that many of his pilots would not have fuel enough to find their way back in the dark. Within minutes, 215 planes had taken off from eleven carriers. There had been little time to devise a logical attack plan, so it was left to individual flight commanders to choose their own targets. In a twenty-minute period beginning at 1840, the Americans conducted a complex series of bombing and torpedo attacks that sank the carrier *Hiyo* and two oiler tankers. The carriers *Zuikaku, Chiyoda,* and *Ryujo,* as well as the battleship *Haruna,* were damaged, and eighty more Japanese planes were shot down.

The major problem facing Mitscher and the pilots in the attacking squadrons was how to get the planes back to the carriers and retrieve them. Task Force 58 was 250 miles away, and with no moon it became pitch-dark by the time the returning aircraft were only one-third of the way back. Very soon, some of the planes began to splash down, out of fuel. Mitscher then took a calculated risk: he ordered all the carriers to turn on their truck lights, running lights, and the glow lights used to outline the flight decks. Each flagship pointed a searchlight at the sky to act as a homing beacon. Cruisers and destroyers also turned on their running lights, and when the first planes showed up at about 2045, fired star shells to help illuminate the fleet. Night fighters were ordered aloft to help guide planes to the carriers.

The actual recovery was hectic. Although most pilots landed successfully, some planes crash-landed on the darkened decks. Others, too short of fuel to fly in the landing pattern, ditched close by ships. The final tally of eighty planes destroyed in various accidents that evening was four times the number lost in combat during the two-day battle. Rescue work by ships and planes that evening and on subsequent days saved most of the crewmen; only forty-nine aviators were never found.

Ozawa, with only thirty-five operational aircraft left, ordered his fleet to retire at full speed toward Okinawa. Spruance pursued the retreating Japanese, but had little chance of catching them. By the evening of the twenty-first, with fuel running low, Spruance called off the search. He and Mitscher had engineered a great victory, utterly destroying the Japanese carrier-based air force. The Japanese navy was still a potent force, but in all subsequent operations it would be forced into action without adequate air cover. Spruance's victory was marred by almost immediate accusations that he had once again been too cautious. Some observers later charged that by restraining Mitscher on the nineteenth, Spruance had thrown away the best chance of destroying most of Ozawa's fleet. He was also accused of misreading Japanese intentions after Ozawa divided his force. Others believed that Spruance did not start the pursuit soon enough and that he had restrained Lee from quickly following up the air strikes of the twentieth. Spruance later reminded his critics that he considered his primary duty to be protecting the land forces on Saipan. This prevented him from more aggressively going after the Japanese carriers sooner.

While the crucial naval air battle was unfolding, marine and army troops secured most of southern Saipan. By midmorning on the eighteenth, the 165th Infantry and elements of the 4th Marine Division's 25th Marines had taken the Aslito airfield. By the close of the day both marine and army units were almost to Magicienne Bay. On the 4th Division's left, the marshy area around Lake Susupe had been cleared of Japanese, and the 2d Division waited for the 4th to reach the east coast and complete its wheeling movement for the drive north. This maneuver was completed by the twentieth, and the marines held a line across the island just south of the hills adjacent to Mount Tapotchau.

In the meantime, four battalions of the 105th and 165th Infantry Regiments were given the task of reducing Japanese opposition in the Nafutan Peninsula. This area, more heavily wooded than most of Saipan, was full of ravines and ridgelines concealing a number of caves. The army units advanced slowly and steadily there in the face of a stubborn Japanese delaying action similar to the one conducted earlier on Biak.

Holland Smith was convinced there were only two or three hundred Japanese in Nafutan, whereas Ralph Smith, the army commander, believed there were at least eight hundred defenders. The marine commander, eager to begin the drive north, and acting on the assumption that only a few Japanese remained in Nafutan, ordered most of the troops out, leaving at first only two battalions to mop up. He could not understand why the army forces were advancing so slowly, and, believing what he saw on his inadequate maps of the area, he did not appreciate the difficulty the GIs were having rooting the Japanese out of the rugged terrain. Although he later blamed the army for allowing the Japanese to break out from Nafutan on 27 June, the simple fact was that the one battalion left on line after the withdrawal of still more troops was not enough to contain them. More than 360 Japanese died in the breakout attempt. A later count of Japanese bodies found on the peninsula showed that there had been at least 1,250 men in the Nafutan area on 18 June.

The army's 165th and 106th Infantry Regiments were ordered to move into position in the center sector between the 2d and 4th Marine Divisions to support the attack north. Because of later allegations made by Holland Smith, it is important to note the situation on 22 June. The 4th Division held the line from the central valley between Mount Tapotchau and the hills overlooking Magicienne Bay, while the 2d Division, on the extreme left, had the unenviable task of having to move north in the shadow of Mount Tapotchau.

Holland Smith and his chief of staff, Brig. Gen. Graves B. Erskine, using maps that did not accurately depict the terrain, assigned optimistic goals for both divisions. Despite the heroic efforts of all the marine assault battalions, those goals were not reached until the sixth day of the attack.

All of the 4th Division's battalions were committed, but only a few yards had been gained by the end of the first day. At about 1600, Erskine informed Ralph Smith that he should move the 106th and 165th forward to relieve 4th Marine Division units holding the center of the line and prepare to take part in a general offensive scheduled the next day. Erskine was not certain exactly when the attack would begin, but told Ralph Smith that it might be 1000. He then drew rough boundaries between the divisions on Smith's overlay. Unfortunately, the left boundary cut through the eastern foothills of Tapotchau. The army commanders who relieved the marines were not properly briefed on enemy strong points in the area, and the marine lines had been pulled back because of Japanese counterattacks during the night. Holland Smith's charts thus indicated that the front line was actually many yards in front of its actual location. This meant that the army units had to fight to recover ground that

Holland Smith's headquarters believed was already held. This misunderstanding was one of the reasons Holland Smith later accused the 27th Division of performing poorly.

Sandwiched between the two marine divisions on 23 June, the two army regiments, still unaware of the operation's scheduled start time, finally began their advance later than corps headquarters wanted. As the GIs moved into a partially wooded open plain dominated in the west by Mount Tapotchau and in the east by a series of low hills, the Japanese—ensconced in caves on either side of the plain—poured a withering fire on their attackers. Only minimum artillery support was available because of fear of striking the 4th Marine Division units advancing to the east. Holland Smith later made much of the army's failure to maintain flank contact. However, by his own order, it was the 4th Marine Division's responsibility to maintain contact in the east, and the western boundary Erskine had drawn for Ralph Smith passed through a series of ravines and hills that made it impossible to keep flank contact there. The 2d Marine Division made good progress along the western coast road, and the 4th Division, after a stiff fight, seized a portion of Hill 600 overlooking the Kagman Peninsula. Still, neither marine unit reached its assigned objectives.

By the evening of the twenty-third the line was in the shape of a shallow U because the army units had been halted after little gain. Incensed by their perceived failure, Holland Smith made one of the most controversial decisions in the Central Pacific theater. The 27th Division, facing some of the most concentrated defenses on the island, had been in the line for only one day. Furthermore, no one from corps had visited the area or discussed the tactical problem with Ralph Smith. Still, Holland Smith decided to relieve the army commander and replace him with Maj. Gen. Sanderford Jarman, who was scheduled to be the garrison commander when the fighting stopped. Jarman had no previous combat experience in World War II.

For more than forty years the only details of the events leading up to Ralph Smith's relief came from a book and articles Holland Smith wrote after the war. These were repeated by a generation of journalists. The stories blackened the reputation of Ralph Smith and the 27th Division. Later evidence points to the self-serving nature of Holland Smith's remembrances. When he first reported his dissatisfaction with Ralph Smith to Admiral Spruance, he offered no specific charges. Spruance, although unwilling to override the wishes of his senior land commander, nevertheless wanted specifics.

General Erskine later supplied the admiral with three reasons for the relief. The first would have been trivial under differing circumstances. It concerned the issuance of two orders by Ralph Smith to units still under corps command because the corps staff was slow in alerting units of impending attacks. The second charge was that the battalion left in Nafutan did not advance rapidly enough. Erskine failed to mention that this unit was under corps control at the time. The third reason concerned the division's failure to attack on time on the twenty-third, for which all the blame was placed on Ralph Smith. Erskine neglected to mention the lack of cooperation of the marine units or the foul-up getting troops into the line because the 4th Division did not provide guides during the early morning hours. The fact that the 27th was a National Guard division was much later used by Holland Smith and others to explain its presumed lack of effectiveness. However, that argument had little merit. National Guard units distinguished themselves in both the Pacific and European theaters of action.

When informed of his relief on the twenty-fourth, Ralph Smith was shocked. There had been no prior intimation such a move was coming. Nevertheless, he cordially briefed General Jarman on plans for the proposed attack the next day. The maneuver was designed to flank the hills to the east of the division's sector, a plan Jarman faithfully carried out.

Such detail about an otherwise minor event is necessary not just because the relief was unjustified. Harding's relief at Buna and Fuller's at Biak were also unjustified. But Ralph Smith's relief was important because it symbolized the festering differences between the army, the navy, and the Marine Corps in the Central Pacific theater. General Marshall and the Central Pacific theater commander, Lt. Gen. Robert Richardson, had never been satisfied with the command relationships under Nimitz. They argued that marine commanders had never practiced large-scale operations and that overall ground command should rest with the army. Ralph Smith's summary dismissal for what appeared to be no valid reason brought the issue into the open.

Ralph Smith had little part in what followed, having exchanged commands with Maj. Gen. George W. Griner Jr., who was appointed to command the 27th. Smith took over Griner's 98th Division in Hawaii. General Richardson convened a board of inquiry headed by Lt. Gen. Simon Buckner to evaluate the charges against Ralph Smith. After an exhaustive investigation, the Buckner Board concluded that while Holland Smith had the authority to relieve the 27th Division commander, the relief was in no way justified. The disagreement over the Saipan affair later reached the highest levels, pitting General Marshall against Admiral King. When Admiral King appeared unwilling to accept Buckner's report, General Marshall buried it for the sake of interservice cooperation. The subject then remained dormant until revived by Holland Smith's postwar inflammatory articles. However, true to his word, General Marshall made certain that Holland Smith never again commanded army troops.

The 27th Division change in command fortunately had little effect on the outcome of the campaign. By 28 June the Japanese remaining along the ridges and valleys and on Hill Able began to withdraw as the 27th broke into open country. General Griner was surprised when he took over from Jarman to find that, instead of three full regiments, he controlled only four battalions. The rest were under corps command, and Holland Smith informed Griner that he would have to "earn" back the rest of his division. Griner did not get control of all the division's units until 6 July.

While the controversy over command was agitating higher headquarters, the decimation of Saito's forces continued. As the 27th broke out of Death Valley, the 1st and 2d Battalions of the 8th Marines clambered up the slopes of Mount Tapotchau under heavy fire. By the time the crest was secured, the 1st Battalion had been reduced to only two hundred effectives. Possession of this highest point on the island deprived the Japanese of an excellent observation post and conversely gave American artillery spotters a view of the entire island. Other 2d Marine Division units advanced along the coast road, and on 3 July captured the ruined capital city of Garapan. The 4th Marine Division spread out across the Kagman Peninsula, and on 6 July captured the heights of Mount Petosukora.

Corps then decided to pull the 2d Division back into reserve when the advancing troops reached the narrow part of the island. The 27th Division thus occupied the western sector, with the 4th Marine Division in the east for the final advance toward Marpi Point.

General Saito, who had seen his last defensive line collapse and who had only a small portion of his original force left, requested Imperial Headquarters's permission to launch a *gyokusai*—an all-out suicide attack. This was planned for the early morning hours on 7 July. Saito exhorted his troops to take "seven lives to repay our country." Old and infirm, Saito returned to his headquarters after issuing the order and committed suicide on 6 July. His naval counterpart, Admiral Nagumo, once the proud leader of Japan's victorious carrier forces, dined with Saito the evening of the fifth and shortly afterward also committed suicide.

The Japanese attack should not have caught Holland Smith's staff unaware. On 4 July, an army Nisei interrogator learned from a Japanese civilian that such an attack was being planned. Still more information about the Japanese plan was obtained from a Japanese prisoner the evening of the sixth. Colonel W. M. Van Antwerp, the 27th Division's G2, informed the corps G2 of this, and he also alerted individual commanders of the possibility of an all-out attack.

On the afternoon of 6 July, corps headquarters, despite protests by General Griner, ordered the 1st and 2d Battalions of the 105th Infantry to advance along the west coast. Holland Smith believed that a general warning to Griner to look out for an attack would make up for the battalions' potentially precarious situation. By late afternoon, Col. William O'Brien, commander of the 1st Battalion, had made his dispositions for the night. There was a three-hundred- to four-hundred-yard gap caused by a deep gulch between his right flank and the 3d Battalion's left. Perturbed by this, O'Brien requested reinforcements but was told that none were available. He then tried to cover the gap with antitank weapons and machine guns.

Beginning at 0400 on 7 July, an estimated five thousand Japanese, some armed only with sharpened sticks, struck the 105th's lines. Within thirty minutes they had overrun both the 1st and 2d Battalions and begun streaming down the gulch. A marine artillery unit approximately five hundred yards behind the line was also overrun. The army and marine troops exacted a terrible toll but were nevertheless forced back. Several small units banded together to form a strong defensive perimeter in the village of Tanapag. The 27th Division's artillery fired more than twenty-five hundred rounds of ammunition in the first hours of the engagement, indicating the severity of the attack. Still, General Griner was slow to respond to the situation, and it was four hours before a major relief effort was mounted by two battalions from the 106th Infantry.

Griner at first reported to Holland Smith that about fifteen hundred Japanese had attacked. Smith did not accept the report, choosing to believe that there were only two hundred to three hundred attackers. He refused to send up tanks to support the 106th's counterattack, and in a staff conference openly called army personnel "yellow bastards." Early on the seventh, the corps commander finally authorized the attachment of the 3d Battalion, 6th Marines, to assist the 106th Infantry's relief column advancing along the coast. By nightfall, most of the ground lost had been retaken, and on the eighth the units within the Tanapag perimeter were removed by amtracs.

Despite his later protestations, Holland Smith was partially responsible for the success of the *gyokusai*. As already noted, his staff ignored earlier warnings and he gave the order to place the two army battalions forward without adequate reserves. Even worse, he chose to believe that two battalions of "yellow bastards" could not halt the attack of a small number of Japanese. His subsequent recommendation that a Presidential Unit Citation be awarded to the marine artillery unit which was overrun gave credence to the story that the Japanese were halted only by the heroic action of a handful of marine gunners.

The facts were much more complicated, however. The 105th Infantry lost 405 men killed and 512 wounded in twelve hours of fighting, and it was the 105th that halted the Japanese. Two of those killed, Colonel O'Brien and Sgt. Thomas Baker, were posthumously awarded the Medal of Honor. Despite Holland Smith's belief that it was only a small attack, the Japanese lost 4,300 men killed, of whom only 322 were found near the marine artillery unit's position.

Smith again added fuel to the fires of interservice rivalry by ordering the 27th Division back into corps reserve and replacing it with elements of the 2d Marine Division.

The *gyokusai* had so weakened the Japanese defense that the 6th Marines, after passing through the 27th's lines on 8 July, had little difficulty eliminating the last organized Japanese resistance near the coast. Meanwhile, the 8th Marines and the 1st Battalion, 165th Infantry, fought their way through the remnants of the Japanese force in the interior, and the 24th and 25th Marines of the 4th Division advanced to a point near Makunska village from which that division took over all offensive action in the north. By 8 July the 2d Marines of the 2d Division, which had been attached to the 4th, reached the heights above the extreme northern plain. The following day General Schmidt attacked northward with three regiments on line and by that evening reached Marpi Point, the northernmost part of the island. Admiral Turner lost no time announcing the next day that Saipan was secure.

Although Saipan may have been declared secure, the dangerous task of discovering individual Japanese hidden in the ravines and caves went on. The two marine divisions were pulled back to the center and southern part of the island on 13 July to prepare for the Tinian operation and the task of pacification was left to the army. From the time Admiral Turner declared the island secure until the 27th Division left in early August, an additional 1,972 enemy soldiers were killed.

Even before the 4th Division reached Marpi Point, there was a concerted effort to convince soldiers and civilians hiding in caves to come out and surrender. Saipan was the first island encountered by the Allies on which there was a large Japanese civilian population. Government propaganda had portrayed the Americans as monsters who would murder the men and rape and kill women and children. The naval and air bombardments, followed by three weeks of hard fighting, did nothing to dispel civilian fears. Urged on by the military, many chose suicide rather than submission. In the two days before the marines reached the north coast, hundreds of civilians made their way to the top of a sheer bluff overlooking the plain and hurled themselves to the rocks below. This orgy of self-destruction was repeated on other cliffs near Marpi Point. Despite their best efforts, the marines were helpless to stop men, women, and children from leaping into the sea or passively wading into the surf to drown. A number used hand grenades to blow themselves apart. No accurate count could ever be made of the unfortunate civilians who preferred to join their soldiers in death.

The cost of the battle for Saipan was high. When the final tally of casualties was completed in early October, it showed that V Amphibious Corps had lost 3,119 men killed—divided almost equally between the three divisions engaged. In addition, 10,992 men were wounded or missing. The Japanese, on the other hand, lost almost their entire garrison of more than 20,000 men. More importantly, they lost an island only 1,250 miles from Tokyo. Aslito airfield, renamed Isley Field, received its first American plane, a damaged TBF, on 20 July. After engineers repaired and lengthened the runway, it was able to handle heavy bombers, and by early September B-24s were flying strikes against the Bonin Islands. Engineers and navy construction battalions also built another field capable of handling the huge B-29 Superfortress before the end of the year, as well as two smaller fighter fields. The first raid by B-29s from Saipan was flown against Truk in October. Saipan also later became an important navy base, particularly for submarines operating in Japanese home waters.

With the Saipan operation officially over, Admiral Spruance turned to the task of liberating the large island of Guam, the former American possession that had been occupied by the Japanese on 8 December 1941. As noted earlier, the initial plan for seizing the Marianas had optimistically called for General Geiger's III Amphibious Corps to land on Guam on 18 June. But Spruance's decision to commit the 27th Division on Saipan postponed that invasion. The 3d Marine Division and the 1st Marine Provisional Brigade, the assault units, were transported back to Kwajalein and Eniwetok to await the arrival from Hawaii of the army's 77th Division, the necessary reserve unit. Some of the marine units were cooped up on board the transports for fifty-five days before they landed on W day, 21 July. Despite the boredom suffered by the troops, the delay was fortunate as it gave the navy time to systematically work over Guam's western coast. Admiral Conolly, in tactical command of the southern operations, lived up to his nickname

"Close-in." Destroyers and cruisers bombarded Apra Harbor on 27 and 30 June, but those strikes were minor compared to the action that began on 8 July. For thirteen days, the navy blasted beaches and inland targets. By the time the troops went ashore on 21 July, three cruiser divisions and six battleships had pulverized the defenses adjacent to the beaches, destroying most of the Japanese heavy coastal artillery and killing hundreds of soldiers. Japanese airpower on the island had been destroyed earlier by Admiral Mitscher's pilots during the preliminaries to the Philippine Sea battle.

Lieutenant General Takeshi Takashina, the Japanese commander, still had a formidable defensive force, although he was forced to fight the battle without air or naval support. Initially, before the sustained naval bombardment, he had a number of large-caliber coastal defense guns, and each of his regiments were supported by 75mm and 105mm artillery pieces. There was also a tank regiment on Guam, and the Japanese commander used these vulnerable light vehicles with caution—normally to set up ambushes along the narrow forest trails. All in all, Takashina had about 18,500 army and naval troops —which he deployed carefully but incorrectly because he expected the invasion to take place at Tumon Bay where there was a wide, two-and-one-half-mile-long beach.

As they had on Saipan, the American planners correctly guessed the Japanese commander's intention, and instead decided to bring LVTs and DUKW amphibious trucks over the reefs and land on two beaches farther south. Fronting these beach areas were sheer bluffs, in some places over two hundred feet high, beginning a few yards inland from the beaches. Central Guam is a high plateau guarded by rugged hills and cliffs in the west. These provided excellent defensive positions, as did the heavily wooded areas of northern Guam. Unbeknownst to the Americans, General Obata, commander of the Thirty-first Army, was on the island after finding it impossible to reach his headquarters on Saipan. He stepped in and assumed direct command of the Japanese defense after Takashina was killed on 28 July.

At 0530 on 21 July, the navy began its heavy preinvasion bombardment. Soon after that, the LSTs had unloaded the LVTs and DUKWs for their runs across the reef. At about 0830, the first elements of Maj. Gen. Allen Turnage's 3d Marine Division landed between Asan Point and Adelup Point, south of the main town of Agana. The beach there is narrow, as little as two hundred yards wide. Despite considerable small-arms and machine-gun fire from the heights above the beach, the three regiments quickly pushed inland, and the division's heavy equipment soon began to arrive. By midafternoon, all of the division's artillery was ashore.

The 9th Marines, operating in front of Blue Beach on the right,

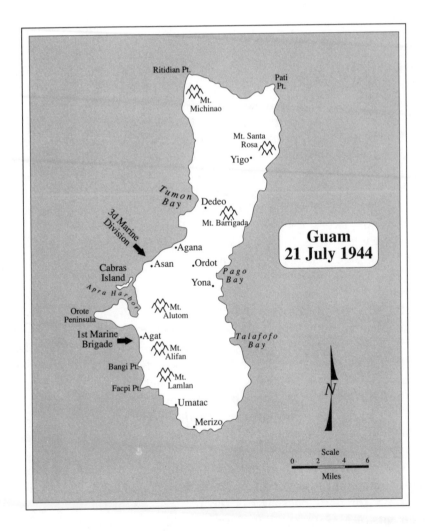

Ritidian Pt.

Pati Pt.

Mt. Michinao

Mt. Santa Rosa

Yigo

Tumon Bay

Dedeo

Mt. Barrigada

3d Marine Division

Guam 21 July 1944

Agana

Cabras Island

Asan

Ordot

Pago Bay

Yona

Apra Harbor

Orote Peninsula

Mt. Alutom

1st Marine Brigade

Agat

Talafofo Bay

Mt. Alifan

Bangi Pt.

Mt. Lamlan

Facpi Pt.

Umatac

Merizo

N

Scale
0   2   4   6
Miles

took Asan Point by 1700, while the 21st Marines on their left seized the high ground above Green Beach. The most difficult task was in the 3d Marines's area inland from Red Beach, where Chonito Cliff and its sixty degree incline temporarily blocked any further advance. Tanks were brought up to support the companies clambering up the cliff. Fortunately the long bombardment had destroyed many of the Japanese emplacements there, and by noon the marines had secured the position. Shortly thereafter, other companies from the 3d Marines seized Adelup Point. By the evening of the first day, the marines had a precarious but firm toehold at Asan.

Meanwhile, Brig. Gen. Lemuel C. Shepherd Jr.'s 1st Marine Provisional Brigade had landed south of Orote Peninsula near the village of Agat. The marines there had more maneuvering room and, despite very heavy losses, the 4th Marines soon seized Bangi Point and, with the aid of tanks, took prominent Hill 600. A battalion from the 4th Marines also moved to secure the important road leading through Maanot Pass into the interior. At the same time, the 1st Battalion, 22d Marines, moved north up the coast road and seized Agat village, while the 2d Battalion began a maneuver designed to seal off the Japanese occupying Orote Peninsula. Like the 3d Division marines at Asan, Shepherd's men at the close of the day held only a shallow lodgment, and at best had established footholds on only the first line of ridges.

Both marine commanders were fortunate that Takashina had no detailed plans for massive counterattacks against the marine perimeters that night and thus threw away his best chance to inflict maximum damage on their units. The only attack of note that night was made against the 4th Marines when Col. Tsunetaro Suenaga, commander of the 38th Regiment, led a series of futile banzai charges that accomplished nothing, but cost the Japanese many casualties. The next morning the marines in both sectors resumed the attack against a basically static defense.

On the Asan front, the major problem was seizing Bundschu Ridge and the adjacent highlands. Major General Kiyoshi Shigematsu, the Japanese commander there, zeroed in all his available mortars and artillery on that area. The 3d Marines made little headway in the face of such stubborn resistance, and the regiment was unable to occupy the high ground until late on the twenty-third.

Meanwhile, on the right flank, the 9th Marines took Piti Navy Yard and landed on Cabras Island the next day.

Although the high ground immediately adjacent to the beaches had been secured, the marines did not have a solid front. There were gaps in the line caused partially by terrain and partially because the front was too long to be held by the weary marines, who had already suffered 1,650 casualties.

At Agat, General Shepherd sent the 4th Marines farther inland to seize the area around Mount Alifan, while the 22d Marines attacked through the rice paddies against stiffening opposition to secure an important road junction east of Orote Peninsula. Shepherd decided he needed more support, and on 22 July asked Maj. Gen. Andrew D. Bruce, commander of the 77th Division, to land the 305th Infantry Regiment. During the next two days the rest of the army troops came ashore. Like their 27th Division counterparts on Saipan, the men in each of the 77th Division's regiments had to wade ashore from outside the reef because of the shortage of LVTs and DUKWs. However, General Bruce and his staff understood the logistical problem and the fact that Shepherd was busy attempting to expand the beachhead. Unlike on Saipan, there was never any serious friction between army and marine commanders. General Geiger never doubted the valor or ability of army troops. He asked for and received the fullest cooperation from Bruce, and did not interfere in the tactical disposition of army units any more than he did with the marine divisions.

There was a general lull in the fighting on 25 July as the marine and army units regrouped. The exception was in the 1st Marine Provisional Brigade's sector. General Shepherd sent the bulk of his two regiments north to extend control over the base of Orote Peninsula as far as Apra Harbor. They made contact with the 9th Marines by nightfall, and approximately twenty-five hundred Japanese were isolated on the peninsula. The 77th Division in turn moved to relieve the eastern-facing marine positions farther inland. This enabled Shepherd to concentrate on reducing the navy and army troops trapped on the peninsula, where they operated from the best defensive positions on the island. General Geiger resisted pressure from Holland Smith to begin a general breakout in the Asan area before Orote Peninsula was secure.

The battle for Guam was greatly simplified by General Takashina's decision to authorize two banzai charges, one against Shepherd's brigade and the other, larger attack against the 3d Division. The marines on Orote Peninsula became aware of the possibility of an attack when they heard the shouts of drunken troops coming from the Japanese lines. Shortly after midnight on 26 July, a battalion from Comdr. Asaichi Tomai's force wildly assaulted the 22d Marines's line near the Agat-Sumay road junction. A combination of corps 155mm guns and the 77th Division's medium artillery blew the attackers apart before they reached the dug-in marines. Despite the near destruction of the battalion, Tomai ordered a second attack. It, too, was repulsed before dawn. Japanese losses in these fruitless attacks amounted to more than five hundred men, significantly weakening the Orote defenses.

Three hours later, after a series of probing attacks, Takashina launched his well-planned assault on the stretched-out 3d Division lines where, in one sector, a battalion of the 21st Marines tried to cover a two-thousand-yard front with just 250 men. The attack on the regiment was only partially disrupted by artillery fire, and the front disintegrated into a series of deadly hand-to-hand combats. Some Japanese broke through and rushed down a ravine toward the beach, only to be destroyed by tank-infantry teams. Another major attack found the half-mile-wide gap between the 4th and 9th Marines, and the Japanese there temporarily seized the high ground adjacent to the beach as others invaded the division headquarters area. Marine service personnel quickly formed, counterattacked, and drove the attackers back.

Meanwhile, on the extreme left end of the line, the 3d Marines were hit by the Japanese 48th Brigade. Artillery and mortar fire destroyed large numbers of attackers, and most of those who reached the marine positions were dispatched in desperate hand-to-hand fighting. The attack was over by dawn, and marine patrols began to ferret out enemy troops who had been left behind. Although the exact number of Japanese killed in this series of attacks will never be known, Geiger's headquarters estimated Japanese losses at thirty-five hundred—including a large number of senior officers. The banzai attacks gained nothing for the Japanese and made the conquest of Guam much easier.

The marines' breakout from the beachheads and pursuit of the Japanese remaining on the island did not begin immediately. Generals Geiger and Turnage were uncertain about Takashina's intentions, and the tired marines needed rest after repelling the suicidal charges. So the 3d Division was pulled back to consolidate the front, and the 77th Division relieved the 1st Marine Provisional Brigade, enabling Shepherd to concentrate both of his regiments against the excellent defenses the Japanese had constructed on Orote Peninsula.

On 27 July the 307th Infantry began to move toward Mount Tenjo, located two miles inland from Apra Harbor, while the 305th pushed ahead against scattered resistance to link up with the 3d Marine Division by the evening of the twenty-eighth. The 3d Division also resumed the offensive on the twenty-seventh, and quickly seized Mount Chachao and Mount Alutom. Patrols from the 77th Division probing the overgrown hilly country of southern Guam found only a few Japanese, thus confirming the corps headquarters's conclusion that the main Japanese force was in the north. Geiger halted the general advance on the twenty-eighth and waited for Orote Peninsula to be cleared.

Backed by corps and 77th Division artillery augmented by naval gunfire, the 1st Marine Provisional Brigade began its offensive on Orote Peninsula at 0700 on 26 July. The 22d Marines's advance on the right was channeled down the Agat-Sumay road. The regiment was slowed by swampy ground, whereas the 4th Marines moved rapidly ahead against light resistance. The attack the next day bogged down as both regiments advanced slowly against concerted mortar and machine-gun fire. Despite support from tanks, the marines gained only five hundred yards. However, there were indications of a breakdown in Japanese morale when some of the defenders broke and ran. On the twenty-eighth, resistance against the 22d Marines collapsed; the old marine barracks area was taken, and by evening the destroyed village of Sumay was captured. Meanwhile, the 4th Marines ran into the strongest defensive line on the peninsula and needed tank support before forcing the defenders back to a ridgeline. The final drive began the next day. The airfield was captured, and most of the defenders began to commit suicide while a few tried to escape by attempting to swim to the reef line.

Once Orote Peninsula had been taken, the general advance to the north could proceed. The 77th Division moved across the island to form the right wing of the northern advance, with the 3d Division on the left. The 1st Marine Provisional Brigade consolidated its position and sent patrols into the southern districts to eliminate the few Japanese there. The 3d Division, moving to secure the left flank of the proposed northern drive, seized the Fonte Plateau while the 77th Divison took up positions extending from the center of the island to Pago Bay. General Takashina was killed in the fighting for the Fonte positions, and tactical command devolved on Obata, who ordered a general withdrawal toward Mount Santa Rosa.

Commanding approximately eighty-five hundred men from a number of shattered units, Obata established two strong defensive positions, one in the east near Mount Barrigada and the other in front of the 3d Division at Finegayan. The week-long fighting after the general advance began on 2 August consisted primarily of small-unit encounters. The Japanese would set ambushes along the few trails, inflict casualties, and then fall back. Unlike most Marine Corps actions in the Pacific, the movement north was a cautious advance through very difficult terrain. In some areas, particularly along the eastern flank, contact could not be maintained because of the dense forest and underbrush. Nevertheless, the army units captured Mount Barrigada on 3 August and advanced toward the final Japanese defenses near Mount Santa Rosa. The 3d Division cleared the Finegayan area by 6 August and the next day General Geiger inserted the 1st Marine Provisional Brigade between the two divisions for the final drive to the north coast. Mount Santa Rosa fell to the army on 8 August, and advance elements of the 1st Marine Provisional Brigade reached Ritidian Point, the northernmost part of the island, the same day.

On 9 August a patrol from the 9th Marines located a brush-lined hollow with many caves in the 306th Infantry's sector. The next day, the regiment's 1st Battalion destroyed the defenses of what had been General Obata's command post. Obata himself committed suicide before the battle for the caves had been concluded. During the next few months, vigorous large-scale patrols continued to search out and destroy the remnants of the Japanese garrison.

The cost of liberating Guam had been high: 7,714 casualties, including 1,190 marines and 177 army personnel killed in action. No specific figures could be established for casualties to Guam's Chamorro population, which had maintained its steadfast loyalty to the United States throughout the long ordeal of occupation. The maltreatment of the native population increased after news of the invasion of Saipan reached Guam. Most of the Chamorros were kept in neglected concentration camps. As the Japanese retreated, some took out their frustrations on the Chamorros, wantonly murdering hundreds of civilians. The condition of the liberated Chamorros served as an added incentive to destroy as many Japanese soldiers as possible.

The last of the Mariana Islands to be targeted was Tinian. The campaign's planners decided to simply bypass Rota, the other major island in the chain. An invasion of Tinian, located only three miles across the channel from Saipan, had been included in the overall strategy, but aside from the 27th Division's contingency plans, little detailed work had been done. With the Saipan campaign concluded, corps headquarters decided to seize the island primarily because of the airfield located at its northern end.

A change of command occurred on 12 July when General Schmidt replaced Holland Smith as commander of the V Amphibious Corps. Major General Clifton Cates succeeded Schmidt as commander of the 4th Marine Division. On that same day, Turner, Schmidt, and RAdm. Harry Hill, the new Northern Attack Force commander, met and agreed to launch the assault on 24 July. This left only a very brief time for the many details of the amphibious operation to be worked out. Nevertheless, within a week the major elements of the plan had been agreed upon.

Tinian was sparsely occupied, the bulk of the population living in Tinian town on the southwest coast adjacent to the only good harbor and beach area. Elsewhere, cliffs that rose directly from the coast either precluded or made any attempted landing extremely hazardous. However, there were two very narrow beaches on the northwest coast, and after considerable discussion, the planners chose to have the marines land there instead of at Tinian town. In addition to the naval gunfire and air support that could be brought to bear, the beaches there could be covered by heavy artillery emplaced in southern Saipan. Finally, intelligence officers confirmed that most of the nine thousand Japanese army and naval troops on the island were concentrated in the south, where they expected the invasion to occur.

The final plans called for two 2d Marine Division regiments, covered by a large naval force, to feint toward Tinian town. The actual landings would be made by the 4th Marine Division's 24th and 25th Regiments. One battleship, two cruisers, and four destroyers were assigned to provide fire support off Tinian town, while the other four sectors of the island would be covered by two battleships, four cruisers, and twelve destroyers. Five light carriers and five squadrons of army planes operating from Isley Field on Saipan were available to provide air cover.

The invasion, which Holland Smith described as the perfect amphibious operation, went like clockwork. The demonstration group of seven transports carrying the 2d and 8th Marines, protected by the battleship *Colorado* and escorts, began its run toward the beach at Tinian town at 0730 on 24 July. Colonel Kiyochi Ogata's troops remained frozen in the south by the 2d Division feint. By the time the landing craft had returned to their transports, the 4th Division's troops had safely landed in the north. The Japanese were cheered when their 5-inch coastal guns took the *Colorado* under fire and scored twenty-two hits. The destroyer *Norman Scott* was also hit, killing nineteen sailors and wounding forty-seven. But the volume of fire from the naval vessels soon quieted most of the Japanese shore batteries.

Meanwhile, in the north, where the 24th Marines were assigned a narrow beach with flanking cliffs, only eight LVTs could land abreast. It took an hour to land two battalions. Fortunately there was no large Japanese force to oppose them.

The 25th Marines had a broader beach that allowed twice the number of LVTs to land at the same time. At 0830 the regiment's two assault battalions were ashore and moving inland against only sporadic resistance. By midafternoon the bulk of the 23d Marines—the reserve regiment—was also ashore, and the attached tank and half-track companies landed before nightfall. By then there were more than fifteen thousand men ashore, and the beachhead was one mile deep by one and three-fourths miles wide.

The Japanese responded by launching a series of uncoordinated infantry assaults on the marine lines. On the left, the 24th Marines repulsed banzai charges by naval troops, while the 25th Marines in the center and the 23d on the right fought off similar attacks. By the next morning, more than twelve hundred Japanese had been killed.

After the demonstration off Tinian town, the transports moved

north and began landing the 2d Division's 6th and 8th Marines behind the 4th Division units already ashore. Both regiments moved
immediately to holding areas five hundred yards inland before taking up positions along the east coast. Meanwhile, the 4th Division
pressed south. The 23d Marines employed a double envelopment to
take rugged Mount Mfaga, and the 25th Marines reached the base
of Mount Lasso, which fell on the twenty-sixth. The 8th Marines
captured Ushi Field that same day, and army P-47 close support
aircraft were soon operating from it.

Both divisions advanced southward cautiously despite the light
opposition they encountered. Generals Watson and Cates did not
order their units to move until the objectives had been smothered
by the division artilleries' battalions, corps' big guns on Saipan, and
the naval support vessels. By 29 July the 4th Division had reached
the outskirts of Tinian town. The 25th Marines first cleared caves
on the right, and then the 24th's battalions entered the rubbled town
the next day. Keeping in step, the 2d Division seized the heights
adjacent to Masalog Point with only scattered opposition from the
Japanese defenders. By then the marines held four-fifths of the island, but they had destroyed only one-third of the Japanese garrison. Stretching before them was a mile-long flat plain rising
abruptly to heavily wooded heights that could not be assaulted from
the east because of the steep escarpment. It was on that high ground
that Colonel Ogata had concentrated the remainder of his force.

On 31 July, two battleships and three cruisers bombarded the
high ground for two hours, and more than a hundred planes from
Isley Field, many using napalm, worked over the area. In the 4th
Division sector, the two assault regiments, aided by artillery and
tanks, gained the top of the cliffs by evening, thus penetrating the
last good defensive position in the southwest part of the island.
Meanwhile, the 2d Marine Division regiments advanced across the
bush-covered plain against savage enemy fire. Late in the day, two
battalions from the 8th Marines reached the top of the bluff line,
where they survived two large-scale banzai charges during the night.

On 1 August, the last day of organized Japanese resistance on
Tinian, men of the 4th Division advanced across a flat plateau,
reaching the southern tip of the island by midafternoon. In the east,
the 6th and 8th Marines advanced abreast through heavy under-

growth and routed the Japanese from numerous caves before reaching the cliffs above Marpi Point. Surveying the situation with satisfaction, General Schmidt declared the island secure just before nightfall.

Schmidt's declaration did not mean the end of fighting on Tinian, however. The following day, a last-gasp banzai charge penetrated to the command post of the 3d Battalion, 6th Marines, and was beaten off by headquarters troops who killed 119 Japanese. Small numbers of Japanese continued to make localized attacks for several days thereafter.

Beginning on 31 July, large numbers of civilians began coming out of their hiding places, and the marines used loudspeakers to try to convince those remaining that they would not be harmed. This was only partially successful; many women chose to throw their children off the cliffs before jumping themselves. Some were pushed by Japanese soldiers and many more were blown up by troops using hand grenades.

Although there was no hope of victory, individual Japanese soldiers vowed to kill at least one American before they died. Some hid in huge caves that defied demolition, while others waited in ravines and smaller caves. Clearing them out took five nerve-racking months. The 4th Division was ordered to Maui before the end of August, and soon after most of the 2d Division withdrew to Saipan, leaving behind the 8th Marines to deal with the remaining Japanese. By the time that regiment departed on 1 January 1945, it had killed an additional 542 Japanese while suffering 163 casualties.

Within a few months the Marianas became the home of the newly created Twentieth Air Force. Its B-29s soon began subjecting Japan to unremitting air attacks. Admiral Nimitz, wanting to be closer to the action, chose Guam as his headquarters for the final months of the war.

For the Japanese, the immediate effect of their defeats in the Marianas was a deepening pessimism and a growing belief that they could not win the war. The disastrous Philippine Sea battle, followed by the loss of Saipan, created a crisis at the highest level of the Japanese government. Prime Minister Tojo's ministry had become increasingly unpopular with both the general public and leading political and military figures. Many believed that, as prime minister and minister of war, he was responsible for Japan's losses. Liberals within the establishment, such as Prince Konoye, had never given Tojo their unwavering support. They believed that the only hope of negotiating a peace lay in changing the government, and they did not want to wait until Germany was defeated. Military radicals, on the other hand, blamed Tojo for mismanaging the war. Admiral Sokichi Takagi and his group, concluding that only force would suffice to rid them of Tojo, began plotting his assassination.

The loss of Saipan brought the liberals and moderate military critics together. Alarmed by their growing opposition, Tojo consulted with Marquis Koichi Kido, the Privy Seal and one of the emperor's closest advisers. Tojo learned that the emperor was annoyed by the concentration of power in Tojo's ministry, particularly the authority Tojo had given to Adm. Shigetaro Shimada, the navy minister and chief of staff. Tojo's belief that he had lost the emperor's confidence was reinforced on 17 July by the action of the *jushin,* the emperor's high-level advisory body. Not satisfied with Shimada's resignation, they demanded that Tojo also resign. Bowing to the inevitable, Tojo received the resignations of his ministers and then met with the emperor the following day to offer his own. After considerable discussion, the *jushin* recommended Gen. Kuniaki Koiso, commander of troops in Korea, to become prime minister, and Adm. Mitsumasa Yonai became navy minister. Stripped of most of his power, Tojo became a member of the *jushin.*

Despite the changes in government, no concrete move was made toward seeking a favorable peace. The liberals were not powerful enough to force the military to admit the obvious. Despite the reality of Japan's position, the reluctance of its leaders to admit publicly that the war was lost meant the conflict would continue indefinitely.

Chapter 12

Return to the Philippines

GENERAL MACARTHUR WAS convinced that the Joint Chiefs had ignored the Southwest Pacific theater. He later complained that he had to beg like a rug merchant for the supplies and men he needed. A closer examination, however, reveals that despite the "Germany first" mindset in Washington, MacArthur had been given all that he reasonably could have expected. By mid-1944 he had Krueger's Sixth Army, the powerful Fifth and Thirteenth Air Forces, and a small fleet directly under his command. Although Admiral King refused to quit lobbying for an invasion of Formosa, it was a foregone conclusion after the July conference with President Roosevelt in Hawaii that MacArthur's proposed Philippines operation would have first priority. The Marianas landings did not detract from preparation for the Philippines effort because war planners believed that MacArthur, in order to guarantee success, would not mount an invasion there until late in the year.

Preliminary plans called for a stepping-stone approach, first capturing Halmahera in the Moluccas, and then landing at Sarangani Bay on Mindanao, 350 miles distant. These plans were radically altered after intelligence sources reported that the Japanese, who had no intention of giving up their key base in the Moluccas, had stationed some thirty-seven thousand men there. Furthermore, there was a shortage of landing craft because of the Normandy invasion. The last straw was Nimitz's refusal to release his fast carriers to cover the long jump from Hollandia and Biak to Halmahera. Faced with all these negatives, MacArthur's staff reluctantly decided to substitute Morotai, a boggy island 44 miles long and 25 miles wide, located 10 miles off the northern coast of Halmahera, almost 850 miles from Biak.

The Japanese had concluded that Morotai would not be suitable for an airfield and thus neglected to provide a substantial defense force. The American invasion, scheduled for 15 September, thus became a prime example of overkill. MacArthur allocated twenty-eight thousand combat troops from Maj. Gen. Charles Hall's XI Corps for the operation. More than twelve thousand service and construction troops would follow them in as soon as the island was secure and begin construction of airfield and port facilities. Air cover was to be provided by RAdm. Thomas L. Sprague's six light carriers, supplemented by Fifth Air Force planes from Biak. This massive display of power must have awed the fewer than five hundred Japanese on the island. Not surprisingly, the landings were unopposed and the small Japanese garrison was eliminated by 4 October.

On the day following the initial landings, ships began unloading heavy equipment and construction personnel. Despite the swampy conditions, two airfields were constructed and medium bombers and fighters were using them in early October to strike Mindanao. The runways were later extended so that heavy bombers could help support the Leyte landings. In addition, dock and service facilities were constructed for motor torpedo boats, which interdicted Japanese barge traffic and protected the Morotai garrison from raids from Halmahera and the eastern Celebes. The Australian I Corps later used Morotai as a base for the invasion of Borneo in April 1945.

The next step before a Philippines invasion was to be a two-corps assault on islands in the Palau group of the western Carolines, ostensibly to protect MacArthur's eastern flank. Major General John Hodge's XXIV Corps, consisting of the 7th and 96th Divisions, was to land simultaneously on Babelthuap, Yap, and Ulithi. General Geiger's III Amphibious Corps, composed of the 1st Marine

Division and the army's 81st Division, was slated to seize the southern Palau islands of Peleliu and Angaur. The timetable for the various assaults was set at the Octagon conference of the Combined Chiefs, held in Quebec on 11 September. The various Palau landings were scheduled for 5 October, to be followed by landings on Mindanao on 15 November and Leyte on 20 December.

In May 1944 Admiral Nimitz, who wanted Spruance to share top billing with Halsey, altered the command structure of the Central Pacific fleet. This change, which took effect after the Marianas operation, did not affect the ships assigned. When the fleet operated under Spruance, it continued to be known as the Fifth Fleet. When Halsey assumed command, the force became the Third Fleet. After the Marianas campaigns, Spruance and most of his senior commanders turned over Central Pacific operations to the Third Fleet. Therefore, Halsey commanded the covering force for the Palau operations.

From the beginning, Halsey was critical of the overall Palau plan and concurred with Nimitz's cancellation of the assault on Babelthuap. In preparation for the operation, the Third Fleet sortied from Pearl Harbor on 24 August, directed by Halsey from the new fast battleship *New Jersey*. A task group led by Mitscher was detached for a strike against the Bonin Islands while the rest of the fleet proceeded to the western Carolines. For three days beginning on 6 September, Halsey's planes ranged up and down the island chain, destroying large numbers of Japanese aircraft and rendering airfields useless to the enemy. The fleet then proceeded to the Philippines, striking targets on Mindanao and the Visayan Islands, destroying an estimated two hundred more Japanese planes.

Halsey's opposition to the planned Carolines invasion increased. He contacted Nimitz and suggested that the Palau operation be called off and that, considering the lack of Japanese airpower, the Philippines invasion date be moved forward. Nimitz passed Halsey's suggestions to the Combined Chiefs, who were still meeting in Quebec. After receiving MacArthur's approval, they concurred on a plan to postpone the invasion of Mindanao and instead assault Leyte on 20 October. The proposed landings on Yap and Ulithi were canceled, and XXIV Corp was shifted to MacArthur's control for the Leyte operation. MacArthur was also promised the

Third Fleet to back up his smaller Seventh Fleet. All available shipping in the Pacific was to be diverted to MacArthur to carry Krueger's Sixth Army to the Philippines. Inexplicably, despite Halsey's recommendation, Nimitz did not call off the planned III Amphibious Corps operation against Peleliu and Angaur, thus setting the stage for one of the bloodiest debacles of the entire war.

Of the two southern islands targeted by the planners, the most formidable was Peleliu, whose airfield was believed necessary to support the Philippines invasions. Shaped like a fishhook, it is seven miles long and two miles across at its widest point. In the southeast is a shallow inlet that ends in swampy terrain. The narrow northern part of the island is intersected by another larger inlet protected by coral reefs. The southern half of the island is generally flat and covered with scrub brush except in the areas cleared for the airfield. Narrow coastal plains on the east and west border the most dominating part of the island, the Umurbrogol heights. These are composed of a number of low, rugged limestone hills riddled with natural caves. These were augmented by manmade caves of varying sizes. The largest, constructed by the navy on the north end of the island, was five stories deep. Colonel Kunio Nakagawa had sited his artillery and the bulk of the thirteen thousand defenders in the heights. Expecting no assistance from the larger garrison on Babelthuap, he planned to contest every yard of ground and make his final stand in the Umurbrogol. There would be no banzai charges.

Angaur, the southernmost of the Palau Islands, is six miles southwest of Peleliu. Only two and one-half miles long, it is generally flat. Although Angaur was the most profitable of all the islands in the chain because of its phosphate deposits, Lt. Gen. Sadae Inoue, in charge of defending the Palau group, concluded the island was strategically unimportant. Unwilling to weaken the Babelthuap garrison to reinforce Angaur, Inoue left the island commander, Maj. Ushio Goto, with only fifteen hundred men to defend Angaur. Although Goto planned to fight the same type of delaying action as Nakagawa, it was a foregone conclusion that if the Americans landed in force the fight would be over quickly.

The plan for the Peleliu assault was deceptively simple. Vice Admiral Theodore Wilkinson would oversee the landing of the veteran 1st Marine Division on five beaches opposite the airfield. The army's 81st Division, commanded by Maj. Gen. Paul J. Mueller, was scheduled to land two regiments on the north coast of Angaur. However, the 81st would remain in floating reserve until it was first determined that the division would not be needed on Peleliu. Naval gunfire support would be supplied by RAdm. Jesse B. Oldendorf's task force consisting of five battleships, eight cruisers, and fourteen destroyers. Rear Admiral Ralph A. Ofstie's seven light carriers would supply combat air support for the operation.

The action against Peleliu began on 10 September with Oldendorf's ships zeroing in on all discernible targets. It appeared to naval observers that nothing survived the bombardment prior to the landings. Unfortunately for the marines, the shelling was halted prematurely; the bulk of the Japanese defenders remained untouched in their caves. Major General William Rupertus, the 1st Marine Division commander, was also overly optimistic. In a message broadcast to his men prior to the landings, he promised a dirty but quick campaign that would be over more quickly than Tarawa.

General Rupertus's hopes for a quick victory were dashed early on 15 September when the first assault units reached the reef line. Accurate, preplanned artillery and mortar fire began to take a heavy toll of the LVTs and DUKWs, and by the end of the day, the Japanese had knocked out sixty vehicles. On the division's left flank, Col. Lewis "Chesty" Puller's 1st Marines were pinned down all along the beach soon after landing at 0830. The Japanese there, dug in along a ridgeline not shown on any maps, prevented any significant advance for the entire day. Colonel Harold D. Harris's 5th Marines had an easier time on the two center beaches, and by midafternoon had taken the southern part of the airfield. Amphibious Sherman tanks swam in with the fourth wave, providing invaluable close-in support—particularly to the elements of the 1st and 5th Marines that managed to reach the airfield. At 1650, Nakagawa ordered twenty of his light tanks to try to break through the lines there, but all were destroyed by fire from bazookas and the Shermans. On the right flank, two battalions from Col. Herman Hanneken's 7th Marines advanced slowly toward the southeastern peninsula in the face of heavy fire from ruined buildings and a large concrete blockhouse.

By evening, the marines had secured a precarious lodgment measuring roughly three thousand yards wide and five hundred yards deep. Losses had been heavy—more than eleven hundred men—and they had not yet reached the Umurbrogol hill mass.

For the next four days, the marines, backed by the awesome firepower of naval guns and aircraft, slowly expanded the perimeter. The 7th Marines cleared the southeastern peninsula by the seven-

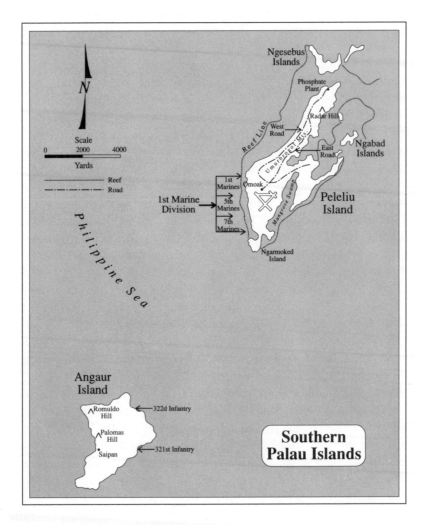

teenth, while the 5th Marines pushed the Japanese from the Lobster Claw, a jut of land east of the main east road. Puller's 1st Marines had the most difficult task, however. His left flank battalion withstood a major counterattack on the evening of the sixteenth, killing an estimated 350 Japanese. Then, reinforced by a battalion from the 7th Marines, his regiment the next day began to assault the southern section of the Umurbrogol, called Bloody Nose Ridge by the marines. If the airfield was to be used, it was necessary to control the heights to keep the Japanese from shelling it.

The high humidity and one-hundred-degree temperatures took a heavy toll as the weary marines launched attack after attack with only minimal success. When Puller asked for reinforcements on the sixteenth, he was told none were available. Despite the desperate situation facing the marines, Admiral Wilkinson, on the advice of Rupertus, had released two regiments of the 81st Division for the Angaur operation. By 21 September, Rupertus's optimism had faded as it became obvious that the 1st Marines, having gained only slight footholds on the Umurbrogol, could go no further. When relieved by the 7th Marines, the regiment had suffered almost 60 percent casualties in the combat battalions. General Geiger, who had decided to relieve the 1st Marines on 21 September, alerted General Mueller on Angaur to begin loading the 321st Infantry Regiment for action on Peleliu.

The 81st Division's assault of Angaur on the sixteenth went very smoothly. The 322d Infantry landed in the north and pushed southward following the rail line to link up with the 321st, which had landed on the eastern beaches. The Japanese offered little resistance; Major Goto was evidently content with simply withdrawing to the highlands in the northwest section of the island. On 20 September, with most of the island under U.S. control, General Mueller declared Angaur secure. However, it took another month for the 322d to clear the rugged, cave-pitted Japanese positions. Despite this, there was little danger to the construction crews who came in almost immediately and began work on the airfield. Nor was there any need to keep the 321st on the island, especially when the marines were taking such heavy casualties on Peleliu.

The 81st Division's third regiment, the 323d, had been kept in floating reserve and perhaps might have been committed to the fight on Peleliu had it not been involved in the capture of Ulithi Atoll. On 16 September, Admiral Nimitz ordered Wilkinson to seize Ulithi, with its great harbor, as quickly as possible with the forces already at his disposal. Wilkinson responded by sending RAdm. William H. G. Blandy northward with a convoy of thirty-one ships, and on 21 September Blandy landed the army troops on the first of the atoll's many islands. In all, the invaders found only two dead Japanese. Thus, at a time when men were desperately needed on Peleliu, an entire regiment was committed to seizing an undefended atoll. Nevertheless, the capture of Ulithi was a major accomplishment because its lagoon could provide safe berthing for hundreds of ships. Within weeks it was serving as an advanced fleet base, and Admirals Halsey and Mitscher used it as an anchorage for part of TF 38, which launched a major attack on Formosa in early October.

Even before the 1st Marines had ceased to be an effective fighting force on Peleliu, Generals Geiger and Rupertus realized the futility of frontal infantry assaults. They knew they needed to change their tactics, and with this knowledge came an admission that there would be no quick victory. The highlands had to be taken yard by yard by bringing to bear concentrated firepower on small sections after the Umurbrogol had been sealed off. To do this, the recently arrived 321st Regiment moved north astride the West Road on the twenty-third. The regiment took Gareboru village halfway up the coast and gained access to a trail leading east into the Umurbrogol. The regiment then shifted the axis of its attack eastward as the 5th Marines moved through its lines and began to clear out the Japanese in the north and on adjacent Ngesebus Island. This was accomplished within three days, thus isolating the remnants of Nakagawa's force in a pocket nine hundred yards long by four hundred yards wide. With the Americans in control of nine-tenths of the island, General Geiger declared it secure on 27 September.

But the fighting on Peleliu was far from over. The Japanese were ensconsed in the most difficult terrain of the Umurbrogol, and elements of the 5th and 7th Marines were assigned the difficult task of rooting them out. Aided by division and corps artillery and low-flying F4U Corsair fighter-bombers from the 2d Marine Air

Wing based at the Peleliu airfield, they had reduced the pocket to only half its size by mid-October when most of the marine units were relieved by the 321st Infantry, whose commander, Col. Robert F. Dark, assumed tactical control of the operation. The 1st Marines had already left the island, and on 22 October the 7th Marines followed. A week later, the 5th Marines were removed to the Russell Islands. The quick and dirty campaign Rupertus had promised had turned into a nightmare in which each of the marine regiments suffered almost 50 percent casualties. More than thirteen hundred marines were killed in action.

During the final phase of the Peleliu operation, General Mueller employed classic siege warfare techniques. No infantry attack was made until the targeted area was thoroughly worked over by light and heavy artillery, tanks, and Corsairs carrying conventional bombs and napalm. The reduction of the pocket was slowed by torrential rains every day, as well as by a typhoon. The fighting continued to be intense, although the Japanese force had been reduced to only a few hundred men. The various strong points were taken one by one. Finally, on 27 November, the last Japanese position on the height called the China Wall was captured. By that time Nakagawa and his superior, Maj. Gen. Kenjiro Murai, had committed suicide. Despite the very conservative approach to capturing the Umurbrogol, the 81st Division suffered 827 casualties in the period after 20 October.

In retrospect, the bloody fighting on Peleliu produced few positive results. Although both the Peleliu and Angaur airfields were operational in time for the Leyte landings, they played no crucial role in that operation. Japanese airpower in the southern Philippines had all but been destroyed by the earlier carrier strikes, and planes from the Third and Seventh Fleets supplied all the air support MacArthur's troops needed until airfields could be seized on the island.

Admiral Nimitz never gave a detailed explanation of why he failed to call off the Peleliu operation at the same time that he canceled the proposed actions farther north. Nothing would have been lost if the Japanese garrisons on Peleliu and Angaur had been bypassed, as was the case with the much larger force on Babelthuap. Ironically, the operation that cost no American lives proved to be the most valuable. Ulithi's excellent harbor, which could shelter the bulk of Nimitz's blue-water fleet, became an important forward staging area and was used continually throughout the remainder of the war.

With Peleliu secure, Admiral Halsey next moved to neutralize Japanese airpower on northern Luzon, Okinawa, and Formosa. He divided TF 38 into three groups, and planes from the task force penetrated Japan's inner defense lines, striking Okinawa on 10 October. The naval aviators destroyed a number of smaller ships and approximately a hundred aircraft. The following day, two of the carrier task groups moved south and hit Japanese facilities at Aparri in northern Luzon. On 12 October the fleet moved into positions around Formosa and launched over thirteen hundred sorties.

Admiral Soemu Toyoda, the commander of the Combined Fleet, was on the island, and together he and VAdm. Shigeru Fukudome prepared for a major air confrontation. They stripped their four big carriers of planes to augment the seven hundred planes Fukudome already had in his Sixth Base Air Force. This gave the Japanese more than a thousand planes with which to oppose those from Halsey's nine fleet carriers. But the poorly trained Japanese pilots were no match for the Americans. At the close of the first day, almost all of Fukudome's fighters had been destroyed, and great damage had been inflicted on ground installations.

Task Force 38 did not escape unscathed during the six-day operation against the Ryukyus, Luzon, and Formosa. Mitscher lost a total of eighty-nine planes and sixty-four pilots and crewmen. In addition, the new heavy cruiser *Canberra* took an aerial torpedo on the thirteenth, and the next day the light cruiser *Houston* was knocked out of action. However, in one of the great salvage feats of the war, both ships were towed to safety and eventually repaired.

The lack of heavy naval attacks on the fourteenth was offset by China-based B-29s from the Twentieth Air Force. More than a hundred of the huge bombers hit the Takao area on Formosa, dropping almost the same tonnage of bombs in one mission as Halsey's planes had in three days. The B-29s returned to Formosa on each of the next three days, despite the problems they had getting fuel supplies over the Himalayas from India. Bombers and fighters from the

Fourteenth Air Force also aided in disrupting the Japanese by attacking installations in Hong Kong. Despite this assistance from land-based aircraft, the real victory belonged to TF 38. The destruction of ships, factories, hangars, and ammunition dumps was important, but the primary objective was the destruction of Japanese airpower in the region. In all, TF 38 pilots engaged more than a thousand planes and destroyed at least five hundred. Although there would be air attacks on the American landings on Leyte, particularly by kamikazes, Japan's air strength was so depleted by the Formosa air battle that only a limited number of planes could be sent from there to the Philippines at any time during the campaign.

The Japanese penchant for exaggerating enemy losses convinced many senior naval officers in Japan and the Philippines that what was in reality a stunning defeat was a Japanese victory in which the U.S. Third Fleet lost eleven carriers, two battleships, and four cruisers. The emperor issued a special proclamation celebrating Japan's glorious victory, and some senior army officers were lulled into believing that MacArthur's long-expected invasion of the Philippines would be canceled.

The decision to postpone the invasion of Mindanao and move up the Leyte landings by two months caused considerable modifications to the plan for General MacArthur's triumphal return to his beloved islands. The navy had little time to collect the ships needed to transport the two hundred thousand men of General Krueger's Sixth Army, but despite the difficulties, the armada, the largest ever assembled in the Pacific, departed mainly from Manus and Hollandia a week before the Third Fleet struck at Formosa.

Admiral Kinkaid, who was in overall command while the ships were at sea, accompanied TF 77, which consisted of the bombardment and carrier groups. The main power of TF 77 was in its eighteen escort carriers with a total complement of more than five hundred planes, and its escort of six battleships and eight cruisers. Task Force 78, commanded by Admiral Barbey, carried Maj. Gen. Franklin Sibert's X Corps, composed of the 1st Cavalry and 24th Infantry Divisions. The targets for this northern group were the two beach areas on the western side of San Pedro Bay south of Leyte's capital city, Tacloban. Admiral Wilkinson's TF 79 carried General

Hodge's XXIV Corps, which included the 7th and 96th Divisions. Its goal was the broad beaches off the village of Dulag. Until air bases had been seized and were operational, air cover had to be provided by TF 77 and Halsey's TF 38.

Leyte is the eighth largest island in the Philippines chain, measuring 115 miles long by 45 miles across at its widest point in the north. Inland from Dulag it is only fifteen miles across. Some observers have compared its shape to a large, elongated molar with the roots pointing south. Leyte guards the eastern approaches to the Visayan Sea. To the south, Mindanao lies across the Surigao Strait, and Samar is to the north across the narrow San Juanico Strait. East of the island is Leyte Gulf. Entrance into the gulf was guarded by small Japanese detachments on three islands: long, thin Dinagat, Homonhon, and tiny Suluan. The most notable geographic feature on Leyte is the heavily forested central mountain range that separates the narrow western plain from the broader Leyte Valley in the east. Excellent beaches line the shores of Leyte Gulf and San Pedro Bay, but the inland terrain is marred by swamps, rice paddies, and a number of streams. The water table is quite high, so much of the ground in eastern Leyte is mushy and not able to support heavy equipment. Adding greatly to the myriad problems facing an invader are the incessant autumn rains and the ever-present danger of typhoons. The few roads then on the island connected Tacloban with towns to the south as well as to Palompon and Ormoc in the west. Movement any distance from these roads and the forest trails was difficult, thus allowing the Japanese defenders to concentrate forces to block them.

The Japanese did little during the long years of the war to correct the deficiencies in their command structure. The army, navy, and air forces operated as separate entities in the field. Unity of command existed only when the representatives of the individual services at Imperial Headquarters were in agreement or when field commanders had good personal relationships.

In light of this, it is fair to say the command situation in the Philippines on the eve of the American invasion was complex in the extreme. Field Marshal Count Hisaichi Terauchi, who commanded the Southern Army and whose jurisdiction stretched to Burma, had his headquarters in Manila. The unit primarily responsible for the defense of the Philippines was the Fourteenth Army on Luzon, and Imperial Headquarters chose this crucial time to replace its commander, Lt. Gen. Shigenori Kuroda, with the hero of the conquest of Malaya, Gen. Tomoyuki Yamashita. Yamashita arrived in Manila on 6 October, just two weeks before the Leyte landings. Added to the nearly insurmountable difficulty of defending the islands against the overwhelming might of the American forces was the fact that he inherited a staff and commanders with whom he was unfamiliar. The senior naval officer in the Philippines at that time was Admiral Toyoda, commander of the Combined Fleet, who directly controlled the major naval element, the First Mobile Fleet, which remained separate from VAdm. Gun'ichi Mikawa's Southwest Area Fleet. What was left of Japanese airpower in the Philippines was divided between the navy's Fifth Base Air Force and the Fourth Air Army. There were general agreements between the commanders, but there was no overall plan for combined air operations. General Yamashita was in the uncomfortable position of being unable to control the activities of either the substantial naval forces in the region or Lt. Gen. Kyoji Tominaga's air army. Furthermore, as long as Field Marshal Terauchi was in Manila, Yamashita was his subordinate and, although given primary field responsibility, he did not control the Thirty-fifth Army in the southern Philippines.

Further complicating Yamashita's problems was Imperial Headquarters's indecisiveness. The initial plan for the defense of the Philippines, Sho-1, called for only token resistance on the southern or central islands. Luzon was to be the major battleground, and most of the Japanese land force was stationed there. Nevertheless, the Thirty-fifth Army commander, Lt. Gen. Sosaku Suzuki, whose responsibility was defending Mindanao and the Visayas, commanded a large force estimated at approximately one hundred thousand men. Leyte was garrisoned by the Thirty-fifth Army's 16th Division, which had been involved in the infamous Bataan Death March twenty-seven months earlier. The Leyte commander, Lt. Gen. Shiro Makino, had about twenty thousand men available for the island's defense—more than enough to carry out his responsibilities under the original Sho-1 Plan. Suzuki also alerted his 1st Division on Cebu to be ready to move to Leyte to support the 16th.

Once the euphoria from the perceived Formosa victory wore off,

Tokyo began to rethink its Philippines defense plans. Imperial Headquarters rejected Terauchi's and Yamashita's pleas to leave the original plan intact, and on 20 October Yamashita was informed that Suzuki was expected to resist an invasion with all the force available to him. If necessary, Yamashita was to send troops from Luzon to support Suzuki. However, not knowing the exact time or place for the invasion, Toyoda could not have his naval units in position to attack the American transports during their most vulnerable phase. He had to wait until the landing force was already in Leyte Gulf before he could order his fleet to move. Thus the Americans met only local opposition and their lodgment was secure by the time Japanese naval units attacked on 24 October.

As the main elements of Admiral Kinkaid's force proceeded slowly northward, others forged ahead. These included minesweepers and ships bearing underwater demolition teams, and Admiral Sprague's light carrier force. The burden of providing air support for the landings fell to Sprague's pilots because Halsey had halted the Third Fleet northeast of Luzon. His fleet carriers did not arrive until after the invasion began. Beginning on 18 October, Sprague's pilots flew 450 sorties in three days, striking facilities on Cebu, Negros, North Mindanao, and Leyte. There was hardly any air opposition as the Japanese had abandoned the rain-drenched Leyte airfields. Meanwhile, men of the 6th Ranger Battalion landed on Suluan and Dinagat Islands early on the seventeenth. Homonhon Island was secured the next day, clearing the way for Admiral Oldendorf and his Fire Support Unit South to move to Leyte Gulf, followed later that night by RAdm. G. L. Weyler's Fire Support Unit North. By the nineteenth, six battleships, five cruisers, and fifteen destroyers were in position to support the landings scheduled for the next day. Finally convinced of the place and approximate time of the landings, Admiral Toyoda alerted all of his naval units, including Admiral Kurita's powerful 1st Attack Force at Lingga Roads near Singapore. The Sho-1 Plan was to be implemented as soon as possible.

On 20 October, according to plan, TF 78 divided into three sections and landed X Corps on the three beaches south of Tacloban. Prior to the landings, which began at approximately 0930, the support group built around the battleships *Mississippi, Maryland,*

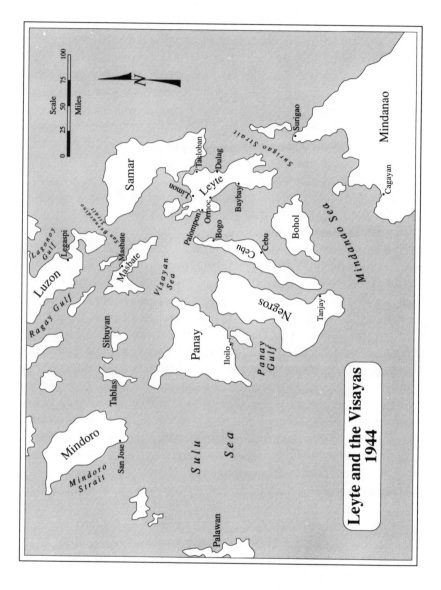

Leyte and the Visayas
1944

and *West Virginia* pounded the surrounding area for more than two hours. Major General Verne D. Mudge's 1st Cavalry Division landed near the village of San Ricardo, while Maj. Gen. Frederick Irving's 24th Division landed on a broad beach fifteen hundred yards to the south, near the village of Palo. Within minutes, elements of the 24th Division had driven inland almost a quarter of a mile, and members of the 19th Regiment scrambled up the slopes of Mount Guinhandong, the only major height in the vicinity, before its defenders could recover from the heavy shelling. The 1st Cavalry, like the 24th, was relatively unopposed, receiving only a few rounds of mortar fire. By 1530 the Cataisan Peninsula across from Tacloban had been cleared.

Meanwhile, TF 79 duplicated the success of Admiral Barbey's northern landings. After heavy naval and air bombardment, XXIV Corps's two divisions landed on four excellent beaches near the village of Dulag. Major General James L. Bradley's 96th Division went ashore on the two northernmost beaches and moved inland, taking the only high ground in the vicinity within forty minutes. That accomplished, the division's right flank units began a pivoting movement in order to link up with X Corps. Major General Archibald V. Arnold's 7th Division landed farther south and took Dulag by noon. The ease with which all units moved after getting ashore was due to General Suzuki's decision not to contest the landings. Knowing he had only a fraction of the men available to Krueger, Suzuki ordered the 16th Division to hold the forward areas as long as possible before falling back to the main defense line at the foot of the mountains to the north and west. Thus, by the end of the first day, all combat elements from the two corps were ashore—along with much of their equipment and supplies.

One memorable event occurred during the Leyte landings that was recorded for posterity by prepositioned army cameramen. General MacArthur had sailed from Hollandia on the cruiser *Nashville* and, despite objections from his staff, decided to go ashore immediately. Early in the afternoon his landing craft grounded a few yards from the surf's edge on Red Beach, and, very much aware of the historic nature of his act, MacArthur stepped off into the water and waded ashore. Later on the beach, accompanied by President Sergio Osmeña and surrounded by his staff and selected members of Osmeña's cabinet, MacArthur solemnly announced, "I have returned." The general then called on Filipinos to rally to him and rise up against the Japanese. After the 1st Cavalry Division took Tacloban on the twenty-third, MacArthur and Osmeña again went ashore, this time to proclaim the reestablishment of civil government in the Philippines. Although somewhat premature given the long, difficult task of fully liberating the islands, MacArthur had symbolically fulfilled his promise made in Australia two and one-half years before.

The Americans at Leyte were fortunate that earlier air strikes had done such damage to the Japanese air forces. The few air raids made on American ships were very successful. On the first afternoon of the landings, a single plane torpedoed the cruiser *Honolulu,* blasting a huge hole in its side and killing sixty men. The next day, a Japanese pilot crashed his plane on the venerable Australian cruiser *Australia,* causing severe damage and killing the captain and nineteen men. Both ships were withdrawn and escorted back to Manus.

In the four days after the initial landings, planes from Sprague's escort carriers flew more than eight hundred sorties and destroyed many more Japanese planes on the ground. Aircraft from the Third Fleet repeatedly hit the Visayan airfields, and bombers from Kenney's Far Eastern Air Force worked over Japanese airfields on Mindanao. At the same time, the Dulag and Tacloban airfields were captured, and engineers began frantically working to lay down dirt and sand on the marshy runways to enable army planes to use the fields. Both were ready for use as emergency strips by the twenty-fifth.

After taking Tacloban, elements of the 1st Cavalry Division pushed up the western shore of San Juanico Strait while other units were loaded on landing craft and threaded through the narrow straits to seize the northern end. Landings were also made at La Paz on Samar. These operations secured control of the straits and blocked the movement of Japanese reinforcements to eastern Leyte. The 24th Division pushed northwest to overcome the Japanese defenses on two hills west of the village of Palo, and by the twenty-fifth was preparing for a major drive into Leyte Valley. Farther south, the 96th Division launched a two-pronged attack. Units on one axis drove to the village of Tanauan and on the twenty-fifth made contact with the 24th Division, thus linking XXIV Corps with X Corps to the north. The other attacking units drove straight ahead through swampy terrain south of Catmon Hill, taking the village of Tabontaban on the twenty-seventh. In the extreme south, the 7th Division, after capturing Dulag, pushed up the road paralleling the Marband River and on the twenty-fourth captured the village of Burauen, eleven miles from the landing beaches and on the edge of the mountain chain. The thousand-foot-high Catmon Hill was by-passed. It was finally taken on 29 October after heavy naval and artillery bombardment.

Several days after the initial landings, the focus of action shifted from land operations to the certainty of a major naval engagement. Allied intelligence officers, aware of the movement of some Japanese naval units, had concluded that the Japanese would once again attempt to alter the course of the war with a stunning naval victory. Admiral Toyoda's order to execute the Sho-1 Plan began a series of events that culminated in the largest naval battle of the Pacific war. The main outlines of the plan were drawn up before the disastrous aircraft losses in Formosa and the Philippines, and therein lay its fundamental weakness, as Admiral Ozawa later admitted. Although the Japanese were outnumbered by at least four to one in ships, it was their lack of experienced carrier pilots that foredoomed the operation. Admiral Fukudome on Formosa tried to compensate by sending all available planes to the Philippines, but even with these there were probably no more than two hundred land-based aircraft available in the islands on 25 October.

As was the case with all major Japanese naval operations, this one, designed to destroy the American amphibious forces and fire support ships off Leyte, was complex. It called for Admiral Ozawa, leading a decoy force consisting of the fleet carrier *Zuikaku*, the light carriers *Zuiho, Chitose,* and *Chiyoda,* and the half carriers *Ise* and *Hyuga,* screened by three cruisers and eight destroyers, to leave the Inland Sea on 20 October and proceed into the Philippine Sea north of Luzon. Its sole purpose was to lure the main elements of the Third Fleet north, and thus expose the beaches and support ships to the power of the 1st Attack Force. After receiving Toyoda's orders, the main force sailed on the afternoon of the eighteenth, refueled at Brunei, and then headed for the Palawan Passage northeast of Borneo on the twenty-second. Commanded by Admiral Kurita aboard the cruiser *Atago,* the 1st Attack Force's main element was the two largest battleships in the world, the *Musashi* and *Yamato,* each mounting nine 18.1-inch guns as their main battery. The force also included the older battleships *Nagato, Kongo,* and *Haruna,* and a screen of twelve cruisers and thirteen destroyers.

A second element, the Central Force under VAdm. Shoji Nishimura—which included the battleships *Yamashiro* and *Fuso,* one cruiser, and four destroyers—left Lingga the same day and made a wide detour into the Sulu Sea with Surigao Strait as its objective.

Vice Admiral Kiyohide Shima's 2d Attack Force, consisting of two cruisers and eight destroyers, left Japan on 22 October to support Nishimura, but the manner of that support was left up to him. Strangely, he made no attempt to contact Nishimura or even catch up with him.

Two Seventh Fleet submarines, the *Darter* and *Dace,* operating off the southern end of the Palawan Passage, sighted Kurita's force early on the twenty-third, pinpointing its location for Halsey. They moved into the attack, and Comdr. David McClintock on the *Darter* fired six torpedoes at Kurita's flagship, the *Atago,* from a thousand yards. He immediately loosed four more from his stern tubes at the second cruiser in the column, the *Takao.* Four of the first torpedoes fired struck the *Atago,* which sank almost immediately. The hits on the *Takao* were enough to force it out of the battle line. Admiral Kurita and his staff were rescued, but almost half of the *Atago*'s complement were lost. While *Darter* was striking the lead ships in the left column, Comdr. Bladen Claggett maneuvered the *Dace* for a run at the right column. Shortly before the *Atago* went down, he fired four torpedoes at the heavy cruiser *Maya.* The *Maya* exploded and sank immediately. Later, while trying to finish off the *Takao,* the *Darter* ran aground. Despite attempts by the crews of both submarines to free the boat, *Darter* had to be abandoned. Nevertheless, the two subs had sunk a pair of Japan's best heavy cruisers and seriously damaged a third. Even more important,

Halsey and Kinkaid had been alerted to the approach of the main Japanese striking force.

By the afternoon of the twenty-third, Halsey knew that three enemy forces were closing in on Leyte Gulf. He had three task groups immediately available, and he recalled a fourth, Admiral John McCain's TG 38.1, and had it refueled at sea. At a few minutes past 0800 on 24 October, a search plane located Kurita's force, obviously bound for San Bernardino Strait. Because the strait was presumably heavily mined, Admiral Nimitz had forbidden entry into it without his permission. Halsey thus arranged his task groups in a fanlike manner, with RAdm. Frederick C. Sherman's TG 38.3 to the north, RAdm. Gerald F. Bogan's TG 38.2 off San Bernardino Strait, and RAdm. Ralph E. Davison's TG 38.4 about sixty miles from Samar.

Before the Americans could launch any air strikes, the Japanese on Luzon sent three waves of land-based naval aircraft against Sherman's group. Each of these raids, consisting of approximately fifty planes, was, with one exception, beaten off by fighters from *Langley, Essex, Princeton,* and *Lexington.* A lone Aichi D4Y3 "Judy" dive-bomber broke through at about 0930 and dropped a 550-pound bomb on the flight deck of the *Princeton.* Despite heroic efforts by the crew and firefighters from other ships, the flames reached the torpedo storage area and the carrier blew up, seriously damaging the cruiser *Birmingham,* which was alongside. Early that evening, the *Princeton* was sunk by torpedoes from the cruiser *Reno.*

Kurita's force was located by planes from Bogan's TG 38.2 a few minutes after 0800 on the twenty-fourth. He immediately launched forty-five aircraft from the carriers *Intrepid* and *Cabot,* which two hours later attacked the Japanese. A second strike of equal strength was launched at 1045, and a smaller force including planes from the *Essex* and *Lexington* reached Kurita's fleet by 1330. In all, 259 sorties were made against the Japanese with a loss of only eighteen planes. The attackers concentrated on the superbattleship *Musashi.* The giant ship was hit by four bombs and a torpedo during the initial strike. Later attacks pumped seventeen bombs and ten more torpedoes into the stricken vessel. Falling behind the fleet, the pride of the Japanese navy finally went down at 1930, taking more than a thousand men with it. The battleships *Yamato, Nagato,* and *Haruna* were also hit but none seriously enough to put them out of action. The heavy cruiser *Myoko* was damaged and forced to retire.

During the air battle, Admiral Fukudome on Luzon insisted on hoarding his remaining planes to strike directly at the American carriers later. By midafternoon, Kurita, operating without air cover, decided to retire, regroup, and hope for air support when he again attempted to reenter the strait. He reversed his fleet's course and proceeded to the west for two hours before resuming his eastward movement. But the Sho-1 Plan had been compromised; he would not meet Nishimura in Leyte Gulf as planned.

Admiral Ozawa's force approaching from the north was to act as bait to lure the main American forces away from the straits. By 1130 on the twenty-fourth he was only 230 miles from the northern elements of the Third Fleet. He launched seventy-six planes, half of his aircraft strength, at 1145 to attack Sherman's TG 38.3. When the attack failed, the surviving pilots sought safe haven on Luzon.

Late that afternoon Halsey's scouts located Ozawa's carriers. Believing that Kurita's fleet had been so badly mauled that it was not a threat, Halsey concluded that Ozawa's force was the main enemy threat and that Kinkaid had enough planes on his escort carriers to protect the beachhead and landing force. Halsey, who had earlier assumed tactical control of Admiral Mitscher's TF 38, generally ignored its commander. Although Halsey learned just before midnight that Kurita's battle group was moving through San Bernardino Strait, he did not detach Admiral Lee's battleships to await it. When Kurita's force broke out of the strait, he discovered the way was clear and headed south to attempt a rendezvous with Nishimura.

Shortly after noon, Kinkaid alerted all ships to prepare for a night action. A cordon of destroyers was set up around the twenty-eight Liberty ships in the gulf, and Admiral Oldendorf, in command of the fire support section, was advised to prepare for a surface action in Surigao Strait. Oldendorf immediately initiated a plan he hoped would result in the destruction of Nishimura's force. After organizing his force into three groups, Oldendorf moved his ships into blocking positions just north of the Hibuson Islands and had them steam on parallel east-west tracks. Oldendorf led five cruisers and nine destroyers on the southern flank, and RAdm. Russell S. Berkey had three cruisers and thirteen destroyers on the north flank. A battle line of six battleships and six destroyers commanded by Admiral Weyler was sandwiched in between. To the south, in the Mindanao Sea, thirty-eight PT boats monitored the Japanese approach. Nishimura had sent two separate forces to scout ahead of his battleships. Forty miles southwest of Surigao Strait, the first PT boat sections made contact with Nishimura's advance forces shortly after midnight on 25 October. As the Japanese ships plowed on, the PT boats attacked with little effect. But their sighting reports kept Oldendorf informed of the Japanese movements.

A destroyer division of seven ships commanded by Comdr. J. G. Coward patrolled the strait itself. Learning of the Japanese approach, he left two destroyers on picket duty and divided his force into two sections for an attack. He planned to strike from the east with three destroyers while Comdr. R. H. Philips led two destroyers on an attack from the west. At about 0300, Coward's destroyers launched twenty-seven torpedoes from a range of nearly eight thousand yards. One struck the battleship *Fuso,* the largest ship in the van, which slowed down and dropped out of the battle line. It sank forty-five minutes later. Shortly thereafter, Philips's squadron let loose fifteen torpedoes. Three destroyers were hit; two sank, and one dropped out of the battle. The destroyers also scored a hit on the admiral's flagship, the *Yamashiro.*

Nishimura's force then encountered two more destroyer squadrons. Squadron 24's six destroyers attacked at 0330. A torpedo from the *Killen* struck the *Yamashiro,* slowing the battleship down to only a few knots, but Nishimura continued to head northward. Oldendorf next sent in Squadron 56. Although most of the squadron's torpedoes missed their targets, four more struck the *Yamashiro.* During Squadron 56's attack, the Japanese gunners found the range on the *Newcomb,* which took a large number of hits but survived the action. Meanwhile, Nishimura, seemingly oblivious to his losses, continued to steam ahead—directly into Oldendorf's battle line. It was the answer to a battleship admiral's dream: crossing the T. *West Virginia* opened up with its 16-inch guns from twenty-six thousand yards at 0353, and was soon followed by the *Tennessee* and *California,* each operating with the latest radar. *Maryland* and *Mississippi,* with older fire control systems, were not as accurate.

At twenty thousand yards, Admiral Berkey's cruisers added the weight of their main batteries. Thousands of shells of all calibers were fired at Nishimura's three surviving ships. *Yamashiro* absorbed the most hits, but the cruiser *Mogami* and destroyer *Shigure* were badly damaged.

Oldendorf ordered a cease-fire to sort out his formations when some of his ships began taking friendly fire. The pause allowed the *Mogami* and *Shigure* to escape. The *Yamashiro* sank thirty minutes after the main action began, taking Admiral Nishimura and most of the crew with it. In the short span of four hours, Nishimura lost two battleships and three destroyers sunk, and one heavy cruiser and one destroyer were badly damaged.

Admiral Shima's 2d Attack Force was approximately forty miles behind Nishimura's Central Force when the action in Surigao Strait began. He moved ahead as rapidly as possible with his force of three cruisers and four destroyers, only to have the light cruiser *Abukuma* torpedoed south of Panaon Island by a PT boat. At a few minutes past 0400, Shima sighted what was left of the battleship *Fuso* and very soon concluded that Nishimura's force had been destroyed. Realizing that his inferior force stood little chance of succeeding where Nishimura had failed, Shima informed higher headquarters that he was retiring to plan further actions.

At 0545, Adm. Thomas Sprague sent planes from his escort carriers to attack the retreating Japanese. They found both Shima's force and the battle-damaged *Mogami*. *Mogami* was repeatedly torpedoed, and sank soon after. The limping *Abukuma* was caught and sunk by planes from the Fifth and Seventh Air Forces on 27 October. In addition, a Japanese transport unit carrying reinforcements to Ormoc was caught by Sprague's planes in the Visayan Sea, and the light cruiser *Kinu* and destroyer *Kitagami* were sunk. Later that day, a seaplane tender was attacked and sunk. An air raid on Manila by planes from *Lexington* on 4 November caught and sank the cruiser *Nachi* in the harbor. The disaster was complete. Of the ships in Nishimura's and Shima's forces that had entered Surigao Strait, only the cruiser *Ashigara* and five destroyers survived.

While the action in Surigao Strait was unfolding, Kurita's force, which had broken out into the Philippine Sea, had an opportunity to destroy the bulk of the American escort carrier group. Admiral Sprague had divided his force into three sections, code-named Taffy

1, 2, and 3. Taffy 3, commanded by RAdm. Clifton A. F. Sprague, was closest to the oncoming enemy. Rear Admiral Felix B. Stump's Taffy 2 lay farther south off the entrance to Leyte Gulf. Kurita's decision to reverse course caught the escort carriers off guard; none of the commanders had expected to encounter the main portion of the Japanese battle fleet.

Kurita, too, was surprised when he did not encounter any opposition on his second run through San Bernardino Strait. His force was in the process of a routine maneuver when the American carriers were sighted and he issued his attack order. Fortunately for Taffy 3, the resultant confusion reduced the striking power of Kurita's major ships. All of the escort carriers in Taffy 2 and 3 launched as many planes as possible, but the surprise of having the Japanese fleet within striking range also caused confusion on board the carriers. Nevertheless, Adm. Clifton Sprague ordered his destroyer screen to attack the Japanese battleships and cruisers. These attacks, combined with air strikes, minimized the damage done by Kurita's heavy guns.

The confused action that began off Samar at 0700 lasted for two and one-half hours, dominated at first by attacks by the destroyers from Taffy 3's screen. These were highlighted by the *Johnson* torpedoing the cruiser *Kumano,* forcing it from the battle, and the *Hall*'s and *Heermann*'s uneven contests with the battleships *Haruna* and *Yamato* and the heavy cruiser *Chikuma*. A combination of poor gunnery by the Japanese and aggressive actions by the destroyers, and later by the even smaller destroyer escorts, kept American losses to a minimum. Ultimately, however, the greater firepower of the Japanese took its toll, sinking the *Johnson* and *Hall* and the destroyer escort *Roberts*. But their hour-long counterattack helped confuse the Japanese and kept Kurita's ships from concentrating fires on Taffy 3's vulnerable escort carriers.

In attempting to evade torpedoes the captain of the *Yamato* turned the giant ship due north, a maneuver which effectively took that supership out of the battle. But the four Japanese cruisers continued south and engaged Clifton Sprague's Taffy 3. The *Kolanin Bay* was struck by a total of thirteen 8-inch shells, *Fanshaw Bay* took four 8-inch hits, and *White Plains* was hit by several 6-inch shells, but none of these carriers was put out of action. The most exposed ship, the *Gambier Bay,* was struck by a dozen shells, went dead in the water, and sank at a few minutes past 0900. It was the major U.S. casualty of the battle.

The Japanese did not escape unscathed. The heavy cruiser *Chokai* was heavily damaged by the destroyer attacks and sunk by planes from *Kitkun Bay.* Torpedo planes from Stump's Taffy 2 caught the *Chikuma* and sank that heavy cruiser at approximately 0900. Shortly afterward, Kurita signaled to all ships to break off the action. For the next three hours his ships reassembled and waited outside San Bernardino Strait while the admiral decided what to do next. Finally, influenced by reports that Halsey's force was close by, he decided not to enter Leyte Gulf and notified higher headquarters at 1230 that he was retiring through the strait. The Battle of Samar was over. Despite having the element of surprise in his favor, Kurita had lost three heavy cruisers while sinking only one escort carrier and allowing four to escape relatively unscathed.

As the northern escort carriers fought their desperate battle with Kurita's 1st Attack Force, Taffy 1 off northern Mindanao encountered a chilling new Japanese tactic: kamikazes. Organized suicide attacks on American ships were the brainchild of VAdm. Takijiro Onishi, commander of the First Air Fleet. There had been an earlier attempt, during the Battle of the Philippine Sea, for designated suicide pilots to attack American ships, but all of their planes were destroyed before they could attack Spruance's fleet. Because of this, American commanders were not aware of the kamikaze threat until the Leyte actions. Onishi had concluded correctly that Japan's lack of trained pilots, combined with the overwhelming numbers of American planes and ships, meant that conventional air attacks could not blunt the enemy's advance. However, a suicide dive on a warship could be made by even an inexperienced pilot. There was no problem enlisting volunteers who, in discharging their duty to family and emperor, saw an opportunity for a glorious death. The Japanese military leaders who approved the plan believed the sacrifice of these young heroes would lift morale on the home front and at the same time confuse the Americans.

Onishi had hoped to have his suicide units prepared to coordinate with the main Sho attacks. However, it was not until most of the battles had been lost that he finally committed the suicide squadrons. The first of these struck at Taffy 1. At about 0745 on 25 October, a Japanese plane from Davao crashed onto the deck of the carrier *Santee,* causing damage to the flight deck and killing sixteen men. The carrier *Petrof Bay* narrowly escaped when its antiaircraft batteries destroyed a would-be martyr. At the same time, a plane crashed on the *Suwannee*'s flight deck. Shortly thereafter, five aircraft from Luzon struck at Taffy 3 while the ships were busy recovering aircraft. One Zero crashed through the flight deck of the *St. Lo,* igniting torpedoes and bombs on the hangar deck. The ship was a blazing wreck within thirty minutes and later sank. *Kitkun Bay, White Plains,* and *Kalinin Bay* also were struck by kamikazes, but their fires were soon brought under control. Early in the afternoon, another suicide plane hit the *Suwannee,* causing even more damage. After these attacks, a forewarning of things to come, the kamikaze pilots left the major ships alone, concentrating instead on shipping in Leyte Gulf.

Admiral McCain's TG 38.1, ordered by Halsey to support Kinkaid's pursuit of the retreating Kurita, launched an attack at extreme range early in the afternoon on the twenty-fifth. This strike did no significant damage to the Japanese fleet. Kurita's ships also escaped the sixth sortie of the day from Stump's Taffy 2 planes. McCain was joined the next day by Bogan's group, and together they launched a total of 250 planes. The main Japanese ships again escaped damage, but the cruiser *Noshiro* was sunk and serious damage was inflicted on the cruiser *Kumano.* It was sunk a month later near Lingayen Gulf. The destroyer *Shiranuhi,* from Shima's force, was also sunk. Despite these attacks, as well as raids by B-24s from Morotai, what was left of Kurita's main force safely reached Brunei Bay in Borneo.

While the battles of Surigao Strait and Samar were in progress, Halsey's massive force, built around five fleet and five light carriers and bolstered by Admiral Lee's TF 34 of six fast battleships, was closing in on Ozawa's decoy fleet. The Japanese admiral, after sending off his few planes to attack Sherman's group on the twenty-fourth, was disappointed that Halsey had not taken the bait. Then, when he learned that Kurita had retreated, Ozawa turned north, apparently abandoning the plan. Informed of Kurita's later movements, he once again turned south. It was at that point that Halsey's force, once again under the tactical control of Admiral Mitscher, located the Japanese two hundred miles northeast of Cape Engaño on Luzon. Even before the sighting at 0700 on 25 October, Mitscher had launched a number of planes, and these were waiting to attack.

The first strike against the Japanese was by aircraft from *Essex, San Jacinto,* and *Intrepid.* The large carrier *Zuikaku,* a veteran of Pearl Harbor, was struck by a torpedo that destroyed its communications system. A number of bombs hit the carrier *Chitose* and the destroyer *Akatsuki;* both ships quickly sank. Mitscher's second strike, made up of planes from the *Franklin* and *Lexington,* left the carrier *Chiyoda* burning. It was finally sunk in the afternoon by gunfire from an American cruiser. The third strike, made up of planes from *Essex, Langley,* and *Lexington,* was launched just before noon and caught the *Zuikaku* and *Zuiho* fleeing northward. Three more torpedoes blew the *Zuikaku* apart, and it sank at a few minutes past 1400. The *Zuiho* was attacked by planes from *Essex* and struck a number of times. The Japanese carrier was later hit by waves of attackers from the fourth strike, and sank at 1530. Hits were also registered on the converted battleship *Ise,* but it survived, as did four of Ozawa's cruisers. Ozawa still had twelve of his ships afloat, and, although pursued by American submarines, most of these were able to escape into the Inland Sea. However, on the evening of the twenty-fifth, the submarine *Jallao* torpedoed and sank the fleeing light cruiser *Tamu,* the last of Ozawa's force to be destroyed.

Early in TF 38's action with Ozawa, Kinkaid informed Halsey of the battle off Samar and requested Halsey's aid. Halsey responded by instructing McCain to reinforce Thomas Sprague's light carriers. He did not detach TF 34, Lee's battleships, immediately because he planned to move them in later to destroy the remaining ships in Ozawa's force—and he had calculated that they could not cover the four hundred miles to Samar in time to be of any use. However, at about 1000, Halsey received another plea from Kinkaid and, almost simultaneously, a communication from Nimitz. The latter threw him into a rage. It queried: "Where is Rpt Where is Task Force 34 RR The World Wonders." Staff officers sought to calm their commander by pointing out that the phrase "the world wonders" was merely padding and not intended as a criticism. Much later, Halsey learned that a junior officer had put in the first "Where is Rpt," (repeat), giving the message a peremptory tone Nimitz had not intended. Stinging from the perceived rebuke, Halsey believed he had no choice but to detach Lee's battle line and send it south to aid Kinkaid, giving up the chance to destroy Ozawa's force. As Halsey had suspected, Lee's fast battleships arrived too late to take part in the battle.

The naval victory in the four separate but connected battles was perhaps not as noteworthy as Midway, but it was nevertheless a stunning success. The Japanese naval command was aware of the Sho-Go (Victory Operation) Plan's desperate nature, and the planners themselves must have realized that their navy was already defeated. After the actions at Leyte Gulf, however, the situation was no longer debatable; Japanese ships never again posed a significant threat to American dominance of the seas.

Halsey's actions, on the other hand, were sharply criticized. Despite the stunning victories, many faulted him for not leaving a portion of the Third Fleet to cover San Bernardino Strait. Yet much of that criticism was after the fact. Halsey, acting on the intelligence regarding Japanese fleet movements he had available on the twenty-fourth, made three assumptions. The first was that Kurita's ships had been badly damaged and were retreating. The second was that Ozawa's carriers were the main force. Finally, he assumed that the Seventh Fleet was strong enough to deal with any future developments. Kurita's success against the escort carriers was due to the laxity of their commanders in not conducting more thorough searches. That they were surprised was not Halsey's fault. It is difficult not to agree with Halsey that the only significant mistake he made was ordering Lee's battle line south when he had Ozawa's damaged fleet under his guns.

The multiple victories over the Japanese fleets did not end the tasks of the naval support groups. Although the army had captured five airfields in eastern Leyte, they were unusable for bombers, and the continuing bad weather delayed further construction. It was not until 27 October that thirty-four P-38s flew into Tacloban, the only serviceable airfield, and these were kept busy fighting off the revived Japanese air forces. Halsey thus kept three task groups to provide close air support for the army and to attack shipping and airfields as far away as Luzon.

Surprisingly, during the last week of October, Japanese army and naval air units achieved near parity with American forces by bringing in aircraft from Luzon, Formosa, and Kyushu. Many of these were designated for use as kamikazes. The carriers *Intrepid, Franklin,* and *Belleau Wood* were all seriously damaged by suicide attacks and forced to retire for repairs. The Seventh Fleet was also a target, and by the thirtieth one destroyer had been sunk and five others damaged. The kamikaze activity did not halt the buildup of men and supplies, and it had the negative effect of helping to destroy available Japanese aircraft. The kamikaze losses, coupled with attrition from aggressive American air action, had by the first week in November reduced Japanese airpower in the region to a negligible force. Nevertheless, MacArthur insisted that Halsey's carriers continue to give air support, and Nimitz and Halsey reluctantly agreed.

On land, operations by Krueger's Sixth Army were slowed by torrential rains that lasted for more than three weeks. The already soggy ground became swampy, streams flooded, and the few roads became almost impassable. Nevertheless, significant gains were made. The main objective after consolidation of the perimeter was the town of Carigara on the north coast. If this area was secured, then the 1st Cavalry and 24th Infantry Divisions could reverse the axis of attack southward into the Ormoc Valley of western Leyte and assault the major town of Ormoc.

General Suzuki also recognized the importance of Carigara. He pulled back the bulk of his 16th Division into northern Leyte and rushed reinforcements to the town as soon as they became available. Despite protests from Field Marshal Terauchi and General Yamashita, Imperial Headquarters in Tokyo insisted upon making Leyte a major battleground. Not only were hard to replace aircraft thrown into the action, but Yamashita had to order troops he wanted to save for the Mindanao, Cebu, and Luzon campaigns into the fighting. Bombing and strafing by American naval and army planes claimed a number of ships and barges in the straits between Leyte and Cebu. On 11 November, the worst day for the Japanese rein-forcements, planes from the Third Fleet sank three transports and four destroyers. Nevertheless, an estimated forty-five thousand men had been landed by that date, the most important being the fresh 1st Division from Shanghai.

General Sibert of X Corps, aware of the strength of the defenses at Carigara, sent several 1st Cavalry Division units in an amphibi-ous end run to secure the northeastern coastline adjacent to the town. He then waited until the 24th Division, advancing from the south, was on line. That division had a difficult transit because of weather, swampy conditions, and Japanese resistance. By 29 Octo-ber, after smashing a Japanese regiment, the 24th had taken Jaro, an important road junction ten miles south of Carigara. Sibert was at last prepared for his general attack.

In the meantime, XXIV Corps was responsible for clearing south-ern Leyte and then moving westward through the mountains. It was soon apparent to General Hodge that only scattered forces were in the south, since Suzuki had chosen to make his stand in the north. While the 96th Division scoured the south, the 7th Division at-tacked west toward Dagami, the last Japanese stronghold east of the mountains. Any attack against that town was funneled along the road from the town of Burauen because of the swamps on either side. To the north of the swampy area, the Japanese had constructed pillboxes, trenches, and machine-gun pits. The 7th Division took very heavy casualties before it could clear this maze of defenses and enter Dagami on 30 October. When scouts located a narrow winding trail across the mountains, elements of the 7th Division moved across to western Leyte, seizing the village of Baybay, south of Ormoc, on 3 November. There were too few men available to attempt an assault on Ormoc, and, realizing the threat posed by American troops so close to Ormoc, Suzuki sent reinforcements to block the coast road.

On 1 November, General Sibert launched his delayed attack on Carigara. The 34th Infantry Regiment spearheaded the move from Jaro, and by nightfall was within two miles of the town. The following day, a heavy artillery barrage was laid down as the 1st Cavalry Division attacked from the west. Units of both divisions entered the town and secured it by midafternoon. There was little

Japanese resistance, as local commanders had decided to withdraw after part of their main defenses were outflanked by the amphibious operation. The plan was to pull back into the hills, reconstruct the shattered 41st Infantry and reinforce it with the newly arrived lst Division, and then launch a major counterattack that would clear the Americans from the town and reestablish Japanese control over northern Leyte.

But Suzuki's plan was based on false information. He was not aware that all of Sibert's corps was present in the area and that elements of the lst Cavalry Division were already pushing westward. Lieutenant General Tadasu Kataoka, commanding the lst Division, soon discovered these facts and the plan was altered to contest the American movement toward Ormoc along the highlands guarding the main road south.

General Krueger, believing that he had insufficient forces to guard against a seaward threat to northern Leyte and begin a major offensive against Ormoc, ordered X Corps to halt on 4 November and secure the Carigara Bay area. This move, however necessary it may have seemed to Krueger, gave Kataoka time to organize his defenses along a long, steep ridge astride the road into Ormoc Valley.

General Suzuki, taking advantage of his central position, was able to send reinforcements to plug gaps as fast as they appeared in his highland defenses. The 24th Division's 21st Infantry Regiment, fighting the miserable weather and the determined Japanese defenders on each hill and ridge, took very heavy losses. However, by mid-November they had inflicted more than two thousand casualties on their adversaries and controlled all of what had become known as Breakneck Ridge. Meanwhile, the 19th Infantry Regiment seized the high ground east of the ridge and moved southwest to establish a roadblock on the main road leading south to Ormoc. Elements of the 34th Infantry rode amtracs to the west shore of Carigara Bay, where they landed and seized a ridge overlooking the road. These actions prevented the Japanese from using the road to supply troops maintaining a perimeter northeast of Ormoc.

Krueger earlier had been provided with Kataoka's captured attack plan, and he circumvented it by ordering Sibert to send units from the lst Cavalry Division southwest of Carigara to seize other highlands. The lst Cavalry carried out this mission in terrible weather against only sporadic enemy resistance. By 15 November, most of the high ground between northern Leyte and Ormoc Valley was in American hands.

There was heavy fighting during the first two weeks of November in XXIV Corps's area. The 96th Division, advancing westward, was delayed by remnants of Lt. Gen. Shiro Makino's 16th Division. The Japanese had some prepared defenses, but in general they used natural terrain features to contest every hill, ridge, and valley. Like their comrades in the north, the Japanese in this sector seldom retreated, and they had to be rooted out of their positions. Each day there were localized counterattacks, and at night small numbers of Japanese would infiltrate the American lines. Nevertheless, by mid-November infantrymen of the 96th Division had eliminated all major Japanese positions west of Dagami.

The 7th Division was dispersed on search and destroy missions throughout southern Leyte, although the bulk of the 32d Infantry Regiment, which had earlier crossed the mountains and seized Baybay, was beginning to probe northward toward Ormoc by 15 November.

At this time, Krueger proposed to MacArthur an amphibious landing near Ormoc by the uncommitted 32d Division. Admiral Kinkaid advised against it, however, because the Seventh Fleet was short of landing craft, and he feared that the possible loss of shipping to kamikazes in such an endeavor would jeopardize the proposed invasions of Luzon and Mindanao. MacArthur concurred and Krueger abandoned the plan temporarily.

General Yamashita decided in early November to change Japanese strategy. He ordered Suzuki to shift the bulk of the Thirty-fifth Army southward, abandoning the idea of counterattacking in the Carigara region. By the time Suzuki received his orders on the thirteenth, the Japanese situation had deteriorated to such an extent that it was no longer feasible to move the army south. A further complication was the arrival on 14 November of the 32d Division, whose fresh troops replaced those of the tired and weakened 24th Division in the Tacloban area.

Meanwhile, in Manila, Yamashita and his Fourteenth Army staff again tried without success to convince higher authority to give up the Leyte fight and instead concentrate all available forces for the expected invasion of Luzon. Rebuffed, he did not countermand Suzuki's order sending the 26th Division to Leyte. The bulk of that division landed safely, although most of its heavy weapons, ammunition, and equipment were lost to American air strikes. By 23 November, four of its battalions confronted the 7th Division's 32d Infantry along the so-called Shoestring Ridge north of Baybay and began well-coordinated attacks that continued for five days. This action drew in most of the Japanese 26th Division, and Maj. Gen. Archibald Arnold was in turn forced to commit the bulk of his 7th Division.

At this point—at the height of the rainy season, when much of the land resembled a marsh—Krueger, with the addition of Maj. Gen. Joseph M. Swing's 11th Airborne Division, planned a concerted drive in XXIV Corps's area against the remnants of the Japanese 16th Division west of Dagami. Sibert's X Corps would simultaneously attempt to break into the Ormoc Valley from the north. The scheduled date for the new offensive was 5 December. Yamashita was also planning a bold stroke designed to seize four of the American-held airfields in eastern Leyte. Lieutenant General Koyji Tominaga, commander of the Japanese Fourth Air Army, had suggested a hit-and-run attack by a small number of parachute troops on these fields simply to destroy planes and equipment. Yamashita seized upon this idea and ordered a full-scale assault by the 2d Parachute Brigade. This attack, code-named Wa, would be coordinated with an eastward thrust by the 26th Division that, if successful, would drive a wedge between the American forces. Tominaga's small-scale parachute attack on 26 November on Buri and Byung Fields went ahead as planned and was a disaster. Three of the four transport planes crashed, and most of the survivors were quickly captured or killed.

Operation Wa also went ahead as planned on 5 December. Unfortunately for the Japanese, coordination between the paratroopers and General Makino's 16th Division, attacking toward Buri Field, was poor. The paratroopers also missed two of the targeted airfields. Nevertheless, the attacks surprised the small local garrisons, Air Corps, and construction personnel, and the Japanese gained complete control of San Pablo Field. Krueger ordered a newly arrived regiment from the 38th Division to help General Swing's airborne troops, and the airfield was recaptured by evening of the next day.

Lieutenant General Tsuyuo Yamagata's depleted 26th Division sent elements across the mountains to attack the Americans in the Burauen area. In four days of fighting, these were almost destroyed by 11th Airborne Division units. The rest of the 26th Division troops were scattered in small bands throughout the mountains. The few hundred men left alive in the paratroop brigade and the 16th Division men caught east of the mountains did not reach the northwest coast until February 1945.

During the two weeks of fighting after 25 November, Admiral Fukudome and General Tominaga brought into action the largest part of the Japanese air force on southern Luzon. The Fourth Air Army's planes struck at Sixth Army anchorages, shipping in the gulf, and airfields. The navy planes attacked ships of both the Third and Seventh Fleets. On 25 November, suicide planes damaged four of Admiral Halsey's carriers, and this convinced him to do what he had wanted to three weeks before: retire temporarily from the Leyte area.

Despite the failure of the Wa operation, Suzuki continued to receive reinforcements. The 68th Brigade was scheduled to land at Ormoc on 8 December with five thousand men. But the convoy was caught by Kenney's planes, which did considerable damage and forced it to land the troops at San Isidro Harbor. After losing most of its artillery, the brigade struggled over a tortuous route to join the 1st Division and had little effect on the battle for Ormoc.

At the same time the Japanese were attempting to land troops at Ormoc, the Americans were landing in the same area. General Krueger in late November finally received the necessary amphibious craft to carry out his earlier plan. Major General Andrew Bruce's 77th Division, which had been reorganized after the Guam invasion and kept in reserve, reached Leyte on 23 November and was alerted a week later for the Ormoc landing.

Ormoc had been stripped of most of its defenders for tactical operations elsewhere, so the 77th Division's landings south of the town on 7 December were hardly opposed. Despite efforts by kamikazes, which sank the destroyers *Mahan* and *Ward,* by evening the 77th had seized the town of Ipil and established a beachhead two miles wide and a mile deep. By 8 December, Maj. Gen. Yoshiharu Tomochika, chief of staff of the Thirty-fifth Army, had pulled back nearly two thousand troops to defend the southern approaches to Ormoc. Yamashita also ordered the five hundred remaining paratroopers from the ill-fated 2d Parachute Brigade still on Luzon to jump into the area of the airfield still controlled by the Japanese. Two troop convoys, one from the Camotes Islands and a larger one from Manila, were intercepted by army and marine pilots who sank two destroyers and a number of transports. Only a small portion of the reinforcements landed.

That same day General Bruce ordered an immediate advance toward Ormoc before Japanese reinforcements could arrive. Sporadic resistance from Japanese dug in along the wooded ridges failed to halt the 77th Division, and by evening its units were within sight of the town. The attack continued on 9 December against stiffening Japanese resistance. However, supporting artillery firing white phosphorus and high explosives cleared the way for the infantry. Despite having to fight off several banzai charges, Bruce's troops were in position for a final assault on the town by evening. On the tenth, every gun and mortar in the 77th opened up on the town as the 307th Infantry Regiment attacked directly north. The 306th Infantry was sent on a wide flanking movement to the east, and by midafternoon it had turned the Japanese flank. The remaining defenders retreated northward and by evening Ormoc, the last major Japanese supply port, had fallen. General Bruce announced its capture by reporting to Krueger, "Have rolled two sevens in Ormoc." Even more significant than the loss of the port, the Japanese troops operating to the south and east were cut off from those operating in the north. Outnumbered and trapped, the situation of the scattered remnants of the Japanese Thirty-fifth Army was hopeless.

Krueger's forces next proceeded to crush the last of the major organized units on Leyte. The 7th Division drove north against diminished resistance toward Ormoc, and the 77th Division pushed north of the town. By the fifteenth the 77th had forced the Japanese north of Valencia, and on 21 December made contact with X Corps troops. Meanwhile, X Corps had finally shattered the defenses in the northwest and destroyed most of the Japanese 1st, 30th, and 102d Divisions. Elsewhere in XXIV Corps's area, the 7th Infantry and 11th Airborne Divisions had trapped General Yamagata's large Japanese force between them.

Imperial Headquarters in Tokyo, failing to comprehend that the desperate fight for Leyte was lost, ordered Yamashita to prepare for a counterlanding at Carigara. This foolhardy plan was discarded only because of the American invasion of Mindoro and Fourteenth Army fears of an early landing on Luzon. It was not until 20 December that General Sugiyama informed Premier Koiso that Leyte had been abandoned in preparation for the decisive battle on Luzon.

The last major battle on Leyte was the combined operation from 23 December to Christmas Day to secure the port of Palompon and force Suzuki and the remnants of the Thirty-fifth Army into the wooded hills to the north. In accordance with previous plans, General Eichelberger and his newly activated Eighth Army headquarters took over the Leyte operation on 26 December, relieving Krueger to conduct the larger and more difficult task of subjugating Luzon. General MacArthur then declared that, except for minor mopping-up operations, the campaign was officially over. As with many of MacArthur's pronouncements, this was not completely accurate. There were still some fifteen thousand Japanese holding out in a number of pockets in the mountains of central and northern Leyte, and the grim, dangerous task of reducing these lasted until mid-February 1945.

The Leyte campaign, although lasting much longer than MacArthur and Krueger had imagined, brought unexpected results. The Third and Seventh Fleets had effectively destroyed most of what remained of the once mighty Japanese fleet. The losses of planes and pilots from Fukudome's Sixth Base Air Force and Tominaga's Fourth Air Army trying to defend Leyte could never be replaced. The Japanese army units committed on Leyte were among the best in the Philippines, and almost all of the estimated sixty-five-thousand-man force was destroyed at a cost to the Americans of thirty-five hundred dead.

Admiral Yonai, the Japanese navy minister, summed up the Leyte defeat by noting that the island's loss ultimately meant the loss of the entire Philippines chain. Effectively cut off from its sources of raw materials in the East Indies and Southeast Asia, Japan did not have the means to prevent Allied forces from carrying out any operations they chose. Japan could, by suicidal resistance, only delay the inevitable.

Chapter 13

Advance to Luzon

THE LEYTE OPERATION was but a prelude to the larger and much more difficult tasks of invading Luzon and ultimately clearing the Japanese from the dozens of islands in the southern Philippines. Luzon was the major objective. Irregular in shape and approximately 450 miles long from San Bernardino Strait in the south to Babuyan Channel in the north, Luzon was then populated by more than seven million persons. The bulk of the population lived on the flat western coastal plain south of Lingayen Gulf. Midway on the west coast is Manila Bay, one of the finest landlocked harbors in the world. The city of Manila is one of the largest in Asia. Radiating out from Manila was a good road system linking the capital with all the major towns on the island.

Before invading Leyte, General MacArthur issued operational orders for the Luzon and Mindoro landings, assigning the task to the Sixth Army and the Seventh Fleet. By 15 November 1944, General Krueger's staff had completed plans for the initial landings on Luzon. The landing sites chosen were at the base of Lingayen Gulf, very near to where the Japanese had landed at the beginning of the war. An alternate plan to land troops simultaneously at Aparri in the north was given up in favor of concentrating forces in western Luzon with the objective of seizing Manila. A secondary landing was planned south of the city after the Lingayen beachhead had been secured.

The Luzon operation was originally set for 20 December, but problems providing air cover for the projected earlier landing on Mindoro, combined with the relative success of the kamikaze attacks off Leyte, caused MacArthur to postpone both operations. The Mindoro operation was rescheduled for 15 December and the Lingayen landings for 9 January 1945.

The Luzon campaign was the longest and most difficult of the entire Pacific war. The Lingayen landings eclipsed in size the invasions of North Africa, Sicily, and southern France. Krueger's Sixth Army, reconstituted for the Luzon operation, would operate initially with Maj. Gen. Oscar Griswold's XIV Corps and Maj. Gen. Innis Swift's I Corps. The XIV Corps, composed of the 37th and 40th Divisions, was assigned beach areas adjacent to the town of Lingayen. I Corps, with the 6th and 43d Divisions, would land farther north near the town of San Fabian. Krueger had the 25th Division, the 158th Infantry Regiment, and the 13th Armored Group in reserve. Ultimately the 32d, 33d, and 38th Infantry Divisions and the lst Cavalry Division would also be involved. In all, Krueger had more than two hundred thousand troops available for the assault. General Eichelberger, still conducting operations on Leyte, had the Americal and 96th Divisions and the 11th Airborne Division. The Seventh Fleet and General Whitehead's Fifth Air Force, operating from Leyte and Mindoro, were assigned to cover the massive operation. Elements of Halsey's Third Fleet would also provide some air cover, but its main contribution would be air strikes on installations on Luzon and Formosa to keep the Japanese there from supporting Yamashita. Formosa was also targeted by the Fourteenth and Twentieth Air Forces, and Admiral Lockwood's submarines prowled the waters in great numbers throughout the Philippines.

No longer hampered by interference from Field Marshal Terauchi, General Yamashita had been given a free hand in defending the Philippines. However, this did not mean a unified command. The twenty-five thousand naval troops obeyed their own commanders, who often ignored Yamashita's instructions. This was particularly true with regard to the defense of Manila. The heavy losses of men in the defense of Leyte had reduced Yamashita's potential for resisting the attack he knew was coming. He had one armored and seven infantry divisions totaling approximately two hundred sixty thousand men. The number of aircraft available on 15 December, including both army and navy air units, has been estimated at 450. But the combination of air attacks by Halsey's planes on the still functioning airfields, combined with losses from kamikaze attacks, reduced air strength to fewer than a hundred planes by mid-January. Faced with these facts, the ever-pragmatic Tiger of Malaya decided to offer only token resistance to the landings, to pull his troops out of Manila, and retire to three defensible areas in the mountains. From there he hoped to tie down as many American troops as possible for as long as possible. This decision meant that after they were ashore, the Americans could quickly occupy the western coastal plain.

Before attacking Luzon, MacArthur wanted to seize the island of Mindoro, which lies just 15 miles south of central Luzon. The island, 60 miles wide by 110 miles long, occupies a strategic location. All sea traffic from Leyte and Mindanao to central and northern Luzon had to pass close to Mindoro; Manila is only 90 miles to the north. Fifth Air Force planes based on Leyte were in no position to cover the Luzon operations, but aircraft flying from Mindoro could provide the needed support, thus relieving many of the naval units for strikes elsewhere.

The plan was to send a regiment from the 24th Division and the 503d Parachute Infantry Regiment—a total of almost twelve thousand combat troops—to land on the southwest coast to seize the flat lands and the town of San Jose. These and 16,500 air force and construction troops were carried by RAdm. Arthur D. Struble's Visayan attack force, which consisted of three cruisers, ten destroyers, twenty-three PT boats, and a number of smaller craft escorting seventy-three landing craft. Farther south, in the Sulu Sea, was a covering force and carrier group that included three battleships, three cruisers, six light carriers, and eighteen destroyers.

The landings on 15 December went smoothly because there were fewer than five hundred Japanese on Mindoro. Brigadier General William C. Dunckel's force quickly moved to occupy San Jose, and construction crews began work to repair the main field there. The first P-38s flew in from Leyte on 23 December and took part in fierce air actions initiated by the Japanese. Later, on 2 January, an amphibious operation secured the northwest section of the island, and by 30 January the entire coastal area was controlled by U.S. forces. On 3 January another small amphibious operation was mounted against the neighboring island of Marinduque, which was secured within a week.

However easy the occupation of Mindoro was, it was fraught with danger for the ships supporting the landings. The air-sea battle began on the thirteenth when a Val bomber from Cebu broke through and crashed into the cruiser *Nashville* as the convoy entered the Sulu Sea, damaging it severely and killing 133 men. Another suicide plane seriously damaged the destroyer *Haraden* that same day.

Japanese air attacks from fields in Cebu, Panay, and Luzon increased as the convoy neared Mindoro. A major effort was mounted on the fourteenth when forty-nine kamikazes and escort fighters took off from Luzon for Mindoro. Fortunately they were intercepted by planes from TF 38, which destroyed most of the would-be attackers. Beginning on the fourteenth, Halsey's fleet suppressed the Japanese air units on Luzon with what Admiral Nimitz referred to as the BBB: the big blue blanket, a defensive aerial umbrella over all the fields on Luzon. As a result of this two-day operation, only the failed attack on the fourteenth was launched from Luzon. An estimated two hundred planes were destroyed on the ground or intercepted, many of these being replacements from Formosa. The ability of TF 38 to continue to strike the Luzon fields was seriously compromised by the damage done by a typhoon that caught the fleet unprepared on the eighteenth. The storm scattered the fleet over a sixty-mile area, destroyed many planes on the carriers, and sank the destroyers *Hull* and *Spence*. Most of the Third Fleet retired to Ulithi for repairs and did not return to the Philippines until 29 December.

After the Mindoro landings, army fighters and SBDs from Marine Air Group 12 flying from Leyte in support of the Seventh Fleet's escort carriers provided almost continuous air cover. Despite this aerial superiority, one-quarter of the attacking kamikazes managed to break through. Two LSTs were sunk on 15 December, and one PT boat was destroyed on the nineteenth. Another two LSTs were sunk and one Liberty ship was hit on the twenty-first. Suicide attacks continued throughout the following week, claiming another Liberty ship and LST on the twenty-eighth, and registering hits on three destroyers. By the end of the year, the Japanese had lost more than a hundred planes, seriously weakening their air efforts against the Lingayen convoys. Even the heaviest air attacks failed to keep the convoys from bringing supplies to Mindoro. These attacks moderated in early January as what was left of the Japanese air force on Luzon prepared for the invasion there.

Mindoro was also the scene of a futile naval attack the day after Christmas. Field Marshal Terauchi in Saigon, completely out of touch with the realities of the Philippine situation, recommended to Imperial Headquarters a counterattack on Mindoro. This foolhardy suggestion was opposed by Yamashita. However, Imperial Headquarters decided that something should be done to show the flag. A bombardment mission was organized in Camranh Bay under the command of RAdm. Masatomi Kimura. His force consisted of two cruisers and six destroyers, and it was to sink any American shipping it encountered on the way to the Philippines, then, once off Mindoro, bombard the American beachhead and airfields in a manner reminiscent of the attacks on Guadalcanal. It is probable that Japan's newest aircraft carrier, the 27,000-ton *Unryu*, would have been assigned to Kimura, but it had been sunk in the China Sea on the nineteenth by the American submarine *Redfish*.

Kimura's force almost achieved the surprise he sought. There were no major American ships in the immediate vicinity of Mindoro when he came within range of his targets on the evening of the twenty-sixth. However, his small flotilla suffered nearly constant air attacks, and Kimura bombarded the target area for only forty minutes before hastily withdrawing. The shelling caused little damage, and all of Kimura's ships suffered at least some damage from the air attacks. Several PT boats attacked the retreating Japanese, and one managed to torpedo and sink a destroyer. Kimura's futile raid, although causing American commanders momentary concern, achieved nothing and showed once again how weak the once-powerful Japanese navy was after three years of war.

By January 1945, when it resumed its tasks of pinning down Japanese airpower on Luzon and destroying aircraft on Formosa, the Third Fleet was the most powerful naval force ever assembled. The latter task was extremely important because Formosa was the staging ground for all replacement aircraft headed for Luzon. Japanese factories more than compensated for Japan's appalling aircraft losses in 1944. Japanese aircraft production reached its peak in June, when more than two thousand aircraft were built. Even after the Americans began bombing the home islands, Japanese aircraft factories still churned out planes, producing some fourteen hundred in January 1945. Many of these were sent to Formosa to stage for the Philippines.

With the shift of emphasis to suicide missions, Japan's need for qualified pilots was significantly reduced. The kamikazes were expected simply to fly their planes to Formosa and then on to Luzon, where they would be in a position to intercept and destroy American shipping. But the air strikes by Halsey's fliers on Formosa on the third, fifth, and ninth, as well as those on the Luzon airfields on the sixth and seventh, interrupted the supply of suicide planes to Luzon.

Despite the Third Fleet's best efforts, the convoys headed for the Lingayen and San Fabian beaches had to run a gauntlet of suicide attacks even more damaging than those off Mindoro. The lead element in this massive assault was Admiral Oldendorf's Fire Support Unit of six battleships, six cruisers, and fourteen destroyers. Twelve light carriers were also on hand to provide air cover before and after the preliminary bombardment of the beach areas.

In the late afternoon of 4 January, seventy-five miles west of Panay, a twin-engine bomber undetected by any of Oldendorf's ships crashed into the carrier *Ommaney Bay,* its bombs exploding on the hangar deck. Within the hour, the carrier went down. The following day, while still 150 miles west of Luzon, the fleet suffered massive air attacks in the morning. Wildcat fighters from the light carriers beat off the attackers, but later in the day kamikazes scored hits on the light carrier *Manila Bay,* the American cruiser *Louisville,* and the Australian cruiser *Australia.*

On 6 January, Oldendorf began his preliminary bombardment at approximately 1100 while under attack by kamikazes. Planes from TF 38 were prevented from helping because of heavy overcast east of Luzon. An aircraft from the first wave of attackers struck the bridge of the *New Mexico,* the flagship of the San Fabian attack group. Admiral Weyler, the task group commander, and the British Pacific commander, Adm. Sir Bruce Fraser, survived, but the ship's captain, R. W. Fleming, and Lt. Gen. Sir Herbert Lumsden, Winston Churchill's personal representative to MacArthur's command, were killed. Later, kamikazes scored hits on the battleship *California,* the cruisers *Columbia, Louisville,* and *Australia,* and the destroyers *Allen Sumner, O'Brien, Southland,* and *Long.* The *Long* sank soon after it was struck. In all, Oldendorf lost one ship in the afternoon's attacks, and eleven were damaged. Nevertheless, all damaged ships remained on station and continued to pound the shore installations. The following day the destroyer *Palmer* took a series of hits, as did the *Australia,* which was so badly damaged it was at last forced to retire.

In the meantime, the main landing forces, Admiral Berkey's San Fabian group and Wilkinson's Lingayen group, entered Mindanao Strait on the seventh. Fortunately, the Japanese were so busy attacking Oldendorf's ships that they ignored the forty-mile-long convoy until the eighth. Early that morning, the kamikazes began systematic attacks on the escort carriers. One hit the *Kadashan Bay,* and the damage was so serious that the carrier had to retire. The convoy was joined off Leyte by General MacArthur and his staff on the *Boise,* and Admiral Kinkaid on the *Wasatch,* so they could observe the landings. If the example of the disaster on the *New Mexico* was not enough to illustrate the dangers to high-ranking officers, the damaging attack on the evening of the eighth on Admiral Ofstie's flagship, *Kitkun Bay,* emphasized the point.

Preliminary bombardment of all targeted beach areas began at 0700 on 8 January, and by 0930 on the ninth, the largest landing of troops in the Pacific theater was under way. The Lingayen operation called for an initial landing of two corps containing four assault divisions landing abreast on twelve separate beaches.

The XIV Corps landed along a four-thousand-yard strip midway between Lingayen town and Dagupan with Maj. Gen. Rapp Brush's 40th Division on the right and General Beightler's 37th Division on the left. There was no opposition; General Yamashita's plan did not call for contesting the landings, so none of the beach defenses were manned. Elements of the 40th Division moved west toward Port

Sual, located on the southwest corner of the gulf, and then to Alminos, an important road junction twelve miles beyond. By noon, a battalion from the 185th Infantry Regiment was six miles west of the beaches and another had pushed through Lingayen town. The 160th Infantry crossed the Calmay River and was four miles inland by nightfall. Meanwhile, the 37th Division's 148th Infantry Regiment was ferried across the Calmay in the early afternoon. On the corps's left, elements of the 129th Infantry moved into the town of Dagupan while others pushed eastward to the mouth of the Dagupan River and made contact with the 6th Division on I Corps's right. By evening, XIV Corps held a beachhead twenty miles wide and nearly four miles deep. The next two days saw the two divisions moving cautiously but quickly inland against only sporadic resistance. Only the 160th Infantry suffered any losses, and those were light—only fifteen casualties. By 12 January all corps units had reached the Final Beach Line. Their next objective was to continue southward and secure crossings of the Agno River.

The initial tasks in the I Corps sector were more difficult. The two landing beaches midway between the Dagupan and Buled Rivers were separated from each other, and the area assigned to I Corps for the first few days was larger than XIV Corps's sector. However, there was no opposition to Maj. Gen. Edwin Patrick's 6th Division, which landed on the right flank beaches. By dusk, the division's lead units were four miles inland and had made contact with troops from the 37th Division. The only significant fighting during the first three days of the operation was in Maj. Gen. Leonard F. Wing's 43d Division sector. Three tiers of ridges were located approximately three miles inland on the division's right, and the Japanese had set up a few defensive positions there. The 169th Infantry Regiment, harassed by mortar and artillery fire, moved east toward the highest hill but was unable to launch an assault on it until the following day. This defensive position was not taken until midday of the eleventh. Meanwhile, the 103d Infantry had taken the village of San Fabian and struck southeastward. The last of the 43d Division's infantry regiments, the 172d, took two other key hills in the center. The division's losses were light, 55 killed and 185 wounded, but the Japanese opposition was enough for Krueger to commit two regiments of the Sixth Army's reserve in the I Corps sector. By 12

January, I Corps's beachhead was firmly established and its units were moving eastward toward the main Japanese defenses.

The route to Manila was hardly contested because Yamashita had positioned the bulk of his forces in three mountain strongholds. The most important of these was located north-northeast of Lingayen, and Yamashita—from his headquarters in the mountain town of Baguio—retained direct command of the 152,000-man force, which was called the Shobu Group. The second largest concentration was

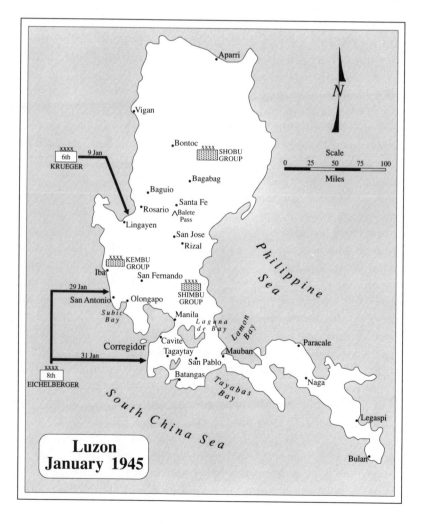

Luzon
January 1945

in the south, where Lt. Gen. Shizuo Yokoyama commanded the Shimbu Group, a force of about 80,000 men. Although Yokoyama's defense area included all of southern Luzon, his main concentration was in the hills east and northeast of Manila. The third redoubt area was in the Zambales Mountains on the west side of the Central Plain, where delaying action could prevent the Americans from using Clark Field. The element stationed there, the Kembu Group, was a mixed force of 30,000 men commanded by Maj. Gen. Rikichi Tsukada. Yamashita had stockpiled supplies in these areas and was content to stand on the defensive, exacting the maximum possible casualties from the attackers. His orders to General Yokoyama were to put up only token resistance in the Manila area while bringing out as much food and equipment as possible during the withdrawal from the city. However, the naval commander disagreed, believing Manila should be strongly defended. Before he left for Baguio, VAdm. Denshichi Okochi, commanding the Southwest Area Fleet, placed his subordinate, RAdm. Sanji Iwabachi, in charge of the Special Naval Base Force with orders to defend the city. This confusion in command was not cleared up until after it was too late to evacuate the twenty thousand mostly naval troops from Manila. The defense of Manila ran counter to Yamashita's plans, but by the time he was aware of what was happening, Krueger's forces had blocked all exits from the city.

The terrain and stubborn Japanese defense in I Corps's area worried General Krueger and the XIV Corps commander, General Griswold. Griswold's units were moving rapidly south against little opposition, and at one point a thirty-mile gap opened between the two corps. Before launching his attack on the Kembu Group, Griswold sent several probes into I Corps's area to determine Japanese strength there. He held up the 40th Division until he was convinced that the threat of a Japanese attack from the northeast was minimal. Then, on the twenty-fourth, he ordered the 40th Division to change the axis of its attack 90 degrees and advance westward toward the ridges and hills overlooking Clark Field.

To counter the Americans, General Tsukada had arranged his defense in three eastward facing lines. The first, his outpost line, took advantage of a series of ridges and hills that stretched for almost ten miles. The second, his main line of resistance, was located approximately five miles to the west along another set of ridgelines, anchored in the north by a thousand-foot-high ridge. Two miles to the west he had stationed naval troops in his last stand position. The major strength of the Kembu Group was the terrain it occupied. The American infantry would have to attack straight ahead and be forced into the time-consuming role of clearing each ravine and cave. Although Tsukada did not have heavy artillery, he was well supplied with mortars, machine guns, and antiaircraft guns being used for ground defense. The major Japanese weakness was the morale of the troops, many of whom were Formosan or laborers from Okinawa.

General Griswold, believing the Clark Field area to be lightly held, at first designated only the 160th Infantry Regiment to begin the drive westward on the twenty-fourth. When it made minimal gains in the first two days, he committed the 108th Infantry on the right. The 108th quickly seized three key hill positions, but by the twenty-sixth the battle had become one of short, slow advances in the face of heavy mortar and machine-gun fire. Artillery and air concentrations permitted the 160th to advance steadily through the many draws and ravines, and by the end of the day Tsukada's first line was crumbling. The 108th turned southwest on the twenty-seventh, and by day's end had gained almost a thousand yards. This success reduced the Japanese first line to only isolated strong points. Elsewhere, other elements of the 40th Division secured the Manila railroad and Route 3 from Bamban to Mabalacat. The 37th Division, which was guarding the corps's eastern flank, moved up to capture Mabalacat airfield and an important road junction with Route 4.

General Griswold's major task was to capture the four airstrips in the Clark Field area. To accomplish this, he moved the 37th Division south of the Socobra River to engage the Japanese Eguchi Detachment. North of the river, the 40th Division was to engage the Takaya and Takayama Detachments and secure the eastern foothills of the Zambales Mountains. Facing only sporadic resistance, the 145th and 129th Infantry Regiments took Clark Field by the evening of the twenty-eighth, and captured the Fort Stotsenburg area the next day. The 37th Division troops continued westward, and by the end of January had taken the heights from which the Japanese bombarded the airfield with artillery fire.

To the north, operating in more rugged terrain, the 40th Division managed to gain footholds in the hills, threatening Tsukada's main line of resistance. Although the remnants of the Kembu Group were still a force to contend with, by 1 February they were no longer a threat to XIV Corps's narrow corridor leading to Manila. General Krueger thus felt safe in moving the 37th Division from the Clark Field area in order to aid in the capture of the city.

Before the invasion, General MacArthur, in an overly optimistic pronouncement, said that his troops would capture Manila within two weeks. He was now pressuring Krueger to push ahead rapidly toward the city. Krueger successfully argued that he feared for XIV Corps's exposed flank and wanted to await the arrival of reinforcements. The first of these, the 1st Cavalry Division, the 32d Infantry Division, and the 112th Cavalry Regiment, arrived at Lingayen on the twenty-seventh. Two days later, Maj. Gen. Charles Hall's XI Corps, thirty thousand strong, landed in Zambales Province without opposition. Cooperating with Philippine guerrillas, elements of the corps moved eastward, ultimately sealing off the Bataan Peninsula. Finally, on 31 January, the 11th Airborne Division landed on the western coast at Nasugbu, twenty-five miles south of Cavite, and soon was prepared to move north toward Manila. By 1 February, Krueger was able to muster three corps composed of eight combat divisions and numerous attached units. He could at last satisfy MacArthur by closing in on Manila.

On 30 January, Krueger ordered Griswold to move part of the 37th Division south and cross the Pampanga River within two days. At the same time, General Swift's I Corps was to continue its steady pressure on Yamashita's westerly defense lines and begin an offensive to capture the important road and rail center of San Jose. The XI Corps was to move east and link up with XIV Corps, thus completely sealing off the Bataan Peninsula. The recently arrived 1st Cavalry Division, commanded by Maj. Gen. Verne Mudge, was attached to XIV Corps and ordered to dash down Route 5, enter Manila, and free prisoners at San Tomás University. It was then to press southward into the heart of the city. The two regiments assigned for this mission, the 2d and 5th Cavalry, were to be accompanied by the 44th Tank Battalion. Air support would be provided by the 32d and 24th Marine Air Groups. Meanwhile, the 11th Airborne Division, still under Eighth

Army command, was to move as quickly as possible to enter Manila from the south using Route 17.

MacArthur's and Krueger's plans were extremely complex, calling for elements of the Sixth Army to attack in three different directions on six fronts. How quickly the offensive succeeded was contingent on Yamashita's decision, conveyed to Yokoyama, to concede Manila and the coastal areas to the Americans.

The lst Cavalry Division began its dash a few minutes past midnight on 1 February and, utilizing Route 5, moved quickly to the northern outskirts of Manila. The cavalrymen found a bridge over the Bulacan River intact, and by midafternoon of the third a Sherman tank from the 44th Tank Battalion had broken down a wall of San Tomás University, which the Japanese had converted into a prison. After liberating approximately thirty-seven hundred prisoners, the 8th Cavalry pushed on and seized old Bilibid Prison and Malacañan Palace. The cavalry units were stopped short of the Quezon Bridge over the Pasig River by a roadblock, giving a Japanese demolition team time to blow up the bridge.

On the fourth, the 37th Division's 148th Infantry Regiment entered Manila to the west of the cavalry and set free more than a thousand prisoners held on the Far Eastern University.

Meanwhile, the 11th Airborne Division, which had landed on 2 February, took the town of Aga by midafternoon. The following day, three air drops by the 511th Parachute Regiment cut off the defenders of Tagaytay Ridge, the strongest defensive position blocking the northern advance. The rest of the 11th Airborne moved quickly to confront the Japanese Genko line, which had been established to defend the narrow Hagonoy Isthmus. The defenders made a brief stand at Imus, but the paratroopers broke through and captured Nichols Field. General Eichelberger, who accompanied the paratroopers, notified MacArthur on 5 February that they had entered southern Manila. On 7 February, MacArthur declared the city secure. But it was far from it; Admiral Iwabachi's naval troops could not escape, and he had no intention of surrendering. The battle for the city, which lasted until 4 March, was just beginning.

While the focus of concern in MacArthur's headquarters was Manila, I Corps was testing the front edge of Yamashita's defenses in the mountains east of Lingayen Gulf. The most difficult task in the corps area fell to the 43d Division, which had to capture the town of Rosario, secure the junction of Routes 11 and 3, and extend Sixth Army's lines along the coast as far as Damoritis. Beginning on 18 January and continuing for ten days, the 172d Infantry Regiment struggled to take three large hills north of Rosario. The town was finally occupied on the twenty-eighth. At the same time, to the south, the 63d Infantry seized Hill 1500, Question Mark Hill, and Benchmark Hill. These successes, combined with the earlier occupation of the town of Pozorrubio, secured the division's supply route along Route 3, a good concrete highway, and protected the Lingayen beachhead from attacks from the north and northeast.

Major General Charles L. Mullin Jr.'s 25th Division, operating in open ground just south of the 43d, had the advantage of a good road network. Its first objective was the town of Binalonan, which was situated on a road junction and guarded by only 350 troops. The 161st Infantry Regiment advanced on 17 January and, with the aid of tanks, beat off uncoordinated Japanese attacks and captured the town on the eighteenth.

Next, the 25th Division was given the task of securing crossings over the southerly flowing Agno River. Major General Isao Shigemi, with more than a thousand troops, some light artillery, and forty-five tanks in the vicinity of San Manuel on the 25th's left flank, decided to make a stand at heavily fortified San Miguel. The battle there began on 23 January when the 161st seized key high ground north of the town. In a vicious five-day battle, the 161st's three battalions, backed by tanks and artillery in close support, inched their way through San Miguel. The last major encounter occurred in the early morning of the twenty-eighth when a Japanese tank-infantry counterattack hit the regiment's center. By evening, the town was cleared and the division could advance across the Agno without worrying about attacks on its left flank. General Shigemi and 750 of his men were killed, and all of his tanks, artillery, and light weapons were either captured or destroyed.

The 6th Division, operating on the right side of the I Corps sector, was confronted on 17 January by the Cabaruan Hills, which covered a four-square-mile area defended by more than fifteen hundred Japanese. These were dug into a series of hills, some of which were over two hundred feet high. General Patrick, the division commander, not knowing the enemy strength, ordered his 20th Infantry Regiment to conduct a frontal attack, hoping that it would quickly overcome Japanese resistance. Once that was accomplished, he could comply with General Krueger's order to have his division occupy a line stretching from the town of Bactad in the north to Cuyapo in the south by the twentieth. At first it appeared the schedule could be met. By the nineteenth, the regiment seemed to have cleared out most of the Japanese defenders, and Patrick pulled out two of the attacking battalions, leaving only a reinforced battalion supported by a tank battalion to mop up. But the main Japanese defenses had not been taken, and for the next three days the defenders beat off all attempts to root them out. Patrick finally sent in a battalion from the lst Infantry, and together the two battalions waged a three-day battle that breached the Japanese lines. With help from yet another battalion, the hills were at last cleared on 28 January. The Japanese Omori Detachment, like Shigemi's force, fought to the death, losing almost all fifteen hundred of the defenders.

Meanwhile, the lst Infantry occupied Bactad after being held up briefly at the village of Urdaneta. As soon as Patrick relieved the 20th Infantry in the Cabaruan Hills, its battalions moved southeast against light resistance, and by the end of January held a line extending from Victoria eastward to Route 5, about five miles distant. Thus, while the lst Cavalry and 37th Infantry Divisions were closing in on Manila, I Corps troops had secured their flanks and were also in a position to begin the long, harsh, bloody task of confronting Yamashita's main mountain defenses.

An integral part of the complex planning for the conquest of Luzon was the clearing of Manila Bay as soon as possible. This meant forcing the Japanese out of the Bataan Peninsula. The task became the responsibility of General Hall's XI Corps, which had landed at San Narciso on 29 January and quickly captured the airfield at San Marcelino and the town of Olongapo on Subic Bay. The XI Corps's main forward element was Maj. Gen. Henry L. C. Jones's 38th Division. Jones, encountering little Japanese resistance, pushed his troops eastward quickly at first. Neither he nor Hall had any concrete knowledge of the number of Japanese or the nature of their defenses along the corps's axis of advance. They discounted a report from Lt. Col. Gyles Merrill, commanding the guerrillas in the area, who estimated that more than two thousand men defended the winding portion of Route 7—which later became known as Zigzag Pass. Hall believed fewer than nine hundred Japanese blocked his way to sealing off the Bataan Peninsula. He should have listened to Merrill; the Japanese commander, Col. Sanenobu Nagayoshi, had almost twenty-eight hundred men guarding the three-mile section of Route 7. On either side of the highway, dense jungle covered the extremely rough terrain. Nagayoshi, well supplied with food for his troops and ammunition for his light artillery and mortars, had established a series of pillboxes in key positions. He realized that the terrain that made it impossible to maintain flank contact was his ally, channeling the American attacks.

The 152d Infantry Regiment was at first given the task of flanking Nagayoshi's positions, and General Hall, insulated in corps headquarters, could not understand why this had not been done by the evening of 2 February. But the rugged terrain prevented the regiment from making contact with the Japanese until the next day. General Hall, meanwhile, had dispatched the 149th Infantry to seize the town of Dinalupihan, whose capture would seal off the peninsula. Moving north of Route 7 through difficult terrain, it finally seized the town on the fifth. But the main resistance was at Zigzag Pass, and Hall pressed Jones to use his last regiment, the 151st, to quickly sweep the Japanese aside. Despite heroic efforts, the regiment made little progress and took heavy casualties. Hall then passed the 24th Division's 34th Infantry Regiment through to the central part of the front. Even with two regiments backed by division artillery and P-47 strikes from San Marcelino, the Americans failed to crack the Japanese defenses.

By 5 February, the division had suffered 465 casualties, and Jones and Hall began arguing over tactics. Jones wanted to halt the attacks and blast the Japanese defenses for two days with every gun in the corps's arsenal. Hall, persisting in his belief that the division was lethargic, replaced Jones with Maj. Gen. William Chase on the sixth. As was true in most such cases, the change altered very little. Finally, Hall ordered the 149th Infantry to begin attacking westward toward the pass while the other two regiments continued to put pressure on the Japanese defenses. Hall belatedly accepted the advice of his departed subordinate and had corps and division artillery pound the Japanese before launching major attacks. The slow advance on two fronts frustrated Hall. It was not until 14 February, almost two weeks after his troops first tried to take the pass, that the final Japanese strong point was overrun.

The capture of Zigzag Pass allowed General Hall to concentrate on the destruction of all Japanese troops on the peninsula. To help facilitate this, the 151st Infantry boarded landing craft at Olongapo on 14 February and landed at Mariveles at the southern tip of Bataan the next day. The regiment immediately sent patrols northward along both the east and west coasts. Meanwhile, the 6th Division's 1st Infantry Regiment left Dinalupihan on the twelfth and followed the eastern coastline to Pilar, about twenty-five miles south. The 1st was joined by the 149th Infantry on the sixteenth.

The deployment of a division equivalent on Bataan was based on the erroneous intelligence estimate of approximately nine thousand defenders. In reality there were fewer than two thousand, and the local commander, with only two exceptions, did not contest the advance of either American force. Elements of the 1st Infantry moving south met the 151st near the town of Limay on the eighteenth. Other 1st Infantry troops set out over the main road from Pilar to Bagac on the west coast. They encountered only sporadic fire from stragglers, and reached the sea on 21 February. The remaining Japanese on Bataan, estimated at a thousand men, retreated to the jungle slopes of Mount Natib north of the cross-island road. They were hunted down by 38th Division troops assisted by Filipino guerrilla forces.

With Bataan cleared, the first step in MacArthur's plan to open up Manila Bay had been achieved. The next objective was the tadpole-shaped island of Corregidor, where General Wainwright's troops had made their last stand in 1942. The island is approximately seven thousand yards long by twenty-five hundred yards at its widest point. Most of the permanent buildings and facilities were located to the west in the wide area called Topside. Near the island's midsection is 350-foot Malinta Hill, which concealed the complex of tunnels that had sheltered headquarters and hospital facilities during the 1942 siege. Although the Japanese had five thousand naval troops on the island, they posed no real threat to the Sixth Army's actions elsewhere. When Yamashita decided to concede the coastal plain, he made possession of the island superfluous.

But Corregidor had symbolic value, and MacArthur wanted it captured quickly and flamboyantly. MacArthur met with Krueger in mid-January and stated that he wanted the "Rock" seized as soon as possible by a combined airborne and amphibious assault. Although the operation would be conducted by XI Corps, Krueger's staff devised a plan that would involve the 503d Parachute Infantry Regiment then on Mindoro. Colonel George M. Jones, the 503d's commander, wanted to target the only good landing site, Kindley Field, on the tail of the island. Krueger vetoed this because the paratroopers would be too far away from the main installation's Topside and might have to fight their way through the two good approaches, thus losing the element of surprise. Instead, the 3d Battalion was ordered to drop on the small expanse of the parade ground and golf course. There were only enough C-47 transports available to handle the 3d Battalion and a battery of artillery in the first lift. This meant the first group to land would be without reinforcements for nearly five hours. Two hours after the initial drop, troops from the 24th Division's 34th Infantry Regiment would land near the middle of the island and move to secure Malinta Hill before linking up with the paratroopers.

Very early on the morning of 16 February, twenty-four B-24 heavy bombers and forty-two medium bombers joined the eight cruisers and fourteen destroyers bombarding the island. Later, just before the landings, seventy A-20s strafed and bombed suspected gun positions. At about 0830, the first C-47s appeared and the 3d Battalion jumped, completely surprising the Japanese. However, almost 25 percent of the men were injured during the jump, and many paratroopers missed the drop zone entirely. Before the Japanese could mount a serious counterattack, the 34th Infantry's 3d Battalion landed, and within thirty minutes had seized Malinta Hill. The Topside perimeter was expanded and was relatively secure by the time the 503d's lst Battalion jumped at 1240.

A fortunate accident ultimately contributed to the relatively quick defeat of the Japanese on Corregidor. Captain Akira Itagaki and his party, while inspecting a defensive position ostensibly in a safe area, encountered several paratroopers who had missed the drop zone. Itagaki was killed in the ensuing firefight, apparently confusing the Japanese, who failed to offer any coordinated resistance after his death.

The fight for the island became a complex series of small-unit actions in which the paratroopers and infantrymen systematically reduced the Japanese bunkers and underground defenses. Air assaults with napalm paved the way for attacks on strong points. Artillery was also used, firing at caves and bunkers at point-blank range. The Japanese attempted night infiltration but with little success. Their banzai charges were no more successful. The last major banzai attack was on the morning of the nineteenth, when four hundred Japanese broke through the line and almost reached the old barracks area Topside before they were destroyed.

American commanders feared that the Japanese committing suicide in the tunnels would blow up their underground ammunition sites in hopes of killing as many attackers as possible. On the evening of the twenty-first, in conjunction with an attempt by some two thousand Japanese to break out of the Malinta complex, a series of explosions rocked the hill but caused few American casualties. Most of the Japanese who tried to escape were killed.

By 24 February, XI Corps controlled all of the island except the last three thousand yards of the tail. The final desperate suicidal act by the Japanese occurred on the morning of the twenty-sixth when they detonated an underground arsenal beneath a hillock close to Kindley Field. The ensuing explosion killed more than 200 Japanese and 50 Americans, as well as wounding another 150. The fierce but futile resistance, combined with suicides, eliminated almost the entire garrison. Only twenty prisoners were taken during the operation. By the end of the month, MacArthur had his symbolic victory; Colonel Jones formally presented "Fortress Corregidor" to the supreme commander at a ceremony on 2 March.

The final clearing of Japanese defenses in Manila Bay targeted three small islands: Caballo, El Fraile, and Carabao. Since these presented no threat—and operations in Manila proper held the attention of Sixth Army—there was no rush to capture them. On 27

March General Chase finally received permission to assault Caballo, the largest of the islands lying southeast of Corregidor. After a heavy bombardment, the 2d Battalion, 151st Infantry, landed and quickly gained control of most of the island. The four-hundred-man garrison retired into prewar mortar pits and tunnels that were placed so that tank and artillery fire did little damage to them. The Americans finally discovered a single ventilator shaft and pumped twenty-five hundred gallons of diesel oil into the tunnels. The fuel was then ignited with white phosphorus and the ensuing explosion killed all the defenders. The same tactic was used on El Fraile, a coral reef that before the war had been transformed into a fortress with three-foot-thick walls and renamed Fort Drum. The fort had only one entrance, and the walls were unscalable. On 13 April, the 113th Engineers built a ramp on the superstructure of an LCM that men carrying hoses scrambled across onto the top of the fort. They pumped oil down a vent, then tossed in a timed TNT charge. The resulting fire caused the magazine to explode, again killing all the defenders. The last island, Carabao, was repeatedly attacked by bombers and fighters. Finally, on 16 April, the 1st Battalion/Infantry, 151st Regiment, landed and found no Japanese present. The 350-man garrison had already withdrawn to the mainland two miles away.

However symbolic the capture of Corregidor may have been, it was relatively unimportant in comparison to the developing battle for Manila. Iwabuchi's decision to stand and fight meant that MacArthur and Krueger would be forced into an urban battle. The Japanese had not heavily contested the areas north of the Pasig River, and troops of the 1st Cavalry Division on 8 February captured Novaliches Dam, one of the city's main water sources. Soon afterward, the cavalrymen got a taste of what would later develop when they entered the New Manila subdivision covering a half square mile area. Opposed by the Japanese 1st Independent Naval Battalion, it was necessary to have both division and corps artillery reduce the buildings to rubble before the remnants of the Japanese unit retired eastward across the Marikina River.

By the evening of the eighth, the 1st Cavalry and 37th Infantry Divisions had cleared all of Manila north of the Pasig and moved up to that broad river. Krueger then ordered XIV Corps troops to cross the river and seize the Privisor Island generating plant. Because the retiring Japanese had blown all the bridges, the 148th Infantry Regiment had to use LVTs and small assault boats to cross and gain a lodgment in the Malacañan Gardens area. Between 8 and 10 February, the regiment cleared the adjacent Pandacan region and the Paco District farther west. There was heavy fighting before strong points at the railroad station, Paco School, and Concordia College were overcome. Nevertheless by the evening of the tenth, the 148th had reached the Estero de Paco, a north-south, canal-like stream. The previous day, one company had been ferried across the Estero de Tonque to Privisor Island. There, a company-size Japanese force held the boiler plant and four adjacent buildings. Each of these had to be assaulted—but not until after corps and division artillery silenced most of the Japanese guns targeting the island. By then the restrictions imposed on artillery fire, which had prevailed in the early stages of the battle for Manila, had been lifted, clearing the way for the understrength 37th Division, its troops exhausted from almost continual fighting, to begin the assault on the Japanese final defense lines in the old city.

The 11th Airborne Division's advance from the south had been relatively unimpeded—except at Nichols Field—and Cavite had been bypassed. On 8 February, lead elements of the division made contact with 5th Cavalry Regiment troops moving westward. This juncture completed the encirclement of the Japanese Naval Defense Force, which found itself pressed into a narrow perimeter one-half mile wide and two miles long. Two days later, the 11th Airborne was attached to Griswold's XIV Corps. Griswold halted the division's northern movement and instead gave it the task of clearing the Cavite Navy Yard and Nichols Field to the east. A two-regiment attack on Nichols Field on the twelfth cleared the Japanese from the area. At the same time, the 8th and 12th Cavalry Regiments crossed the Pasig, bringing the 1st Cavalry Division abreast of the 37th Division for the final push into Manila.

Iwabuchi was hopelessly trapped. General Yokoyama, unaware of the desperate situation in the city, organized a two-regiment attack against the Novaliches Dam area and Route 3 north of Manila and ordered Iwabuchi to break out. The attacks began on 15 February and lasted for three days. The 7th and 8th Cavalry Regiments halted the Japanese with minimal losses, while the Japanese lost an estimated one thousand men. Adding to the futility of Yokoyama's attack was Iwabuchi's refusal to even attempt to break out.

The 11th Airborne Division cut off the 750-man Abe Battalion south of the city and destroyed it in five days. On the eighteenth, in combination with units from the 1st Cavalry Division, the paratroopers moved against Fort McKinley—only to discover that most of the thousand-man garrison had escaped to the east.

While this relatively minor action was taking place, the 37th Division and the main elements of the 1st Cavalry were involved in a series of hard-fought small-unit actions against a number of strong points held by the Japanese Central Force. Although each action had its own deadly scenario, they all had similarities. The Japanese had occupied a number of multistoried, reinforced concrete buildings. Chief among these were the post office, city hall, numerous hotels, the central police station, the hospital, and various buildings of the university. A complicating factor for the attackers was the large number of civilians caught up in the fight. At the other extreme, as the Japanese situation worsened, discipline broke down and atrocities mounted against the hapless Filipino population.

The tenacity of the defenders meant that advances in all sectors were slow and depended on the massive use of corps and division artillery. Tanks and heavy mortars added to the firepower of 105mm and 155mm guns firing point-blank at selected targets. The destruction of the Central Force took ten days. In the southern sector, it took elements of the 5th and 12th Cavalry Regiments nearly a week to occupy LaSalle University, the stadium, and Santa Escolastica College. Farther north, in the center of the city, the 148th Infantry—reinforced later by elements of the 5th Cavalry—fought a series of desperate small-unit actions to occupy the four wings of the hospital. Finally, with the aid of corps and division firepower, they seized the various university buildings by 23 February. Another major task for the 37th Division's 129th and 148th Infantry Regiments was to rout the Japanese from the new police station and adjacent buildings in the northeast sector of the city. They were taken only after a battalion of 105mm guns, supported by tanks and mortars, had reduced the concrete buildings to rubble. Farther north, within a few blocks of the fortress of Intramuros, was the city hall, and just south of the Pasig River was the general post office. The buildings' solid construction made taking them very difficult for the men of the 145th Infantry. At city hall, approximately 250 Japanese stopped the attackers cold until a massive concentration of heavy and light artillery enabled them to enter what was left of the building. The post office building absorbed a three-day artillery pounding before troops from the 145th entered through a second-story window and systematically, floor by floor, eliminated the defenders.

With, the battle for the strong points over and the bulk of the Central Force destroyed, Griswold's troops prepared to confront the last organized resistance in Manila. The remnants of Iwabuchi's defense force were entrenched in the confines of Intramuros, an old fortress with walls that were forty feet thick. The Japanese had also built an elaborate tunnel system linking various buildings within the walls. The southeastern portion of the fortress was covered by enfilading fire from a number of large government buildings just outside. The weakest part of the fortress defense was in the northeast, where the ancient walls ended near Quezon Gate.

General Beightler's plan of attack called for a battalion from the 37th Division to cross the Pasig River on 23 February and force its way into the northern section while two other battalions attacked from the east through a breach in the wall. Beightler and Griswold wanted air strikes on targets within the walls, as well as close air support for the assault forces once the attack began. General Krueger agreed, but knowing of MacArthur's love for the city, decided not to order air strikes without the supreme commander's approval. It was not granted. MacArthur feared the destruction that such generalized strikes would produce and the untold number of civilian casualties they would cause. But he did not restrict the use of artillery, so Krueger made sure that the attacking troops had massive artillery support.

The artillery preparation began on 17 February. Soon the 8-inch howitzers had opened a large breach in the east wall and 155mm guns firing from eight hundred yards had opened a hole in the north wall close to Quezon Gate. The methodical barrage continued until the morning of the twenty-third. In all, more than eight thousand rounds were fired into the relatively small area of Intramuros.

An amphibious assault by the 3d Battalion, 129th Infantry, in conjunction with attacks from the east by two battalions from the 145th, surprised the already stunned defenders. Both attacks were relatively unopposed. The northern assault was temporarily slowed when the Japanese released approximately three thousand civilian prisoners. Most of these were women and children; the bulk of the male Filipino prisoners had been butchered by their captors. Despite the distraction, the 37th Division, supported by mobile artillery and tanks, had established control of the eastern half of Intramuros by the end of the day. The next day, Fort Santiago, located in the northwest corner of the enclave, was captured and the remaining defenders in the walled city were compressed into an area around the aquarium. Within hours the last resistance there had also been overcome.

Thanks to the heavy artillery support, American casualties were quite low—20 men killed and 240 wounded. However, all the major buildings within the enclave were seriously damaged or destroyed, and an unknown number of Filipino civilians killed. The bulk of the estimated 1,700 Japanese defenders also died.

The last serious Japanese resistance within Manila proved to be the most tenacious. A complex of government buildings southeast of and adjacent to Intramuros, including the Philippine legislative building, the Department of Agriculture complex, and the one which had housed the Bureau of Finance, provided good defensive positions for an estimated five hundred Japanese. The scenario for capturing these was the same as at Intramuros. The reinforced concrete buildings were pounded by artillery for two days before a coordinated attack by units of the 148th Infantry and 5th Cavalry Regiments began on 26 February. All the early attacks by the cavalrymen on the agricultural building were stopped by the Japanese—even after the Americans managed to get inside. Not until 1 March were they able to clean out the defenders on all the floors. Troops of the 148th managed to enter the Legislative Assembly on the twenty-sixth but were confined to the first floor for more than a day. During the next two days they systematically cleared the top three floors. The same kind of fanatical resistance was found at the finance building, the last in the complex to be attacked. The Japanese did not surrender even after the entire building collapsed. Only then could the cavalry troops wipe out the last resistance.

Late in the afternoon of 3 March, General Griswold reported to General Krueger that all opposition in Intramuros and the government buildings had been eliminated. MacArthur could finally sense the triumph that his 6 February communique had so confidently reported and for which he had received congratulations from Churchill, Curtin, and Chiang Kai-shek. *Time* and *Newsweek* magazines had also headlined the liberation. However, the predicted "complete destruction" of the Japanese had taken another four weeks—and Manila was destroyed in the process. There would be no triumphal parade through the rubble-strewn streets of the Pearl of the Orient. Three-quarters of the residential district in the southern part of the city had been destroyed. Utilities were almost nonexistent, and the business district was obliterated.

The city's Filipino population suffered unbelievable horrors. Although many became casualties of the fighting, even worse had been the orgy of torture, rape, and murder by the doomed Japanese defenders—actions that later caused Yamashita to be condemned to death. Although no accurate count has ever been made, an estimated one hundred thousand Filipinos died before Manila was liberated.

While the fighting in Intramuros was raging, MacArthur, true to his promise, formally restored the Commonwealth government to President Osmeña and his cabinet on 27 February. The new government faced the difficult task of deciding what actions to take against José Laurel's puppet regime headquartered in Baguio.

XIV Corps, although deeply involved in the Manila operation, also had orders to move against the Shimbu Group to the northeast in order to secure adequate water supplies for the city. Once again MacArthur's and Krueger's intelligence agencies, despite the services of Filipino guerrillas, sadly misinterpreted the situation. They estimated that General Yokoyama had only 20,000 troops, whereas in reality he had almost 50,000. He had divided his front into three sections. The Kawashima Force, with 9,000 men, guarded the north end of the line in the Ipo Dam region. To the south of this force was the 12,000-man Kobayashi Force, covering a ten-mile front centered on the Wawa Dam. Finally, the 9,000-man Noguchi Force defended a line from just north of the town of Antipolo to the shore of Laguna de Bay, twelve miles farther south.

Griswold, meanwhile, assigned only the 6th Division and 2d Cavalry Brigade the task of pushing back the Japanese and securing Manila's water supply. Adding to their woes was the fact that intelligence officers also incorrectly identified the city's chief water source. The heavily defended Wawa Dam should not have been the main target since the city received very little water from it. The main objective should have been the Ipo Dam, guarded by the smaller Kawashima Force.

On 20 February, leading elements of the 2d Cavalry Brigade crossed into the Marikina Valley south of the Wawa Dam in an effort to turn the Noguchi Force's flank. The cavalrymen met only slight opposition until they reached the foothills northwest of Antipolo and encountered the main defenses. Noguchi had his troops dug into the hillsides and had masked his artillery by hiding the guns in caves. The cavalry units were under constant fire as the Japanese launched localized counterattacks to prevent significant gains. After two weeks of fighting, the 2d Cavalry Brigade units were still more than a mile from Antipolo. They had suffered 375 casualties, including General Mudge, the 1st Cavalry Division commander, who was wounded by a grenade.

The 6th Division, which had crossed the Marikina River on 22 February, encountered a series of grassy hills north of Marikina town. The Japanese defenses there were anchored on Mount Pacawagan and Mount Mataka and in a deep, seven-mile-long gully that links the two hills. Despite heavy artillery support and air strikes, the infantrymen, like their cavalry counterparts to the south, made little headway.

Griswold finally halted the attacks along the fifteen-mile front and regrouped his understrength units. He then decided to attack on a narrower front, concentrating on the Noguchi Force. On 8 March the 2d Cavalry Brigade, after three days of hard fighting, took Antipolo. At the same time, units of the 6th Division managed to slip between the Kobayashi and Noguchi Forces. Threatened by what appeared to be a double envelopment, Yokoyama prepared a complex counterattack plan that he executed on the twelfth. Air and artillery fire cut the attacking Japanese to pieces. The only tangible result of the Japanese counterthrust was the significant weakening of Yokoyama's forces.

By the twelfth, General Griswold had replaced the depleted cavalry units with the 43d Division, recently arrived from northern Luzon. Two days later, XI Corps took over the campaign to secure the Wawa Dam. The 6th Division was to keep pressure on the Kobayashi Force's left by attacking directly toward Mount Benicayan. The division, which gained little in its five-day attempt to breach the Japanese defenses, lost its commander, General Patrick, who was killed by machine-gun fire on the fourteenth. However, in the south, the 43d Division's 103d Infantry Regiment outflanked the Noguchi Force's left on the twenty-first and forced its remnants and the left-flank elements of the Kobayashi Force to fall back to new positions in the hilly area east of Montalban. It took two more months of a grinding war of attrition before the Japanese finally gave up the Wawa Dam and were forced back to a line farther east anchored by Mount Hapanong and Mount Pamitinan. By the end of March, 435 GIs were dead and more than 1,400 had been wounded. An estimated 7,000 Japanese troops were killed.

Southeast of Manila, the Japanese commander, Col. Masatochi Fujishige, led thirteen thousand men in the defense of the northern shore of the Visayan Passage. His major task, however, was to make certain that the Shimbu Group's left flank was not turned. There was relative quiet in this sector while the battle for Manila was under way. The one major event was the Los Baños raid on 24 February. This well-planned, daring operation by a battalion of the 188th Glider Infantry, aided by Filipino guerrillas and elements of the 511th Parachute Infantry, freed 2,147 U.S. prisoners. Striking through enemy-held territory, troops from the 188th approached the prison on Laguna de Bay from the west while others rode ashore in amtracs and paratroopers dropped into the camp proper. The 250-man Japanese garrison was disposed of, the prisoners loaded aboard amtracs, and the assault troops were away and back in friendly territory before Fujishige could react.

From the opening moves to secure the Lipa corridor to southern Luzon, General Griswold had only the 11th Airborne Division and the understrength 158th Infantry Regiment, a force roughly equal in size to Fujishige's. Nevertheless, he ordered General Swing to start the operation on 7 March. The 187th Glider Infantry moved down from the southern slopes of Tagaytay Ridge southeast of Nosugbu and advanced eastward south of Lake Taal. The glider men encountered little opposition until they reached Mount Macolod, where the Japanese had well-established defenses. Meanwhile, the 511th Parachute Infantry had advanced from the town of Real on the south shore of Laguna de Bay down Route 19 toward Santo Tomas. The Japanese defenses on Mount Bijiang, which controlled movement along Route 1, were negated, but the regiment was not strong enough to overcome Japanese defenses in the Santo Tomas-Tanauan region. The paratroopers instead contented themselves with mopping up bypassed elements in the areas they controlled. On 23 March the 1st Cavalry Division relieved the 11th Airborne Division, which was shifted around Lake Taal to replace the 158th Infantry. Within a week, the two divisions began clearing the remaining Japanese from southern Luzon.

While XIV Corps assaulted the Wawa Dam region and began moving into southern Luzon, other Sixth Army elements began a slow, determined move from the west coast of Lingayen Gulf toward the important highland city of Baguio. For operations in northern Luzon, Krueger at first had the 25th, 32d, and 33d Divisions. These were later augmented by the 37th Division. In addition, he could count on the UAFIP(NL), the Northern Luzon Filipino volunteer organization.

The UAFIP(NL) was organized by Col. Russell W. Volckmann, who had taken to the hills rather than surrender in 1942. By the time of the invasion, his force numbered approximately eight thousand men. By the end of February 1945, it had grown to more than eighteen thousand—armed with weapons provided by Sixth Army or captured from the Japanese. It even had its own artillery units, equipped with mixed-caliber pieces taken from the enemy. Volckmann organized his force into twenty-nine-hundred-man regiments and, much to Krueger's delight, these Filipino units had cleared much of the west coast of Luzon north of the town of San Fernando by the end of February. In addition, the guerrillas dominated the north coast west of Aparri and denied use of two of the major northern highways to Yamashita's forces.

General Krueger decided in late February that his main effort against the Shobu Group in the north would be along the front guarding the approaches to the town of Bambang (Bayombong) at the head of the Cagayan Valley. He planned to use the 25th and 32d Divisions for this attack. The 33d Division, commanded by Maj. Gen. Percy W. Clarkson, would be confined to holding actions and vigorous patrolling until the 37th Division could be brought up from Manila to support the proposed attack on the northern flank.

The offensive began in early March with the 33d Division's 123d and 130th Infantry Regiments slowly advancing into the highlands and along Route 11 in the southern sector. A battalion from the 123d waged a hard-fought battle for the village of Pugo seven miles inland, then attacked along a trail toward Baguio from there. By 27 March that advance had bogged down five miles southwest of Baguio. The advance from the coastal town of Caba was halted just west of the village of Asin. In the 37th Division's zone, the 129th Infantry, moving toward Baguio along Route 9, was stopped by well-entrenched defenders nine miles northwest of its objective. At the end of March, Yamashita's defenses along the Baguio front were holding, forcing Krueger and Swift to regroup before they began a three-pronged offensive on 12 April.

South of the Baguio area Krueger had Maj. Gen. William Gill's 32d Division and Maj. Gen. Charles Mullin's 25th Division along a front roughly parallel to Route 5 to the east. The ultimate objective of I Corps in this sector was Bambang. The immediate objective, however, was to secure Route 5 and capture the key town of Santa Fe. In order to do this, the two divisions would have to fight their way across hilly terrain and through two heavily defended passes. General Swift, the I Corps commander, believed that the 32d could move quickly eastward using the Villa Verde Trail, which connected the town of San Nicolas to Route 5. At the same time, the 25th would drive north along Route 5, breaking the Japanese defenses south of Santa Fe and catching the Japanese remnants between the two divisions. This plan ignored a number of harsh realities. The terrain favored the defense, the weather was terrible, the attacking troops were tired, and the regiments, particularly the 32d Division's, were understrength.

At first it appeared that the 32d Division would be able to carry out its mission quickly when, on 24 February, its 127th Infantry Regiment broke through the Japanese forward defenses. But a quick victory was not to be. Major General Haruo Konuma, surprised by the 127th's early success, quickly began to reinforce the three-mile-long Salacsac Pass leading to Santa Fe. With the addition of the 2d Tank Division, by 1 March he had over ten thousand men facing the 127th. Furthermore, Konuma had established a complex system of mutually supporting defensive positions, mostly in caves, from which his artillery and automatic weapons could cover every bend of the trail.

On 7 March, the 127th Infantry began a series of monotonous, time-consuming flanking movements. This maneuver proved costly, and the gains were minimal: it took two weeks to advance the front line a thousand yards. By 23 March, the regiment had suffered 335 battle casualties and lost 500 more men to sickness and battle fatigue. When it was finally relieved by the 128th Infantry, it was 1,100 men understrength. At the close of the month there was stalemate not only along the trail, but also in the river valleys to the north, where the 126th Infantry had been active.

The second part of the I Corps plan also seemed destined for early success. The 25th Division's advance north along Route 5 started on 23 February. Mullin, unlike General Gill, could deploy all three of his regiments to converge on the village of Puncan. Moving swiftly, the division captured the town on 4 March and declared the route from San Jose, to the village of Digdig secure. This had been accomplished with only two hundred casualties, whereas an estimated thirteen hundred Japanese had been killed. The division resumed the attack on 5 March and within three days, advancing over difficult terrain, had captured the village of Putlan, six miles away. The Japanese began to slow the 25th's advance as it moved close to the thirty-five-hundred-foot-high Balete Pass just south of Santa Fe. Once again the terrain aided the defenders, and very soon there was a virtual stalemate.

After two months of fighting, the Sixth Army had won great successes. The central plain had been captured, Manila Bay cleared, and the city of Manila, although badly damaged, had been liberated. But the bulk of Yamashita's forces were in the mountainous regions northeast of the capital, and the keys to the entrances into this fortress were still under Japanese control. It had become obvious that the campaign there would be a long, arduous, and costly one. It would be necessary to deploy more troops, and if any gains were to be made there, they would be the result of time-consuming, frustrating actions against a skilled and determined enemy.

By the early spring of 1945, the Philippines had become superfluous to the ultimate goal of defeating the Japanese. Although more than 250,000 Japanese troops still occupied the mountains of Luzon and most of the important southern islands, the war had passed them by. At Yalta in February, Roosevelt, Churchill, and Stalin had agreed on the general strategy to be pursued once Germany had been defeated. A portion of the agreement called for the Soviet Union to enter the war in order to pin down the Kwantung Army in Manchuria and other forces in Korea. No specific details of the proposed invasion of Japan were discussed, but Roosevelt and the U.S. Joint Chiefs assumed that MacArthur would not undertake any further action in the Philippines while planning and gathering strength for the final assault on the Japanese home islands. Nevertheless, without a directive from Washington, MacArthur authorized General Eichelberger's Eighth Army to begin operations against the southern islands. For one who prided himself on his "wither on the vine" strategy, MacArthur in the final months of the war ordered operations of dubious merit not only in the Philippines but in another backwater region: the Dutch East Indies.

However questionable these major actions were, there could be no argument against the concurrent actions in Nimitz's theater of operation. The decision to bomb Japan from the Marianas made it imperative that secondary air bases along the route be secured. Iwo Jima in the Bonins was a logical target, as was the larger island of Okinawa, only 850 miles from Tokyo. Okinawa could provide not only valuable airfields, but also serve as a major staging ground for the invasion of Japan.

Chapter 14

The Noose Tightens: Iwo Jima and Okinawa

THE PACIFIC WAR took a turn in early 1945 with the arrival of growing numbers of sleek, long-range Boeing B-29 bombers. Prior to that time, Allied energies had been focused upon the necessity of seizing land for air bases needed to support offensives aimed at recovering territory the Japanese had conquered in 1942. With the exception of the April 1942 Doolittle raid, it was not until the late summer of 1944 that the Japanese home islands were brought under attack. Even then, only a comparative handful of B-29s flying from China were available, and Admiral Halsey's plans to strike Japan proper had to be put on hold because of the necessity of providing air cover for the Philippines operation. Thus, until the early months of 1945, the Japanese people remained relatively untouched directly by the war—and undoubtedly most of them, aided by government control of the media, still believed that Japan was winning. However, the more thoughtful senior officers in the Japanese armed forces believed that Japan lost the war when the Marianas were taken because airfields sited there brought all of Japan's major cities within range of the B-29s.

The construction of airfields on Guam was delayed when Admiral Nimitz decided to move his headquarters there from Hawaii. Because the navy controlled allocations of men and materiel and determined priorities, work on naval facilities took precedence. No such problem existed on Tinian and Saipan, however. Bombers from Brig. Gen. Haywood S. Hansell Jr.'s XXI Bomber Command began the first small-scale high-altitude attacks on Japanese industrial plants from those islands in December 1944. The attacks grew in size and intensity after the command passed to Maj. Gen. Curtis E. LeMay in early January. LeMay and his superior in Washington, General Arnold, brought pressure to bear on the navy to redefine priorities and thus sped up completion of the three airfields on Guam, which became operational in late February 1945.

By early March, LeMay was able to send three hundred B-29s to Tokyo in the most devastating air attack of the war. However, these attacks were not without cost, particularly after LeMay, dissatisfied with results from high-level bombing, ordered the B-29s down to lower altitudes. Japanese antiaircraft defenses were heavily concentrated around all the major cities, and although the fire was often erratic, it took its toll on the bombers. Japanese fighters, although manned by relatively unskilled pilots, also exacted a price. Emergency airfields north of the Marianas were needed to provide relief for aircraft too badly damaged to make it back to a base in the Marianas. The new long-range fighter, the P-51 Mustang, could also be based on advanced airfields and used to escort the B-29s, protecting them from Japanese interceptors. The answer to these needs was a volcanic rock called Iwo Jima, located in the Bonin Islands 660 miles south of Tokyo.

Iwo Jima's importance was recognized even before any of the Marianas were secured. General Arnold in July 1944 recommended to the joint planners that Iwo be seized, and they agreed—provided that the island's capture did not interfere with more important operations. The Joint Chiefs of Staff, in their 3 October 1944 directive authorizing MacArthur's invasion of Luzon, also instructed Admiral Nimitz to occupy one or more positions in the Bonins on 20 January 1945. Iwo Jima was chosen over the larger, more northerly Chichi Jima because it would take too long to construct airfields on the latter, whereas Iwo already had two completed fields. The October directive also targeted Okinawa in the Ryukyus for invasion on 1 March 1945.

The date for the assaults on Iwo and Okinawa were later changed when the invasion of Luzon was postponed from 20 December until 9 January because the fast carrier forces, either TF 38 or TF 58, could not adequately cover operations in the Philippines and the Bonins at the same time. The new date fixed for the Iwo Jima assault was 19 February.

Major General Harry Schmidt's V Amphibious Corps, consisting of the 3d, 4th, and 5th Marine Divisions, was given the mission of taking the island. It would be directly supported by a huge naval armada commanded by RAdm. William Blandy, whose force included a dozen light carriers, six battleships, five cruisers, and sixteen destroyers. Task Force 58, once again commanded by Mitscher and divided into five task groups, was scheduled to strike hard at targets in Japan and on both Chichi and Iwo Jima. It would then stand by and provide air cover and close air support to the marines as they moved inland.

Iwo Jima is a small, lamb-chop-shaped volcanic island only four and one-half miles long by two and one-half miles wide. Its most significant feature is Mount Suribachi, an inactive volcano rising 550 feet above sea level at the shank end of the island. Most of the shoreline is rocky or has steep cliffs. The only beaches suitable for landings are adjacent to Mount Suribachi. These beaches extend over two miles and consist of deep, black volcanic sand. The footing is so difficult there that steel mats were needed even for tracked vehicles. The northern plateau on which the two airfields were built has little vegetation. There are no streams; the inhabitants depended on cisterns for drinking water. Prior to early 1944 there were approximately eleven hundred civilians on the island in addition to a five-thousand-man garrison. The larger neighboring island of Chichi Jima was more heavily fortified and had a larger garrison because Imperial Headquarters considered it the more valuable of the two.

The Japanese began to strengthen Iwo's defenses in early March 1944. Civilians were shipped to Japan against their will, and the first of the big guns began to arrive. Until the end of May, responsibility for defending the island rested with the navy. Transporting troops from Chichi Jima to Iwo was very hazardous, particularly after the Marianas invasion. American submarines and surface craft sank a number of ships. The most celebrated sinking was the USS *Cobia*'s torpedoing of the *Nisshu Maru* in July. All of the tanks belonging to the 26th Tank Regiment were lost when the ship went down. In all, approximately fifteen hundred troops lost their lives in the shuttle operation. Nevertheless, by early September there were almost fifteen thousand troops on the island.

Because of the rapid buildup, the army assumed responsibility for Iwo's defenses in early June. The man chosen to command the defenders was Lt. Gen. Tadamichi Kuribayashi, a veteran of the China war and commander of the Imperial Guard in Tokyo. He was Tojo's personal choice. Ironically, Kuribayashi had openly opposed war with the United States because, as a deputy attache in Washington in the 1920s, he had traveled widely and had been impressed with America's industrial potential. Nevertheless, he accepted the task of overseeing Iwo's defenses, knowing full well he could not hope to keep American forces from ultimately conquering the island. His defensive plan reflected this fatalism: He sought only to inflict the maximum possible damage on the attackers.

In the months following Kuribayashi's arrival, he set his troops to work constructing pillboxes, blockhouses, and bunkers built close to the ground with thick walls and ceilings made of reinforced concrete. Most were covered with sand and then carefully camouflaged. Natural caves were enlarged, and many new ones were blasted out of Suribachi. The Japanese constructed large underground chambers, some as much as five stories deep. These served as storage and hospital areas, as well as safe havens for troops during air and naval bombardments, and were connected by miles of tunnels with a large number of surface openings.

Kuribayashi at first did not want to contest the beaches, but after many discussions with his naval counterpart, RAdm. Toshinosuke Ichimaru, he agreed to build a series of strong points covering the landing areas. The many well-camouflaged 120mm and 6-inch guns were sited so that their fire could enfilade the beaches. His smaller-caliber artillery, antiaircraft guns, and mortars were also well hidden and located where only a direct hit could destroy them. Kuribayashi's orders to his forces in January were that they were to defend to the death.

Long before the invasion, Iwo was subjected to regular air and naval bombardment because it was the staging ground for air attacks on Saipan. The most damaging of these attacks was on Christmas Day 1944, and the pace picked up thereafter. Major General Willis H. Hale's Seventh Air Force, headquartered on Saipan, was widely dispersed throughout the Central Pacific. The main targets for its B-24s had been the various bypassed islands although it did stage a number of raids on Iwo in September and October. Then Lt. Gen. Millard Harmon, in charge of the strategic air forces in the Central Pacific, ordered Seventh Air Force raids on all secondary islands to cease in order for the bombers to concentrate on Iwo. From December onward, weather permitting, Iwo was visited every day by heavy bombers. At times, the Seventh's strikes were coordinated with attacks by B-29s and naval bombardment. By 16 February 1945, Iwo Jima had been pounded with the heaviest preinvasion bombardment of any Pacific island.

An adjunct to the naval support of the Iwo Jima operation was a two-day attack on Honshu, the largest of Japan's home islands. The honor of commanding this first naval air strike since the Doolittle raid in 1942 went to Admiral Spruance. In late January Halsey relinquished command, Third Fleet elements were redesignated Fifth Fleet, and Admiral Mitscher replaced Admiral McCain in charge of the fast carrier force, once again renamed TF 58. There had been significant additions to the main fleet since the Marianas operations. Spruance now had five task forces, the main elements of which were eleven fleet carriers, five light carriers, and eight fast battleships. This vast armada sortied from Ulithi, and by dawn on 16 February was 125 miles southeast of Tokyo.

Despite threatening weather, a total of five fighter sweeps were launched against airfields near Tokyo in an effort to prevent Japanese interception of the planned bombing attacks. The first of these strikes was met by more than a hundred planes, of which forty were reported destroyed. Later, the Japanese pilots seemed reluctant to engage the hundreds of American fighters. A lowering fog caused Mitscher to launch his bombers before he had planned. They took off in the early afternoon on the sixteenth and struck at a number of industrial plants near Tokyo. The attacks were repeated the next day, but further missions were called off because of the weather and the necessity to provide protection for V Amphibious Corps's invasion of Iwo.

The results of the foray were disappointing. A few small ships and one large transport were sunk, and a number of direct hits were made on engine and airframe factories. The greatest damage had been done to the intercepting aircraft and those caught on the ground. At least five hundred Japanese planes were reported destroyed. American combat losses were heavy: sixty aircraft in combat and twenty-eight to other causes.

Moving southward, RAdm. Ralph Davison's *Lexington* TG 58.2 and Admiral Sherman's *Essex* TG 58.3 were soon on station sixty-five miles northwest of Iwo, prepared to support the marines' attack.

Admiral Blandy's TF 54 was off Iwo by dawn on 16 February and, despite the bad weather, began bombarding the island. The next day was clear and the six battleships and assorted cruisers and destroyers began an all-day bombardment. Maps of the island had been gridded, and fire control, utilizing spotter planes flown by specially trained pilots, was excellent. The saturation naval fire continued on the eighteenth, joined by heavy bomber strikes flown by the Seventh Air Force. Twelve LCI gunships were sent in close to shore to cover underwater demolition teams operating off the landing beaches. The gunships were taken under fire by the Japanese gunners and all were hit. Some of the crews suffered up to 60 percent casualties. Believing that the main attack had begun, Kuribayashi exposed a number of his hidden big guns. These were immediately engaged by the battleships, some of which had closed to within three thousand yards. The major concentration of fire was on the flanks of the invasion beaches.

The final preinvasion bombardment by Blandy's force, augmented by two fast battleships and three cruisers from TF 58, began at 0630 on 19 February. After eighty-five minutes of continuous fire, the naval bombardment ceased so planes from TF 58 could bomb and strafe. The ships then resumed firing, continuing to shoot even after the first wave of marines approached shore. The navy then provided a rolling barrage, shifting fires at two-hundred-yard intervals. Although it had been sharply criticized for its performance at Tarawa and Peleliu, no such charges could be made of the naval support given at Iwo. No other island in the Pacific war was so thoroughly saturated with metal and high explosives. However, Kuribayashi's scheme of burrowing his men and weapons in caves, tunnels, and blockhouses meant that despite the pounding from ships and bombers most of Iwo's defenses survived intact.

The first assault waves from Maj. Gen. Clifton Cates's 4th and Maj. Gen. Keller E. Rockey's 5th Marine Divisions were loaded on

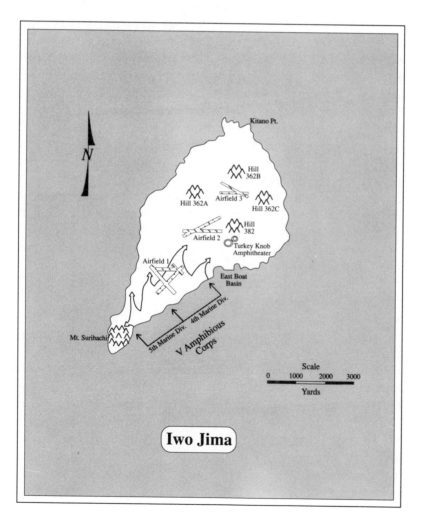

five hundred LVTs. Covered by aircraft and with the navy blasting away at Iwo's defenses, the LVTs sustained few hits during the run to the beaches. The landings were made at approximately 0905 in both division areas. In the south, the 5th Division landed two regiments, the 27th and 28th Marines. The plan was for the 27th Marines to drive straight across the island at its narrowest part while the 28th secured a lodgment and then turned south toward Mount Suribachi. The 4th Division's goal was the high ground northeast of its beaches.

The marines in all sectors, but especially in the 4th Division area, were at first pinned down on the beaches by very heavy Japanese fire, and each regiment took severe casualties before it could move inland. In addition to concentrated enemy fire, the marines faced a number of natural obstacles. It was nearly impossible to dig a foxhole in the shifting sand, which meant that as long as the marines were on the beaches, there was no protection from the withering fire. Rapid movement in the soft volcanic sand was impossible, even for tracked vehicles. Finally, the landing beaches were paralleled by three terraces caused by storms. In some places these were more than ten feet high, further restricting movement inland.

One major reason why the marines were able to extricate themselves from the beaches was the high volume of fire from the battleships and cruisers. Directed by marine fire control personnel on the ground or in LCIs offshore, the navy continued to pour shells onto the terrain directly ahead of the marines. By 1000 the first tanks had arrived. Although many were knocked out of action by antitank fire and mines, those that survived provided the hard-pressed marines with additional firepower. Despite all this assistance, the main effort came from individual marine rifle squads. Because most of Kuribayashi's rifle and mortar positions were so well hidden, they had to be taken out with satchel charges, hand grenades, or flamethrowers.

To the south, the 28th Marines, despite massed fire from the front and from Suribachi, had reached the mountain's foothills by 1500. North of them, the 27th Marines reached the southern part of Airfield No. 1 by noon. By midafternoon the 27th had reached the western coast, thus effectively cutting off the Japanese on Suribachi from the rest of the island's defenders.

The heaviest fighting on the nineteenth was in the 4th Division sector, where enfilading fire from higher ground caused heavy casualties. The 23d Marines were able to move only five hundred yards inland by noon, and by midafternoon had gotten only as far as the edge of Airfield No. 1. The 25th Marines, attacking the high ground to the northeast, struggled to reach the first ridges behind the boat basin by the close of the day.

The initial advance was far behind the V Amphibious Corps staff's optimistic schedule. The marines held a lodgment approximately four thousand yards long by seven hundred yards deep in the north, and eleven hundred yards deep in the south. They suffered 2,420 casualties that day, including 560 killed. However, the bulk of both divisions were on shore—nearly 30,000 men—and although equipment and supplies were piled up on the beaches, the mess would be sorted out over the next few days. There was no doubt at the end of the first day that V Amphibious Corps would eventually secure Iwo Jima.

The fighting was initially divided into two almost distinct operations. Kuribayashi had developed his main defense line across the island based upon the highland areas adjacent to Airfield No. 2. In the extreme south were the complex defenses leading to and on Mount Suribachi. This was considered a separate sector even before it was isolated on the nineteenth. Colonel Kanehiko Atsuchi had approximately two thousand men on the mountain, and Kuribayashi told Atsuchi that he expected every soldier there to make Suribachi his tomb and to kill as many of the enemy as possible. Atsuchi placed most of his men in caves, pillboxes, machine-gun positions, or mortar pits around the base of the mountain. Suribachi itself was honeycombed with caves, and all marine movement could be seen from the many observation posts above the plain. Atsuchi's major problem was the incessant bombardment, particularly by naval guns, which could reach every slope. In addition, bombers and fighters from the two task forces plastered Suribachi.

The task of taking the mountain was given to Col. Harry Liversedge's 28th Marines. The assault got under way at 0820 on 21 February after the Japanese main defense line had been subjected to heavy naval bombardment and a forty-plane strike. Advancing on a seven-hundred-yard front, the regiment's three battalions moved under continuous fire from all types of weapons, suffering heavy losses before even reaching the Japanese positions. The lst Battalion reached the base of Suribachi and swung south around it along the coastline. The deadliest fighting occurred in the center, where the Japanese had constructed the most complex defenses. Despite the lengthy naval and air bombardment, most of the Japanese positions were untouched. The marines of the 3d Battalion encountered stiff resistance and, disregarding the heavy fire, set about rooting the enemy out of each position. By midafternoon the Japanese defense line had been breached. The rest of the day and throughout the next, the marines, pelted by heavy rain, cleared the remaining bunkers, spider holes, and caves in preparation for climbing the mountain's steep slopes.

The easiest way to the top of Suribachi was along the northeast slope, and the task was given to Easy Company, 2d Battalion, 28th Marines. The company's executive officer, lst Lt. Harold G. Schrier, was given a small flag to emplace on the summit by Lt. Col. Chandler W. Johnson, the battalion commander. The ascent to the crater was very difficult; in places the marines had to crawl on their hands and knees. But the Japanese offered no concerted opposition, and the marines reached the crater's rim by 1000. At first there were no Japanese in sight, but soon they appeared from holes and caves in various parts of the crater. Most were systematically killed.

Marines from Lieutenant Schrier's patrol discovered a piece of discarded pipe, attached the small flag to it, and raised it at 1020. The flag could be seen by marines and naval personnel on the plain below, and this simple act was a tremendous morale booster. By then, however, other marines had moved up—accompanied by three photographers. One of the marines had a large four-by-eight-foot flag that had been found in one of the LSTs. This large flag was attached to a longer piece of pipe, and as the smaller flag was lowered, six marines raised the new one in its place. Joe Rosenthal, an Associated Press photographer, had taken a number of photographs of the activities in the crater, including the first flag raising. He had no idea that his picture of this second flag raising would become the most famous single photograph of the Pacific war and would later come to symbolize the heroism of the Marine Corps. Secretary of the Navy James V. Forrestal, who had landed on Iwo for an inspection just minutes before, caught sight of the flag and observed to Lt. Gen. Holland Smith that its appearance over Suribachi would ensure that the Marine Corps would last for five hundred years.

However uplifting the Suribachi episode was, it was a minor part of the battle for the island. By the third day, the marines controlled one-third of the island and were attacking northward. Two battalions from the 5th Division were moving on line in the western sector while the 4th Division attacked the center and in the east. Part of the center of the marine line was occupied on 22 February by the 21st Marines from the 3d Division, which was the corps's floating reserve. The regiment's commitment had been delayed because Smith wanted to save the 3d Division for the upcoming Okinawa operation.

The heaviest fighting over the next three days was around Airfield No. 2. Attacking against heavily fortified slopes south of the field on 22 February, the units gained only about a hundred yards. There were literally thousands of bunkers, pillboxes, caves, trenches, mortar pits, machine-gun nests, and hull-down tanks located adjacent to the field. The assault continued the next day with no appreciable gain. The same situation prevailed on both flanks, resulting in a near stalemate. One observer viewing the attacks on the center described the scene as hell with the fire out.

On 24 February, the battleship *Idaho* and cruiser *Pensacola* bombarded the ridge north of Airfield No. 2. Their fires were soon augmented by air strikes. The 3d Battalion, 21st Marines, made three different attacks across the field before finally securing it in the late afternoon. The 26th Marines advanced about eight hundred yards on the left, while the 27th Marines, moving along the west coast, was held up by Japanese occupying a ridge controlling the valley through which the regiment had to pass. In the 4th Division zone, the 24th Marines had blasted their way to a major ridgeline northeast of the airfield. By the close of the day the marines controlled almost half of the island, but the combat efficiency of most units was down to 60 percent and the casualty toll had mounted to eight thousand men.

General Schmidt, after consulting with Holland Smith, reluctantly decided to commit the 3d Division's 9th Marines. Smith then ordered the 3d Marines back to the Marianas. Even Smith's most ardent defenders later concluded that the decision to hold back the rest of the 3d Division was a mistake. General Schmidt, reflecting the attitude of the hard-pressed regiments on shore, believed the entire division's commitment would have been a welcome relief and would have expedited the final reduction of the Japanese defenses.

Further activity in the center of the marines' line was postponed until the 9th Marines could relieve the exhausted men of the 21st. Most of 25 February was given over to firmly securing Airfield No. 2. In the east, the 4th Division encountered the Japanese 2d Mixed Brigade, commanded by Maj. Gen. Sadasue Senda. His mutually supporting defenses were anchored on a series of landforms—Hill 382, a shallow bowl known as the Amphitheater, and a bald height nicknamed Turkey Knob. On the latter was a large concrete blockhouse. This entire area was later called the Meat Grinder by the marines.

The attack on Hill 382 began on 25 February and, despite concentrated fire from all types of weapons, it took five days of bitter, costly fighting before it was captured by the 23d Marines. Little further progress in the Meat Grinder region was made by the end of February.

In the western sector, 5th Division marines had reached a key position, Hill 362A, and the 3d Division finally broke through the main central defenses and advanced forward approximately a thousand yards, capturing a part of the unfinished airfield. The 3d Division's right-wing elements then attacked due east toward the coast, only fifteen hundred yards away.

However tired and dispirited the marines may have been, the Japanese were in significantly worse condition. On 27 February, Kuribayashi reported to Imperial Headquarters that more than half the island had been lost and more than half of his force destroyed, including two-thirds of his officers.

The U.S. Navy did yeoman service throughout the battle, providing big-gun support on call for the ground forces and blanketing Iwo with air strikes from various carrier task groups. This was not accomplished without cost. During the night of 20–21 February, the

Japanese made thirteen unsuccessful attacks on Sherman's and Davison's ships. The next day, however, six kamikazes flying from Hachijo Jima attacked the *Saratoga* at 1650. Two crashed in the water near the waterline, blasting holes in the hull, and two others struck the flight deck. Damage control had hardly put out the fires when, two hours later, five more planes attacked and a bomb hit the forward flight deck. The *Saratoga* was so badly damaged that it was ordered back to Eniwetok. The crew lost 123 sailors killed and 192 wounded. At about the same time, the escort carrier *Bismarck Sea* was hit by a lone kamikaze. The explosion started gasoline fires and detonated the ammunition magazine. The carrier sank three hours later, taking 218 crewmen with it. There were also isolated reports of Japanese coastal defense guns in the north engaging ships and causing some damage.

Despite these attacks, the Fifth Fleet was so powerful that Mitscher was able to take part of TF 58 north for raids on Tokyo and Nagoya. After achieving only minimal success because of bad weather, the task force moved on to Okinawa, achieving complete surprise. Planes from the carriers roamed at will over the island, and cruisers and destroyers made three firing runs before departing. Even more valuable than the destruction of planes and equipment during this raid were the aerial photographs taken. The pictures helped the planners then at work on the Okinawa invasion to pinpoint Japanese strong points and installations.

Meanwhile, the bitter battles continued on Iwo, each day a repetition of the previous as the three divisions made slow progress in their advance northward. In the 4th Division sector, the Japanese held tenaciously to the Amphitheater and Turkey Knob despite daily poundings by artillery and tanks. By 3 March, the division's combat efficiency was down 50 percent. While the right flank elements fought directly ahead, units on the left were swinging to the east, threatening to trap the enemy. General Senda, the senior Japanese officer in this sector, defied Kuribayashi by ordering a massive banzai charge for the evening of 8 March. The center of this attack fell on the 23d Marines, which destroyed the attackers. By dawn the next day, more than eight hundred Japanese corpses littered the field—all for nothing. On 10 March, General Cates's troops finally overcame organized resistance in the Amphitheater, on Turkey Knob, and at Minami village and joined the 3d and 5th Divisions for the final assault on Kuribayashi's last defenses.

The 3d Division, operating in the center sector, had encountered fanatical resistance in an area the marines called Cushman's Pocket. The pocket was not overrun until 16 March, and it took three weeks of desperate fighting before the last organized resistance in front of the division's right flank was broken. However, some division elements broke through to the sea on 9 March, splitting the Japanese defenders.

The 5th Division in the meantime had reached a gorge five hundred yards south of Kitano Point, the northernmost tip of the island. There, some fifteen hundred Japanese, including Kuribayashi, planned to fight to the last man. In a final gesture acknowledging his valiant defense of Iwo, Imperial Headquarters on 16 March promoted Kuribayashi to full general. The fighting in the 5th Division sector continued for more than a week. Finally, conceding the inevitable, Kuribayashi committed suicide on the twenty-sixth. By then, the 3d Division had taken over the northern sector and the other two battered marine divisions had left the island.

A formal flag raising ceremony attended by most of the senior commanders had been held on 13 March, evidence that higher authority had become impatient with the length of the campaign— which lasted five weeks longer than the most optimistic estimates. The fighting continued even after the last of the 3d Marine Division units were replaced by the army's 147th Infantry Regiment. During operations against the bypassed enemy troops still concealed in caves and tunnels, the army regiment would kill 1,602 Japanese and take 867 prisoners.

The Iwo operation, however important it might have been originally considered, was the most costly in Marine Corps history. Kuribayashi's defense had cost the lives of most of the 20,000-man Japanese garrison. The marines lost 6,821 killed and 19,207 wounded. Iwo Jima joined a growing roll of bloody marine successes. The award of twenty-seven Medals of Honor attested to the heroism evinced by men of the three marine divisions. Uncommon valor became a common commodity on that miserable, forlorn volcanic island.

In return for the marines' sacrifices, the United States gained two serviceable airfields within six hundred miles of Japan. Long before the fighting ended, the Seabees had built roads on the southern part of the island, repaired the two airfields, and erected radar stations atop Mount Suribachi. The first crippled B-29 made an emergency landing on Iwo on 4 March, and two days later, Brig. Gen. Ernest C. Moore brought in the first complement of army fighter planes from the Marianas.

Despite the ongoing Philippines operations, Admiral King did not easily give up on his desire to invade Formosa. However, arguments by Generals Harmon and Richardson and Admiral Spruance convinced Nimitz that an invasion of Okinawa in the Ryukyu Islands would be more advantageous. This was the genesis of the September 1944 decision to substitute Okinawa for Formosa in the plans for operations in the coming year. The operation, code-named Iceberg, was tentatively set for 1 March 1945, but the actual date for the assault depended upon the Iwo Jima operation. Because the reduction of the Japanese garrison on Iwo took much longer than envisioned, the invasion of Okinawa had to be postponed until 1 April, Easter Sunday.

Okinawa is the largest of the Ryukyu Islands, which extend in an arc from Kyushu to Formosa. The island is approximately sixty miles long and oriented on a southwest to northeast axis. In the north, the Motobu Peninsula extending into the East China Sea is eighteen miles across, the widest part of the island. To the south, halfway down the island, is the Ishikawa Isthmus, only two miles wide. The island then widens in the Katchin Peninsula to fifteen miles. The northern two-thirds of Okinawa is mountainous, with some peaks rising to fifteen hundred feet. There are only a few small streams in this section, and the terrain is generally heavily wooded. The few roads there were close to the coastline, making cross-country maneuvering very difficult. Only a fraction of the total population resided in the north. By contrast, the south, which is heavily cultivated, is mostly open, rolling country with a few low-lying hills. This part of the island was the most densely populated, particularly near the largest cities, Naha and Shuri. In 1940 the population was estimated at one-half million. Most of the people were native Okinawans who, despite being under Japanese control after 1871, still maintained their old customs and language. There was a good road net in the south with an excellent stone road connecting the major cities. The Japanese had also constructed a number of airfields there.

As with so many Japanese-held islands, Okinawa was not heavily defended until it became obvious to Imperial Headquarters that the outer defense ring was in danger of collapse. In April 1944 the Thirty-second Army was established there and, from that time onward, troops were steadily brought in from Japan, China, and Manchuria. This process was fraught with danger because American submarines were very active in the waters near Okinawa. The heaviest loss suffered during these reinforcement attempts occurred on 23 June 1944 when the *Tayama Maru* was sunk, taking five thousand troops with it.

In August, the former commander of the Japanese Military Academy, Lt. Gen. Mitsuru Ushijima, took command of the island's defenses. He and his chief of staff, Lt. Gen. Isamu Cho, following the example of other Japanese commanders, decided not to contest any landings but to instead concentrate their defenses in the south. There, Ushijima constructed an intricate system of artillery and mortar positions, blockhouses, and pillboxes. By the time the Americans invaded, the ravines and hills were also honeycombed with man-made caves. In March 1945, Ushijima had only thirty-five aircraft, and these were soon destroyed. Nevertheless, Imperial Headquarters assured him that sea and suicide air attacks launched from Japan would protect the island from the American fleet. In all, Ushijima had more than 65,000 regular army and 8,800 naval personnel under his command. In addition, in the months immediately preceding the invasion, the Japanese inducted approximately 20,000 Okinawans into the Thirty-second Army. Including service personnel converted to infantry, Ushijima was able to muster more than 100,000 defenders when the Americans landed.

In the weeks prior to the invasion, women and children were ordered north, but many ignored the order and remained in what would be the battle zone. The main elements of Ushijima's force were the 44th Infantry Mixed Brigade and the 24th and 62d Divisions. The Japanese were artillery rich, having two medium artillery regiments with forty-four 150mm guns. In addition, there were six antiaircraft artillery battalions and many 75mm and 47mm weapons attached to various units. The Japanese had always been extremely competent with mortars, and on Okinawa they had twenty-four "flying ashcans"—huge 320mm pieces—and ninety-six standard 81mm tubes. The gunners, hidden in concealed positions, were ordered not to fire on American ships but rather to conserve ammunition for use on the attacking infantry.

The American force designated for the Okinawa operation was the newly formed Tenth Army commanded by Lt. Gen. Simon Buckner. It consisted of two corps, General Geiger's III Marine Amphibious Corps and the army's XXIV Corps, commanded by Maj. Gen. John Hodge. The units that made up this army were scattered over the South and Southwest Pacific theaters. The main components of III Amphibious Corps were the veteran 1st Marine Division, commanded by Maj. Gen. Pedro del Valle, and the 6th Marine Division, commanded by Maj. Gen. Lemuel Shepherd. The XXIV Corps consisted of Maj. Gen. Archibald Arnold's 7th Division, and Maj. Gen. James Bradley's 96th Division. Until mid-December, the 96th had been deeply involved in the Philippines fighting, and its officers and men had little time to prepare for the invasion. The other assault divisions had been able to rest for more than six months. In addition, Admiral Turner held in reserve the 2d Marine Division, which was scheduled to fake a diversionary landing on southern Okinawa, and the army's 77th Division. The latter was slated to occupy the Kerama Islands, a small group off Okinawa's southwest coast. The army's 27th Division was held in floating reserve.

The final plan was deceptively simple. III Amphibious Corps would land on ten beaches on the western side of the island north of the Bishi Gawa River, and XXIV Corps would land on eleven beaches south of the river. The marines would then push inland, taking Yontan Field, after which some units would continue to drive across the island while others would turn and begin to suppress the Japanese in the north. Hodge's XXIV Corps was ordered to seize Kadena Field and, once the island had been cut in two by the eastward advance, begin to move south against General Ushijima's main defenses. As an adjunct to the landings, heavy artillery would be off-loaded on some of the Kerama Islands and on neighboring Keise Shima in order to provide counterbattery fire.

Prior to the invasion, Admiral Mitscher led his powerful TF 58 northward to attack the many airfields and installations on Kyushu. For two days, beginning on 19 March, hangars, barracks, airfields, and targets of opportunity were hit. Seventeen ships, including the superbattleship *Yamato,* were also damaged. The Japanese commit-

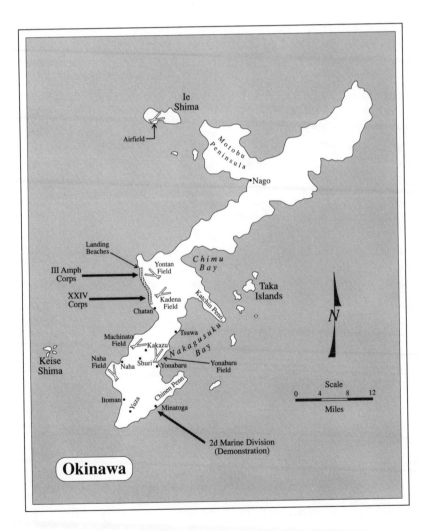

ted a large number of planes to defend the island with little effect. At the conclusion of the operation, American fliers claimed more than five hundred planes destroyed either on the ground or in the air. The Japanese later reported that two hundred were lost. Whatever the exact figure, the Japanese ability to attack the Okinawa invasion force was severely impaired by Mitscher's air strikes. Facilities on Kyushu were later targeted by B-29s from the Marianas on the twenty-seventh and thirty-first.

A portent of the future, however, was the kamikaze attacks on TF 58 during the Kyushu raid. Admiral Ugaki committed more than a hundred suicide planes, most of which were destroyed before they could cause any damage. Still, a few managed to get through the fighter and antiaircraft defenses. The carriers *Intrepid* and *Yorktown* were both slightly damaged by kamikazes on the nineteenth. But the worst was yet to come. The following day a suicide plane struck the carrier *Wasp*, penetrated the hangar deck, started fires that took some time to contain, and killed 101 sailors. Even worse was the damage done to the carrier *Franklin*, which sustained hits on both the flight and hangar decks. These caused six huge explosions, and fire ravaged the ship's interior. Heroic efforts by the crew kept the carrier afloat, although it was listing badly when taken under tow. The kamikaze attack killed 732 men and wounded 265. The remaining crewmen took the wounded carrier on a twelve-thousand-mile voyage by way of Pearl Harbor, where the damage was determined to be too extensive for repairs to be done there, and then on to a shipyard in New York.

Despite individual successes, the Japanese air attacks failed to prevent the bulk of TF 58 from moving into position to support the Okinawa landings. A welcome addition was the British Pacific Fleet commanded by Adm. Sir Bruce Fraser. His force, consisting of two battleships, four carriers, six cruisers, and fifteen destroyers operating under Spruance's overall command, was designated TF 57 and dispatched to conduct attacks on Japanese installations on islands between Formosa and Okinawa beginning on 26 March.

That same day the 77th Division began landing on the Kerama Islands, which were to be used as supply and repair bases in support of the larger Okinawa operation. The 77th's three regiments encountered only sporadic resistance as they executed a complex series of amphibious operations. Surprisingly, 121 prisoners were taken, although most of the troops in the small garrison resisted to the end. A total of 530 Japanese were killed in the operations. More than five hundred Japanese suicide boats were also captured or destroyed. An important adjunct to the Kerama Islands operation was the seizure of nearby Keise Shima by a battalion of the 306th Infantry. The 420th Field Artillery Group began landing its 155mm guns on the thirty-first, and by evening had begun registering on selected Japanese positions in southern Okinawa.

The huge invasion fleet was in position off the western landing beaches by 0330 on 1 April. Its thirteen hundred vessels included ten battleships, nine cruisers, and twenty-three destroyers. Meanwhile, the 2d Marine Division was positioned for a mock diversionary landing on the other side of the island off the Minatoga beaches. The fire support ships blasted the main landing area for over two hours before 135 fighters and bombers raked the beaches and adjacent areas.

The landings were anticlimactic. The four-thousand-yard run to the beaches brought down very little fire on the landing craft, and by 0900, six waves of amtracs were ashore in both corps' sectors. Shortly after the initial landings, LVT(A)s raced ahead to give fire support, and by midmorning tank and division artillery units were ashore. By 1530 the guns were in place and registered.

No one was more pleasantly surprised by the relative lack of Japanese opposition than were the infantrymen conducting the assault. Marines from the 6th Division moved unopposed toward Hanza town and met only scattered resistance as they advanced on Yontan, where they captured the airfield by noon. There was no resistance at all in the 1st Marine Division sector, and leading units had advanced almost two miles inland by the end of the day. The XXIV Corps experienced similar success. Kadena Field was captured by 1000, and both army divisions penetrated more than three thousand yards inland. By the close of the day, General Buckner had fifty thousand troops crammed into a lodgment fifteen thousand yards long by four thousand yards deep. Casualties were extremely light, particularly in comparison to the bloody landings at Peleliu and Iwo Jima: there were only 132, including 28 men killed in action.

The advance continued on 2 April, impeded only by local defense and service troops, many of whom did not even have rifles. By nightfall elements of the 1st Marine Division were at the base of the Katchin Peninsula and 7th Division troops had reached the east coast, effectively severing the island. The 6th Marine Division, moving through very difficult terrain, secured the hill masses north of Yontan Field and was ready to push into the Ishikawa Isthmus by the evening of 3 April.

Thanks to the lack of concerted opposition, Tenth Army was eleven days ahead of schedule. The Yontan airstrip's three runways were quickly made usable and became fully operational by 8 April. But when the army divisions swung south, opposition increased as they reached the first of General Ushijima's main lines of defense.

Before that time, most of the fighting was in the 6th Marine Division sector in northern Okinawa. The marines there were operating in extremely rugged wooded country with few roads. Colonel Takehiko Udo, commanding in the north, had hinged his defense on 1,200-foot-high Mount Yaetake, where he had approximately thirteen hundred men dug in and all the approaches covered by machine guns, mortars, and artillery. While two of the marine division's regiments probed the surrounding area, the 29th Marines began the assault on the mountain on 12 April. It soon became apparent that the task was beyond the capabilities of just one regiment, so the 4th Marine Regiment was committed. Attacking eastward while the men of the 29th forced their way west under the protection of division artillery and the big guns of the navy fire support ships, the Japanese were systematically cleared from the mountain. Organized resistance in the northern sector of Okinawa did not end until 20 April, and the 6th Marine Division continued searching out guerrilla bands there until early May.

Meanwhile, to the south, XXIV Corps had unmasked strong defensive positions north of Shuri by 5 April. The 96th Division discovered a series of fortified positions protected by minefields and covered by many mortars and machine guns in the western half of the corps zone. Chief among the strong points was a position on what was called Cactus Ridge. Japanese tank-infantry counterattacks delayed capture of this key objective until elements of the 383d Infantry Regiment threw the enemy off the ridge with a series of frontal assaults.

To the east, the 7th Division gradually pulled even with the 96th to provide a consistent line across the island. The major outpost in the 7th's sector was a height called the Pinnacle. There the Japanese had dug trenches and had the entire front covered by medium and heavy artillery, which delivered very accurate fire. Nearby Naha had been the site of a Japanese artillery school, and almost every yard of southern Okinawa had been surveyed, allowing the Japanese gunners to pinpoint every attack. Despite such support and determined Japanese resistance, the 184th Infantry finally took the Pinnacle on 8 April after three bloody attacks. Two other major strong points, Triangulation Hill and Tomb Hill, fell the next day, and it became obvious to General Hodge that they had found the main Japanese defenses. From that time onward, maneuver was very difficult and most of the attacks were channeled directly into the most heavily defended positions.

The 7th Division reached the northern outskirts of Ishin and Ouki villages and there its southern movement was halted. The corps's main effort on 9 April was in the 96th Division zone, where two ugly, squat hills made up the Kakazu hill mass. The Japanese there had constructed one of the strongest defensive positions on the island. One company from the 383d managed to gain the top of Kakazu West but was forced off. The regiment seized it the next day, but all attempts to take the saddle and the eastern hill failed. Concentrations of Japanese medium and heavy artillery fire stalled the last of this series of attacks on 12 April.

General Ushijima at first resisted the pleas of his more aggressive officers to launch a counterattack to drive the Americans from southern Okinawa, but on 9 April he finally agreed to a general attack by elements of two divisions. The tactical plan called for massive infiltration of the American lines by six battalions, after which troops would attack the 7th and 96th Divisions' positions from the rear.

The Japanese counterstrike began at dusk on the twelfth after a heavy preparatory bombardment. Although the 7th Division was involved, the main attack fell on the 96th in the lightly held sector between Tombstone Hill and Kakazu Ridge. Heavy support by division artillery and naval gunfire helped the infantrymen to thwart the attackers. By dawn, all was over. A few small bands of Japanese were caught behind the lines, but these were quickly eliminated. A less ambitious attack was mounted that evening, but it, too, was broken by a combination of artillery and small-arms fire. The Japanese gained nothing for the loss of more than five hundred killed in the two abortive actions.

Even before the Japanese attack, General Buckner had planned to commit the 27th Division. He was fully aware of the increasing opposition and the mounting losses in Hodge's two battered divisions. One 27th Division regiment, the 105th, had already been in action. After a thorough reconnaissance of the islands off Okinawa's east coast showed that Tsugen Shima was occupied, the 105th's 3d Battalion landed there on 10 April. Within a day it had wiped out the 230-man Japanese garrison. The bulk of the 27th Division landed at Kadena on 9 April and moved into the line west of the 96th Division for Hodge's major attempt to crack the Shuri defenses on 19 April.

The plan was for the 96th to drive directly ahead while the fresh 27th moved to secure Kakazu Ridge and the 7th advanced to the Naha-Yonabaru road. On the night of the eighteenth, engineers built a 128-yard-long footbridge, two Bailey bridges, and one pontoon bridge across the inlet on the extreme right flank west of Uchitomari village. By midnight, men of the 27th Division's 106th Regiment had crossed over and were ready to advance to the Urasoe-Mura Escarpment.

Early morning of the nineteenth witnessed the greatest artillery concentration of the Pacific war. Twenty-seven battalions of corps and division artillery—joined by the big guns on six battleships, six cruisers, and fifteen destroyers—blasted away at the Japanese positions. The bombardment was followed by massive navy and marine air strikes. At 0640, army troops began to advance all along the line. Despite the hellish pounding, the Japanese defenses remained intact. The 27th Division's 105th Infantry was halted in front of Kakazu Ridge. Farther west, the 106th, which had gained positions on the escarpment, could not move south. The regiment was hit by intense fire from cave, tunnel, and tomb positions. Thirty tanks, attacking between the Kakazu and Nishibaru Ridges, reached Kakazu village, but they were stopped by antitank fire and Japanese suicide squads armed with satchel charges. Only eight tanks managed to extricate themselves. To the east, the 96th Division's 382d Infantry was halted by concentrated fire from many mutually supporting dug-in positions along Tombstone Ridge. The adjoining 381st Infantry had momentary success as one of its companies drove over Nishibaru Ridge to the village beyond. However, these gains could not be maintained. In the 7th Division sector, despite the use of flamethrower tanks, the assaults on Ouki Hill and Skyline Ridge proved fruitless. By the close of the day, Tenth Army had accomplished very little—at a cost of 720 casualties. Ushijima's first defense line still held.

While the land battles for southern Okinawa raged, there were two developments elsewhere that, although not directly affecting the campaign, had far-reaching implications for the conduct of the latter stages of the war.

The first of these came on 6 April when the Joint Chiefs, after much debate, moved to regularize command relationships in the Pacific. Although not yet conceding the need for a supreme commander, they recognized that with the war closing in on Japan, all army and navy units operating in the two theaters should be controlled by a commander from their respective branches. This plan gave MacArthur, recently appointed to the new rank of General of the Army, control over all army units. Nimitz, who had been likewise honored with promotion to Fleet Admiral, gained command over all naval units. Because the Okinawa operation had been planned and was being carried out by Nimitz's headquarters, MacArthur, by then deeply involved with planning for the invasion of Japan, decided not to interfere in the general conduct of the campaign. A related decision of considerable importance was the recognition of the Twentieth Air Force as an operational entity directly under the Army Air Forces commander, General Arnold.

The second development, the death of President Roosevelt on 12 April, dealt a devastating psychological blow to civilians and military personnel alike. His successor, Vice President Harry S Truman, a little-known Missouri politician, was handed the difficult task of helping to decide the future of Europe as Germany teetered on the verge of collapse. Ultimately, he would also be called upon to make the most momentous decision of the Pacific war.

While the Tenth Army was making only slow progress on shore against determined suicidal Japanese resistance, the navy was engaged in its most serious challenge of the war. Although kamikazes had caused considerable damage to the fleet off the Philippines, those attacks paled in comparison to the well-organized hordes that struck Turner's support fleet and TF 57 and TF 58 during the month of April. Admiral Toyoda's plan, code-named Ten-Go, called for massing two thousand planes on Kyushu, Formosa, and other islands in the Salishima Gunto, half of which would be suicide aircraft. Although the goal was not met, Toyoda had seven hundred planes in position by 6 April. He also planned to send submarines carrying Kaiten manned torpedoes. These craft were guided by loyal sailors bent on wreaking havoc on the American fleet. In conjunction with all these attacks, he ordered the largest kamikaze of all, the super battleship *Yamato*—with fuel for only a one-way trip—to bombard the American positions on Okinawa. Nothing in the closing months of the war showed the desperation and fatalism of the Imperial high command better than the dispatch of their showpiece battleship on a suicide mission that, even if successful, would not have altered the situation on Okinawa.

The first of the kamikaze attacks was launched on 31 March against the radar picket ships. At first there were random attacks by fewer than twenty planes, but beginning on 6 April the Japanese employed massed attacks called *kikusui* (floating chrysanthemum). These varied in size from as many as 355 planes on 6 April to as few as 45 planes on 22 June. More than nineteen hundred sorties were launched against U.S. naval forces, including the ten *kikusui* attacks. The ships of the destroyer picket lines received the worst pounding. Accurate antiaircraft fire and action by navy and army fighters kept the damage to the major ships of the Fifth Fleet to a minimum. The picket line destroyers, equipped with the latest radar, manned sixteen positions in designated areas ranging from fifteen to a hundred miles distant from Okinawa. The first attacks on the picket ships damaged three destroyers, and the Kerama anchorages were also hit. The British carriers in VAdm. Sir Philip Vian's TF 57 were attacked on 1 April while their aircraft flew suppression strikes in the Sakishima Gunto. The carrier *Indefatigable* was struck but, thanks to its armored flight deck, sustained only minor damage. The destroyer *Ulster* was hit and very seriously damaged.

The first major Japanese suicide attack came on 6 April. Despite excellent air cover and precision antiaircraft fire, twenty-two attacking planes got through and struck their targets. Along the western picket line the destroyers *Bush* and *Calhoun* were sunk and the *Morris, Witter, Howorth,* and *Hyman* were damaged. Kamikazes sank the destroyer *Emmons* and badly damaged the *Purdy, Mullany,* and *Rodman* off Okinawa's east coast. Two ammunition ships were hit in Kerama Harbor, as was a fully loaded LST. Turner's ships and planes claimed 182 destroyed, and the fliers from TF 58 said they shot down 249. The disparity between claims and the actual number of kamikazes involved, 355, can best be attributed to the confusion of combat.

After a brief lull, the attacks resumed on 9 April when a kamikaze damaged the destroyer *Sterett.* Three days later the destroyers *Cassin, Young, Purdy, Lindsey, Zellars,* the destroyer escort *Whitehurst,* and the battleship *Tennessee* were all hit. A Baka (a twenty-foot-long manned rocket bomb carrying more than a ton of explosives) launched from a bomber struck the destroyer *Abele,* which sank within five minutes. A *kikusui* assault directed at TF 58 resulted in damage to the carriers *Enterprise* and *Essex,* the battleship *Missouri,* and the destroyer *Kidd.*

A third *kikusui* was launched on 16 April, once again mainly on the picket line. The carrier *Intrepid* was slightly damaged, the destroyer *Laffey* sustained serious damage after surviving twenty-two separate attacks, and the minesweeper *Harding* was struck. On the twenty-seventh the destroyers *Ralph Talbot* and *Rathburn* were hit, and the ammunition ship *Canada Victory* was blown apart. The next day three more destroyers, the *Daly, Twiggs,* and *Brown,* sustained heavy damage.

In all, 820 planes were counted in the mass attacks on the Fifth Fleet in April. In early May, after a new group of pilots and planes were moved into position on Kyushu, the strikes resumed. Continuing efforts by TF 58 aircraft and Army Air Forces heavy bombers failed to halt the buildup.

The attitudes that motivated the kamikaze pilots were reflected in the fatalistic decisions of the most senior Japanese army and naval officers. There is no better illustration of this than the decision to send the *Yamato* on its one-way voyage to Okinawa.

The *Yamato* left harbor on the afternoon of 6 April accompanied by a pitifully small escort: a light cruiser and eight destroyers. Admirals Spruance and Mitscher were alerted by a submarine of the presence of the Japanese ships, which were then tracked by submarine and air patrols. Mitscher ordered all four task groups to take up intercept positions northeast of Okinawa. In addition, RAdm. Morton L. Deyo led six older battleships, seven cruisers, and twenty-one destroyers from Turner's fire support group north to prevent a breakthrough.

Deyo's squadron never got into the fight. Two of Mitscher's carrier task groups, Clark's TG 58.1 and Sherman's TG 58.3, were in position to attack at 1000 on 7 April, and the carriers launched 280 planes, including 98 torpedo bombers. One of the Japanese destroyers was sunk at 1245. It was soon followed by the cruiser *Yahagi*, which took twelve bomb hits before it went down. The *Yamato* was also struck at about 1245. The huge battleship took two medium bombs and one torpedo hit but continued to plow southward at reduced speed. Three more of the destroyer escorts were sunk while the *Yamato* was attacked by thirty planes, which in thirty minutes scored three bomb and nine torpedo hits. Finally, at approximately 1423, the *Yamato* sank, taking with it more than twenty-five hundred men. This futile last-gasp effort by the once proud Imperial Navy cost the lives of thirty-six hundred men.

The battle against the kamikazes continued at sea throughout the campaign, but the most desperate fighting was on land as the Tenth Army continued to assault Ushijima's defenses in actions reminiscent of the costly World War I debacles on the western front.

Despite XXIV Corps's growing problems in the south, General Buckner decided on 10 April to use the 77th Division to capture the island of Ie Shima, located approximately three and one-half miles off the western tip of the Motobu Peninsula. This island, only five miles long and two miles wide, at the time was dominated by two features—one man made, the other natural. The central portion of the island contained an airfield, and behind the town of Ie rose the Pinnacle, a 640-foot-high hill. The Japanese commander, aided by the civilian population and his three-thousand-man garrison, had constructed elaborate defenses in the town and along the slopes of the Pinnacle. In addition to the hundreds of natural caves in the area, the defenders constructed pillboxes, converted houses in the town and ancestral tombs into defensive positions, and sowed thousands of mines.

Ie Shima is ringed by coral reefs, thus providing few good landing areas. Major General Andrew Bruce, the 77th Division's commander, decided to land the 305th Infantry Regiment on the narrow southern beaches while at the same time the 306th Infantry went ashore on the western beaches. The plan was for the 305th to swing eastward, capturing the high ground south of the town, while the 306th took the airfield and then drove on to the eastern end of the island.

The landings were executed as planned on 16 April. The 306th met only slight resistance and quickly seized the airfield. By nightfall, elements had penetrated three miles inland and were in position just north of Ie town. The men of the 305th had no such luck. They encountered heavy enemy concentrations in caves and fortified tombs and advanced only eight hundred yards. That night the Japanese launched a major counterattack that rocked the 305th.

General Bruce held back the 306th the next day and landed his reserve, the 307th Infantry, southwest of the town. After coordinating with the 305th, it moved into Ie, where the Japanese had constructed a defense in depth using abandoned houses. By evening the infantrymen had advanced as far as Government Hill and a ridge in the center of town later aptly named Bloody Ridge. Both regiments made repeated attempts to take these two prime objectives on 18 and 19 April.

On the eighteenth, a jeep carrying famed war correspondent Ernie Pyle and the 307th's commander, Lt. Col. Joseph Coolidge, was engaged by a concealed machine gun. Pyle was killed—a tragic end to the combat career of the dogface soldier's beloved spokesman.

A company from the 307th managed to reach the top of Bloody Ridge on the nineteenth but could not hold it. Meanwhile, the 306th had reached the eastern coastline and was in position north of the Pinnacle. Bruce decided to shift the main effort to that sector, and on the twentieth troops from the 306th gained the northern slopes of the hill. The other two regiments, advancing yard by yard, finally secured Government Hill and Bloody Ridge that same day. On the twenty-first,well-coordinated attacks by all three regiments brought an end to organized resistance on Ie Shima. Flushing the remaining Japanese from the caves and tunnels took many more days, but the island was secure.

The six-day battle had cost the 77th Division 1,100 casualties. More than 4,700 Japanese died, including an estimated 1,500 civilians dressed in Japanese uniforms and supplied with arms by the regular troops. The engineers quickly moved in and the airfield was soon operable. On 10 May a fighter group was stationed there. It was joined within a month by a night-fighter squadron.

On 19 April General Hodge launched a major offensive on Okinawa all along the relatively static XXIV Corps front. In the east, elements of the 7th Division attacked Skyline Ridge, which blocked movement south along the coast, and Ouki Hill. The action there was a repetition of earlier operations: a massive artillery preparation followed by tank-infantry attacks against well-defended positions. At first the advance was measured in yards against the veteran thousand-man 11th Independent Infantry Battalion. However, by 23 April, men of the 32d and 184th Infantry Regiments had captured both objectives and killed more than half the defenders. In the central sector, the 96th Division attacked Nishibaru Ridge with little initial success. By the twenty-second, the 382d Infantry was reduced to 50 percent efficiency. It was replaced by the 383d, which, after two more days of inching forward, captured the ridge. In the 27th Division sector to the west, the way to Machinato Field was blocked by heavy Japanese defenses in an area called the Item Pocket and along Ryan Ridge—named after Capt. Bernard Ryan, the 165th Infantry Regiment company commander whose men finally took the ridge. While the 96th and 7th Divisions had made deep penetrations into Ushijima's first line of defense, the battle for the pocket and ridge led by the 165th Infantry raged until 27 April.

With his front broken and his 62d Division having suffered 50 percent casualties, Ushijima began withdrawing his troops to his second line of defense. The strong point on Kakazu Ridge that had caused so much trouble was taken on the twenty-fourth; the attackers met no resistance. By the end of the month the central and eastern units of XXIV Corps had moved ahead approximately a thousand yards, and the strongest Japanese resistance in the west had been smashed. One of the reasons for the success of the five-day American offensive was that the bulk of the Japanese 24th Division and 44th Independent Mixed Brigade were in the south, where Ushijima feared an amphibious landing on the Minatoga beaches. Generals Hodge and Bruce both had urged such a maneuver on Buckner, but he refused to attempt it because of the difficulty of supplying the force. Buckner feared the possibility of the landing becoming a debacle like the one at Anzio.

Beginning on 1 May, both sides began shifting forces. Buckner moved the lst Marine Division into line, replacing the 27th Division on XXIV Corps's extreme right, and brought the 77th from Ie Shima to take over the center from the battered 96th. Its 381st Infantry had taken more than five hundred casualties during the last four days of April in a series of abortive attempts to take Kochi Ridge. The 7th Division remained on the left until it was relieved ten days later. Lieutenant General Isamu Cho, chief of staff of the Japanese Thirty-second Army, sided with the field commanders and convinced Ushijima to order the 24th Division into position on the eastern end of the Japanese defense line. The 44th Infantry Mixed Brigade was also shifted from the south, to the Asa River line north of Naha.

Despite these changes, the nature of the fighting remained the same. Each major American attack would be preceded by a heavy artillery and mortar preparation and then the infantry, supported by tanks, would move out against the Japanese defenses along the ridgelines and in the hills. The marines launched an immediate attack southward against the complex Japanese defenses. It proved to be as unsuccessful as earlier attacks by the 27th Division. The 7th Division was locked in a ferocious five-day battle with the Japanese entrenched on Kochi Ridge and on the hills east of Kochi. In the center of the line the 77th Division was involved with equally stubborn Japanese defenders on the Maeda Escarpment. Finally, the 307th Infantry took the key positions there on 4 May.

The stubborn Japanese defense was working all too well, but such tactics did not suit some of Ushijima's subordinate commanders who wanted to take the offensive and drive the Americans back to the beaches. These differences were argued out at a staff conference at Thirty-second Army headquarters on 2 May. Ushijima and Cho finally gave in and authorized a major counterattack, which would be coordinated with heavy kamikaze attacks on the fourth. Two small-scale amphibious attacks were planned to strike behind the American lines. The soldiers who landed would carry satchel charges and do as much as possible to disrupt the rear areas.

The operation began with Japanese naval air force units operating from Kyushu taking off at dusk on 3 May. In this fifth *kikusui* attack, the destroyer *Aaron Ward* was severely damaged and its fellow picket, the *Little,* was hit repeatedly and sank almost immediately. Two LSMs were also damaged. Continuing attacks on the fourth sank the destroyers *Luce* and *Morrison* and damaged the *Ingraham* and *Shea.*

The Japanese land operations were not as successful. The two amphibious landings during the night of the third were fiascoes. Most of the Japanese suicide engineers were killed in their boats. In the 7th Division sector, the Japanese infiltrated in great numbers and at 0500 on 4 May began a general attack toward the ruined towns of Onaga and Ishin. The 32d and 184th Infantry Regiments beat off successive attacks during the day.

The main attack was in the center, where the Japanese 32d Regiment was to punch a hole in the American defense line so the 44th Infantry Mixed Brigade could pass through and turn west in order to cut off the 1st Marine Division, which at that time was deeply committed to its own offensive. Artillery and automatic weapons from the 77th Division's 306th Infantry cut the attacking forces to pieces as they attempted to regain the escarpment. The Japanese light tanks supporting the attack were all destroyed.

During the night of 4–5 May, approximately four hundred Japanese broke through and recaptured Tanabaru town, one mile behind the XXIV front. From there they were a threat to the 7th Division's supply route. It took two days of hard fighting to destroy them.

To support the offensive, the Japanese finally brought many of their field pieces into the open. Counterbattery fire from the superior American artillery destroyed an estimated sixty medium field pieces. By midnight on 5 May Ushijima was aware that his offensive had failed. It had gained nothing, and he had lost approximately five thousand troops sorely needed for the continued defense of Naha, Shuri, and Machinato. To make up for these heavy losses, Ushijima began to mix service troops with his regular infantry.

General Buckner planned to take advantage of the Japanese losses by beginning a general assault on 11 May. To prepare for this, General Hodge ordered the 1st Marine Division to secure a small knob called Hill 60 and then move south of the Asa River. The marines secured the hill after a three-day fight and were situated just north of the town of Dakeshi on the west coast. In the center, the 77th Division inched ahead from the Maeda Escarpment with heavy air, artillery, and tank support. By 10 May the division was within a mile of Shuri. In the eastern sector, the 7th Division, which had begun the attack on the hill defenses around Kochi on 26 April, was relieved by the 96th Division and ordered into reserve. By the tenth, the 96th had almost completely occupied the hills.

Although Hodge's attacks had not succeeded in accomplishing all of his optimistic goals, Tenth Army was in good position to begin reducing Ushijima's main defenses. Buckner, after taking direct command of the land battle, inserted the 6th Marine Division on the extreme right of the line, giving him two corps abreast.

The general offensive that began on 11 May soon broke down into a series of localized battles for strong points. Despite the specter of annihilation, the Japanese defended every hill, ridge, and gulch.

In the west, the 6th Marine Division crossed the Asa River and reached the north bank of the Asato River on the twelfth. The 29th Marines, moving southeast, fought a four-day battle before a key position, Sugar Loaf Hill, was captured. Continuing onward, the regiment was halted by heavy fire from the Shuri Heights in the 1st Marine Division area. In just ten days of fighting for important but minimal gains, the 6th Division took twenty-six hundred casualties.

The 1st Marine Division faced the Shuri Heights, composed of many ridges and draws, as well as fortified positions in the town of

Dakeshi. South of Dakeshi were the Wana Ridge and Wana Gorge. Ushijima had reinforced this sector by bringing up reinforcements to support the remnants of his 62d Division, which was down to six hundred men. By the time the tank-infantry teams from the 7th Marines began their attack on the eleventh, the Japanese had sixty-seven hundred men in the sector with orders to die in place. Despite this fanatical defense, the marines had taken most of the northern part of Wana Ridge by the fourteenth. However, it required more than two weeks of additional fighting before the rest of the ridge and the gorge were captured.

The 77th Division's assault in the center on 17 May began with an attack on the important Ishimmi Ridge northeast of Shuri. A company from the 307th Infantry infiltrated Japanese lines and seized the heights. Despite heavy losses—156 of 204 men killed or wounded—they held the ridge for three days in the face of artillery, mortar, and infantry attacks. They were reinforced on the twentieth by other elements from the 307th. Meanwhile, the 305th Infantry continued inching its way toward Shuri along Route 5. Beyond Ishimmi town, in a seemingly never-ending series, were hills called Chocolate Drop, Wart, and Flat Top. The 306th and 307th Infantry Regiments managed to eliminate opposition on the Chocolate Drop, the most tenaciously defended hill, by the twentieth.

On the Tenth Army's left, the 96th Division fought for ten days past Zebra Hill to Dick Hill on the division's right. On the extreme left the 381st and 383d Infantry Regiments assaulted Conical Hill, the major height northeast of Yonabaru. By the evening of the twenty-first, the hill's eastern slopes had been captured, allowing Buckner to commit the 7th Division to an attack down the corridor past Nakagusuku (Buckner) Bay without danger of fire from the right flank. This opened the possibility of enveloping the enemy forces to the west.

Unfortunately for the Americans, the weather, which had been unseasonably good, became a major factor in the final days of May. Beginning on the twenty-first, a week of very heavy rain turned the battlefield into a quagmire. Even tanks and amphibious tractors could not move to support the infantry. The hellish conditions already prevalent along the front were made worse by the decomposing bodies of Japanese soldiers. Sanitation became a real problem, and disease swept through the ranks. Faced with such conditions, the American drive literally bogged down in the center.

Elsewhere, the front remained static during the last week of May. The 77th Division was also halted by the mud, rain, and continued heavy fire from the heights overlooking Shuri. The same lack of forward movement prevailed in the 96th Division sector. But there was movement at each end of the American line.

In the west, General Shepherd shifted the 6th Marine Division attack that had stalled in the Sugar Loaf complex south toward Naha. During the night of the twenty-fourth, engineers bridged the swollen Asato River and the marines crossed and entered Naha early the next day. The largest city in Okinawa, Naha offered no particular tactical advantage except as a gateway to movement farther south. The marines encountered no significant opposition until they crossed the canal into eastern Naha and drove toward the Kokuba Hill line. Despite the rain and increasing opposition from the 44th Infantry Mixed Brigade, Shepherd's men had by the end of the month taken the village of Machisi near their boundary with the 1st Marine Division.

At the other end of the American line, the army's 7th Division, taking advantage of the collapse of Japanese defenses around Conical Hill, moved south and west hoping to envelop the Japanese in Shuri. The 184th Infantry, despite abortive counterattacks, captured Yonabaru and by 30 May had moved almost two miles south of the city.

All hopes of a quick envelopment faded when the 32d Infantry ran into a complex defense system west of Yonabaru. Without tank support, the attack stalled. Then the weather broke, allowing the 32d to take the key hills and move near Chan village by the end of the month.

After almost two months of fighting on Okinawa, the major prizes of Naha, Yonabaru, and Shuri had eluded the Tenth Army. All elements were still battling an enemy who controlled most of the heights protecting the major concentrations along the Shuri perimeter. III Amphibious Corps had sustained almost eleven thousand casualties, and XXIV Corps, which had borne the brunt of the fighting, had suffered almost fifteen thousand casualties. The attrition rate on vehicles was very high. More than 60 percent of all the light and medium tanks committed were either destroyed or damaged. All the troops were exhausted, and illness was rampant. However bad the situation was for the Americans, the Japanese condition bordered on hopeless. The 62d Division had been almost completely wiped out; an estimated sixty-two thousand Japanese were dead. Despite these losses, there was no sign of slackening in the tenacious defense. The Japanese fought until they were killed.

Tenth Army intelligence in the last week of May had concluded that the Japanese would make a final stand along the Shuri line. However, at a staff meeting on the twenty-first, Ushijima and Cho decided to withdraw the bulk of their remaining forces southward, leaving only a rear guard to hold the hills around Shuri. Aerial observers relayed messages to Buckner's headquarters of a great amount of seemingly confused movement behind the lines. Not until 30 May did higher headquarters concede that Shuri might be held by fewer troops than suspected. That same day, elements of the lst Marine Division northwest of the city moved through a gap in the Japanese line to seize Shuri ridge. The castle there, built in 1544 for the kings of Okinawa but by then a ruin, lay one-half mile in front of the marines. After receiving permission to encroach on 77th Division territory, a battalion from the 5th Marines occupied the castle by midmorning. A number of Japanese remained in caves underneath the fortress and had to be carefully rooted out.

On the thirtieth the 77th Division's 307th Infantry took a major defensive position, Dorothy Hill, burning out three levels of caves in the process. Later, other elements captured three more hill positions. In the east, the 96th had been halted for nine days by Japanese defenses on two large hill masses northeast of Shuri. Using grenades and satchel charges, infantrymen of the 382d Infantry finally secured those positions. The Japanese shell was finally cracked open when the 77th Division moved from Wana Ridge into northern Shuri on the thirty-first, meeting elements of the lst Marine Division that had moved north from the castle. Shuri, Okinawa's second largest city, was finally in American hands—but it was almost destroyed in the process. An estimated two hundred thousand high-explosive rounds were pumped into the city before Ushijima decided to move most of his remaining troops south.

* * *

Offshore, the navy was heavily engaged during the entire month of May with individual and organized kamikaze attacks. There were four more *kikusui* attacks, each involving more than a hundred planes of all types. The most dangerous were by two-engined bombers crammed with bombs or torpedoes. Despite continuous air cover by navy and army fighters and excellent vectoring by the radar picket ships, some Japanese aircraft always managed to break through. Antiaircraft fire took a extensive toll of the suicide planes but the few that survived did terrible damage.

The sixth *kikusui*, a 150-plane strike on 11 May, lost two-thirds of its number before reaching the ships. Nevertheless, the destroyers *Evans* and *Hadley* were so badly damaged that they had to be towed to Kerama. Nor did TF 58 escape. Mitscher's flagship, the *Bunker Hill*, took two hits and sustained damage second only to that suffered by the *Franklin*. The suicide planes caused 353 deaths on the carrier. Three days later, the *Enterprise* was damaged so badly that it, too, had to be sent to a major West Coast shipyard. These serious losses were in contrast to the British aircraft carriers *Formidable, Indomitable,* and *Victorious,* all of which were struck by kamikazes but whose armored decks kept damage to a minimum. Individual attackers damaged the destroyer *Bache* on the thirteenth and the *Fox* on the fifteenth.

The seventh *kikusui*, launched over a three-day period from 23 to 25 May, was the last in which the Japanese committed more than a hundred planes. The continued pounding of Kyushu and Shikoku by TF 58, coupled with the heavy attrition of the kamikazes, dramatically lowered the number of planes available. In this attack the destroyers *Stormes, Anthony,* and *Braine* were so seriously damaged that they had to be towed to Kerama.

The last major organized attack of the month occurred on the twenty-eighth. It coincided with a changeover in the U.S. fleets as Halsey again replaced Spruance and McCain took over from Mitscher. This attack cost the third Fleet the destroyer *Drexler,* which was blown apart, and the destroyers *Anthony, Braine,* and *Shubrick,* all heavily damaged.

Suicide planes also attacked fixed installations on Kerama and at the airfields at Kadena, Yontan, and on Ie Shima. One of the most bizarre episodes in the entire kamikaze campaign occurred on the evening of 24 May at Yontan Field. Five two-engined bombers were spotted approaching the field from the direction of Ie Shima. Four of these were shot down but the fifth, although damaged, did a wheels-up landing on the airstrip. Ten heavily armed Japanese leaped from the plane and began throwing grenades and incendiaries at parked aircraft. Before they were killed, these suicide troops had destroyed seven planes and damaged twenty-six others. In addition, they ignited a fuel dump and seventy thousand gallons of gasoline went up in flames.

It began to rain heavily on 1 June as the marines and army infantry pursued the retreating Japanese. The 7th Division was held up only briefly by sporadic defense of two hills before moving into the rugged Chinen Peninsula. Fortunately, Ushijima had not ordered elaborate defenses constructed in this region, and the fleeing Japanese did not put up a concerted defense. Late in the afternoon of the third, the 184th Infantry reached the southeast coast near the town of Hyakuna. To the west, 96th Division soldiers—moving as fast as the ankle deep mud would allow—by 6 June had come within a few hundred yards of the Yaeju Dake Escarpment, which was defended by the remnants of the Japanese 24th Division and the 44th Infantry Mixed Brigade. After overcoming supply problems, the 1st Marine Division took up positions facing the western side of the escarpment.

The 6th Marine Division, advancing on Tenth Army's extreme right, was given the task of securing the Oroku Peninsula, which was guarded by the remnants of the ten-thousand-man Naval Base Force commanded by RAdm. Minori Ota. General Shepherd mounted an amphibious operation with the 4th Marines, sending the regiment across the estuary south of Naha to the northern tip of the peninsula on 4 June. The division's other two regiments landed farther west and began tightening the ring around Ota's headquarters. The Japanese, well supplied with automatic weapons and occupying well-prepared defensive positions—many of them underground—held off the marines for ten days. Although Ota and many of his officers and men committed suicide, the marines took 159 prisoners, the first large group to surrender on Okinawa.

By 4 June Ushijima had successfully repositioned approximately eleven thousand men in and behind the Yaeju Dake Escarpment, a four-mile height rising two hundred feet above the valley floor. The line was anchored in the east on a hill near the village of Han-agusuka, where the 7th Division on 9 June began to try to envelop the main positions located farther west. The 32d Infantry, backed by medium and flamethrowing tanks, managed to secure positions along the base of the hill and a small portion of the escarpment proper by the twelfth. A night attack by the 17th Infantry seized even more ground and the defenders were finally burned out. At the same time, the 96th Division—attacking directly ahead against the main defenses on the escarpment—managed to flank the peak in the 7th Division zone, and continuous pressure from both divisions collapsed the eastern defenses by the evening of the thirteenth.

Along the western end of the Japanese line, remnants of the Japanese 24th Division held up a regiment from the 96th Division and the lst Marine Division along Kunishi Ridge for five days. Tanks and artillery finally shattered that section of the line, and on 14 June the Japanese forces ceased to be an organized army. Some units continued to fight savagely as they retreated farther south and established two defensive perimeters. Japanese casualties continued to mount as individuals and small units tried to escape. An estimated nine thousand Japanese were killed between 19 and 21 June.

From the beginning of the campaign, Tenth Army had dropped more than eight million leaflets urging the Japanese to surrender. These had little effect until the collapse of the Yaeju Dake defenses. At that point, the leaflets, combined with appeals by Japanese-American linguists and captured Japanese, convinced hundreds of soldiers to surrender each day. In all, more than 7,400 soldiers and 3,300 laborers capitulated.

Fresh troops from the 2d Marine Division, which had landed in early June, were used to reduce the final semiorganized defenses in the extreme south. While watching one of these actions from a forward command post on 18 June, General Buckner was wounded during a Japanese barrage and died before he could be evacuated. He was succeeded by General Geiger, who became the first marine ever to command a U.S. field army. That exalted status lasted only five days before Gen. Joseph W. Stillwell arrived to take over Tenth Army. On 22 June, one day after General Geiger declared Okinawa secure, Generals Ushijima and Cho committed ritual suicide outside a cave on the southeast coast.

Tenth Army established a blocking line between Naha and Yonabaru and both corps moved steadily northward, systematically sealing caves and rooting out Japanese who had earlier escaped detection. During this week-long operation highlighted by bloody skirmishes, 8,900 Japanese troops were killed and 2,900 more prisoners were taken.

Pacification operations were begun in the north in May when the 27th Division was pulled out of the southern line, put under island command, and ordered to conduct a series of sweeps that continued until the end of July. These small-unit actions over difficult terrain resulted in the deaths of more than a thousand Japanese and turned up more than five hundred prisoners.

The battle for Okinawa lasted much longer than originally expected, but the struggle taught the American high command lessons that should have been learned long before. With each step closer to Japan proper, defenses improved and Japanese leaders and their troops seemed more dedicated than ever. Ushijima and his field commanders had skillfully utilized terrain to inflict maximum casualties. Tenth Army and naval casualties totaled 49,451, including 12,520 dead or missing. The organized and individual kamikaze attacks wreaked havoc on the supporting fleet. They sank 36 ships and damaged 368 more. More sailors—a total of 4,907—died in these attacks than in the four army divisions, which lost 4,582 killed. Marine casualties amounted to 2,938 dead. In addition, 763 planes were lost during the campaign.

Japanese losses were much greater. The Thirty-second Army was destroyed. An estimated 110,000 Japanese were killed, and, surprisingly, 7,400 prisoners were taken. The kamikaze attacks that proved so successful against the Fifth Fleet had nevertheless cost Japan an estimated 7,800 aircraft. Okinawa's cities and towns were leveled and more than 80,000 civilians died, a portent for the future if the home islands had to be invaded.

In the impersonal calculus of war, despite the carnage and destruction, this most expensive of all Central Pacific operations was worth the sacrifice. Later, some critics characterized Buckner as a butcher and claimed that he should have established a line in the extreme south and let Ushijima and his men starve. This after-the-fact analysis could be applied to a number of other campaigns, including Peleliu, Bougainville, Saipan, and Luzon. Such criticism cannot deflect from the importance of the conquest of the island. Okinawa provided excellent fleet anchorages, and planes flying from the improved and lengthened runways of its airfields could attack Japan directly with minimal fear of retaliation. By July four heavy and five light and medium bomber groups were operating from these fields on a daily basis. B-29s began arriving in July, and plans called for twelve B-29 groups to operate from Okinawa by the time of the planned invasion of Japan. Furthermore, Tenth Army remained on the island and prepared for its part in Operation Coronet, scheduled for the spring of 1946.

Chapter 15

The Killing Time

LONG BEFORE THE Okinawa operation was concluded, the Joint Chiefs of Staff had instructed MacArthur and Nimitz to plan for the invasion of the Japanese home islands. During the preliminary stages of planning, the differences between army and navy strategists became apparent. Admirals King and Spruance wanted to seize positions on the south China coast and from there intensify the bombardment of Japan, as well as draw the blockade tighter. They argued that such a strategy might preclude the need to invade Kyushu and Honshu. MacArthur was openly critical of such undertakings. Any invasion of the China mainland would not be without cost, and the stepped-up bombing campaign and blockade might take years to bring about Japan's surrender. Admiral King abandoned his arguments for the China venture only after Nimitz joined MacArthur in recommending a two-step invasion of Japan. The Joint Chiefs responded on 25 May 1945 by issuing a directive that spelled out in general terms the responsibility of the army and navy in the projected invasion.

MacArthur's staff had already begun planning for the complex operation. Code-named Downfall, it was divided into two parts: Olympic and Coronet. For Olympic, Krueger's Sixth Army would invade southern Kyushu on 1 November 1945. The larger and more complex operation, Coronet, the conquest of Honshu, was planned for the spring of 1946 and would involve Eichelberger's Eighth Army and Gen. Courtney H. Hodges's First Army, which was to be transferred from Europe in the autumn of 1945. All the military and civilian planners—including President Truman, who approved the operation in June—were aware of the heavy casualties that would likely be incurred in an invasion of the Japanese home islands.

Major General Curtis LeMay, who had taken charge of XXI Bomber Command on 19 January after commanding XX Bomber Command in the China-Burma-India theater, was one who came to believe that an invasion of Japan might be unnecessary. Although the B-29s got off to a slow start from bases in the Marianas in the fall of 1944, LeMay continued the high-altitude raids on industrial targets begun by his predecessor, Brig. Gen. Haywood Hansell. By mid-February he was sending more than two hundred bombers on each mission. One such raid on 25 February 1945 convinced LeMay to change drastically the methods of attack and target selection. Although minimal damage was caused on that raid by 500-pound high-explosive bombs, poststrike photoreconnaissance showed that almost a square mile of Tokyo had been ignited by incendiaries.

LeMay, with General Arnold's approval, decided to load the B-29s with oil and napalm incendiaries, and ordered the attacks to be made at only five thousand to ten thousand feet altitude. He further decided to strip the bombers of guns and ammunition in order to increase their payload. Finally, he decided to launch full-scale attacks against Japan's five largest cities at night. This experiment ignored the notion so long held by American airmen of the efficacy of daylight precision bombing. If the experiment worked, XXI Bomber Command would be employing the same tactics as had the British in Europe: saturation area bombardment.

The American bombing campaign against Japan in 1945 was not motivated primarily by the desire to kill civilians. Rather it was a recognition of the impossibility of separating purely residential areas from neighboring factories. In addition, much small-scale manufacturing was done by shadow factories hidden among the dwellings, and much of the piecework was done by civilians in their homes. The Japanese people would pay a severe price for the demographics of their industry.

The first major raid following LeMay's new directives was on the night of 9–10 March, when 334 B-29s lifted off from four airfields in the Marianas and set course for Tokyo. Flying through inaccurate antiaircraft and night-fighter fire, the bombers set Tokyo aflame. The bombs and ensuing firestorm killed more than 83,000 people and wounded 41,000. The probability is that the casualties were actually much higher than these official figures. Intelligence later discovered that 267,000 buildings, one-fourth of Tokyo, had been destroyed and a million persons left homeless. No other single raid of the war, not even the atomic bomb attacks, was so destructive of life and property.

LeMay followed the Tokyo raid with four other massive strikes. The B-29s struck Nagoya on the night of 11–12 March, Osaka the next night, Kobe on the sixteenth, and Nagoya was hit again on the nineteenth. Eight square miles of Osaka were destroyed, almost one-fifth of Kobe was burned out, and four square miles of Nagoya burned. The March raids cost XXI Bomber Command only twenty B-29s destroyed and an additional seventy-five damaged. Most of these losses were from antiaircraft fire. Japanese pilots appeared reluctant to close with the big bombers even though some were flying the latest fighter aircraft, such as the army's Nakajima Ki-84 Frank, and the replacement for the Zero, the navy's Mitsubishi J2M Jack.

LeMay and Arnold reluctantly gave up the strategic air offensive at MacArthur's and Nimitz's request to aid the Okinawa offensive by hitting airfields in Kyushu, Shikoku, and Formosa. Not until 11 May did LeMay's bombers return in force over Honshu. However, the March raids proved conclusively that Japan's cities lay helpless before the planes of the Twentieth Air Force. Within a month the continuing attacks on Japan's five most important cities had destroyed 105 square miles of a total of 257. The number of B-29s lost was minimal compared to the destruction they wrought.

In late July, Army Air Forces command relationships in the Pacific were further reorganized. The Twentieth Air Force, until then directly controlled by General Arnold in Washington, was placed under Gen. Carl A. Spaatz, formerly commander of U.S. Strategic Air Forces, Europe. His headquarters was established on Guam. LeMay became Spaatz's chief of staff in early August, and Maj. Gen. Nathan Twining took over the Twentieth Air Force from LeMay, who had been given its command only a month earlier.

Before the projected invasion of Japan, XX Bomber Command was shifted from China to Okinawa to become part of the Eighth Air Force, recently arrived from England. In addition, VII Fighter Command, the bulk of whose planes were P-51s, was located on Iwo Jima. General Kenney's Far East Air Forces, headquartered on Okinawa, would continue to supply direct tactical and strategic support for MacArthur's operations. Washington expected coordination between the army air forces and the navy to be achieved by agreements between MacArthur, Spaatz, and Nimitz.

One example of cooperation predated the new command arrangements. Halsey's Third Fleet was drawing a noose around Japan. Naval air strikes on harbor and air facilities complemented those of the B-29s, and Admiral Lockwood's submarines were operating openly in the Sea of Japan and the China Sea against what was left of the Japanese merchant marine. Responding to Nimitz's request, the B-29s began to lay mines in the main channels leading to the key ports of the Inland Sea. As early as May 1945, more Japanese ships were sunk by mines than by submarine action. In July and August Japanese shipping losses amounted to 409,000 tons, nearly half by mines.

By July Japan was virtually cut off from mainland Asia, its major source of food and raw material. Most crucial was the lack of petroleum products. The remains of the fleet were immobilized; only nineteen destroyers and thirty-eight submarines with restricted range were available to counter the expected American landings. Shortages of gasoline hampered the air defenses, making it much easier for the B-29s and naval aircraft to bomb Japan at will.

Although the large-scale bombing raids, combined with naval air and sea operations, had isolated Japan from its far-flung empire and devastated its economic infrastructure, there were few signs that the Japanese government was even contemplating surrender. During the first four months of 1945, Imperial General Headquarters made a number of substantive changes to meet the American invasion expected by November. Six new area armies were to be formed and a call-up of the last of Japan's reserves would create forty-two new divisions. In mid-March the four remaining first-line divisions were recalled from Manchuria, leaving the Kwantung Army with only twelve divisions and no armor. Finally, on 15 April, the General

Defense Command headquarters was abolished and its strategic responsibilities were given to the army section in Imperial General Headquarters.

Operational command for the defense of Japan, code-named Ketsu-Go, was divided between Field Marshal Hajime Sugiyama, commanding the First General Army, and Field Marshal Shunroku Hata, commander of the Second General Army. Sugiyama controlled the Eleventh, Twelfth, and Thirteenth Area Armies, which had thirty infantry divisions, two armored divisions, twelve independent mixed brigades, and four tank brigades available for the defense of Honshu. Hata was expected to confront the projected first invasion on Kyushu with the Fifteenth and Sixteenth Area Armies, composed of twenty-three divisions, four independent mixed brigades, and three tank brigades. In all, Hata would have available more than six hundred thousand men to counter the invasion.

An Air General Army commanded by Gen. Masakazu Kawabe was formed in April 1945. Although hampered by the near destruction of the aircraft industry, Kawabe planned to have eight hundred army fighters and bombers supplemented by three thousand kamikazes to cooperate with the local army commands in their attempts to halt the Kyushu invasion on the beaches.

Even during this crucial planning stage, there was no supreme commander. The navy continued to jealously guard its separate status. The Naval General Command simply sought to settle differences with the army and air force by a series of agreements. The navy defined its role in the defense of Japan as trying to destroy as many enemy ships as possible. The navy planned to meet the American fleet at sea with five thousand aircraft, of which twenty-five hundred were training planes converted to kamikazes. Closer to shore, a second-line fleet composed of midget submarines (Koryu), suicide boats (Shinyo), and human torpedoes (Kaiten) awaited the invasion force.

All communications throughout the island nation were placed under a central agency, and civilians were expected to help defend their homeland. Civilian volunteers were recruited in the country districts and trained in the spring for guerrilla operations. Special suicide squads made up of military personnel and civilians were formed. Their objective was to knock out enemy tanks whose armor was too thick for the guns of the inferior Japanese tanks.

*   *   *

By the end of July plans for Operation Coronet were almost complete. Prior to the invasion, the general plan called for Kenney's Far East Air Forces on Okinawa and Ie Shima, in cooperation with the fast carrier forces, to destroy Japan's naval and air forces, port facilities, and sea and land communications. Spaatz's B-29s would continue to attack Japanese cities, concentrating after August upon those not yet targeted.

The rapid growth of the Pacific Fleet permitted Nimitz to reorganize it for the Kyushu invasion. Where previously there had been only one fleet in the theater, there would be two fleets—each larger than the single fleet operating prior to the Iwo Jima invasion. Halsey's Third Fleet was to be redesignated the 2d Fast Carrier Force and, as a preliminary to the landings, was to operate against the Kuriles, Hokkaido, and Honshu. Spruance's Fifth Fleet would become the 1st Fast Carrier Force, and included Turner's Amphibious Landing Force. The area assigned to Spruance's carriers included the western part of Honshu, Kyushu, and Shikoku. Air cover for the landings was to begin on D-minus-8 and was to be provided by fourteen fleet carriers, six light carriers, and thirty-six escort carriers. The Gunfire and Covering Force, consisting of thirteen older battleships, twenty-four cruisers, and thirty-eight destroyers, was also to begin firing on Honshu on D-minus-8.

Sixth Army's goal was to establish a defensible line in the south anchored on the city of Sendai in the west and Tsumo in the east. This would assure control of Kagoshima Bay, where port facilities were available for continuous supply of the defending troops. A series of airfields would be built behind this line in order to provide close air support for the invasion of Honshu early in 1946.

Krueger would command four corps with fourteen divisions. II Corps, made up of the 3d, 4th, and 5th Marine Divisions, was to land in the west just south of the town of Kushikuno. IX Corps, composed of the 81st and 98th Infantry Divisions, would be used as a decoy force, feinting as if to land near the entrance to the bay. The corps would then become the army's floating reserve. XI Corps, made up of the 43d, Americal, and 1st Cavalry Divisions, was to land on southeastern beaches on the shores of Ariake Bay. Farther north, I Corps, with the 25th, 33d, and 41st Divisions, would land at Miyazaki. If the fourteen divisions were not sufficient to secure southern Kyushu, Krueger could expect reinforcements of three divisions per month taken from the Honshu invasion force. Many of the Eighth Army units scheduled for action on the larger island would be combat divisions redeployed from Europe during the fall and winter of 1945.

Although the attention of high-level American planners in Washington, Guam, and Manila was focused primarily upon the air war and the projected invasion of Japan, there were still major campaigns being mounted against enemy-held territory in the Southwest Pacific. General Yamashita, who still commanded more than sixty-five thousand men in the hilly region northeast of Manila on Luzon, could not be ignored. It was obvious that Krueger's offensive against the Japanese redoubt had to continue until Yamashita's forces were destroyed.

There were three other areas where MacArthur either instigated or condoned operations which, at that stage of the war, were questionable. Chief among these was the southern Philippines, where Eichelberger's Eighth Army was conducting a complex series of amphibious operations. During the earlier New Guinea operations, MacArthur had followed a proven strategic policy of bypassing huge Japanese garrisons when these could not interfere with his main strategic goals. The Japanese in the southern Philippines, devoid of air and naval support, posed no threat to any action MacArthur planned either in completing the Luzon campaign or in launching Operation Coronet. But MacArthur saw the liberation of the Philippines as a debt of honor. He had promised the Filipino people that he would free them, and he did not intend for them to suffer any longer than necessary under Japanese control. It is not clear if the Joint Chiefs were aware that MacArthur intended to carry out the liberation until the operation was too far developed to interfere. Later explanations for MacArthur's decision referred to the necessity of projecting land-based airpower farther west to sever Japanese lines of communication and to act as cover for his projected campaign in the Dutch East Indies, yet another questionable plan.

Eichelberger, whose Eighth Army at the time included the Americal, 24th, 31st, 40th, and 41st Infantry Divisions and the 503d Parachute

Infantry Regiment, planned to make maximum use of Filipino guerrillas. There were an estimated thirty-three thousand guerrillas on Mindanao, and smaller yet effective groups on other islands. Air support would be provided by the Thirteenth Air Force from Morotai and Leyte, the Fifth Air Force from Mindoro, and four Marine Air Groups were available for close air support. The one major problem was the shortage of landing craft and close support vessels. Most of the light carriers and all the battleships had been returned to Nimitz and were being employed at Iwo Jima. The shortage of landing craft meant that the amphibious operations had to be executed sequentially. Fortunately, General Suzuki's Thirty-fifth Army units were not present in any great number on any of the islands except Mindanao, where he intended to make a stand with approximately forty-three thousand troops. The remainder of his 105,000 menwere scattered in smaller garrisons throughout the islands.

On 6 February Eichelberger was ordered to secure the island of Palawan. A week later he received instructions directing him to secure the Zamboanga Peninsula on Mindanao and the Sulu Archipelago, thus drawing a ring around the rest of the Japanese garrisons in the southern Philippines.

The first target, Palawan, is a large island 270 miles long by 20 miles wide. Intelligence reported fewer than two thousand Japanese troops there, concentrated in the hills around the town of Puerto Princesa. General Sibert, the X Corps commander, assigned the Palawan operation to the 41st Division's 186th Infantry Regiment. Landing unopposed on the northern shore of Puerto Princesa harbor, the leading elements quickly seized the town. The Japanese commander withdrew at first to the hills ten miles north of town but, because of lack of good defenses, was quickly driven farther into the interior.

By mid-April the 186th controlled most of Palawan and a number of smaller offshore islands. Construction crews had begun work on a new airfield but abandoned the work because of the nature of the soil and instead concentrated on improving the older Japanese airstrip. This was not completed in time to aid in operations against Mindanao. However, planes from there later struck at Japanese installations in southern China and Indochina.

The next objective for General Doe's 41st Division was the Zamboanga Peninsula. Supported by Marine SBDs flying from a prewar airstrip on the north side of the peninsula, the 162d Infantry landed on 10 March virtually unopposed. The Japanese commander withdrew his estimated eighty-nine hundred troops from Zamboanga city to the high ground three miles inland. The 162d entered the city the following day and began to pursue the Japanese. Filipino guerrilla forces blocked the east coast road and, after two weeks of heavy fighting, the Japanese defenses crumbled. Organized resistance ceased on 25 March as the Japanese were driven from the Mount Capisan area farther into the wild interior. Of the five thousand Japanese troops involved in the long retreat, only thirteen hundred survived the war.

On 2 April, before the Zamboanga operation ended, a battalion of the 163d Infantry Regiment landed on Sanga Sanga Island in the Tawitawi group in the Sulu Sea. The small Japanese garrison was quickly eliminated. Very soon, airfields on this island two hundred miles southwest of Zamboanga and only forty miles from Borneo would prove very helpful in covering the North Borneo invasion.

Eighth Army next launched three interconnected operations in the latter part of March. The first target was Panay, which was garrisoned by approximately 2,750 troops, most of whom guarded Iloilo town. Filipino guerrillas controlled the bulk of the island, and on 18 March the 40th Division's 185th Infantry landed west of Iloilo and quickly occupied it. In what was becoming a typical scenario, the Japanese retreated into the jungle-covered hilly interior. But the Americans did not follow the script. They instead turned over all operations on Panay to the guerrillas, who were still fighting the remaining Japanese at the close of the war.

The 40th Division's next objective was Negros, an island located south of Panay. Lieutenant General Takeshi Kono commanded a force of about 13,500 men there. On 29 March the 185th Infantry left Panay and landed on the west side of Guimaras Strait. It was later joined by the 160th Infantry. Kono had withdrawn the bulk of his forces approximately five miles into the interior and established two defensive lines. Although the Filipino guerrilla forces controlled more than two-thirds of the island, it took almost two months of heavy fighting in mountainous terrain before the Japanese defenses were broken. Even then, Kono withdrew farther into the interior. By early June Kono had lost an estimated four thousand men killed. When the Japanese finally surrendered in September, an additional thirty-three hundred had died of disease and starvation. Nevertheless, more than six thousand Japanese continued the struggle until they were finally convinced that Japan had lost the war.

The third major operation before the eastern Mindanao invasion was the attack on Cebu, a 150-mile-long island lying some thirty miles east of Negros. On the eastern side, Cebu city, the second largest city in the Philippines, was in ruins. Its harbor was large and excellent. MacArthur planned to use Cebu as a staging area for the Americal, 44th, and 91st Divisions for the invasion of Japan. General Suzuki, commander of the Thirty-fifth Army, was on Cebu but he delegated tactical command to Maj. Gen. Takeo Manjome, who deployed the bulk of his 14,500-man force near Cebu city.

Two infantry regiments, the 132d and 182d, of Maj. Gen. William H. Arnold's Americal Division, landed southwest of Cebu city near the town of Talisay on 26 March. The attack was halted briefly along the beaches by extensive minefields, but there was little opposition. General Manjome did not try to defend Cebu city, and elements of the 132d liberated it the following day.

The Japanese defenses in the hills to the north were bolstered by a great number of antiaircraft guns, and the defenders fought off a series of frontal attacks by the 182d Infantry. Although driven back an average of one mile in the central sector, the Japanese line held. On 10 April, Arnold committed the 164th Infantry to an attack on Manjome's right flank. At the same time, the 132d hit hill positions on the Japanese left flank as the 182d continued its frontal assault. The Japanese defenses finally collapsed and Manjome began withdrawing his remaining seventy-five hundred men on the seventeenth. Pursued by the guerrillas and two regiments from the Americal, the Japanese were broken up into small groups.

By mid-June the Americal was withdrawn from action to prepare for the invasion of Japan, and the guerrillas were left to harry the scattered Japanese. Fighting against a Japanese force of equal size, the Americal Division had not only secured most of Cebu, but at a cost of only 410 men killed. An estimated 5,500 Japanese died. There were still 8,500 Japanese on the island when the war ended.

As an adjunct to the campaign on Cebu, General Arnold sent a battalion of the 164th to nearby Bohol Island on 11 April. A reinforced company of approximately 350 Japanese attempted to hold a hill line against the Americans but most had been killed by 23 April. The survivors were pursued into the interior by regular infantry and guerrilla troops. In the meantime, the rest of the 164th made another amphibious landing on southern Negros on 26 April and began working with a Filipino guerrilla regiment. By mid-May the Japanese garrison of approximately 1,300 men had been almost totally destroyed. The remnants escaped into the interior where 800 would survive to surrender in August.

These two minor operations concluded Eighth Army activities in the central Visayan Islands. Whether one disagrees or not with the necessity of the Visayan operations, their success is unquestioned. The three main islands, each larger than any of the Caroline, Marshall, or Mariana Islands, had been secured with a loss of 835 killed and 2,300 wounded. The Japanese lost more than 10,000 men killed in action, and an additional 4,000 later died of disease and starvation.

The final large-scale Eighth Army operation in the southern Philippines was against the major Japanese concentration on Mindanao east of the Zamboanga Peninsula. There the Japanese had a force estimated at more than forty-three thousand men, the main elements of which were the 100th Division, the 32d Division, and the 32d Naval Special Base Force. Fortunately for X Corps, the Japanese command structure was a shambles. General Suzuki had been killed en route from Cebu, and his death left Lt. Gen. Gyosaku Morozumi in command. Morozumi chose to remain in tactical control of the 32d Division, leaving Lt. Gen. Jiro Harada to exercise separate operational control over the 100th Division and the naval troops defending the Davao area.

The U.S. 24th Division landed on 17 April near Parang on Illana Bay, a hundred miles west of Davao, and quickly moved east along one of the main highways and the Mindanao River. The division drove the Japanese from the key road junction at Kabacan on 23 April, effectively dividing the Japanese forces. After the 31st Division landed, General Sibert ordered a two-pronged attack. He sent the 124th Infantry up the Sayre Highway to capture Kibawe, forty-five miles to the north, as well as to investigate whether a trail from Kibawe led southeastward to Davao. If so, he intended to attack Harada's defenses from the rear. Sibert also sent the 34th and 19th Infantry Regiments east along Highway 1 toward the coastal town of Digos south of Davao.

The 124th encountered little resistance during its advance, and the 34th Infantry took Digos on 27 April. Much to MacArthur's surprise, it took only ten days for the 24th Division to fight its way across the island in the longest sustained land advance of the Pacific war. The 19th Infantry quickly passed through the 34th's lines and began to move northward along the coast toward Davao. Instead of attempting to hold the city, General Harada pulled back the bulk of his troops to a hill defense line approximately four miles inland, and the 19th Infantry moved into the bombed out shell of the city on 2 May.

Reinforced by the 162d Infantry, which had recently completed the Zamboanga operation, Sibert changed the axis of his attack to confront Harada's main defenses west of Davao. The renewed attack began on 30 April as elements of the 24th Division tried to break through the defenses in the hills overlooking the airport. After two weeks, the main Japanese defenses in the sector still held although the airport and a portion of the main highway were under American control. The 19th Infantry, after consolidating its control over the Davao area, attempted without success to clear the Japanese from their strong positions west of the Davao River. The 34th Infantry replaced the 19th and began a three-battalion frontal attack on 17 May. Farther west along the main highway, the 21st Infantry had begun to move north from the town of Mintal. Neither of these offensives produced significant gains, but Sibert persisted with his frontal assault. Very costly small-unit engagements occupied both regiments for the next two weeks. By the close of May, Harada's first line had been breached and he had lost half of his effectives in the sector.

Attacks against Harada's defenses east of the Davao River began on 29 May when the 19th Infantry struck westward against the naval unit's position at Mandog. By 9 June the last organized resistance along that line ended with the remaining Japanese retreating into the hills, where Filipino guerrillas were given the responsibility of mopping up. The 21st Infantry, operating on X Corps's left flank, seized the town of Wangon, the western anchor of Harada's line. By 10 June Harada's defenses had been overrun along a ten-mile front, and what was left of the 100th Division was in full retreat northward into the mountains. By then the Japanese had suffered 4,500 killed at a cost to the 24th Division of 350 dead and 1,600 wounded.

On 27 April General Eichelberger ordered Maj. Gen. Clarence Martin's 31st Division to move north against the Japanese 30th Division by advancing up the largely unfinished Sayre Highway. This was no easy task as it meant using landing craft to cross the Pulangi River, after which the advance would be hampered by deep gorges as the troops moved up to the higher plateau. The Japanese destroyed bridges as they fell back, forcing the engineers to build sixteen Bailey bridges and sixty-five wooden structures. Despite the problems of terrain and Japanese harassment, Kibawe town was captured within a week.

General Morozumi was surprised by the speed with which the 124th Infantry moved, but he counterattacked and pinned down its lead elements fifteen miles north of Kibawe for over a week until, on 12 May, U.S. artillery was brought up to end the stalemate. The Japanese battalion obstructing the advance had bought time for Morozumi to concentrate his forces around the town of Malaybalay preparatory to withdrawing into the Agusan Valley to the east.

General Eichelberger, worried about the problem of supplying the 31st Division, ordered the 40th Division's 108th Infantry Regiment to land on the southern end of Macajalar Bay on 10 May and to advance southward along the highway and link up with the 155th Infantry, which had replaced the exhausted 124th. On 15 May the 108th encountered a strong blocking force eighteen miles inland, where the road descends into a deep canyon. It took four days for the Japanese to be cleared from their defenses there. Finally, on 23 May, the two divisions made contact.

Morozumi had not employed his troops to best advantage along the highway, but that changed as he retreated into the mountains. He conducted a stubborn defense in that area, as did Harada to the southeast, against elements of the 24th, 31st, and 40th Divisions and organized Filipino guerrilla units. Although combat patrols continued to encounter Japanese elements until the close of the war, General Eichelberger declared eastern Mindanao secure on 30 June. As late as August, 22,250 Japanese troops were still operating in the interior. During the long Mindanao campaign, more than 10,000 Japanese were killed and an estimated 8,000 more succumbed to disease and starvation.

The complex conquest of the southern Philippines, for all practical purposes, was completed by the time of General Eichelberger's announcement. It had been a planning triumph for Eichelberger and his staff, and all army units had performed in an exemplary fashion. Considering the many difficulties involved, the cost of conquering the southern islands had been relatively light. The Eighth Army lost 2,070 men killed and 6,990 wounded.

The Eighth Army campaign was conducted at the same time as the final stages of the conquest of Luzon by Sixth Army. On 22 March, even before the invasion of Palawan, troops from the 1st Cavalry Division in southern Luzon had begun to swing east from Lake Taal to capture Mauban on Lamon Bay. The 11th Airborne Division's 511th PIR moved eastward along the south shore of Lamon Bay, and by 14 April had entered the Bicol Peninsula. Pursuit of the Japanese continued as far as the town of Naga, west of Mount Isarog. There the 511th was joined by the 158th Infantry Regiment, which had landed at Legaspi on 1 April. The two regiments cleared southern Luzon of all organized resistance by 2 May. Meanwhile, the 182d Infantry, operating in the Eighth Army zone of action, secured northwestern Samar, and a battalion from the 108th Infantry neutralized Masbate Island.

The campaign against Yamashita's Shobu Group in northern Luzon remained the most difficult and time consuming of all the operations in the Philippines. The breakthrough by I Corps at Santa Fe in early May caused Yamashita to speed up his plans to withdraw most of his troops over back roads and trails into the Cordillera Central. In order to achieve this, he left skeleton forces to deny Sixth Army the Cagayan Valley as long as possible.

Krueger's plan was to move the 37th Division up through Bambang into the valley as elements of the 11th Airborne Division made a drop farther north. After a composite task group moved into extreme northern Luzon paralleling the west coast and entered Aparri unopposed on 15 June, the paratroopers moved south against very little opposition and linked up with the 37th Division on 26 June. By then, except for pursuit and mopping up, all of northern Luzon was controlled by I Corps.

Meanwhile, the 25th Division kept the remnants of Yamashita's 10th Division from joining him. Thrusting southeastward from Aritao, the 25th inflicted heavy losses on the Japanese, forcing them deep into the Sierra Madre Mountains between Highways 4 and 11. That was the situation when MacArthur removed both Sixth Army and I Corps headquarters from further operational responsibility in order for Krueger's and Swift's staffs to begin planning for the invasion of Kyushu. Responsibility for the destruction of Shobu Group thus fell to Eichelberger's Eighth Army and Griswold's XIV Corps.

The final attacks on Yamashita's defenses began in early July in the middle of the rainy season. With the 32d division attacking from the southwest, the 6th from the east along Highway 4, and the USAFIP(NL) moving eastward along the same route, the Japanese enclave was slowly reduced in a series of desperate small-unit actions. Yamashita had chosen well the position for Shobu Group's last stand. The terrain was among the most difficult encountered on Luzon, with steep hills, deep ravines, and gullies. The Japanese troops were still dangerous, and when cornered would fight to the end. But they were on the edge of starvation. Their supplies had almost run out, and prisoners told of the deterioration of morale. By mid-August the area in the Asin Valley still controlled by the Japanese was only seven miles wide by nine miles long. Approximately fifty-two thousand troops, a much larger number than American intelligence had estimated, were forced into this enclave at the time of the Japanese surrender. Indicative of the Shobu Group's will to resist the three divisions pressing in on them was the high toll the Americans paid during the last month of the war, when U.S. casualties on Luzon amounted to 1,650 men.

As Yamashita walked out of the Asin Valley to surrender on 15 August, he must have been aware that he had achieved all the goals he had established for the Fourteenth Army prior to the American landings. Although his casualties were massive—approximately

95,000 of his 150,000 men—he still had a large force in being after seven and one-half months of combat. His Fourteenth Army had pinned down four U.S. infantry divisions, one separate regiment, an armored group, a parachute division, the USAFIP(NL), and thousands of Filipino guerrillas. Even in August, Eichelberger had to commit three reinforced divisions to the attack on the Asin enclave. Yamashita's forces inflicted 37,870 casualties on MacArthur's armies, including 8,310 killed in action. It took the emperor's decision to surrender to force Yamashita's capitulation.

As American forces completed the occupation of the Philippines, secured Iwo Jima and Okinawa, and prepared to invade Japan, there was yet another active theater of operation far from the forward action. Thousands of Japanese troops had been bypassed in New Guinea, New Britain, and Bougainville. Their major preoccupation in the last year of the war was to find enough food to stay alive. Except for encounters with patrols, these units posed no danger to the Allied bases established on those islands, and conquest of the areas under Japanese control would not contribute in the slightest to ending the war.

Despite the inconsequential nature of the Japanese presence in these once key areas, the Australian high command ignored the American policy of simply maintaining a strong perimeter defense around the lodgments they had established. Instead, the Australians ordered full-scale offensives against the surviving main elements on the three islands. General Blamey, defending this policy after the war, claimed that it was preferable to allowing the Australian army to vegetate, a decision that was hardly applauded by the Australian infantrymen called upon to fight the jungle, rain, and disease in addition to the Japanese—who were likewise forced into battles they did not want.

The attitude of Australia's senior military leaders appears to have been a reaction to the secondary role assigned Australian troops after 1943. After having promised to use Australian troops on Leyte, MacArthur changed his mind and left the two Australian armies to guard what had become strategic backwaters. MacArthur and his staff, primarily interested in the Philippine campaign and later the planning for the Kyushu invasion, left Blamey and the Australians to their own devices and did not interfere with their aggressive plans.

On New Guinea, Lt. Gen. Sir Vernon Sturdee, commander of the First Army, had two divisions in the general area where contact with the Japanese could be expected: the 5th Division at Madang and the 6th at Aitape. The latter unit, commanded by Maj. Gen. Sir Jack Stevens, was used to destroy what was left of the Japanese Eighteenth Army. The 6th Division's three brigades had by mid-November 1944 relieved the last elements of the American XI Corps and begun aggressive patrolling southward from the main coastal base at Aitape.

The Japanese commander, General Adachi at Wewak, had three greatly understrength divisions: one located twenty miles inland at Bolif, another at But, twenty-five miles west of Wewak, and a third in and around Wewak. He had no air force or naval support, and his store of ammunition was slight. Medical supplies were almost nonexistent, and huge areas in the immediate interior were brought under cultivation to maintain survival rations for his thirteen-thousand-man army.

The Australian forces did not suffer from these problems, but there were other factors that made the coming campaign an ordeal for the Australian foot soldiers. New Guinea's terrain, vegetation, insects, and rain adversely affected all the troops who fought there. However, the Americans had been able to capitalize on their amphibious capability and thus bypass much of the rugged interior. But Stevens had no landing craft when he began his offensive toward Wewak. So his troops had to hack their way overland to their objective.

The first major actions in the seven-month campaign were conducted south of Aitape in an effort to cut the Japanese supply line between the villages of Malin and Amani and ultimately to Bolif. By the end of January, the 17th Brigade had secured its immediate objectives around the village of Walum and forced the elements of two Japanese regiments farther to the east. During the next two months the brigade sent company-sized probes deep into the Torecelli Mountains, forcing the Japanese to regroup near Marpik village. Marpik fell on 12 April after some severe fighting. An airstrip was quickly constructed and this enabled supplies to be more efficiently and quickly brought forward to the lead units.

In the meantime, the 16th Brigade reached Abai on the coast after relieving the 19th Brigade and continued to advance against only slight Japanese resistance. The town of But, which had housed Adachi's headquarters, was taken in mid-March and the Australians quickly crossed the Dagua River. The scale of the fighting can be judged by the fact that when the 16th was relieved by the 19th Brigade in early May, it had lost only 85 killed and 192 wounded in three months of fighting. An estimated 900 Japanese were killed during the same period.

The Australians were finally in a position to assault Wewak, which they believed would be vigorously defended. Stevens and his subordinate commanders were pleasantly surprised at the ease with which this one-time Eighteenth Army headquarters town was captured on 9 May. Adachi, after deciding that he did not have sufficient forces to defend Wewak, had begun to pull out even before the Australians attacked. After finding a few landing craft, Stevens sent a portion of the 19th Brigade by sea to Dove Bay to cut off the Japanese retreat to the east. The maneuver forced the Eighteenth Army away from the coast and into the hilly areas to the south. At the close of the war, Adachi's forces were defending an arc facing northwest, still only about twenty miles from Wewak.

One restriction on more ambitious Australian activity was the condition of the attacking units. Although the 6th Division lost only 442 killed and 1,141 wounded, from the time it relieved the U.S. XI Corps until the close of the war, disease took a terrible toll: more than 16,000 men were admitted to the hospital during that period.

The end of the questionable Wewak offensive came when General Adachi, whose reluctant defense had cost an additional 9,000 Japanese lives, came out of the hills on 13 September to surrender his remaining force to Maj. Gen. Sir Horace Robertson at Cape Wom.

A further example of Australian aggressiveness that accomplished little was the New Britain offensives. Located northeast of New Guinea, the 320-mile-long island is dominated by a mountain chain whose peaks rise to eight thousand feet, separating the wide northern coastal plain from its more narrow counterpart to the south. There are few good landing areas along the north shore; the best ones are found in the numerous bays at the southern end of the island. Rabaul, the once dominating air and naval base, is located in the extreme east on the Gazelle Peninsula, a fifty-square-mile extension described by Open Bay to the north and Wide Bay to the south. The monsoon season, which lasts from December through April, inundates the jungle with heavy daily rains. The U.S. marines who seized the Allied footholds at Cape Gloucester and Arawe in the west considered operations on New Britain to be more difficult than on Guadalcanal. After seizing bases in the west, American forces were generally content to establish firm defenses around their lodgments and to rely upon their patrol activity and Australian-led native guerrillas to keep them informed of Japanese activities in the midpart of the island. The American 40th Division's main concentration was at Cape Gloucester, but there was a regiment in the Talasea-Cape Hoskins area on the north coast and a battalion at Arawe. The major forces of the Japanese and Americans were thus separated by three hundred miles—and neither wished to upset the status quo. All this changed when the Australian 5th Division replaced the 40th.

The Australian commander, Maj. Gen. Sir Alan Ramsay, faced the same problems as his counterpart on New Guinea. The lack of sufficient landing craft made it very difficult to undertake large-scale amphibious operations, so his three brigades would be forced to conduct long, exhausting land operations. Such considerations did not deter Ramsay or his superiors. Believing that Gen. Hitoshi Imamura had only thirty-five thousand troops, most of whom were on the Gazelle Peninsula, Ramsay planned to force the Japanese from the long stretch then separating Allied and Japanese bases. In November 1944 he mustered enough naval support to land a battalion at Jacquinot Bay, two hundred miles east of Arawe. This became his major forward base, and an airstrip was constructed there in May 1945. On the north shore, Ramsay moved elements forward to the village of Ea Ea on Hison Bay. Operating from these positions, the Australians then secured the bays to the north and south of Gazelle Peninsula. In late February 1945 the northern and southern Australian forces linked up and began conducting aggressive patrols that isolated the peninsula. In the meantime, native guerrilla forces were conducting a campaign to exterminate small Japanese outposts in the middle of the island.

Once his forces reached the Gazelle Peninsula, General Ramsay ordered two minor offensives along the coast. Finding the Japanese positions well defended, he contented himself with aggressive patrolling in all sectors for the final four months of the war. One reason for this newfound reticence was the revised estimate of fifty thousand Japanese troops on the island. This estimate, which was still much too low, no doubt gave the Australian command reason to pause as the 5th Division had fewer than twenty thousand effectives.

One of the great mysteries of the South Pacific campaigns is General Imamura's quiescence. Elsewhere, Japanese commanders had maintained a spirited defense despite suffering crushing losses. When the war ended, Imamura controlled four army divisions and the equivalent of another division of naval troops. Yet Imamura did not launch any significant counterattacks. He deployed fewer than fifteen hundred men forward of his defensive line. Fortunately for the Australians, Imamura was content to wait out the war in the Gazelle Peninsula. In the end, 53,200 soldiers and 16,200 naval personnel surrendered to the Australians.

Although the Australian soldiers on New Britain had acquitted themselves as well as their counterparts in any theater, the situation there in August 1945 would have been the same if they had simply continued the American policy of containment.

At about the same time that General Stevens's 6th Division was replacing American forces on New Guinea, Blamey sent Lt. Gen. Stanley G. Savige's Australian II Corps to Bougainville. American forces had established a defensible perimeter around Empress Augusta Bay, and in early 1944 the Americal and 32d Divisions had fought off a major Japanese effort to dislodge them. Suffering heavily in the attempt, General Hyakutake's forces retreated southward. From that time on, except for patrol clashes, the Americans and Japanese on Bougainville maintained an unofficial truce. General Griswold, the U.S. XIV Corps commander, understood that all strategic objectives on Bougainville had been met and he was not prepared to sacrifice lives for nothing. General Hyakutake, with his army cut off from outside supplies, ordered more than half of his available force to cultivate large areas near his headquarters in the large southern town of Buin. He, too, was satisfied with the status quo.

General Savige, who had participated in the tactical planning for the use of Australian troops in the Southwest Pacific, implemented a more aggressive policy immediately after assuming command of the island on 22 November. On 23 December Savige ordered a three-pronged offensive. He planned to force the Japanese back to the Bonis Peninsula in the north while conducting vigorous patrols aimed at cutting the Japanese lines of communication running through the highlands in the central region. The main arena would be in the south, however, where the bulk of the Japanese forces were located.

The offensive in the central section of the island began on 30 December. Within two days, Pearl Ridge, a key objective, had been reached. From there the Australians could observe both coasts and begin their long-range combat patrols. These, combined with the use of native troops, secured most of the central highlands west of Keita by mid-1945.

In early January the 11th Brigade began its offensive in the northwest. Strong Japanese resistance slowed the brigade's advance, but by 6 February these defenses, too, had been broken. In a series of small-unit actions in the interior over the next two weeks, the Australians cut off escape routes to the south. Land and amphibious attacks against Soraken Point were eventually successful, and by the end of March the Japanese had been forced back to the base of the Bonis Peninsula, where they held their lines until the end of the war.

The main Australian effort was directed southeastward along the western coastline with the ultimate objective of destroying the Japanese main force and capturing Buin. That offensive was hampered more by the terrain and weather than by the Japanese defenses. Between the Pagana River and Buin were nine large rivers, swampland, and intermittent jungle. There were only two reasonably good roads paralleling the coast, and the Australian advance kept close to these. Australian engineers, even before the rains, were kept busy bridging the streams and widening and cording the roads so that heavy equipment could be brought up.

Lieutenant General Masatane Kanda, who succeeded Hyakutake

in February, decided not to contest the Australian advance north of the Pagana River and offered only token resistance until the enemy had advanced as far as the Hongorai River. Nevertheless, the Australian 7th Brigade, after a month of operations in the swamps and dense undergrowth, had gone only twelve miles. Then, with air support from RAAF planes based at Torokina, the brigade broke into the open and took Mosigetta town, one of the key initial objectives, on 11 February. The subsequent advance to Toko ten miles south on the coast was rapid, and that town became the Australians' major forward supply base.

General Kanda mounted a series of counterattacks against the brigade's positions astride the coastal road on 30 March. Although threatening, the attacks were contained—as were another series that began on 5 April. These failures cost the Japanese approximately six hundred dead. Since the beginning of the offensive, the Australians had destroyed almost two entire Japanese regiments. After being checked on 5 April, Kanda pulled his forward elements back to his Hongorai River defense line.

Savige halted his own offensive to allow engineers to improve the roads, after which he brought up an armored regiment equipped with Mark II Matilda medium tanks. When operations resumed at the end of April, the Australians launched two parallel movements. By 17 May they had reached the upper Hongorai, where Savige replaced the worn-out 7th Brigade with the relatively fresh 15th Brigade. These troops breached the Hongorai defenses and by 24 June were at the Miro River, less than twenty miles from Buin. Kanda pulled in all available troops and positioned them in a horseshoe-shaped perimeter around Buin.

Savige and his staff scheduled the final offensive to begin on 10 July but nature intervened. Rain, which had been a daily occurrence and had inconvenienced the Australians, halted all offensive activity. Beginning on 3 July the downpour continued for four weeks. Almost all the bridges so laboriously built were washed away, and the roads became seas of mud. The tired infantrymen, many of whom had already questioned the need for this aggressive campaign, became even more miserable. The offensive was rescheduled for the latter part of August, but the end of the war nullified the plan and saved thousands of Australian and Japanese lives.

Nevertheless, the Australian offensive had taken a heavy toll of lives for the small advantage gained. After March 1944, who controlled the most territory on Bougainville was of absolutely no consequence. When Kanda surrendered there were still 15,000 army and 6,000 naval personnel on the island, all that was left of an original garrison of more than 65,000 troops. Savige's six-month campaign cost the Japanese an estimated 18,000 men who were killed outright or died of wounds and disease. Australian casualties amounted to 516 dead and 1,572 wounded.

If the decision to carry forward questionable offensive actions on New Guinea, New Britain, and Bougainville can be attributed primarily to General Blamey and the Australian War Cabinet, such was not the case with the Borneo operation. At first conceived by Churchill and the British Imperial General Staff to aid in the ultimate reconquest of Malaya and Singapore, it was later embraced fully by MacArthur's headquarters. On 3 February 1945 MacArthur informed General Marshall, when requesting a greater allotment of ships and landing craft, that he considered the seizure of the Borneo oil fields to be of utmost importance. MacArthur was informed that more shipping could not be made available until the war in Europe ended. Marshall then made the trenchant observation that a Borneo campaign would have little effect on the outcome of the Pacific war. But MacArthur persisted, pointing to the advantage of restoring the territory to the Netherlands East Indies authorities. The British by then had gone on record opposing the use of men and materiel in Borneo because Brunei Bay, which was proposed as a naval base, was too far from the main action and would not be ready for use until early 1946. Nevertheless, with more transport available, the Combined Chiefs of Staff in April approved a plan to land the Australian I Corps on Tarakan Island on 1 May, Brunei Bay on 10 June, and at Balikpapan in the southeast on 1 July.

The discussions between various commands concerning Borneo brought out latent problems between MacArthur and Blamey that also involved the Australian government. Beginning in the fall of 1943, Prime Minister Curtin's government was under pressure to cut back on the number of troops. Gradually, the size of the Australian army was reduced from a high of twelve divisions in 1942 to six infantry divisions and two armored brigades by the spring of

1945. MacArthur in turn ordered Blamey to commit all of these to continuous operations on Borneo. Curtin and the War Cabinet were perturbed by this.

Although he finally agreed to MacArthur's East Indies strategy, Blamey was outraged by the proposed command structure. Lieutenant General Sir Leslie Morshead's I Corps was to be placed directly under the American Eighth Army headquarters, which would direct the campaign. Blamey, appointed as commander of Allied ground forces in the theater in 1942, had been ignored by MacArthur after the Lae campaign. Although he retained the title, Blamey actually exercised command only over Australians. But even that authority was to be taken away from him for the Borneo campaign. Still smarting over broken promises concerning the use of Australian troops in the Philippines, Blamey met with MacArthur in Manila on 14 March and effected a compromise. Morshead's troops, for operational purposes, would not come under Eighth Army but would be placed directly under MacArthur. Blamey's headquarters would be responsible for all administrative details. Although this confrontation in retrospect may appear minor, the compromise effectively gave the Australians full tactical control of the Borneo operation since MacArthur's staff was more concerned with winding down the Philippines operations and planning for the Kyushu invasion.

The first target in the East Indies was the pear-shaped island of Tarakan, located a few miles off the northwest coast of Borneo. The island is fifteen miles long and eleven miles wide. The only major town was Tarakan, located two miles from the three proposed landing beaches at Lingkas. The major objective was the airfield sited four miles away. The island's interior was heavily overgrown and the two thousand Japanese infantry there could take advantage of numerous hills and ravines.

On 30 April a commando detachment seized the small island of Sadau west of Tarakan, and a battalion of artillery moved in and set up its guns to help support the landings. Prior to the landings, the beach areas were pounded by escort ships, and the air force flew three hundred interdiction sorties. The Australian 2d Brigade Group, some thirteen thousand strong, began landing at 0800 on 1 May. Despite sporadic resistance, by the end of the day it had consolidated its hold on a secure lodgment south of the town. By 5 May

Tarakan town and the airfield had been taken, and Netherlands East Indies civil affairs personnel moved in.

True to form, the Japanese commander on Tarakan moved the bulk of his force into the interior and contested every major hill. By mid-May the entire southern part of the island had been captured, but it took another month to clear the interior. The Australian infantry patrols engaged in these deadly small-unit engagements cooperated well with tactical air, which at times included low-flying B-24 bombers.

Conquest of the island cost the Australians 225 killed and 669 wounded. Almost the entire Japanese garrison was wiped out—a total of 1,540 killed. In return, the Allies gained an airfield that was in such bad condition that it could not be repaired in time to support subsequent landings.

The next objective in Borneo was Brunei Bay, the best harbor in the northwestern part of the island. The thirty-mile-wide bay is protected by a group of small islands of which Labuan is the largest. The region is the most heavily populated in all of north Borneo. A light railway connected it to Jesseltown to the north. There were few roads at the time; the easiest routes into the interior were by the many rivers, but these are normally bordered by swamp land. The interior regions are also hilly and heavily forested. All of this limited Australian activity.

But the interior was populated by native Dyaks who hated the Japanese. In late 1943, groups of Dyaks led by Chinese from the Brunei Bay region rebelled. The uprising had been put down with typical Japanese ferocity. By 1945 there were four organized guerrilla bands led by British officers operating against Japanese outposts and lines of communication. They had even cleared underbrush and trees for a small airfield.

Labuan was a major target not only because of its location, but because of its airfield and petroleum storage facilities. The major Allied objectives in this area of British Borneo were Brunei town and the oil fields at coastal Seria and inland at Miva. Once the bay and oil fields were secure, a defensive perimeter would be established and the main work of recontructing the port and oil production facilities could begin.

Defense of the Brunei Bay area was the responsibility of the 56th

Independent Mixed Brigade, a part of Lt. Gen. Masao Baba's Thirty-seventh Army. The main part of the brigade was located at Jessel-town, over a hundred miles northwest of the bay. The Japanese had only fifteen hundred troops in the vicinity of Brunei town. The Australian unit chosen for the operation, code-named Oboe 6, was the veteran 9th Division commanded by Maj. Gen. George Wootten. The landings on 10 June were made on schedule and with only slight opposition. Landing beaches for the 24th Brigade were at Victoria Harbor on Labuan, while part of the 20th Brigade cleared Muana Island and the rest made the main effort on two beaches on the southern hook of the bay. Using Brunei River, the Australians reached the airfield by the twelfth and the following day occupied battered Brunei town. In the first four days, one battalion moved seventeen miles northward along the bay while another probed the immediate interior.

Meanwhile, the 24th Brigade had landed on Labuan with little opposition and seized the airfield and Labuan town as the Japanese defenders retreated northward. General MacArthur, taking a grand tour of the southern Philippines aboard the cruiser *Boise,* decided to proceed farther south to watch the Labuan landings. While driving toward the town with General Morshead on the first day ashore, MacArthur was informed that two Japanese hiding in a culvert along their route had been killed just minutes before. Without further mishap, and satisfied with the progress of the Australians, he left the same day for Manila. By 12 June, tanks had been landed and within two days all of the island had been cleared of Japanese except for a twelve-hundred-by-six-hundred-yard area west of the main road that the Australians called the Pocket. The Australians pounded the area with artillery and naval gunfire for two days. Finally, on 21 June, two infantry companies moved into the Pocket to eliminate most of the dazed defenders. Engineers and construction crews moved onto the island within days, and by the last week of July a wharf for Liberty ships, ten large oil storage tanks, and a runway had been constructed, and the roads in southern Labuan had been improved.

On the mainland, the 20th Brigade advanced into the interior along the rail line and up the rivers. One of the main objectives, the town of Beaufort, located twenty miles inland on the Padas River, was taken on 27 June. Although defended by an estimated one thousand troops, there was little fighting as the Japanese withdrew farther into the interior. The Australians set up a firm perimeter and from then onward contented themselves with vigorous patrolling.

In early July a battalion was sent northward along the coast to establish an outpost twenty miles north of Cape Nosang, while other units took the town of Seria, sixty miles to the south, and later the port town of Lutong. Seria was the site of a major oil field and, before retiring, the Japanese set fire to thirty-seven of the wells. It took three months' labor by more than two thousand troops to extinguish the fires. The older Miva field was captured intact.

By early July the Japanese had conceded Brunei Bay and its immediate area to the Australians. General Wootten had no intention of pursuing them into the interior with large forces. Instead, regular patrols and actions by native guerrillas sufficed to keep the lodgment safe. The British Borneo civil affairs unit began rebuilding the shattered towns and providing services for more than seven thousand civilians. Among these were many freed prisoners of the Indian army who reported on the savage treatment accorded them during their captivity and the wanton killings by Japanese troops even as they retreated.

While the 9th Division was still engaged at Brunei Bay, the third phase of the Borneo operation, code-named Oboe 2, began. Blamey had protested vehemently that the seizure of the Balikpapan area in southern Borneo was unnecessary, particularly after the Combined Chiefs canceled plans to invade Java later. The Japanese were being systematically destroyed in more active areas. The Okinawa and Philippines operations were almost finished, Gen. Sir William J. Slim's Fourteenth Army had taken Rangoon, and LeMay's bombers continued to devastate Japan. MacArthur, however, was adamant, so the Australian 7th Division, not active since the Ramu Valley campaign on New Guinea in 1944, was transported to Morotai in preparation for the largest Australian amphibious operation of the war.

The Japanese had an estimated four thousand troops in the vicinity of Balikpapan, and fifteen hundred more near Samarinda in the immediate interior. Despite the eighteen big coast defense guns and a large number of dual-purpose and antiaircraft guns mounted in the hills and ridges overlooking the harbor, it was obvious to the Japanese commanders that they could not hold out long against the overwhelming Australian force. Instead, they planned to briefly contest the Australian moves toward the southern towns of Klandasan and Balikpapan before retiring into the hinterland.

The 7th Division, commanded by Maj. Gen. E. J. Milford, would ultimately number over thirty-three thousand men with attached troops. Besides a full complement of artillery, it also had two squadrons of Matilda tanks and one of Frogs (flamethrowing tanks). Vice Admiral Barbey commanded the attack force, which, in addition to the troop transports, included five American, one Netherlands, and two Australian cruisers, and nine destroyers. A task group of three carriers and their escorts provided air cover for the landings, while the Fifth and Thirteenth Air Forces supplied strategic support.

The sixteen-day saturation by Allied cruisers was the longest sustained naval bombardment of the war. Five days before the landings, B-24, B-25, and P-38 aircraft began systematic bombing and strafing attacks in the invasion area. The navy also undertook the difficult task of removing mines from the entrance to Balikpapan harbor, the most heavily mined area in the Southwest Pacific.

As planned, three brigades began landing on three beaches just east of Klandasan at 0900 on 1 July 1945 after a final tremendous preinvasion bombardment. One battalion of the 18th Brigade quickly moved westward along the coast against minor resistance and captured Klandasan, then turned north to enter Balikpapan. Another battalion attacked a major hill complex southeast of the port and quickly captured the heights and the cracking station. Balikpapan fell on 3 July. Meanwhile, two battalions from the 25th Brigade moved north and east, securing the inland hill lines and the Sepinggang airstrip. By the evening of the third the Australians had captured both major towns, two airstrips, and held a lodgment five miles wide by one mile deep.

A drenching rain fell as elements of the 21st Brigade moved five miles eastward up the coast to secure the Manggar airfield. Despite the many pillboxes and fortified caves, Japanese resistance was minimal largely because of the continuous pounding of these positions by bombers, division artillery, and the big guns of the supporting cruisers.

Most of the fighting after 5 July was along the two main roads, the Milford Highway leading north and the Vasey Highway leading east. By 9 July all major objectives had been secured, and on the twenty-first General Milford decided to halt. Aggressive patrolling became the order around the perimeter, and this resulted in a number of sharp clashes with small groups of Japanese. The last such engagement took place in the eastern area on 9 August.

The very quick collapse of the Japanese defenses was a pleasant surprise for the Australians, who had expected heavier casualties than they sustained. The operation was well handled, with excellent cooperation between all the forces involved. However, the Balikpapan operation, conducted so much later than the other Borneo operations, was even more questionable than those at Tarakan and Brunei Bay. Furthermore, after cancellation of plans to invade Java, the entire Borneo campaign became redundant and strategically useless.

The bombing assaults against Japan's major cities by the Twentieth Air Force and Nimitz's two huge naval task forces continued while MacArthur's forces wrapped up the Philippines campaigns and the Australians assumed the offensive farther south. Although MacArthur visited with Eichelberger on Mindanao and with Morshead on Labuan and at Balikpapan, he remained primarily concerned with overseeing the development of plans for the coming invasions of Japan. However necessary the projected invasions, the assaulting troops would confront hundreds of thousands of soldiers backed by a patriotic and aroused civilian population—all prepared to die defending their homeland. Allied casualties, based upon a similar loss ratio to that experienced on Okinawa, were projected at over one million. Japanese military and civilian casualties would likely be many times more. Whether or not that dark forecast was accurate will never be known. Thanks to events far from the Pacific theater, all the plans for the massive assault on Japan would soon be shelved.

Chapter 16

Unconditional Surrender

DESPITE FRENZIED PREPARATIONS by the Japanese to meet the expected American invasion, there was no adequate defense against the B-29s. The Japanese high command was hoarding the last of its aircraft for kamikaze attacks on the landing force. After being released from interdiction raids against Japanese bases on Formosa, Honshu, and Shikoku, on 17 June LeMay's planes again began bombing Japanese cities.

There were few viable targets left in Tokyo, Yokohama, Kobe, Osaka, and Nagoya, so the huge bombers were turned loose on Japan's secondary cities. Planes would fly over the targeted areas before a raid and drop leaflets to inform civilians of the projected bombing so that as many as possible could escape. Normally, four cities would be attacked at night simultaneously, with a wing of B-29s assigned to each city. Between the end of June and 14 August there were sixteen such attacks on fifty smaller industrial towns, the bombers dropping fifty-four thousand tons of incendiaries.

Some indication of the effectiveness of these raids can be seen by viewing the destruction in four of these towns. Tsu was 54 percent destroyed, Aomori 64 percent, and Ichinomiya 75 percent. On 1 August Toyama, a city of 125,000 persons, was 99.5 percent destroyed. So successful were the B-29 raids that LeMay concluded that if the bombers maintained the pace, the Twentieth Air Force would have no viable targets after October.

The Third Fleet imposed a veritable blockade of Japan after surviving a major typhoon in early January. Three task groups from TF 38, each built around three *Essex*-class carriers and two light carriers, began systematic strikes on exposed Japanese targets on 1 July. On 10 July planes from Admiral McCain's task force hit the dozen or more airfields located on the Tokyo plain. Although damaging facilities, very few aircraft were destroyed because the Japanese had carefully concealed their remaining planes. Three days later northern Honshu and southern Hokkaido, heretofore immune from major attacks, were heavily bombed, and a large number of coal-carrying ferries and colliers were sunk.

At the same time, a part of McCain's task force made up of three battleships and two cruisers bombarded the iron works at Kamaishi, halting production. Another segment of the battle fleet blasted the large iron and steel complex at Wanishi on Hokkaido. Other surface ships destroyed a large part of the radar and electronics center at Hitachi.

On 24 July, and again four days later, planes from TF 38 attacked the Kure and Kobe naval bases, sinking the battleships *Haruna, Ise,* and *Hyuga,* and damaging two cruisers and three of Japan's remaining aircraft carriers.

Bad weather prevented the task force from striking during the first week in August. However, on 9 August, devastating naval strikes against a concentration of suicide bombers hidden away in northern Honshu resulted in the destruction of an estimated 250 enemy planes. Japan was being battered to pieces by sea and air even before the first atomic bomb was dropped.

That awesome weapon was the crowning achievement of American science and technology. Its antecedents are found in the work of theoretical physicists mainly in Europe during the interwar period. In October 1939, two expatriate scientists, Leo Szilard and Eugene P. Wigner, aware of the destructive potential of the newly discovered process of nuclear fission, persuaded Albert Einstein to write a letter to President Roosevelt suggesting the possibility of constructing a bomb with tremendous destructive power. The president appointed a committee of scientists to investigate. However, little was done until reports from Europe in mid-1941 indicated that the Germans were working on such a device and that a team of scientists led by Werner K. Heisenberg were considerably ahead of researchers in Britain and the United States. Vannevar Bush, one of the president's most important scientific advisers, confirmed that a fission bomb might be constructed by early 1945.

In December 1941 the Office of Scientific Research and Development was established, and in August 1942 the Manhattan Project—which nuclear research and governed the construction of an atomic bomb—was begun. The man chosen to administer this most costly scientific program of World War II was Brig. Gen. Leslie R. Groves, an engineer known for his administrative ability.

The project left the theoretical sphere on 2 December 1942 when Enrico Fermi's team, operating in a laboratory under the football field at the University of Chicago, created the first controlled nuclear chain reaction. Groves, aided by the scientific community, recruited the finest scientists and engineers for the top secret project. The complex task of working out the manifold details of creating the bomb was left to J. Robert Oppenheimer's team, which he established at the remote site of Los Alamos, New Mexico. Two major industrial complexes, one at Hanford, Washington, and the other at Oak Ridge, Tennessee, were built to produce the crucial ingredients for the necessary chain reaction. Two different methods were developed for causing the necessary release of energy. One system utilized U235, a rare uranium isotope; the other employed the synthetic element plutonium. The Hanford plant produced plutonium, whereas Oak Ridge produced enriched uranium. Ultimately, more than 120,000 people working in thirty-seven facilities throughout the United States and Canada were involved in work related to the Manhattan Project, which cost over two billion dollars.

Although by mid-1945 it was believed that the device constructed at Los Alamos would work, there were many questions concerning the ultimate safety of the bomb. Some scientists worried that the weapon's detonation might start a chain reaction in the atmosphere that would destroy all life on the planet. All such doubts concerning the bomb's destructive potential were answered on 16 July 1945. At a remote section of Alamogordo Air Base in New Mexico, the scientists placed the prototype bomb in a tall tower and detonated it. The flash of light caused by the explosion of this first atomic device could be seen sixty miles away. Oppenheimer, who had contributed so much to its design and construction, witnessing the explosion from six miles away, was so awed that a phrase from the *Bhagavad Gita* came to his mind: "Now I am become Death, the destroyer of worlds."

President Truman, only three months into his presidency and on his way to meet with Churchill and Stalin at Potsdam, was thus presented with the most awesome weapon ever devised. It would be his decision when or if the bomb would ever be used. However, his freedom of action was complicated by decisions made earlier by President Roosevelt. At the Casablanca meeting with Churchill in February 1943, Roosevelt had surprised the prime minister with a statement that there would be no discussion of terms with the enemy. Only unconditional surrender would be accepted. What may have been at first an offhand statement designed for the press and to convince the Germans of the seriousness of Allied aims became the stated goal for ending hostilities in Europe and Asia. It is possible that had unconditional surrender not been the only alternative, the Germans might have decided not to fight to the bitter end. Although that scenario remains unproven speculation, Truman and most of his advisers embraced the unconditional surrender dictum, and that demand did indeed prolong the war with Japan.

As early as the fall of 1943, State Department experts had recommended that Emperor Hirohito be retained as titular head of state in any postwar reorganization. Later, military members of a special interdepartmental committee concurred—provided that the emperor would submit to control by Allied civil authorities. In February 1945 at Malta, just prior to the Yalta conference, Churchill had pressed Roosevelt to modify the demand for Japan's unconditional surrender if this would shorten the war. General Marshall and Adm. William D. Leahy expressed similar views to the president. However, many hardliners—among them Roosevelt's close friend and personal emissary, Harry Hopkins—expressed contrary opinions. Those in the government who wanted to deal with Hirohito as a war criminal reflected the attitude of the American people, most of whom wanted the emperor either imprisoned or executed. Undersecretary of State Joseph Grew, former ambassador to Japan, approached President Truman a number of times, urging him to make a public statement assuring the Japanese that surrender would not mean the loss of the imperial system or harm to Hirohito. Truman, who at that time had been president for only a month, did not think he could make such an announcement without more detailed information. He appointed a committee composed of the secretaries of war and navy and Undersecretary Grew to investigate the problem and provide him with a written statement that he could take to the Potsdam conference.

The committee provided the president with a draft surrender demand just before he boarded the cruiser *Augusta* for the conference. The wording of the section dealing with the possible future government of Japan held out the promise of a constitutional monarchy. The committee members obviously expected Japanese officials to read between the lines and conclude that the imperial system, however modified, would survive. During the voyage, however, Truman's new secretary of state, James F. Byrnes, convinced the president that it would be politically inexpedient to make such a declaration, no matter how vague. To him, the political repercussions of flaunting the obvious will of the American public were too serious to allow the wording to stand. Thus the wording of that section was changed to the promise to withdraw occupation forces when "there has been established a peacefully inclined and responsible government."

At the earlier Yalta conference in February, with the war against Germany almost won, the fate of postwar Europe had been largely decided. Some of the agreements made between the Anglo-American Allies and Stalin would later be harshly criticized. One of those that later came under attack was Roosevelt's eliciting a promise from Stalin that the Soviet Union would renounce its nonaggression pact with Japan and, within three months of the end of the war in Europe, declare war on Japan.

Unlike Roosevelt's demand for unconditional surrender, which had so surprised Churchill and many Allied military advisers, the agreement on Russia's entry into the Asian war was welcomed by most observers. Later, in the 1950s, General MacArthur would attempt to distance himself from his earlier endorsement of the agreement. On a number of official and unofficial occasions, he expressed his opinion of the absolute necessity for Soviet troops to pin down the imagined powerful Kwantung Army in Manchuria. But President Truman's closest military advisers, knowing that the atomic bomb worked, had concluded that Soviet entry in the conflict was not necessary to end the war. Furthermore, they were suspicious of Stalin, believing that his intent was to secure the Kurile Islands, southern Sakhalin Island, and a special position in Manchuria and Korea. Whether Soviet intervention was necessary became moot: Stalin intended to honor the bargain he'd made at Yalta. At Potsdam the Soviet chief of staff informed Marshall that the Russian armies would be prepared to move into Manchuria by mid-August.

The Potsdam meeting between Stalin, Truman, Churchill, and Clement R. Attlee, who succeeded Churchill as British prime minister on 28 July, was called primarily to address some of the problems in Europe left unanswered by the Yalta conference. However, a considerable amount of time was devoted to the Japanese problem by both the heads of state and their military advisers. The draft declaration calling for unconditional surrender had been drawn up in Washington earlier. On 18 July, Churchill and Truman discussed the wording of what would be called the Potsdam Declaration and agreed that it should be communicated to the Japanese government as soon as possible. The draft was submitted to Chiang Kai-shek, who gave his approval on 26 July. Stalin and his military advisers had no part in drafting the declaration because Russia was still neutral. However, the Soviet premier was informed of the contents of those sections representing Allied views.

Soviet Foreign Minister Vyacheslav M. Molotov asked that transmission of the declaration be delayed. He secretly feared that the demands might prompt Japan to capitulate before the Soviet Union could enter the war. Truman, knowing that the bomb worked and that fissionable material was on its way to Tinian and would be ready for use as early as 4 August, denied the Soviet request. In doing so, the president casually mentioned to Stalin that the United States had "a new weapon of unusual destructive force." Stalin passed over this information as if it were not important, simply mentioning that he hoped it would be put to good use. It later became apparent that Klaus Fuchs, an exiled German scientist working at Los Alamos, had kept the Soviets informed about the development of the plutonium bomb.

The fall of Saipan had convinced many Japanese leaders that the war could not be won, and dissatisfaction with Tojo's policies led to his replacement soon after the loss of the Marianas. His replacement, Kuniaki Koiso, although ambivalent, was influenced by navy minister Mitsumasa Yonai, who favored an early ending of the war, and by some members of the *jushin,* such as Prince Konoye. Even Marquis Koichi Kido, the Privy Seal and Hirohito's closest adviser, came to view surrender as necessary if Japan was not to be totally destroyed. However, the militarists in the Supreme Council were still in the majority, and Koiso felt he had no choice but to continue to support the army leaders in the hope of winning a decisive victory and thus bettering Japan's position at the peace table. In September 1944 Foreign Minister Shigemitsu searched out the possibility of sending a special envoy to Moscow in order to obtain, among other things, Kremlin mediation. This, the first of many attempts to convince the Soviet government to intervene, failed.

That same month, Konoye, acting on his own, asked the Swedish ambassador to forward to London a series of proposals for ending the war. Among them was the promise to give up all conquered territory, including Manchuria, if peace terms could be arranged. The Allied reply was noncommittal, but it implied that the only acceptable way to halt hostilities was unconditional surrender. Koiso's government then attempted to use Chiang as a medium to end the war by negotiating with an agent purporting to be empowered to deal with ending hostilities on the Asian mainland. This ended in a fiasco, embarrassing the Koiso government and, together with the announcement of the American landings on Okinawa, helped bring it down on 4 April 1945.

The new premier was Kantaro Suzuki, a retired admiral who had barely escaped assassination in 1937. Although basically neutral toward the idea of a quick cessation of hostilities, he chose Shigenori Togo, an outspoken critic of the war, to be his foreign minister. However, in the Supreme War Council, Gen. Yoshijiro Umezu and Admiral Toyoda, chiefs of staff of the army and navy, and the army minister, Gen. Korechika Anami, were adamantly against peace. Premier Suzuki was neutral in the discussions but would not at that time accept unconditional surrender. One of Togo's first acts was to follow up on Shigemitsu's talks with the Swedish ambassador. Togo wanted Sweden to act as a mediator with the Allies. The Swedish government's position was that it would not act unless formally and officially asked to do so by Japan. Togo, who did not have the support in the Supreme Council for this, decided once more to approach the Soviets.

In the spring of 1945 there were two efforts by Japanese nationals overseas to get Japanese officials to discuss ending the war with Allen Dulles, head of the American Intelligence Service in Switzerland. Dulles had played a crucial role earlier in negotiating the surrender of German forces in Italy. The first of the Japanese contacts was orchestrated by a former naval attache in Berlin. After discussions with Dulles's agents, he suggested that the navy minister, Admiral Yonai, arrange to have a senior official sent to confer with Dulles. Although Yonai personally approved of this idea, he was vetoed by Togo. The second and more important of these contacts was initiated in June by Lt. Gen. Seigo Okamoto, one-time Japanese military representative in Berlin. He informed Dulles that the main impediment to peace was fear that the Allies would not retain the imperial system. He also indicated that Japan wanted to retain Formosa and Korea. Dulles told Okamoto that only Allied leaders could make such decisions. Dulles also encouraged Okamoto to accelerate Japanese peace efforts before Russia entered the war. President Truman learned of this peace overture before the issuance of the Potsdam Declaration. The Switzerland discussions were also reported to Togo, but it was too late to pursue that particular effort.

The loss of Okinawa and the continual bombing convinced the militants in the Supreme Council that no time should be lost trying to secure peace. Unfortunately, they accepted Togo's conclusion that the best hope lay in using the good offices of the Soviet government. After Togo announced the abandonment of the Anti-Comintern Pact of 1936 and tried to begin negotiations to replace the Neutrality Act, Molotov made it clear that Russia did not intend to enter into a new agreement.

On 6 June the chiefs of the armed services presented the Supreme Council with a memorandum on the future conduct of the war, calling for continued mass mobilization of the population to resist invasion. Another memorandum, however, showed that Japan did not have the power to bring the struggle to a successful conclusion. Nevertheless, on 8 June the Supreme Council, in the presence of Hirohito, accepted the first memorandum and concurred in the decision "to pursue the war to the bitter end." Marquis Kido, deeply concerned by this attitude, conveyed his feelings to the emperor and to other members of the government. On 18 June six members of the War Council met and recommended that further attempts be made to get Stalin to intercede with the Allies. Hirohito summoned the council to another meeting on 22 June and indicated his growing, although belated, concern with the peace process. He ordered the council to quickly attempt to restore peace and ignore the bellicose announcement of 8 June. On 7 July Hirohito again asked the Supreme War Council to negotiate for peace.

Given Japan's desperate condition in July, it is remarkable that Japanese leaders proceeded with their deliberations in such an unhurried manner. Even more surprising, despite rumors of an upcoming Allied meeting in Germany, Togo insisted upon attempting to get the Soviets to mediate. Despite previous rebuffs, on 12 July Togo instructed the Japanese ambassador in Moscow, Sato Naotake, to get Molotov to agree to accept Prince Konoye as a special envoy. Konoye would bring a letter from Hirohito stressing Japan's wish for a speedy end to the war, although unconditional surrender remained anathema. This proposal did not reach Stalin and Molotov until the Soviet delegation was already at Potsdam. On 18 July the Japanese ambassador was informed that no definite reply could be given because the message contained nothing specific and because Konoye's mission was not spelled out.

Togo tried twice more to explain to the Soviets what the Konoye mission was about, but it should have been obvious that the Soviets were not interested in aiding Japan. It is also strange that apparently no one in the Japanese Foreign Ministry suspected Russia was on the verge of attacking—despite evidence of massive Russian troop movements to Manchuria's borders. As the Potsdam Declaration made clear, the Japanese government had no choice but to accept unconditional surrender or continue the war.

President Truman and his cabinet were kept fully informed of Togo's desperate attempts to get more favorable terms. American code breakers were reading the messages between Tokyo and Moscow and were fully aware of Japan's desire for peace. A comprehensive intelligence analysis informed the cabinet of Japan's readiness to conclude a peace based upon the principles of the Atlantic Charter. But it also noted that the government was still attempting to secure peace through Russia and did not consider unconditional surrender to be an acceptable alternative to continued resistance. President Truman at any time during and after the Potsdam conference could have secured an end to the war if the unconditional surrender demand so lightly tossed off by President Roosevelt at Casablanca had been modified to accept the continuation of the imperial line. However, most of his advisers, hardened by almost four years of brutal war and with the memory of Pearl Harbor still fresh, had no intention of being lenient with the perfidious Japanese.

In the summer of 1944 General Arnold decided that a special unit would be needed to deliver the atomic bomb if that ever became necessary. The 509th Composite Group, commanded by Col. Paul W. Tibbets Jr., a veteran of the European air war, was created for that purpose. This seventeen-hundred-man outfit had only a single combat element, the 393d Bombardment Squadron. Tibbets, who was the only man in the squadron aware of its mission, put the men through months of grueling practice in their specially modified B-29s at Wendover Field, Utah, honing their skills at high-level bombing. In May 1945 the unit began moving to Tinian in the Mariana Islands, and by early July the entire group was located at North Field. On 20 July it began flying combat missions. The presence of the new unit, which was assigned "milk runs" (easy missions), caused feelings of resentment among some crews in the regular bombardment groups. LeMay much later commented that all the special training was not needed, that any number of Twentieth Air Force bomber crews could have carried out the mission. Despite the curiosity, and perhaps resentment, the 393d continued to practice while a special air-conditioned hut was constructed to house the atomic bomb.

On 26 July the cruiser *Indianapolis* delivered the materials needed to make "Little Boy"—a uranium bomb—operative. The bomb's assembly was completed by 1 August. The sinking of the *Indianapolis* on 29 July while en route from Tinian to the Philippines has led to much nonhistorical speculation. Would it still have been necessary to use atomic weapons on Japan if the Japanese submarine I-58 had sunk the *Indianapolis* on its way *to* Tinian? Whatever one may think, it is doubtful, despite the desires of the emperor, that Japan would have agreed to make peace before the more powerful plutonium bomb arrived.

When apprised of the details of the Potsdam Declaration on 27 July, Prime Minister Suzuki and Foreign Minister Togo did not see in it a dictate of unconditional surrender. The emperor concurred and ordered that it be treated with the "utmost circumspection." Suzuki wanted to gain clarification of the most crucial issue: the fate of the imperial dynasty. However, he tragically decided not to make a formal reply, expecting a follow-up from the Allies that never came. Nevertheless, many of the major Japanese newspapers, probably on orders from the military, ran editorials critical of the declaration and called for its rejection. Forced by these reports into making a public announcement, Suzuki commented on the afternoon of 28 July that the Potsdam Declaration was nothing but a rehash of earlier statements and that the government would ignore it. The word he used was *mokusatsu*, one definition of which is to "treat with contempt." American newspapers ran headlines proclaiming that Japan had officially turned down the Potsdam call for surrender. Although this misunderstanding later was used as further justification for using the bomb, it played little part in the decision to do so. Only a rapid reply from the Japanese government could have prevented its use, and Suzuki and his ministers were not prepared to act that quickly.

General Spaatz, who like LeMay believed that Japan could be forced to surrender by bombing alone, received permission on 1 August to use the first bomb anytime between the third and tenth. He was authorized to bomb one of four cities: Kokura, Nagasaki, Niigata, or Hiroshima. Many in the administration wanted Tokyo to head the list, and Kyoto, the site of considerable industrial development, was initially included on the target list, but Secretary Stimson reminded Truman of its central place in Japanese history and the president concurred in its removal. Spaatz finally decided that Hiroshima, the site of shipbuilding factories, electrical works, and other assorted war industries, as well as headquarters of the Second General Army, should be the target.

On 6 August 1945 weather planes reported to Colonel Tibbets that Hiroshima was clear. Accompanying Tibbets and his crew aboard the *Enola Gay* were two other B-29s loaded with scientific and military observers. Once the *Enola Gay* cleared four thousand feet, Capt. William S. Parsons, a naval atomic expert, inserted the detonating device, thus completing the circuit. The bomb was armed.

According to survivor accounts, the Japanese paid little attention to the approaching B-29s. The military, as well as the general population, had become so accustomed to reconnaissance flights by a few aircraft that the *Enola Gay*'s approach was not considered unique. The dropping of seven hundred thousand leaflets urging the civilian population to evacuate had produced results, however. More than a hundred thousand persons left the city before the sixth. Those who remained probably felt relatively secure because Hiroshima had largely been spared from the massive Twentieth Air Force raids.

But they were not safe; they were to be the first victims of a new form of mass destruction. When the bombadier released "Little Boy" at 0815, the entire nature of war was changed. Within seconds of release, the bomb detonated at an altitude of 660 yards and Hiroshima ceased to exist. More than 80 percent of all buildings were destroyed. The official count of the dead was 71,379—fewer than in the Dresden and Tokyo firestorms, but this destruction was caused by just one bomb. In all probability that count was low, as was the estimate of approximately 80,000 wounded. To these casualty figures must be added the thousands who later died because of their exposure to radiation.

President Truman was informed of the attack while at sea aboard the *Augusta* on his way back from the Potsdam conference. He authorized Stimson to release a prepared statement indicating the power of the new weapon and again calling for the Japanese to surrender.

Even after hearing of the destruction wrought at Hiroshima, Foreign Minister Togo continued to seek Soviet support. He cabled Ambassador Naotake, instructing him to immediately call on Molotov to ascertain if the Soviet attitude had changed. On 8 August Sato finally gained an audience and was handed a long note informing him that, effective 9 August, the Soviet Union was declaring war on Japan. One and a half million troops under Field Marshal Aleksander M. Vasilevskii had already invaded Manchuria and were advancing on three fronts. Stalin had honored his pledge to enter the war and, due to the reluctance of the Japanese government to accept the inevitable, Truman had lost his gamble to end the war before Russia could get into it. After the war, Admiral Yonai claimed that the Soviet action had a more profound effect upon him and his colleagues than did the atomic bombing. It dashed the hopes of Suzuki, Togo, and the other moderates in the Supreme War Council that somehow the Soviets would force the Allies to withdraw their unconditional surrender demand.

Suzuki was outraged by the Soviets' duplicity and, when informed of Russia's declaration of war, told Togo that Japan must end the conflict. Given the opposition of the military leaders, he sought the emperor's approval. This was communicated via Kido on the morning of the ninth. An emergency meeting of the *jushin* was called for 1100. Suzuki and Togo, aided by Yonai, argued that peace was the only alternative. However, Anami, Umezu, and Toyoda, although they knew of Japan's hopeless situation, still refused to accept the inevitable. Suzuki reported to Kido that he believed the emperor would have to make the decision. This conclusion was confirmed at the divided cabinet meeting that afternoon when the military members still refused to acknowledge that the war was lost and nothing could be gained by waiting. Despite the knowledge that a second atomic device had been dropped on Nagasaki, Anami, speaking for the rest of the officers, stated that Japan "must fight to the end."

When there was no reply to Truman's 6 August statement, preparations to drop a second atomic bomb continued. On Saipan, sixteen million propaganda leaflets urging civilians to evacuate were written in more modern Japanese than earlier versions. They were then dropped on the target cities. On the eighth, Maj. Charles W. Sweeney, who had flown the instrument plane, the *Great Artiste,* on the Hiroshima raid, was notified that he would fly the second mission. Instead of his own plane, he was scheduled to fly another B-29, Capt. Frederick Bock's *Bock's Car.*

The second bomb, nicknamed "Fat Man," was different from the Hiroshima weapon. It was a spherical plutonium type, theoretically of much greater destructive power. It did not need to be armed in flight but was fully operational at takeoff.

Sweeney's primary target when he took off from Tinian early in the morning on 9 August was Kokura, a port on the northeast coast of Kyushu. He had problems rendezvousing with the two B-29s carrying the scientific observers, and after flying around for two hours, Sweeney decided to head for the target with only one escort. When *Bock's Car* reached Kokura, it was partially obscured by smoke and haze. Sweeney, who had been instructed to bomb visually, proceeded to the secondary target, Nagasaki, a city of two hundred thousand. That target also was partially obscured, and after one unsuccessful run, Sweeney decided to try once more before aborting the mission.

Unfortunately for the people of Nagasaki, the bombadier found his aiming point and released Fat Man at 1101. The bomb, which exploded at a higher altitude than had Little Boy at Hiroshima, was not as destructive as scientists had projected. Nevertheless, the central city was destroyed. American sources estimated the death toll to be 35,000, whereas Japanese officials claimed 74,800 died. As at Hiroshima, many of the wounded later died, and the latent effects of radioactivity continued to claim lives for many years.

Even after news of the Nagasaki bombing reached them, senior Japanese officials were either reluctant to act decisively or, like Anami, the most vocal of the military leaders, were prepared to resist to the last. An imperial conference was convened in the afternoon on the ninth and, after a brief recess, continued through the evening. Ten minutes before midnight the emperor appeared, took a seat on the dais, and listened to presentations of the various viewpoints. The militants were still violently opposed to accepting the terms of the Potsdam Declaration. Premier Suzuki followed the militants with an impassioned plea for Hirohito's intervention.

As he spoke, the impassioned Suzuki made a serious error in protocol. He stepped away from his chair and approached the emperor directly, advancing very close to the dais. The emperor ignored the breach of etiquette and, soon after Suzuki finished, stood up and offered his opinion. He said that continuing the war meant "destruction of the nation and a prolongation of bloodshed," and concluded by saying, "I swallow my own tears and give my sanction to the proposal to accept the Allied proclamation on the basis outlined by the Foreign Minister." Hirohito had at last intervened. Had he not been so concerned with maintaining the proper distance from the policy makers, he could have acted long before, when it first became apparent that Japan had lost the war. Later that morning, the tenth, the emperor's decision was approved by the entire cabinet.

Surprisingly, Hirohito's statement did not end the controversy. Togo transmitted the decision immediately through regular diplomatic channels to Switzerland and Sweden. The note, however, qualified the acceptance with the proviso that this would not "prejudice the prerogatives" of Hirohito.

President Truman received the Japanese note before noon on 10 August. He and his closest advisers were uncertain about the accuracy of the report. The top Pentagon civilians, Secretaries Stimson and Forrestal, were in favor of a clear statement to Japan that the emperor would be allowed to continue as head of state. They also wanted an immediate halt to the bombing as a gesture of goodwill. Secretary of State Byrnes held out for no modification to the Potsdam Declaration. He was supported by the president. Truman did not order a halt to the bombing of Japanese cities until the twelfth. Spaatz had planned to drop a third bomb, preferably on Tokyo, as a symbolic gesture in repayment for Pearl Harbor. However, delivery of the materials for a plutonium weapon could not be shipped until 13 August and the earliest it could be used was the seventeenth. When no definite reply had been received, the president authorized General Arnold to resume the incendiary strikes. Spaatz sent over a thousand bombers of all types to strike at Tokyo and other key cities. Half of Kumagaya and one-sixth of Isesaki were destroyed in this massive raid.

Secretary of State Byrnes had drafted a reply to the Japanese note that restated the Allied position but was ambivalent with regard to the key question of imperial rule. However, the Byrnes note did leave open the possibility for Hirohito to continue as emperor.

It was then circulated to all the Allied powers for approval. This was received at midnight on 12 August and the note was immediately dispatched to Japan.

There were five different Japanese cabinet meetings on the twelfth, and in each the military chiefs, despite Hirohito's earlier pronouncement, were adamantly against ending the war on Allied terms. The Byrnes note, with its vague language on the salient point, gave Anami and others in meetings the next day a chance to argue against acceptance. However, Suzuki concluded by midafternoon that the Byrnes note left the emperor's position intact and therefore announced his acceptance. The main problem was how to inform the army leadership of the decision and control unruly officers and minimize a potential violent conflict between elements of the armed forces.

Early on the morning of 14 August, Hirohito again made known his position, instructing the government to accept the terms. He indicated his willingness to do anything to end the war and to persuade the army and navy to lay down their arms peacefully. Anami and the other military chiefs finally stated their acceptance of this divine command and left to convey the decree to their staffs and senior officers. Later that day a simple two-paragraph statement accepting the Potsdam Declaration and promising to issue orders to all commanders to cease hostilities was drafted. It was soon signed by all members of the cabinet, and Hirohito quickly affixed his signature to the document, thus ending the disastrous war that had begun so promisingly for Japan forty-five months before. There would later be amplifications of the surrender and a formal ceremony, but the note transmitted to the Japanese legation in Switzerland that evening effectively marked Japan's capitulation.

The emperor accepted Kido's and Suzuki's suggestion that he broadcast the surrender message to the nation. It was considered unthinkable that he should do this directly, so arrangements were made for him to record his speech. In the speech, which marked the first time his people would hear his voice, Hirohito explained at length his reasons for agreeing to capitulate. He spoke of the "most cruel bomb" used by the Allies, and stated his fear of the "obliteration of the Japanese nation" unless the enemy's demands were met. Hirohito's voice was not completely clear on the first recording, so the emperor obligingly made a second one. The two ten-inch discs were then locked away in an office in the Household Ministry to forestall any attempt to steal them. It was still not known what the reaction in the military services would be once they had been informed of the proposed surrender.

There was a highly confused situation at the War Ministry following the cabinet meetings on the fourteenth. The army chief of staff, General Umezu, was still reluctant to obey the surrender order, but General Anami could not imagine opposing the emperor's wishes and made his position very clear to a group of younger officers who sought his advice and support for action to prevent the surrender. To stop any precipitous actions by high-ranking officers Anami, Hata, Sugiyama, and Umezu later signed a terse statement circulated to senior commanders stating that the army would support the imperial decision. Anami then convened a meeting of all the section chiefs and announced his support of the emperor and ordered them to do likewise. These actions meant that any reaction to the surrender decision would be left to midranking officers. A number of them, led by Maj. Kenji Hatanaka and Lt. Col. Masataka Ida, were formulating plans to seal off the Imperial Palace and search out and destroy the recordings, thus giving them more time to convince their superiors to continue the struggle.

Hatanaka, the zealous leader of the coup attempt, lied in an effort to convince a number of regimental commanders that Anami and Umezu supported them. The key figure in their plot was Lt. Gen. Takeshi Mori, commander of the Konoye Division, and whose responsibility was guarding the palace grounds. At first Mori had raged against those who had betrayed the nation, but by afternoon had calmed down—although he was still not certain what action he should take. When confronted by a group of young officers led by Hatanaka, he put off giving them assurances of support and told them to wait while he went to the Meiji shrine to contemplate. One overzealous air force officer drew his sword and advanced on Mori, ostensibly to demand an immediate response. This led to violence. Mori's brother-in-law was cut down and Hatanaka shot Mori. Increasingly desperate, the conspirators used Mori's seal to alert the Konoye Division to block all entrances to the palace grounds. Hatanaka and other officers searched for the recordings but could not find them. The romantic, desperate actions of the conspirators came to an end when Gen. Shizuchi Tanaka, commander of the Eastern Army, refused to honor their appeals and ordered them to leave the palace and return the troops to their barracks. Realizing that all was lost, the coup leaders complied. Hatanaka later committed suicide.

Other military leaders reacted with almost universal despair to the news of the proposed surrender. While no senior officials were involved in the coup, many were sympathetic and some began to kill themselves even before the emperor's broadcast. Anami and Onishi, creator of the kamikaze forces, were among the first. Admiral Ugaki, then commander of the kamikaze units, flew from Ota air base with six other pilots, seeking to end their lives by destroying one more Allied ship. None of the planes apparently ever got within striking distance of any American warships. Despite such heroics and the obvious desire of the majority of military officers to continue the fight, the emperor's broadcast went on as planned. Precisely at noon on 15 August, just after the playing of the national anthem, the Japanese heard their emperor addressing them as "Our Good and Loyal Subjects" and explaining why he decided to "effect a settlement of the present situation."

After approving Hirohito's acceptance offer, President Truman appointed General MacArthur to be Supreme Commander of Allied Powers. Within certain limits, MacArthur was allowed to plan for and conduct the official signing of the surrender, as well as the occupation of Japan and later Korea. MacArthur notified the Japanese that he wanted a delegation of sixteen members to meet with him on 17 August.

A new government had been chosen in Japan, replacing Suzuki, Togo, and the other members of the cabinet who resigned on the fifteenth. Prince Toshihiko Higashikuni became prime minister and Mamoru Shigemitsu returned as foreign minister. MacArthur's demand was the first key test of the government, and it was with great difficulty that sixteen willing and qualified people could be found to serve on the peace delegation. The delegation was ultimately headed by the army's deputy chief of staff, Lt. Gen. Torashiro Kawabe, and flew to Ie Shima on board two Mitsubishi bombers. There the members were transferred to C-54s and flown to Manila.

Met by Maj. Gen. Charles A. Willoughby, MacArthur's intelligence chief, they were treated with great courtesy. MacArthur chose not to meet the delegation but sent General Sutherland, his chief of staff, to conduct the ceremony. All went well until the surrender document was presented. This shocked the Japanese, not because it called for capitulation, but by the way it referred to the emperor. It used the pronoun *watakushi* for I instead of *chin,* a word that was specifically reserved for the emperor when referring to himself. MacArthur's chief interpreter allowed the delegation to make the correction. With this change the documents were accepted and the delegation flew back to Japan on the twentieth.

There was considerable apprehension in both MacArthur's and Nimitz's headquarters that the overwhelming number of Japanese soldiers might be maneuvered by diehard officers to oppose the Allied occupation. This did not occur; the emperor's word was obeyed and there were no incidents.

On 26 August C-54 aircraft began ferrying 11th Airborne Division troops to Atsugi airport, and two days later the first infantry contingent began landing. Admiral Halsey had moved a large part of the Third Fleet into Sagami Sea and began landing Marines at Yokosuka on the thirtieth. He maintained his carriers outside the bay to provide air cover if needed. In all, there were 258 ships of all kinds anchored in or near the bay—including the Royal Navy contingent. Admiral Spruance's Fifth Fleet was still patrolling along the western coastline and Kinkaid's Seventh Fleet was preparing to escort the troop transports that would land U.S. forces in the southern part of Korea. General Eichelberger arrived on the thirtieth to take charge of land operations. Despite the potential danger, MacArthur's personal plane, the *Bataan,* touched down at Atsugi only two hours after Eichelberger's.

In the two weeks following Hirohito's submission, senior military leaders of all the Allied powers began to converge on Japan in order to represent their nations at the official surrender ceremony. MacArthur allowed Nimitz to choose the location. The admiral chose Halsey's flagship, the fast battleship *Missouri,* a choice that obviously pleased the president, a native Missourian.

The ceremony was scheduled for midmorning on 2 September, and an ordinary mess table covered with green baize cloth was set up on the *Missouri*'s veranda deck. Two sets of surrender documents—one in English, the other in Japanese—were placed on the table. The flag that had flown over the Capitol in Washington on 7 December 1941, was raised at Morning Colors. Distinguished visitors began to arrive shortly after 0700, and within an hour the Allied representatives were all on board. Shortly after 0800 Nimitz arrived, followed by MacArthur at 0843. At 0856 the Japanese delegation, headed by Foreign Minister Shigemitsu, began mounting the gangway. Shigemitsu had lost a leg in an assassination attempt years before, and his artificial leg pained him so much that he had difficulty with the steps. Behind him came Umezu, who detested the foreign minister for his pacifist views. Umezu had threatened to kill himself rather than take part in the degrading ceremony. Only Horohito's intervention convinced Umezu to take part. Shigemitsu got no help from the general. Once on board, the civilians, dressed in top hats and formal morning dress, were directed to a position facing the table. In front and on both sides were representatives of the Allied governments and flag officers of the American army and navy. MacArthur appeared at a few minutes past nine, accompanied by Nimitz and Halsey.

Flanked by Lt. Gen. Jonathan Wainwright and Lt. Gen. Sir Arthur Percival, both symbols of earlier defeats, MacArthur opened the ceremony with a brief statement praying that "from this solemn occasion a better world shall emerge out of the blood and carnage of the past." He then motioned for the Japanese delegates to come forward and sign the surrender documents. Shigemitsu, fumbling with his hat, seemed to be in pain as he tried to find where to sign. MacArthur ordered Sutherland to show Shigemitsu the place and at 0904 he affixed his signature to the documents, officially ending the Pacific war. After the Japanese, MacArthur signed, accepting the surrender on behalf of all the Allies. Nimitz then signed for the United States, followed by military representatives from each of the Allied powers.

MacArthur concluded the ceremony with another brief statement: "Let us pray that peace be now restored to the world and that God preserve it always. These proceedings are now closed." On cue, a flight of 450 naval planes and hundreds of army bombers and fighters swept low over the ships of the Third Fleet, further showing the Japanese the awesome might of the Allied forces.

The war was officially over, but it took months to receive the surrender of the hundreds of Japanese garrisons scattered throughout Asia and the Pacific. The Russians did not abide by the cease-fire, but instead continued their operations in Manchuria. Some die-hard elements in the interior of a number of Pacific islands also continued to fight. They did this not because of a desire to disobey the emperor, but because of poor communications. When finally informed of the surrender, the officers brought their men in and laid down their arms. Hirohito's word represented the honor of the Japanese nation and, although defeat was bitter, they accepted their fate.

The tragedy that must have haunted the very decent man who by accident of birth was considered a god by one hundred million people was that he did not use that latent power until his nation was in ruins and his country occupied.

MacArthur, eloquently as always, expressed the relief of his countrymen after 1,364 days of bloody conflict when he declared, "The entire world is quietly at peace. The holy mission has been completed."

Selected Bibliography

Official Records and Oral Histories

There are three main depositories for declassified records relating to the Pacific war. Each of these is located either in or near Washington, D.C. Those record groups related to the navy's role are found at the U.S. Naval Historical Center at the Washington Naval Yard. Nearby is the Marine Corps Archives, where all materials relating to the corps are either housed or can be called up from storage. The Modern Military Records Branch of the National Archives, located in Suitland, Maryland, is the repository for records pertaining to army ground and air operations.

Each service branch has diligently collected oral histories. Most of the oral memoirs of senior army officials are located at the U.S. Army Military History Institute at Carlisle Barracks, Pennsylvania. The extensive Marine Oral History Collection is at the Marine Corps Archives, and the recollections of naval leaders are at the Naval Historical Center.

Memoirs

Arnold, H. H. *Global Mission.* New York: Harper, 1949.

Barbey, Daniel. *MacArthur's Amphibious Navy.* Annapolis, Md.: Naval Institute Press, 1969.

Churchill, Winston. *History of the Second World War.* Vol. 3, *The Grand Alliance.* Boston: Houghton Mifflin, 1950.

_____. *History of the Second World War.* Vol. 6, *Triumph and Tragedy.* Boston: Houghton Mifflin, 1953.

Eichelberger, Robert L. *Our Jungle Road to Tokyo.* New York: Viking, 1950.

Hull, Cordell. *The Memoirs of Cordell Hull.* New York: Macmillan, 1948.

Kenney, George C. *General Kenney Reports.* New York: Duell, Sloan, and Pearce, 1949.

Kimmel, Husband R. *Admiral Kimmel's Story.* Chicago: Henry Regency, 1955.

King, Ernest J. *Fleet Admiral King: A Naval Record.* New York: Norton, 1952.

Krueger, Walter. *From Down Under to Nippon.* Washington, D.C.: Combat Forces Press, 1953.

Layton, Edwin T. *And I Was There.* New York: Morrow, 1985.

LeMay, Curtis, and MacKinlay Kantor. *Mission With LeMay.* Garden City, N.Y.: Doubleday, 1965.

MacArthur, Douglas. *Reminiscences.* New York: McGraw-Hill, 1964.

Malloné, Richard C. *The Naked Flagpole: Battle for Battaan.* Novato, Calif.: Presidio, 1980.

Potter, E. B., and Chester W. Nimitz. *Triumph in the Pacific.* Englewood Cliffs, N.J.: Prentice Hall, 1963.

Sakai, Saburo, Martin Caidin, and Fred Saito. *Samurai.* New York: Dutton, 1958.

Smith, Holland M., and Percy Finch. *Coral and Brass.* New York: Scribners, 1949.

Stimson, Henry L., and McGeorge Bundy. *On Active Service in Peace and War.* New York: Harpers, 1948.

Truman, Harry. *Memoirs by Harry S Truman.* Vol. 1. Garden City, N.Y.: Doubleday, 1955.

Ugaki, Matome. *Fading Victory: The Diary of Admiral Matome Ugaki, 1941–1945.* Edited by Donald Goldstein and Katherine Dillon. Pittsburgh, Pa.: University of Pittsburgh Press, 1991.

Wedemeyer, Albert C. *Wedemeyer Reports.* New York: Holt, 1958.

Biographies

Agawa, Hiroyuki. *The Reluctant Admiral.* Tokyo: Kondansha International, 1989.

Barker, A. J. *Yamashita.* New York: Ballantine, 1973.

Buell, Thomas. *Master of Seapower: A Biography of Admiral Ernest J. King.* Annapolis, Md.: Naval Institute Press, 1976.

————. *The Quiet Warrior: A Biography of Admiral Raymond Spruance.* Boston: Little, Brown, 1974.

Butow, Robert. *Tojo and the Coming of the War.* Princeton, N.J.: Princeton University Press, 1961.

Dallek, Robert. *Franklin Roosevelt and America's Foreign Policy, 1932–1945.* New York: Oxford University Press, 1979.

Dyer, George C. *The Amphibians Come to Conquer: The Story of Admiral Richmond Keley Turner.* Washington, D.C.: Government Printing Office, 1972.

Forrestel, E. P. *Admiral Spruance, USN: A Study in Command.* Washington, D.C.: Navy Department, 1966.

Halsey, William F., and Joseph Bryan. *Admiral Halsey's Story.* New York: Whittlesey, 1947.

Hoyt, Edwin. *How They Won the War in the Pacific: Nimitz and His Admirals.* New York: Weybright & Talley, 1970.

James, D. Clayton. *The Years of MacArthur.* Vol. 2. New York: Houghton Mifflin, 1972.

Larabee, Eric. *Commander in Chief.* New York: Harper and Row, 1987.

Leutze, James. *A Different Kind of Victory: A Biography of Admiral Thomas C. Hart.* Annapolis, Md.: Naval Institute Press, 1981.

Manchester, William. *American Caesar.* Boston: Little, Brown, 1987.

Pogue, Forrest C. *George C. Marshall, Ordeal and Hope, 1939–1945.* New York: Viking, 1966.

_____. *George C. Marshall, Organizer of Victory.* New York: Viking, 1973.

Potter, E. B. *Bull Halsey.* Annapolis, Md.: Naval Institute Press, 1985.

_____. *Nimitz.* Annapolis, Md.: Naval Institute Press, 1976.

Potter, John D. *Yamamoto.* New York: Paperback Library, 1967.

Sherwood, Robert. *Roosevelt and Hopkins.* New York: Harper, 1948.

Official Histories

Allison, David. *New Eye for the Navy: The Origin or Radar at the Naval Research Laboratory.* Washington, D.C.: Naval Research Laboratory, 1981.

Appleton, Roy, et al. *U.S. Army in World War II. Okinawa: The Last Battle.* Washington, D.C.: Historical Division, Department of the Army, 1948.

Arthur, Robert, Kenneth Cohlmia, and Robert Vance. *The Third Marine Division.* Washington, D.C.: Infantry Journal Press, 1948.

Craven, Wesley, and James Cate, eds. *The Army Air Forces in World War II*. Vol. 1, *Plans and Early Operations, January 1939 to August 1942*. Chicago: University of Chicago Press, 1958.

———. *The Army Air Forces in World War II*. Vol. 4, *The Pacific: Guadalcanal to Saipan, August 1942 to July 1944*. Chicago: University of Chicago Press, 1950.

———. *The Army Air Forces in World War II*. Vol. 5, *The Pacific: Matterhorn to Nagasaki*. Chicago: University of Chicago Press, 1953.

Crowl, Philip. *U.S. Army in World War II: Campaign in the Marianas*. Washington, D.C.: Historical Division, U.S. Army, 1960.

———. *U.S. Army in World War II: Seizure of the Gilberts and Marshalls*. Washington, D.C.: Historical Division, U.S. Army, 1955.

Dexter, David. *Australia in the War of 1939–45, Army*. Vol. 6, *The New Guinea Offensives*. Canberra: Australian War Memorial, 1961.

Dod, Karl C. *The Corps of Engineers: The War Against Japan*. Washington, D.C.: Office of the Chief of Military History, 1966.

Edmonds, Walter. *The Story of the Army Air Force in the Southwest Pacific, 1941–1942: They Fought with What They Had*. Boston: Little, Brown, 1951.

Frank, Benis, and Henry Shaw. *History of U.S. Marine Corps Operations in World War II*. Vol. 5, *Victory and Occupation*. Washington, D.C.: Historical Division, Headquarters, U.S. Marine Corps, 1968.

Garand, George, and Truman Strobridge. *History of U.S. Marine Corps Operations in World War II*. Vol. 4, *Western Pacific Operations*. Washington, D.C.: Historical Division, Headquarters, U.S. Marine Corps, 1971.

Hata, Ikuhiko, and Yasuho Izawa. *Japanese Naval Aces and Fighter Units in World War II*. Annapolis, Md.: Naval Institute Press, 1989.

Heinl, Robert. *The Defense of Wake*. Washington, D.C.: Historical Section, U.S. Marine Corps, 1947.

Hoffman, Carl. *Saipan: The Beginning of the End*. Washington, D.C.: Historical Division, Headquarters, U.S. Marine Corps, 1950.

_____. *The Seizure of Tinian.* Washington, D.C.: Historical Division, Headquarters, U.S. Marine Corps, 1951.

Hough, Frank, Verle Ludwig, and Henry Shaw. *History of Marine Corps Operations in World War II.* Vol. 1, *Pearl Harbor and Guadalcanal.* Washington, D.C.: Historical Division, Headquarters, U.S. Marine Corps, 1966.

Kirby, S. Woodburn. *The War Against Japan.* 4 vols. London: H.M.S.O., 1957–1965.

Long, Gavin. *Australia in the War of 1939–45, Army.* Vol. 7, *The Final Campaigns.* Canberra: Australian War Memorial, 1963.

McCarthy, Dudley. *Australia in the War of 1939–45, Army.* Vol. 5, *South-West Pacific Area—First Year: Kokoda to Wau.* Canberra: Australian War Memorial, 1959.

Maurer, Maurer, ed. *Air Force Combat Units of World War II.* Washington, D.C.: Government Printing Office, 1960.

Miller, John. *U.S. Army in World War II, Cartwheel: The Reduction of Rabaul.* Washington, D.C.: Office of the Chief of Military History, 1959.

Milner, Samuel. *U.S. Army in World War II: Victory in Papua.* Washington, D.C.: Office of the Chief of Military History, 1957.

Morison, Samuel Eliot. *History of United States Naval Operations in World War II.* Vol. 3, *The Rising Sun in the Pacific.* Boston: Little, Brown, 1961.

_____. *History of United States Naval Operations in World War II.* Vol. 4, *Coral Sea, Midway and Submarine Actions.* Boston: Little, Brown, 1949.

_____. *History of United States Naval Operations in World War II.* Vol. 5, *The Struggle for Guadalcanal.* Boston: Little, Brown, 1949.

_____. *History of United States Naval Operations in World War II.* Vol. 6, *Breaking the Bismarcks Barrier.* Boston: Little, Brown, 1950.

_____. *History of United States Naval Operations in World War II.* Vol. 7, *Aleutians, Gilberts, and Marshalls.* Boston: Little, Brown, 1951.

_____. *History of United States Naval Operations in World War II.* Vol. 8, *New Guinea and the Marianas.* Boston: Little, Brown, 1962.

_____. *History of United States Naval Operations in World War II*. Vol. 12, *Leyte*. Boston: Little, Brown, 1958.

_____. *History of United States Naval Operations in World War II*. Vol. 13, *The Liberation of the Philippines: Luzon, Mindanao, the Visayas*. Boston: Little, Brown, 1959.

_____. *History of United States Naval Operations in World War II*. Vol. 14, *Victory in the Pacific*. Boston: Little, Brown, 1961.

Nichols, Charles, and Henry Shaw. *Okinawa: Victory in the Pacific*. Washington, D.C.: Historical Branch, G3 Division, Headquarters, U.S. Marine Corps, 1955.

Shaw, Henry, and Douglas Kane. *History of U.S. Marine Corps Operations in World War II*. Vol. 2, *Isolation of Rabaul*. Washington, D.C.: Headquarters, U.S. Marine Corps, 1963.

Shaw, Henry, Bernard Nalty, and Edwin Turnbladh. *History of U.S. Marine Corps Operations in World War II*. Vol. 3, *Central Pacific Drive*. Washington, D.C.: Office of the Chief of Military History, 1953.

Smith, Robert Ross. *U.S. Army in World War II: Triumph in the Philippines*. Washington, D.C.: Office of the Chief of Military History, 1963.

U.S. War Department. *The Capture of Makin*. Washington, D.C.: Historical Division, War Department, 1946.

_____. *Guam, Operations of the 77th Division*. Washington, D.C.: Historical Division, War Department, 1946.

_____. *Papuan Campaign*. Washington, D.C.: Historical Division, 1989.

Secondary Works

Anderton, David. *American Fighters of World War II*. New York: Crescent, 1987.

Andrews, Phillip, and Leonard Engel, eds. *Navy Yearbook*. New York: Duell, Sloan and Pearce, 1944.

Barker, A. J. *Midway: The Turning Point*. New York: Ballantine, 1976.

Batchelor, John, Anthony Preston, and Louis Casey. *Sea Power*. New York: Exeter, 1979.

Belote, James H., and William Belote. *Titans of the Sea*. New York: Harper and Row, 1975.

_____. *Typhoon of Steel: The Battle for Okinawa.* New York: Harper and Row, 1970.

Berry, Henry. *Semper Fi Mac.* New York: Arbor House, 1982.

Blair, Clay, Jr. *Silent Victory.* New York: Lippincott, 1975.

Buchanan, A. Russell. *The United States and World War II.* Vols. 1 and 2. New York: Harper and Row, 1964.

Calvacoressi, Peter, and Guy Wint. *Total War.* New York: Pantheon, 1972.

Clausen, Henry C., and Bruce Lee. *Pearl Harbor: Final Judgement.* New York: Crown, 1992.

Coletta, Paolo. *The American Naval Heritage.* Lanham, Md.: University Press of America, 1987.

Costello, John. *The Pacific War.* New York: Quill, 1982.

Cronin, Francis. *Under the Southern Cross: The Saga of the Americal Division.* Washington, D.C.: Combat Forces Press, 1951.

Dower, John W. *War Without Mercy: Race and Power in the Pacific War.* New York: Pantheon, 1986.

Dull, Paul S. *The Imperial Japanese Navy, 1941–1945.* Annapolis, Md.: Naval Institute Press, 1968.

Falk, Stanley. *Bloodiest Victory: Palaus.* New York: Random House, 1974.

_____. *Decision at Leyte.* New York: Norton, 1966.

Feifer, George. *Tennozoan: The Battle of Okinawa and the Atomic Bomb.* New York: Ticknor and Fields, 1992.

Feis, Herbert. *Japan Subdued: The Atomic Bomb and the End of the War in the Pacific.* Princeton, N.J.: Princeton University Press, 1961.

_____. *The Road to Pearl Harbor: The Coming of the War between the United States and Japan.* Princeton, N.J.: Princeton University Press, 1950.

Fuchida, Mitsuo, and Masatake Okumiya. *Midway.* Annapolis, Md.: Naval Institute Press, 1955.

Gailey, Harry A. *Bougainville, 1943–1945: The Forgotten Campaign.* Lexington, Ky.: University Press of Kentucky, 1991.

_____. *"Howlin' Mad" vs. the Army: Conflict in Command, Saipan 1944.* Novato, Calif.: Presidio, 1986.

_____. *The Liberation of Guam, 21 July–10 August 1944.* Novato, Calif.: Presidio, 1988.

_____. *Peleliu: 1944*. Annapolis, Md.: Nautical and Aviation, 1983.

Garfield, Brian. *The Thousand-Mile War: World War II in Alaska and the Aleutians*. Garden City, N.Y.: Doubleday, 1969.

Gow, Ian. *Okinawa, 1945*. Garden City, N.Y.: Doubleday, 1985.

Griffith, Samuel. *The Battle for Guadalcanal*. Annapolis, Md.: Nautical & Aviation, 1979.

Hammel, Eric. *Guadalcanal: The Carrier Battles*. New York: Crown, 1987.

_____. *Munda Trail*. New York: Orion, 1989.

Heinl, Robert. *Victory at High Tide*. Annapolis, Md.: Nautical & Aviation, 1979.

Hayashi, Saburo, and Alvin Coox. *Kogun: The Japanese Army in the Pacific War*. Quantico, Va.: Marine Corps Assoc., 1959.

Hough, Frank O. *The Island War: The United States Marine Corps in the Pacific*. New York: Lippincott, 1947.

Hoyt, Edwin P. *Japan's War: The Great Pacific Conflict, 1853–1952*. New York: McGraw-Hill, 1986.

_____. *MacArthur's Navy*. New York: Orion, 1989.

_____. *Storm Over the Gilberts*. New York: Mason/Charter, 1987.

_____. *To the Marianas*. New York: Avon, 1983.

Huber, Thomas. *Japan's Battle of Okinawa, April–June 1945*. Leavenworth Papers No. 18. Fort Leavenworth, Kans.: Combat Studies Institute, 1991.

Inoguchi, Rikihei, Tadashi Nakajima, and Robert Pineau. *The Divine Wind*. New York: Ballantine, 1958.

Iriye, Akira. *The Origins of the Second World War in Asia & the Pacific*. New York: Longmans, 1987.

Isley, Jeter, and Philip Crowl. *The U.S. Marines and Amphibious War*. Princeton, N.J.: Princeton Unversity Press, 1951.

Jablonski, Edward. *Airwar*. 2 vols. Garden City, N.Y.: Doubleday, 1971.

Jackson, Donald. *Torokina*. Ames: Iowa State University Press, 1989.

Johnston, Richard. *Follow Me: The Story of the Second Marine Division in World War II*. New York: Random House, 1948.

Karig, Walter, Russel Harris, and Frank Manson. *Battle Report: The End of An Empire*. New York: Holt, Rinehart and Winston, 1948.

Keogh, E. G. *The South West Pacific 1941–45*. Melbourne: Grayflower, 1965.

Kerr, E. Bartlett. *Flames Over Tokyo: The U.S. Army Air Forces' Incendiary Campaign Against Japan, 1944–1945*. New York: Fine, 1991.

Kirby, S. Woodburn. *The War Against Japan*. London: H.M.S.O., 1969.

Leary, William M. *We Shall Return: MacArthur's Commanders and the Defeat of Japan*. Lexington: University Press of Kentucky, 1988.

Leckie, Robert. *Strong Men Armed*. New York: Bantam, 1963.

Lewin, Ronald. *The American Magic: Codes, Ciphers and the Defeat of Japan*. New York: Farrar, Straus and Giroux, 1982.

Lord, Walter. *Day of Infamy*. New York: Bantam, 1987.

_____. *Incredible Victory*. New York: Harper and Row, 1967.

Love, Edmund G. *The 27th Infantry Division in World War II*. Washington, D.C.: Infantry Journal Press, 1949.

McMillan, George. *The Old Breed: A History of the First Marine Division in World War II*. Washington, D.C.: Infantry Journal Press, 1949.

Marshall, S. L. A. *Island Victory*. Washington, D.C.: Infantry Journal Press, 1944.

Meyers, Max. *Ours to Hold High: The History of the 77th Division in World War II*. Washington, D.C.: Infantry Journal Press, 1987.

Morrison, Wilbur H. *Above and Beyond*. New York: St. Martins, 1983.

_____. *Point of No Return: The Story of the 20th Air Force*. New York: Times Books, 1979.

Mueller, Paul J. *The 81st Infantry Division in World War II*. Washington, D.C.: Infantry Journal Press, 1948.

Musicant, Ivan. *Battleship at War*. New York: Avon, 1988.

Okumiya, Masatake, and Mitso Fuchida. *Midway: The Battle That Doomed Japan*. Annapolis, Md.: Naval Institute Press, 1955.

Okumiya, Masatake, Mitso Fuchida, and Jiro Horikoshi. *Zero*. New York: Dutton, 1956.

Pacific War Research Society. *Japan's Longest Day*. New York: Kondansha International, 1990.

Pomeroy, Earl. *Pacific Outpost: American Strategy in Guam and Micronesia*. Palo Alto, Calif.: Stanford University Press, 1951.

Prange, Gordon W. *At Dawn We Slept.* New York: Penguin, 1982.
_____. *Miracle at Midway.* New York: Penguin, 1982.
Preston, Anthony. *Aircraft Carriers.* New York: Grosset and Dunlap, 1979.
Proehl, Carl W., ed. *The Fourth Marine Division in World War II.* Washington, D.C.: Infantry Journal Press, 1946.
Reynolds, Clark. *The Fast Carriers: The Forging of an Air Navy.* New York: McGraw-Hill, 1968.
Shaw, Henry. *Tarawa: A Legend Is Born.* New York: Ballantine, 1969.
Sheek, Patrick, and Gene Cook. *The U.S. Marines in the Pacific, 1942–1945.* New York: Sloan, 1947.
Sherrod, Robert. *History of Marine Corps Aviation in World War II.* Washington, D.C.: Combat Forces Press, 1952.
_____. *On to Westward.* New York: Duell, Sloan and Pearce, 1945.
_____. *Tarawa.* New York: Duell, Sloan and Pearce, 1945.
Simmons, Edward H. *The United States Marines.* New York: Viking, 1976.
Sledge, E. B. *With the Old Breed at Peleliu and Okinawa.* Novato, Calif.: Presidio, 1981.
Smith, S. E. *The United States Marine Corps in World War II.* 2 vols. New York: Ace, 1973.
Spector, Ronald H. *Eagle Against the Sun: The American War with Japan.* New York: Free Press, 1985.
Tillman, Barrett. *The Wildcat in World War II.* Annapolis, Md.: Nautical and Aviation, 1983.
Toland, John. *Infamy: Pearl Harbor and Its Aftermath.* Garden City, N.Y.: Doubleday, 1982.
_____. *The Rising Sun.* 2 vols. New York: Random House, 1970.
Wheeler, Richard. *Iwo.* New York: Lippincott and Cowell, 1980.
_____. *A Special Valor: The U.S. Marines and the Pacific War.* New York: Harper and Row, 1983.
Willmott, H. P. *Empires in Balance.* Annapolis, Md.: Naval Institute Press, 1982.
Y'Blood, William. *Red Sun Rising: The Battle of the Philippine Sea.* Annapolis, Md.: Naval Institute Press, 1980.

INDEX

Aaron Ward, 437
ABDACOM, 124–26, 131–32, 134–35
ABDAFLOT, 125, 129
Abe, RAdm. Hiroaki, 165, 199–200
Abele, 432
Abukuma, 359
Adachi, Lt. Gen. Hatazo, 274, 284–87, 463
Adak, 154, 157, 170
Admiralty Islands, 274, 278
Agat, 327–28
A-Go Plan, 281, 308
Ainsworth, RAdm. Walden L., 231–32
Air Command Solomons (AirSols), 228, 235–36, 240, 244, 275
Akagi, 78, 81, 90, 142, 152, 159, 163–65
Akatsuki, 363
Akiyama, RAdm. Monzo, 264
Alabama, 40
Albacore, 43, 314
Aleutians, 153–54, 157, 165, 245, 250, 253–54
Allen Sumner, 381
Amboina, 129–30
American Volunteer Group (AVG), 24, 62
Anami, Gen. Korechika, 291, 484, 489–90, 493–94
Angaur, 16, 340, 343
Anglo-Japanese Treaty, 14–15
Anthony, 442

Aoba, 192
Arashi, 164
Arizona, 92, 94, 96
Arnold, Gen. Henry H., 51, 88, 112, 190, 301, 408, 430, 448, 486
Arnold, Maj. Gen. Archibald V., 352, 369
Arnold, Maj. Gen. William H., 456–57
Asan, 326–27
Ashigara, 116
Aslito airfield, 316
Astoria, 166, 182
Atago, 65, 355
Atlanta, 199
Atsuchi, Col. Kanehiko, 415
Attlee, Clement R., 482
Attu, 154, 157–58, 170, 250–53
Augusta, 480, 488
Austen, Mount, 179, 198, 204–5
Australia, 130, 134, 138, 140–41, 144, 146, 174, 209, 215; air force (RAAF), 141, 213, 215, 223, 279, 283, 468; army units, corps: I, 338, 469–70; II, 272, 466; divisions: 3d, 225; 5th, 463, 465–66; 6th, 140, 214, 463–64, 466; 7th, 140, 209, 217, 222, 226, 473–74; 8th, 140–41; 9th, 141, 222, 225, 473; brigades: 2d Group, 470–71; 7th, 214, 468; 11th, 467; 16th, 216–17; 17th, 463–64; 18th, 212, 214, 216, 219–20;

19th, 464; 20th, 472; 21st, 212, 217, 226, 474; 24th, 472; 25th, 214–16, 226; 26th, 226; naval forces, 142, 295
Australia, 132, 142, 182, 353, 380–81

Baba, Lt. Gen. Masao, 472
Babelthuap, 340, 345
Bache, 442
Bairoko Harbor, 231, 233
Baker, Sgt. Thomas, 322
Balete Pass, 404
Balikpapan, 129, 469, 473–75
Baltimore, 300
Barber, Lt. Rex, 230
Barbey, RAdm. Daniel E., 222, 225, 272–74, 282, 287, 347, 474
Barton, 200
Bataan, 495
Bataan, 116–21, 386, 388–91; Death March, 121–22, 349
Batavia, 125, 138–39
Beightler, Maj. Gen. Robert S., 233, 242, 381, 397
Belleau Wood, 312, 365
Benham, 201
Berkey, RAdm. Russell S., 358–59, 381
Berryman, Maj. Gen. Frank H., 272
Betio, 255–56, 259
Biak, 287–89, 290–95, 309, 338
Birmingham, 356
Bismarck Sea, 419
Black Force, 139
Blackburn, Brigadier A. S., 139

Blamey, Gen. Sir Thomas A., 145, 215, 225–26, 271–72, 287, 462–63, 466, 469–70
Blandy, RAdm. William H. G., 344, 409, 412
Bloch, RAdm. Claude C., 84, 91
Bock, Capt. Frederick, 490
Bock's Car, 490
Bogan, RAdm. Gerald F., 305, 309, 356, 362
Boise, 129, 192, 381, 472
Bonin Islands, 109, 324, 339, 405, 408
Borneo, 83, 123, 127, 130, 455, 469–70
Bougainville, 142, 173, 235–38, 242–46, 287, 466–69
Bradley, Maj. Gen. James L., 352
Braine, 442
Bratton, Col. Rufus S., 80, 85–87
Brereton, Maj. Gen. Lewis H., 51, 110, 112–13, 125, 132–33, 135
Brett, Lt. Gen. George H., 125, 132–33, 142, 145, 209, 215, 222
Brockman, Comdr. William H., 164
Brooklyn, 40
Brown, 432
Brown, Maj. Gen. Albert E., 252
Brown, VAdm. Wilson E., 102, 143, 146, 148
Brownson, 275
Bruce, Maj. Gen. Andrew D., 328, 370–71, 434, 436
Brunei, 127, 362, 469, 471–73, 475
Brush, Maj. Gen. Rapp, 381

Buckner, Lt. Gen. Simon B., Jr., 250, 320, 423, 426, 429, 433, 436, 441, 444–45
Bulolo Valley, 141, 223
Buna, 210, 212–13, 216, 218, 220–22
Bunker Hill, 241, 263, 311, 313, 442
Burke, Capt. Arleigh A., 241
Bush, 432
Bushido, 20, 54
Butaritari Island, 255–56
Byrnes, James F., 481, 491–92

Cabot, 356
Cactus Air Force, 186, 203
Calhoun, 432
California, 39, 92, 94, 96, 358, 381
Callaghan, RAdm. Daniel J., 199–200
Canada Victory, 432
Canberra, 142, 182, 346
Cape Gloucester, 223, 272, 274–76, 465
Cape Torokina, 236, 238
Carlson, Lt. Col. Evans F., 255
Caroline Islands, ll, 47, 249, 288, 308, 339
Carpender, VAdm. Arthur S., 209, 304
Cassin, 95–96, 432
casualties: Australian, 214, 221, 287, 469, 471; Filipino, 122, 398; Japanese, 121, 184, 188, 201, 207, 214, 217, 220, 224, 234, 243, 246, 253, 261, 265, 285–87, 290, 295, 297, 304, 322–24, 329, 333, 335, 343, 357, 372, 388, 393, 398, 410, 419–20, 433, 435–37, 441, 445, 449, 456–57, 459–60, 462, 464, 469, 488, 490; U.S.: army, 220–21, 253, 265, 294, 296, 322, 324, 331, 345, 366, 382, 390, 398, 401, 404, 427, 430, 435–37, 440, 445, 456–57, 459–61; Marine Corps, 192, 203, 205, 207, 261, 265, 275, 324, 328, 331, 335, 345, 415, 420, 438, 440, 445; navy, 101–2, 138, 204, 234, 246, 256, 261, 333, 346, 419, 425, 445
Cates, Maj. Gen. Clifton B., 176, 179, 332, 413, 419
Cavella, 311
Cebu, 349, 365, 378, 455–56
Celebes, 127, 130
Chaffee, Brig. Gen. Adna R., Jr., 33
Chalan Kanoa, 302–3, 305, 307
Chamorros, 109, 303, 331–32
Chase, Maj. Gen. William C., 277, 390
Chiang Kai-shek, 22, 61, 299, 398, 482–83
Chi-Ha, 60
Chicago, 142, 182
Chichi Jima, 77, 310, 409
Chikuma, 90, 159, 168, 196, 360–61
China, 2, 3, 5, 7, 9, 11–12, 14, 16, 18–23, 26, 53, 55–56, 59, 70, 72–73, 78, 300–l, 447
Chitose, 124, 127, 130, 185, 311, 354, 363

Chiyoda, 311, 315, 354
Cho, Lt. Gen. Isamu, 422, 436–37, 441, 444
Choiseul, 235–37
Chokai, 182
Christie, Capt. Ralph W., 269
Churchill, Prime Minister Winston, 25, 124, 249, 381, 398, 404, 469, 480, 482
Chuyo, 67
Claggett, Comdr. Bladen, 355
Clark Field, 110, 384–86
Clark, RAdm. Joseph, 311, 433
Clarkson, Maj. Gen. Percy W., 403
Cleveland, President Grover, 9, 37
Clowes, Maj. Gen. Cyril A., 213–14
Cobia, 410
Collins, Maj. Gen. J. Lawton, 194, 205–6
Colorado, 39, 333
Columbia, 381
Combined Chiefs of Staff, 124–25, 221, 339
Condor, 90
Conolly, RAdm. Richard L., 262–63, 302, 324–25
Coolidge, Lt. Col. Joseph, 434
Coolidge, President Calvin, 14
Corlett, Maj. Gen. Charles H., 253–54, 262, 264
Corregidor, 119–20, 122–23, 391–94
Coward, Comdr. J. G., 358
Cowpens, 313
Crace, RAdm. John C., 148–50
Crutchley, RAdm. Victor A. C., 181–82, 271

Culin, Col. Frank L., 252–53
Cunningham, Brig. Gen. Julian W., 285
Cunningham, Comdr. Winfield Scott, 104–5, 108
Curtin, Prime Minister John, 144, 398, 469–70
Curtiss, 96
Cushing, 199

Dace, 355
Daly, 432
Dark, Col. Robert F., 345
Darter, 355
Darwin, 129, 134
Davao, 110, 124, 127–28, 362, 458
Davison, RAdm. Ralph E., 356, 412, 419
De Ruyter, 130, 136–37
del Valle, Maj. Gen. Pedro A., 187–88, 202
Devereux, Maj. James P. S., 104–5, 107–8
Dewey, Commodore George, 10, 38
DeWitt, Lt. Gen. John L., 250
Dobodura, 210, 222, 225
Doe, Brig. Gen. Jens A., 288–89, 455
Dönitz, Adm. Karl, 48
Doolittle, Lt. Col. James H., 146
Doorman, RAdm. Karel W. F. M., 130–32, 134–37
Downes, 95–96
Draemel, RAdm. Milo F., 98
Dreadnought, 14, 38–39
Drexler, 442
Driniumor River, 284–86

Dulles, Allen, 484
Duncan, 192
Dunckel, Brig. Gen. William C., 377
Dusenbury, Lt. Col. C. C., 86
Dutch, army: 126–27, 131–34; 2d Division, 139; 1st Regiment, 140; 6th Regiment, 139; naval actions, 129–31, 137
Dutch East Indies, 24–26, 51, 68–69, 73, 80, 85, 109–110, 123–124, 133–40, 453, 469–70
Dutch Harbor, 157–58

Earhart, Amelia, 17
École de guerre, 32
Edson, Col. Merritt A., 44, 187–88, 191, 193, 260
Eggert, Lt. Joseph, 312
Eichelberger, Lt. Gen. Robert L., 215–16, 278, 282, 294, 372, 376, 405, 448, 454, 459–62, 475, 495
Einstein, Albert, 478
Eisenhower, Gen. Dwight D., 32
El Fraile, 393–94
Elkton plans, 227–28, 235
Ellice Islands, 254
Ellis, Earl H., 17
Elrod, Capt. H. T., 106
Embick, Lt. Gen. Stanley D., 47
Emmons, 432
Emmons, Lt. Gen. Delos C., 103, 190
Empress Augusta Bay, 236–37
Encounter, 138
Engebi, 263, 265, 267
Eniwetok, 265, 267, 302, 309
Enola Gay, 488

Enterprise, 41, 98, 102, 105, 146, 155, 160, 162, 165, 168–69, 178, 185, 196–97, 199–101, 228, 236, 263, 314, 432, 442
Erskine, Brig. Gen. Graves B., 317, 319
Espíritu Santo, 148, 238
Essex, 42, 249, 263, 310–13, 356, 363, 432, 478
Eta Jima, 56
Eurocentric policy, 18, 25–26, 48, 72, 194, 337
Evans, 442
Evertsen, 138
Ewa Field, 94
Exeter, 131, 136–38
Ezaki, Col. Yoshio, 277

Fanshaw Bay, 360
Farragut, 40
Fechteler, RAdm. William M., 287, 295, 297
Fermi, Enrico, 479
Fife, Capt. James R., 269
Fiji Islands, 145, 174–75, 178
Finschhafen, 224, 226, 271
Fitch, RAdm. Aubrey W., 102, 148, 150, 228
Fleet Marine Force, 44
Fleming, Capt. R. W., 381
Fletcher, RAdm. Frank J., 102–4, 143, 146–51, 156–57, 160, 165–67, 170, 178–79, 183–85, 195
Florida Island, 181
Fonte Plateau, 331
Ford, 129
Ford Island, 90, 92
Formidable, 442
Formosa, 5, 19, 58, 110, 113, 299,

337, 346–47, 349, 354, 365, 380, 431, 477
Forrestall, James V., 417, 491
Fort Shafter, 87, 91
Four-Power Treaty, 15
Fox, 442
France, 5, 25, 29, 32–34, 48, 68–69
Franklin, 363, 365, 425, 442
Fraser, Adm. Sir Bruce, 381, 425
French Frigate Shoal, 154
Fubuki, 65, 192
Fuchida, Comdr. Mitsuo, 75, 77, 89–90, 92, 97
Fuchs, Klaus, 482
Fujishige, Col. Masatochi, 401
Fukudome, VAdm. Shigeru, 69–70, 230, 346, 354, 370, 372
Fuller, Maj. Gen. Horace H., 282, 291–94
Fuller, Maj. Gen. J. F. C., 33
Furlong, RAdm. William R., 92
Fuso, 153, 355, 358–59

Gambier Bay, 361
Gar, 42
Gato, 42
Gay, Ens. George H., 162
Gazelle Peninsula, 465–66
Geelvink Bay, 287, 290
Geiger, Brig. Gen. Roy S., 186, 195, 242–43, 303, 328–30, 334–35, 444
Genda, Comdr. Minoru, 75, 77, 89, 97
Gentleman's Agreement, 14
Germany, 5, 11–12, 25, 32, 48, 68, 70, 72, 479–80, 484

Gerow, Brig. Gen. Leonard T., 80, 86–87
Ghormley, VAdm. Robert L., 144, 175, 178, 181, 185–86, 190–91, 194–95
Gilbert Islands, 246, 249, 255
Gill, Maj. Gen. William H., 283–84, 404
Ginder, RAdm. Samuel P., 263
Glassford, VAdm. William A., 125, 129, 134, 137–38
Gona, 210, 216–17
Goodenough Island, 213, 216
Goto, Maj. Ushio, 340
Goto, RAdm. Aritomo, 109, 147, 150, 192
Graf Spee, 131
Grampus, 42
Great Artiste, 490
Great Britain, 12, 15, 18, 25–26, 32, 38, 57, 68–69, 74, 85, 136; Royal Navy, 136–38, 148, 425, 432, 442
Great White Fleet, 2, 38
Green Islands, 244
Grew, Ambassador Joseph, 21, 24, 73, 480–81
Griner, Maj. Gen. George W., Jr., 320–21
Griswold, Maj. Gen. Oscar W., 233, 243, 376, 384–86, 397, 400–401, 461, 466
Groves, Brig. Gen. Leslie R., 479
Guadalcanal, 45, 173–207, 227, 237–38, 240
Guam, 10–11, 18, 46, 49, 109, 301–3, 309, 311, 324–32, 335, 407, 449, 453

Gwin, 232

Hadley, 442
Haguro, 136
Hale, Maj. Gen. Willis H., 411
Haleiwa Field, 94
Hall, 360
Hall, Maj. Gen. Charles P., 284–86, 338, 389–91
Halmahera, 291, 294, 337–38
Halsey, Adm. William F., Jr., 84, 88, 98, 102, 155–56, 195–96, 227–28, 233–35, 240–41, 250, 278, 339, 344, 346, 350, 356–57, 361–65, 370, 376, 378, 380, 407, 411, 495–96
Hammann, 166
Hanihara, Ambassador Masano, 13
Hanneken, Col. Herman H., 44, 194, 198, 341
Hansell, Brig. Gen. Haywood S., Jr., 408, 448
Hara, Adm. Chuichi, 149–51
Harada, Lt. Gen. Jiro, 457–59
Haraden, 378
Harding, 432
Harding, Maj. Gen. Edwin F., 215, 217, 219
Harmon, Maj. Gen. Millard, 191, 195, 204, 228, 233, 411, 421
Harrill, RAdm. William F., 311
Harris, Col. Harold D. 341
Hart, Adm. Thomas C., 51, 108, 110, 112, 115, 125, 129, 132
Haruna, 64, 116–17, 152, 159, 192, 195, 199, 315, 355, 478

Hata, Field Marshal Shunroku, 451, 493
Hatanaka, Maj. Kenji, 493
Hatsukaze, 240
Hawaiian Islands, 9, 15, 46, 48, 78, 82, 84, 87, 89, 99, 102, 145
Hayashi, Gen. Senjuro, 20
Hayate, 106
Hearst Press, 9, 12–13
Heermann, 360
Heisenberg, Werner K., 479
Helena, 96, 197, 232
Helfrich, VAdm. Conrad, 132–33, 136
Henderson Field, 183, 187, 195, 199, 203, 215
Hepburn, RAdm. Arthur J., 49
Herring, Lt. Gen. Edmund F., 215
Hester, Maj. Gen. John H., 230, 233
Hickam Field, 88, 90, 92, 94–95, 98
Hiei, 64, 76, 153, 195, 200
Higashikuni, Prince Toshihiko, 493
Higgins, Andrew, 45
Hill, RAdm. Harry W., 228, 256, 265, 267, 332
Hirohito, 19, 74, 480–81, 485, 487, 490–92, 494–97
Hiroshima, 487–88
Hiryu, 75–76, 107, 130, 152, 160, 165, 167
Hitler, Adolf, 25, 48, 68, 99
Hiyo, 67, 199, 201, 311, 315
Hobart, 142

Hodge, Maj. Gen. John R., 236, 338, 366, 423, 428, 435–36, 438
Hodges, Gen. Courtney H., 448
Hokkaido, 452, 478
Holcomb, Lt. Gen. Thomas, 195
Holland, 72–73
Hollandia, 276, 278–79, 281, 289, 347, 352
Holtz Bay, 170, 250, 253
Homma, Lt. Gen. Masaharu, 109–10, 116, 119–22, 124
Honolulu, 76, 95–96
Honolulu, 232, 353
Honshu, 154, 411, 448–49, 452, 477–78
Hoover, RAdm. John E., 248, 264
Hopkins, Harry L., 99, 480
Horii, Maj. Gen. Tomitaro, 109, 141, 174, 188, 210, 212, 214–16, 226
Horikoshi, Jiro, 63
Hornet, 42, 146–47, 155, 160, 162, 165, 168–69, 190, 196–97, 310–11, 313
Hosho, 66, 167
Hosogaya, VAdm. Boshiro, 153, 157–58, 169–70
Houston, 110, 130, 134, 137–39; (new), 346
Howorth, 432
Hull, 378
Hull, Cordell, 24, 71–73, 76, 78, 81, 84–85, 88
Humboldt Bay, 278, 282
Hyakutake, Lt. Gen. Haruyoshi, 183, 188, 190, 193–94, 198, 203, 205, 207, 210, 237, 242, 244, 246, 466–67

Hyman, 432
Hyuga, 153, 354, 478

I-168, 166, 168
I-175, 257
I-26, 186
Ichiki, Col. Kiyono, 184
Ichimaru, RAdm. Toshinosuke, 410
Ida, Lt. Col. Masataka, 493
Idaho, 39, 252, 417
Ie Shima, 433–36, 442–43, 452, 494
Ilgen, Maj. Gen. G. A., 139
Ilu River, 174, 184
Imamura, Lt. Gen. Hitoshi, 138, 140, 203, 205, 223, 465–66
Immigration Act of 1924, 14, 20
Inada, Maj. Gen. Masazumi, 282–83
Indefatigable, 432
Independence, 241, 249
Indiana, 40
Indianapolis, 486–87
Indochina, 72, 81, 131
Indomitable, 442
Ingraham, 437
Inoue, Gen. Sadae, 340
Inoue, VAdm. Shigeyoshi, 58, 109, 150–51
Intramuros, 397–98
Intrepid, 363, 365, 425
Inukai, Prime Minister Tsuyoshi, 21
Iowa, 266
Irving, Maj. Gen. Frederick A., 282, 352
Ise, 153, 354, 363, 478

Ishii, Viscount Kikuyiro, 12
Itagaki, Capt. Akria, 292
Iwabachi, RAdm. Sanji, 384, 387, 395, 397
Iwasa, Maj. Gen. Shun, 245
Iwo Jima, 310, 405, 408-9, 412-21

Jallao, 363
Jaluit, 102, 268
Japan: aircraft production, 62; army organization, 57; army training, 3-4, 55; atrocities, 12, 23, 147, 244, 296, 332, 396; capitulation, 492-94; Chinese war, 21-24, 53, 55-56, 59-61, 69-70, 73-74, 78, 81, 300; economic policies, 3, 5, 16, 18-19, 59; espionage, 78-80, 89, 95, 380; government system, 2-3, 19-21; Imperial General Headquarters, 58-59, 203, 205, 288, 350, 365, 379, 418, 450-51; imperialism, 1-2, 4-8, 11-13, 15-16, 20-27, 52, 67-72; interservice rivalry, 56-59; Liaison Committee, 59, 70, 72, 74, 77-78, 81; naval organization, 57-58; naval training, 4, 55-56; naval rivalry with U.S., 14-15; peace proposals, 483-87, 489, 491; Pearl Harbor attack, 77-78, 89-98; Pearl Harbor planning, 68-70, 73-78, 81; pilot training, 63-64; relations with Axis, 67-68, 70; submarine operations, 115, 154, 168, 190, 200, 257, 487; surrender arrangements, 495-97; ultra-nationalism, 20-21, 23, 54-55; U.S. diplomatic relations 1941, 71, 73-74, 76, 78-79, 81, 84-88; U.S. embargo, 68-69, 73-74, 78, 81

Japanese air strikes: Cape Gloucester, 275; Ceylon, 146; Coral Sea, 150-51; Darwin, 134; Dutch East Indies, 131, 134, 136, 138; Dutch Harbor, 158; Guadalcanal, 180, 185-86; Guam, 109; Hollandia, 282-83; Iwo Jima, 419; Midway, 159-61; Okinawa, 425, 431-33, 437, 442; Pearl Harbor, 77-78, 89-98; Philippines, 113-14, 353, 356-57, 361-63, 365, 370; Philippine Sea, 312-24; Salamaua, 143; Wake, 105-6

Japanese army units: armies: 1st General, 451; 2d General, 451; 2d Area, 279, 288, 298; 8th Area, 203; 11th, 12th, 13th, 15th, and 16th Area, 451; 4th Air, 349, 369-70, 372; 14th, 349, 368-69, 372; 15th, 109; 16th, 134, 369; 17th, 188, 210; 18th, 274, 279, 286, 464; 32d, 436-37, 457; 35th, 349, 368, 371, 454, 456; 37th, 472; 100th, 457, 459; Eastern, 494; Kwantung, 450, 482; Southern, 281, 348; divisions: 1st, 349, 372; 2d, 139, 188, 193; 4th, 120; 16th, 109-10, 349, 352, 365, 369-70; 21st, 120; 26th, 369-70; 30th, 372, 459; 32d, 437;

38th, 109, 188; 41st, 367; 43d,
304; 48th, 109–10, 115, 119,
139–40; 51st, 223; 61st, 109;
62d, 422, 436, 439, 441; 102d,
372; Konoye, 493; brigades:
2d Para, 369, 371; 35th, 184,
187; 44th Mixed, 436–37, 440,
443; 48th, 329; 56th Mixed,
472; 65th, 109, 119; 68th, 370;
regiments: 23d, 241; 26th Tank,
410; 222d, 291; 230th, 139–40
Japanese miscellaneous units: 2d
Attack Force, 115; 56th Group,
139; Aoba Detachment, 213–
14; Eguchi Detachment, 385;
Iwasa Unit, 245; Kawashima
Force, 399–400; Kemba Group,
384–86; Kobayoshi Force, 400–
401; Magata Unit, 245; Muda
Unit, 245; Noguchi Force, 400–
401; Omori Detachment, 389;
Shimbu Group, 384, 399, 401,
403; Shobu Group, 383, 403,
460–62; South Seas Detachment, 109, 141–42, 212; Special Landing Force, 226; Takaya
Detachment, 528; Takayama
Detachment, 528
Japanese naval units: fleets: 1st,
58; 2d, 58, 110, 169, 184, 240;
3d, 58, 110; 4th, 58, 142; 8th,
181, 233; 1st Air, 66, 75, 281,
361; 1st Mobile, 152, 308–10,
349–50; 2d Mobile, 153, 240;
Carrier, 58; Combined, 58, 74,
156–69, 170, 252, 267, 281,
293, 301, 305, 308; Southeast
Area, 73; miscellaneous organizations: 1st Attack Force, 361;

5th Base Force, 349; 5th Car-
rier Division, 75; 5th Landing
Force, 153, 157, 184; 6th Base
Force, 346, 372; 7th Landing
Force, 255, 256; Ichiki Detach-
ment, 153; Special Naval Base
Forces, 255, 384, 443, 457
Japanese-Soviet Neutrality Pact,
26
Jarman, Maj. Gen. M. Sanderford,
319
Java, 51, 70, 126, 130–40, 474
Java, 137
Jintsu, 186, 232
Johnson, 360
Johnson, Lt. Col. Chandler W.,
416
Joint Planning Board, 45–46
Jones, Col. George M., 392–93
Jones, Maj. Gen. Albert M., 117
Jones, Maj. Gen. Henry L. C.,
389–90
Juneau, 200
Junyo, 67, 165, 195, 199, 311
Jupiter, 137
jushin, 336, 483

Kaga, 76, 142, 152, 159, 162–64
Kagoshima, 75
Kaiten, 431, 451
Kajioka, RAdm. Sadamichi, 105–
8
Kakuta, RAdm. Kakuji, 158, 311
Kalinin Bay, 362
kamikaze, 361–62, 365, 370–71,
376–81, 419, 425, 431–33, 437,
451
Kanda, Lt. Gen. Masatane, 245–
46, 468

Kaneohe Naval Air Station, 90
Kataoka, Lt. Gen. Tadasu, 367
Katchin Peninsula, 421, 427
Kawabe, Gen. Masakazu, 451
Kawabe, Lt. Gen. Torashiro, 494
Kawaguchi, Maj. Gen. Kiyotake,
    184, 187–88, 215
Kawase, VAdm. Shiro, 251, 253
Kelly, Capt. Colin P., 116
Kenney, Maj. Gen. George C.,
    145, 215, 218, 222, 225, 241,
    244, 272, 450, 452
Kerama Islands, 424–25, 432, 442
Kidd, 432
Kido, Marquis Koichi, 336, 483,
    485, 489
kikusui, 431–32, 442
Killen, 358
Kimmel, Adm. Husband E., 49–
    50, 79–80, 82–83, 88, 91, 101–
    4, 117
Kimura, RAdm. Masatomi, 379
King, Adm. Ernest J., 39, 103–
    4, 145, 174–75, 182, 248–49,
    299, 421, 447
King, Maj. Gen. Edward P., Jr.,
    122–23
Kinkaid, RAdm. Thomas C., 149,
    195–96, 200, 204, 251–52, 272,
    277, 347, 350, 357, 363–64,
    368, 381, 495
Kinryu Maru, 186
Kinu, 359
Kirishima, 64, 76, 152, 201–2
Kisaragi, 106
Kiska, 154, 157–58, 170, 250–
    51, 253–54
Kita, Ikki, 20
Kitagami, 359

Kitkun Bay, 361–62, 381
Knox, Secretary of the Navy Frank,
    83, 86, 88, 99, 102–3, 194
Kodiak, 157–58
Kodo-Ha, 19–20, 23
Koga, Adm. Mineichi, 171, 230,
    237–41, 244, 252–53, 266–67,
    281
Koiso, Gen. Kuniaki, 336, 372, 483
Kokoda Trail, 210, 212, 214–17,
    274
Kolanin Bay, 360
Kolombangara, 230, 232–34
Kondo, VAdm. Nobutake, 110,
    134, 154, 165, 168, 170, 184–
    85, 195, 197, 199, 201
Kongo, 64, 153, 192, 195, 199,
    355
Kono, Lt. Gen. Takeshi, 455
Konoye, Prime Minister Fumimaro,
    21–22, 25, 68, 72–74, 77, 81,
    336, 483, 485
Konuma, Maj. Gen. Haruo, 404
Korea, 5–8, 19–20, 495
Korteneer, 137
Kramer, Lt. Comdr. Alwin D.,
    80, 85
Kriegsakademie, 32
Krueger, Lt. Gen. Walter, 272–
    73, 284, 286, 288–93, 297, 337,
    340, 352, 365, 368–70, 372,
    375–76, 382, 384, 386–87, 389,
    392, 397–98, 403, 447, 453,
    460
Krulak, Lt. Col. Victor H., 236–
    37
Kumano, 195, 360
Kuribayashi, Lt. Gen. Tadamichi,
    410, 413, 415, 418–20

Kurile Islands, 77–78, 452
Kurita, Adm. Takeo, 168, 199, 313, 350, 355–57, 359, 361–64
Kuroda, Lt. Gen. Shigenori, 349
Kuropatkin, Gen. Aleksey N., 6
Kuroshima, RAdm. Kameto, 70
Kurusu, Ambassador Saburo, 81, 84, 88
Kusaka, RAdm. Ryunosuke, 77
Kusaka, VAdm. Jin'ichi, 173, 205, 223
Kuzume, Col. Naoyuki, 291–93
Kwajalein Atoll, 106, 302, 309
Kyoto, 487
Kyushu, 365, 421, 424, 431–32, 442, 447, 449, 452–53, 470

Lae, 141–42, 217, 223–27
Laffey, 199
Lamphier, Capt. Thomas G., Jr., 230
Landing Operations Doctrine, 44
Landrum, Brig. Gen. Eugene M., 252–53
Langley, 41, 110, 136; (new) 356, 363
Lansing, Secretary of State Robert, 12
Layton, Lt. Comdr. Edwin T., 79–80, 155
League of Nations, 16–19, 21
Leahy, Adm. William D., 480
Leary, VAdm. Herbert F., 142, 145
Lee, RAdm. Willis A., Jr., 200, 202, 267, 311, 313, 316, 357, 362, 364
Lejeune, Maj. Gen. John A., 43

LeMay, Maj. Gen. Curtis E., 408, 448–49, 473, 487
Lend-Lease Act, 26, 48
Leslie, Lt. Comdr. Maxwell F., 163–64
Lexington, 41, 50, 98, 101–2, 142–43, 148, 150–51, 311–13; (new) 356, 359, 365
Leyte, 300, 338–39, 347–54, 365–72, 375–78
Leyte Gulf, 350, 356–57, 360–61, 364
Liaotung Peninsula, 5–7
Lindsey, 432
Lindsey, Lt. Comdr. Eugene E., 162
Lingayen Gulf, 111, 115–16, 362, 375
Liscombe Bay, 257
Liversedge, Col. Harry B., 230–31, 233, 415
Lockwood, RAdm. Charles A., 269, 314, 376, 450
London Naval Treaty, 39
Long, 381
Long Island, 183
Los Baños, 401
Los Negros, 276–77
Louisville, 380
Luce, 437
Lumsden, Lt. Gen. Sir Herbert, 381
Luzon, 46, 111, 113, 115–21, 124, 299, 346, 349, 365, 369, 372, 375–77, 381–405, 453, 460–62

MacArthur, Gen. Douglas, 50–51, 87, 110–14, 116–23, 132,

143–45, 174–76, 190, 209–10,
212–13, 219, 221, 224, 227,
235–36, 247–50, 271–72, 276–
78, 283, 287, 290–91, 293–95,
297–300, 302, 337, 339–40,
345, 347, 352–53, 365, 368,
372, 381, 387, 392–94, 397,
405, 430, 447, 450, 453, 456,
462, 469, 472, 475, 494–97
Madang, 226, 274, 279, 463
Magata, Col. Isashi, 245
"Magic," 71
Mahan, 371
Mahan, RAdm. Alfred Thayer, 4
Majuro Island, 262
Makassar Strait, 130
Makin, 254–57
Makino, Lt. Gen. Shiro, 349, 369
Malaya, 24, 26, 69, 73, 80, 85,
141, 469
Malinta Hill, 122, 391–92
Maloelap, 255
Manchuria, 2, 5, 7–8, 20–22, 26,
59, 405, 482–83, 489, 497
Manhattan Project, 479
Manila, 46, 375–77, 384, 386–
87, 394–99, 405, 453, 494
Manila Bay, 50, 122, 375, 404
Manila Bay, 115, 380
Manjome, Maj. Gen. Takeo, 456
Manus, 276–78
Marblehead, 129–30
Mariana Islands, 11, 17, 246, 278,
281, 301–2, 304, 308, 324, 335,
337, 407
Markham Valley, 225, 272, 274
Marshall Islands, 11, 47, 246, 249,
261–62, 268, 302–3
Marshall, Gen. George C., 31,

33, 50, 80, 83, 86–87, 119,
125, 250, 319–20, 469, 480
Martin, Maj. Gen. Clarence A.,
284, 459
Maruyama, Lt. Gen. Masao, 188,
191, 193, 196
Maryland, 39, 92, 94, 96, 350, 358
Massachusetts, 40
Massacre Bay, 252
Massey, Lt. Comdr. Lance E., 163
Matsuda, Maj. Gen. Iwao, 274
Matsuoka, Foreign Minister
Yosuke, 25–26, 68, 72
Maya, 355
McCain, RAdm. John S., 175–
78, 362–63, 411, 442, 478
McClintock, Comdr. David, 355
McClusky, Lt. Comdr. Wade, 161–
62, 164, 167
McKinley, President William, 9–
10
McMillin, George J., 108
McMorris, RAdm. Charles H.,
84, 251–52
Meiji Revolution, 2–3, 53
Merrill, Lt. Col. Gyles, 390
Merrill, RAdm. A. Stanton, 240
Merritt, Maj. Gen. Wesley, 10
Midway Island, 18, 50, 97, 146,
155–56
Mikawa, VAdm. Gun'ichi, 181–
83, 199–201, 213–14, 349
Mikuma, 138, 169
Miles, Brig. Gen. Sherman, 80,
82–83, 86
Milford, Maj. Gen. E. J., 474–75
Milne Bay, 209–10, 212–14
Mindanao, 111–13, 337, 339, 347,
350, 365, 377, 454, 457–60

Mindoro, 372, 376–79, 454
Minneapolis, 98, 204
Mississippi, 39, 350, 358
Missouri, 432, 495–96
Mitchell, Brig. Gen. William, 35–36
Mitchell, Lt. Comdr. Samuel G., 162
Mitchell, Maj. John W., 228
Mitchell, Maj. Gen. Ralph, 244
Mitscher, RAdm. Marc A., 228, 263, 266, 310–12, 314–15, 325, 339, 344, 357, 363, 419, 424, 433, 442
Mizuho, 130
Mogami, 40, 138, 169, 359
Mokmer Field, 293
Molotov, Vyacheslav M., 482, 484–85
Mono Island, 236
Monssen, 200
Montgomery, RAdm. Alfred E., 241, 311
Moore, Brig. Gen. Ernest C., 421
Moosbrugger, Comdr. Frederick, 234
Mori, RAdm. Kokichi, 226
Mori, Lt. Gen. Takeshi, 493
Morotai, 291, 298, 300, 338, 362
Morozumi, Lt. Gen. Gyosaku, 457, 459
Morris, 432
Morrison, 437
Morshead, Lt. Gen. Sir Leslie, 272, 470, 475
Mountbatten, Adm. Lord Louis, 293
Muda, Col. Toyhorel, 245

Mudge, Maj. Gen. Verne D., 352, 386, 400
Mueller, Maj. Gen. Paul J., 341, 343, 345
Mullany, 432
Mullin, Maj. Gen. Charles L., Jr., 388, 403–4
Munda, 203, 227, 230–32
Murai, Maj. Gen. Kenjiro, 345
Murray, RAdm. George D., 196
Musashi, 266, 355
Mutsuhito, Emperor, 2, 53
Mutsu, 64, 153
Mutsuki, 186
Myoko, 127, 357

Nachi, 136, 359
Nafutan Peninsula, 303, 316–17
Nagano, Adm. Osami, 57, 69, 70, 205
Nagasaki, 487, 489–90
Nagato, 64, 153, 355, 357
Nagayoshi, Col. Sanenobu, 390
Nagoya, 419, 449, 477
Nagumo, VAdm. Chuichi, 58, 70, 75–78, 82, 89, 91, 96, 104, 126, 134, 146–147, 152–55, 160–61, 164–65, 167, 185, 196–97, 203
Naha, 421, 438, 440
Nakagawa, Col. Kunio, 340–41, 345
Nanking, 12, 23
Naotake, Sato, 485, 489
Nashville, 352, 378
Nassau, 252
National Defense Act of 1920, 33
Natsushio, 130

Nautilus, 161, 164
naval battles: Bali, 135; Balikpapan, 129; Bismarck Sea, 223–24; Cape Engaño, 362–64; Cape Esperance, 192; Coral Sea, 97, 148–52, 174, 210; Eastern Solomons, 185–86; Empress Augusta Bay, 240; Guadalcanal, 199–202; Java Sea, 136–37; Kolombangara, 232; Kula Gulf, 232; Leyte Gulf, 354–62; Makassar Strait, 130; Midway, 97, 144, 156–69, 174; Philippine Sea, 311–14, 325, 335, 361; Samar, 360–61; Santa Cruz Island, 196–97; Savo Island, 182–83; Tassafaronga, 204; Tsushima, 7, 67, 90, 308; Vella Gulf, 234
Naval Expansion Act of 1938, 41–42
Negros, 455–56
Nelson, Col. Leroy E., 204–5
Neosho, 148–49, 151
Neutrality Act, 24
Nevada, 92, 94–96, 252
New Britain, 141, 173, 225, 242, 272, 288, 464
New Caledonia, 144–45, 174–75
New Georgia, 141, 186, 227–28, 230–31, 233–34, 247, 250
New Guinea, 147, 152, 175, 209–27, 238, 271–300
New Ireland, 142, 173, 244, 276
New Jersey, 266–67, 339
New Mexico, 39, 381
New Orleans, 95, 204
New Zealand, 145, 178; army units:

3d Division, 236; 8th Brigade, 236; 14th Brigade, 244
Newcomb, 358
Ngesebus Island, 344
Nimitz, Adm. Chester W., 42, 47, 103, 142, 144–45, 147–48, 152–56, 169–70, 175, 179, 191, 227–28, 247–48, 250, 266–67, 278, 299–300, 302, 319, 335, 338–40, 345, 356, 378, 407–8, 430, 447, 450, 454, 495–96
Nine-Power Treaty, 15–16, 24
Nishibaru Ridge, 429
Nishimura, VAdm. Shoji, 135, 355, 357–59
Nisshu Maru, 410
Noemfoor Island, 295–97
Nomura, Ambassador Kichisaburo, 78, 84, 86, 88
Norman Scott, 333
North Carolina, 40, 178, 185, 190
Northampton, 204
Noshiro, 362
Noumea, 185, 195, 200
Numata, Lt. Gen. Takazo, 292

O'Brien, 190
O'Brien, Col. William, 321–22
Oahu, 47, 89–90, 92, 98, 102, 154
Obata, Lt. Gen. Hideyoshi, 304, 325, 331
Obayashi, RAdm. Sueo, 311–13
Office of Naval Intelligence (ONI), 80
Ofstie, RAdm. Ralph A., 341, 381
Ogata, Col. Kiyochi, 333–34
Oglala, 92, 96

Oka, Col. Akinosuka, 194
Okada, Prime Minister Keisuke, 21
Okamoto, Lt. Gen. Seigo, 484
Okinawa, 346, 405, 408–9, 417, 421–22, 426–31, 433, 435–46, 452, 475, 483
Oklahoma, 92, 96
Okochi, VAdm. Denshichi, 384
Oldendorf, RAdm. Jesse B., 341, 350, 357–59, 380–81
Ommaney Bay, 380
Open Door Policy, 11, 12
operations: Catchpole, 265; Coronet, 446–48, 452–53; Cyclone, 296; Downfall, 447; Flintlock, 262; Galvanic, 249; Hurricane, 291–92; Oboe, 473; Olympic, 447; Typhoon, 297; Watchtower, 175, 178–79
Oppenheimer, J. Robert, 479–80
Orange Plan, 45–47, 50, 67, 97, 111, 117, 247, 249–50
Orote Peninsula, 109, 327–28
Osaka, 449, 477
Osmeña, President Sergio, 352–53, 398
Ostfriesland, 35
Ota, RAdm. Minori, 443
Outerbridge, Lt. William W., 90–91
Owen Stanley Mountains, 174, 210, 216, 223
Oyama, Field Marshal Iwao, 7
Ozawa, VAdm. Jisaburo, 131, 135, 203, 308–10, 312–16, 354, 357, 362–64

Palau Islands, 17, 281, 339–40
Palawan, 454
Palembang, 134
Pallister, RAdm. A. F. E., 134
Palmer, 381
Panay, 378, 455
Panay incident, 23
Parker, Maj. Gen. George M., Jr., 116, 119
Parrott, 129
Parry Island, 265
Parsons, Capt. William S., 488
Patch, Maj. Gen. Alexander M., Jr., 195, 203–5
Patrick, Maj. Gen. Edwin D., 289, 295, 382, 388-89, 401
Paul Jones, 129
Pearl Harbor, 1, 17, 22, 30–31, 45–46, 52, 59, 61, 66, 68, 71, 76, 78, 81, 101–3, 146, 154; attack, 77–78, 82–98
Peleliu, 340–46, 413
Penguin, 108
Pennsylvania, 92, 95–96, 256
Pensacola, 40, 204, 417
Perch, 42, 65
Percival, Lt. Gen. Arthur E., 126
Perth, 136–38
Petrof Bay, 362
Phelps, 151
Philippines, 16, 18, 45–46, 48, 50–51, 69–70, 83, 87, 99, 109–24, 140, 144, 151, 276, 298–99, 358; army units: divisions: 11th, 112, 114, 116; 21st, 112, 121; 31st, 112, 116; 51st, 116; 71st, 112, 116; UAFIP (NL) Vol-

unteer, 402, 461; 26th Cavalry Regiment, 116; Scouts, 122; guerrillas, 391, 402–3, 455, 458
Philipps, VAdm. Tom, 126
Philips, Comdr. R. H., 358
Pike, 42, 65
Platt, Capt. W. M., 107
Poindexter, Gov. Joseph B., 99
Pope, 129, 138
Port Arthur, 5–7
Port Moresby, 141–44, 147–48, 152, 173–75, 188, 209–10, 212, 214–16
Portland, 98, 200
Potsdam Conference, 480, 482, 486; and Declaration, 482, 485, 487, 489–90
Pownall, Gen. Sir Henry, 125
Pownall, RAdm. Charles A., 248
Preston, 201
Prince of Wales, 126
Princeton, 236, 356
Puller, Lt. Col. Lewis B., 44, 191, 193, 341
Purdy, 432
Purple code, 79
Putnam, Maj. Paul A., 105
Pye, VAdm. William S., 88, 92, 103–4, 155
Pyle, Ernie, 434

Quebec Conference, 339
Quezon, President Manuel L., 121
Quincy, 182

Rabaul, 109, 142–43, 147, 173, 175, 179–80, 183, 187, 203,

206, 217, 224, 227, 238–39, 241, 244, 246, 268, 272–73, 465
Rainbow plans, 48–49, 82
Raleigh, 96
Ralph Talbot, 432
Ramsey, Maj. Gen. Sir Alan, 465–66
Ramu Valley, 272, 274
Ranger, 41
Rathburn, 432
Redfish, 379
Reeves, RAdm. John W., 263, 311
Rendova, 231
Reno, 356
Repulse, 126
Richardson, Lt. Gen. Robert C., Jr., 248, 319, 421
Richardson, RAdm. James O., 47
Roberts, 360
Robertson, Maj. Gen. Sir Horace, 464
Rochefort, Comdr. Joseph J., 155
Rockey, Maj. Gen. Keller E., 413
Rockwell, RAdm. Francis W., 251–52
Rodman, 432
Roi-Namur, 105, 255, 262–63, 268
Roosevelt, President Franklin D., 18, 23–26, 69, 71, 73, 85–86, 88, 124, 132, 147, 249, 299, 337, 404, 430, 478, 480, 486
Roosevelt, President Theodore, 2, 10, 38
Root, Secretary of War Elihu, 30–31, 38

Rosenthal, Joe, 416
Row, Brigadier R. A., 236
Rowell, Maj. Gen. Sydney F., 210–12, 214
Rupertus, Maj. Gen. William H., 180, 341, 343–44
Russia (see also Soviet Union), 2, 4–7, 55, 60–61, 67, 72, 74, 85
Russo-Japanese War, 2, 4, 6–8, 46, 55
Ryan, Capt. Bernard, 435
Ryujo, 110, 124, 131, 135, 138, 153, 165, 167–68, 185, 311, 315
Ryukyu, 346

Saipan, 17, 301–5, 307–8, 316–23, 332, 411, 483
Saito, Lt. Gen. Yoshitsugu, 304, 307–8, 321
Salamaua, 141–43, 217, 223–26
Salmon, 42
Salt Lake City, 40
Samar, 360–61, 460
Samoa, 145, 174, 190
Sampson, RAdm. William T., 38
San Bernardino Strait, 309, 356–57, 361, 364, 375
San Francisco, 192, 197, 199–200
San Jacinto, 363
San Tomás University, 386–87
Sanananda, 217, 220–21, 223
Sangamon, 228
Sano, Lt. Gen. Tadayoshi, 188
Santa Cruz Islands, 175
Santee, 362

Santo Tomas, 115, 402
Saratoga, 49, 101–2, 151, 155, 169, 178, 185–86, 228, 236, 263, 419
Sarawak, 127
Sargo, 42
Sasaki, Maj. Gen. Noboru, 231–32, 234
Savige, Lt. Gen. Stanley, 466–68
Savo Island, 180, 182, 187
Schilling, Maj. Gen. Willem, 140
Schmidt, Maj. Gen. Harry, 262, 302, 309, 323, 332, 335, 409, 417
Schofield Barracks, 94
Schouten Islands, 287
Schrier, lst Lt. Harold G., 416
Scott, RAdm. Norman, 182, 192, 199
Sea Witch, 136
Seawolf, 115
Sebree, Brig. Gen. Edmund B., 202
Seeadler Harbor, 276–77
Selfridge, 235
Senda, Maj. Gen. Sadasue, 418–19
Sendai, 240
Shanghai, 21, 120
Shantung Province, 5, 12, 16
Shaw, 96
Shea, 437
Shepherd, Maj. Gen. Lemuel C., Jr., 327–28, 440, 443
Sherman, RAdm. Forrest P., 263, 412, 419, 433
Sherman, RAdm. Frederick C., 240–41, 356–57

Shibasaki, RAdm. Keiji, 255
Shigematsu, Maj. Gen. Kiyoshi, 327
Shigemi, Maj. Gen. Isao, 388
Shigemitsu, Foreign Minister Mamoru, 483–84
Shigure, 359
Shikoku, 442, 449, 452, 477
Shima, VAdm. Kiyohide, 355, 359, 362
Shimada, Adm. Shigetaro, 74, 336
Shimizu, Col., 296
Shiranuhi, 362
Sho-1 Plan, 349–50, 354, 357, 361, 364
Shoho, 150–51
Shokaku, 67, 75, 95, 147, 150–52, 185, 195–96, 311, 314
Short, Lt. Gen. Walter C., 82–83, 91, 95, 103, 117
Shortland Islands, 186, 188, 199, 201, 203, 235, 239
Shoup, Col. David M., 259–60
Shubrick, 442
Shuri, 421, 429, 438–41
Sibert, Maj. Gen. Franklin C., 290, 347, 366–67, 369, 454, 458
Sims, 149, 151
Sims, Adm. William S., 15
Singapore, 69, 73, 126, 133, 281, 350, 469
Sino-Japanese War, 5
Slim, Gen. Sir William J., 473
Smith, 196
Smith, Maj. Gen. Holland M., 44, 248, 256–57, 259, 261–62, 264–65, 302–3, 316–20, 322, 328, 333, 417–18

Smith, Maj. Gen. Julian C., 256, 260
Smith, Maj. Gen. Ralph C., 256–57, 302, 309, 316–20
Solomon Islands, 142–43, 147, 174, 183
Somerville, Adm. Sir James F., 146
Sorido, 293
Soryu, 67, 75–76, 95, 107, 130, 152, 163–64
South Dakota, 40, 196, 201–2, 312
Southland, 381
Soviet Union, 8, 26, 70, 405, 481–82, 485, 489, 497
Spaatz, Gen. Carl A., 449–50, 452, 487–88, 491
Spanish-American War, 9–10, 30–31, 45
Spence, 378
Sprague, RAdm. Clifton A. F., 360
Sprague, RAdm. Thomas L., 338, 350, 359, 363
Spruance, RAdm. Raymond A., 155, 166–70, 247, 265–67, 302, 305, 309–11, 315–16, 339, 411, 421, 425, 433, 442, 447, 495
St. Lo, 362
St. Louis, 95, 232
Stalin, 404, 480–81, 485
Stark, Adm. Harold R., 78–79, 83, 86–87, 103–4
Starkenborg-Stachouwer, Gov. Gen. A. W. L. T., 133, 140
Sterett, 432
Stevens, Maj. Gen. Sir Jack, 463–64, 466

Stilwell, Gen. Joseph W., 444
Stimson, Secretary of War Henry
    L., 21, 73, 78, 81, 86, 487, 491
Stirling Island, 236
Stormes, 442
Struble, RAdm. Arthur D., 377
Stump, RAdm. Felix B., 360, 362
Sturdee, Lt. Gen. Sir Vernon, 463
Sturgeon, 129
Suenaga, Col. Tsunetaro, 327
Sugiyama, Gen. Hajime, 69, 205,
    372, 451, 493
Sumatra, 74, 126, 131–34
Sumiyoshi, Gen. Tadashi, 193
Suribachi, Mount, 409, 414–17,
    421
Surigao Strait, 358–59
Sutherland, Maj. Gen. Richard
    K., 112, 145, 213, 496
Suwannee, 362
Suzuki, Prime Minister Kantaro,
    483, 487, 489–90, 492
Suzuki, Lt. Comdr. Suguru, 76
Suzuki, Lt. Gen. Sosaku, 349–
    50, 352, 366–67, 370, 454, 456
Sweeney, Maj. Charles W., 489–
    90
Swift, Maj. Gen. Innis P., 277,
    376, 461
Swing, Maj. Gen. Joseph M., 369,
    402–3
Swordfish, 129
Szilard, Leo, 478

Taft, President William, 11
Tagami, Lt. Gen. Hachiro, 288–
    90
Taiyo, 67, 311, 314

Takagi, Adm. Sokichi, 336
Takagi, RAdm. Takeo, 136–38,
    147, 149–51
Takahashi, VAdm. Ibo, 110
Takao, 355
Takashina, Lt. Gen. Takeshi, 325,
    327, 329, 331
Takasu, VAdm. Shiro, 154
Talbot, Comdr. Paul, 129
Tambor, 42, 169, 269
Tamu, 363
Tanahmerah Bay, 278, 281–82
Tanaka, Gen. Shizuchi, 494
Tanaka, RAdm. Raizo, 124, 184–
    87, 190–92, 199, 201–2, 204
Tanapag, 321–22
Tankan Bay, 78, 81
Tapotchau, Mount, 303, 316
Tarakan Island, 126–27, 469–71,
    475
Tarawa, 254–55, 257–61, 341
Tassafaronga, 192, 201
Tatsuta, 106
Tayama Maru, 422
Taylor, Lt. Ken, 89, 94
Tennessee, 39, 92, 96, 358, 432
*Tentative Manual for Landing
    Operations,* 44
Tenyru, 106
ter Poorten, Maj. Gen. Hein, 125,
    130, 133, 140
Terauchi, Field Marshal Count
    Hisaichi, 109, 348–49, 365, 376,
    379
Teshima, Lt. Gen. Fusataro, 279,
    283
Thach, Lt. Comdr. John S., 163
Thailand, 25, 69, 83

Theobald, RAdm. Robert A., 157–58, 250–51
Thomas, Lt. Comdr. Francis, 95–96
Tibbets, Col. Paul W., Jr., 486, 488
Tinian, 301–3, 305, 332–35, 486–87, 490
Tippecanoe, 148
Tjilatjap, 131
Togo, Adm. Marquis Heihachiro, 4, 6–8, 67, 90
Togo, Foreign Minister Shigenori, 81, 86, 484, 487, 489, 491
Tojo, Prime Minister Hideki, 25, 54, 57, 77–78, 81, 335–36, 483
Tokyo, 81, 183, 405, 419, 449, 491
Tomai, Comdr. Asaichi, 329
Tominaga, Lt. Gen. Kyoji, 349, 369–70, 372
Tomochika, Maj. Gen. Yoshiharu, 371
Tomonaga, Lt. Joichi, 161
Tone, 90, 159–61
Towers, VAdm. John H., 248
Toyoda, Adm. Soemu, 230, 279, 281, 293, 346, 349–50, 354–55, 431
Toyoda, Foreign Minister Teijiro, 72
Treasury Islands, 235–36
Treaty of Portsmouth, 7
Treaty of Shimonosiki, 5
Trenchard, Air Marshal Hugh M., 35
Tripartite Pact, 18, 68, 81

Trobriand Islands, 222, 225
Tromp, 130
Trout, 304
Truk, 16–17, 105, 109, 142, 147, 184, 197, 237, 241, 255, 266, 268, 278–279, 324
Truman, President Harry S, 430–31, 448, 480–81, 486, 488, 491, 494
Tsingtao, 12
Tsukada, Maj. Gen. Rikichi, 384–85
Tulagi, 143, 148, 173–75, 179, 182–83, 232
Turnage, Maj. Gen. Allen H., 242, 325
Turner, RAdm. Richmond Kelly, 83, 176, 178–79, 181–83, 186, 190, 192, 195, 198, 234, 248, 256, 302, 309, 323, 330, 432, 452
Twenty-One Demands, 12, 16
Twiggs, 432
Twining, Maj. Gen. Nathan F., 235, 449

Udo, Col. Takehiko, 427
Ugaki, VAdm. Matome, 230, 309, 425, 494
Ulithi, 339, 344, 346, 411
Ulster, 432
Umezu, Gen. Yoshijiro, 483, 493, 496
United States: code breaking, 51, 79–80, 85, 87, 155; diplomatic relations 1941, 71, 73–74, 76, 78–79, 81, 84–8; embargo, 68–69, 73–74, 78, 81; immigra-

tion policies, 13–14; isolationism, 18, 25, 29–30; Joint Chiefs, 227, 337, 405, 408, 430, 447, 453; naval rivalries, 14–15, 49, 67–68; peace proposal, 480, 482, 486; Pearl Harbor attack, 77–78, 82–89; prewar policies, 2, 8–11, 17–18, 23–27, 45–48, 67–69; surrender arrangements, 481–82, 486–87, 491–92, 495–97

Unryu, 379

Unyo, 67

U.S. air operations: B-29 raids, 335–36, 448–51, 477–78, 488, 490–91; Balikpapan, 474; Biak, 294; Bougainville, 230; Doolittle raid, 146–47, 407, 411; Dutch East Indies, 127–28; Guadalcanal, 186; Iwo Jima, 411; Los Negros, 277; Marshalls, 263, 268; Midway, 160–61; Milne Bay, 213; New Guinea, 144–45, 223–24, 281; Noemfoor, 295; Philippines, 112, 114–15, 353, 359, 370, 392; Rabaul, 227, 241; Vogelkop, 297; Wewak, 225

U.S. Army: air corps training, 32, 35–37; Air Transport Command, 37; armored units, 32–34; officer corps, 31–33; reforms, 30–31; War College, 31–32, 34, 47; War Department, 52, 86

U.S. Army Air Forces units: 5th Air Force, 215, 217–18, 222–24, 237, 241, 277, 297, 337–38, 359, 376–77, 454, 474; 7th Air Force, 249, 268, 359, 411–12; 8th Air Force, 450; 11th Air Force, 250–51, 253–54; 13th Air Force, 228, 237, 298, 337, 454, 474; 14th Air Force, 347; 20th Air Force, 335, 346, 430, 449, 477–78, 486; 339th Fighter Squadron, 228; 393d Bombardment Squadron, 486; 509th Composite Group, 486; VII Fighter Command, 450; XX Bomber Command, 448–49; XXI Bomber Command, 408, 448–49; Far Eastern Air Force, 353, 450, 452

U.S. Army units: armies: Alamo Force, 274, 288, 293, 295; 1st, 448; 6th, 337, 340, 347, 365, 370, 376, 382, 392, 404, 447, 452, 460; 8th, 298, 372, 386, 405, 448, 453–55, 457, 460, 470; 10th, 423, 427, 430–31, 438, 444–45; corps: I, 144, 215, 219, 278, 376, 382–84, 386–89, 403–4, 452, 460–61; X, 347, 350, 352, 354, 366–67, 369, 371–72, 457, 459; XI, 284, 338, 386, 463–64, 389, 401, 452; XIV, 203, 243, 246, 381–82, 386, 394–95, 399, 402, 461, 466; XXIV, 338–39, 348, 352, 354, 366, 368–69, 372, 376, 384, 423, 426–27, 433, 435, 437; divisions: Americal, 175–76, 191, 202, 206, 236, 243, 246, 452; Composite Army-Navy (CAM), 206–7; lst Cavalry, 273, 277, 347, 352–53,

365–67, 386, 394, 400, 402, 452, 460; 6th, 290, 297–98, 376, 382, 388, 400–401, 461; 7th, 252–53, 338, 352, 366, 368–69, 371–72, 423, 427–29, 435, 437, 440, 443–44; 11th Airborne, 369–70, 372, 376, 386, 395–96, 402, 460; 21st, 278; 24th, 293, 347, 352–54, 365–67, 377, 390, 392, 453, 457–58; 25th, 194, 203, 205–6, 228, 233, 376, 388, 403, 452, 461; 27th, 256, 265, 303–4, 318–21, 323–24, 328, 423, 429, 436; 31st, 290, 453, 457, 459; 32d, 144, 215–16, 218–19, 273, 284, 368, 376, 386, 403–4, 461; 33d, 376, 403; 37th, 194, 229, 233, 242–43, 246, 381, 385–87, 389, 394–95, 398, 403, 460–61; 38th, 370, 376, 389, 391; 40th, 381, 384–85, 453–55; 41st, 144, 215, 220, 225, 278–79, 289, 291–92, 294, 453–55; 43d, 195, 228, 230, 233, 284–86, 376, 382, 388, 401; 44th, 456; 77th, 324, 328, 330, 370–71, 423, 425–26, 433–35, 438-39, 441; 81st, 339, 341, 343, 345; 91st, 456; 96th, 338, 352–53, 366–67, 376, 407, 423, 428–29, 435, 438, 441, 443–44; brigades: 2d Cavalry, 400; 5th Cavalry, 277; regiments: lst, 298, 389, 391; 5th, 7th, 8th, and 12th Cavalry, 387, 395–96; 17th, 252–53, 264; 19th, 352, 367, 458; 20th, 389; 21st,

367; 24th, 392; 27th, 232, 235; 31st, 144; 32d, 252, 283, 368, 435, 437, 440; 34th, 293, 366–67, 390, 458; 35th, 206; 63d, 288; 103d, 231, 382; 105th, 310, 316, 321–22, 429; 106th, 262, 265, 267, 310, 317, 322, 429; 108th, 385, 459; 112th Cavalry, 273, 284–86; 124th, 284–85, 457–59, 126th, 216–17, 219, 273; 127th, 219–20, 283–85, 404; 128th, 216, 219, 284, 404; 129th, 382, 385, 403; 132d, 204–5, 456; 145th, 233, 385, 398; 147th, 175, 198, 420; 148th, 233, 245, 342, 387, 396, 398; 149th, 390–91; 151st, 390, 391, 394; 152d, 283; 158th, 289, 295, 376, 460; 160th, 382, 385, 455; 161st, 233, 388; 162d, 282–83, 292–94, 455, 458; 163d, 220, 279, 283, 288–89, 292, 455; 164th, 192–93, 198, 202, 456–57; 165th, 256–57, 309–10, 316–17, 323, 435; 169th, 231; 172d, 231, 382, 388; 182d, 202, 245–46, 260; 184th, 264, 428, 434–35, 437, 440, 443; 185th, 382, 455; 186th, 282, 292, 294, 454; 188th Glider, 401; 305th, 330, 434, 439; 306th, 331, 371, 426, 439; 307th, 330, 371, 434–35, 439, 441; 321st, 343–44; 322d, 343; 323d, 343–44; 381st, 430, 436, 439; 382d, 441; 383d, 428, 439; 503d Para., 225, 296, 453; 511th Para., 387, 401, 460; Ted Force, 286;

Tornado Force, 288; Urbana Force, 218, 220; Warren Force, 218–19

Ushijima, Lt. Gen. Mitsuru, 422–23, 427–28, 435–39, 441, 443–45

U.S. Marine Corps, 43–45, 96, 104–8, 228, 455

U.S. Marine Corps units: aviation: 1st Wing, 44; 2d Wing, 44, 237, 344–45; Group 3, 186; Group 12, 378; Group 24, 386; Group 32, 386; Fleet Marine Force, 44; I Amphibious Corps, 242; II Amphibious Corps, 452; III Amphibious Corps, 303, 324, 338, 423, 440; V Amphibious Corps, 302, 324, 332, 409, 415; divisions: 1st, 176, 178, 203, 228, 272, 339–40, 423, 436, 438–41, 443–44; 2d, 197, 206, 257–61, 302, 307–8, 316–18, 320–21, 323, 332–33, 423, 426; 3d, 228, 236, 242–43, 262, 309, 324–25, 327–28, 330–31, 417–18, 420, 452; 4th, 302, 307–8, 316–18, 320, 332–35, 413–14, 417, 419, 452; 5th, 413–14, 417–18, 420, 452; 6th, 423, 426–27, 438, 443; brigades: 1st Provisional, 309, 324, 327–28, 330–31; regiments: 1st, 44, 179, 202, 341, 343–44, 437; 2d, 333; 3d, 237–29, 409; 4th, 44, 112, 122, 327, 329–30, 409, 427; 5th, 44, 176, 179, 197–98, 275, 341, 343–45, 409, 441; 6th, 205, 261, 307, 334; 7th,

44, 176, 190–91, 198, 274–75, 341–45; 8th, 194, 202, 205, 307, 333–35; 9th, 237–38, 326–29, 331, 417–18; 12th, 238; 21st, 240, 327, 329, 417, 418; 22d, 265, 267, 327, 329–30; 23d, 263, 307, 333–34, 419; 26th, 417; 27th, 414, 417; 28th, 414–16

U.S. Navy: aircraft carrier design, 41-42; Asiatic Fleet, 51; General Board, 38, 41, 48; interwar developments, 39–43; Pacific Fleet, 49, 67, 76, 79, 83, 85; prewar organization, 38–39; submarine operations, 42–43, 48, 90–91, 129–30, 169, 269–70, 289, 304, 310, 314, 355, 363, 379, 450

U.S. Navy air operations: Coral Sea, 148, 150–51; Formosa, 380; Guadalcanal, 185–86, 187; Iwo Jima, 415; Japan, 411–12, 419, 424–25; Lae & Salamaua, 143; Marianas, 305–6; Marshalls, 263; Midway, 160–67; Okinawa, 346, 419, 433, Philippines, 350, 353, 360, 363, 366, 378; Philippine Sea, 311–15, 346; Rabaul, 241; Tarawa, 259; Tokyo, 146–47; Truk, 266

United States Navy units: fleets: 3d, 247, 335, 340, 345, 347, 353–54, 364, 366, 370, 376, 379–80, 411, 452, 478, 495, 497; 5th, 170, 247, 261, 266, 305, 339, 411, 431, 452, 495;

7th, 272, 276, 302, 340, 345, 355, 364, 368, 370, 376, 495; task forces: TF 8, 157–58; TF 11, 148; TF 15, 200; TF 16, 155–56, 161, 251; TF 17, 147–48, 155, 160, 196; TF 32, 228, 234; TF 38, 236, 240, 344, 346–48, 356–57, 363, 378, 409, 478; TF 39, 236, 240; TF 50, 241; TF 54, 412; TF 58, 263, 279, 281, 305, 308, 409, 411–12, 419, 425, 431–33; TF 61, 178, 181, 196; TF 64, 192; TF 67, 204, 228; TF 68, 228; TF 77, 347–48; TF 78, 279, 281, 283, 347, 350, miscellaneous organizations: VII Amphibious Force, 222, 225, 272; Northern Amphibious Force, 252; Makin Force, 256; Marshalls Force, 262, 264; Tarawa Force, 256
Utah, 96

Van Antwerp, Col. W. M. 321
Van Volkenburgh, Brigadier Robert, 145
Vandegrift, Maj. Gen. Alexander A., 176, 178–80, 184, 186, 191–95, 197–98, 202–3
Vasey, Maj. Gen. George A., 217, 226
Vasilevskii, Field Marshal Aleksander M., 489
Vella Lavella, 234, 241
Versailles peace conference, 12, 29
Versailles Treaty, 29

Vestal, 96
Vian, VAdm. Sir Philip, 432
Vincennes, 182
Visayan Islands, 111–12, 339, 349, 457
Vladivostok, 5, 7
Vogelkop, 295, 297
Volckmann, Col. Russell W., 402
Victorious, 442

Wagner, 1st Lt. Boyd D., 114
Wainwright, Maj. Gen. Jonathan M., 112, 116, 121–23, 496
Wakde Island, 281, 287–89
Wake Island, 18, 49–50, 84, 88, 101–8, 169
Waldron, Lt. Comdr. John C., 162
Walke, 201
Ward, 90–91, 371
Wasatch, 381
Washington, 40, 201–2
Washington disarmament conference, 14–16, 20
Washington Treaty, 20, 64, 66, 122
Wasp, 41, 178, 185, 190, 313
Watson, Maj. Gen. Thomas E., 265, 267, 302
Wau, 223, 225
Wavell, Field Marshal Sir Archibald P., 125–26, 129–33
Welch, Lt. George, 89, 94
Welles, Sumner, 78, 81
West Point, 32, 34
West Virginia, 40, 92, 94, 96, 352, 358
Wewak, 273–74, 278–79, 281, 284, 287, 463–64

Weyler, RAdm. G. L. 350, 358, 381
Wheeler Field, 88, 94–95
White Plains, 360
Whitehead, Maj. Gen. Ennis C., 272, 376
Whitehurst, 432
Wigner, Eugene P., 478
Wilkinson, RAdm. Theodore S., 86, 234, 340, 343–44, 381
Willoughby, Maj. Gen. Charles A., 495
Wilson, President Woodrow, 16
Windeyer, Brigadier Victor, 226
Winds Messages, 85
Wing, Maj. Gen. Leonard F., 382
Witter, 432
Wood, Gen. Leonard, 46
Woodlark Island, 222, 225
Wootten, Maj. Gen. George F., 219, 274, 472–73
World War I, 11–12, 30, 32, 35, 38, 42
Wotje, 255, 268
Wright, RAdm. Carleton H., 204

Yahagi, 433
Yalta Conference, 405, 480–81
Yamada, Maj. Gen. Kunitaro, 226
Yamagata, Lt. Gen. Tsuyuo, 372
Yamaguchi, RAdm. Tamon, 161, 165, 167
Yamamoto, Adm. Isoroku, 51, 57–58, 64, 66–70, 73–75, 96–98, 145-46, 151–54, 165, 167–71, 174, 184, 195
Yamashiro, 153, 355, 358–59
Yamashita, Lt. Gen. Tomoyuki, 109, 126, 131, 349–50, 365, 368–69, 371, 376–77, 379, 381, 383–84, 387, 392, 405, 453, 460–62
Yamato, 65, 165, 355, 357, 360, 424, 431, 433
Yamazaki, Col. Yasuyo, 252–53
Yayoi, 186
Yazawa, Col. Kiyomi, 216
Yokayama, Col. Yosuka, 217
Yokosuka, 4, 75
Yokoyama, Lt. Gen. Shizuo, 384, 387, 399, 400–01
Yonai, Adm. Mitsumasa, 68, 336, 372–73, 483–84, 489
Yorktown, 41, 143, 148, 150–51, 155–56, 160, 163–67, 425
Yoshohito, Emperor, 19
Young, 432
Yubari, 105

Zamboanga, 453–54
Zellars, 432
Zhukov, Gen. Georgy, 61
Zigzag Pass, 390–91
Zuiho, 167–68, 196, 311, 354, 363
Zuikaku, 76, 95, 147, 150, 152, 185, 195–96, 311, 314–15, 354, 363